Systems and Software Development, Modeling, and Analysis:

New Perspectives and Methodologies

Mehdi Khosrow-Pour
Information Resources Management Association, USA

A volume in the Advances in Systems Analysis,
Software Engineering, and High Performance
Computing (ASASEHPC) Book Series

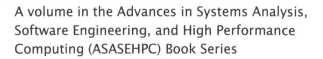

Information Science
REFERENCE
An Imprint of IGI Global

Managing Director:	Lindsay Johnston
Production Editor:	Jennifer Yoder
Development Editor:	Erin O'Dea
Acquisitions Editor:	Kayla Wolfe
Typesetter:	John Crodian
Cover Design:	Jason Mull

Published in the United States of America by
Information Science Reference (an imprint of IGI Global)
701 E. Chocolate Avenue
Hershey PA 17033
Tel: 717-533-8845
Fax: 717-533-8661
E-mail: cust@igi-global.com
Web site: http://www.igi-global.com

Library of Congress Cataloging-in-Publication Data

Systems and software development, modeling, and analysis : new perspectives and methodologies / Mehdi Khosrow-Pour, editor.
    pages cm
 Includes bibliographical references and index. ISBN 978-1-4666-6098-4 (hardcover) -- ISBN 978-1-4666-6099-1 (ebook) --ISBN 978-1-4666-6101-1 (print & perpetual access) 1. Computer software--Development. 2. Computer systems--Design and construciton. I. Khosrow-Pour, Mehdi, 1951- editor.
 QA76.76.D47S954 2014
 005.3--dc23
                                2014007988

This book is published in the IGI Global book series Advances in Systems Analysis, Software Engineering, and High Performance Computing (ASASEHPC) (ISSN: 2327-3453; eISSN: 2327-3461)

Advances in Systems Analysis, Software Engineering, and High Performance Computing (ASASEHPC) Book Series

Vijayan Sugumaran
Oakland University, USA

ISSN: 2327-3453
EISSN: 2327-3461

MISSION

The theory and practice of computing applications and distributed systems has emerged as one of the key areas of research driving innovations in business, engineering, and science. The fields of software engineering, systems analysis, and high performance computing offer a wide range of applications and solutions in solving computational problems for any modern organization.

The **Advances in Systems Analysis, Software Engineering, and High Performance Computing (ASASEHPC) Book Series** brings together research in the areas of distributed computing, systems and software engineering, high performance computing, and service science. This collection of publications is useful for academics, researchers, and practitioners seeking the latest practices and knowledge in this field.

COVERAGE

- Computer Graphics
- Computer Networking
- Computer System Analysis
- Distributed Cloud Computing
- Enterprise Information Systems
- Metadata and Semantic Web
- Parallel Architectures
- Performance Modeling
- Software Engineering
- Virtual Data Systems

IGI Global is currently accepting manuscripts for publication within this series. To submit a proposal for a volume in this series, please contact our Acquisition Editors at Acquisitions@igi-global.com or visit: http://www.igi-global.com/publish/.

Titles in this Series

For a list of additional titles in this series, please visit: www.igi-global.com

Handbook of Research on Innovations in Systems and Software Engineering
Vicente García Díaz (University of Oviedo, Spain) Juan Manuel Cueva Lovelle (University of Oviedo, Spain) and
B. Cristina Pelayo García-Bustelo (University of Oviedo, Spain)
Information Science Reference • copyright 2015 • 723pp • H/C (ISBN: 9781466663596) • US $515.00 (our price)

Handbook of Research on Architectural Trends in Service-Driven Computing
Raja Ramanathan (Independent Researcher, USA) and Kirtana Raja (IBM, USA)
Information Science Reference • copyright 2014 • 759pp • H/C (ISBN: 9781466661783) • US $515.00 (our price)

Industry and Research Perspectives on Embedded System Design
Alessandra Bagnato (Softeam R&D, France) Leandro Soares Indrusiak (University of York, UK) Imran Rafiq
Quadri (Softeam R&D, France) and Matteo Rossi (Politecnico di Milano, Italy)
Information Science Reference • copyright 2014 • 434pp • H/C (ISBN: 9781466661943) • US $245.00 (our price)

Contemporary Advancements in Information Technology Development in Dynamic Environments
Mehdi Khosrow-Pour (Information Resources Management Association, USA)
Information Science Reference • copyright 2014 • 320pp • H/C (ISBN: 9781466662520) • US $205.00 (our price)

Systems and Software Development, Modeling, and Analysis New Perspectives and Methodologies
Mehdi Khosrow-Pour (Information Resources Management Association, USA)
Information Science Reference • copyright 2014 • 400pp • H/C (ISBN: 9781466660984) • US $215.00 (our price)

Handbook of Research on Emerging Advancements and Technologies in Software Engineering
Imran Ghani (Universiti Teknologi Malaysia, Malaysia) Wan Mohd Nasir Wan Kadir (Universiti Teknologi Malaysia, Malaysia) and Mohammad Nazir Ahmad (Universiti Teknologi Malaysia, Malaysia)
Engineering Science Reference • copyright 2014 • 478pp • H/C (ISBN: 9781466660267) • US $395.00 (our price)

Advancing Embedded Systems and Real-Time Communications with Emerging Technologies
Seppo Virtanen (University of Turku, Finland)
Information Science Reference • copyright 2014 • 308pp • H/C (ISBN: 9781466660342) • US $235.00 (our price)

Handbook of Research on High Performance and Cloud Computing in Scientific Research and Education
Marijana Despotović-Zrakić (University of Belgrade, Serbia) Veljko Milutinović (University of Belgrade, Serbia) and Aleksandar Belić (University of Belgrade, Serbia)
Information Science Reference • copyright 2014 • 476pp • H/C (ISBN: 9781466657847) • US $325.00 (our price)

IGI GLOBAL
DISSEMINATOR of KNOWLEDGE

www.igi-global.com

701 E. Chocolate Ave., Hershey, PA 17033
Order online at www.igi-global.com or call 717-533-8845 x100
To place a standing order for titles released in this series, contact: cust@igi-global.com
Mon-Fri 8:00 am - 5:00 pm (est) or fax 24 hours a day 717-533-8661

Table of Contents

Detailed Table of Contents

Remigijus Gustas, Karlstad University, Sweden
Prima Gustiene, Karlstad University, Sweden

Managing evolutionary changes, identification of discontinuities, and separation of concerns is not an easy task in the area conceptual modeling in information system development. One of the fundamental problems is that most conventional conceptual modeling techniques deal with the collection of loosely linked meta-models, which are defined by different types of diagrams. Typically, system development methods project interactive, behavioral, and structural aspects of information systems' conceptual representations into disparate views. Therefore, the semantic integrity of various architecture dimensions is difficult to achieve. In this chapter, the authors present a semantically integrated conceptual modeling method. The advantage of this method is stability and flexibility of the diagrams to manage the constant changes of system requirements. This method provides the possibility to visualize the interplay among structural, interactive, and behavioral aspects. This is very important for the control of semantic integrity and to maintain a holistic representation where external and internal views of service conceptualizations are visualized together. Such visualization is also important for separation of concerns, which provides foundation for creation of modeling patterns. Modeling patterns are important for several reasons. First, they can be used for demonstration of the interplay of fundamental constructs that are used for system analysis and design. Secondly, modeling patterns are important for the evaluation of the expressive power of semantic modeling languages. It is demonstrated by case studies that sequential, underlying, enclosing, overriding, and overlaying interaction loops between actors provide the foundation for the composition of complex scenarios, which span across organizational and technical system boundaries.

Raymon R. Bruce, Embry-Riddle Aeronautical University, USA & University of Electrical
Systems and Technology of China, China

This chapter traces the origin of the concept of work in five staged sections. The first section examines the question, what is work? Work originally referred to "doing," that is, work organization, synergy, and energy. The second section develops the Greek word family for work into a dynamic model of doing. The third section shows how nature guides working change through energy exchange. It examines how a work as re-organization model would function in nature's jurisdictional domain of guiding energy exchanges. Nature's laws provide guidance for self-governing latitude to energy jurisdictional domains' evolutionary change. The fourth section examines policymaking as human guidance imitating nature. Policymaking limits individual self-governance to guide a specified social community of people (polis) doing work. Policymaking is explored to see how humans use policymaking to govern themselves and their cultural social groups including governments by using nature's use of laws as guidance. Policymaking is also a form of laying down basic parameters of work as re-organization through energy exchanges in the ambient environment. Policies are human artifacts designed help a social group work well together. Part five presents an issue analysis as an invited Organization Development consultant to help find ways for the Sri Lankan government, the University of Moratuwa, and the apparel and textile industry to work together in their extreme makeover of human resource development of their apparel and textile industry. Action training and research, stakeholder management, and wicked problem issue analysis are the organization development methods used to demonstrate this field theory of work re-organization through energy exchange.

Chapter 3

Context Awareness is the ability of systems and applications to sense the environment and infer the activity going on in the environment. Context encompasses all knowledge bounded within an environment and includes attributes of both machines and users. A context-aware system is composed of context gathering and context inference modules. This chapter proposes a Context Inference Engine (CiE) that classifies the current context as one of several known context activities. This engine follows a Minkowski distance-based classification approach with standard deviation-based ranks to identify likeliness of classified activity of the current context. Empirical results on different data sets show that the proposed algorithm performs closer to Support Vector Machines (SVM) while it is better than probabilistic reasoning methods where the performance is quantified as success in classification.

Chapter 4

This chapter examines the established Systems Dynamics (SD) methods applied to software projects in order to simplify them. These methods are highly non-linear and contain large numbers of variables and built-in decisions. A SIMULINK version of an SD model is used here and conclusions are made with respect to the initial main controlling factors, compared to a NASA project. Control System methods are used to evaluate the critical features of the SD models. The eigenvalues of the linearised system indicate that the important factors are the hiring delay time, the assimilation time, and the employment time. This illustrates how the initial state of the system is at best neutrally stable with control only being achieved with complex non-linear decisions. The purpose is to compare the simplest SD and control models available required for "good" simulation of project behaviour with the Abdel-Hamid software project model. These models give clues to the decision structures that are necessary for good agreement with reality. The final simplified model, with five states, is a good match for the prime states of the Abdel-Hamid model, the NASA data, and compares favourably to the Ruiz model. The linear control system model has a much simpler structure, with the same limitations. Both the simple SD and control models are more suited to preliminary estimates of project performance.

Chapter 5

This chapter presents a System Dynamics (SD) simulation model that not only replicates self-organizing system uncertainty results but also looks at self-organization causally. The SD simulation and model analysis results show exactly how distributed control leads positive feedback to explosive growth, which ends when all dynamics have been absorbed into an attractor, leaving the system in a stable, negative feedback state. The chapter's SD model analysis helps explain why phenomena of interest emerge in agent-based models, a topic crucial in understanding and designing Complex Adaptive Self-Organizing Systems (CASOS).

Chapter 6

In this chapter, the authors inch towards better understanding of the notion of informational infrastructure and the role of standards in the development of infrastructures in the new information age. Specifically, the authors consider the standardization process as pertaining to informational infrastructure development. They focus on two particular aspects of standardization: temporal dynamics and the social organization. Using Bauman's concept of liquid modernity, the authors argue that standards often become hybrids of solid and liquid modernities linking together different scales of time, space, and social organization. To better illustrate theoretical concepts, they draw on practical examples from the development of informational standards, infrastructures, and services, particularly from the domain of Cognitive Radio Systems (CRS), a new generation of "paradigm changing" communication technologies and services. The aim of this chapter is to offer the scholars of standards and innovation a fresh, non-mainstream perspective on the social and temporal dynamics of standardization and infrastructure development processes, to bring forth new understandings of the complexity of relationships between business, technology, and regulatory domains in the formation of informational infrastructure.

Chapter 7

During last decade, the world watched a social acceptance of computing and computers, enhanced information technology devices, wireless networks, and Internet; they gradually became a fundamental resource for individuals. Nowadays, people, organizations, and the environment are empowered by computing devices and systems; they depend on services offered by modern Pervasive Information Systems supported by complex software systems and technology. Research on software development for PIS-delivered information, on issues and challenges on software development for them, and several other contributions have been delivered. Among these contributions are a development framework for PIS, a profiling and framing structure approach, and a SPEM 2.0 extension. This chapter, revisiting these contributions, provides an additional contribution: a pattern to support the use of the development framework and profiling approach on software development for PIS. This contribution completes a first series of contributions for the development of PIS. This chapter also presents a case study that allowed demonstrating the applicability of these contributions.

Chapter 8

Artificial Neural Networks (ANN) are used for statistical modeling of spatial events in geosciences. The advantage of this method is the ability of neural networks to represent complex interrelations and to be "able to learn" from known (spatial) events. The software advangeo® was developed to enable GIS users to apply neural network methods on raster geodata. The statistic modeling results can be developed and displayed in a user-friendly way within the Esri ArcGIS environment. The complete workflow is documented by the software. This chapter presents five case studies to illustrate the current possibilities and limitations of spatial predictions with the use of artificial neural networks, which describe influencing factors and the selection of known events of the phenomenon to be modeled. These applications include: (1) the prognosis of soil erosion patterns, (2) the country-wide prediction of mineral resources, (3) the vulnerability analysis for forest pests, (4) the spatial distribution of bird species, and (5) the spatial prediction of manganese nodules on the sea bottom.

Chapter 9

Analytical processing (OLAP) tools typically only deal with relational data. Hence, the analytical processing systems on XML data do not have all the functionality provided by OLAP tools to traditional data (i.e. relational). In addition, current commercial and academic OLAP tools do not process XML data that contains XLink. Therefore, there is a need to develop a solution for OLAP systems in order to assist in the strategic analysis of the organizational data represented in XML format. Aiming at overcoming this issue, this chapter proposes an analytical system composed by LMDQL (Link-Based Multidimensional Query Language), an analytical query language; XLDM (XLink Data Metamodel), a metamodel given to model cubes of XML documents with XLink and to deal with syntactic, semantic, and structural heterogeneities commonly found in XML documents; and XLPath (XLink Path Language), a navigation language for XML documents connected by XLink. As current W3C query languages for navigating in XML documents do not support XLink, XLPath is discussed in this chapter to provide features for the LMDQL query processing and a prototype system enabling OLAP queries over XML documents linked by XLink and XML schema. This prototype includes a driver, named sql2xquery, which performs the mapping of SQL queries into XQuery in a relational OLAP server. In order to validate the proposed system, a case study and its performance evaluation are presented to analyze the impact of analytical processing over XML/XLink documents.

Chapter 10

Cloud computing addresses the use of scalable and often virtualized resources. It is based on service-level agreements that provide external users with requested services. Cloud computing is still evolving. New specific collaboration models among service providers are needed for enabling effective service collaboration, allowing the process of serving consumers to be more efficient. On the other hand, Scout

Movement or Scouting has been a very successful youth movement in which the collaboration of its members can be observed. This motivated a previous work aiming to design MAS-Scout, a framework that defines Multi-Agent Systems based on the principles of Scouting. In this chapter, MAS-Scout is used to design a system to deal with service collaboration in a cloud computing environment focusing on the premise that Scouting has been a very successful social movement in the world and that collaboration is part of its principles. The results presented in this chapter show that MAS-Scout, which is based on the Scouting principles, can be satisfactorily used to automate cloud computing needs.

Chapter 11

Asheesh K. Singh, Motilal Nehru National Institute of Technology Allahabad, India
Rambir Singh, Inderprastha Engineering College, India

This chapter presents the design approach of an Improved Approximated Simplest Fuzzy Logic Controller (IASFLC). A cascade combination of simplest 4-rule Fuzzy Logic Controller (FLC) and an nth degree polynomial is proposed as an IASFLC to approximate the control characteristics of a 49-rule FLC. The approximation scheme is based on minimizing the sum of square errors between the control outputs of a 49-rule FLC and a simplest 4-rule FLC in the entire range of Universe Of Discourse (UOD). The coefficients of compensating polynomial are evaluated by solving instantaneous square error equations at various test points in the entire UOD. This IASFLC maps the output of a 49-rule FLC with absolute deviation of less than 5%. The proposed IASFLC is used to control the dc link voltage of a three-phase shunt Active Power Filter (APF). A detailed analysis is performed during transient and steady state conditions to check Power Quality (PQ) and dynamic performance indices under randomly varying balanced and unbalanced loading conditions. The performance of proposed IASFLC is compared with a 49-rule FLC and Approximated Simplest Fuzzy Logic Controller (ASFLC) based on minimization of the deviation at central values of Membership Functions (MFs). It is found comparatively better for harmonic and reactive compensation with a comparable dynamic response. The memory requirement and computational time of proposed IASFLC are even lesser than the ASFLC.

Preface

With the rise of service-oriented architecture and multi-vendor system integration, computer systems and software have become increasingly complex. This increasing complexity calls for a multi-faceted approach to not only the development process but also the modeling and analytical processes, taking into special consideration the functionalities best suited for the evolving needs of the end-user. *Systems and Software Development, Modeling, and Analysis: New Perspectives and Methodologies* discusses the issues, challenges, and standards associated with systems and software development, the dynamic modeling methods required for successful system analysis and design, and the analytics tools used to identify tendencies and standards that must be considered in order to yield a relevant, high-quality end product.

The book is organized into 11 chapters. A brief description of each of the chapters can be found below:

In chapter 1, "Semantically Integrated Conceptual Modeling Method and Modeling Patterns," Remigijus Gustas and Prima Gustiene discuss the management of evolutionary changes, identification of discontinuities, and separation of concerns in information system development. The chapter presents one of the fundamental problems faced by information system developers today: that most conventional conceptual modeling techniques deal with the collections of loosely linked meta-models, which are defined by the different types of diagrams. In this chapter, the authors present the semantically integrated conceptual modeling method. They posit that the advantage of this method is stability and flexibility of the diagrams to manage the constant changes of system requirements. Through case study examples, the authors show that sequential, underlying, enclosing, overriding, and overlaying interaction loops between actors provide the foundation for the composition of complex scenarios.

Raymon R. Bruce traces the origin of the concept of work in the second chapter of this book, titled "Founding a Field Theory of Work: Re-Organization through Energy Exchange." In five sections, the author provides an answer to the question, what is work?, develops the Greek word family for work into a dynamic model of doing, shows how nature guides work change through energy exchange, examines policymaking as human guidance imitating nature, and presents the author's issue analysis as an invited Organization Development consultant who helps the Sri Lankan government, the University of Moratuwa, and the apparel and textile industry find ways to work together in their extreme makeover of human resource development of their apparel and textile industry. Action training and research, stakeholder management, and wicked problem issue analysis were the organization development methods used to demonstrate this field theory of work re-organization through energy exchange.

In "Context Inference Engine (CiE): Classifying Activity of Context using Minkowski Distance and Standard Deviation-Based Ranks," the third chapter of this book, Umar Mahmud and Muhammad Younus Javed define context awareness and context-aware systems. They propose a Context Inference Engine (CiE) that classifies the current context as one of several known context activities.

Chapter 4, "Simple System Dynamics and Control System Project Models," examines the established Systems Dynamics (SD) methods applied to software projects in order to simplify them. A SIMULINK version of an SD model is used in the chapter, and conclusions are made with respect to the initial main controlling factors, compared to a NASA project. Control system methods are used to evaluate the critical features of the SD models.

Nicholas C. Georgantzas and Evangelos Katsamakas present a System Dynamics (SD) simulation model that replicates self-organizing system uncertainty results and looks at self-organization causally in chapter 5, "Modeling a Simple Self-Organizing System." The authors use SD simulation and model analysis results to show how distributed control leads positive feedback to explosive growth, leaving the system in a stable, negative feedback state. The chapter's SD model analysis helps explain why phenomena of interest emerge in agent-based models, a topic crucial in understanding and designing Complex Adaptive Self-Organizing Systems (CASOS).

In chapter 6, "The Role of Standards in the Development of New Informational Infrastructure," Vladislav V. Fomin and Marja Matinmikko inch towards a better understanding of the notion of informational infrastructure and the role of standards in the development of infrastructures in the new information age. Specifically, the authors consider standardization processes as pertaining to informational infrastructure development. They focus on two particular aspects of standardization: temporal dynamics and social organization. Using Bauman's concept of liquid modernity, they argue that standards often become hybrids of solid and liquid modernities linking together different scales of time, space, and social organization. To better illustrate theoretical concepts, they draw on practical examples from the development of informational standards, infrastructures, and services, particularly from the domain of Cognitive Radio Systems (CRS) with the overall aim of offering scholars of standards and innovation a fresh, non-mainstream perspective on the social and temporal dynamics of standardization and infrastructure development processes.

In chapter 7, José Eduardo Fernandes and Ricardo J. Machado revisit the contributions of Pervasive Information Systems (PIS) researchers to provide a pattern that supports the use of the development framework and profiling approach on software development for PIS. Their chapter, "Development Framework Pattern for Pervasive Information Systems," completes the first series of research contributions for the development of PIS and presents a case study that demonstrates the applicability of these contributions.

Andreas Barth, Andreas Knobloch, Silke Noack, and Frank Schmidt present five case studies to illustrate the current possibilities and limitations of spatial predictions with the use of artificial neural networks in chapter 8, "Neural Network-Based Spatial Modeling of Natural Phenomena and Events." Applications presented by the authors are: (1) the prognosis of soil erosion patterns, (2) the country-wide prediction of mineral resources, (3) the vulnerability analysis for forest pests, (4) the spatial distribution of bird species, and (5) the spatial prediction of manganese nodules on the sea bottom.

In chapter 9, titled "Multidimensional Data Analysis Based on Links: Models and Languages," Paulo Caetano da Silva addresses the need for a solution for OLAP systems in order to assist in the strategic analysis of the organizational data represented in XML format. Aiming at overcoming this issue, the author proposes an analytical system composed by LMDQL (Link-Based Multidimensional Query Language), an analytical query language; XLDM (XLink Data Metamodel), a metamodel given to model cubes of XML documents with XLink and to deal with syntactic, semantic, and structural heterogeneities commonly found in XML documents; and XLPath (XLink Path Language), a navigation language for XML documents connected by XLink. As current W3C query languages for navigating in XML documents do not support XLink, the author also discusses XLPath to provide features for the LMDQL query processing and a prototype system enabling OLAP queries over XML documents linked by XLink and XML schema. In order to validate the proposed system, a case study and its performance evaluation are presented to analyze the impact of analytical processing over XML/XLink documents.

In "A Scouting-Based Multi-Agent System Model to Deal with Service Collaboration in Cloud Computing," Mauricio Paletta discusses MAS-Scout, a framework that defines Multi-Agent Systems based on the principles of Scouting. In this chapter, MAS-Scout is used to design a system to deal with service collaboration in a cloud computing environment focusing on the premise that Scouting has been a very successful social movement in the world and that collaboration is part of its principles. The results presented in this chapter show that MAS-Scout, which is based on the Scouting principles can be satisfactorily used to automate cloud computing needs.

The last chapter, "Power Quality Improvement using Improved Approximated Fuzzy Logic Controller for Shunt Active Power Filter," authored by Asheesh K. Singh and Rambir Singh, presents the design approach of an Improved Approximated Simplest Fuzzy Logic Controller (IASFLC). The chapter authors propose a cascade combination of simplest 4-rule Fuzzy Logic Controller (FLC) and an nth degree polynomial as an IASFLC to approximate the control characteristics of a 49-rule FLC. The proposed IASFLC is used to control the dc link voltage of a 3-phase shunt Active Power Filter (APF). A detailed analysis is performed during transient and steady state conditions to check Power Quality (PQ) and dynamic performance indices under randomly varying balanced and unbalanced loading conditions. The performance of proposed IASFLC is compared with a 49-rule FLC and Approximated Simplest Fuzzy Logic Controller (ASFLC) based on minimization of the deviation at central values of Membership Functions (MFs).

Mehdi Khosrow-Pour
Information Resources Management Association, USA

Chapter 1
Semantically Integrated Conceptual Modeling Method and Modeling Patterns

Remigijus Gustas
Karlstad University, Sweden

Prima Gustiene
Karlstad University, Sweden

ABSTRACT

Managing evolutionary changes, identification of discontinuities, and separation of concerns is not an easy task in the area conceptual modeling in information system development. One of the fundamental problems is that most conventional conceptual modeling techniques deal with the collection of loosely linked meta-models, which are defined by different types of diagrams. Typically, system development methods project interactive, behavioral, and structural aspects of information systems' conceptual representations into disparate views. Therefore, the semantic integrity of various architecture dimensions is difficult to achieve. In this chapter, the authors present a semantically integrated conceptual modeling method. The advantage of this method is stability and flexibility of the diagrams to manage the constant changes of system requirements. This method provides the possibility to visualize the interplay among structural, interactive, and behavioral aspects. This is very important for the control of semantic integrity and to maintain a holistic representation where external and internal views of service conceptualizations are visualized together. Such visualization is also important for separation of concerns, which provides foundation for creation of modeling patterns. Modeling patterns are important for several reasons. First, they can be used for demonstration of the interplay of fundamental constructs that are used for system analysis and design. Secondly, modeling patterns are important for the evaluation of the expressive power of semantic modeling languages. It is demonstrated by case studies that sequential, underlying, enclosing, overriding, and overlaying interaction loops between actors provide the foundation for the composition of complex scenarios, which span across organizational and technical system boundaries.

DOI: 10.4018/978-1-4666-6098-4.ch001

INTRODUCTION

Every enterprise system can be seen as a composition of the organizational and technical components, which are viewed as various types of enterprise actors (Gustas & Gustiene, 2007). Although many requirements can be attributed to an individual component, still there are many requirements that impact many components. Such requirements cut across components and a called crosscutting concerns (Jacobson & Ng, 2005). Conventional information system (IS) analysis and design methods are restricted in their ability to distinguish among crosscutting concerns, which span across various types of diagrams. It does not matter whether designers apply structured analysis and design (SAD) methods (Gane & Sarson, 1979), (Yourdon & Constantine, 1979), object-oriented or component based methods (OMG, 2010): their expressive power is limited in separating various concerns. To break down a problem into smaller parts is called separation of concerns (Jacobson & Ng, 2005). Disability to manage separation of concerns is one of the reasons why the way systems are currently built is rather primitive and meet a lot of problems. Consequently, managing the complexity of specifications in software engineering is the problem that can be attributed to various limitations of traditional IS modeling and design methods. To obtain value from the graphical representations they must be integrated and semantically correct.

In the traditional areas of engineering, developers are able to present their design decisions by using a finalized computation-neutral representation. This is not a case in the area of system engineering. The limitations of conventional system modeling methods result in two side effects, which in aspect-oriented software development (Jacobson & Ng, 2005) are known as tangling and scattering. Tangling occurs when the software component or class, instead of fulfilling a particular concern, encapsulates a diverse set of concerns. If a particular concern is spread across multiple components, then this situation is called scattering. When the requirements caused by that concern are modified, the designer must identify all related components and to find out how these components are affected by introduced changes. Especially, modifying requirements, which are related to a big number of diagrams, become quite problematic. Poor understanding of concerns makes it difficult to make even simple evolutionary extensions of IS specifications. Separation of crosscutting concerns (Gustas & Gustiene, 2012) is the first fundamental problem, which cannot be solved without modifying modeling foundation in system analysis and design. In this paper, we introduce a new way of modeling and decomposition principles, which suggest a new and more natural way of managing complexity in system engineering. We also present four modeling patters that we constructed using this semantically integrated conceptual modeling method (SICM).

The declarative nature of value flow exchanges help technical system designers to analyze underlying business events, which are quite comprehensible for such stakeholders as business process modeling experts, enterprise architects, and users. Diagnosing value flows among different organizational components in IS engineering is important for solving the alignment problem (Wieringa, 2008), (Wieringa & Gordijn, 2005) of value models (Gordijn & Akkermans, 2000) with the behavioral effects and structural changes in various classes of objects. Value exchanges and related coordinating events can be used as the guidance for system designers to move smoothly from system analysis to design, without a requirement to represent a complete solution. By sending and receiving value flows, the actors enter into commitments regarding their privileges, rights, responsibilities and obligations. One of the reasons why the conventional system analysis and design methods are not suitable for modeling the deontic aspects of organizations (Wagner, 2003), such as commitments and claims (Chopra et al., 2010), is that they not able to capture value and coordinating flows among organizational subsystems. Interaction-based thinking has proved to be fruitful in the area of enterprise engineering (Dietz, 2006). However, there is a paradigmatic mismatch between the traditional object-oriented IS modeling methods and system analysis approaches, which are based on the modeling of interactions between actors. The paradigmatic differences are an obstacle in finding an elegant solution for the alignment problem of business process design with IT operations (Wieringa, 2008). So, the second fundamental problem is unclear principles of blending between the traditional system and enterprise engineering methods. Our intention is to introduce semantically integrated modeling method, which allows combining interaction dependencies between actors with the conventional semantic relations in the area of system analysis and design.

A human limited mind allows focusing on a particular concern at a time in isolation without paying too much attention to other concerns. One particular concern usually comprises static and dynamic aspects of IS specifications. However, it is common to all conventional system analysis and design methods to separate disparate dimensions of enterprise architecture (Zachman, 1987). Therefore, most conventional IS design methods have the problem of bridging between static and dynamic aspects of different concerns. The analysis of the static and dynamic aspects of IS specifications in isolation creates difficulties in conceptual modeling of IS specifications. The consequence of such analysis is that additional semantic modeling assurance procedures are necessary to introduce in order to establish integrity across multiple diagrams. Integrity problems imply semantic inconsistency and incompleteness of conceptual representations on various levels of abstraction. Nearly all object-oriented modeling techniques deal with the collections of models (Glinz, 2000). One of the major flaws of the conventional information system modeling has been unclear semantic integration principles

between static and dynamic aspects of system conceptualizations. A starting point in the traditional modeling approaches is typically the specification of static dependencies between concepts, which can be represented by relations between various classes of objects. Data flow modeling in terms of Data Flow Diagrams (DFD) was the strength of SAD methods. UML also supports various types of associations between actors and use cases. But modeling of data flows between subsystems is awkward in UML. It is not completely clear how coordinating data flows, which are necessary for the initiation of value flows, can be explicitly defined by the conventional IS analysis and design methods.

One of the benefits of the DEMO method (Dietz, 2006) is the focus on modeling organizational interactions. The actor transaction diagram and the process structure diagram provide a solid foundation for interaction-based thinking, because these diagrams show in a concise form the essential model of enterprise construction and operation. Conventional modeling approaches have difficulties to capture the essential interactions of organization. Interaction dependencies are crucial for visualization of information, decision and resource exchange activities among enterprise subsystems. The understanding of interactions is important for keeping track of desired continuity and for the detecting semantic incompleteness, which result in business or software process breakdowns across organizational and technical system boundaries. Analyzing interactions is very important in redesigning and reengineering organizations (Hammer, 1990), (Gustas, 2010b). The advantage of modeling organizational interactions is that they remain stable over time. It helps stakeholders to comprehend the essential business model before and after radical change. However, significant efforts are necessary for aligning evolutionary changes of interactions with the corresponding modifications of static and dynamic aspects of IS specifications. So, the challenge is how to improve the flexibility of conceptual modeling representations for introducing evolutionary changes and continuous innovations of enterprise system architectures.

All the fundamental IS modeling problems above-mentioned are interrelated. More research efforts are necessary in developing a solid theoretical foundation for managing complexity, integration, alignment and evolution of system conceptualizations. The goal of this paper is to introduce a new way of modeling for the separation of crosscutting concerns in terms of simple interaction loops. The way of modeling based on interactions is important for constructing various scenarios in a more comprehensive way. If system architects are not able to separate concerns, the complexity of analysis and design task increases exponentially and it is difficult to meet evolving needs of stakeholders. Semantic integration and evolution of different diagram types in system analysis are the core interrelated problems. Most conceptual modeling languages are plagued by the paradigm mismatch between various constructs of diagrams. Alignment and management of system development complexity are practical tasks, which cannot be solved without developing a more comprehensive and semantically integrated conceptual modeling foundation. Achieving integrity among interactive, behavioral and structural aspects is not trivial, because typically the constructs of different modeling traditions do not fit each other. In such situation, designers are forced to deal with semantically inconsistent or incomplete diagrams. In this paper, we present Semantically Integrated Conceptual Modeling (SICM) method, which provides a more flexible way of modeling for managing complexity and dealing with evolutionary changes of IS conceptualizations. Integrated way of modeling allows us to construct modeling patterns which are important for business process modeling. The advantage of these modeling patters is that they enable visualization and integration of static and dynamic aspects. Traditional modeling patters present just dynamic aspects of business processes, no data.

INTERACTION-BASED WAY OF MODELING

The way of modeling that enables explicit modeling of interaction flows (Gustas & Gustiene, 2009) is critical for the identification of discontinuity in IS specifications and to comprehend the details of crosscutting concerns between different enterprise subsystems (Papazoglou, 2008). Business process scenarios can be conceptualized by identifying essential workflows, which can be expressed as a set of purposeful interactions between organizational or technical components. Technical components are enterprise subsystems such as machines, software and hardware. Organizational components can be human individuals, organizations and their divisions. Components are represented by the roles they play that are called actors. Interaction dependencies among actors are important for identification of business events as well as for separation of crosscutting concerns. By following interaction dependencies, it is possible to explore various ways in which enterprise system components can be used. In this section, we are going to demonstrate how interaction flows can be composed into workflow loops (Denning & Medina-Mora, 1995). A workflow loop is considered as a basic element of various scenarios, which describe interplay between various actors that could be seen as service requesters and service providers (Gustiene & Gustas, 2011). In its most generic form, a workflow loop is viewed as a response to request that provides some value to requester (Gustas, 2010b).

We distinguish between actors and passive concepts. An actor can only be represented by an active concept (Wagner, 2003). An instance of an actor is an autonomous subsystem. Its existence can be motivated by a set of interaction dependencies with other actors that keep this subsystem viable. Interaction dependency R(A⇢B) between two active concepts indicates that the actor A is an agent, which can perform action R on one or more recipients, which are represented by actor B.

Actions are able to manipulate objects and their properties that are represented by the passive concepts (see next section). The graphical notations of three different types of interaction dependencies between actors are presented in Figure 1.

Actors are denoted by square rectangles and actions are represented by ellipses. Solid rectangles are used for the denotation of resource flows and light boxes indicate information flows. Interaction dependencies (⋯→) are indicated graphically by broken arrows. They represent moving flows such as information, decision, or resource. Actors may view all moving flows either as coordination flows (Dietz, 2006) or value flows (Gordijn & Akkermans, 2000) such as materials, financial resources, etc.

The event flows of business process scenarios can be analyzed as compositions of service interaction loops. Service loops are very useful to analyze discontinuity of value creation process, which capture service value in an exchange between two or more parties. Each service description can be defined by interaction flows into opposite directions between a service requester and service provider (Gustas & Gustiene, 2008). Both requests and responses can be viewed as elementary interactions. Such understanding of requests and responses is consistent with the ontological

foundation of service process (Ferrario & Guarino 2008). According to Ferrario and Guarino, services cannot be transferable, because they are events, not objects. Service providers are actors who receive service requests and transform them into service responses, which are sent to service requesters. This idea is illustrated graphically in Figure 2.

The presented simple interaction loop is a basic element, which is used in a very early conceptual modeling phase for the analysis of crosscutting concerns in terms of service requests and service responses among organizational and technical components. Service responses cannot be delivered without triggering service requests. A response can be viewed in a number of ways. It can be represented by a promise to deliver a desirable result to service requester. It can also be a production action, which brings a desired product to service requester. Two actors can be loosely coupled by interaction dependencies into two opposite directions by the following expression:

If Request (Service Requester ⋯→ Service Provider)

then Response(Service Provider ⋯→ Service Requester).

Figure 1. Three types of interaction dependencies

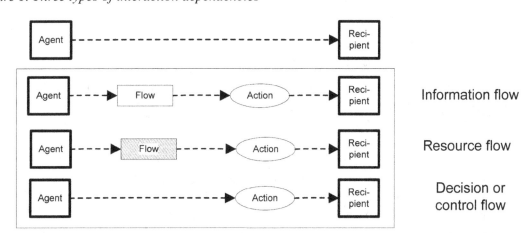

Figure 2. Basic interaction loop

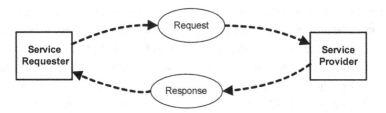

Every business or technical use-case functionality in essence can be defined by a scenario. The flow of interaction events is important for understanding the structure of scenario, which can be described in terms of request and response events between actors. For example, Create Reservation event is viewed as a promise in connection to Request Room event. Pay event can be understood as a response in exchange to Provide Hotel Room event. Events are triggered by communication actions. Legal sequences of actions represent possible event flows for actors to communicate with each other. Service interaction loops can be delegated to various organizational and technical components. For instance, two interaction loops among different actors, which represent the technical component such as Hotel Reservation System and three organizational components, are represented in Figure 3.

The diagram represents interaction possibilities, which are available to four actors. Actors can be related by inheritance, composition and classification dependencies (Gustas, 2010b). These dependencies are used for reasoning about various ways in which interaction loops can be composed, merged or overlaid on the top of each other. Available actions can be also viewed as rights, responsibilities, obligations and claims. A customer has a right to Request Room by informing a Hotel Reservation System about Room Requirements. If the requested type of room is available, then a Hotel Reservation System has responsibility to Create Reservation for Customer. By taking advantage of the available actions, the actors may enter into commitments regarding their obligations. For instance, the effect of successfully executed Create Reservation action is the new commitment to provide a hotel room for a customer. Interaction

Figure 3. Two interaction loops in a Hotel Management System

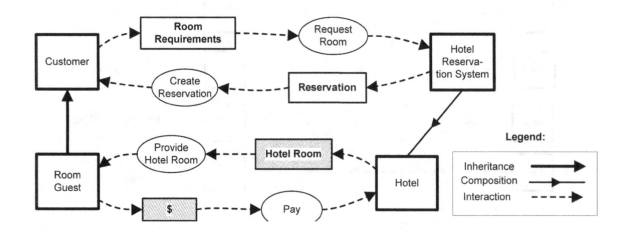

dependencies are inherited by the more specific actors and they are propagated to compositional wholes according to the special inference rules (Gustas, 2010a). For example, Create Reservation is a derived responsibility of Hotel. If Hotel creates a Reservation, then it is obliged to Provide Hotel Room for a particular Room Guest. On the other hand, if Hotel is obliged to Provide Hotel Room, then Room Guest is entitled to claim a hotel room. Most traditional IS analysis and design methods do not provide enough reasoning about commitments and claims.

BASIC ELEMENTS OF SEMANTICALLY INTEGRATED CONCEPTUAL MODELING (SICM) APPROACH

The interpretation of the modeling concepts for the representation of a problem domain is very important (Boman et al., 1997), because the concepts determine the semantic correctness of requirements specification (Gustiené, 2010). This process of requirements specification concerns the modeling of stakeholders' requirements, which are defined during the requirements determination phase (Maciaszek, 2005). The content presented in the requirements statements is important for expressing static and dynamic relations among different concepts of a problem domain. The analysis of these concepts is critical as these concepts represent information of a problem domain and which are of the main interest (Gustafsson & Höglund, 2009).

The ontological principles developed by Bunge (Bunge, 1979) are important for understanding the rational of a core conceptual modeling construct in the SICM method. Bunge suggests that world is composed of things. Things can be composed into subsystems, which are viewed as interacting components. When two subsystems interact, they cause certain things to change. Changes to things are manifested via properties. Any subsystem can

be viewed as a passive object, but not every object can play role an active subsystem. According to the ontological principles of Bunge (Bunge, 1979), just interacting things (which cause objects to change) can be viewed as subsystems. It is quite beneficial to analyze interactions between subsystems for keeping the track of crosscutting concerns and for justification why a subsystem is useful. Interaction dependencies between two concepts indicate that these concepts should be interpreted as actors. An actor represents a collection of subsystems, which are characterized by the same set of rights, responsibilities and commitments. For example, the consequence of the Create Reservation event (se Figure 3) results in the commitment to provide a hotel room for a specific guest. By accepting the consequences of the Provide Hotel Room action, Room Guest enters into the commitment to Pay for the hotel.

Conceptual modeling focuses on representing certain aspects of human perceptions about things. Ontology distinguishes between concrete things and conceptual things (Wand et al., 2000). Concrete things are objects and systems. Every autonomous subsystem can be viewed as a system on its own. Objects may be either physical or conceptual. If object represents a set, it can only be a concept. Whether an object is an individual or a set is relatively unimportant. What is an individual in one context may become a set in another context and vice versa. Any system can be interpreted as an object, but not every object is a system. Two interacting subsystems can be viewed as an entirely new system. Possible interpretations of concepts in the SICM method are represented in Figure 4.

Actors are active concepts, which are characterized by interaction dependencies. Organizational actors can be represented by humans or by organizational subsystems, which are composed of humans. Technical actors are represented by artifacts of a physical world (software or hardware components). A concept can be passive and active at the same time. There is no clearly defined criterion for distinguishing between these

Figure 4. Interpretation of concepts

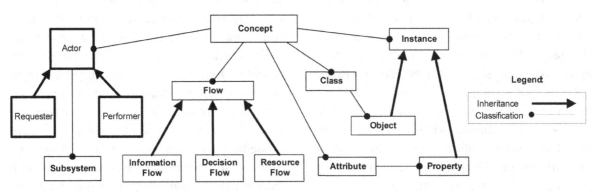

two types of modeling artifacts in conceptual modeling languages. Typically, passive concepts are represented by classes or entities, which are characterized by attributes, relationships and state changes. In the presented modeling approach, interactions between active concepts may affect instances of passive concepts. The interaction effects can be expressed by creation and termination actions, which describe structural changes in various classes of objects (Gustas, 2011a). An actor is a special instance of concept characterized by a unit of functionality, which is exposed to the environment. It depends on the privileges of an individual actor, what type of value or coordination flow he/it is entitled to initiate or to receive. In the DEMO theory (Dietz, 2006), initiators and executers are viewed as active elements, which are represented by individuals or subjects. In service-oriented approach, such actors are entitled as service requesters and service providers (Gustiene & Gustas, 2011). In the SICM method, we will refer to these actors correspondingly as requesters and performers. Any value flow typically requires initiation of some coordinating interactions, which are necessary for provision of value flows. The DEMO approach distinguishes between two kinds of actions: production acts and coordination acts. Coordination acts are normally initiated by requesters. Coordination acts are necessary to make commitment regarding the corresponding production act, which is supposed to bring a value flow

to service requester. Production acts are normally performed by performers. Therefore, they should be always associated with some value flows.

The behavioral and structural dimensions of interactions can be analyzed in terms of creation, reclassification and termination effects of communication actions. The internal changes of objects can be expressed by using transition links between various classes of objects. The reclassification of object is defined in terms of communication action that is terminating an object in one class and creating a new object in another class. Sometimes, objects may pass several classes, and then they are terminated. Graphical notation of the reclassification construct is graphically represented in Figure 5(a).

Unbroken arrows represent control flow of creation and termination events. Object classes may denote a persistent or transient set of objects. Fundamentally two kinds of changes are identified during any reclassification event: termination and creation of an object. A creation event is denoted by the outgoing transition arrow to an initial class. Graphical notation of the creation (◄——) construct is represented in Figure 5(b). A termination (——►) construct is represented by the transition dependency directed from a final class. Before an object can be terminated, it must be created. The graphical notation of the termination construct is represented in Figure 5(c).

Figure 5. Graphical representation of three types of modeling constructs

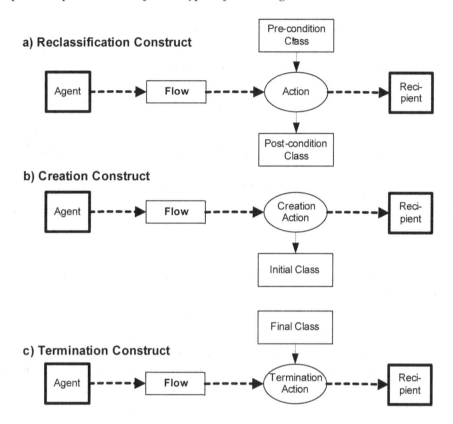

When two subsystems interact one may affect the state of each other (Evermann & Wand, 2009). Structural changes of objects can be defined in terms of object properties (Bunge, 1979). Any communication action typically prescribes manipulation of one or more objects. Otherwise, this action is not purposeful. Object property changes may trigger objects transitions from one class to another. Structural changes of objects are manifested via static and dynamic properties. Dynamic properties are represented as actions, which are connected to classes by the creation and termination links. Static properties of objects are represented by mandatory attributes. Both single-valued and multi-valued attribute dependencies denote static properties. Graphical notation of various cases of static dependencies is represented in Figure 6.

One significant difference in SICM is that the association ends of static relations are nameless. Motivation of such a way of modeling can be found in some other papers (Gustas, 2011a). Semantics of static dependencies is defined by cardinalities, which represent a minimum and maximum number of objects in one class (B) that can be associated to objects in another class (A). Single-valued dependency can be represent by the following cardinalities: $(0,1;1,1), (0,*;1,1)$ and $(1,1;1,1)$. Multi-valued dependency denotes either $(0,1;1,*)$ or $(1,1;1,*)$ cardinality. Static dependencies are not defined yet in the interaction diagram in Figure 3. Therefore, this diagram does not provide any semantic details about possible options of a control flow in which communication actions must be triggered. The diagram shows only interactive dependencies of a business scenario. Both interaction events and transitional effects

Figure 6. Notation of static dependencies

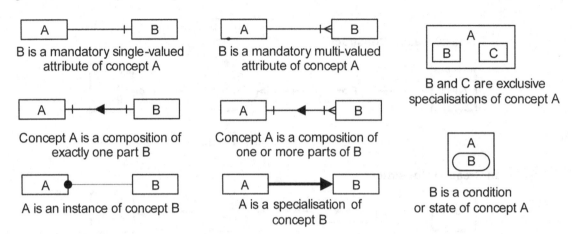

are necessary to describe the behavior fully. The actions such as Request Room, Create Reservation, Provide Hotel Room and Pay should also specify the acceptable ways for structural changes to occur in different classes of objects. For instance, Create Reservation event requires the creation of Hotel Reservation with the specific properties such as Identified (Logged-in) Customer and minimum one Reserved Hotel Room. Moreover, Create Reservation is a noteworthy event, which is terminating a Hotel Reservation Request with the property of Type of Room[Desirable]. Examples of one creation and one reclassification event are presented in Figure 7.

A simple interaction loop between requester and performer can be viewed as the basic construct of any communication process (Denning & Medina-Mora, 1995). In carrying out the work, a performer may in turn initiate further interactions. In this way, a network of the loosely coupled actors with various roles comes into interplay to fulfill the original service request. To put it in other terms, the interacting loops can be composed together into more complex interaction webs by using creation and termination actions. If the object transition effects cannot be conceptualized by using different pre-condition and post-condition class properties, then the communication action

Figure 7. Example of simple interaction loop

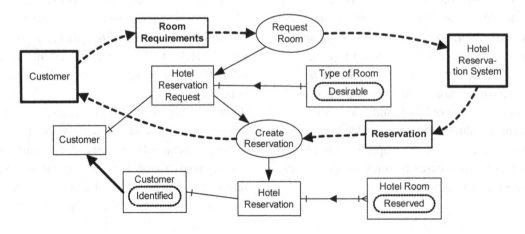

is not purposeful. Interaction dependencies with not purposeful actions are highly questionable. In SICM method (Gustas & Gustiene, 2012), simple interaction loops are used as a natural way for the separation of concerns in complex business scenarios. The network of loops thus can be interpreted as rights, responsibilities, obligations or claims among various actors involved in any business process. If such deontic elements are unclear or missing, then they may cause breakdowns in business scenarios. Modeling based on interactions facilitates control of business process continuity and semantic integrity. The identification of discontinuity is important as it helps to find breakdowns in IS specifications.

BASIC EVENTS OF INTERACTION-BASED APPROACHES

Interaction dependencies are extensively used in a foreground of enterprise engineering methods (Dietz, 2006). These methods are rooted in the interaction pattern analysis and the philosophy of language. The underlying idea of interaction pattern analysis can be explained by a well-known conversation for action schema (Winograd & Flores, 1986). The purpose of introducing this

schema was initially motivated by the idea of creating computer-based tools for conducting conversations. Our intention is to apply the interaction dependencies as they are defined by the SICM method in combination with conventional semantic relations, which are used in the area of system analysis and design. Interaction loops can be expressed by interplay of coordination or production events, which occur in a particular pattern. This pattern is represented in Figure 8.

The idea behind a conversation for action schema can be explained as turn-taking. Any service interaction pattern can be characterized by the same four types of main events:

1. Request,
2. Promise,
3. State and
4. Accept.

Requester (R) initiates a request (R:Request) action and then is waiting for a particular promise (P:Promise) or a service provision (P:State) action from Performer (P). Request, promise and acceptance are typical coordination actions, which are triggered by the corresponding types of basic events. Coordination events are always related to some specific production event. Both

Figure 8. Conversation for action schema (Winograd and Flores, 1986)

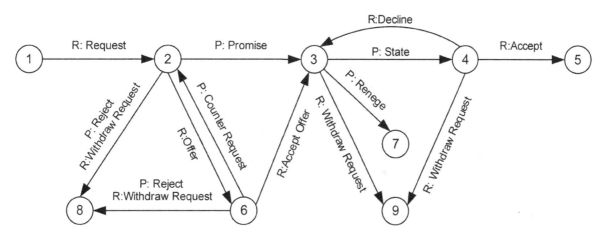

coordination and production events can be combined together into scenarios, which represent an expected sequence of interactions between requester and performer. We will show how creation, termination or reclassification constructs of the SICM method can be used to define the new facts, which result from the main types of events of the basic transaction pattern (Dietz, 2006). Four basic events and related reclassification effects are represented in Figure 9.

New facts resulting from four basic events are instantiated by such classes of objects as Request, Promise, Stated Result and Accepted Result. Two interaction loops between Requester and Performer of the basic transaction pattern are composed together. A promise is created in the first interaction loop. It can be consumed in the next interaction loop. Created or terminated objects and their properties can be interpreted as facts, which represent requests, promises and statements about delivered or accepted results. For instance, the Create Reservation action in Figure 3 can be

interpreted as a promise to Provide Hotel Room. Request Room and Create Reservation are typical coordination actions, which can be viewed as triggering events for a corresponding production action. For example, the sequence two different interaction loops can be defined as follows:

1. If Request Room(Customer ⸱⸱⸱➤ Hotel) then Provide Hotel Room(Hotel ⸱⸱⸱➤Customer).
2. If Provide Hotel Room(Hotel ⸱⸱⸱➤Room Guest) then Pay(Room Guest ⸱⸱⸱➤Hotel).

It is obvious from the presented example that the Provide Hotel Room business event is viewed as a production event. It creates effects, which can be associated with the transition P: State in the conversation schema (see Figure 8). Production event creates the new fact of Stated Result (see Figure 9). For example, the Provide Hotel Room business event can be analyzed as Hotel Room exchange for money. Production events are triggered by the resource exchange actions (Provide

Figure 9. The basic pattern of a transaction

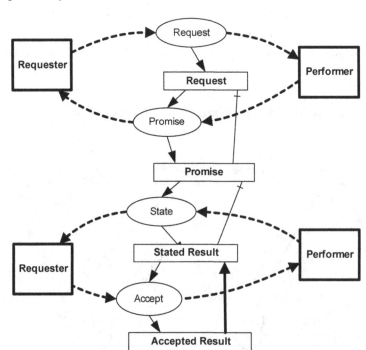

Hotel Room and Pay). According to the diagram in Figure 10, a Room Guest pays in the exchange to Hotel's service, which is represented by the action Provide Hotel Room. An assigned hotel room is supposed to create a value for a Room Guest. It is often the case in practice that the promise or acceptance actions are missing, because they are performed tacitly. For example, there is no explicitly represented acceptance action for the production action Provide Hotel Room and Pay in two interaction loops, which are presented in Figure 3 and 10.

The pattern, which was illustrated in Figure 13, defines the case when Requester and Performer are consenting to each other's communication actions. For a communication action to be successfully performed at least two conditions should be met:

1. A requester initiates the interaction flow by triggering a communication action,
2. A performer agrees to accept the interaction flow, which is generated by communication action.

Any enterprise system can be analyzed as the composition of autonomous interacting components, which may not necessarily consent with each other. Actors can be involved in various interaction loops for different purposes; because they want to get rid of problems or to achieve their goals. Analysis of goals, problems and opportunities (Gustas, 1998), (Gustas & Gustiene, 2008), (Horkoff & Yu, 2010), (Chopra et al., 2010) may help to understand why different actors act, react or not act at all. For instance, a requester may not be interested to initiate any interaction, or a performer may refuse to accept the interaction flow. There are many other alternative events, which may take place when one of two presented conditions is violated. Alternative actions can be introduced to handle possible breakdowns in the basic interaction pattern. These alternatives can be represented by such transitions as Reject, Withdraw Request, Offer, Decline in the conversation for action schema (see Figure 8). They are necessary for actors involved in the business process to deal with unexpected situations. For instance, a performer may fail to deliver a desired result on time.

MODELLING PATTERNS USING SICM METHOD

Analysis patterns are groups of concepts that represent common constructions in business model-

Figure 10. Two production actions in resource exchange between Room Guest and Hotel

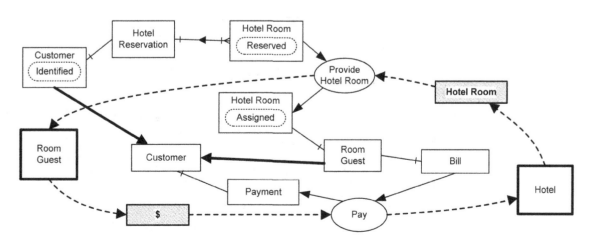

ing (Fowler, 1997). These patterns are similar to workflow patterns, which were established with the aim to define business process modeling on a recurring basis (Russell et al., 2006). Usually workflow patterns are defined using Business Process Modeling Notation (BPMN) (2004) for business process diagram and UML activity diagram from the Object Management Group (2009). The problem is that both notations are able to express process behavior, but do not take into account the static part (data) of the business process (Gustiene, 2010). It does not explicitly show what changes take place with the objects when some activity is processed. The analysis of the static and dynamic aspects of IS specifications separately creates fundamental difficulties in conceptual modeling of IS. If just dynamic aspects are taken into consideration, then the quantity of patterns increases and their usage becomes more complicated for business process change management. Verification of semantic integrity between business processes and business data in such a situation becomes very difficult. This leads to integrity problems, which imply semantic inconsistency and incompleteness of conceptual representations on various levels of abstraction. Integrated models should contribute to the process of validation and verification (Chester & Athwall, 2002).

Constructs based on SICM method were used for the construction of the following four analysis patters (Gustas & Gustiene, 2009) presented in this paper. The advantage of such constructs is that it combines the intersubjective and objective perspectives using just s single diagram type, which helps to place focus on the integration of static and dynamic aspects. Various combinations of the static and dynamic dependencies used are able to express the main workflow control patterns such as sequence, synchronization, selection, search and iteration. Comprehensibility and visual recognition of the fundamental patterns is necessary in constructing more specific pattern variations by composing them in different ways.

SEQUENCE PATTERN

The sequence pattern is defined by an ordered series of activities. One activity starts after a previous activity has completed. The sequence pattern can be defined by using a composition of two or more reclassification actions. Since a creation and termination action is a special case of reclassification, it can be used instead of a reclassification action. An example of a sequence pattern is represented in Figure 11.

Figure 11. Sequence pattern

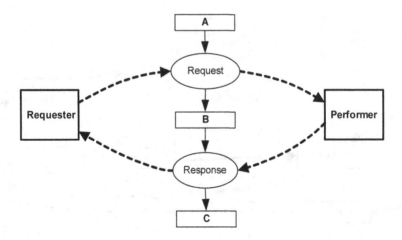

The example of this sequence pattern is presented in Figure 12.

In the presented example, the sequence of three creation actions is used to express the sequence pattern: *Send Bill*, *Pay*, and *Transfer Money*. *Pay* action can be executed only if *Send Bill* action has been completed and *Transfer Money* action can be processes only if the process of payment has been completed. The changes that take place with the objects present the static aspects of the system (objective perspective). When *Travel Agency* sends *Bill* to *Customer*, *Send Bill* action creates a new object *Reservation* in state [Bill Sent], which is a specialization of object Reservation, which was created in previous interaction loop. The object has two specific attributes: Reservation[Bill Sent] and Bill. When *Customer* gets bill and evokes the process of payment, action *Pay* creates a new object Reservation[Paid] with a specific attribute *Payment*. When *Bank* sends payment to *Travel*

Figure 12. Example of sequence pattern

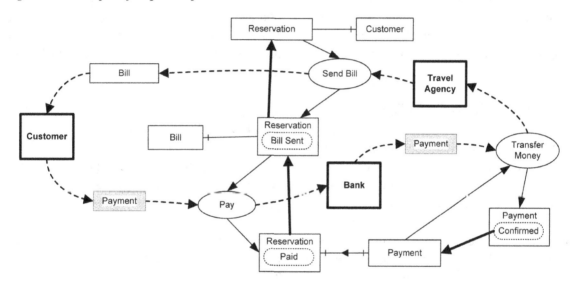

Figure 13. Synchronization pattern

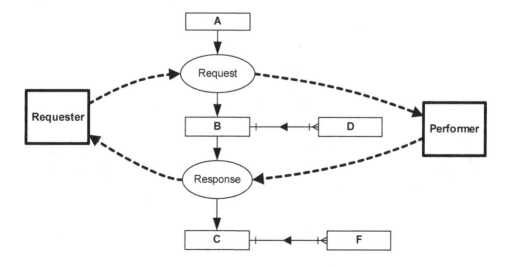

15

Agency evoking the process of *Transfer Money,* a new object Payment[Confirmed], which is a specialization of the object Payment (inheritance).

Every action is responsible for the removal of the attribute object links that are associated with the pre-condition class and for the creation of attribute object links with post-condition class. It cannot be responsible for any changes of object links of more general classes or for object links of the attributes. Creation, reclassification and removal of objects in more general classes, and in the attributes that are viewed as classes with their own attributes, should occur in an earlier sequence. For instance, for the *Send Bill* action to be triggered, a *Reservation* object is required to be created in advance by another service.

SYNCHRONIZATION PATTERN

Sometimes, some activities must be performed concurrently rather than serially. A synchronization pattern combines the path of these activities. It is important that the final set of activities be completed before the next process can continue. The synchronization pattern is presented in Figure 13.

This pattern illustrates that an action is responsible for the removal of object A and all its parts B. Creation of D requires the creation of at least one object of E. Compositional attribute objects must be created, reclassified or terminated by the same action, because a part and a whole have identical life cycles. If an object is created, then the links with the compositional part are created as well. If an object is deleted, then the links are deleted / disconnected at the same time. That is the reason why an action propagates according to the class composition links from a whole to a part and vice versa. Propagation of actions is a useful property, because it allows modeling synchronization in a natural way. The synchronization pattern example is illustrated in Figure 14.

Supply action propagates to parts: termination of *Order* and *Order Items*, and creation of *Delivery* and *Delivery Items*. *Food* (material flow) means the delivery of a set of items, which were *Order Items*.

SELECTION PATTERN

A Selection pattern can be expressed using a composition of two different sequences between the same two actors. The selection represents two alternative outcomes of a service request that can be selected by service provider. Two ways of replaying by service provider are mutually exclusive. Typically, only one type of response is desirable by requester. The selection pattern is represented graphically in Figure 15.

Figure 14. Example of synchronization pattern

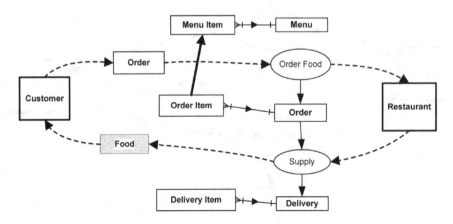

Figure 15. Selection pattern

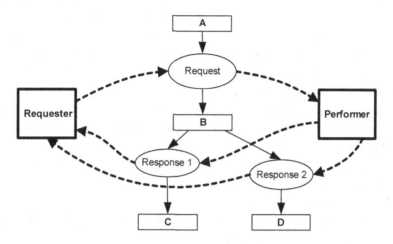

Note that Response 1 and Response 2 are exclusive. If Response 2 is triggered, then precondition class object B is removed and response 1 cannot be triggered and vice versa. The example of selection pattern is represented in Figure 16.

For instance, if *Person* (service requester) applies (*Apply*) for a job by sending application (*Application Data* flow) to *Company* (service provider), then *Company* has two alternatives to choose between: to employ a *Person* or reject an *Application*. The *Apply* action should create an *Application* object, which is associated to one *Applicant*. Every *Applicant* object can be composed of one or many applications. In the case of an *Employ* action, *Applicant* object should be reclassified to *Employee*. Otherwise, the *Reject* action should terminate *Application* object.

Figure 16. Example of selection pattern

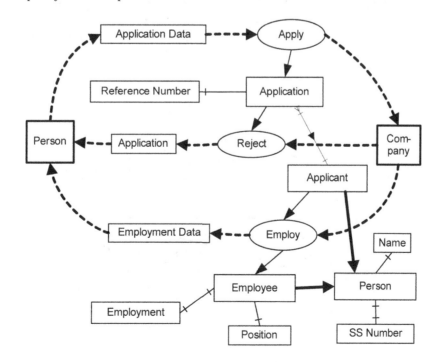

SEARCH PATTERN

A search pattern can be defined using a composition of sequence and iteration patterns. An iteration pattern with a missing pre-condition class for Request and post-condition class for response would express a special case of a search pattern, where a found object (B) is created and then consumed in a response action, which is presented for requester. A search pattern is represented graphically in Figure 17.

A post-condition of request action can be represented by using an exclusive specialization of two classes of objects (D and E), where depending on failure or success one of the objects will always be created. In the case of a failure, an object (D) is terminated by performer (Response 1) and search pattern can be again reiterated by requester. In case of a success, a requested object is found (E) and then reclassified by displaying it to a requester (Response 2). The object (C) is created. The example with search pattern is represented in Figure 18.

The search pattern in the presented example can be explained in the following way: the post-condition of *Request Flight* action is an exclusive specialization of two objects Flight Request[Not Fulfilled] and Flight Request [Fulfilled]. If the flight request was fulfilled, then the compositional

object of Flight[Found] was created and *Reservation* flow is sent to *Customer* by invoking operation *Create Reservation*. If the *Flight Request* was not fulfilled then the flow with rejected request is sent to the *Customer* by invoking operation *Reject Request*. In that case, the *Customer* has possibility to reiterate the search again. Note: The object of *Flight* will not be terminated in the case where the request was rejected, because it will be necessary in the next interaction loops.

ALTERNATIVE BEHAVIOR

The alternative actions are necessary to handle breakdowns in the basic pattern of a transaction. Actors representing autonomous subsystems act in different positions, which are driven by different set of goals. If coordination and production actions are triggered, they generate noteworthy events, which can be defined by creation, termination or reclassification effects in various classes of objects. We have already illustrated how turn-taking, which is prescribed by conversation for action schema, is expressed by composing two interaction loops into a sequence (see Figure 9). Requester (R) typically triggers request (R:Request) and then is waiting for a particular promise (P:Promise) or service response (P:State) from a Performer

Figure 17. Search pattern

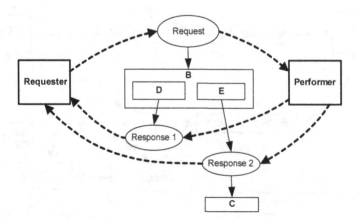

Figure 18. Example of search pattern

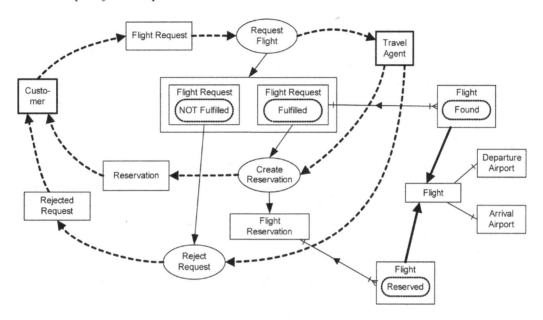

(P). However, a performer may dissent. Instead of promising or delivering requested product, a performer may respond by rejecting request. Some of possible alternatives are demonstrated in the conversation for action schema (see Figure 8). Various interaction alternatives between two actors can be also defined by interaction dependencies, which may produce different, similar or equivalent behavioral effects. Two dynamic properties, which represent the termination effects of concept A and the creation effects of concept B, are represented in Figure 19.

Graphical notation of two alternative termination actions is indicated in Figure 19(a). Graphical notation of two alternative creation actions is represented in Figure 19(b). Both actions are

exclusive. It means that termination of A or creation of B can be performed only once. Either Action1, or Action2 can be triggered. For instance, a performer may either promise (action1) or reject (action2) request (see Figure 21). Three different alternatives for handling a Hotel Reservation Request that are denoted by Create Reservation, Handle Waiting List and Reject Request actions are represented in Figure 20.

Create Reservation action is an event of the main, expected scenario. It can be performed successfully on a condition that Hotel Reservation is created. In case of failure, to compose the Hotel Reservation of at least one Hotel Room [Reserved], would cause a breakdown in the basic transaction pattern. Breakdowns require definition

Figure 19. Graphical notation for representation of alternative actions

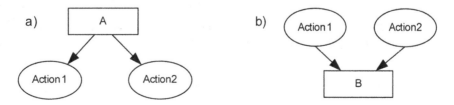

Figure 20. Three alternative ways of handling Hotel Reservation Request

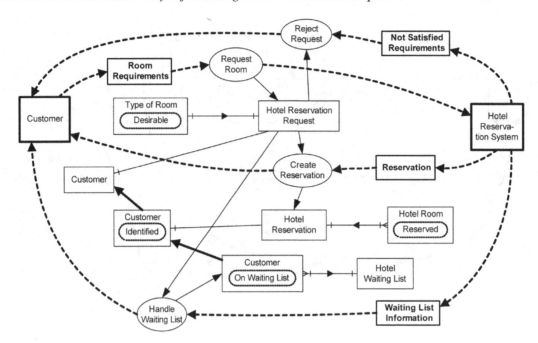

of the alternative events. The first alternative is represented by Handle Waiting List action, which defines the reclassification effects of Hotel Reservation Request object. The second alternative is termination of Hotel Reservation Request by Reject Request action. This option may be caused by a failure of the Handle Waiting List action. Please note that Customer [On Waiting List] object can be created just in case the Customer agrees to Accept Waiting in the underlying interaction loop (see more specific diagram in Figure 26). In our example, the condition of failure to Create Reservation can be specified by the underlying interaction loop (see next chapter).

A performer may experience difficulties in satisfying a request. For example, Hotel Reservation System may Reject Request, because it is simply incorrect or incomplete. Instead of promising, a performer may respond by rejecting request. Requester may also express disappointment in stated result and decline it. Decline is represented by the termination of Stated Result and creation of Declined Result object. For instance, the Hotel

Guest may decline the assigned hotel room, which was assigned by the Provide Hotel Room action. The basic transaction pattern can be complemented with two dissent patterns. This extended schema is known as the standard pattern (Dietz, 2006). Two described alternatives together with the basic transaction pattern are represented in Figure 21.

In practice, it is also common that either requester or performer is willing to completely revoke some events. For example, the requester may withdraw his own request. There are four cancellation patterns (Dietz, 2006), which may lead to partial or complete rollback of a transaction. Every cancellation action can be performed if the corresponding fact exists. For instance, the Withdraw Request action can be triggered, if a request was created by the Request action. In our previous example, Withdraw Request action is missing in Figure 12. Nevertheless, it is reasonable and should be introduced. For instance, Withdraw Reservation Request action can be added for the termination of a Hotel Reservation Request. Request cancellation event may be triggered when the customer finds a

Figure 21. The standard transaction pattern

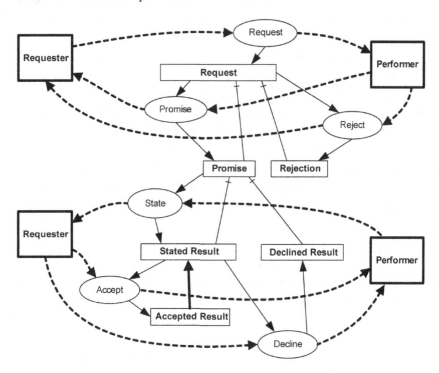

better or cheaper room alternative in another hotel. A Withdraw Promise action may take place if a Promise for some reason cannot be fulfilled by Performer. For instance, a Hotel Room was damaged by the former room guest. The requester may agree or disagree to accept the consequences of the Withdraw Promise action. It should terminate the Promise and to preserve the Request. The third cancellation event can be represented by the option Cancel Result. It should be initiated by Performer to avoid Decline action by the requester. The requester typically allows canceling result, because after this action the Promise is still not terminated. The forth cancellation event may take place when the whole transaction was completed, but the requester discovers some hidden problem and he regrets his acceptance. For instance, the customer may try to Cancel Acceptance of the Hotel Room for the reason that wireless Internet access is not working properly in his room. The possibility to superimpose four cancellation patters on the standard pattern is not the only advantage

of the presented modeling approach. The SICM method has sufficient expressive power to cover other special cases, which are not matching the standard pattern and four described cancellation patterns. For instance, it is unclear how the DEMO approach would cope with the Handle Waiting List alternative, which is represented in Figure 20. This option is also excessive in comparison with all legal transitions, which are defined by the conversation for action schema (Winograd & Flores, 1986).

MODELING SEQUENTIAL, ITERATIVE AND SYNCHRONIZED BEHAVIOR

Every interaction loop can be analyzed separately as it is required by the principle of separation of concerns. A simple interaction loop is viewed as a fundamental element for composition of scenarios. Interaction loops can be composed into more complex interaction webs. Therefore, interaction loops provide a natural way for separation of concerns. The interplay of static and dynamic aspects is crucial to understand a concern composition mechanism. Two dependent interaction loops can be interrelated by created or terminated objects of overlapping classes. Combining different interaction loops together is an excellent mean for analyzing integrity and continuity of interactions in complex business scenarios. Two interaction loops can be composed together to express sequential, alternative, iterative or synchronized behavior. In our studies, we identified five different ways of interaction loop composition: a) sequence, b) underlying, c) enclosing, d) overriding and e) overlaying. In this section, we will present the examples of sequence, underlying and enclosing loops. The cases of overlaying (Gustas, 2011b) and overriding will be demonstrated in the next section.

Interaction loops can be composed into a sequence when a created object in the first interaction loop is consumed in the second interaction loop. In some cases, requests and responses can

be delegated to more specific actors or their parts. For example, two interaction loops, which are presented in Figure 7 and 10, can be composed into a sequence, which is represented in Figure 22.

This diagram represents two interaction loops composed into a sequence between four different actors. Hotel Reservation System is part of a Hotel and Room Guest is a specialization of Customer. The Provide Hotel Room action consumes Hotel Room[Reserved] object, which is part of the Hotel Reservation. The corresponding Reservation object must be created in the previous interaction loop (see Create Reservation action). The Provide Hotel Room action also creates a Hotel Room[Assigned] object with the property of Room Guest. A preliminary Bill object must be generated for every Room Guest. The Bill object is consumed in the Pay action, which is necessary for creation of Payment. According to the presented diagram, the second interaction loop can be reiterated more than once, because Hotel Reservation is defined as composition of one or more Hotel Room[Reserved]. Each reserved hotel room can be assigned to a different room guest.

Figure 22. Sequence of two interaction loops

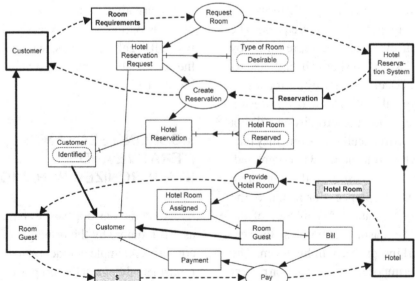

The primary interaction loop can be composed of the more specific loop on a lower level of granularity. In this case, the interaction loop on a lower layer of decomposition is viewed as an underlying interaction loop. Execution of the underlying loop must be synchronized with the primary interaction loop. Example of an underlying interaction loop is represented in Figure 23.

In this example, the underlying loop is superimposed with the Create Reservation action from the primary interaction loop, which is represented in Figure 18. The underlying interaction loop describes Customer's response to Hotel Reservation System's request. If customer expects to receive Reservation flow from the Hotel Reservation System, it is necessary for him to reply to the service request from the technical component in the underlying loop. The request and reply in the underlying loop is specified as follows:

If Offer Rooms (Hotel Reservation System ⋯→ Customer),

then Select Room(Customer ⋯→ Hotel Reservation System).

The actions of underlying loop are synchronized with the primary interaction loop. According to the presented description, Create Reservation is reclassification action, which is composed of Select Room and Offer Rooms actions on the lower granularity level. The Select action cannot be triggered prior to Offer Rooms action. Select action can be performed several times for each Hotel Room[Available]. The Create Reservation action is synchronized with the Select action, which is supposed to create such parts as Hotel Room[Reserved] of the compositional object Hotel Reservation. So, the underlying loop is necessary for offering available rooms, selection of desirable rooms and providing necessary data about the expected room guest. In this example, the object creation and reclassification effects represent the important semantic details of unambiguous scenario in which two interaction loops are composed together.

Enclosing one loop into another is similar to inclosing of a transaction (Dietz, 2006). The main element of enclosing is a primary interaction loop between requester and performer. In carry-

Figure 23. Synchronized underlying interaction loop

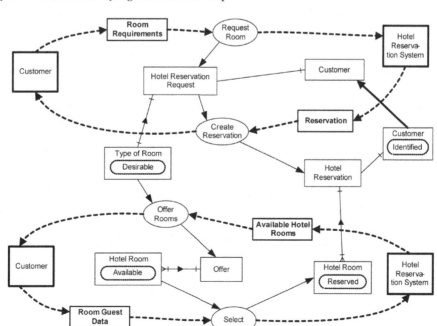

ing out the work, a performer may play the role of requester in the secondary interaction loop by initiating further interactions. In this way, a network of loosely coupled actors with various roles comes into interplay to fulfill the original service request. Organizational systems may be composed of several interaction loops, which are delegated to more specific components. For example, the Hotel may implement the Provide Hotel Room action (see Figure 22) by delegating Check-in and Check-out functionality to its parts such as Hotel Counter Staff (organizational component) and Hotel Reception System (software component). If Room Guest is willing to Check-in, he needs to Present Reservation to the Hotel Counter Staff. The Room Guest is also able to provoke the Check-out event from a Hotel Reception System by triggering the Return Key action. There are two enclosing and two secondary enclosed interaction loops, which are represented in Figure 24.

The primary interaction loop between Room Guest and Hotel Counter Staff encloses the second interaction loop between the Hotel Counter Staff and Hotel Reception System. It is necessary for checking in the reserved room and assigning it to the Room Guest. This is done by creating Hotel Room[Assigned] object and connecting it with the Room Guest and Bill objects. The enclosed loop on the top corresponds to a computerized process, which creates Hotel Room[Assigned] object. The third interaction loop between Room Guest and Hotel Counter Staff on the bottom encloses the fourth interaction loop between the Hotel Counter Staff and the computerized Hotel Reception System. It is necessary for finding an assigned hotel room and reclassifying it to Hotel Room[Empty]. It is not difficult to see that Check-out is enclosing Find Assigned Room and Release Room actions, which terminate Hotel Room[Assigned] object prior to termination of Room Guest object. So,

Figure 24. Two enclosing interaction loops

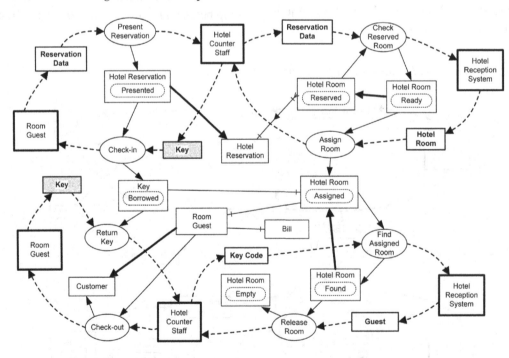

basically the manual Check-out event is composed of two enclosed events, which are triggered during the interaction with a Hotel Reception System.

CASE STUDY EXAMPLE: INTERPLAY BETWEEN GRAPHICAL SCENARIOS TO USE CASE DIAGRAM

Interaction loops consisting of coordinating interactions or separate production actions can be used as a mechanism for the separation of concerns in complex business process scenarios. In this section, we will demonstrate how various fragments of diagrams of the presented case study can be interpreted as the conceptual representations of use-case scenarios. In practice, use-case descriptions are written by using a natural language text (Cockborn, 2000), (Dennis, et al., 2010). Consequently they are translated into use-case diagrams. A use-case description is supposed to contain all necessary information for building UML diagrams. The problem is that the narrative text, which defines the flow of events, can be ambiguous, incomplete and inconsistent with the remaining concurrently defined use-case descriptions. The verification of semantic consistency between different business scenarios, which are written by using a natural language text, is extremely

difficult. So, instead of using a narrative text for specification of use-case scenarios, we replace it by conceptual representations, which are defined by a number of interaction loops.

We analyze slightly modified scenario, which was presented by Jacobson and Ng (Jacobson & Ng, 2005). Our initial focus is on the business scenario, which is represented in Figure 22. Its functionality can be captured by using one use-case diagram. In practice, a separate use-case diagram can be developed for representing interactions between human actors and one autonomous computerized subsystem. The primary coordinating loop in this business scenario (see Figure 7) can be considered as a separate use-case, which is represented by the Reserve Room use-case in Figure 25. Each production action, such as Provide Hotel Room and Pay, denote separate transactions as well. So, they can be viewed as two separate use-cases, which, in our case study, exclusively represent functionality of a technical system.

The more precise scenario of the Reserve Room use-case is represented in Figure 25. It also contains the underlying sub-flow of the expected scenario, which demonstrates the normal flow of events. The Offer Rooms action can be performed successfully if and only if one or more desirable rooms are available. The possibility of failure to create an Offer with at least one Hotel

Figure 25. Use-case diagram

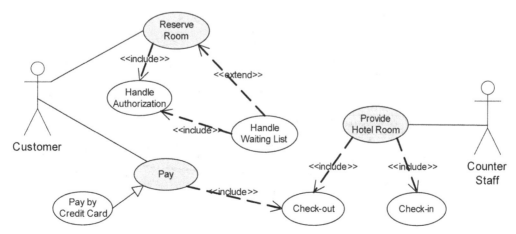

Room[Available] requires definition of the alternate flow of events, which is represented by the Handle Waiting List action in Figure 20. The alternative scenario is represented by the extension use-case. It is triggered when the desired type of room is not available. The extension use case must have a reference to some extension point indicating when the extension use-case flow will be inserted. The alternative scenario, which defines the Handle Waiting List use-case, is represented in Figure 26. Please note that the Reserve Room and Handle Waiting List are linked by <<extend>> relations, which indicate the existence of an extension flow in the Reserve Room use-case.

Handle Waiting List action is synchronized with the underlying loop, which consists of two more specific actions such as Offer Waiting List and Accept Waiting. It means that the Handle Waiting List use-case extends the Reserve Room

use-case when at least one Room[Available] cannot be created in the composed Offer, because a desirable hotel room is not available. In this case Type of Room[NOT Available] object can be created, which preserves from the termination (see inheritance) properties of desirable type of room in the Hotel Reservation Request. Reject Request is the third alternative (see Figure 20). This option may be caused by a failure of the Handle Waiting List action, because the Customer[On Waiting List] object cannot be created. Please note that Customer[On Waiting List] can be created just in case a Customer agrees to Accept Waiting. If Customer triggers the Reject Waiting action, then this object is not created and the Handle Waiting List action in the primary loop will fail.

Joint points are useful for the specification of overlaying interaction loops that must be included across many different scenarios. One example

Figure 26. Alternate flow of events with the underlying interaction loop

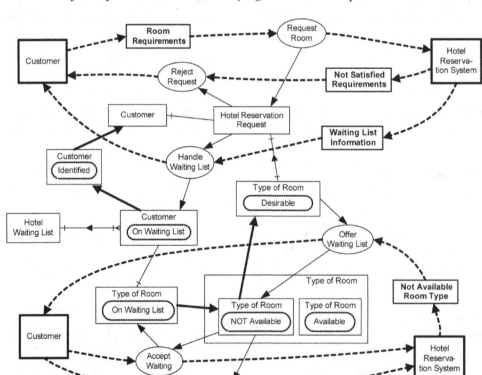

of such interaction loop is represented by the handle authorization use-case. Please note that the Handle Authorization use-case is connected by <<include>> relation to Reserve Room use-case as well to Handle Waiting List use-case. Creation of object properties in the dependent classes or creation of objects in the more general classes can be understood as such joint points for inclusion of the mandatory sub-flows, which must be executed across different scenarios. The authorization sub-flow in the Handle Authorization use-case must be inserted into the main flow of events of two different scenarios such as Handle Waiting List and Reserve Room. It is necessary for creation of Customer[Identified] object. The semantics of the authorization flow is defined by one overlaying interaction loop, which is defined in Figure 27.

The overlaying interaction loop (Handle Authorization) is synchronized with the creation of Customer[Identified] object. According to the presented diagram, the creation of

Customer[Identified] object can take place prior to creation of the Hotel Reservation object as well. It is also possible to say that the Handle Waiting List use-case is overlaid with the Handle Authorization flow of events, because the creation of Customer[On Waiting List] object takes place during the execution of the alternative flow of events, which are represented by the Handle Waiting List action (see Figure 26). Customer[Identified] class represents a subset of logged in customers. Since objects of this class are required to be created in two different scenarios, the Customer[Identified] class is viewed as a joint point. These two alternative scenarios require the Handle Authorization use-case to be completed. In aspect-oriented software development (Jacobson & Ng, 2005), the notion of point cut is similar to the alternatives in the SICM method. Alternatives are useful for the identification of extension flows. The <<extend>> relation is typically specified in use-case diagrams for the representation of extension points.

Figure 27. Overlaying Reserve Room with the Handle Authorization interaction loop

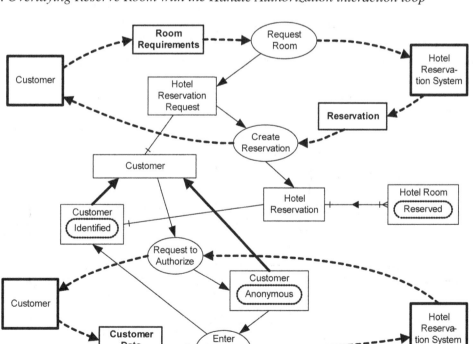

Extension flows of use-case scenarios correspond to the alternative interaction loops. The overlays are similar to joint points in aspect-oriented software development.

Up till now, we haven't explained the fifth case of interaction loop composition, which was entitled to as overriding. More specific interaction loops, which represent finer granularity interactions, may override more generic interaction loops. Overriding helps designers to introduce more specific details by refining conceptual representations of scenarios on the more generic levels of abstraction. Overriding loops can be defined by introducing the more specific communication actions, which are consistent with the communication actions in more abstract interaction loop. Consistent communication action terminates or creates at least one object of more specific class. For example, Provide Hotel Room action in the resource exchange in-teraction loop (see Figure 10) can be overridden by four more specific interaction loops, which are represented in Figure 24. Two enclosing interaction loops, which specify the Check-in and Check-out use-cases, are linked to some complimentary classes of objects such as Reservation[Presented], Hotel Room[Ready], Key[Borrowed], etc. They represent the more specific static properties of pre-condition and post-condition classes in the Provide Hotel Room action (Hotel Room[Assigned] and Hotel Room[Reserved]). So, these two enclosing interaction loops are consistent with Provide Hotel Room action. The second example of overriding is represented by Pay by Credit Card action, which is represented in Figure 28.

Pay by Credit Card action on the lower level of decomposition can be also viewed as a consistent alternative to the Pay (in cash) action. It is used to reclassify Bill into Credit Card Payment. Since

Figure 28. Overriding Pay action with the interaction loop on the lower level of abstraction

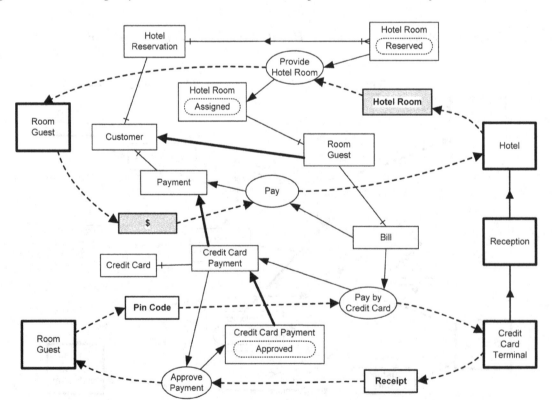

Bill is a property of Room Guest, the termination of Bill object is causing termination of Room Guest and his Hotel Room[Assigned]. The Room Guest termination is represented by Check-out action in Figure 24. This action is synchronized with a computerized interaction loop, which can be used to understand the semantics of Check-out use-case. Check-out is necessary for finding an assigned hotel room and reclassifying it to Hotel Room[Empty]. It encloses Find Assigned Room event and Release Room event, which terminate Hotel Room[Assigned] object prior to termination of Room Guest object. So, the action Pay, which can be overridden with Pay by Credit Card action, also includes the Check-out action (see Figure 25). It should be noted that the semantic power of UML diagrams is insufficient for combining such semantic details of manual and computerized flows of events. Parallel, sequential, exclusive or iterative use case behavior can be specified by using UML activity diagrams, but normally this type of specification is not associated with use case diagrams. It creates difficulties in detection discontinuities and inconsistencies in conceptual representations of business scenarios, because the knowledge on interaction loop composition is difficult to visualize in UML.

CONCLUSION

Different business scenarios can be conceptualized by identifying the essential business events, which are expressed as a set of interactions between organizational or technical components. Separation of crosscutting concerns by decomposing conceptual representations of scenarios into simple interaction loops suggests a flexible way for introducing evolutionary extensions to meet evolving needs of stakeholders. We have demonstrated the main principles of semantically integrated conceptual modeling approach (SICM), which allows designers to construct scenarios in a more comprehensible way. The way of model-

ing built on interaction loops can be gradually enhanced or replaced on demand on the lower levels of decomposition.

In this paper, we have demonstrated how SICM method was used for creation of constructs the advantage of which is that these constructs enables visualization and integration of static and dynamic aspects across organizational and technical system boundaries. It was also demonstrated how the expressive power of static and dynamic aspects is sufficient for defining four modeling patterns such as sequence, selection, synchronization and search.

Traditionally, system designers focus on business use-case modeling. A use case is described in computation-free terminology. Initial use-case descriptions are specified by using natural language text, which can be ambiguous, incomplete and inconsistent. We have demonstrated a graphical way for defining scenarios by integrating interactive, behavioral and structural aspects of information systems (IS) conceptualizations. In this paper, we presented the case study examples in which complex use-case scenario specifications were replaced by the graphical conceptual representations. It was also demonstrated how scenario flows, sub-flows and alternate flows of software and business processes can be composed together. Sequences, underlying, enclosing, overriding and overlaying interaction loops between actors provide the foundation for composition of complex scenarios.

Conventional conceptual modeling methods are developed for the analysis of business processes and business data in isolation. In this situation, it is difficult to achieve the semantic integration of static and dynamic aspects when several crosscutting concerns are combined together. Inability to detect integrity problems among concerns in early system development stages is one source of errors in IS specifications. In the software engineering community, many scholars believe in use-case-driven approach as a technique for the separation of crosscutting concerns, since the realization of use cases touches several classes. Nevertheless, it is very difficult to integrate concerns by using use case diagrams, because the static and dynamic aspects of the system are not presented in use cases.

Interaction dependencies, which define the interplay of coordination or production events, are lying in the foreground of the presented SICM method. It was demonstrated how interaction dependencies can be analyzed in interplay with the traditional semantic relations in the area of system analysis and design. An enterprise system is defined as the composition of autonomous interacting components, which may not necessarily consent with each other. Possible breakdowns in the basic pattern of a transaction can be avoided by designing the alternative interaction loops. Alternatives help designers to meet evolving needs of stakeholders. It was demonstrated how the standard transaction pattern can be used for reasoning about the conceptual representations of scenarios. The predefined communication patterns provide a strong foundation for the developing of conceptual models with a more comprehensible structure. The networks of interaction loops may span several organizations, partnerships or alliances. If the alternative scenarios are not designed into the system, it increases working overload and give rise to customer complaints. Breakdowns in scenarios, which define software processes, can be viewed as hidden requirement defects. Such incomplete requirements may accidentally inject new defects. Unexpected breakdowns in business process scenarios may interfere with organizational goals.

The expressive power of most conventional information system design methodologies is insufficient for defining interaction dependencies, which are crucial for capturing the deontic features of conceptual models. In this paper, it was demonstrated how to integrate non-traditional DEMO constructs with the structural and behavioral aspects of conceptual models. Various types of UML diagrams are difficult to integrate in a straightforward way. Structural analysis methods provide some possibilities for modeling components, data flows and processes on different levels of decomposition, but resulting hierarchies are becoming clumsy. The alternative flows of events are typically difficult to capture in the traditional IS modeling approaches, the principles for separation of crosscutting concerns are unclear. We have demonstrated various examples of sequential, iterative, parallel and alternative behavior by composing interaction loops in different ways. Keeping interaction loops separate helps designers to analyze complex scenarios. If concerns cannot be separated in terms of basic interaction loops, the complexity of a system analysis and design task increases exponentially. Separate concerns, which are expressed by the semantically integrated conceptual models, are much easier to understand, extend and maintain. The SICM method provides a comprehensible and constructive way to conceptualize systems, because it is rooted in the philosophy of system thinking, where a system maintains its existence through the interactions of its subsystems.

Our future research ambition is to apply the SICM method for systematic modeling of privacy enhancement and security assurance mechanisms (Gustas & Gustiene 2013). Since security and privacy enhancement mechanisms must be designed into the enterprise system, the new method should provide integration of interactive, behavioral and structural aspects of system conceptualizations, which are critical for personal data analysis (Weber & Gustiené, 2013). Data cannot be analyzed separately not taken into account the processes that cause the changes of data. This is especially relevant for management of such fundamental principle of privacy as data minimization as well as for other principles such as data life cycle management and privacy assurance and negotiation.

REFERENCES

Blaha, M., & Rumbaugh, J. (2005). *Object-Oriented Modeling and Design with UML*. Pearson.

Boman, M., Bubenko, J., Johannesson, P., & Wangler, B. (1997). *Conceptual Modeling*. New York: Prentice-Hall.

Booch, G., Rumbaugh, J., & Jacobson, I. (1999). *The Unified Modeling Language User Guide*. Addison Wesley Longman, Inc.

BPMN. (2004). *Business Process Modelling Notation*. Retrieved June 9, 2009, from http://www.bpmn.org

Bunge, M. A. (1979). Treatise on Basic Philosophy, vol. 4, Ontology II: A World of Systems. Reidel Publishing Company.

Chester, M., & Athwall, A. (2002). *Basic Information Systems Analysis and Design*. London: McGraw-Hill.

Chopra, A. K., Mylopoulos, J., Dalpiaz, F., Giorgini, P., & Singh, M. P. (2010). Requirements as Goals and Commitments Too. In *Intentional Perspectives on Information System Engineering*. Springer. doi:10.1007/978-3-642-12544-7_8

Cockburn, A. (2000). *Writing Effective Use Cases*. Addison-Wesley Professional.

Denning, P. J., & Medina-Mora, R. (1995). Completing the Loops. *Interfaces*, *25*, 42–57. doi:10.1287/inte.25.3.42

Dennis, A., Wixom, B. H., & Tegarden, D. (2010). *Systems Analysis and Design with UML* (3rd ed.). Wiley.

Dietz, J. L. G. (2006). *Enterprise Ontology: Theory and Methodology*. Springer. doi:10.1007/3-540-33149-2

Dori, D. (2002). *Object-Process Methodology: A Holistic System Paradigm*. Springer. doi:10.1007/978-3-642-56209-9

Evermann, J., & Wand, Y. (2009). Ontology Based Object-Oriented Domain Modeling: Representing Behavior. *Journal of Database Management*, *20*(1), 48–77. doi:10.4018/jdm.2009010103

Ferrario, R., & Guarino, N. (2008). Towards an Ontological Foundation for service Science. In *Proceedings of First Future Internet Symposium*. Vienna, Austria: Springer.

Fowler, M. (1997). *Analysis Patterns: Reusable Object Models*. Menlo Park, CA: Addison-Westley.

Gane, C., & Sarson, T. (1979). *Structured System Analysis*. Prentice Hall.

Glinz, M. (2000). Problems and Deficiencies of UML as a Requirements Specification Language. In *Proc. of the 10-th International Workshop on Software Specification and Design*. Academic Press.

Gordijn, J., Akkermans, H., & van Vliet, H. (2000). Business Process Modeling is not Process Modeling. [LNCS]. *Proceedings of Conceptual Modeling for E-Business and the Web*, *1921*, 40–51. doi:10.1007/3-540-45394-6_5

Gustafsson, J., & Höglund, J. (2009). The Common Model of an Enterprise's Value Objects: Presented in Relevant Business Views. In A. Persson & J. Stirna (Eds.), Lecture Notes in Business Information Processing: Vol. 39: The Practice of Enterprise Modeling: Second IFIP WG 8.1 Working Conference, PoEM 2009, (pp. 23-37). New York: Springer.

Gustas, R. (1998). Integrated Approach for Modelling of Semantic and Pragmatic Dependencies of Information Systems. In *Proceedings of 17th International Conference on Conceptual Modeling (ER'98)*. Singapore: Springer.

Gustas, R. (2010a). A Look behind Conceptual Modeling Constructs in Information System Analysis and Design. *International Journal of Information System Modeling and Design, 1*(1), 79–108. doi:10.4018/jismd.2010092304

Gustas, R. (2010b). Conceptual Modeling and Integration of Static and Dynamic Aspects of Service Architectures. In *Proceedings of International Workshop on Ontology, Conceptualization and Epistemology for Information Systems, Software Engineering and Service Sciences*. Hammamet, Tunisia: Springer.

Gustas, R. (2011a). Modeling Approach for Integration and Evolution of Information System Conceptualizations. *International Journal of Information System Modeling and Design, 2*(1), 45–73. doi:10.4018/jismd.2011010103

Gustas, R. (2011b). *Overlaying Conceptualizations for Managing Complexity of Scenario Specifications*. Paper presented at the IFIP WG8.1 Working Conference on Exploring Modeling Methods for Systems Analysis and Design. London, UK.

Gustas, R., & Gustiene, P. (2008). Pragmatic-Driven Approach for Service-Oriented Analysis and Design. In *Information Systems Engineering - from Data Analysis to Process Networks*. IGI Global. doi:10.4018/978-1-59904-567-2.ch005

Gustas, R., & Gustiene, P. (2009). Service-Oriented Foundation and Analysis Patterns for Conceptual Modelling of Information Systems. In C. Barry, K. Conboy, M. Lang, G.Wojtkowski, & W. Wojtkowski (Eds.), *Information Systems Development: Towards a Service Provision Society: Proceedings of the 17th International Conference on Information System Development* (ISD2008), (pp. 157-165). New York: Springer.

Gustas, R., & Gustiene, P. (2012). Conceptual Modeling Method for Separation of Concerns and Integration of Structure and Behavior. *International Journal of Information System Modeling and Design, 3*(1), 48–77. doi:10.4018/jismd.2012010103

Gustiené, P. (2010). *Development of a New Service-Oriented Modelling Method for Information Systems Analysis and Design*. (Doctoral Thesis). Karlstad University Studies.

Gustiene, P., & Gustas, R. (2011). Modeling Method for Bridging Pragmatic and Semantic Dimensions of Service Architectures. In *Proceedings of International Conference on Information System Development*. Springer.

Gustiene, P., & Gustas, R. (2013). A Method for Data Minimization in Personal Information Sharing. In D. Mouromtsev, C. Pchenichniy, & D. Ignatov (Eds.), *Proceedings of the MSEPS 2013 (Modeling States, Events, Processes and Scenarios) Workshop associated with the 20th International Conference on Conceptual Structures* (pp. 33-34). Mumbai, India: ICCS. Retrieved from http://iccs2013.hbcse.tifr.res.in/workshops/copy_of_text.pdf

Hammer, M. (1990). Reengineering work: Don't Automate, Obliterate. *Harvard Business Review*, 104–112.

Harel, D. (1987). Statecharts: A Visual Formalism for Complex Systems. *Science of Computer Programming, 8*, 231–274. doi:10.1016/0167-6423(87)90035-9

Horkoff, J., & Yu, E. (2010). Interactive Analysis of Agent-Goal Models in Enterprise Modeling. *International Journal of Information System Modeling and Design, 1*(4). doi:10.4018/jismd.2010100101

Jacobson, I., & Ng, P.-W. (2005). *Aspect-Oriented Software Development with Use Cases*. Pearson Education.

Jones, C. (2009). Positive and Negative Innovations in Software Engineering. *International Journal of Software Science and Computational Intelligence*, *1*(2), 20–30. doi:10.4018/jssci.2009040102

Maciaszek, L. (2005). *Requirements Analysis and System Design: Developing Information Systems with UML*. London: Addison-Wesley.

Martin, J., & Odell, J. J. (1995). *Object-Oriented Methods: A Foundation*. Prentice-Hall.

OMG. (2010). *Unified Modeling Language Superstructure, version 2.2*. Retrieved January 19, 2010, from www.omg.org/spec/UML/2.2/

Russell, N., Hofstede, A. H. M., Aalst, W. M. P., & Mulyar, N. (2006). *Workflow Control-Flow Patterns: A Revised View* (BPM Centre Report BPR-06-22). Retrieved September 11, 2008, from http://www.workflowpatterns.com/documentation/documents/BPM-06-22. pdf

Wagner, G. (2003). The Agent-Object-Relationship Metamodel: Towards Unified View of State and Behaviour. *Information Systems*, *28*(5). doi:10.1016/S0306-4379(02)00027-3

Wand, Y., Storey, V., & Weber, R. (2000). An Ontological Analysis of the Relationship Construct in Conceptual Modeling. *ACM Transactions on Database Systems*, *24*(4), 494–528. doi:10.1145/331983.331989

Weber, S. G., & Gustiené, P. (2013). Crafting Requirements for Mobile and Pervasive Emergency Response based on Privacy and Security by Design Principles. *International Journal of Information Systems for Crisis Response and Management*, *5*(2), 1–18. doi:10.4018/jiscrm.2013040101

Wieringa, R. (2008). Operational Business-IT Alignment in Value Webs. In *Proceedings of 2-nd International United Information Systems Conference UISCON*. Springer.

Wieringa, R., & Gordijn, J. (2005). Value-Oriented Design of Service Coordination Processes: Correctness and Trust. In *Proc. of the 20-th ACM Symposium on Applied Computing*. ACM Press.

Winograd, T., & Flores, R. (1986). *Understanding Computers and Cognition: A New Foundation for Design*. Norwood, NJ: Ablex.

Yourdon, E., & Constantine, L. L. (1979). *Structured Design*. Prentice Hall.

Zachman, J. A. (1987). A Framework for Information System Architecture. *IBM Systems Journal*, *26*(3). doi:10.1147/sj.263.0276

Chapter 2
Founding a Field Theory of Work:
Re-Organization through Energy Exchange

Raymon R. Bruce
Embry-Riddle Aeronautical University, USA & University of Electrical Systems and Technology of China, China

ABSTRACT

This chapter traces the origin of the concept of work in five staged sections. The first section examines the question, what is work? Work originally referred to "doing," that is, work organization, synergy, and energy. The second section develops the Greek word family for work into a dynamic model of doing. The third section shows how nature guides working change through energy exchange. It examines how a work as re-organization model would function in nature's jurisdictional domain of guiding energy exchanges. Nature's laws provide guidance for self-governing latitude to energy jurisdictional domains' evolutionary change. The fourth section examines policymaking as human guidance imitating nature. Policymaking limits individual self-governance to guide a specified social community of people (polis) doing work. Policymaking is explored to see how humans use policymaking to govern themselves and their cultural social groups including governments by using nature's use of laws as guidance. Policymaking is also a form of laying down basic parameters of work as re-organization through energy exchanges in the ambient environment. Policies are human artifacts designed help a social group work well together. Part five presents an issue analysis as an invited Organization Development consultant to help find ways for the Sri Lankan government, the University of Moratuwa, and the apparel and textile industry to work together in their extreme makeover of human resource development of their apparel and textile industry. Action training and research, stakeholder management, and wicked problem issue analysis are the organization development methods used to demonstrate this field theory of work re-organization through energy exchange.

DOI: 10.4018/978-1-4666-6098-4.ch002

INTRODUCTION

Whenever physicists get together, they discuss the big questions of physics. (Robert D. Behn, 1995)

We often think that when we have completed our study of one, we know all about two, because 'two' is 'one and one'. We forget that we still have to make a study of 'and'. Secondary physics is the study of 'and' – that is to say, of organization. (S. A. Eddington, 1958)

This chapter proposes a field theory of work as re-organizing energy resources is founded upon the notion that the universe is fundamentally oscillating energy exchange in all its various forms. The paper examines how the appearance of life has adapted Nature's various jurisdictional domains of to evolve along Jay Gould's Pathways of Life for nearly four billion years ago on earth to what is now referred to as the Tree of Life. Finally, the paper examines how humans can be self-governed free energy agents of change by imitating and adapting Nature's guidance model of oscillating energy exchanges described here as duty~cycles to develop and govern their complex cultures.

The paper traces a notion of the work for work back to its origins in the Proto-Indo-European (PIE) culture root language. There we find their PIE Root to be *wĕrg*, meaning: doing. Later the early Greek culture used this PIE root to express a word family of their concepts of (er*gáths*) a worker or agent, (*ergon*); work to be done, (*organon*); tools, instruments, and resources for doing work (*energeia*); and (*synergeia*) for the work outcome. (Partridge, 1958) An example of how these words in Greek relate in the work of Ctesibius' Hydraulic Musial wind instrument, *organon hydraulis* (285–222 BC) These concepts are traced through various PIE family languages to resulting in forms such as work organization, synergy, and energy.

Work as Re-Organization model is analyzed as how it might function in Nature's jurisdictional guidance of its domain of energy. Primarily the

laws of Nature' serve as guides as to how energy can be exchanged in a number of energy jurisdictional domains within Nature. Jurisdictional domain is used here to refer to the extent something or someone has potential capacity to influence change in inter-reacting with the environment. For Nature's jurisdictional domain it is the universe. However, Energy can be said to have jurisdictional domains where its ability to be exchanged may vary. Energy's jurisdictional domains are identified for the purposes of this paper as: cosmic; atomic and sub atomic particles; molecules; organisms, and humans. All energy jurisdictional domains are guided to conform to Nature's base laws of thermodynamics. It could be better name those as laws of ergo-dynamics since *thermo* properly refers only to heat energy. The use of law as guidance is also examined as not explicit absolute directions, but limits that they cannot be safely ignored for long. In other words, there is always room for temporary freedom for doing something a little differently.

People have adapted Nature's guidance model from the need and capacity for doing work to re-organize resources for themselves and for their cultures in order to sustain their lives and communities. Meeting peoples' needs requires them to re-organize the organization of their resources around them, including themselves, in working together to achieve their needed life outcomes. People create jurisdictional rule domains as artifacts to guide individuals and social groups to self-manage their behavior in their evolving cultures.

What is culture? Culture has acquired many meanings. In ancient times Cicero used culture as an agrarian metaphor that related civilization to the cultivation of the inter-reactions between our organic and our rational intellect. In our modern time, Cris Argyris describes it as the dynamic between one's espoused theory of action verses one's enacted theory of action (Argyris, 1997). The crux of the dilemma between our organic forces and our rational forces rests in the nature of the energy and information exchange required of us in doing our work. There is always a gap between deciding what we espouse our needs are and doing the energy/information exchange required to enact meeting those needs. Thus there develops a reality schism between the deciders (policy makers), the doers (people doing the work) and meeting communal needs sharing by the outcomes equitably.

Policymaking is a classic example of this human creation of regimes of norms, rules and laws as guides to evolving human behavior. In so doing human cultures always escort the complexity and danger of calculating the exact nature of our needs relative those outcomes we select to meet those needs.

The last half of the paper provides an onsite practioners analysis of the application of the concepts of the previous sections above. To that end, it is analysis of a nation's effort to derive a planned extreme makeover of the Human Resource development of its most important export industry. In 2002 Sri Lanka was informed that world quota system for apparel and textiles would be eliminated in five years. They faced a serious loss in their apparel and textile industry which provides nearly 50% of the nation's revenue through export of apparel and textile goods. They inaugurated a successful five year extreme makeover of not only their industry but completely expanded the range of their industry services in the global market.

However, the Human Resources Development plan to create a College of Apparel and Textiles (COAT) was left to 2006, when the industry world export quota system was to be removed. A serious disconnect surfaced between the industry, the government, and the main university's apparel and textile department. They could not come to agreement on the policy for creation of a new modern College of Apparel and Textiles similar to those in England and America.

The Sri Lanka's Moratuwa University, the industry's Joint Apparel Association Forum (JAAF) requested and received a Fulbright grant for a Fulbright Senior Specialist in organization development to research their issues and to help them find a path together through this most urgent impasse. In five years they had successfully create a new ultramodern apparel and textile industry, but the prospect of furnishing the future human resource trained to run it into the future was in jeopardy. This case study encompasses and provides inspection the previous four Parts of this chapter.

WHAT IS WORK?

What are organizations that we have so many theories about them? Perhaps one of the main needs for theories on organizations is the fact that organizations have come to play an ever larger role in our public and private lives. Businesses, social groups, and governments abound with organizations and us within in them. What, then, is organization? How does organization evolve? Or has organization always been with us? In their paper, "A future for organization theory: living in and living with changing organizations," James Walsh, Alan Meyer, and Claudia Bird Schoonhoven remark as to the state of our understanding organization:

The field of organization theory is adrift. The press for 'relevance' is but one symptom of a field that has lost its bearings. Scholarship that was once so relevant is now irrelevant (or worse) the answer is to change our research foci. The theories we developed to comprehend the Management Revolution no longer have the traction they once did. Organization and management theory is uniquely positioned to ask and answer questions that speak to the defining characteristics of our new century. The future is ours. We need to seize it. (Walsh, Meyer, & Schoonhoven, 2006, 657–671)

Organization theories tend to be more about organizations and their management than about the nature of *organization* itself. There are many definitions of organizations. Most of them come to a generic base: organizations are people working together for a common outcome (Harmon & Mayer, 1986). Organization theories tend to focus on a particular aspect of organizations in order to address the organization issues of the historical moment. For example, Max Weber's bureaucratic organization focused on economic efficiency, the scientific management approaches of Frederick Taylor and others focused on effectiveness, while the human relations theories of Kurt Lewin and others focused on participation, performance, and learning. (Lewin, et al., 1975) Each new organization theory usually proposes its own framework and much of its own terminology. Although new organization theories are traditionally built upon past theories, they often tend to develop into separate schools, often at theoretical odds with each other. Another view: "There is no such thing as *the* theory of organizations" (Shafritz & Ott, 1996).

A graduate seminar research workshop/symposium on "what is Organization," was conducted by the author in 1995 at Kaunas University of Technology in Lithuania. It included examining Action Training & Research (AT&R) designed by Neely Gardner (Gardner, 1974, 106–115) as it applies to public policy development (Bruce and Wyman, 1998). In selecting a genealogical approach to conduct the participants' research on organization they took note of Nietzsche's warning against using genealogy of language as a method of research: "all concepts in which an entire process is semantically concentrated elude definition, only that which has no history is definable" (Spivak, 1988). Likewise, Benedict Anderson points out the potential value to research using this genealogical approach on language,

First, one notes the primordialness of languages, even those known to be modern. No one can give a date for the birth of any language. Each looms up imperceptible out of the horizonless past. (Insofar as homo sapiens is homo dicens, it can seem difficult to imagine an origin of language newer than the species itself.) Languages thus appear rooted beyond almost anything else in contemporary societies (Anderson, 1991).

Therefore, the workshop/symposium on developing a theory on organization focused on language as a researchable cultural artifact for their object of analysis: *organization*. In selecting a genealogical approach to their research on organization, the workshop was not seeking a definition for *organization*; they had to assume that the word is self-explanatory in that regard. They were merely sampling the genetic traces of the word 'organization' in order to use its simplicity to guide them to see if their genealogical research would lead to insights about policy development. In this, they were following the example of genealogical research set out by Michel Foucault:

The interpreter as genealogist sees things from afar. He (or she) finds that the questions which were traditionally held to be the deepest and murkiest are truly and literally the most superficial. This certainly does not mean that they are either trivial or lacking in importance, only that their meaning is to be discovered in the surface practices, not in mysterious depths. (Dreyfus & Rabinow, 1983)

The approach was to use the Lithuanian language and its rich treasure of retained Proto Indo-European language elements as an instrument for glimpsing insights by probing under the surface nature of organization, as the word rather than seeking some primordial true meaning. Interpreting the meaning of what we see is the genealogical research trap that Nietzsche warns against, because then we will then be mistaking a word's various traces. As scientists, our genealogical research must be in the other direction; we must examine the obviousness of the words' traces, rather than searching the hidden meanings; those we bring to the research project ourselves. (Nietzsche, 1988)

Therefore, the Kaunas University of Technology's graduate workshop/symposium on organization theory conducted their genealogical research guided by Eddington's conjunction 'and,' as indicating secondary research of organization, which linked into Karl Weick's definition of organization as a series of conjunctions:

A shared sense of appropriate procedures and appropriate interpretations, an assemblage of behaviors distributed among two or more people, and a puzzle to be worked on. The conjunction of these procedures, interpretations, behaviors, and puzzles describes what organizing does and what an organization is [emphasis added] (Weick, 1979, 54)

The workshop/symposium participants traced the word *organization* back through several of its genealogical appearances in Western languages. Those traces were used to refine their emerging theory of organization into a simpler model with which they could examine the subsequent changes in the use of organization as it developed over time, particularly as it related to policy making in Lithuania's recent post-Soviet situation.

Using the word *organization* to depict how people associate with one another for some common purpose gained its prominence with the unfolding of the industrial revolution in the nineteenth century, with the rise of corporate capitalism, nationalism, and, in particular, with the sociological writings of Max Weber, Karl Marx, and Emile Durkheim. The word *organization*, of course, has much earlier roots in our language that can inform us about its original nature.

For example, the word *organization* comes to English via French and the Roman Latin name for musical pipe organs: *organum*. The *organum* pipe organ is a loud pneumatic sound instrument used in ancient Roman circus games not too unlike the blast horns used by attendees of the current world soccer cup matches. The actual invention of the pipe organ is usually credited to a Greek engineer, Ctesibius of Alexandria, who created an apparatus called the *organon hydraulis* or water organ depicted in Figure 1, as an experiment during his study of hydraulics in Egypt in the 3rd Century BCE (Encyclopedia Britannica, 2012).

Ctesibius' water *organon* was a wind driven musical instrument using a combination of windmill pneumatics and hydraulics to pressurize and

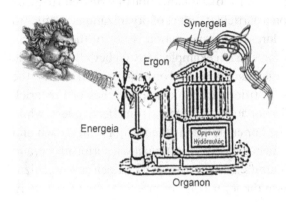

Figure 1. Ctesibus' organon hydraulic and Greek word family for wĕrg

blow air across a set of pipes to create music. O*rganon hydraulis* means literally: an instrument (*organon*) that uses wind power energy (*energeia*) to pump air into a water (*hydro*) chamber to pressurize air, and to bring together the forced air across pipes (*aulos*) resulting in the (*synergeia*) of music as depicted in Figure 1. *Organum* and *organon* were Latin and Greek words, respectably, for instrument or tool used for doing work. In this case the work outcome was sounds synthesized to become music pleasant to the ear. (Bruce, 2011, 734). Ctesibius' water *organon* provides a prototype for the model building in the next section.

Organon was part of a word family for work in classical Greek, e.g.: (*ergon*) work to be done, (e*rgáths*) worker or agent, *(organon)*, tools, instruments for energy exchange, and (*energeia*), energy resources for working, and (*synergeia*)for the work outcome (Partridge, 1958). For example, Aristotle's first books were grouped together by his students under the title of *Organon,* meaning instruments and tools used for intellectual work, i.e., thinking. In *Organon* Aristotle describes our basic instruments of reason, namely how we use language and logic as tools to represent, categorize, and interpret our experiences, and how we can use reason to derive new knowledge from our perceptions in order to develop our personal and social activities to a common good. However, *organon* comes to Greek from the earlier Proto

Indo-European (IE) root *wĕrg* (Figure 2). The Germanic branch of the Proto Indo-European language also uses the same parent language root. The original sound and meaning of *wĕrg*, namely: to work, to do, is still retained in *Werk* (German) and in *work* (English) (Partridge, 1958). The big insight here is that we have gotten organization and work turned upside down. We tend to think of work as a function of organization, while it appears that organization is a function of work.

More importantly, it is clear from Classical Greek, Germanic, and Lithuanian languages that in the West the concept of work is genealogically prior to our use of *organization* in modern times, and in that genealogical precedence, *work* engenders *organization*. Therefore, in order to glimpse the traces in Weick's context of organization as a *conjunction* of people, behaviors, and puzzles to be *worked* on, we need examine perhaps an even bigger question, namely the question regarding the nature of work itself.

BUILDING A DYNAMIC MODEL OF DOING

In his essay, "Science and Reflection" Martin Heidegger asks the question: "What does it mean 'to work'? (Heidegger, 1977, 159-160) He also

traced the etymology of the word for work back to PIE root *wĕrg. But in describing his genealogical research of the word 'work' he cautions us that what is decisive is the way in which the genealogical research of language is undertaken. Heidegger concludes:

The mere identifying of old and often obsolete meanings of terms, the snatching up of these meanings with the aim of using them in some new way, leads to nothing, if not to arbitrariness. What counts, he informs us, is for us to rely on the early meanings of a word and its changes, in order to catch sight of the realm into which the word 'work' speaks. Only in this way does the word speak, and speak in the complex of meanings into which the matter that is named by it, unfolds throughout the history of poetry and thought. Work is doing. (Heidegger, 1977, 159-160)

What work is doing is changing things. And changing is: the transition from one order to another in time. In physics, *erg* is a measure of work, e.g., horse power, defined as the energy that is required to bring about change in the position of, namely lift, a standard mass weight to a standard distance. In chemistry work is the energy measured in the change from one type of chemical reaction into a new chemical compound. These energy exchanges are of Thermal Units (BTU) according to the laws of thermodynamics.

In the biological realm, work seems to be centered on the need of organisms, simple and complex, to sustain themselves through biological energy exchange via the extended food-chain of nutrition, reproducing in kind, and evolving along what Jay Gould called "the pathway of life" (Gould, 2004, 43). Life in all its various forms, if it is to persist, it must grow, and reproduce. Life needs to constantly consume energy-deriving sustenance from its environment, as well as adapt to change in that environment. The base enactment process of how organisms can accomplish this needs is encoded (DNA) into the nature of their physical

Figure 2. Etymology of organization and work

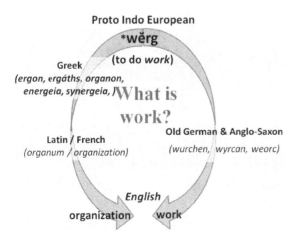

make-up. They have the capacity to apprehend their environment well enough to be able to behave in a way that constantly changes their situation to their benefit or they are lost. The seemingly most obvious rule here may not be the survival of the fittest, but rather all things considered, the survivors are the fittest for the present. Yet, all living organisms are, at best, fit to survive only for a while, and none for very long in cosmic time scales. Still, life persists. Work in the biological realm is organisms doing things to their external and internal environments in order to achieve the best overall outcome for them.

Clearly, this economic aspect furnishes us with one of the most obvious notions of life in general, and of work in particular. If people continue take in less energy than they consume, in a time they will no longer sustain their life. However, the chain of survival of the fittest is non-linear; events can overtake even the fittest individual in the present. Nevertheless, whatever work changes people manage to accomplish in life, the changes may have beneficial effects not only for them but for others as well. In this way change engendering the value of working together for all.

If people can agree on ways to re-organize their work efforts to work together for mutually beneficial outcomes the agreement forms an informal policy for them for prospective future actions It seems apparent that any model of work in the human social realm has to retain the primary elements of life: (1) organisms need, (2) doing things, (3) by exchanging energy resources (4) for outcomes that could benefit them. Therefore, to restate the obvious: work is people doing things to achieve outcomes that they hope will be beneficial to them and theirs. In the Kaunas University of Technology's research workshop a simple model of the Action Training & Research view of work was first constructed around cycles of those three action elements and three phases; stated in their simplest form they are people who:

1. WORK to meet their
2. NEEDS, which they
3. DO by
4. *Performances* capable of RESOURCE
5. RE-ORGANIZATION through
6. *Energy Exchange - - - - - -* during
7. *Inter-Reactions ....* among their
8. *Resources'* capacities to achieve
9. OUTCOMES people
10. *Value* to meet their NEEDS

The relationships between the cyclic action elements indicate the dynamic aspect of the simple work model. These relationships between the work elements transform the model for work into one that is structured along three inter-relational dimensions shown in Figure 3 and developed from the first Lithuanian workshop/symposium Report (Bruce, 1997, pp. 5-14).

This view of the ongoing and dynamic reconciliation among these three dimensions is the fundamental function of the model of work. It is based on realizing that everything is already in a current state of organization. Work purports to create change through performing energy exchanges to re-organize things, i.e., bringing about new outcomes. Therefore, the work theory model

Figure 3. A policy model of work as re-organization

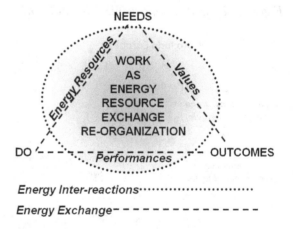

of organization would be, in effect, *Work-as-Re-organization*. What is work for people then?

It seems clear that *wĕrg* was originally used to describe the elements of the process of people doing things to support living for themselves, their family, and their community such as *weaving* for women and *hunting* or *herding* for men. However, as conscious creatures we have a degree of free will or intentionality. We can imagine what we need and want, as well as imagine various possibilities on how to behave and perform in order to get what we need, want, or desire. Although we can imagine and choose what outcomes we want, we, as people, must imagine along these three diverging avenues of intentionality. Therefore, in this view of work, organization is the capacity or capacities of a person through exchanging energies to re-organize their resources into new product outcomes that meet the person's new needs.

Work, as described in the model shown in the Table 1, is comprised of work elements that join in conjunction the three decision dimensions of intentionality to develop a policy change strategy plan. The theory of work and organization is primarily a theory of the three work elements, in conjunction (&) to form the decision dimensions of values & resource re-organization capacities & performance. These "&"s are Weick's conjunctions (and Eddington's *and*) of procedures, behaviors and puzzles to be worked on as well as those conjunctions between the decision dimensions of intentionality. In short the secondary study of

Weick's conjunctions is Eddington's notion of organization. The (&) represents inter-reaction among two or more entities wherein energy is exchanged, resulting in change in some or all of the participants.

To develop a policy strategy plan, requires the study of the '&s'. Each of the three decision dimensions poses a separate question of intentionality, i.e., linking their '&s.' For example, how is the 'people's needs' element to be linked to the 'outcomes' element? More precisely, what are the outcomes needed? First, how are we linked to the outcomes to which we *value*? In order to make the link, we must imagine and select what possible outcomes we intend to pursue. Secondly, and at the same time, how do we evaluate our needs and selected potential outcomes to our element of 'doing'? Namely, what are our best capacities to apply accessible energy to change resources enough to achieve our intended outcomes? What new capacities must we develop? We need to imagine and decide what deeds we intend to perform in order to achieve our selected outcomes. Even with a single person work is a form of policy development.

Whatever we decide to do must naturally correlate some meaningful way with the out come that we have selected to work toward. Finally, how do we link the 'doing' work element with outcome we have selected to achieve? More exactly, how must we *perform* (even with others) to enact the deeds we believe are required to achieve our

Table 1. Work as a basic model of re-organization (& = inter-reactions)

Work Inter-Reaction Phases	Re-Action Elements			Policy- Strategy
1. Needs determine outcome *values*	NEEDS	&	OUTCOMES	What we need/want Issues Analysis: Strategic Plan's problems & opportunities
2. Capacities required to re-organize resources in inter-reactions	DOING	&	NEEDS	What we can do: Project Planning Resource Re-Organization
3 Performance capability to achieve outcomes through energy exchange	OUTCOMES	&	DOING	How we do it: Gathering the Resources and Project Management

chosen outcome? What training or practice do we need to undergo to bring our capacities and performance to the level required to achieve the needed outcomes?

We must imagine our physical selves in constant motion while intentionally trying to perform those deeds as best we can, often in competition with others who may be pursuing to bring about some of the same resources and outcomes for themselves. This performance decision dimension is the most nebulous of the three in that it encompasses the entire risk-for-gain dynamic of work as re-organization for accomplishing needed changes. In the final analysis the complete decision-making process is performance policy in action. Up to now, we had purposefully minimized the use of the word 'action' to describe obvious aspects of the model because it describes this dynamic of the model. That dynamic is all of the work elements and decision dimensions are in action concurrently all the time. We resort to Aristotle's definition of action as being movement in which the outcome is present.

Because of intentionality, that is, our limited degree of free will to enact change through energy exchange in our environment, these three decision dimensions among the elements of work comprise an incredibly convoluted, complex, and inter-related action directed decision-making process. The fundamental dynamic of our espoused values is to achieve an outcome that will effectively meet our needs. The socio-economic value of the outcome to us, we hope, will be greater to us and our social communities than the sum value of our resources required in achieving our intended outcomes. Finally, through our espoused values we hope that our actual performance of action taken enacting those values will be sufficient to bring about the changes in our resources intended as the selected outcome, yet with a minimum of unintended negative outcomes. This non-linear triad of imaginings and intentionality is a distinctively human aspect of work. Linking them to work together (Weick's conjunctions) is a policy

of re-organization of changing things for our perceived benefits. Clearly, the outcomes do not materialize exactly as we had intended in every case, but such is the nature of work.

Needs Determine Outcome Values

People are agents of re-organization. The driving force of the changes people or organizations undertake are their needs. However needs are abstract notions arising from our natures as well as our understanding of what is currently and ongoing on around us. When several people or organizations are involved in needs assessment this can become a very complex process.

Abraham Maslow's theory of motivation depicts the hierarchy of these needs in Figure 4 (Maslow, 1996, 45-56).To begin with the first enigma of work is the potential conflict between one's espoused values for action and the values enacted in their actions. Our physical needs fundamentally drive the entire work process. In addition, this pyramid can be deceptive; because people have concurrent needs for action emanating in constant flux through all levels of Maslow's hierarchy of needs model. They constantly ebb and flow in time with our main focus on our needs shifting as well.

This strange thicket of needs, charged with our cellular chemistry, feelings, and emotions becomes nature's guiding/driving force for work. In addition, our rational thinking and knowledge are also focusing our efforts in regard to our perceived needs. Often, these physical and rational needs are countervailing leading to a state of cognitive dissonance within us. When others are involved cognitive dissonance can lead to the cooperative effort to experience wicked problems where the more that is done to solve them only makes them worse. (Bruce, Cote, 2002, 39-46)

These dynamic rational and restless needs must be encompassed and somehow focused by us upon particular outcomes and goals in the process of our work as re-organization to change things to meet

Figure 4. Maslow's Hierarchy of Needs and Potential for Cognitive Dissonance

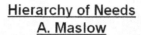

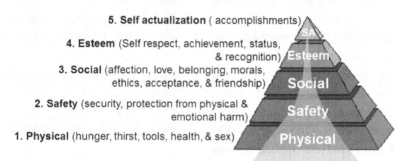

our equally changing needs over time. Together our complex of needs constitute our disposition to effect outcomes that would not otherwise occur without our limited freedom to intervene in the unfolding events of our environmental situation. The use of the word *value* here is a convention to encompass the subset of values/valences that interlink our thoughts, emotions, feelings, needs, wants, desires, etc., which, in turn, urge us to action or inaction. The words *will, disposition, motivation, inclination, goal setting, attitude, or temperament* can also be used to characterize this limited relational needs decision dimension of our work as re-organization for changing things. Clearly, sorting out our intentions and focusing them on specific outcomes in a complex function full of countervailing forces is the stuff of policy making. Sorting out those forces and figuring out what is best for us is how we manage our ongoing behavior. That is, how we self-govern our work as re-organization agents for inter-reacting in our environment.

Doing and Needs: The Decision Dimension of Resource Re-Organization Capacities

Equally complex is the paradox of deciding what resources such as tools, physical resources, and help from other people we have to work with in

order to achieve the outcomes we have selected to pursue. Theories of behavior range from the linear conditioned response approach of behaviorists such as B. F. Skinner to the non-linear humanistic consultative theories of Carl Rogers. For example, to the degree that we do not properly relate our behavior with needs, wants, and other valences of our values, we are simply responding to the latest and strongest stimulation coming to us from our environment. In this case human behavior can be reduced to functional cause-and-effect of Stimulus/ Response. At the other end of the spectrum of behavior theories Carl Rogers' perspective sees the forces that impinge upon even the smallest human effort are so numerous, are non-linear and often countervailing that they seem to defy any analysis at all. (Rogers, 1951)

Doing and Outcomes by Performance through Energy Exchange

A second paradox of work in performance is linked to capacities. One cannot perform proper work without the capacities to do it. At the same time one cannot have the capacity to work if one cannot perform the work. This paradox is resolved through training and through practice called experience as an informal personal policy strategy plan. We cannot say that we really understand the work unless we have acted upon it before.

In work, the performance decision dimension a series of little steps of work as re-organization to change things, each building on the previous and preparing for the next. Work organizes the intended outcomes, the intended behaviors, and the commitment of one's personal resources in performing many actions to achieve the outcome in a successfully and economic fashion that expresses the maker's espoused values. One must learn to accomplish all of the myriad intermediate actions work steps of re-organizing the resources involved and to inter-relate them in production synthesis performance. This learning comes from the experience of trying out each step until it is so instilled in one's physical and mental behavior that they become habitual and can be accomplished well without having to think about them. Experience comes from the Greek words for experience and trying-out (*ex peri*). Part of the outcome of the performance experience is the acquisition of new understanding. In any case, matching the selected outcome with the selected behavior in making changes is the proof of the work. In performance all the work elements and decision dimensions come together in the focus of each moment's actions through energy exchange.

SELF-GOVERNANCE WHILE GUIDED BY NATURE'S LAWS

In general, then, art in a sense completes what nature is unable to finish, and in a sense imitates nature. – Aristotle (384 - 322 BC)

This approach to organization development for change was developed in more detail in a paper presented at COMPACT II (Bruce, 2013) Are Nature's laws absolute or do they allow a degree of leeway for chance of evolutionary novelty in their observance? Charles Saunders Peirce approached this question in the late nineteenth century, "Since

law in general cannot be explained by any law in particular, the explanation must consist in showing how law is developed out of pure chance, irregularity, and indeterminacy," (Peirce, 1888: 277). Later in 1905, perhaps after his conversations with James Clerk Maxwell who had described molecules as a vortex of force fields, Peirce clarified his notion of chance, indicating that natural laws must include relative degrees of latitude for inter-actions involving energy exchange in the dynamic energy environment.

What I mean by saying that if the universe were governed by immutable law there could be no progress. In place of the word progress I will put a word invented to express what I mean, to wit, vari-escence. I mean such a change as to produce an uncompensated increment [evolution] in the elements of a situation. (Peirce in Hardwick, 1977: 143)

What is a duty~cycle? The Laws of Nature are imperatives providing directional guidance in the evolving but not yet determined chance of circumstances. By imperative is meant guidance that cannot be safely ignored for long, for in the long run Nature will out. The guidance takes the form of a duty~cycle of repeated work indicated by the law's imperative direction.

Nature's Laws of Thermodynamics depicted in Figure 5 are a set of instructions that set up the model imperative duty~cycle tasks for any physical energy exchange (work) obligation to include some energy dispersal toward entropy The ~ signifies as the dynamics of 'rest and restart' of the ongoing oscillating cycle: "When astronomers talk about matter being fed into supermassive black holes, they talk about 'duty cycles.' The speed of a black hole duty cycle describes how rapidly it changes back and forth from feeding on matter to sitting quietly," (Sharf, 2012: 36) *The sitting quietly* rest period echoes an earlier creation work duty~cycle described in Genesis. Nature's laws for mortal life employ duty~cycle model to guide organisms in

Figure 5. Nature's model instructions guiding energy and life

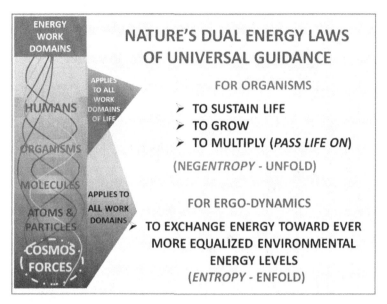

their three phase duty~cycle tasks: to 1) sustain life, in order to 2) grow, and to 3) self-replicate in order to pass their DNA on along what Jay Gould's pathway of life.

As a policy is an agreed upon artificial regime or duty~cycle intended as a guide of action that prescribe, within certain limits of freedom, for people to achieve together particular needed work outcomes. The policy's guidance, as noted above, it is a form of communal duties that urges us to continue our flow of action along designated pathways to needed work outcomes by constantly applying energy exchange efforts to re-organize our resources to achieve the designated results.

For example, in Figure 6, policy choices are shown as a possible blend between regulation control and freedom of action. However, successful robust implementation comes from a proper balance between the inter-reaction of the two as indicated by the Robust Policy Zone.

An policy duty~cycle does provide us enough freedom for us to exchange energy/ information, i.e., inter-react in the environment within discrete adaptive variances and still guided by and observing the imperative directives of the regime, yet with a degree of freedom to adapt our individual

behavior to the evolving situation at hand in the present. These freedoms are manifest as our organization capacities and skills to work, i.e., re-organize our resources. These policy duty~cycles of energy exchange capacities are unique to each person to be adaptive in new encounters in his or her changing environment.

In this way, our cultural and social imperative duty~cycle regimes evolved first into informal regimes reflected, for example, in behavior norms, character ethics, morals, etc., guiding us into productive inclusion role in family, social, community, and national groups. Many of these informal duty~cycle regimes are then subsequently evolved into more formal policies, and the detailed strict rules and laws of self-governance.

There is a major pitfall in our imitating Nature's imperative duty~cycle regimes as a model for humans. As humans we have only a vague notion of the purpose of Nature's laws of imperative duty~cycle regimes. Everything depends on the initial conditions of the changing moment. However, when we develop imperative regimes to govern our cultures and societies then defining the purposes of a policy's imperative regime is problematic.

Figure 6. Variability of policy implementation

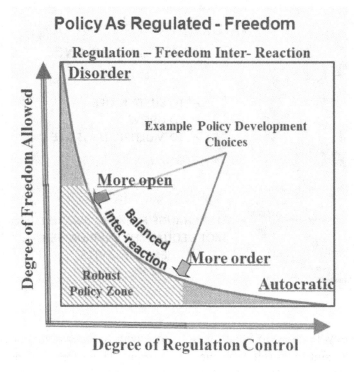

Developing a policy assumes the trustfulness of the stewardship capacities of those governing. At the same time the policy assumes that there is a reciprocal trust on the part of the others that are working to achieve the policy's needed outcomes. It is the trust that connects the individual to work with the many toward a prescribed result.

This stewardship power of imperative duty~cycle regimes is subject to the human flaws inherent in not only the capacities of the people that create and administrate the imperative regime policies, but also by those who are to enact the policy's intended outcomes. History is replete with stewardship inadequacies from both policy maker and policy enactor.

The inherent conflicts in a community about sustainable resource usage for human capacity development relative to the sustainability of the environment can be tractable on the local basis. However, on the stage of nature at large, innovative organizations and processes are required to man-

age an equitable and sustainable balance between freedom of innovation and regulation of resource use for Sustainable Development on a global scale in the future. Our record of accomplishment on that count has been tilted toward regulative exploitation of nature rather than cooperation and sustainability of nature, except where it benefits us. (Keene & Bruce, 2011, 4)

For example, policies as imperative duty~cycle regimes are commonly used to govern how people as individuals and in groups (cities, firms, etc.) organize and develop their Information Communication Technology resources to meet their designated individual and communal needs. Such policies are intended to provide guidance to assist people in both their objective (regulated reasoning) and subjective (freedom heuristic common-sense) judgment in their decision making in the situational moment of action taking to use Information Communication technologies to achieve their needed work outcomes.

A policy is neither a plan nor strategy of action per se; policy provides guidelines for behavior in action within which is prescribed an allowable scope of freedom of behavioral judgment for action, yet with some direction prescribed in terms of work outcomes to work toward. Too much regulation stifles implementation, while too much freedom lacks direction and resource re-organization misapplied away from the policy's intended outcomes. In order for the policy choices (indicated by the red arrows in Figure 6) to achieve a more robust implementation, they would need to find ways to allow more freedom to the implementers to achieve the intended outcomes. They would need to revisit the policies' freedom of action in order to adapt to the changing work situation on the ground. Similarly, the blue arrow policy choices may indicate a need to revise policies to be more realistic of the situation and more useful guidance in the form of duty~cycle guidance to help the implementers better re-organize their resources to achieve the policy's needed outcomes.

How do multiple personal duty~cycles work in a theory of work-as-re-organizing? Such a consideration must include not only Nature's duty~cycles but more importantly it must focus on one's personal duty~cycle artifacts learned and accepted from one's evolving culture.

First, working duty~cycles artifacts have to be learned from Human Agents for Adaptive Change as shown in Figure 7. Therefore the duty~cycles actually reside in the individual person. For example, Nature's thermodynamics and mortal life duty~cycles are resident in the makeup of the person's physical bodies as depicted in Figure 7. The human duty~cycles reside in the form of arrays of learned and accepted cultural duty~cycles of the intellect and performance experience.

However, the effect of these human generated duty~cycles are dependent on the degree that a person actually internalizes them and becomes committed to be guided by their appropriate duty~cycle values in their decisions to risk re-organizing their resources to enact them at any moment.

Figure 7. Personal energized information duty-cycle exchange complex

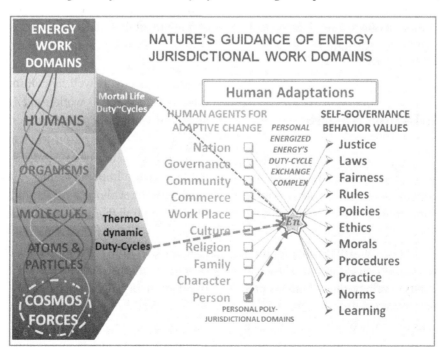

As mentioned above, duty~cycles encounter gaps between a person's espoused values and their enacted values of the moment. Figure 7 shows the network of a person's interconnections of Personal Energized Information Duty~Cycles Exchange Complex. There is an array of human agent social groups that can influence a person by getting them to accept and participate in various social groups' duty~cycles that pertain to the agent social group has developed. It becomes clear that a person can have alliances as a member of some or all of the social agents of adaptive change. At the same time the person may have different versions of some or all of their Personal duty~cycle artifacts relative to which social group is involved in any particular action decision is at hand. Because everything in the network of the Personal Energized Information duty~cycle Exchange Complex can place the person in dilemmas known as wicked problems as they may vie for the person's commitment for action in their behalf. (Rittel, Webber. (1973, 155) This too can lead to cognitive dissonance in the person's action behaviors. Equally, Nature's built in duty~cycles operate at the deeper feelings such as fear, anger, and desire. "For without culture or holiness, which are always the gift of a very few, a man may renounce wealth or any other external thing, but he cannot renounce hatred, envy, jealousy, revenge, and so on. Culture is the sanctity of the intellect." (Ross, 1909, 189)

HUMANS IMITATING NATURE

Policymaking is people and their social jurisdictional domains developing self-governance to guide for people (*polis*) doing work. Looking beyond nature's material and biological imperative duty~cycle regimes, the key human jurisdictional domains are social and cultural imperative regimes with the function of cultural evolution. These are the imperative duty~cycle regimes humans create to shape their communal work behaviors as individuals and as members of various our social and cultural groups. Some of these cultural social duty~cycle regimes include norms, ethics, and morals, as well as policies, laws, administrative regulations. However, policies, by the nature of energized information communications, now take center stage for personal as well as for global cultural development.

The Energized Energy Exchange work element from Table 1 shows that energized information exchange is the exclusive media of action through all work domains. Any work of resource development, i.e., change in any of the work domains is exclusively implemented as an exchange of and energized information. This means that the energies in the energy exchange carry the very information that facilitates the exchange as well as the energy that enacts the change.

At the same time this freedom can lead to a wide variety of harmful abuses and other unwanted uses as depicted in Figure 8. Thus, these confrontations highlight the dilemma of policy choices of how to bring about a better cultural enhancing balance of into the zone of robust policy for positive human development for all.

Policies are our own artifacts that can help us work together. The grand enigma of work in relation to re-organization is this fact that re-organization is fundamentally related to the capacities of each person as a work agent to be able to re-organize changes that are more useful in meeting that individual's needs as well as communal needs of others. That is, each worker-agent is, in effect, an autonomous policy organization that engages in work-as-re-organization to change resources to meet his, or her needs, guided of course by natures' own n imperative duty~cycle regimes.

People's revolving social policies find that by working together, the stakeholders have great advantages toward meeting needs and increasing sustainable cultural development over time and over generations. As mentioned earlier, much of modern organization theories and practices have evolved toward examining and developing the processes of management and organization

Figure 8. Policy development adjustment

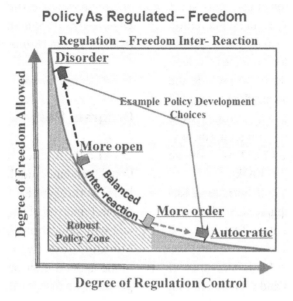

structures for getting many people to work together in a way not only to meet their individual but the collective needs of their organization as well. History is replete with all various sorts of organizational schemas to get people to work together. However, each schema has had to include getting the stakeholders, whether owners or employees, to share 1) their needs, 2) what they must do, and 3) to participate in the benefits of the resulting outcomes.

When people work together there must be enough connection between the individuals' needs to bind them together into organizations such as families, tribes, communities, market firms, and social groups. Trust is the bond that facilitates people working together in cooperative work activities of resource re-organization to meet and share in outcomes that could not be met without working together. Trust in cooperative re-organization is the valuable capacity people have to establish and establish (manage) energized information resource exchanges together to better suit the participants' individual and collective organization needs. However, if the share of the

participants is out of balance mistrust begins to dissolve, and commitment to policies and resource re-organization founders. History is replete with the misguided products of our overreaching human policy artifacts of misguiding imperative regimes of regulated freedoms.

Policymaking has a growing role in managing large inter poly-jurisdictional civil development projects. When disruptive events threaten to bring the whole project to a stop: who is in charge? Who needs to be in on the decisions? How can the impact be minimized by all?

A HUMAN RESOURCE DEVELOPMENT EXTREME MAKEOVER PROJECT: SRI LANKA APPAREL AND TEXTILE INDUSTRY

Background

The Sri Lanka Apparel and Textile industry needed to keep pace with changes in the global trends of the Apparel and Technology global export industry and markets. These changes included the World Trade Organization's abolition of garment export quotas. To keep competitive as an island nation Sri Lanka restructured its Apparel and Textile Industry. However they needed to create a College of Apparel and Textiles in order to provide the expert people they needed to run their upgraded industry. These three stakeholder groups were having irreconcilable problems in agreeing on how best to organize and manage COAT as a college of Apparel and Textiles for Sri Lanka.

Marcus Maurer in his, "Skill Formation Regimes in South Asia: A Comparative Study on the Path-Dependent Development of Technical and Vocational Education and Training for the Garment Industry" was studying Sri Lanka' apparel and textile makeover efforts and pointed out that the stakeholders were, "Keen not to have public training organizations entirely controlled by government agencies, the entrepreneurs envisioned the establishment of a "Council of Apparel and Textile" (COAT) in the form of a private company that was to be given the authority by the government to spend the allocated funds for training purposes. In this context, JAAF also invited two Fulbright consultants[1] specialized in Public Administration, who were virtually taken care of by Sri Lankan Garments, and who briefed the entrepreneurs on similar institutional frameworks in other countries." (Maurer, 2011, 242)

Fulbright Senior Specialists Program
Grant Authorization No. 2320
Raymon Bruce
7620 Vista Cedro CT NE
Albuquerque, NM 87109

Has been selected by the J. William Fulbright Foreign Scholarship Board for a FULBRIGHT SENIOR SPECIALISTS GRANT under the provisions of the Mutual Educational and Cultural Exchange Act of 1961 (as amended.), the FULBRIGHT PROGRAM. This grant is administered by the Bureau of Educational and Cultural Affairs, United States Department of State with the cooperation of the Institute of International Education.

Issue Date: Thursday, November 16, 2006

Program Purpose

COAT is the first attempt in Sri Lanka to set operational mandate/guidelines for an overall systemic framework/operational policy for education in the apparel industry. The project would involve contact with educational institutions, the Education Ministry, Govt. Departments and the key players in the apparel industry. The Govt. has given this project high priority due to the importance of the garment industry in Sri Lanka. Several key apparel manufacturers are spearheading the project due to the need for such a policy body to ensure that the industry education is competitive to face world trends. Participants include a multitude of stakeholders varying from high profile academic to industry experts.

Description

The specialist would interact with a multitude of stakeholders including high profile academics and industry experts, and bring about an effective body that would articulate policy and set standards, with an efficient process in place to achieve the higher focus of COAT. (Fulbright, 2006, 1)

The author's Fulbright Senior Specialist grant to conduct a field issue analysis which as requested by the Government of Sri Lanka, the University of Moratuwa, and the country's Joint Apparel Association Forum to help them work out some agreement on how to best upgrade the Apparel and Textile industries Human Resources. There was agreement on the importance of the need for a college of apparel and textiles, but disagreement on the best way to change from the education, training, and technology resources scattered around the country.

The World Trade Organization had announced in 2002 that it would be removing the quota restrictions on apparel and textiles by 2005 and would later be removing the China quota restrictions in 2008. Global apparel and textile manufacturing firms realized that after 2008 they would have severe difficulty in competing on price point in the global market for manufacturing apparel and textile goods. Since the Apparel and textile industry brings in over 50% of the Sri Lanka's export revenues (see Figure 9) the removal of export quotas by 2005 was a serious economic issue. Therefore, a group of apparel and textile firms in Sri Lanka organized a Joint Apparel and Textile Forum (JAAF) to address this major change in the global export of apparel and textile products. "The formation of JAAF could be considered an innovation in organizational methods given that it fundamentally changed how firms interacted with one another and became the vehicle through which industry interests are now voiced and promoted." (Wijayasiri, 2008, p.14) Janaka Wijayasiri's Case study 3, "The ending of the multi-fibre agree-

ment and innovation in the Sri Lankan textile and clothing industry," is and extensive account of Sri Lanka's reinvention of their apparel and textile industry.

JAAF developed and implemented a five year redevelopment plan. The plan was to restructure their Apparel and Textile Industry from being solely manufacturers of quality apparel and textile products, to become comprehensive suppliers of complete apparel and textile products from fashion design, marketing, research, testing, manufacturing, packaging, and delivering completed products to their business customers abroad. (Hettiarachchi, 7007)

Much of their five year redevelopment plan had been implemented by 2006. What remained to be implemented in the five year plan was the part of the plan for a holistic Human Resource Development to assure that there would be enough qualified employees trained in all the new facets of the currently implemented 'one-stop-shop' apparel and textile business of Sri Lanka. The Human Resource Development phase for the plan included building a comprehensive College of Apparel and Textile, (COAT, a working title) to educate and train the Human Resources now

Figure 9. Sri Lanka apparel and textile industry % of export revenues

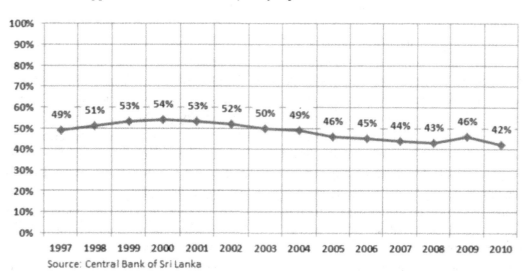

Source: Central Bank of Sri Lanka

needed for the new broader business posture. The Human Resource Development program would include competencies in apparel and fashion design, in product development and testing, in marketing and productivity improvements, and in all the phases of apparel and textile manufacturing technology. [(Joint Association Apparel Forum (JAAF), 2007, p 5-7)

These efforts led the Sri Lankan government to allocate, in the budget proposal for the year 2006. Rs. 250 million (roughly US $3 million) for the establishment of a College of Textiles and Clothing that was to be located in Thulhiriya, far out from Colombo, on the premises of a former textile mill which had been closed down under the previous government. The site had been promised in President Rajapaksa's election manifesto to be re-vitalized at any cost. The government envisioned this college becoming a regional training provider that would attract people from the entire South Asian Association for Regional Cooperation (SAARC), and would link up with relevant international institutes to offer globally recognized degrees and diplomas." (Maurer, 2011)

Methodology Used

The consultant's issue analysis approach included three methods for Sri Lanka's project which focus on the complexity on inter-reaction across poly-jurisdictional domains, in this case the Sri Lanka government, the apparel and textile industry, and the University. First was to use Action Training and Research as developed by Neely Garner. Second was to take a stakeholder management approach to sort out document and get tentative agreement on the disagreements among the key stakeholder's poly-jurisdictional domains. Third was to apply a wicked issue resolving method. A wicked problem can be defined as a problem that always gets worse no matter what is tried in solving it. Wicked issue analysis is a wicked issue resolving method to view the situation as an issue that is problematic and opportunistic. The

analysis deconstructs the issue into problems and opportunities first. The stakeholders then focus on seeking to discover the core of the issue to be resolved. Then the stakeholders can strategize which problems and opportunities to solve.

What is a Stakeholder?

A stakeholder is anyone or organization that has a resources at stake in any change-making and/ or its possible outcome. Rob Llewellyn defines:

A stakeholder is anyone who is:

- Managing the programme of work
- Working within the programme of work
- Directly or indirectly contributing to the programme of work
- Affected by the programme of work or its outcomes (Rob Llewellyn, 2009)

Modern civil development projects such as interstate road building, sustainable water conservation projects, and housing development projects involve a diversified network of stakeholder individuals and their community social groups. Consider that individuals as having poly-jurisdictional aspects to self-governance, their inter-reactive participation behavior with others in many external social jurisdictions. In the case of work projects that involve many social jurisdictions such as public development projects involving private and public jurisdictions the inter-reactions become vastly complex running along an evolutionary time line. However, there is no such thing as a perfect plan in projects that involve projects that not only re-organize people at work, but involve community and infrastructure development efforts. Too many disruptive events will always occur to divert or disrupt the subscribed development project.

By taking the view that individual and the inter-reactive social groups in which they participate are single and together self-governed poly-jurisdictions, when there is a situation involving such multi-jurisdictions of stakeholders working together to managing change there is a complex systems theory dynamic. Each individual stakeholder, as well at the various social stakeholder poly-jurisdiction groups all will have unique vested stakes in not only the change outcome, but in how their participation will need to play out in terms of their capability, capacities, costs, and outcome payoffs impact their respective work re-organization energy exchange of resources in play.

Stakeholder management is a key part of project planning, management, and organization development. Stakeholder analysis is the process of identifying the individuals and groups that are likely to affect or be affected by a proposed action, and sorting them according to their impact on the action and the impact the action will have on them. This information is used to assess how the interests of stakeholders should be addressed in a project planning and implementation or other organized action as shown in Figure 10.

Even assuming good will on all parties, the core change involves ultimately stakeholder resource re-organization. The key resources to be in evolved in re-organization are those of the stakeholder individuals and those of the social poly-jurisdiction in which they are participants. Finally, the resource re-organization occurs in the combined inter-reactions among the stakeholders and their respective resources which besides their material assets, but more importantly their skills, knowledge, capabilities, character, experience, and interpersonal relations, responsibilities, and social status.

Figure 11 depicts the three Sri Lanka stakeholder groups in a COAT project network map. It shows them as shows them as three inter-reacting as poly-jurisdictional domains, including their sub Poly-jurisdictional domains as well. The diversity of purpose, resources, and urgencies has led the project into a wicked problem situation.

What are Wicked Problems?

Horst W. J. Rittel and M. M. Webber originally proposed the concept of "wicked problems" when they saw that in solving some problems, the solution of one aspect of the problem often increased

Figure 10. An imaginary project network map depicting two major government stakeholder's poly-jurisdictional domains and many sub-poly-jurisdictional domains

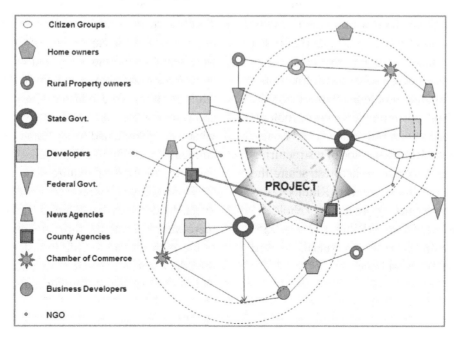

Figure 11. Sri Lanka stakeholder groups in a COAT project network map

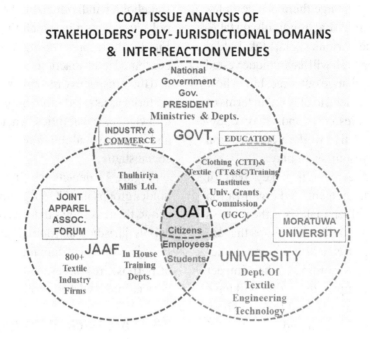

other more difficult aspects of the problem. (Kunz and Rittel et al, 1970, p. 3) Wicked problems are not wicked problems but tamable problems wrapped up in a wicked issue. The issue itself is not solved but is resolved in time with interventions or without them. Wicked Issues cause problems and opportunities. The approach to dealing with a wicked problem is to resolve the issue generating the problem first and then working on trying to solve the problem. (Bruce and Cote, 2002, 39-46)

Once the issue is tamed, the problem is more amenable to being solved with traditional decision-making and problem-solving methods. This approach uses two complementary problem-solving methods in order to tame wicked issues. Participants used Rittel's method of restructuring wicked problems to explore and restructure the wicked problem's issue context. Rittel's "conversation components of issues, stakeholders' positions, and arguments," (Rittel, 19723, p.155) provides the scaffolding to reconstruct the wicked problem's context as an issue.

The AT&R Organization Development Issue Analysis Process

The three host stakeholder groups provided the Fulbright OD Consultant open access in their respective areas to examine the COAT issue among them.by to all the Apparel and Textile firms and the other firms that comprised the Apparel and Textile Industry in Sri Lanka. Instead of localizing the factories in the capital city of Colombo, they were scattered around the island villages for the employees to be able to remain in their villages while working in the industry. The action training and research consulting process was to listen to what these people had to say about the COAT as an idea of a college for Sri Lanka to undertake, and listening for what requirements it must meet.

This issue analysis research approach was conducted to identify what, if any, dysfunctional gaps there were keeping the three stakeholder groups of the Apparel and Textile Industry (JAFF) and the Education and Training organizations (Univ.) and the Ministries of Textiles and of Education

(Govt.) from being so oppositional, while agreeing on the need to stay competitive players in the global markets. After each meeting, we updated our ongoing report and returned the updated copy to the people we interviewed with the option to add anything they thought of later and to remove anything that they may have second thoughts about. This approach had a triple value of gathering information, of sharing what others have already contributed, and of highlighting certain conflicts regarding inter-reaction across boundaries of the three stakeholder groups of identified above as JAAF, Univ., and Govt.

The author used his Gap Analysis Probe (GAP) approach to identify any subset of dysfunctional gaps among the three stakeholders involved in the wicked issue's problem context. A gap refers to a natural separation between entities that serves to differentiate them one from another. (Bruce and Cote, 2002, 39-46)

Therefore, dysfunctions across the gaps are the units of analysis for the COAT issue. Therefore, it is important to present in some detail just what is included in this concept of the gap analysis. In addition, gaps can have multi dimensions of as depicted for the Sri Lanka COAT college project. These three basic gap dimensions are useful in our gap analysis the useful levels in gaps for identifying the key dysfunctional gaps in their complex inter-reactions involved in providing Human Resource Development services are: 1) realm 20 scale; and 3) Transform.

The *Realm* dimension depicted in Figure 12 refers to gaps that exist among inter-reacting jurisdictional domains, In this case there is a three basic realm gaps between the apparel and textile industry (JAFF); the Executive branch and its Ministries of Textile and Education (Govt.) and its main university of Moratuwa (Univ.) Realm gaps are usually gaps of differentiation and identity, involving different general value systems. Finally the gap between the public sector and the private sector gap arises between public sector's bureaucracy and private sector's entrepreneurial and competitive businesses.

The *Scale* dimension refers to the micro/macrocosm or hierarchal scalar shift of focus or point-of-view within the same realm and/or inter-reacting realms. In Sri Lanka's case scalar gaps occur relative to which group's interjurisdictional domain is the regulator of action relative to the interjurisdictional domain group that is to be

Figure 12. Three levels of gaps in inter-reactions between the three stakeholder groups

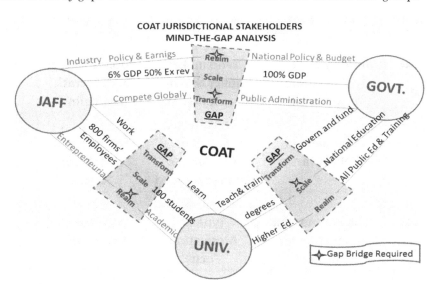

the doer of Human Resource development. For example, the difference between national government administration as regulator and a state university as educator is a scalar gap.

The *transform* gap refers to the differences of work process or development projects between interjurisdictional domains within a realm and/or entities in inter-reacting interjurisdictional domains. There is also the difference between the university's technical department curriculum of education and the private industry firms' interjurisdictional domain's need for new students and employees trained in new technology.

The development of one's performance in a work situation will usually encounter transform gaps between worker and management or even customer. In each case the differentiating gap may involve a preponderance of one or more of the three dimensions as well. All three levels of are present to some degree.

A dysfunctional gap among multiple players is often what makes an issue wicked. If one tries to solve the one dysfunctional gap as a problem, it can easily throw off one or more of the other

gaps as a result, portending a wicked impasse. The more it is worked upon to be solved the more wicked it becomes. For example, a new employee who is being transformed into a team member is also encountering a scalar shift from individual to social group at the same time the group may be experiencing the new employee as a realm gap depending on the background reasons the new employee has been sent to them by the organization.

A GAP Interface Analysis Map shown in Figure 12 was drawn up to identify and analyze the various Gaps that may be causing any difficulties in JAFF moving forward on the COAT project. The three levels of GAP interface, Realm, Scale, and Transform link the major players involved in developing COAT. Through interviews of the people from each of the player organizations we were able to fill in the map as depicted in Figure 12. The analysis surfaced wicked issues among the three major players. The gap analysis revealed the following eight key Dysfunctional Realm Gaps that are also noted in Figure 12. The gap analysis revealed the following eight key Dysfunctional Realm Gaps that are also noted in Table 2.

Table 2. Three dysfunctional gaps between stakeholders

#	STAKE HOLDER	DISCONNECT	COAT Wicked Issues	DISCONNECT	STAKE HOLDER
I.	JAAF	*Industry Policy & Costs and investments*	Realm: Who makes policy & Who Pays for what ?	Public Policy & beaurocratic budgeting	GOVT.
II.	JAAF	Complete in Global Market	Transform: Speed of Response to Change Needed	*Stewardship and Public Service*	GOVT.
III.	JAAF	Entrepreneurial innovation for business	Realm: Type of Motivation Focus	*Academic Knowledge*	UNIV.

Developing COAT Requirements to Restructure the Three Dysfunctional Issue Gaps

In terms of how a COAT college could be set up to work with these education and training issues there seemed to be general agreement that something must be done soon or Sri Lanka would easily be eclipsed by events and competition from other countries. There was diverse ideas on what that should be and what role, if any, COAT could have. Above all, the objective of COAT was to give the college a holistic structure to the integrated model for developing the human resources needed by the apparel and textile industry in Sri Lanka.

COAT: Organization Basic Requirements

Since the COAT initiative did not envision actually erecting a "bricks& mortar" College of Textiles. Rather, it could consider adapting the bankrupt and empty Thulhiriya Mills Ltd., now under the control of the Government Ministry of Commerce and Industry. What was envisioned was a viable organization resource that could effectively integrate the current Apparel and Textile Industry education, training and technology innovation research resources, both private and public. COAT would create a plan to organize together to initiate fundable projects that will keep the development of human skills, knowledge and abilities up to the standard needed for apparel and textile firms to remain competitive in the global market place.

Nevertheless, to resolve whatever institutional structure that was to be considered for COAT must be compared and evaluated by the following basic stakeholder requirements in Table 3:

These requirements were used to evaluate the four alternatives in resolving the issue's dysfunctional gaps creating the three key stakeholders' wicked issue of establishing COAT.

To be effective, Education, Training, and Innovation resource development Technology

Table 3. Stakeholder requirements for COAT (Bruce & Kirk)

1	Open and inclusive to all stakeholders affected who wish to be involved
2	Provide leading edge education and training in the functions and global business and innovative technology of the Apparel and Textile Industry
3	Facility programs should be open to the qualified students in Sri Lanka.
4	Organization structure to be accepted and agreed to by the participating stakeholder partners
5	Transparent decisions and activities throughout operation of the organization
6	Develops consensus on mutually held interests and responsibilities regarding education, training and technological research in the Apparel and Textile field
7	Ready access to support private & public funding by developing professional transparent project proposals that include viable action plans, milestones and accountability
8	Provide a variety of support services to members (for a supporting fee)
9	Sustainable support and funding for the organization and appropriate staff
10	Ready communication access to all stakeholder principals
11	Develop, set and maintain industry requirement standards for education, training, and technology innovation research
12	Links the Industry, education, training, and technology research for innovation into an integrated whole that will be able to citizens of Sri Lanka, namely, employees and students to continually develop themselves as valuable partners in the apparel and textile industry in general and in their own Policy personal development in particular.

Platforms must involve a broad base of stakeholders in defining and implementing their Strategic Research and Development Agendas for integrating the education, training, and innovation Technology resources of the Sri Lanka apparel and textile industry.

The Intervention

A Summit Symposium of the Stakeholder Groups together was titled as "Temporary COAT- a Beginning." The three stakeholder groups as well as other interested organized gathered together in a symposium as a virtual integrated Collegium of Apparel, and Textiles COAT stakeholders. The issues were explored including those examined and discussed already in this case analysis. The consultant's various progress reports were freely shared with the stakeholders in order for each of the stakeholder groups to obtain a clearer vision of their respective stakes at issue in upgrading the education and innovation support to the apparel and textile industry in Sri Lanka.

The symposium constituted a proto COAT that was established as a 24 hour entity: Council of Apparel and Textiles (COAT) of equal partners formed of the symposium attendees, as depicted in Figure 13.

Main Alternative enactments for this COAT to consider were:

1. Create a Public Private Partnership to develop human resources for the Apparel and Textile industry.
2. Create an NGO Human Resource Development Institution for Apparel and Textile

3. The Apparel and Textile Industry should do the research and training for their industry
4. The stakeholder groups develop their own a cooperative structures to work together.

This symposium of a Council of Apparel and Textiles COAT was conducted by professional two local organization change facilitators hired from the Sensei International a firm in Sri Lanka selected by JAAF for facilitating the symposium. The symposium was designed to gather stakeholders interviewed by the author from the Apparel and Textile industry, the Education, Training, and Innovation Technology Research institutions, and the Government Ministries to chart their future path to develop their combined program to integrate their efforts to build and a more effective Human Resource development for the industry.

The premise was to assemble the stakeholder groups as an initial informal Council of Apparel and Textiles (modeled in Figure 10) for them to exchange their concerns and aspirations about the means of working together to assure the success of a modernized Human Resource Development program for the industry. Success was meant to

Figure 13. Proto-COAT organized symposium

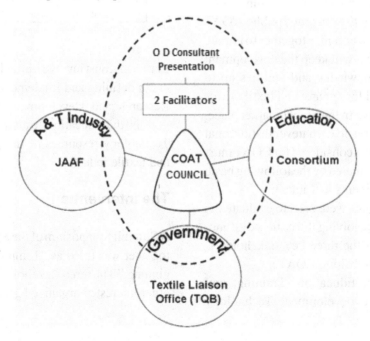

address the common interests and missions of each of the three stakeholder groups. They could evaluate the four alternatives and decide on a joint course of development, or they could also decide to disband the council and chart separate tracks of action among the stakeholders that would achieve the same results to coordinate and integrate their efforts.

After an introduction by Mahesh Amalean, Chairman of Mas Holdings, the Fulbright consultant presented a report in a brief PowerPoint presentation sharing the results of his issues analysis research of the issues in previous discussions with the assembled stakeholders. Next, the Sensei professional process facilitators formed the some 35 stakeholder participants into groups at separate tables. Each group had an even mix of industry, education and government stakeholders.

The facilitators explained the following symposium process: Each group was provided with a chart of the ten COAT Organization Requirements. (Table 3) The four COAT models cited above were arrayed in a column matrix on the chart for the groups to evaluate against the ten COAT Organization Requirements. The stakeholders were also instructed by the facilitators to come to a consensus in the group as to how they ranked the four alternative models as to the models' expected ability to perform each of the ten requirements. The facilitators explained that this was not a decision model, but a means of developing a group consensus about the models' relative strengths and weaknesses.

The groups discussed the requirements and models together for an hour. Each group then totaled the scores of the three models at the bottom of the matrix. Then a spokesperson from each group reported their discussions and consensus results to the assembled participants. As each grouped presented their results the facilitators tallied the ranking scores in a spreadsheet projected on the screen. (Bruce and Kirk, 2007, p. 656)

There was spirited discussion in the mixed groups where participants from the different areas of concern talked across the table with each other, some for the first time. Each group was able to come up with a consensus total ranking for the three COAT organization models. All of the models received good scores, showing that they were viable choices. In their presentations, the group spokespersons expressed the need for a COAT organization and that they should continue working on it. Of course, no one model came out ahead of the other two. At that point the authors explained again that this was not a decision task. All of the models had advantages and weaknesses, some more than others. However, there is a forth model that is not yet defined. That fourth model is the one that the assembled stakeholder groups could design by taking the best of all three models and creating a new design for a veritable as a Human Resource Development COAT for the Apparel and Textile Industry of Sri Lanka.

The facilitators then led the symposium participants to form a working group called, Council of Human Resource Development which would meet within a week to chart out the next steps to bring the development of COAT to the next level of institution building. The participants were then invited by the facilitators to a buffet and cocktails for a more social setting for exchanging their reactions, ideas, and concerns for the future of the COAT project. The symposium could be looked upon as the first gathering of COAT where the stakeholders from the three stakeholder group's areas of concern came to their first tentative consensus together. (Bruce and Kirk, 2007, p. 656)

Findings: Bridging the Three Wicked Issue Dysfunctional Gaps

The COAT symposium's temporary council functioned as a guide to the stakeholder to see the key issue was not so much the separation of government and private industry jurisdictional domain legal mandates but the lack of communication and bridges among them. The groups focused on developing the informal alternative

4. The stakeholder groups develop their own a cooperative structures to work together.

Their informal associations to work together created effective communication ties to provide a comprehensive, quality, and innovative resource for the nation's economy without setting up a formal bureaucratic Council of Apparel and Textiles. The wicked issue arising out of the reality of the reasonable differences between the between the stakeholder groups' dysfunctional gaps between their missions and operations was resolved by building a holistic realignment of inter-reactions among the stakeholder groups around their mutual interests without encroaching on their separate methods of governance and mission operations.

Bridging Dysfunctional Realm Gaps with Two COATS

COAT Bridge I: Who Makes Policy and Who Pays for What?

In March 2006 MAS Investments Ltd. entered into a partnership agreement with the Board of Investment of Sri Lanka to develop the Thulhiriya Textile Park into an Export Processing Zone named MAS Fabric Park. In 2006 the Sri Lanka Government formed partnership agreement with the Sri Lanka's MAS Investments Ltd., a member of JAAF, to redevelop the defunct 175 acre Thulhiriya Textile Mills and revive it into an Export Processing Zone named MAS Fabric Park at a cost of US $100 million. MAS initially invested $25 million to develop the apparel zone. They planned six projects to improve the industry such as developing a training college within the zone. The new industrial park was to work with local and foreign universities to position itself as a knowledge centre for Textile & Garment Technology, Lean Manufacturing, and Corporate Social Responsibility programs for community development.

In 2008, MAS Holdings Ltd opened the MAS Institute of Management and Technology (MIMT). It is located at the MAS Fabric Park, at Thul-

hiriya. The opening of MIMT was conducted by the distinguished patronage of Vice Chancellor, of the University of Moratuwa, Professor Malik Ranasinghe. MAS Holdings Ltd Chairman Deshamanya Mahesh Amalean said: "My vision is to see Sri Lanka recognized as a destination for knowledge and innovation within the next five years. This is one step towards that goal." (MAS Institute of Management and Technology, 2008)

MAS Institute of Management and Technology (MIMT) was created to enhance employment opportunities to the youth of this country and to uplift competencies in the industries in Sri Lanka. There is a particular focus on the Textile, Apparel, Information Technology and Business Process Outsourcing sectors. MIMT now partners with leading training providers to offer a range of programs. The flexibility of working with a network of partners will ensure that MIMT's training will remain relevant to the changing needs of the nation.

MIMT offers customized programs to address the skill shortages in the Apparel and Textile, the Information Technology, and the Business Process Outsourcing, industries. The goal is to develop well rounded candidates by focusing on core competencies and soft skill development. MIMT's own job placement center will help students from MIMT find employment within the MAS Fabric Park and in other industries.

MAS Institute of Management and Technology (MIMT) is a public training institute with exceptional facilities and infrastructure, including a fully equipped auditorium seating 300 people, 17 training rooms with labs for English language, IT, textile processing and sewing machine mechanics and residential facilities for up to 250 people and a technology innovation section.

As an open institution MIMT accepts qualified students from other training and university organizations. It also sponsors internships into industry. In addition MIMT now offers certificate and degree programs. Thus JAFF established the bridge with the stakeholder Moratuwa University. The ceremonial opening of MIMT was conducted under the distinguished patronage of Professor Malik Ranasinghe, Vice Chancellor, of the University of Moratuwa. A superstructure used to bridge the transforming gaps among the three stakeholder groups was a comprehensive 300 page training manual "Competence and Beyond," published and maintained by JAAF to help education providers align their courses with the needs of the clothing industry. The manual outlines the skills, standards and knowledge required for 139 jobs relating to the clothing supply chain, from spinning to customer care. The aim is to ensure that staff working within academic institutions, many of whom have very little practical experience of the industry and how it works, can better align their curricula with the specific needs of the companies who will eventually employ their students.

The guide has been compiled with the help of companies from all sectors of the industry, who teamed up to define the 139 key jobs and the skills required for the various roles. It spans the functions of employee accountability, performance measures, qualifications and experience across a range of jobs at all levels of production, from manager to operator.

JAAF believes 'Competence and Beyond' is the first documentation worldwide to map out all the key job roles in the apparel and textile industries. And it points out that the document is intended to evolve over time, and be updated and refined periodically to keep pace with industry changes.

COAT Bridge II: Speed of Response to Change Needed

Another example of bridging dysfunctional transition gaps was initiated from the (Govt.) stakeholder group. By Parliament Act No.12 of 2009, the Sri Lanka Government re-organized their Apparel and Textile Industrial vocational training resources together under the Ministry of Industry and Commerce. There the ministry created COAT by merging the Institutes of Textile Training & Services Center (TT&SC) with the Clothing Industry Training Institute (CITI) to

become the Sri Lanka Institute of Textile & Apparel (SLITA). It is empowered to award diploma, degrees at graduate and postgraduate level.

SLITA provides a fast track and cutting edge education to professionals for managing the Apparel Industry in a competitive era. The institute has entered into Memorandum of Understanding (MOU) with North Carolina State University's College of Textiles. With synergy of new technology and the knowledge from the industry, Institute mandate is to create of technical and management professional who can understand the dynamics of global business environment for Textile & Apparel Industry.

The various dysfunctional gaps scalar gaps of regulation and autonomy between the three stakeholder groups were bridged by SLITA's Board of Governors current inclusion of members from the Ministries of Industry and Commerce, the Apparel and Textile Industry firms (JAAF), and educators from the University of Moratuwa and the Lyceum International School – Wattala (Univ.) For the stakeholder (Govt.) there are also additional members from the Ministry of Trade & Commerce, the Ministry of Economic Development, the Ministry of State Resources and Enterprise Development, the Ministry of Higher Education, the Department of Fiscal Policy, and Ministry of Finance and Planning.

COAT Bridge III: Type of Motivation Focus

In the process the stakeholders were able to better see that knowledge and markets are also partners as well in the field of innovation. Internships and education program sharing among education institutions were benefiting all. In Sri Lanka there are many fruitful areas for partnering common interests between the apparel and textile industry institutions; the education, the training, and the innovation technology research institutions; and the government ministries. Perhaps the most valuable advance, however, is the openness to solve wicked issues by developing further informal institutions of partnerships-to-partnerships where people involved in the prospective partnership can themselves work together to manage of common interests by developing fruitful, working relationships whether permanent, informal, or temporary.

We have seen a case in Sri Lanka the Apparel and Textile Industry, government, and academia where many of their interests converged into finding several partnership process to communicate more regularly with each other across gaps, natural or dysfunctional, in order to coordinate the industry's Human Resource Development that they need in order to retain and grow their share of the ever changing global economies.

CONCLUSION

By taking a view of energy exchange as the fundamental agency of work to change, the role of people can be seen as self-governed jurisdictional domains in which to participate as inter-reactors to work together for social change and development. By examining together the disconnects in the many gaps that may normally separate them they can discover the wicked problems may be fundamental issues that can create problems and opportunities which are more amenable to solving and to exploitation. Those that are not require innovative and imaginative bridge building in order to work together in a common cause.

REFERENCES

Anderson, B. (1991). *Imagined communities: Reflections on the origin and spread of nationalism* (rev. ed.). London, UK: Verso.

Aristotle, . (1941). *The basic works of Aristotle* (R. McKeon, Ed.). New York, NY: Random House.

Behn, R. D. (1995). The big questions of public management. *Public Administration Review*, *55*(4), 313–324. doi:10.2307/977122

Bruce, R., S Wyman. (1998). *Changing Organizations, Practicing Action Training and Research*. Thousand Oaks, CA: Sage Publications Inc.

Bruce, R. R. (1997). *Work as organization: A theory*. Helsinki, Finland: Hallinnon Tutkimuksen.

Bruce, R. R., & Cote. (2002). Taming wicked problems: theory and practice, a practical lesson in how to tackle the multi-faceted problems in the workplace. *Public Management*, *31*(3), 39–46.

Bruce, R. R., & Kirk. (2007). Three-way partnership for economic development, the public, private and academic sectors, Sri Lanka. In *Proceedings of 2007 international conference on public administration*. Chengdu, China: UESTC Press.

Bruce, R. R. (2011). What is organization: Governing by imperatives of regulated freedoms. In *Proceedings of the 7th Annual International Conference for Public Administration* (Vol. 1, pp. 734-743). Chengdu, China: University of Electrical Science and Technology China Press.

Bruce, R. R. (2013). *New ways of seeing things, Nature's laws for energy evolving toward self-government*. Paper presented at COMPACT Work II Conference on Challenges of Making Public Administration and Complexity Theory Work. La Vern, La Vern, CA.

Cicero, M. T. (45BC). *Tusculan Disputations*. Retrieved from http://www.gutenberg.org/files/14988/14988-h/14988-h.htm#page-7

Dreyfus, H. L., & Rabinow, P. (1983). *Michel Foucault: Beyond structuralism and hermeneutics* (2nd ed.). Chicago, IL: University of Chicago Press.

Durkheim, E. (1993). *The division of labor in society*. New York, NY: Macmillan.

Eddington, S. A. (1958). *The nature of the physical world*. Ann Arbor, MI: The University of Michigan Press.

Encyclopedia Britannica. (2012). *Ctesibius of Alexandria*. Retrieved February 29, 2012, from http://www.britannica.com/EBchecked/topic/145475/

Fulbright Senior Specialist Program. (2006). *Project ID 2303*. University of Moratuwa.

Gardner, N. (1974). Action training and research: Something old and something new. *Public Administration Review*, *34*(2), 106–115. doi:10.2307/974933

Gould, S. J. (2004). The evolution of life on Earth: Dinosaurs and Other Monsters. *Scientific American*, *14*, 93.

Hardwick, C. S. (1977). *Semiotic and significs: the correspondence between Charles S. Peirce and Victoria Lady Welby*. Academic Press.

Harmon, M. M., & Mayer, R. T. (1986). *Organization theory for public administration*. Boston, MA: Little Brown.

Heidegger, M. (1977). *Science and reflection: The question concerning technology and other essays* (W. Lovitt, Trans.). New York, NY: HarperCollins.

Hettiarachchi, P. (2007). *Competence and Beyond a guide providing a holistic understanding of human capital in the apparel and textile industry*. Sri Lanka: Joint Apparel Association Forum.

Keen, W. O., & Bruce, R. R. (2000). *Keeping the public trust: The value of values in government*. Reston, VA: Keen Ideas.

Kunz, W. & Rittel. (1970). Issues as elements of information systems. In *Center for Planning and Development Research* (Working Paper 131). Berkeley, CA: University of California, Berkeley.

Lewin, K. (1997). *Resolving social conflicts and field theory in social science*. Washington, DC: American Psychological Association. doi:10.1037/10269-000

Lewin, K. et al. (1975). *Frustration and Regression: An Experiment With Young Children*. Iowa City, IA: University of Iowa Press.

Llewellyn, R. (2009). Stakeholder Management Overview. *The Project Management Hut*. Retrieved from http://www.pmhut.com/stakeholder-management-overview

Marx, K. (1976). *Capital* (Vol. 1). London, UK: Penguin Books.

Maslow, A. H. (1996). A theory of human motivation. In *Classic readings in organizational behavior* (2nd ed., pp. 45–56). Belmont, CA: Wadsworth.

Maurer, M. (2011). *Skill Formation Regimes in South Asia: A Comparative Study on the Path-Dependent Development of Technical and Vocational Education and Training for the Garment Industr*. Komparatistische Bibliothek / Comparative Studies Series / Bibliotheque d'Etudes Comparatives Ser.

Ministry of Finance and Planning. (2006). *2006 Budget Speech*. Colombo: Ministry of Finance and Planning.

Nietzsche, F. (1988). *Other worlds: Essays in cultural politics* (G. C. Spivak, Ed.). New York, NY: Routledge.

Partridge, E. (Ed.). (1958). *Origins: A short etymological dictionary of modern English*. New York, NY: Macmillan.

Peirce, C. S. (1888). *A Guess at the Riddle: The triad in physics, MS 909, EP1*. Retrieved 4/4/2013, from http://www.cspeirce.com/menu/library/bycsp/guess/guess.htm

Rittel, H. W. (1972). *Second generation design methods*. J. Wiley and Sons.

Rittel, H. W.J., & Webber. (1973). Dilemmas in a General Theory of Planning. *Policy Sciences*, 4.

Rogers, C. (1951). *Client-centered therapy: Its current practice, implications and theory*. London, UK: Constable.

Ross, D. H. (2009). *A Critical Companion to William butler Yeats, A Literary Reference to His Life and Work*. Facts on File.

Shafritz, J. M., & Ott, S. J. (1996). Introduction. In *Classics of organization theory* (3rd ed.). Belmont, CA: Wadsworth.

Skinner, B. F. (1974). *About behaviorism*. New York, NY: Vintage Books.

Taylor, F. (1976). The principles of scientific management. In *Classics of organization theory* (9th ed., pp. 66–67). Belmont, CA: Wadsworth.

Walsh, J. P., Meyer, A. D., & Schoonhoven, C. B. (2006). A future for organization theory: Living in and living with changing organizations. *Organization Science*, 657–671. doi:10.1287/orsc.1060.0215

Weber, M. (1992). *The protestant ethic and the spirit of capitalism*. New York, NY: Routledge.

Weick, K. E. (1979). *The social psychology of organizing* (2nd ed.). New York, NY: Random House.

Wijayasiri, J. (2008). *Case study 3: The ending of the multi-fibre agreement and 713 Ministry of Finance and Planning*. Colombo: Ministry of Finance and Planning.

ENDNOTES

[1] Raymon R. Bruce & Sharon Bruce, *COAT- A Virtual College of Apparel and Textiles (Fulbright Grant #2303)* (Colombo: Joint Apparel Association Forum, 2007) p. 242.

Chapter 3

Context Inference Engine (CiE):
Classifying Activity of Context using Minkowski Distance and Standard Deviation-Based Ranks

Umar Mahmud
National University of Sciences and Technology (NUST), Pakistan

Muhammad Younus Javed
National University of Sciences and Technology (NUST), Pakistan

ABSTRACT

Context Awareness is the ability of systems and applications to sense the environment and infer the activity going on in the environment. Context encompasses all knowledge bounded within an environment and includes attributes of both machines and users. A context-aware system is composed of context gathering and context inference modules. This chapter proposes a Context Inference Engine (CiE) that classifies the current context as one of several known context activities. This engine follows a Minkowski distance-based classification approach with standard deviation-based ranks to identify likeliness of classified activity of the current context. Empirical results on different data sets show that the proposed algorithm performs closer to Support Vector Machines (SVM) while it is better than probabilistic reasoning methods where the performance is quantified as success in classification.

1. INTRODUCTION

Context Aware Systems provide classify the activity of the current context and facilitate service adaptation based on the activity classification. The core of the context aware system is an inference or classification engine. The task of this engine is to classify the activity and of the current contextual data. The contextual data is composed of

all the devices, services and persons present in the environment.

CiE is designed to identify which activity does the current state belong to? A number of approaches have been proposed in the literature including Rule Based Approaches (RBA) and Classification Based Approaches (CBA) as a means to implement context inference engines. CiE follows a CBA using distance measures and

DOI: 10.4018/978-1-4666-6098-4.ch003

standard deviation based ranks. The distance measure is used to identify the similarity among contexts while the standard deviation based ranks are used to measure likeliness of the outcome.

This chapter is an enhanced version of a paper published in IJAPUC in 2012 (Mahmud & Javed, 2012). This chapter introduces more results performed on different data sets. The data sets are further divided into training set and test sets and failure percentage of classification is recorded. In addition the effect of number of variables, the size of sample set and the selection of Minkowski parameter p is presented.

Section 2 presents the evidences of context classification approaches in the literature. Section 3 compares different context classification algorithms found in the literature. Section 4 presents the architecture and process of CiE with test results. The chapter concludes in Section 5.

2. EVIDENCES OF CONTEXT CLASSIFICATION APPROACHES IN LITERATURE

The early context aware systems are designed as applications that consider spatial and temporal factors as the context. These applications follow RBA for classification of the activity of contextual data (Schilit, Hilbert, & Trevor, 2002), (Want, Hopper, Falcao, & Gibbons, 1992), (Cheverst, Mitchell, & Davies, 1999), (Abowd, Atkenson, Hong, Long, Kooper, & Pinkerton, 1997), (Román, Hess, Cerqueira, Campbell, & Nahrstedt, 2002), (Hofer, Pichler, Leonhartsberger, Altmann, & Werner, 2002), (Wang Y.-K., 2004), (de Deugd, Carroll, Kelly, Millett, & Ricker, 2006), (Dey & Abowd, 1999), (Riaz, Kiani, Lee, Han, & Lee, 2005), (Chen, Finin, & Joshi), (Mahmud, Iltaf, Rehman, & Kamran, 2007), (Gu, Pung, & Zhang, 2004), (Fahy & Clarke, 2004), (Guo, Gao, Ma, Li, & Huang, 2008). Use of context matching is an improvement on RBA (Samulowitz, Michahelles, & Linnhoff-Popien, 2001), (Xue, Pung, & Sen,

2013). RBA is an efficient technique but lacks flexibility in terms of learning new axioms and situations. The effort put in by the developer to introduce new axioms or modify them in different software engineering phases is high. Context aware systems are thus restricted to the quantity as well as the quality of the axioms developed.

To model new situations and improve the concepts the context aware system needs to have learning. CBA is an alternative to RBA where the system classifies the current context as one of known activities (Korpipaa, Mantyjarvi, Kela, Keranen, & Malm, 2003), (Mayrhofer, 2004), (Blum, 2005), (Brdiczka, Crowley, & Reignier, 2007), (Yuan & Wu, 2008). The information about the classified activity is then shared with the applications for subsequent adaptation. Supervised learning has shown encouraging results in context activity classification (Korpipaa, Mantyjarvi, Kela, Keranen, & Malm, 2003), (Brdiczka, Crowley, & Reignier, 2007). CBA has been used as a distance measure based classification system in (Mayrhofer, 2004), (Brdiczka, Crowley, & Reignier, 2007), (Yuan & Wu, 2008). These systems identify the activity of the current context as a measure of similarity between the current context and recorded contexts. Priorities have been proposed as a general remedy to resolve conflicts occurring in classification (Mayrhofer, 2004), (Shin & Woo, 2005).

Most of the systems have a rule based context classification component (Chen, Finin, & Joshi), (Mahmud, Iltaf, Rehman, & Kamran, 2007), (Gu, Pung, & Zhang, 2004), (Fahy & Clarke, 2004), (Loke, 2010), (Guo, Gao, Ma, Li, & Huang, 2008), (Lee, Choi, & Elmasri, 2009), (Cao, Klamma, Hou, & Jarke, 2008), (Paganelli, Spinicci, & Giuli, 2008), (Chihani, Bertin, Suprapto, Zimmermann, & Crespi, 2012), (Riboni & Bettini, 2011), (Bernini, Micucci, & Tisato, 2010), (Barbosa & Andrade, 2009), (Ye, Stevenson, & Dobson, 2011). RBA context aware systems are simple to design. These systems activate first order logic based axioms thus providing a fast mapping between perception and its action. RBA is also suitably represented in the form of set theory, state machines and ambient calculus (Ranganathan & Campbell, 2008). RBA has fast response time but exhibit slower performance for large rule sets (Wei & Chan, 2012), (Pantsar-Syvaniemi, Simula, & Ovaska, 2010). Moreover, uncertainty cannot be addressed by employing axioms unless fuzzification of axioms is done (Korpipaa, Mantyjarvi, Kela, Keranen, & Malm, 2003) and (Ghadiri, Baraani-dastjerdi, Ghasem-aghaee, & Nematbakhsh, 2011). RBA can support probabilistic techniques in addition to axioms as in (Bulfoni, et al., 2008), (Feng, Teng, & Tan, 2009).

CBA identifies which activity the current context belongs to (Mayrhofer, 2004), (Blum, 2005), (Brdiczka, Crowley, & Reignier, 2007), (Yuan & Wu, 2008), (Dargie, 2009), (Vladoiu & Constantinescu, 2011), (Perttunen, Kleek, Lassila, & Riekki, 2009), (Könönen, Mäntyjärvi, Similä, Pärkkä, & Ermes, 2010). Current context is gathered from the sensors present in the environment and the activity is classified. This approach is robust and has strong mathematical and probabilistic basis. Among different classification algorithms Growing Neural Gas, Markov models, Support Vector Machine and Instance Based Learning have been used.

MDA is found to be more suitable for developing heterogeneous context aware systems. MDA are non-mathematical approaches that have found usefulness in their ability to construct platform independent software systems. The prime power of MDA is the separation of business logic and application development through PIM and PSM GReAT is an example transformation tool between PIM and PSM (Almeida, Iacob, Jonkers, & Quartel, 2006). Other techniques include (Samulowitz, Michahelles, & Linnhoff-Popien, 2001), (Shin & Woo, 2005), (Loke, 2010). Mereotopology has also been used to provide advanced relations in axiom sets (Ranganathan & Campbell, 2008), (Schmidtke & Woo, 2009). Table 1 gives a comparison of RBA and CBA.

Table 1. Comparison of inference approaches

Features	RBA	CBA
Mathematical Basis	✓	✓
Noise Tolerance	✗	✓
Probabilistic Support	✗	✓
Algorithmic Support	✓	✓
Machine Learning	✗	✓
Adaptability	✗	✓
Scalability	✗	✓

3. CONTEXT CLASSIFICATION ALGORITHMS

The major classification methods are identified as Distance Measure Based Classification (DMBC), Evolutionary Classification (EC), Probabilistic Classification (PC) and Symbolic Classification (SC). Table 2 presents a comparison of these categories (Mitchell, 1997).

EC methods require high training times to identify the concept. The number of epochs required to perform these tasks are in the order of thousands e.g., Artificial Neural networks (ANN). PC methods are highly dependent on prior information experience e.g., Bayesian and Markov classifiers. SC methods suffer from the fact that the scope is proportional to the set of rules identified as in RBA and Decision Trees (Wei & Chan, 2012).

DMBC techniques include Nearest Neighbour Classification and are more suitable for context awareness though they lack probabilistic support. DMBC are lazy learners and can be modified to include confidence intervals to provide a measure of probability. The limitation of DBMC is the high classification time. DBMC demand the visualization of a context space (Padovitz, Loke, & Zaslavsky, 2004). Hartmann has proposed the use of distance to obtain similarity between attributes (Hartmann, Zesch, Mühlhäuser, & Gurevych, 2008).

Table 2. Comparison of Methods to Achieve Context Classification

Features	DMBC	EC	PC	SC
Fast Training Time	✓	✗	✗	✗
Fast Classification Time	✗	✓	✓	✓
Noise Tolerance	✓	✓	✓	✗
Classifying New Cases	✓	✓	✗	✗
Fast Adjustment of Concept	✓	✗	✗	✗
History Support	✓	✓	✓	✗

To find evidences of algorithms used for context classification in the search criteria includes keywords as "Context Aware Systems", "Context Awareness", "Context Classification", "Context Inference", "Context Recognition" and "Context Activity Recognition". In addition to the keywords the selection is made if the research paper includes context classification method. Among the different research papers identified emphasis is placed on International Journal and Conference Papers as well Technical Reports. Also research papers published on or after 2008 A.D. have been given more importance. An arithmetic count is made on the literature to identify the popular trends in context classification as shown in Figure 1. Clearly, RBA has been the popular choice.

3.1 Rule Based Approach (RBA)

RBA use first order logic for context classification (Mahmud, Iltaf, Rehman, & Kamran, 2007), (Loke, 2010), (Lee, Choi, & Elmasri, 2009), (Paganelli, Spinicci, & Giuli, 2008), (Cioara, Anghel, Salomie, & Dinsoreanu, 2009), (Badii, Crouch, & Lallah, 2010), (Chihani, Bertin, Suprapto, Zimmermann, & Crespi, 2012), (Bernini, Micucci, & Tisato, 2010), (Feng, Teng, & Tan, 2009), (Gu, Pung, & Zhang, PerCom 2008, 2008), (Khalil, Ali, & Kotsis, 2008), (Ahn & Park, 2008), (Ahn Y.-A., 2009), (Duggal, Misra, & Srinivasaraghavan, 2012), (Füller, Nüßer, & Rustemeyer, 2012). Fuller identifies that the size of heap space increases linearly with the increase in number of rules (Füller, Nüßer, & Rustemeyer, 2012).

Figure 1. Count of context classification algorithms

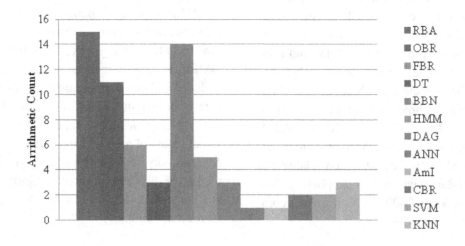

3.2 Ontology Based Reasoning (OBR)

In OBR, axioms are developed and are allied with ontology (Wei & Chan, 2012), (Cao, Klamma, Hou, & Jarke, 2008), (Li, Fang, & Xiong, 2008), (Pantsar-Syvaniemi, Simula, & Ovaska, 2010), (Riboni & Bettini, 2011), (Barbosa & Andrade, 2009), (Ye, Stevenson, & Dobson, 2011), (Strobbe, et al., 2012), (De & Moessner, 2008), (Riboni & Bettini, 2009), (Scalmato, Sgorbissa, & Zaccaria, 2013). OWL associated with Pellet, FACT++, etc provides a realization of OBR. The technique suffers from the scalability issue of the axiom set (Wei & Chan, 2012).

3.3 Fuzzy Based Reasoning (FBR)

Fuzzy reasoning provides fuzzy axioms and allows a degree of probability to be included in an essentially an RBA context aware system (Ghadiri, Baraani-dastjerdi, Ghasem-aghaee, & Nematbakhsh, 2011), (Cheung, Yao, Cao, & Chan, 2008), (Yu, Nakamura, Zhang, Kajita, & Mase, 2008), (Cao, Xing, Chan, Feng, & Jin, 2005), (Lee K., 2010), (Thyagaraju & Kulkarni, 2012). The main drawback is the size of rule set as is the case in OBR as well as fuzzification mechanism (Wei & Chan, 2012).

3.4 Decision Trees (DT)

Decision Trees create statistical based trees to classify query instances based on entropy (Mitchell, 1997). Santos has used Decision Trees to classify context (Santos, Tarrataca, Cardoso, Ferreira, Diniz, & Chainho, 2009), (Singh, Vajirkar, & Lee, 2003).

3.5 Bayesian Belief Network (BBN)

Bayesian Belief Networks use a graphical technique to realize context inference through conditional dependencies. This technique has a strong probabilistic basis through Bayesian Probability (Bulfoni, et al., 2008), (Niklas, Klaus, Sigg, & Beigl, 2010), (Ko & Sim, 2008), (Frank, Röckl, & Robertson, 2008), (Zhang & Izquierdo, 2008), (Krause, Linnhoff-Popien, & Strassberger, 2007), (Zhang, Guan, Zhou, Tang, & Guo, 2008), (Qiao & Li, 2009), (Yordanova, Kruger, & Kirste, 2012), (Min & Cho, 2011), (Rockl, Frank, Hermann, & Vera, 2008), (Wang, Rosenblum, & Wang, 2012), (Song & Cho, 2013). The approximation of probability becomes cumbersome when then the size of BBN is large (Zhang, Guan, Zhou, Tang, & Guo, 2008).

3.6 Hidden Markov Models (HMM)

HMM demand that the inference process should follow the Markov Process. HMM and BBN both are dependent on prior knowledge and the outcome is history biased (Kuo, Lee, & Chung, 2010), (Dargie, 2009), (Cheng, Buthpitiya, Sun, & Griss, 2010), (Kurz, et al., 2011). Xu has given a novel technique for context activity recognition based on Rules, Decision Trees and HMM (Xu, Zhou, David, & Chalon, 2013).

3.7 Directed Acyclic Graphs (DAG)

Graph based algorithms are suggested that use DAG for context classification. This technique is based on graph theory and enjoys visual power (Siebra, Salgado, Tedesco, & Brézillon, 2005), (Nguyen & Choi, 2008). McKeever has used Dempster-Shaffer theory to address uncertainty in contextual data using DAG (McKeever, Ye, Coyle, Bleakley, & Dobson, 2010). The issue with DAG based approach remains the effective conversion of graphs to programming models.

3.8 ANN

ANN has provided an evolutionary approach towards context classification. The task is to identify a weight vector that helps in correctly classifying a query state. ANN suffers from high training times (Guan, Yuan, Lee, & Lee, 2007).

3.9 Ambient Intelligence (AmI)

AmI has been developed from Ambient Calculus and has seen recent employment in context classification. Ambient Calculus is used to describe concurrent systems that exhibit mobility (Cardelli & Gordon, 2001). Context classification through AmI has been used in (Ranganathan & Campbell, 2008).

3.10 Case Based Reasoning (CBR)

CBR are a derivative of RBA and identify the set of rules that lead to the construction of a concept (Mitchell, 1997). CBR has been used for context awareness in (Vladoiu & Constantinescu, 2011), (Lee & Lee, 2008).

3.11 Support Vector Machines (SVM)

SVM provide an unsupervised algorithm that is based on kNN and ANN. SVM construct a hyperplane to identify boundaries between instances of different classes in a hyperspace. SVM is an unsupervised technique and does not require external interaction (Perttunen, Kleek, Lassila, & Riekki, 2009), (Anguita, Ghio, Oneto, Parra, & Reyes-Ortiz, 2012).

3.12 kNN

Distance based algorithms follow kNN approach where a query is classified based on its distance with other instances (Mitchell, 1997). kNN has been used for context classification in (Padovitz, Loke, & Zaslavsky, 2004) (Guan, Yuan, Lee, & Lee, 2007), (Golsa, Troped, & Evans, 2013). The training time of kNN approach is low while the classification time is high. With intelligent feature selection prior to inference process the performance can be enhanced in kNN (Könönen, Mäntyjärvi, Similä, Pärkkä, & Ermes, 2010).

4. CONTEXT INFERENCE ENGINE (CIE)

The core of the context aware system is the classification unit CiE. The task of CiE is to identify whether the activity of the current context is recognized as a recorded activity and with what likeliness? The current context is composed of different attributes. The job is to identify on the basis of distance that which of the recorded contexts are closest to the current context following the theme of kNN (Mitchell, 1997). The distance is measured between the current context and each record in the history. The activity of the closest recorded context is most likely the activity of the current context. Assume S_c is the current context, and S is the set of all recorded contexts then S is defined mathematically in Equation 1 where $S_1, S_2 \ldots S_n$ are the recorded contextsnd n is the total number of recorded contexts.

$$S = \left\{ S_1, S_2, \cdots S_n \right\} \tag{1}$$

Let A_c be the activity of the current context S_c nd A_i e the activity of an arbitrary recorded context $S_i \in S$ Let d_i be the distance between the current context and an arbitrary context S_i hen the activity of the current context is the activity of the closest context as shown in Equation 2. kNN suffers from the noise in the closest context in which case it can output an incorrect activity.

$$A_c = Activity\,of\,\left\{ \min\!\left(d_i \right) \right\} \tag{2}$$

4.1 Distance Measures

Table 3 gives a comparison of different distance measures. These distance measures have their bases in geometry as well as statistics. Among the distance measures listed in Table 3 Chebyshev distance, Hellinger distance, Mahalanobis distance

Table 3. Distance measures

Distance Measure	Basis
Euclidean (Mitchell, 1997)	Straight line between two Cartesian points
Mahalanobis (McLachlan, 1999)	Correlations between sets of variables
Minkowski (Minkowski, 1910)	Line between two points in hyperspace with Minkowski Parameter *p*
Hellinger (Hellinger, 1907)	Between two probability distributions
Bhattacharyya (Bhattacharya, 1943)	Between two probability distributions
Manhattan (Manhattan Distance)	Between two points as sum of absolute distances
Chebyshev (Cantrell, 2000)	Largest difference among two vectors
Hamming (Hamming, 1950)	Between two equal length bit strings

and Bhattacharyya distance are all unsuitable as they require participating vectors or probability distributions (Cantrell, 2000) (Hellinger, 1907) (McLachlan, 1999) (Hellinger, 1907). Context classification demands that distance be measured between a current context and each member of a set of recorded contexts. While in CiE the distance is measured between a single point in a context space and a probability distribution of context space. The Hamming distance loses its effectiveness because it requires equal length bit strings. The recorded contexts may not be equal in length and may also have missing parameters.

If $p=1$ hen Minkowski distance reduces to Manhattan distance and if $p = 2$ hen Minkowski distance reduces to Euclidean distance. Since Euclidean distance and Manhattan distance are specialized form of Minkowski distance, the problem is thus reduced to finding a suitable value of the Minkowski Parameter *p* (Mitchell, 1997), (Manhattan Distance), (Minkowski, 1910).

The Minkowski Distance *d* between two points in a Cartesian plane is given in Equation 3 where *p* is the Minkowski Parameter and Δx s the dif-

fernce between x values of both points and Δy s the difference between y values of both points.

$$d = \sqrt[p]{\left|\Delta x\right|^p + \left|\Delta y\right|^p} \qquad (3)$$

The Minkowski Distance *d* between two points in hyperspace where Δx_i the difference between the ith parameter is given in Equation 4. The total number of parameters is *v*.

$$d = \sqrt[p]{\sum_{i=1}^{v} \left(\Delta x_i\right)^p} \qquad (4)$$

4.2 Density Effect in Distance Measures

Euclidean distance, Manhattan distance, Chebyshev distance and Minkowski distance measure the absolute distance and are not dependent on the density of the data and hence instances having same absolute distance but falling in different data density regions are considered to be equally likely for selection. This is shown in Figure 2 where x_q is the query instance and x_1 and x_2 are two arbitrary instances of the same class. Instance x_1 is in the

Figure 2. Density effect and distance from query instance

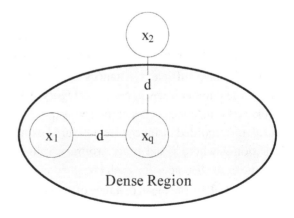

dense region while instance x_2 is in the sparse region. Both are at the same distance d from x_q.

To include the effect of density with Minkowski distance, arithmetic mean and standard deviation can be utilized (McLachlan, 1999). For example, if an instance is within one standard deviation on either sides of the mean then it is in the denser region as compared to an instance that is beyond three standard deviations on either sides of the mean. To measure the density, the mean of the group of similar instances is required. The density assumes that the spread is in an even sphere centred at the mean. For an ellipsoidal spread a measure of direction in the form of a vector is required (McLachlan, 1999). The measurement of the vector requires that distance is measured among probability distribution rather than a single point vs. a probability distribution as in CiE. Hence, the system is constrained that the spread is even, spherical and centred at the mean.

4.3 Conquering Classification Errors in DMBC

1NN can misclassify a query instance if the closest instance has a noise in classification. This is improved in kNN where an odd number of instances are selected and the query is classified according to the number of votes for each possible outcome. Voting thus reduces the precision inherent in 1NN. The number of votes for the highest classification can be considered as the confidence on the outcome.

Assume that a query instance is to be classified among two different categories ct_1 d ct_2 Both categories have sufficient instances i.e $n \geq 30$., ere n is the number of instances per category. The Minkowski distances between query instance x_q and all the recorded instances are measured using Equation 4 where v and p are arbitrary values. The mean of distances for each category is also recorded. Let μ_1 the mean distance of x_q and ct_1

hile μ_2 the mean distance of x_q and ct_2 s shown in Figure 3. It is intuitive that if there is no noise in the closest instance then the classification of mean of the closest category as well as the classification of the closest instance will be same. This is shown in Figure 3 where the classification of closest instance and the classification of mean of the closest category are same. Query x_q is at the origin and the distances are not to scale for illustration purpose. Both axes show absolute distances.

If the closest instance is misclassified then the state would be as shown in Figure 4. Here the classification of the closest instance is not the same as the classification of the mean of the closet category.

Using standard deviation based ranks it could be identified as to which category does the closest instance belong to? Spherical rings are drawn with respect to both μ_1 nd μ_2 Let one ring be within one standard deviation and the outer ring is one and half standard deviation. Then it can be seen that the closest instance is closer to μ_2 an μ_1 It is pertinent that the distances are measured with reference to x_q. It follows from Figure 4 that the closest instance should be an instance of ct_2 it is closer to μ_2

4.4 CiE Algorithm

CiE is based on Minkowski Distance coupled with standard deviation based ranks of the recorded activities of different contexts. The proposed algorithm has two stages: *Distance Measurer* and *Rank Identifier*. The first stage is concerned with measuring Minkowski distances while the second stage is tasked with creating ranks of activities based on standard deviations with reference to the query instance. The architecture of CiE is shown in Figure 5.

Figure 3. Closest instance and mean of closest category with no misclassification

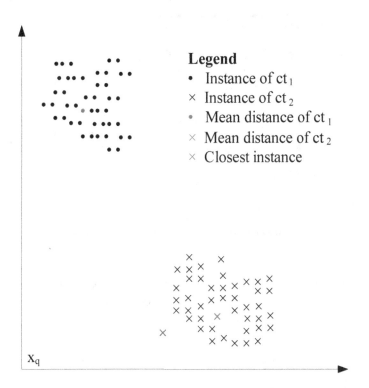

Figure 4. Misclassified closest instance and mean of closest category

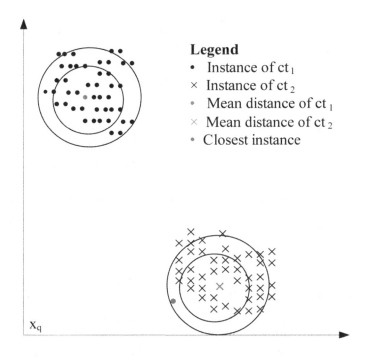

Figure 5. Architecture of CiE

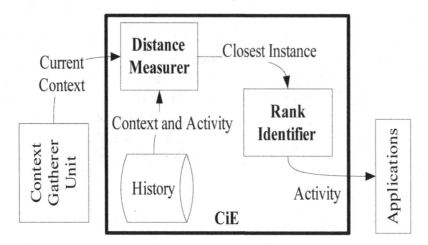

4.4.1 Distance Measurer Stage

The first task is to calculate the Minkowski distances of all the recorded contexts $S_1, S_2 \ldots S_n$ ith respect to the current context S_c The recorded contexts have activity associated with them and can be stored as OWL individuals or as simple files. Let the activity of recorded contexts $S_1, S_2 \ldots S_n$ e $A_1, A_2 \ldots A_n$ espectively. Let there be k distinct activities in the recorded history. The arithmetic mean μ_k f every activity k is calculated. The mean μ_k calculated with respect to S_c Equation 5 shows the arithmetic mean, where m is the total number of recorded contexts per activity k and d_i s the Minkowski distance between S_c nd any arbitrary recorded context S_i

$$\mu_k = \frac{1}{m}\left(\sum_{i=1}^{m} d_i\right) \quad (5)$$

If the activity of the closest recorded context and the activity of the closest mean are same, then the activity of the current context is the activity of the closest recorded context with highest likeliness. This follows Figure 3 and assumes that the closest recorded instance is not misclassified. This situation is also considered as an absolute success.

Table 4 shows the steps of the Distance Measurer stage. The table outlines the variables and shows the asymptotic upper bound for each step.

Step 5 in Table 4 evaluates to a FALSE then standard deviation based ranks are created for the closest recorded context to identify the activity. This case follows Figure 4.

4.4.2 Rank Identifier Stage

It is natural that in a multi-activity context classification environment multiple activities can contest the classification of the closest recorded context. For this likeliness values are generated based on the standard deviation rank. The task of stage two is to identify the likeliness of an activity to be the target activity based on the standard deviation.

The closest context is given standard deviation σ anks from each activity mean as shown in Figure 4. From statistics it is learnt that the smaller the rank the closer is an instance to the mean if it falls within this rank (McLachlan, 1999). Hence, if rank of activity A_1 s smaller than rank of activity A_2 then A_1 s a better choice.

Four ranks of standard deviation, within 1σ o beyond 3σ have been selected. Beyond 3σ he activity is considered to be unlikely as 99.7% f the data items are within 3σ The likeliness is given as static values. The closer the rank the larger is the likeliness. If the ranks are less, the accuracy will be high at the cost of success. Similarly, if ranks are more, the success will be high at the cost of accuracy. Table 5 shows the likeliness values for standard deviation ranks. The likeliness values are flexible and can be changed as per wishes of the user.

The standard deviation σ_k for k^{th} activity is given in Equation 6 where the number of recorded contexts having same activity k s m d_i s the Minkowski distance between i^{th} ecorded context and query context x_q μ_k the mean of Minkowski distances of kth ctivity.

$$\sigma_k = \sqrt{\frac{1}{m}\sum_{i=1}^{m}\left(d_i - \mu_k\right)^2} . \qquad (6)$$

Table 6 shows the Rank Identifier stage of the CiE Algorithm. This stage is constructed as an IF-ELSE-IF block that selects the appropriate activity based on the rank. There is a possibility that multiple distinct activities can be selected as likely due to closer ranks. The algorithm considers this situation as a partial success and returns a short list of likely activities with the closeness of the rank as confidence. A failure in activity classification occurs if the target activity is not among the shortlist identified by the Rank Identifier stage. This is mainly due to noise in the query instance. The failure requires active intervention by the user to select the correct activity.

4.4.3 Symptotic Analysis of CiE Algorithm

In the first stage of CiE algorithm, the barometer instruction is found in Step 1 when Minkowski distances are being calculated, as shown in Table 4. Assume n s the total number of recorded instances, v s the total number of variables in each instance and k s the total number of activities,

then the total asymptotic upper bound for Stage 1 is given in Equation 7.

$$O\left(\text{distanceMeasurer}\right) = O\left(n \times v\right) + O\left(n\right) + O\left(k \times m\right) + O\left(k\right) + O\left(1\right)$$

$$\qquad (7)$$

In the second stage of CiE algorithm, the barometer instruction is found in Step 1 when standard deviations are being calculated, as shown in Table 6. This loop repeats k imes, where k s the total number of activities. The total asymptotic upper bound for Stage 2 is given in Equation 8.

$$O\left(\text{rankIdentifier}\right) = O\left(k \times m\right) + O\left(k\right) + O\left(k\right)$$

$$\qquad (8)$$

For the worst case where the condition in Step 5 of Stage 1 fails, the overall asymptotic upper bound for the CiE algorithm is given in Equation 9.

$$O\left(\text{CiE}\right) = O\left(n \times v\right) + 2\left(O\left(k \times m\right)\right) + 3\left(O\left(k\right)\right) + O\left(n\right) + O\left(1\right)$$

$$\qquad (9)$$

From Equation 9, it is clear that the dominating term is the multiplicative term $O\left(n \times v\right)$ Since the number of instances in the data set tend to be large than the number of categories and the number of variables. Thus, CiE does not perform worse than quadratic time as shown in Equation 10.

$$O\left(\text{CiE}\right) \approx O\left(n^2\right)\big|n\big\rangle v \qquad (10)$$

4.5 Proof of Concept of CiE

The CiE algorithm is implemented in Java language due to platform independent nature of Java. Both the stages of CiE are implemented as Java methods within a class. The evaluation criterion is the correct classification of a context where each recorded context has an associated activity. The outcome is absolute success, with highest likeliness, if both the activity of the mean of the closest activity and the activity of the closest recorded context are the target activity. Otherwise, standard deviation ranks for each activity and the closest recorded context are created. For each rank the likeliness value is determined and the set of all likely activities are identified coupled with their likeliness as a shortlist. If the target activity is part of the shortlist of activities then the case is a partial success. Only if the correct activity is not part of the set of likely activities, the case is

Table 4. Distance measurer stage

Function: *distanceMeasurer()*	
Input: $Current\,context = S_c$, $Set\,of\,recorded\,contexts = S$	
Output: $Activity\,of\,S_c = A_c$, $Likeliness\,of\,activity = l$	
Variables: $Minkowski\,Parameter = p$, $Size\,of\,S = n$	
$Activity\,of\,an\,arbitrary\,recorded\,context = A_j$	
$Total\,number\,of\,variables\,in\,each\,instance = v$	
$Difference\,between\,i^{th}\,attributes\,of\,S_c\,and\,a\,recorded\,context = \Delta x_i$	
$Total\,number\,of\,activities = k$, $Array\,to\,store\,distances = d[n]$	
$Array\,to\,store\,mean\,of\,distances\,of\,activities = \mu[k]$	
$Activity\,of\,the\,minimum\,distance\,instance = A_{min}$	
$Activity\,of\,the\,minimum\,mean = A_{min\mu}$	
$Total\,number\,of\,instances\,per\,recorded\,activity = m$	

Step	Description	Asymptotic Upper Bound

1	//Calculate Minkowski distances
	FOR: $(j=0; j<n; j++)$
	
	$$d[j] = \sqrt[p]{\sum_{i=1}^{v}(\Delta x_i)^p}$$
	
	END FOR
		$O(n \times v)$

2	//Case of absolute success
	$min = Maximum\,Value\,of\,Long$
	FOR: $(j=0; j<n; j++)$
	IF: $(min < d[j])$
	
	$A_{min} = A_j$
	END IF
	END FOR
		$O(n)$

continued on following page

Table 4. Continued

3	//Find mean for all k activities
	FOR: $(j=0; j<k; j++)$
	IF: $(A_k == j)$
	$sum = \sum_{j=0}^{m} d_j$
	END IF
	$\mu[k] = \frac{sum}{k}$
	$k=0$
	END FOR
		$O(k \times m)$

4	//Activity of minimum mean activity
	$minMean = Maximum\ value$
	FOR: $(j=0; j<k; j++)$
	IF: $(minMean < \mu[k])$
	$A_{min\mu} = A_j$
	END IF
	END FOR
		$O(k)$

5	$l = NULL$
	IF: $(A_{min} == A_{min\mu})$
	$A_c = A_{min}$
	$l = HIGHEST$
	OUTPUT $: (A_c, l)$
	//Case of absolute success
	ELSE:
	rankIdentifier();
	END IF
		$O(1)$

considered a failure. The CiE process as a flow model is shown in Figure 6. The test methodology is based on the success in classification by CiE algorithm vs. 1NN algorithm following a supervised approach.

4.5.1 Data Sets for Proof of Concept

To provide proof of concept the two sets compiled by Kristof Van Laerhoven as well as Holger Junker are selected (Laerhoven, 2004) (Junker). These data sets are available free at Institut für Pervasive.

The data set by Kristof Van Laerhoven is a collection of basic activities monitored by 40 sensors tied to both legs of a test subject to monitor activities like sitting standing, walking etc. Nine distinct activities have been recognized by the author and given numerical values with 40 variables. The data set is composed of floating point values with numerical activity identifiers. The population is more than 25000 instances. Uniform sets for both training set and test set are selected.

The data set by Holger Junker is used for locomotion analysis and is a collection of activities including ascending stairs, descending stairs and

Table 5. Likeliness and standard deviation ranks

Standard Deviation Rank	Likeliness
Within 1σ	High
Between 1σ and 2σ	Medium
Between 2σ and 3σ	Low
Beyond 3σ	Unlikely

level walking monitored by sensors tied to legs of a test subject. The tests have been carried out on seven different test subjects. Three distinct activities with 10 variables have been identified by the author and given numerical values. The data set is composed of positive and negative floating point values with numerical activity identifiers. The population is more than 500000 instances.

Table 6. Rank identifier stage

Function: *rankIdentifier()*

Input: $Array\ to\ store\ mean\ of\ distances\ of\ activities = \mu[k]$

$Distance\ of\ closest\ instance = d_i$

Output: $Activity\ of\ S_c = A_c,\ Likeliness\ of\ activity = l$

Variables: $Size\ of\ S = n,\ Total\ number\ of\ activities = k$

$Array\ to\ store\ distances = d[n],\ Activity\ of\ closest\ instance = A_{min}$

$Array\ to\ store\ mean\ of\ distances\ for\ all\ activities = \mu[k]$

$Standard\ deviations\ for\ all\ activities = \sigma[k]$

$Standard\ deviation\ rank\ for\ all\ activities = Rank[k]$

$Activity\ of\ closest\ instance = A_{min}$

$Total\ number\ instances\ having\ same\ activity = m$

$Activity\ of\ an\ arbitrary\ recorded\ context = A_j$

Step	Description	Asymptotic Upper Bound

1	//Standard deviations
	FOR: $(j=0; j<k; j++)$
	IF: $(A_j == k)$
	$$sum = \sum_{i=1}^{m}\left(d[m] - \mu[k]\right)^2$$
	END IF
	$$\sigma[k] = \sqrt{\frac{sum}{m}}$$
	$r=0$
	END FOR
		$O(k \times m)$

continued on following page

Table 6. Continued

| 2 | //Create Ranks
$l = NULL$
FOR: $(j = 0; j < k; j + +)$
IF: $\left(\left(\mu[k] - \left(1 * \sigma[t]\right)\right) < d_i\right)$
$Rank[k] = HIGH$
ELSEIF: $\left(\left(\mu[k] - \left(2 * \sigma[t]\right)\right) < d_i\right)$
$Rank[k] = MEDIUM$
ELSEIF: $\left(\left(\mu[k] - \left(3 * \sigma[t]\right)\right) < d_i\right)$
$Rank[k] = LOW$
ELSE: $Rank[k] = UNLIKELY$
END IF
END FOR | $O(k)$ |
| 3 | FOR: $(j = 0; j < k; j + +)$
IF: $\left(Rank[k] \, ! = UNLIKELY\right)$
OUTPUT : $\left(\textbf{Activity } \textbf{k}, \textbf{Rank}[\textbf{k}]\right)$
ELSE:
OUTPUT : $\left(\textbf{Fail}\right)$
END IF
END FOR | $O(k)$ |

The test machine is an Intel Core 2 Duo 2.0 GHz machine with 2 GB RAM. The Operating system is Windows XP version 5.1 with JRE version 1.7.0. Table 7 shows the statistics of each Test Case. The total size in Table 7 is the summation of sizes of the training set and the test set for initial tests on Kristof Van Laerhoven data set.

4.5.2 Failure Percentage in CiE as Compared With Other Algorithms

To test the effectiveness of CiE a variety of algorithms are implemented and results compared. The algorithms include 1NN using Euclidean Distance (Mitchell, 1997), DWNN using Euclidean Distance (Mitchell, 1997), 1NN based on Minkowski Distance with $p = e^2$ Mitchell, 1997). The CiE is executed with $p = e^2$ Figure 7 shows the failure percentages of each algorithm as a basis of comparison as carried out on Kristof Van Laerhoven data set. The percentage is calculated by dividing the total errors in classification by the size of the test set. Figure 4.6 show that CiE outperforms 1NN and DWNN algorithms. 1NN used with Minkowski Distance with $p = e^2$ follows closely with 1NN using Euclidean except at Test Case Number 4 where it outperforms 1NN with Euclidean. In Test Case Numbers 7 - 9 CiE gives best performance. All the algorithms except CiE are designed to be precise and identify the best activity. CiE reduces the precision to increase the success and associates a degree of likeliness with

Figure 6. CiE Process

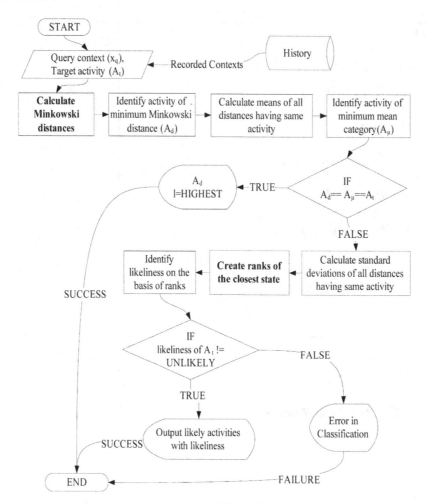

every result. The result show that the technique proposed in CiE is better than pure kNN algorithms.

Figure 8 shows the comparison of percentage errors for CiE algorithm and 1NN as executed on Holger Junker data set. The test configuration is changed for this data set and sizes of training set and test set are given in Table 8. A total of 25 tests cases are generated. It is clear in Figure 4.7 that the proposed CiE algorithm outperforms 1NN. CiE has an average failure percentage of 22.2% s compared to failure percentage of 57.08% y using 1NN. In test case number 7 the performance of both 1NN and CiE is same and has a success rate of 100% since in test case number 7 the clos-

Table 7. Sample and test data sizes for proof of concept on Kristof Van Laerhoven data set

Test Case Number	Sample Set Size	Test Set Size	Total
1	90	40	130
2	90	42	132
3	100	40	140
4	100	42	142
5	90	98	188
6	100	98	198
7	200	40	240
8	200	42	242
9	200	98	298

Figure 7. Failure percentage comparison of algorithms for Kristof Van Laerhoven data set

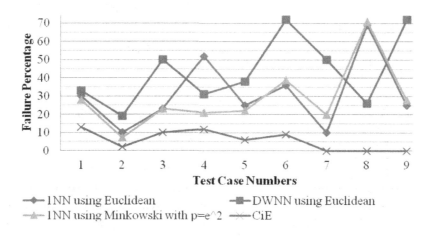

Figure 8. Failure percentage of CiE vs. 1NN on Holger junker data set

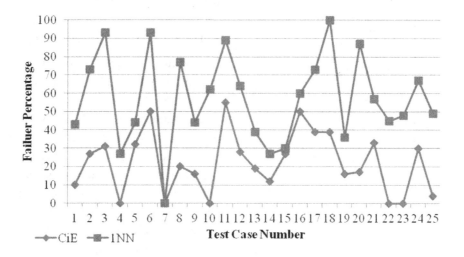

est instance is the target instance for the complete test set.

4.5.3 Situations of Success in CiE Algorithm

CiE successfully classifies current context if the target activity is either the closest or the current context is within sufficient standard deviations of the mean of the target activity. To illustrate the different situations, the sample sets contain equal number of recorded contexts for each activity.

4.5.3.1 Situation of Absolute Success

For the absolute success only the Distance Measurer Stage (Table 4) executes and the result is obtained. The activity of the closest instance A_d the activity of the mean of the closest category A_μ s same as the target activity A_t s represented in Equation 11 and Figure 9. The likeness of success is *HIGHEST* in this situation. This case conforms to the 1NN approach where the activity of the closest recorded instance is the target activity. The 1NN approach is improved by checking the mean of the activity of the closest context

Table 8. Test configurations for Holger junker data set

Test Case No.	1	2	3	4	5	6	7	8	9	10	11	12	13	14	15	16	17	18	19	20	21	22	23	24	25
Trg. Set Size	90	100	90	90	90	100	100	118	100	118	118	118	90	100	173	173	118	173	173	200	200	200	200	173	200
Test Set Size	30	30	42	44	50	42	44	30	50	42	44	50	98	98	30	42	98	44	50	30	42	44	50	98	98

to match the activity of the closest recorded context as well as the target activity.

$$A_d = A_\mu = A_t \tag{11}$$

Figure 9 shows the distance map of the situation of absolute success where the target is activity '9'. Figure 9 shows the distances of a query instance with the instances of the sample set. The distances from the query instance are shown in increasing along the vertical. The distances of the means of each activity are shown on the vertical at point -1 on the x-axis. As is evident the closest instance is from activity '9' and so is the mean of the closest activity. For this case Equation 11 evaluates to true in the algorithm.

4.5.3.2 Situation of Partial Success

If the situation represented in Equation 11 does not hold then Rank Identification Stage (Table 6) is executed. In this case the success is increased at the cost of precision. Activities are given likeliness values with respect to the standard deviation ranks as shown in Table 5. The categories with higher values of likeliness are selected as a shortlist. If the target is part of the short list then the situation is considered a partial success. Figure 10 shows the distance map of the situation of partial success where the target is Activity '4'. Also activities '0', '4' and '9' are close to each other. The activity of closest recorded context is '4' while the activity of the closest mean is '0'. This is the case where misclassification in the sample set leads to an imperfect classification of the query instance. By creating standard deviation ranks it is observed that the query lies within 2σ f activity '2' and activity '4' and within 3σ ctivity '3' as shown in Table 9. These three activities are then shortlisted as probable and given likeliness values. The situation is a success since the target activity is in the short list.

Figure 9. Situation of absolute success

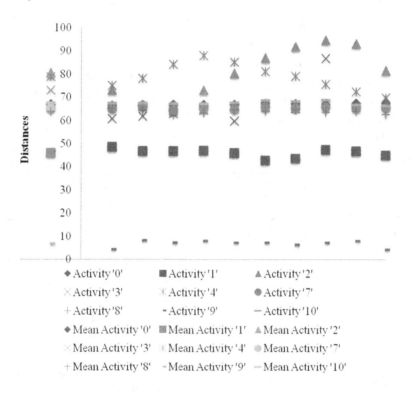

Figure 10. Situation of partial success

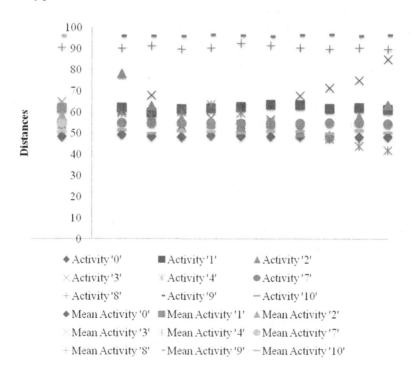

4.5.3.3 Situation of a Failure

If in the outcome of rank identifier stage the target activity has the likeliness value 'Unlikely' then the situation is a classification error and is termed as a failure. This is evident in Figure 11 where the activity of the closest recorded instance is '10' and the activity of the closest mean is also '10'. But Equation 11 does not hold in this situation as the target activity is '0'. By creating standard deviation ranks it is observed that query context lies within 2σ f activity '2' and activity '10' but is beyond 3σ f the activity '0'. This is shown in Table 10. As can be seen that the target activity is at a far distance from the query and hence there is no chance that it may be considered as a probable activity through the CiE algorithm. The reason of failure can be attributed to noise in the query context. Active user interaction is required to resolve this failure.

4.5.4 Time Analysis of CiE Algorithm

The CiE algorithm is executed for each test case on two machines with different specifications. First machine is an Intel Core 2 Duo 2.0 GHz machine with 2 GB RAM. The second machine is Pentium 4, 3.2 GHz with 512 MB RAM. The operating system in both cases is Windows XP version 5.1 with JRE 1.7.0. The test calculates the total time of execution of the CiE algorithm for each test case. The time is measured in nano-

seconds using the *nanoTime()* function in Java. Figure 12 shows the time plot with respect to the test case sizes for Kristof Van Laerhoven data set. The test cases have been ordered in increasing size as shown in Table 7.

It is clear from Figure 12 that the time complexity follows the dominating multiplicative term in Equation 10. The complexity of the CiE algorithm is multiplicative and the worst case will be no poorer than a quadratic curve Here the condition that the sample is larger than the total variables holds true and in all the tests the total number of variables is constant. Figure 13 shows the time plot with respect to the test case size for Holger Junker data set. The test cases have been ordered in increasing size as shown in Table 8. The test is performed on first machine only. As in Figure 12 the time complexity follows Equation 10 for Holger Junker data set as well.

4.5.5 Effect of Minkowski Parameter 'p' on Misclassification

To identify an appropriate value of Minkowski Parameter p est cases are repeated for different values of p o identify failure percentage for different values of p The test data selected is provided by Kristof van Laerhoven (Laerhoven, 2004) and the methodology is to identify the value of p or which the failure percentage is minimum when p s ranged between 0.01 and 100. Table 11

Table 9. Category ranks for situation of partial success

Activity	Mean	SD	Rank	Likeliness
0	48.65	0.33	Beyond 3	Unlikely
1	62.03	1.02	Beyond 3	Unlikely
2	58.18	8.08	2	Medium
3	65.02	9.74	3	Low
4	54.23	7.14	2	Medium
7	54.92	0.14	Beyond 3	Unlikely
8	90.65	0.87	Beyond 3	Unlikely
9	96.3	0.25	Beyond 3	Unlikely
10	50.86	0.58	Beyond 3	Unlikely

Figure 11. Situation of a failure

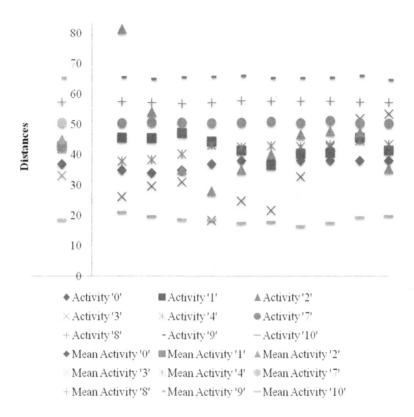

Table 10. Category ranks for situation of a failure

Activity	Means	SD	Ranks	Likeliness
0	36.9	1.5	Beyond 3	Unlikely
1	42.89	3.14	Beyond 3	Unlikely
2	45.1	14.22	3	Low
3	33.28	11.53	2	Medium
4	41.96	2.17	Beyond 3	Unlikely
7	50.63	0.25	Beyond 3	Unlikely
8	57.37	0.28	Beyond 3	Unlikely
9	65.42	0.41	Beyond 3	Unlikely
10	18.66	1.28	2	Medium

shows the total failure on different test set sizes for different values of p Smaller values of Minkowski parameter p ead to more number of misclassifications. Values of 0.01, 0.1 and 0.25 gave worst performance. Higher values of p ive better classification. The value selected in proof of concept of CiE algorithm (i.e $p = e^2$.,)erformed better than Euclidean Distance.

Figure 12. Time analysis of CiE for Kristof Van Laerhoven data set

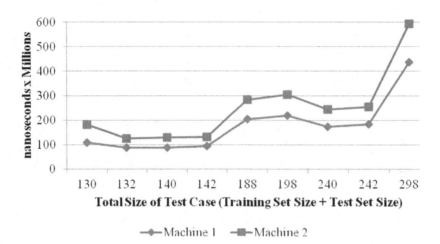

Figure 13. Time analysis of CiE for Kristof Van Laerhoven data set

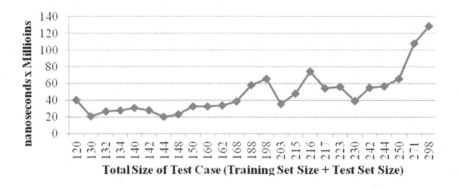

4.5.6 Effect of Minkowski Parameter p and Size of Training Set on Misclassification

The effect of the Minkowski parameter and size of training Set is observed in Figure 14-16 for Kristof Van Laerhoven data set. Test case number 1 has 100 instances in training set, test case number 2 has 118 instances in training set and test case number 3 has 200 instances in training set. The test is executed for different values of Minkowski parameter for a constant test set size. The executions are then repeated for different sample sizes.

The total classification errors are recorded for each test case and plotted. Figure 14-16 show that for larger values of Minkowski parameter and larger training sets, the misclassifications are reduced.

Figure 14 shows the effect of Minkowski parameter and size of training set on misclassification errors when test set size is 30. Figure 15 shows the effect of Minkowski parameter and size of training set on misclassification errors when test set size is 44. Figure 16 shows the effect of Minkowski parameter and size of training set on misclassification errors when test set size is 98. In all the three tests the worst performance is with

Table 11. Effect of Minkowski parameter on misclassification

Sample Size	100	100	100	118	118	118	200	200	200
Test Size	30	44	98	30	44	98	30	44	98
0.01	30	44	98	30	44	98	28	44	98
0.1	30	44	98	30	44	98	28	44	98
0.25	13	14	64	21	16	50	13	11	39
0.5	10	13	49	19	15	32	9	10	27
1	15	17	56	19	15	33	11	8	25
2	17	18	53	19	13	34	11	8	24
e^1.		17	50	18	13	34	11	9	25
3	18	17	50	18	13	34	11	9	25
π.		17	47	18	13	34	11	9	25
4	14	16	43	17	13	34	11	10	24
5	13	13	43	16	13	33	11	11	25
7	13	13	43	16	13	33	11	11	25
e^2.		13	44	16	13	33	11	11	25
8	13	13	49	16	13	33	11	11	25
10	13	13	50	16	10	33	11	11	25
15	14	13	52	20	12	32	11	12	26
25	15	13	55	20	11	31	12	12	27
50	14	13	55	21	12	31	12	12	27
100	14	13	55	21	12	32	12	12	27

Figure 14. Effect of Minkowski parameter and size of training set on misclassification with test data size 30

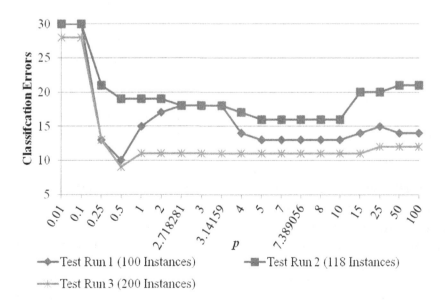

87

Figure 15. Effect of Minkowski parameter and size of training set on misclassification with test data size 44

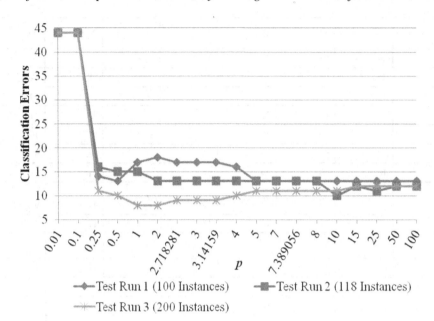

Figure 16. Effect of Minkowski Parameter and size of training set on misclassification with test data size 98

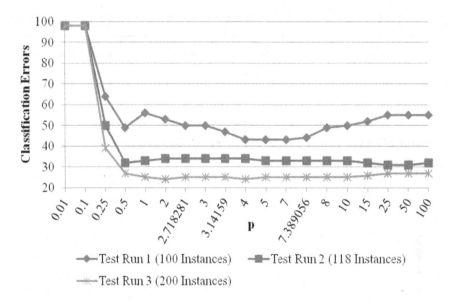

value of p ess than 0.1. The performance is generally constant for values of p reater than 0.5 though with variations to the sample sizes. This shows that value of p should be higher than or equal to 0.5.

4.5.7 Effect of Size of Training Set on Classification Time

The classification time is the time required to classify the current context and is dependent on the total size of the training set i.e. recorded contexts. Figure 17 shows the effect of size of training set on classification time for both Kristof Van Laerhoven data set and Holger Junker data set. The number of variables in Kristof Van Laerhoven data set is 40 while the number of variables in Holger Junker data set is 10. A single query instance is classified for each training set. The size of training sets is shown on X-axis in Figure 17. As is evident from the classification time is a monotonically increasing function of the size of training set. Also with the introduction of more variables the classification time increases as it is larger for Kristof Van Laerhoven data set than Holger Junker data set.

Figure 18 shows the linear least square line of the effect of training set on classification time for Kristof Van Laerhoven data set (Reid). The linear least square equation is given in Equation 12.

$$y = 65000x + \left(2.9\times10^7\right) \qquad (12)$$

Figure 19 shows the linear least square line of the effect of training set on classification time for Holger Junker data set (Reid). The linear least square equation is given in Equation 13.

$$y = 66000x + \left(1.29\times10^7\right) \qquad (13)$$

4.6 Extended Results With Different Test Data Sets

Proof of concept of CiE algorithm shows that the CiE algorithm performs better than 1NN algorithm. It is necessary to identify whether CiE performs better than other algorithms on different data sets. The criterion for selection of data sets includes the gathering of data in context aware setup, the availability of data as a set of attribute-value pairs and activity classification of the data sets. Data sets that provide comparison of different techniques are preferred. Also data sets available as open source are utilized. The selected data sets include OPPORTUNITY Activity Recognition Dataset (ETH Zentrum, Switzerland), (Roggen, et al., 2010), (Lukowicz, et al., 2010), COSAR (Riboni D., 2012), (Riboni & Bettini, 2009), HARUS (Anguita, Ghio, Oneto, Parra, & Reyes-Ortiz, 2012), (Anguita, Ghio, Oncto, Parra, & Reyes-Ortiz, UCI Machine Learning Repository, 2012) and LDPA (Kaluža, Mirchevska, Dovgan,

Figure 17. Effect of size of training set on classification time

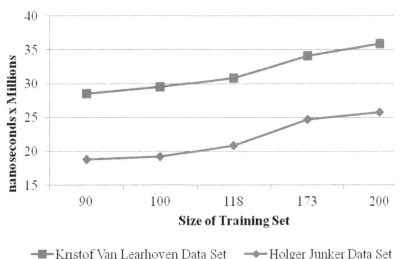

Figure 18. Linear least square line for effect of size of training set on classification time for Kristof Van Laerhoven data set

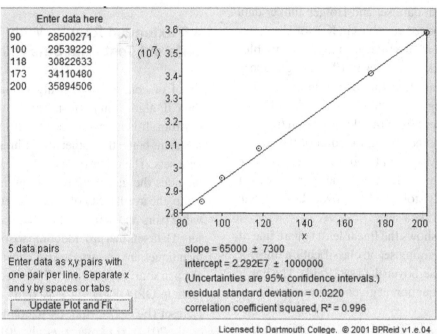

Figure 19. Linear least square line for effect of size of training set on classification time for Holger junker data set

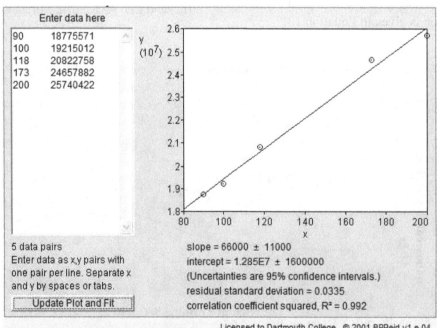

Luštrek, & Gams, 2010), (Kaluža, Mirchevska, Dovgan, Luštrek, & Gams, UCI Machine Learning Repository, 2010).

4.6.1 Test Methodology

For further testing on different data sets training sets and test sets are randomly selected. Some data sets identify the training sets and test sets separately. A total of 25 test cases are performed to reduce the error of experimentation. Initially the training set contains 20 recorded contexts per activity which is then increased to 40 and then 60 while the size of test set remains constant. The reason for the increase is to study the effect of size of training set on the performance. The test cases are repeated for different values of the Minkowski parameter. The values selected are given as a set in Equation 14. The test machine is an Intel Core 2 Duo 2.0 GHz machine with 2 GB RAM. The operating system is Windows XP version 5.1 with JRE 1.7.0.

$$p = \begin{Bmatrix} 0.01, 0.1, 0.25, 0.5, 0.707, \\ 1, 2, e, 3, \pi, 4, 5, 7, e^2, 8, 10, 50, 100 \end{Bmatrix} \quad (14)$$

4.6.2 Failure Percentage of CiE in OPPORTUNITY Activity Recognition Dataset

The opportunity data set uses wearable and environmental sensors to detect daily activities. The data set is multivariate time series with over 2500 instances. Opportunity project is a breakfast scenario that recognizes complex activities in rich sensor environments for four different subjects. The project utilizes 242 different sensors. The opportunity project has different tasks. The tasks selected for CiE evaluation are task A and task C. Opportunity project identifies 30 distinct composite activities including location and gesture of a test subject.

4.6.2.1 Test Results for Opportunity Project Task A

Task A in opportunity project identifies modes of locomotion. There are 114 different variables and the data set is noise free. Training sets and test sets are constructed from the data set provided for task A.

Figure 20 shows the failure percentage for each test case in opportunity project task A with training set size 20 per activity. Figure 20 shows the curves for Minkowski parameter of $0.5, 1$ and 2 The average failure percentage for 0.5 is 2.89% for 1 it is 3.29 and for 2 it is 4.13% In the test cases the best average failure percentage is achieved when Minkowski parameter is 0.5 for training set size 20 per activity.

Figure 21 shows the failure percentage for each test case in opportunity project task A with training set size increased to 40 per activity. Figure 21 shows the curves for Minkowski parameter of $0.5, 1$ and 2 The average failure percentage for 0.5 is 2.09%, or 1 it is 2.75% nd for 2 it is 3.15% In the test cases the best average failure percentage is achieved when Minkowski parameter is 0.5 for training set size 40 per activity.

With further increase of training set size to 60 the average failure percentage of CiE with Minkowski parameter 0.5 reduces to 1.69% or Minkowski parameter 1 reduces to 1.55% hile for Minkowski parameter 2 it is 2.49% For these parameter values of 0.5 and 1 the failure percentage is close. Figure 22 shows that with the increase in number of instances per category the failure percentage reduces.

4.6.2.2 Test Results for Opportunity Project Task C

Task C in opportunity project identifies modes of locomotion with noisy data. There are 114 different variables and the data set includes noise. The authors have introduced NaN ields to simulate missing attributes. Training sets and test sets are constructed from the data set provided for task C

Figure 20. Failure percentage for opportunity project task a with training size 20 per activity

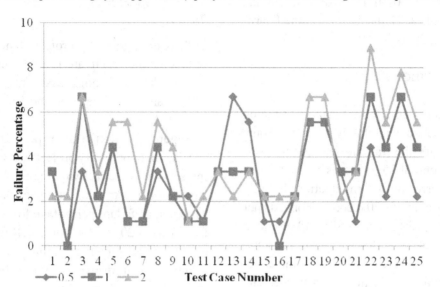

Figure 21. Failure percentage for opportunity project task a with training size 40 per activity

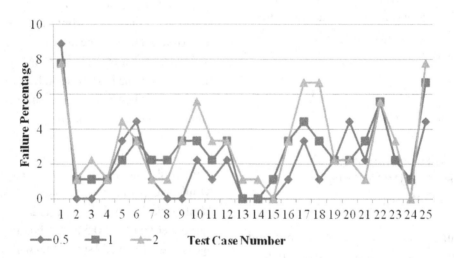

after removal of the Fields bearing NaN ince it does not have a numerical value.

Figure 23 shows the failure percentage for each test case in opportunity project task C with training set size 20 per activity. Figure 23 shows the curves for Minkowski parameter of $0.5, 1 and 2$ The average failure percentage for 0.5 is 35.96% for 1 it is 39.96 and for 2 it is 38.49% In the test cases the best average failure percentage is

achieved when Minkowski parameter is 0.5 for training set size 20 per activity.

Figure 24 shows the failure percentage for each test case in opportunity project task C with training set size increased to 40 per activity. Figure 24 shows the curves for Minkowski parameter of $0.5, 1 and 2$ The average failure percentage for 0.5 is 23.78%, or 1 it is 25.47% nd for 2 it is 24.71% In the test cases the best average failure percent-

Figure 22. Effect of training set size on average failure percentage for opportunity project Task A

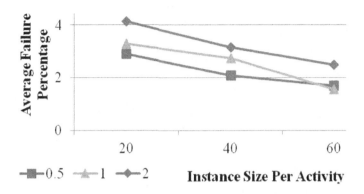

Figure 23. Failure percentage for opportunity project Task C with training size 20 per activity

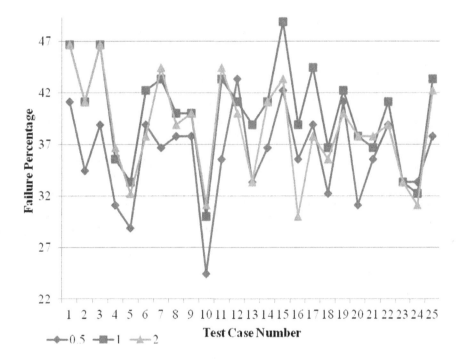

age is achieved when Minkowski parameter is 0.5 for training set size 40 per activity.

With further increase of training set size to 60 the average failure percentage of CiE with Minkowski parameter 0.5 reduces to 17.47% or Minkowski parameter 1 reduces to 17.73% r

Minkowski parameter 2 reduces to 18.98% For these three parameter values the failure percentage is close. Figure 25 shows that with the increase in number of instances per category the failure percentage reduces.

Figure 24. Failure percentage for opportunity project Task C with training size 40 per activity

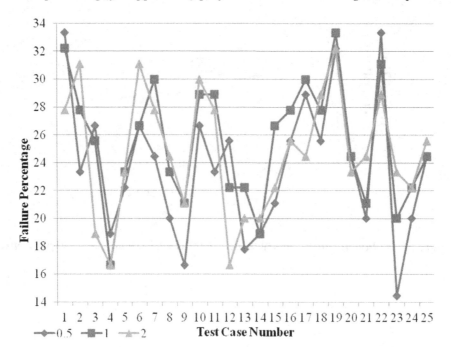

4.6.2.3 Accuracy Comparison of CiE Algorithm with Alternatives on Opportunity Project

The best average accuracy of 98.45% s achieved when the size of the training set is large and Minkowski parameter is 1. The results published by the opportunity project for accuracies of dif-

ferent algorithms on task A are shown in Table 12 (Chavarriaga, Sagha, Roggen, & Ferscha, 2011). It is interesting to note that CiE algorithm performs better than the algorithms given in Table 12. All these algorithms follow CBA.

The best average accuracy of 82.53% s achieved when the size of the training set is large

Figure 25. Effect of training set size on average failure percentage for opportunity project Task C

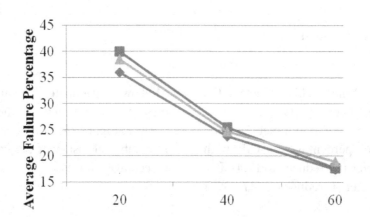

Table 12. Comparison of CiE with different algorithms for opportunity project task a

Classifier	Accuracy
DT	86.89%
SVN+1NN	86.81%
1NN	86.52% and 85.27%
SVM	86.10%
Statistical Comparison	84.18%
C4.5	73.85%
AdaBoost	73.61%

and Minkowski parameter is 0.5 or 1. The results published by the opportunity project for accuracies of different algorithms on task C are shown in Table 13 (Chavarriaga, Sagha, Roggen, & Ferscha, 2011). It is interesting to note that CiE algorithm performs better than the algorithms given in Table 13 and under noise. All the algorithms follow CBA.

4.6.3 Failure Percentage of CiE in COSAR Dataset

The COSAR classifies human activities for a pervasive e-health application (Riboni D., 2012). The data sets classifies 10 distinct activities including brushing teeth, ascending, descending, jogging etc identified on 6 volunteer subjects. The subjects wear accelerometer sensors and GPS sensor on their left pocket and right wrist respectively. The data set is composed of our 5 hrs of data with 18000 instances. The data set is composed of 148 variables. The data set is divided into training sets and test sets by the author. For evaluation of CiE test cases are created for person A and person B.

Table 13. Comparison of CiE with different algorithms for opportunity project Task C

Classifier	Accuracy
HMM	75%
Statistical Comparison	64%

4.6.3.1 Test Results for COSAR Person A

Training sets and test sets are constructed from the data set provided for person A. Figure 26 shows the failure percentage for each test case in COSAR person A with training set size 20 per activity. Figure 26 shows the curves for Minkowski parameter of $0.5, 0.707$ and 1 or which the failure percentage is low. The average failure percentage for 0.5 is 28% for 0.707 it is 28.27 and for 1 it is 32% The average failure percentage for 2 is 50.4% In the test cases the best average failure percentage is achieved when Minkowski parameter is 0.5 for training set size 20 per activity.

Figure 27 shows the failure percentage for each test case in COSAR person A with training set size increased to 40 per activity. Figure 27 shows the curves for Minkowski parameter of $0.5, 0.707$ and 1 The average failure percentage for 0.5 is 7.73%, or 0.707 it is 9.33% nd for 1 it is 12.8% In the test cases the best average failure percentage is achieved when Minkowski parameter is 0.5 for training set size 40 per activity. It can also be seen that in test case numbers 1 and 11 CiE gives 100% uccess with $p = 0.707$ Also in test case number 21 CiE gives 100% success with $p = 0.707$ nd $p = 0.5$

With further increase of training set size to 60 the average failure percentage of CiE with Minkowski parameter 0.5 reduces to 6.4% for 0.707 it reduces to 6.4% or Minkowski parameter 1 reduces to 9.07% Figure 28 shows that with the increase in number of instances per category the failure percentage reduces. The best average success is achieved with $p = 0.5$ nd $p = 0.707$

4.6.3.2 Test Results for COSAR Person B

Training sets and test sets are constructed from the data set provided for person B. Figure 29 shows the failure percentage for each test case in COSAR person B with training set size 20 per activity. Figure 29 shows the curves for Minkowski parameter of $0.5, 0.707$ and 1 or which the failure

Context Inference Engine (CiE)

Figure 26. Failure percentage for COSAR Person A with training size 20 per activity

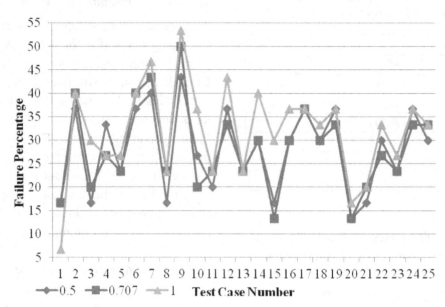

Figure 27. Failure percentage for COSAR Person A with training size 40 per activity

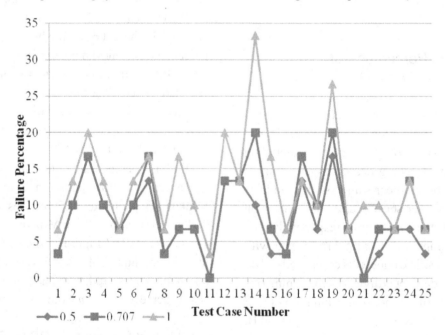

percentage is low. The average failure percentage for 0.5 and 0.707 is 33.2% nd for 1 it is 39.47% The average failure percentage for 2 is 52.67% In the test cases the best average failure percentage is achieved when Minkowski parameter is 0.5 and 0.707 for training set size 20 per activity.

Figure 30 shows the failure percentage for each test case in COSAR person B with training set size increased to 40 per activity. Figure 30 shows the curves for Minkowski parameter of 0.5, 0.707 and 1 The average failure percentage for 0.5 is 34.27%, or 0.707 it is 37.87% nd for 1

Figure 28. Effect of training set size on average failure percentage for COSAR Person A

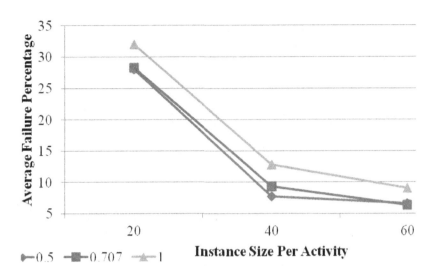

Figure 29. Failure percentage for COSAR Person B with training size 20 per activity

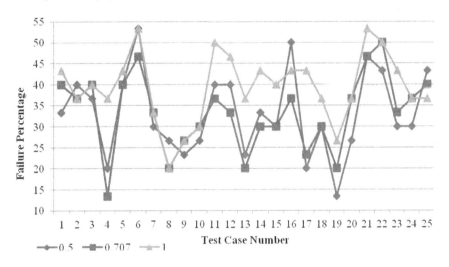

it is 44.27% In the test cases the best average failure percentage is achieved when Minkowski parameter is 0.5 for training set size 40 per activity.

With further increase of training set size to 60 the average failure percentage of CiE with Minkowski parameter 0.5 reduces to 27.73% for 0.707 it reduces to 30.53% for Minkowski parameter 1 reduces to 34.8% Figure 31 shows that with the increase in number of instances per category the failure percentage reduces tough an anomaly occurs when training set size is 40. This anoma-

ly is consistent in all the values of Minkowski parameter selected for the evaluation. The best average success is achieved with $p=0.5$

4.6.3.3 Accuracy Comparison of CiE Algorithm with Alternatives on COSAR Data Set

The best average accuracy of 93.6% s achieved when the size of the training set is large and Minkowski parameter is 0.5 and 0.707 for the data set of person A. While the best average accuracy

Figure 30. Failure percentage for COSAR Person B with training size 40 per activity

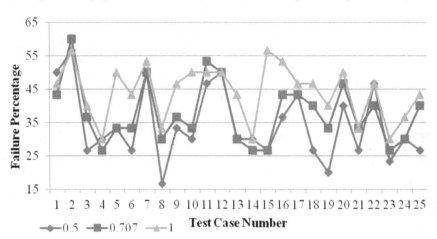

Figure 31. Effect of training set size on average failure percentage for COSAR Person B

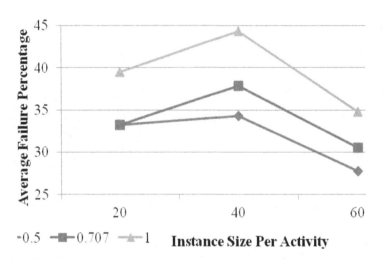

of 72.27% s achieved when the size of the training set is large and Minkowski parameter is 0.5 for the data set of person B. Hence the accuracy ranges between 72.27% − 93.6% r person A and B. Test results published for accuracies of different algorithms on COSAR data set are shown in Table 14 (Riboni & Bettini, 2009). It is interesting to note that using OBR the results are quite close when observing the average upper limit of failure percentage of CiE on person A and person B data sets. Meanwhile the average lower limit of failure percentage on person A and person B data sets is

similar to the results of Bayesian network and SVM.

4.6.4 Failure Percentage of CiE in HARUS Data Set

The HARUS data set classifies activities of daily life while carrying a wait mounted sensor (Anguita, Ghio, Oneto, Parra, & Reyes-Ortiz, 2012), (Anguita, Ghio, Oneto, Parra, & Reyes-Ortiz, UCI Machine Learning Repository, 2012). The data sets classifies 6 activities including walking, ascending, laying down etc on 30 volunteer subjects.

Table 14. Comparison of CiE with different algorithms for COSAR data set

Classifier	Accuracy
Bayesian Network	72.95%
C4.5	66.23%
Multiclass Logistic Regression	80.21%
Naive Bayes Classifier	68.55%
SVM	71.81%
COSAR (ontological reasoning)	93.44%

The data set is composed of 562 variables with over 10,000 instances. The data set is divided into training sets and test sets by the author. For evaluation of CiE test cases are created. The values in the data set are normalized up to 6 decimal places and bounded within the interval $\begin{bmatrix} -1,1 \end{bmatrix}$

4.6.4.1 Test Results for HARUS Data Set

Training sets and test sets are constructed from the data set. Figure 32 shows the failure percentage for each test case in HARUS with training set size 20 per activity. Figure 32 shows the curves for Minkowski parameter of $0.5, 1, 0.707 and 2$ or which the failure percentage is low. The average failure percentage for 0.5 is 21.6% or 0.707 it is 20.9 for 1 it is 20.4 and for 2 it is 22.4% In the test cases the best average failure percentage is achieved when Minkowski parameter is 1 for training set size 20 per activity.

Figure 33 shows the failure percentage for each test case in HARUS data set with training set size increased to 40 per activity. Figure 33 shows the curves for Minkowski parameter of $0.5, 0.707, 1 and 2$ The average failure percentage for 0.5 is 19.6% or 0.707 it is 19.8% or 1 it is 17.38% nd for 2 it is 15.3% In the test cases the best average failure percentage is achieved when Minkowski parameter is 2 for training set size 40 per activity.

With further increase of training set size to 60 the average failure percentage of CiE with Minkowski parameter 0.5 reduces to 18.2% or 0.707 it reduces to 17.1% or Minkowski parameter 1 and 2 both becomes 16.2% The average failure percentage for Minkowski parameter 2 raises for increase in training set size. Figure 34 shows that with the increase in number of in-

Figure 32. Failure percentage for HARUS data set with training size 20 per activity

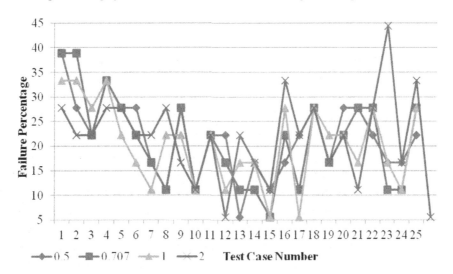

Figure 33. Failure percentage for HARUS data set with training size 40 per activity

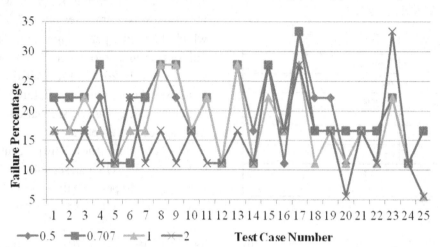

Figure 34. Effect of training set size on average failure percentage for HARUS data set

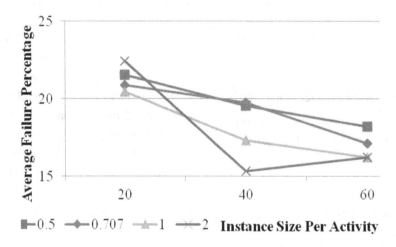

stances per category the failure percentage reduces. The best average success is achieved with $p=1$ nd $p=2$

The best average accuracy of 84.67% s achieved when the size of the training set is 40 instances per activity and Minkowski parameter is 2. Results published for accuracies of alternate algorithms on HARUS data set are shown in Table 15 (Anguita, Ghio, Oneto, Parra, & Reyes-Ortiz, 2012). The authors have used SVM and a hardware friendly version of SVM for activity classification. It is interesting to note that as is the case in COSAR data set, performance of CiE is close to SVM.

4.6.5 Failure Percentage of CiE in LDPA Data Set

The LDPA data set classifies different activities of daily life while carrying wearable sensors (Kaluža, Mirchevska, Dovgan, Luštrek, & Gams, 2010), (Kaluža, Mirchevska, Dovgan, Luštrek, & Gams, UCI Machine Learning Repository, 2010). The data set classifies 11 activities including walking, sitting, falling etc on 5 volunteer subjects. The data set is composed of 8 attributes out of which only 4 are dynamic with over 1,64,000 instances. The dynamic variables include timestamp and x, y and z, coordinate of the person. The timestamp

Table 15. Comparison of CiE with different algorithms for HARUS data set

Classifier	Accuracy
SVM	89.3%
Hardware Friendly SVM	89.0%

information has been excluded from the training set and test sets as it is highly dynamic.

4.6.5.1 Test Results for LDPA Data Set

Training sets and test sets are constructed from the data set. Figure 34 shows the failure percentage for each test case in LDPA data set with training set size 20 per activity. Figure 34 shows the curves for Minkowski parameter of $0.5, 1, 3$ and e^2 or which the failure percentage is low. The average failure percentage for 0.5 is 58.91% or 1 it is 58.06 for 2 it is 59.03 and for e^2 t is 57.7% In the test cases the best average failure percentage is achieved when Minkowski parameter is e^2 for training set size 20 per activity.

Figure 35 shows the failure percentage for each test case in LDPA data set with training set size increased to 40 per activity. Figure 35 shows the curves for Minkowski parameter of $0.5, 1, 2$ and e^2

The average failure percentage for 0.5 is 54.43% or 1 it is 54.67% or 2 it is 54.79% nd for e^2 t is 56.24% In the test cases the best average failure percentage is achieved when Minkowski parameter is 0.5 for training set size 40 per activity.

With further increase of training set size to 60 the average failure percentage of CiE with Minkowski parameter 0.5 increases to 55.76% or 1 it reduces to 54.06% or 2 it reduces to 52.85% nd for e^2 t reduces to 53.46% Figure 36 shows that with the increase in number of instances per category the failure percentage reduces. The best average success is achieved with $p=2$

4.6.5.2 Accuracy Comparison of CiE Algorithm with Alternatives on LDPA Data Set

The best average accuracy of 47.76% s achieved when the size of the training set is 60 instances per activity and Minkowski parameter is 2. Results published for accuracies of alternate algorithms on LDPA data set are shown in Table 16 (Kaluža, Mirchevska, Dovgan, Luštrek, & Gams, 2010). The authors have selected an agent based approach to classify context. The results achieved show that CiE performs poorly. The reason can be attributed to the low number of values.

Figure 35. Failure percentage for LDPA data set with training size 20 per activity

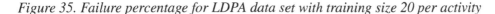
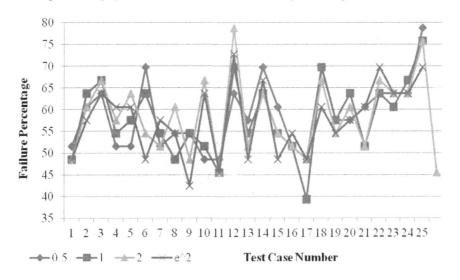

Figure 36. Failure percentage for HARUS data set with training size 40 per activity

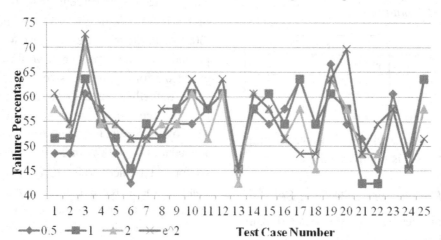

4.6.6 Effect of Number of Variables on Classification Time

As the number of variables grows large, the classification time is also large. So with a rich data description the classification time would be large. Different data sets have been used for evaluation in Sections 4.6.2-4.6.5. The classification time in nanoseconds is recorded is for a success case, a partial success case and a failure. The size of the training set is kept constant at 1000 instances. Table 17 shows the record of time for each data set. It can be observed that the classification time is nearly same for the three cases highlighting that the Distance Measurer stage takes the major amount of time. The number of attributes in each data set is also shown in Table 17.

Figure 37 shows the plot of classification time for partial success cases vs. the number of vari-

ables. It can be seen that the classification time is a monotonically increasing function of the number of variables if the size of the training set is kept constant. This conforms to the dominant term in Equation 10 where by keeping the number of instances constant, the time complexity becomes directly proportional to the number of variables v. i.e., $O\big(CiE\big) \propto v$.

The linear least square line for the classification time and the effect of number of variables is shown in Figure 38 (Reid). The linear least square line equation is given in Equation 14 (see also Figure 39).

$$y = 1489300x + \big(4.22 \times 10^7\big) \qquad (14)$$

4.7 Arbitration

The Arbitrator is part of the Context Classifier and Arbitration Unit. The task of the adapt component in a general architecture of Context Aware System is to make adjustments to the services present in the environment once the activity is identified. This task can be carried out either by the context aware system or by the services present in the environment. Axioms must be supplied that adjust the services based on the activity percept (Russell

Table 16. Comparison of CiE with different algorithms for LDPA data set

Classifier	Accuracy
Machine learning methods	72%
Expert knowledge agents	88%
Meta prediction agents	91.33%

Table 17. Classification time for each data set

Data Set	No of Attributes	Classification Time (nanoseconds)		
		Absolute Success	Partial Success	Failure
LDPA	3	45010190	45200996	45210495
Holger Junker	10	58273328	58731487	59136566
Kristof Van Learhoven	40	106912751	101072622	113922300
Opportunity - Task A	114	206149539	216149539	218728917
COSAR -Person A	148	254696617	259068680	256939359
HARUS	562	878998308	879387744	880503109

Figure 37. Effect of training set size on average failure percentage for LDPA data set

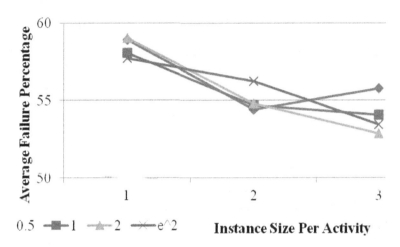

Figure 38. Classification time and effect of number of variables for partial success cases with constant training set size

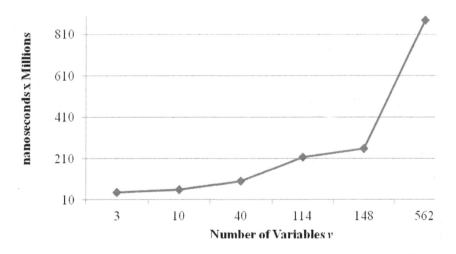

Figure 39. Linear least squares line for classification time and number of variables for partial success cases with constant training set size

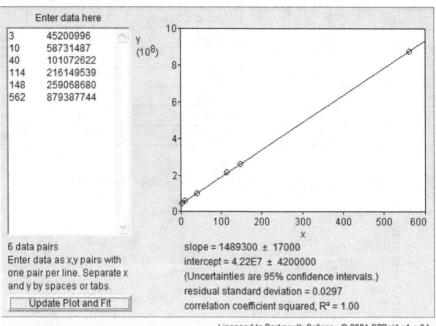

& Norvig, 2010). This thesis recommends that the axioms should be part of the services. The thesis is primarily concerned with activity classification based on the current context.

5. CONCLUSION

A classification based context inference technique is proposed in this chapter. The method is based on distance measure based classification. The current context is taken as input and Minkowski distances are measured among the current context and recorded context. The means and standard deviations of the relative distances are calculated and ranks created for the closest instance. The output of the system is the activity associated with the current context coupled with the likeliness.

The failure percentage of CiE algorithm on different data sets shows that the algorithm is plausible and in some cases has given excellent results. Following a distance based approach the accuracy of the algorithm is close to SVM and it

is better than decision trees, Bayesian learning, HMM and simple statistical learning. The CiE underperforms in the case on OBR and it can be reasoned that the axioms are optimized.

An interesting question is the selection of Minkowski parameter p. As can be observed better results are achieved with $p=0.5$ and $p=1$. But the value is dependent on the structure of the data. It implies that the Minkowski parameter should be selected prior to use of the algorithm based on experiments on the samples. Also CiE can be converted to an adaptable algorithm that adjusts value of p. This is carried-out using Gradient Decent Rule (Mitchell, 1997).

The time complexity shows that CiE is dependent on the number of values and the size of the training set. It can be observed that for small number if values the failure percentage increases. The limitation on due the size of the training set becomes important if the training set is large. Large training set size can lead to consumption of Java heap.

REFERENCES

Abowd, G. D., Atkenson, C. G., Hong, J., Long, S., Kooper, R., & Pinkerton, M. (1997). Cyberguide: a mobile context-aware tour guide. *Journal of Wireless Networks*, *3*(5), 421–433. doi:10.1023/A:1019194325861

Ahn, Y.-A. (2009). *Context awareness inference engine for location based applications. 2009 International COnference on Hybrid Infromation Technology* (pp. 213–216). New York: ACM.

Ahn, Y. A., & Park, J. S. (2008). Spatio-Temporal Context Manager in an Open Context Awareness Framework. *Fourth International Conference on Networked Computing and Advanced Information Management. 2*, pp. 681-684. Gyeongju, Korea: IEEE.

Almeida, J. P., Iacob, M.-E., Jonkers, H., & Quartel, D. (2006). Model-Driven Development of Context-Aware Services. In *Distributed Applications and Interoperable Systems* (Vol. 4025, pp. 213–227). Oslo, Norway: Springer. doi:10.1007/11773887_17

Anguita, D., Ghio, A., Oneto, L., Parra, X., & Reyes-Ortiz, J. L. (2012). Human Activity Recognition on Smartphones Using a Multiclass Hardware-Friendly Support Vector Machine. In *Ambient Assisted Living and Home Care* (Vol. 7657, pp. 216–223). Vitoria-Gasteiz, Spain: Springer. doi:10.1007/978-3-642-35395-6_30

Anguita, D., Ghio, A., Oneto, L., Parra, X., & Reyes-Ortiz, J. L. (2012, 12). *UCI Machine Learning Repository.* Retrieved from UCI Machine Learning Repository: http://archive.ics.uci.edu/ml/datasets/Human+Activity+Recognition+Using+Smartphones

Badii, A., Crouch, M., & Lallah, C. (2010). A Context-Awareness Framework for Intelligent Networked Embedded Systems. *Third International Conference on Advances in Human-Oriented and Personalized Mechanisms, Technologies and Services* (pp. 105-110). Reading, UK: IEEE.

Barbosa, V., & Andrade, M. T. (2009). Multicao: A semantic approach to context-aware adaptation decision taking. *10th Workshop on Image Analysis for Multimedia Interactive Services* (pp. 133-136). London, UK: IEEE.

Bernini, D., Micucci, D., & Tisato, F. (2010). A platform for interoperability via multiple spatial views in open smart spaces. *2010 IEEE Symposium on Computers and Communications (ISCC)* (pp. 1047-1052). Riccione, Italy: IEEE.

Bhattacharya, A. (1943). On a measure of divergence between two statistical populations defined by their probability distributions. *Bulletin of the Calcutta Mathematical Society*, *35*, 99–109.

Blum, M. L. (2005). *Real-time Context Recognition.* Zurich: Swiss Federal Institute of technology (ETH).

Brdiczka, O., Crowley, J. L., & Reignier, P. (2007). Learning Situation Models for Providing Context-Aware Services. In *Universal Access in Human-Computer Interaction. Ambient Interaction* (pp. 23–32). Beijing, China: Spinger. doi:10.1007/978-3-540-73281-5_3

Bulfoni, A., Coppola, P., Mea, V. D., Gaspero, L. D., Mischis, D., Mizzaro, S., et al. (2008). AI on the Move: Exploiting AI Techniques for Context Inference on Mobile Devices. *18th European Conference on Artificial Intelligence* (pp. 668-672). Amsterdam, The Netherlands: ACM.

Cantrell, C. D. (2000). *Modern Mathematical Methods for Physicists and Engineers.* Cambridge, UK: Cambridge University Press.

Cao, J., Xing, N., Chan, A. T., Feng, Y., & Jin, B. (2005). Service adaptation using fuzzy theory in context-aware mobile computing middleware. *11th IEEE International Conference on Embedded and Real-Time Computing Systems and Applications* (pp. 496-501). Hong Kong: IEEE.

Cao, Y., Klamma, R., Hou, M., & Jarke, M. (2008). Follow Me, Follow You - Spatiotemporal Community Context Modeling and Adaptation for Mobile Information Systems. *9th International Conference on Mobile Data Management* (pp. 108 - 115). Beijing, China: IEEE.

Cardelli, L., & Gordon, A. D. (2001). Mobile Ambients. In *Foundations of Software Science and Computation Structures* (pp. 140–155). Lisbon, Portugal: Springer.

Chavarriaga, R., Sagha, H., Roggen, D., & Ferscha, A. (2011). Opportunity activity recognition challenge: Results and conclusions. *2011 IEEE International Conference on Systems, Man, and Cybernetics (IEEE SMC 2011)*. Anchorage, USA: IEEE.

Chen, H., Finin, T., & Joshi, A. (2003). An Intelligent Broker for Context-Aware Systems (CoBrA). *Proceedings of Ubicomp, 2003*, 12–15.

Cheng, H.-T., Buthpitiya, S., Sun, F.-T., & Griss, M. L. (2010). *OmniSense: A Collaborative Sensing Framework for User Context Recognition Using Mobile Phones. Proceedings of HotMobile 2010* (p. 1). Annapolis: ACM.

Cheung, R., Yao, G., Cao, J., & Chan, A. (2008). A fuzzy service adaptation engine for context-aware mobile computing middleware. *International Journal of Pervasive Computing and Communications, 4*(2), 147–165. doi:10.1108/17427370810890256

Cheverst, K., Mitchell, K., & Davies, N. (1999). Design of an Object Model for a Context Sensitive Tourist GUIDE. *Computers & Graphics, 23*(6), 883–891. doi:10.1016/S0097-8493(99)00119-3

Chihani, B., Bertin, E., Suprapto, I. S., Zimmermann, J., & Crespi, N. (2012). Enhancing Existing Communication Services with Context Awareness. *Journal of Computer Networks and Communications, 2012*, 1–10. doi:10.1155/2012/493261

Cioara, T., Anghel, I., Salomie, I., & Dinsoreanu, M. (2009). A generic context model enhanced with self-configuring features. *Journal of Digital Information Management, 7*, 159–165.

Dargie, W. (2009). Adaptive audio based context recognition. *IEEE Transactions on Systems, Man, and Cybernetics, 39*(4), 715–725. doi:10.1109/TSMCA.2009.2015676

De, S., & Moessner, K. (2008). Ontology-based context inference and query for mobile devices. *IEEE 19th International Symposium on Personal, Indoor and Mobile Radio Communications* (pp. 1-5). Cannes: IEEE.

de Deugd, S., Carroll, R., Kelly, K. E., Millett, B., & Ricker, J. (2006). SODA: Service-Oriented Device Architecture. *IEEE Pervasive Computing / IEEE Computer Society [and] IEEE Communications Society, 5*(3), 94–96. doi:10.1109/MPRV.2006.59

Dey, A. K., & Abowd, G. D. (1999). *The Context Toolkit: Aiding the Development of Context-Aware Applications. SIGCHI conference on Human factors in computing systems* (pp. 443–441). Pittsburgh, USA: ACM.

Duggal, A., Misra, M., & Srinivasaraghavan, R. (2012). Categorising Context and Using Short Term Contextual Information to Obtain Long Term Context. *11th International Conference on Trust, Security and Privacy in Computing and Communications* (pp. 1771 - 1776). Liverpool, UK: IEEE.

Fahy, P., & Clarke, S. (2004). CASS: A Middleware for Mobile Context-Aware Applications. *Second International Workshop on Context Awareness* (pp. 1-6). Boston, USA: ACM.

Feng, Y. H., Teng, T. H., & Tan, A. H. (2009). Modelling Situation Awareness for Context-aware Decision Support. *Expert Systems with Applications, 36*(1), 455–463. doi:10.1016/j.eswa.2007.09.061

Frank, K., Röckl, M., & Robertson, P. (2008). The Bayeslet Concept for Modular Context Inference. *Proceedings of the 2008 The Second International Conference on Mobile Ubiquitous Computing, Systems, Services and Technologies* (pp. 96-101). Valenica: ACM.

Füller, M., Nüßer, W., & Rustemeyer, T. (2012). Context driven process selection and integration of mobile and pervasive systems. *Pervasive and Mobile Computing, 8*(3), 467–482. doi:10.1016/j. pmcj.2011.03.002

Ghadiri, N., Baraani-dastjerdi, A., Ghasem-aghaee, N., & Nematbakhsh, M. A. (2011). A Human-Centric Approach To Group-Based Context-Awareness. *International Journal of Network Security and its Applications, 3* (1), 47-66.

Golsa, M. P., Troped, P. J., & Evans, J. J. (2013). Environment feature extraction and classification for Context aware Physical Activity monitoring. *IEEE Sensors Applications Symposium (SAS)* (pp. 123-128). Galveston, TX, USA: IEEE.

Gu, T., Pung, H. K., & Zhang, D. Q. (2004). A Middleware for Building Context-Aware Mobile Services. *IEEE 59th Vehicular Technology Conference. 5*, pp. 2656-2660. IEEE: Los Angeles, USA.

Gu, T., Pung, K. H., & Zhang, D. (2008). Peer-to-Peer Context Reasoning in Pervasive Computing Environments. *Sixth Annual IEEE International Conference on Pervasive Computing and Communications* (pp. 406-411). Singapore: IEEE.

Guan, D., Yuan, W., Lee, S., & Lee, Y.-K. (2007). Context Selection and Reasoning in Ubiquitous Computing. *The 2007 International Conference on Intelligent Pervasive Computing* (pp. 184-187). Jeju City: IEEE.

Guo, H., Gao, G., Ma, J., Li, Y., & Huang, R. (2008). *Reserach of an Adaptive System in Mobile Learning Environment*. Biejing, China: R&D Center for Knowledge Engineering, Beijing Normal University.

Hamming, W. R. (1950). Error Detecting and Error Correcting Codes. *The Bell System Technical Journal, 26*(2), 147–160. doi:10.1002/j.1538-7305.1950.tb00463.x

Hartmann, M., Zesch, T., Mühlhäuser, M., & Gurevych, I. (2008). Using Similarity Measures for Context-Aware User Interfaces. *Proceedings of the 2008 IEEE International Conference on Semantic Computing* (pp. 190-197). Washigton DC, USA: IEEE.

Hellinger, E. (1907). *Die Orthogonalinvarianten quadratischer Formen von unendlichvielen Variablen*. University of Göttingen: University of Göttingen.

Hofer, T., Pichler, M., Leonhartsberger, G., Altmann, J., & Werner, R. (2002). Context-Awareness on Mobile Devices – The Hydrogen Approach. *Proceedings of the 36th Annual Hawaii International Conference on System Sciences* (pp. 292-302). Hawaii: IEEE.

Junker, H. (n.d.). *Context Database*. Retrieved from Institut für Pervasive Computing: http://www.pervasive.jku.at/Research/Context_Database/viewSubmission.php?key=5&action=View&keyname=b4a4&table=c0b0ad8dc8d0&db=9e8f8772

Kaluža, B., Mirchevska, V., Dovgan, E., Luštrek, M., & Gams, M. (2010, 11). Retrieved from UCI Machine Learning Repository: http://archive.ics.uci.edu/ml/datasets/Localization+Data+for+Person+Activity

Kaluža, B., Mirchevska, V., Dovgan, E., Luštrek, M., & Gams, M. (2010). An agent-based approach to care in independent living. *Proceedings of the First international joint conference on Ambient intelligence AmI'10* (pp. 177-186). Malaga, Spain: ACM.

Khalil, I., Ali, F. M., & Kotsis, G. (2008). A Datalog Model for Context Reasoning in Pervasive Environments. *International Symposium on Parallel and Distributed Processing with Applications* (pp. 452-459). Sydney, Austrailia: IEEE.

Ko, K.-E., & Sim, K.-B. (2008). Development of context aware system based on Bayesian network driven context reasoning method and ontology context modeling. *International Conference on Control, Automation and Systems* (pp. 2309-2313). Seoul, Korea: IEEE.

Könönen, V., Mäntyjärvi, J., Similä, H., Pärkkä, J., & Ermes, M. (2010). Automatic feature selection for context recognition in mobile devices. *Journal of Pervasive and Mobile Computing*, 6(2), 181–197. doi:10.1016/j.pmcj.2009.07.001

Korpipaa, P., Mantyjarvi, J., Kela, J., Keranen, H., & Malm, E. J. (2003). Managing Context Information in Mobile Devices. *IEEE Pervasive Computing / IEEE Computer Society [and] IEEE Communications Society*, 2(3), 42–51. doi:10.1109/MPRV.2003.1228526

Krause, M., Linnhoff-Popien, C., & Strassberger, M. (2007). Concurrent Inference on High Level Context Using Alternative Context Construction Trees. *Proceedings of the Third International Conference on Autonomic and Autonomous Systems* (pp. 1-7). Athens, Greece: IEEE.

Kuo, Y.-M., Lee, J.-S., & Chung, P.-C. (2010). A visual context-awareness-based sleeping-respiration measurement system. *IEEE Transactions on Information Technology in Biomedicine*, 14(2), 255–265. doi:10.1109/TITB.2009.2036168 PMID:19906594

Kurz, M., Holzl, G., Ferscha, A., Calatroni, A., Roggen, D., & Troster, G. etal. (2011). The OPPORTUNITY Framework abd Data Processing Ecosystem for Opportunistic Activity and Context Recognition. *International Journal of Sensors. Wireless Communication and Control*, 1(2), 102–125.

Laerhoven, K. V. (2004). *Context Database.* Retrieved 2011, from Institut für Pervasive Computing: http://www.pervasive.jku.at/Research/Context_Database/viewSubmission.php?key=1&action=View&keyname=b4a4&table=c0b0ad8dc8d0&db=9e8f8772

Lee, H., Choi, J. S., & Elmasri, R. (2009). A classification and modeling of the quality of contextual information in smart spaces. *IEEE International Conference on Pervasive Computing and Communications* (pp. 1-5). Galveston, TX: IEEE.

Lee, J., & Lee, H. (2008). A Sensor based context-aware inference algorithm for ubiquitous residential environments. *13th International Conference on Computer Aided Architectural Design Research in Asia*, (pp. 93-102). Chiang Mai.

Lee, K. (2010). Context recognition from incomplete situation with uncertainity management. *4th International Conference on New Trends in Information Science and Service Science* (pp. 481-484). Gyeongju: IEEE.

Li, Y., Fang, J., & Xiong, J. (2008). A Context-Aware Services Mash-Up System. *Seventh International Conference on Grid and Cooperative Computing* (pp. 707-712). Shenzhen: IEEE.

Loke, S. W. (2010). Inceremental Awareness and Compositionality: A Design Philosophy For Context-Aware Pervasive System. *Journal of Pervasive and Mobile Computing*, 6(2), 239–253. doi:10.1016/j.pmcj.2009.03.004

Lukowicz, P., Pirkl, G., Bannach, D., Wagner, F., Calatroni, A., Foerster, K., et al. (2010). Recording a Complex, Multi Modal Activity Data Set for Context Recognition. *23rd International Conference on Architecture of Computing Systems (ARCS)* (pp. 1-6). Hanover, Germany: IEEE.

Mahmud, U., Iltaf, N., Rehman, A., & Kamran, F. (2007). *Context-Aware Paradigm for a Pervasive Computing Environment (CAPP). WWW\Internet 2007* (pp. 337–346). Villa Real, Portugal: IADIS.

Mahmud, U., & Javed, M. Y. (2012). Context Inference Engine (CiE): Inferring Context. [IJAPUC]. *International Journal of Advanced Pervasive and Ubiquitous Computing, 4*(3), 13–41. doi:10.4018/japuc.2012070102

Manhattan Distance. (n.d.). (NIST) Retrieved 10 2011, from NIST: http://xlinux.nist.gov/dads//HTML/manhattanDistance.html

Mayrhofer, R. (2004). An Architecture for Context Prediction. *2nd International Conference on Pervasive Computing (Pervasive 2004)* (pp. 65-72). Vienna, Austria: Austrian Computer Society (OCG).

McKeever, S., Ye, J., Coyle, L., Bleakley, C., & Dobson, S. (2010). Activity recognition using temporal evidence theory. *Journal of Ambient Intelligence and Smart Environments, 2*(3), 253–269.

McLachlan, G. J. (1999). Mahalanobis Distance. *Resonance, 4*(6), 20–16. doi:10.1007/BF02834632

Min, J.-K., & Cho, S.-B. (2011). A Hybrid Context-Aware Wearable System with Evolutionary Optimization and Selective Inference of Dynamic Bayesian Networks. In *Hybrid Artificial Intelligent Systems* (Vol. 6678, pp. 444–451). Wroclaw, Poland: Springer. doi:10.1007/978-3-642-21219-2_56

Minkowski, H. (1910). *Geometrie der Zahlen*. Leipzig: Teubner.

Mitchell, T. (1997). *Machine Learning*. Maidenhead, UK: McGraw-Hill.

Nguyen, T. V., & Choi, D. (2008). Context Reasoning Using Contextual Graph. *Proceedings of the 2008 IEEE 8th International Conference on Computer and Information Technology Workshops* (pp. 488-493). Sydney, Austrailia: IEEE.

Niklas, K., Klaus, D., Sigg, S., & Beigl, M. (2010). DAG Based Context Reasoning: Optimised DAG Creation. *23rd International Conference on Architecture of Computing Systems* (pp. 1-6). Hannover, Germany: IEEE.

Padovitz, A., Loke, S. W., & Zaslavsky, A. (2004). Towards a Theory of Context Spaces. *Proceedings of Second IEEE Annual Conference on Pervasive Computing and Communications Workshop* (pp. 38-42). Orlando, Florida, USA: IEEE.

Paganelli, F., Spinicci, E., & Giuli, D. (2008). ERMHAN: A Context-Aware Service Platform to Support Continuous Care Networks for Home-Based Assistance. *International Journal of Telemedicine and Applications, 2008*, 1–13. doi:10.1155/2008/867639 PMID:18695739

Pantsar-Syvaniemi, S., Simula, K., & Ovaska, E. (2010). Context-awareness in smart spaces. *IEEE Symposium on Computers and Communications (ISCC)* (pp. 1023 - 1028). Riccione: IEEE.

Perttuncn, M., Klcek, M. V., Lassila, O., & Riekki, J. (2009). An Implementation of Auditory Context Recognition for Mobile Devices. *Tenth International Conference on Mobile Data Management: Systems, Services and Middleware* (pp. 424-429). Taipei, Taiwan: IEEE.

Qiao, X., & Li, X. (2009). Bayesian Network-Based Service Context Recognition Model. *International Journal of Distributed Sensor Networks, 5*(1), 80–80. doi:10.1080/15501320802571830

Ranganathan, A., & Campbell, R. H. (2008). Provably Correct Pervasive Computing Environments. *2008 Sixth Annual IEEE Conference on Pervasive Computing and Communications (PERCOM '08)* (pp. 160 - 169). Hong Kong: IEEE.

Reid, B. P. (n.d.). *Linear Least Squares*. Retrieved from http://www.dartmouth.edu/~chemlab/info/resources/linear/linear.html

Riaz, M., Kiani, S. L., Lee, S., Han, S.-M., & Lee, Y.-K. (2005). Service Delivery in Context Aware Environments: Lookup and Access Control Issues. *11th IEEE International Conference on Embeded and Real-Time Computing Systems and Applications* (pp. 455-458). Hong Kong: IEEE.

Riboni, D. (2012, January). *Human activity recognition.* Retrieved from EveryWhere Lab: http://everywarelab.di.unimi.it/palspot

Riboni, D., & Bettini, C. (2009). Context-Aware Activity Recognition through a Combination of Ontological and Statistical Reasoning. *Proceedings of the 6th International Conference on Ubiquitous Intelligence and Computing UCI '09* (pp. 39-53). Brisbane, Austrailia: ACM.

Riboni, D., & Bettini, C. (2011). OWL 2 modeling and reasoning with complex human activities. *Journal of Pervasive and Mobile Computing, 7*(3), 379–395. doi:10.1016/j.pmcj.2011.02.001

Rockl, M., Frank, K., Hermann, P. G., & Vera, M. (2008). Knowledge Representation and Inference in Context-Aware Computing Environments. *The Second International Conference on Mobile Ubiquitous Computing, Systems, Services and Technologies* (pp. 89-95). Valencia: IEEE.

Roggen, D., Calatroni, A., Rossi, M., Holleczek, T., Forster, K., Troster, G., et al. (2010). Collecting complex activity datasets in highly rich networked sensor environments. *2010 Seventh International Conference on Networked Sensing Systems (INSS)* (pp. 233 - 240). Kassel: IEEE.

Román, M., Hess, C., Cerqueira, R., Campbell, R. H., & Nahrstedt, K. (2002). Gaia: A Middleware Infrastructure to Enable Active Spaces. *IEEE Pervasive Computing / IEEE Computer Society [and] IEEE Communications Society, 1*(4), 74–82. doi:10.1109/MPRV.2002.1158281

Russell, S., & Norvig, P. (2010). *Artificial Intelligence: A Modern Approach* (3rd ed.). Berkley: Pearson Education.

Samulowitz, M., Michahelles, F., & Linnhoff-Popien, C. (2001). CAPEUS: An Architecture for Context-Aware Selection and Execution of Services. *Third International Working Conference on New Developments in Distributed Applications and Interoperable Systems* (pp. 23-40). Kraków, Poland: Springer.

Santos, A. C., Tarrataca, L., Cardoso, J. M., Ferreira, D. R., Diniz, P. C., & Chainho, P. (2009). Context Inference for Mobile Applications in the UPCASE Project. *Lecture Notes of the Institute for Computer Science. Social Informatics and Telecommunications Engineering, 7*, 352–365.

Scalmato, A., Sgorbissa, A., & Zaccaria, R. (2013). Describing and Recognizing Patterns of Events in Smart Environments With Description Logic. *IEEE Transactions on Cybernetics, 43*(6), 1882–1897. doi:10.1109/TSMCB.2012.2234739 PMID:23757579

Schilit, B. N., Hilbert, D. M., & Trevor, J. (2002). Context-Aware Communication. *IEEE Wireless Communication, 9*(5), 46–54. doi:10.1109/MWC.2002.1043853

Schmidtke, H. R., & Woo, W. (2009). Towards ontology-based formal verification methods for context aware systems. In *Pervasive Computing* (pp. 309–326). Nara, Japan: Springer. doi:10.1007/978-3-642-01516-8_21

Shin, C., & Woo, W. (2005). *Conflict Resolution Method utilizing Context History for Context-Aware Applications.* S. Korea: GIST U-VR Lab.

Siebra, S. A., Salgado, A. C., Tedesco, P. A., & Brézillon, P. (2005). *A Learning Interaction Memory using Contextual Information*. Retrieved 03 28, 2014, from http://www.cin.ufpe.br/~mbjn/D1.pdf

Singh, S., Vajirkar, P., & Lee, Y. (2003). Context-Based Data Mining Using Ontologies. In *Conceptual Modeling - ER 2003* (pp. 405–418). Chicago, IL, USA: Springer. doi:10.1007/978-3-540-39648-2_32

Song, I.-J., & Cho, S.-B. (2013). Bayesian and behavior networks for context-adaptive user interface in a ubiquitous home environment. *Expert Systems with Applications*, *40*(5), 1827–1838. doi:10.1016/j.eswa.2012.09.019

Strobbe, M., Laere, O. V., Ongenae, F., Dauwe, S., Dhoedt, B., & Turck, F. D. etal. (2012). Novel Applications Integrate Location and Context Information. *Pervasive Computing*, *11*(2), 64–73. doi:10.1109/MPRV.2011.60

Thyagaraju, G. S., & Kulkarni, U. P. (2012). Rough Set Theory Based User Aware TV Program and Settings Recommender. *International Journal of Advanced Pervasive and Ubiquitous Computing*, *4*(2), 48–64. doi:10.4018/japuc.2012040105

Vladoiu, M., & Constantinescu, Z. (2011). U-Learning Within A Context-Aware Multiagent Environment. [IJCNC]. *International Journal of Computer Networks & Communications*, *3*(1), 1–15. doi:10.5121/ijcnc.2011.3101

Wang, X., Rosenblum, D., & Wang, Y. (2012). Context-Aware Mobile Music Recommendation for daily activities. *Proceedings of the 20th ACM international conference on Multimedia MM'12* (pp. 99-108). Nara, Japan: ACM.

Wang, Y.-K. (2004). Context Awareness and Adaptation in Mobile Learning. *The 2nd IEEE International Workshop on Wireless and Mobile Technologies in Education* (pp. 154-158). Taiwan: IEEE.

Want, R., Hopper, A., Falcao, V., & Gibbons, J. (1992). The Active Badge Location System. *ACM Transactions on Information Systems*, *10*(1), 91–102. doi:10.1145/128756.128759

Wei, E. J., & Chan, A. T. (2012). CAMPUS: A Middleware for Automated Context-Aware Adaptation Decision Making at Run Time. *Pervasive and Mobile Computing*, *9*(1), 35–56. doi:10.1016/j.pmcj.2011.10.002

Xu, T., Zhou, Y., David, B., & Chalon, R. (2013). Supporting Activity Context Recognition in Context-Aware Middleware. *27th AAAI Conference on Artificial Intelligence* (pp. 61-70). Califoria: AAAI Press.

Xue, W., Pung, H. K., & Sen, S. (2013). Managing context data for diverse operating spaces. *Pervasive and Mobile Computing*, *9*(1), 57–75. doi:10.1016/j.pmcj.2011.11.001

Ye, J., Stevenson, G., & Dobson, S. (2011). A top-level ontology for smart environments. *Pervasive and Mobile Computing*, *7*(3), 359–378. doi:10.1016/j.pmcj.2011.02.002

Yordanova, K., Kruger, F., & Kirste, T. (2012). Tool Support for Activity Recognition with Computational Casual Behaviour Models. *35th German Conference on Artifical Intelligence* (pp. 108-112). Saarbrücken, Germany: Springer.

Yu, Z., Nakamura, Y., Zhang, D., Kajita, S., & Mase, K. (2008). Content Provisioning for Ubiquitous Learning. *Pervasive Computing*, *7*(4), 62–70. doi:10.1109/MPRV.2008.69

Yuan, J., & Wu, Y. (2008). Context-Aware Clustering. *IEEE Conference on Computer Vision and Pattern Recognition* (pp. 1-8). Anchorage, AK: IEEE.

Zentrum, E. T. H. Switzerland. (n.d.). *Opportunity*. Retrieved from http://www.opportunity-project.eu/

Zhang, D., Guan, H., Zhou, J., Tang, F., & Guo, M. (2008). iShadow: Yet Another Pervasive Computing Environment. *International Symposium on Parallel and Distributed Processing with Applications* (pp. 261-268). Sydney, Austrailia: IEEE.

Zhang, Q., & Izquierdo, E. (2008). Bayesian learning and reasoning for context exploitation in visual information retrieval. *5th International Conference on Visual Information Engineering* (pp. 170-175). Xian, China: IEEE.

Chapter 4
Simple System Dynamics and Control System Project Models

A. S. White
Middlesex University, UK

ABSTRACT

This chapter examines the established Systems Dynamics (SD) methods applied to software projects in order to simplify them. These methods are highly non-linear and contain large numbers of variables and built-in decisions. A SIMULINK version of an SD model is used here and conclusions are made with respect to the initial main controlling factors, compared to a NASA project. Control System methods are used to evaluate the critical features of the SD models. The eigenvalues of the linearised system indicate that the important factors are the hiring delay time, the assimilation time, and the employment time. This illustrates how the initial state of the system is at best neutrally stable with control only being achieved with complex non-linear decisions. The purpose is to compare the simplest SD and control models available required for "good" simulation of project behaviour with the Abdel-Hamid software project model. These models give clues to the decision structures that are necessary for good agreement with reality. The final simplified model, with five states, is a good match for the prime states of the Abdel-Hamid model, the NASA data, and compares favourably to the Ruiz model. The linear control system model has a much simpler structure, with the same limitations. Both the simple SD and control models are more suited to preliminary estimates of project performance.

INTRODUCTION

Software projects, as reported in the Chaos reports (Standish group 2009), *still* have a low success rate in terms of reliability, meeting due dates and working within assigned budgets (Smith 2002, Yeo 2002, Royal Academy of Engineering 2004), despite recent disputes (Glass 2005, Eveleens and Verhoef 2010) about the accuracy of the Chaos report descriptions. Factors, which determine successful project management (Abdel-Hamid and Madnick 1989), may be related to technical production processes, time scheduling in a dynamic environment and individual differences in project managers, members and team processes. Capers Jones (1996) has estimated that such projects only have a success rate of 65%. Projects may be considered as a system in which demands are

DOI: 10.4018/978-1-4666-6098-4.ch004

made (the requirements) and an internal project organisation, is controlled to produce the software goals, while being disturbed by the external environment.

The cost of such disasters such as the UK National Air Traffic System, Health Service computerisation and the London Ambulance Service computerisation is high in both money and human terms.

Despite these failures significant progress has been made in the use of System Dynamics (SD) methods to describe the operation of software projects (Rodrigues and Bowers 1996). Other workers such as Lin & Levary (1989) describe computer aided software design using System Dynamics, expert systems and a Knowledge based management system used in the design of a space station. More recently Häberlein (2004) has discussed the common structures involved in SD models. He contrasted the Abdel–Hamid model, which uses tasks completed with an approach based on requirements. Although we do not use this here the idea has considerable merit as the Abdel-Hamid approach has difficulty including requirements phases. His approach would be more suitable to use when modelling agile methods for example. This point was made by him in referring to the universality of the model. Rodrigues & Bowers *loc. Cit.* and Lyneis & Ford (2007) have established the role of System Dynamics in project management, pointing out the dominating effect of rework and the way factor such as quality or productivity affects project performance. Rahmandad and Weiss (2009) describe work investigating the dynamics of concurrent software development, illustrating the feedback loops dominating inter-project dynamics and tipping points. An excellent presentation by David Ford (2009) highlights in a very clear way the essential feedback processes arising in all projects, not just software development, illustrating how the projects run into problems as indicated by the SD models, leading to very clear solutions with regard to the tipping points on the project. Earlier in 2007 David

Ford and James Lyneis have given an excellent state–of-the-art synopsis of where SD methods had placed project research, indicating how SD models had been used in litigation after project failures. They made a plea for better post project analysis and use of SD methods for estimation of costs and manpower planning. A significant milestone has been the use of an SD model in agile software development by Cao, Ramesh and Abdel-Hamid (2010). This will show the software community that thought SD project models were only applicable to Waterfall processes that they were incorrect. Trammell et.al. (2013) has used SD methods to analyze the effects of funding fluctuation on software development. A recent comprehensive analysis by Mingers and White (2009) of Systems Thinking and its' contribution to Management Science reviews the contribution of SD to many fields of study but doesn't stress the very important contribution that SD project analysis has made, possibly the greatest financial contribution of any Systems methodology. System Dynamics models are now widely used in construction (Zhang et. al. 2014) to assist with planning, risk management (Boateng et.al. 2012) and defense project control (Cantwell 2012).

Some of the earliest attempts at creating project models by Roberts (1964) led to the very successful SD models of operation of the software development process models of Abdel-Hamid & Madnick (TAH) (1991). These TAH models use equations relating levels such as the *number of perceived errors*, or *the number of reworked errors* and relate them to rates such as *the error detection rate* or *the rework rate, significant features of these models included the decision processes.* These models were validated against NASA project data for a medium size project and the agreement is strikingly good. The SD model structure is highly non-linear with a number of theoretical assumptions, for example about how the errors in the coding are propagated. These structural assumptions do not allow for System Dynamics models to enable any general rules to be developed by academics to allow managers to make sound judgements based on good analysis. The distinction with models of inventory processes, which are related, is the rationale for this research programme. Early SD inventory models developed by Forrester (1961) were also non-linear and contained a number of factors, such as employment rate, that made the problem too complex for simple rules to be developed. Towill's group at Cardiff (Disney & Towill 2002) and others devised linear control system models to enable operational rules to be investigated and optimal solutions to be found as well as stability margins to be obtained (White & Censlive 2006). Part of the simplification of the Project Model is being tackled in the USA by the newer control system models of software testing (Cangussu et al 2002) and the approach to control by White (2006) is reviewed by White (2012). The whole purpose of this research application is to develop simple control system models of the project development process, as in inventory analysis, and obtain rules for stability. This should include the newer evolutionary and agile Project Management methods of Gilb (2005) and others.

Human Organisation Effects

Recent research has identified the importance of the managerial and organisational contexts that create the latent conditions for error and failures. This lack of transfer to and impact on industry is related to an insufficient consideration of system development problems and poorly documented error modelling techniques (Johnson 1999). Other studies in this field have considered the significance of pre-project activities for developing effective team working and management (Jiang et al, 2002), post-project reviews of process-related factors for competence building in project teams (von Zedtwitz, 2002) and leadership styles for managing group dynamics (Lewis, Welsh and Dehler, 2002). Few reliable SD models have been derived in this area and no fully validated models are available.

This is particularly difficult with present SD models of projects where 32 states or levels are being modelled simultaneously with over 100 feedback loops.

In order to succeed the Project manager must have a mental model of how the project system operates to achieve the system goals.

It is also important to realise that no matter how successful we are at controlling the external disturbances the goal of a successful project cannot be achieved if the internal processes are not stable. This is only possible if a good internal model is used and the best model available extant is that of Abdel-Hamid.

Industrial use at BP (Johnson et al. 2006) has been to focus attention on using SD models to aid in project planning and *model-in-the-loop* execution, while academic use has shown the efficacy of using the models as e-learning devices to aid understanding (Rodriguez et.al. 2006).

The purpose of this section is to set out an analysis of the system dynamics model from a control engineering point of view illustrating how the initial state of the system is at best neutrally stable. It will show how the reduced system is stable, but with control only being achieved with the complex non-linearity's applied. The intended use of these simplified models is to provide a vehicle for initial project feasibility studies to be estimated. To this purpose models that require less empirical constants and organisation specific information are required. The final model described is a control–theoretic model using no nonlinear data tables, unlike the SD models included here.

System Dynamics Model

Software development lifecycles are described by Ruparelia (2010), where he discusses the Waterfall, B, Spiral and V models as well as iterative and agile methods. The Model derived from that of Tarek Abdel-Hamid (TAH) consists of four main sections (Figure 1) and although widely thought to

Figure 1. Software development subsystems (from Abdel-Hamid)

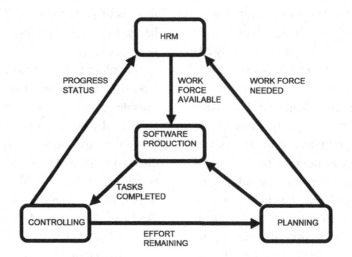

be a waterfall model only can be readily modified to represent all the methods mentioned.

The main functions set up in the model are an input block supplying information such as the size of the task, the estimate of the size etc. The blocks are Human Resource management, Production, Planning and control subsystems. Each of these has sub-subsystem blocks for example the production sub-system has the Manpower Allocation System (MAS) (Figure 2), the Software Development System(SDS), the Software Testing System (STS) and the Quality Assurance System (QAS). Each sub-subsystem has individual components with decisions built in as a representation of how management decisions were made (Figure 3).

Validation of the TAH Model

Data from a NASA project producing 24.4K Delivered Source Instructions (DSI) was used by Tarek Abdel-Hamed (TAH) with quite good information and a very good degree of agreement as shown in Figure 3. It also shows the flexibility of the model to add in overtime at a particular stage of the project to see what effect this has on overall completion date and cost.

The SIMULINK implementation of the TAH model is seen to give good agreement with the original Dynamo model but also with the observed data despite using slightly different implementation of some decisions. This difference in these two sets of data is that the NASA data includes an amount of overtime, not available in detail. The NASA data lies between the simulated values of zero and full overtime, ctrlsw=0 and ctrlsw=1, respectively.

The non-linearity is obvious when the convoluted decisions are incorporated in the model. This is quite typical of SD models in general. It is also the case that if the completion time predicted by the SD model is put back in as one of the initial trial values then the new completion time is not the same as originally predicted. This is also true of the other values that are initially guessed such as the size of the software. This is a result we might expect from such a nonlinear model. It does not make the predictions incorrect just that we must be sure what we are using in the first place. This model does not predict the size of the final project ab initio. Knowledge of the likely underestimate in size must be known in advance. Although the model is validated using the only public data avail-

Figure 2. Manpower allocation system in SIMULINK

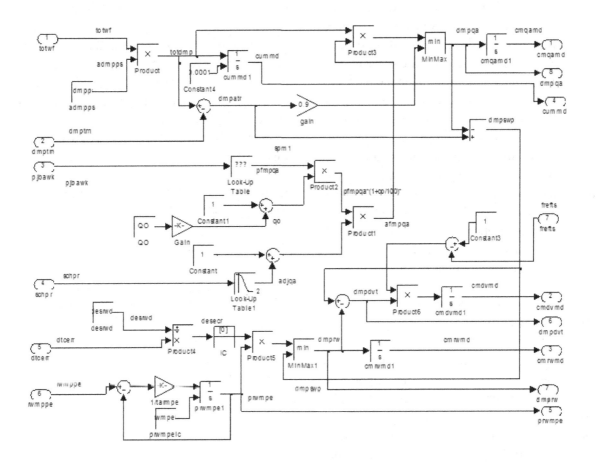

Figure 3. Simulated costs versus NASA actual costs/staff days

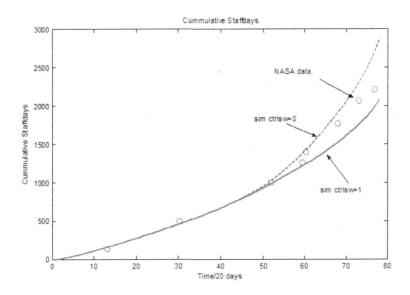

able, it is known that many larger projects have been validated using private company data by the System Dynamics software vendors. Our future research is to compare the model predictions with developments of different software projects. The size of the project is not material in the model to it's' operation except that since it is a nonlinear model the times and other results do not scale.

The initial size of the project is injected into the system by using a step function at time zero. To allow for changing requirements we can input a further change in size of the project with another step input at a specified time. We can change the rate of error generation throughout the project or simulate the addition of extra labour or the rate of burnout of that workforce.

Control System Analysis of the TAH Model

The project system being examined is a closed loop controlled system. Due to its' importance only the initial behaviour of the project will be considered here. The model was initiated by a step change in the required number of Delivered Source Instructions to be generated. This is the initial estimate. The programme modifies this in light of detected errors. The SD model was linearised, by hand algebraically, around the conditions at time =0 to enable a grasp of what factors governed the starting trends in the model. For times later in the development process the linearization was achieved using the functions in MATLAB. This yield a normal state-space set:

$$\dot{\mathbf{x}} = \mathbf{A}\mathbf{x} + \mathbf{B}\mathbf{u}$$
$$\mathbf{y} = \mathbf{C}\mathbf{x} + \mathbf{D}\mathbf{u} \tag{1}$$

$$\mathbf{x} = nx1, \mathbf{y} = mx1, \mathbf{u} = rx1,$$
$$\mathbf{A} = nxn, \mathbf{B} = nxr, \mathbf{C} = mxn, \mathbf{D} = mxr$$

The number of states n =32, the number of outputs is m=2, and the number of inputs here is r=1

$\mathbf{x}$ are the states; $\mathbf{y}$ are the outputs; $\mathbf{u}$ are the inputs to the system; $\mathbf{A}, \mathbf{B}, \mathbf{C}, \mathbf{D}$ are matrices describing the linear system.

The results of linearising the model at t=0 are an extremely sparse matrix.

The eigenvalues of this linearised model at time =0 are:

[0, 0, 0, -0.0045, 0, 0, -2.000, 0, -0.0320, 0, 0, -0.0325, -0.0065, 0, 0, -0.1000, 0, 0, 0, 0, 0

-0.0500, 0, 0, 0, 0, 0, 0, 0, 0, 0, 0]

The initial model is stable or more correctly neutrally stable, but the dominant eigenvalue is given by:

$$\lambda_{31} = \frac{1}{2c_1c_3c_6} \left(\begin{matrix} -c_1c_3 - c_1c_6 - c_3c_6 - \\ \left(\begin{matrix} c_1^2c_3^2 - 2c_1^2c_3c_6 - 2c_1c_3^2c_6 + \\ c_1^2c_6^2 - 2c_1c_6^2c_3 + c_3^2c_6^2 \end{matrix} \right)^{0.5} \end{matrix} \right) \tag{2}$$

where c_1 is the hiring delay; c_3 is the assimilation delay; and c_6 is the average employment time. In other words the initial rate of progress in the project depends only on how quickly you get staff to work on the project, not on the size of the project. If this initial trajectory is poor then overruns are more difficult to correct. Thus initially at least, the most important part of the business are the HR and training departments. The overall stability of the project is only achieved by the nonlinear decisions built into the model. These are meant to represent typical practice and were the subject of intense investigation by Abdel-Hamid and others. If you examine each decision then the implementation is quite logical but whether people under pressure always act in these ways is debatable. They are however, the best descriptions we have at present.

A system is said to be controllable if at time t_o we can transfer the system by means of a control vector from the original state to any final state and a system is said to be observable if a system is in state $\mathbf{x}(t_o)$ and we can determine the state from observations of the output over a finite time interval.

If we look at the controllability and observability of this model we find that 26 states are unobservable and 27 states are uncontrollable at t=0.

This demonstrates the problem for the software project manager. They cannot at the beginning of the project observe how well the project is proceeding, in fact not before the first cycle of trainees reaches the production team. The fact that the project is therefore uncontrollable in the linear sense should not surprise us because if we cannot observe what is happening it cannot be controlled. It was usually stated that this problem was due to the lack of recognition of how much software had been written, but this problem starts before this it is due solely to the delays in the company in obtaining any information before a certain time delay has occurred. This means that setting the project on the right trajectory is exceptionally important as we have open loop control with no real feedback until the non-linear decisions start to provide the requisite feedback and control. The penalties would mean that extra resources would have to be provided later in the project to complete tasks (other than the rework). To minimise the delays in reporting should be the prime aim of any project manager, in particular the initial data is crucial to the onwards trajectory and the first corrections. It is like a launch of a vehicle into outer space. If we do not correct the initial direction there will not be enough fuel (staff effort) at the end to pull the project back on target. Results shown by Lyneis, Cooper & Ells (2001), for the Peace Shield project, show that staffing policies and better hiring conditions reduce the

completion time. Their results also hint at differing initial trajectories in those cases.

The model can be reduced in order using the minreal function (Moore 1981) in MATLAB to eliminate the states that are uncontrollable and unobservable [22]. This is performed using all the data reported by Abdel-Hamid (1991). The reduced order model gives:

$$
\mathbf{A} = \begin{bmatrix}
-0.13054 & -0.018518 & 0.03171 & 0 \\
0.98733 & 0.079177 & -0.13558 & 0 \\
-0.14178 & 0.019294 & -0.033039 & 0 \\
-0.0018893 & 0.031924 & -0.0088642 & -0.03204
\end{bmatrix}
\tag{3}
$$

$$
\mathbf{B} = \begin{bmatrix}
0.11863 \\
0.004758 \\
-0.0081475 \\
8.395
\end{bmatrix}
\tag{4}
$$

$$
\mathbf{C} = \begin{bmatrix} 0 & 0 & 0 & 1 \end{bmatrix}
\tag{5}
$$

$$
\mathbf{D} = \begin{bmatrix} 0 \end{bmatrix}
\tag{6}
$$

With eigenvalues:

-0.0422 + 0.1224i

-0.0422 - 0.1224i

0.0000

-0.0320

The eigenvalues contain one zero root, one negative root and two complex conjugate roots. This makes the system neutrally stable.

We can compare the linear output with the fully nonlinear model in Figure 4.

The linearised curve was computed using the initial eigenvalues determined for time equals zero.

The reduced order linear model does not predict the experimental data nor does it follow the simulation of the nonlinear model. This is because important feedback paths have been eliminated in the model reduction process but it is not a reasonable fit to the experimental data. It is a poor predictor of the final cost in staff days largely because it does not cater for the rework. Rework is perhaps the single most important factor in lengthening the completion of the project (Lyneis & Ford 2007). The initial rate of cumulative staff days for the linear system is greater than that of the nonlinear system.

The Human Resource policies that need to be implemented to cater for these observations include a more rapid initial recruitment and a speeded up training programme. This will enable the whole project to be put on track more quickly, to reduce the time to the first errors being detected, to the subsequent rework being identified earlier and hence fixed earlier.

This will reduce the overall 'lost' time in the project. The major lesson from the Tarek Abdel Hamid work is to reduce time constants for detecting all parametric values associated with development from training to error detection, to reacting to staff shortages.

SIMPLE PROJECT MODELS

The main disadvantage of using The Tarek Abdel-Hamid model is the amount of information incorporated into the model as empirical data and also the data to be inputted as constants to enable a system to be modelled for a particular project. What we were seeking here is a simplified model to enable predictions of costs and resources to be made at the start of any project without assumptions about detailed performance to be known in advance.

Figure 4. Project model 9

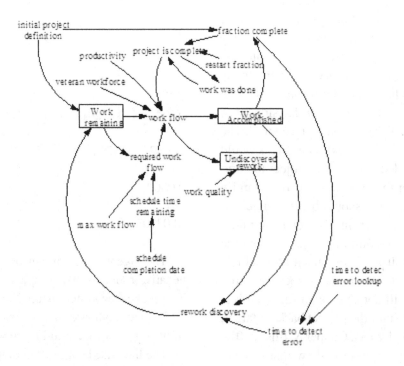

Houston *et.al.* (2001) have shown using sensitivity analysis that Project duration; Project cost; the number of staff and rate of generation of errors are key issues in software project management. They looked at the work of four models those of Abdel-Hamid, Madachy's own, Tvedt and Sycamore. They then examined factors that exhibited less than 1% effect on the outcomes. All models showed extreme sensitivity to job size. All are described as being wedded to the Waterfall process although this is not entirely correct. Houston comments that the response patterns from the four models are so different it is questionable that they represent the same process. In this light we are looking for the underlying main features to include in a simulation model. Initially we used two simple models (Ventana 1999), which have only three states and less than twenty eight equations in the system model while the better of the two, project 9, has a limited set of equations defining the workforce. Ruiz et al. (2001) used a simplified TAH model but with only half the complexity of the original. It would appear that they started from the other direction of this work by reducing the TAH model eliminating feedback loops found to have a smaller degree of importance. It is not clear how many states or levels were used in their model. While this model here used 27 variables Ruiz used 67. They achieved a verified similar behaviour of their model and as good an agreement to the TAH performance as our simpler model. The simpler model (Ventana 1999), in common use in System Dynamics texts, was chosen to include the effect of rework. The simpler of the two, project model (Figure 4) model 9, has a limited addition of work force data, no error generation, no control function, no QA policy, no overtime, fatigue or effects of late discovery of extra work.

The main TAH model includes most realistic parameters that affect project handling. The main quibble with it is the data used and the way decisions are mechanised. The two lower order models were examined to see how well they reproduced

the overall model predictions using the NASA data e.g. Figures 5 & 6. The more complex of the two models is shown in Figure 7. It is clear that the simple models should only be able to give a general prediction of the main three states that they include.

The complexity of the TAH model representation can cause chaotic behaviour, although the causal relationships that are responsible are uncertain. The TAH model is divided into sections as in Figure 1 but each of these sections is further subdivided. Figure 2 shows one sixteenth of the whole system and is larger than the two simpler models, figures. 4 & 7, shown here. The illustrative section of the larger model is the manpower allocation subsystem. This has fourteen equations to describe the subsystem whereas project model 9 has only two that cater for staff involvement. Despite this very simplified description the results are impressive. Using the data from the NASA project the responses, where possible, are compared in Figures 5 & 6.

The comparison of the three model responses for the 610 task Initial Project Development (IPD) shows that the cumulative tasks developed (cmtkdv) are in surprisingly good agreement, certainly up to 250 days into the project. The simpler project 9 outputs disagree early in the project, when recruitment is an issue but later are in good agreement. After 250 days the TAH project model detects and adjusts for the increased workload discovered and goes on to complete more tasks. A limit is reached at 310 days for projects 9. These models do not allow the number of tasks discovered to be incorporated into the overall size of the project. The tasks in the Abdel-Hamid model are more than the two simpler models, not only because the model recognises the new tasks discovered in more detail but also the perceived values are not necessarily in line with true values due to the delays incorporated in the model.

At 250 days the perceived tasks are at the peak compared to the simpler cases and this agrees with the picture in Figure 7. Project 9 has a lag due to

Figure 5. Project model 9 compared to TAH model for cumulative tasks

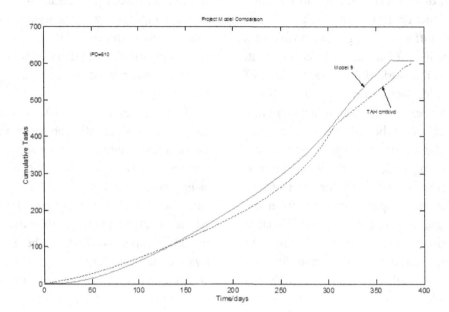

Figure 6. Comparison of tasks discovered

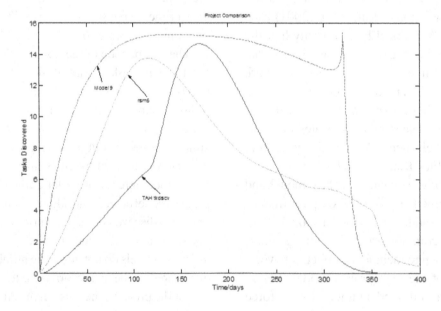

recruitment and this is even greater in the Abdel-Hamid model. At the end of the project the rate of change is nearly identical in all models. This is where no effect is felt from staffing changes. Overtime decisions in the Abdel-Hamid model have already been implemented.

Figure 6 shows how the number of tasks discovered, tkdscv, vary for the three project models. The overall values are not hugely different, although for the simpler models, the undiscovered rework for Project 9 are larger, with the peak values for the simpler models occurring very close to the end of

Figure 7. Model rsm6

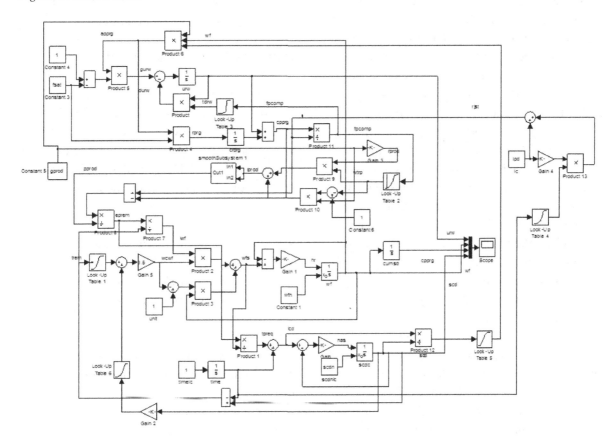

the project. The peak value for the Abdel-Hamid model occurs near the middle of the project. The problem of choosing the correct number of tasks at the beginning of the project is the key to making good predictions. .

In this example we have an initial project size guess that is 35% less than the number of task eventually found to be needed. If we input the number of tasks known at the end of the project we get Figure 1 where we see a much better correspondence between the three project models. The agreement between Project 9 and the Abdel-Hamid model is very good. For Project 9 the initial rate depends on the staffing recruitment. The key to getting this close agreement is to use values for error generation and productivity that are realistic. The interesting observation is that the cumulative number of tasks developed is nearly an

s-shaped curve and fits a number of real processes observed by Sterman (2000). This would lead to the idea that a number of dominant processes in the project process obey quite simple rules and the complexity of the Abdel-Hamid model may not be necessary for good-enough prediction of project tasks completed. The staffing levels, the number of reworked tasks and other factors not shown here are not as easily predicted.

It is clear from the results given earlier that simple models do give a reasonable prediction to the cumulative number of tasks developed versus time, although not predicting the final number of tasks from an, initial, underestimate. They do not give an accurate picture of the number of reworked tasks, while not agreeing in shape the overall peak values are not greatly in error. The tasks remaining to be developed follow a similar curve but the values indicated by the Abdel-Hamid model are larger at each time interval and continue for longer. This relates to the error generation prediction mechanism and work rates required.

The basic structure of project models needs to incorporate the effects of rework but needs to add in the number of tasks to be reworked in the correct sense, unlike the two models shown here.

The next feature that needs to be modified includes the generation of errors, which is done in these models by a mechanism that is too simple. This does not mean that we have to go to the level of detail in the Abdel-Hamid model as in that case over half of the variables are dummy quantities. Although it useful to have these expressed only a small number of these are essential to the manager's understanding of the management problem. For example there are nine equations that relate productivity in some fashion to similar variables.

Feedback in the Abdel-Hamid model is complex, most of the sensory data is not real but perceived. Since it is very difficult to know whether any DSI is actually finished, there is going to be some uncertainty about when particular parts of the whole software are completed. However the feedback/feed forward paths number in the hundreds and the feedback paths in project 9 number eighty six.

The way these loops individually affect the response has yet to be tested. In effect the project models need to be tuned to give data to the manager that is useful but does not cause such complexity that the model becomes uncontrollable. This feedback that is most needed is what time the project can be deemed complete.

This relies on two main pieces of data, one is the number of tasks to be completed and the second is what staff work output is needed to complete these extra tasks. Information such as fatigue does not have to be put into the model in as sophisticated a form as the Abdel-Hamid

model. It would suffice to have the ability to input a maximum output or as a minimum.

Improved Reduced Model

The final simplified nonlinear model (Figure 7) was based on the project model from Roberts (1964). This model was altered so that the tables were obtained as closely as possible from the TAH data set. This model has 5 states and is less than half as complex as the Ruiz model. The states represented are:

- Cummulative real progress(tasks)
- Cummulative staff days
- Scheduled completion date
- Undiscovered rework(tasks)
- Workforce

This model rsm6 shows a considerable better match to the TAH data as indicated in Figures 9 to 12.

The level of rework now agrees more closely to the TAH plot of tasks discovered (tkdscv), peak values are quite close but the models are greater early in the project. The final scheduled completion date now agrees with the NASA data; however these predictions increase over the true vales at about 200 days. The cumulative predictions of Staff days needed are slightly higher but are close at the end of the project. The Full Time Equivalent (FTE) staff prediction is good until right at the end of the project. This model has no provision for overtime. The data for cumulative staff days is close to the experimental data at a point after 300 days but exceeds the real values before that by up to 20%. However the agreement is better than other methods such as COCOMO. The predictions of FTE staff days follow the shape of the experimental data up to 250 days and are

Figure 8. Control System model

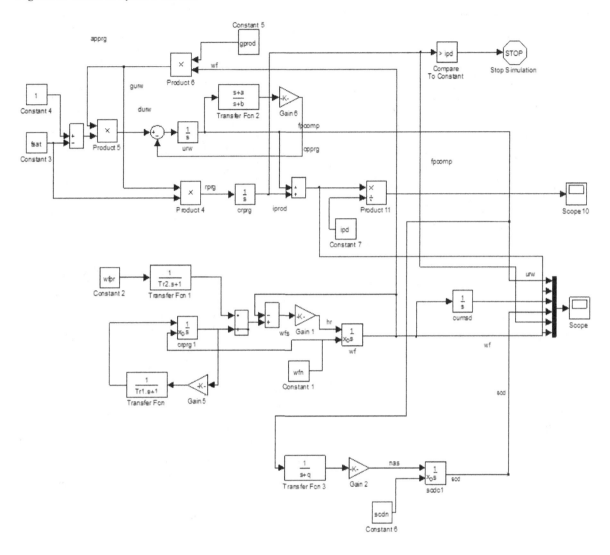

close at the end of the project. This is certainly adequate for initial planning calculations.

Control System Model

Developments of this simplified model led to the Control System model described in White (2012). This model is a completely linearised simplification of model rsm6 (Figure 8).

The equations that describe the model are shown below:

$$\dot{x} = Ax + Bu$$

$$y = Cx + Du \tag{7}$$

$$x = 9*1, A = 9*9, B = 9*1, C = 1*9, D = 0$$

x are the states; **y** are the outputs; **u** are the inputs to the system; **A, B, C, D** are matrices describing the linear system (see Box 1).

Box 1.

$$A = \begin{pmatrix}
0 & 0 & 0 & 0 & 0 & 0 & 1 & 0 & 0 \\
0 & 0 & 0 & 0 & 0 & 0 & fsat\ gprod & 0 & 0 \\
0 & 0 & -b - 1/tdrwm & 0 & 0 & a/tdrwm & (1-fsat)gprod/tdrwm & 0 & 0 \\
0 & 0 & 0 & -q & 0 & 1/tms & 0 & 0 & 0 \\
0 & 0 & 0 & 1 & 0 & 0 & 0 & 0 & 0 \\
0 & 0 & -1 & 0 & 0 & 0 & (1-fsat)grpod & 0 & 0 \\
0 & 0 & 0 & 0 & 0 & 0 & -1/wfat & 1/wfat & 1/wfat \\
0 & 0 & 0 & 0 & 0 & 0 & 0 & -1/Tr2 & 0 \\
0 & 0 & 0 & 0 & 0 & 0 & 0 & 0 & 1/tdwfs
\end{pmatrix} \tag{8}$$

$$B = \begin{pmatrix} 0 \\ 0 \\ 0 \\ scdn \\ 0 \\ 0 \\ wfn \\ wfpr \\ Tr2 \\ wfn \end{pmatrix} \tag{9}$$

$$\mathbf{C} = \begin{pmatrix} 1 & 1 & 0 & 0 & 1 & 1 & 1 & 0 & 0 \end{pmatrix} \tag{10}$$

where

$$x = \begin{pmatrix} CUMSD \\ CRPRG \\ DURW \\ NAS \\ SCD \\ URW \\ WF \\ WFSb \\ WFSa \end{pmatrix} \tag{11}$$

The dominating eigenvalues depend on the hiring delay, the assimilation delay and the time of employment. This means that the whole performance of the project is dominated by the HR policies of the company. The required action by the HR department should be to speed up the hiring process. Staff moving from another project must be released from that project at the earliest possible opportunity. The training process should be speeded considerably and the number of staff allocated to training from the main project staff should be reduced and sophisticated software means of keeping staff up to date used.

It is possible to allow for changes in requirements in this version of the model and also allow any changes to staffing fatigue etc. while the project is being run.

One of the virtues of the control system model is that it allows the use of powerful control theory analysis to find critical behaviour in systems. In this case we can use sensitivity analysis to compute how much a particular variable is affected by another during the system response. If we compute how the sensitivity ratio of cumulative staff days to *tdwfs* or the time constant of varying the workforce we obtain a value of +7 dB. This means that the final value of Staff days is very dependent of the rate of hiring staff. Similarly the sensitivity of cumulative staff days is -60dB or a very small dependence on the initial value of staff for the project.

Figure 9. FTE staff comparison

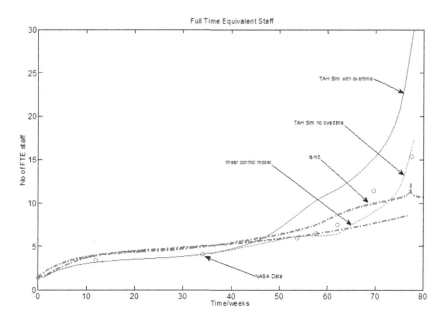

Figure 10. Scheduled completion date

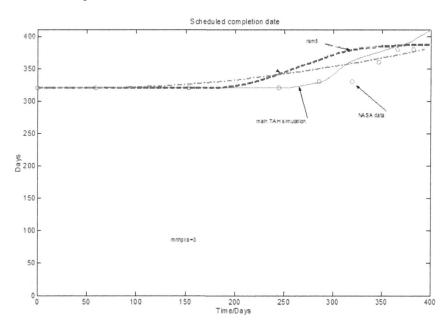

Figure 11. Tasks discovered

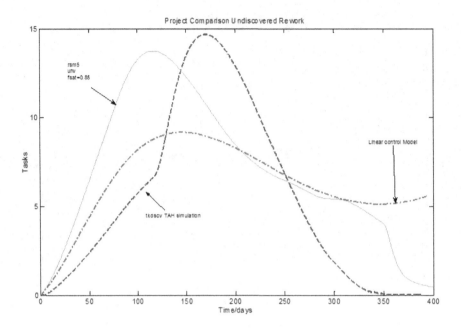

Figure 12. Cumulative staff cost

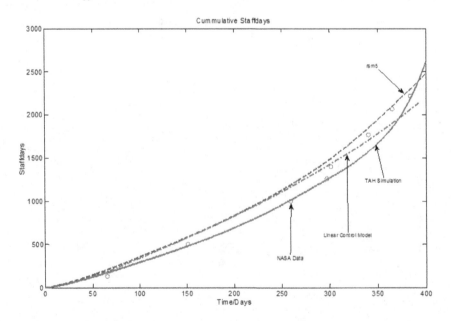

CONCLUSION

The SIMULINK model derived from Tarek Abdel–Hamid's Dynamo implemented System Dynamics gives good agreement with the NASA data for a 24.4K DSI project. The model was linearised so that a state-space representation for the closed loop system could be written to apply at the origin t=0. This version was shown to be neutrally stable but unobservable and uncontrollable. The significance of this result is that the initial behaviour of the system as dictated by the eigenvalues is more important than for stable systems where there are inbuilt restoring forces to force the trajectory back to the chosen path if a disturbance pushes the system away from its' initial trajectory. In the SD project models the non-linear human decisions are necessary to provide those restoring forces. The linear model however gave a poor prediction of the response of cumulative staff days in the cost of the development. It under predicts due to not accounting properly for rework.

The major dominating eigenvalues depend on the hiring delay, the assimilation delay and the time of employment. This provides analytical support to the commonly held view that the whole trajectory of the project is dominated by the HR policies of the company. The required action by the HR department should be to speed up the hiring process at least initially by reducing the time to approve new posts, reduce the time to advertise and curtail the internal delays. Another important feature is retention of staff. If the staff are transferred from another project they must be released from that project early or at least on time. The training process should be speeded up by at least 50% and the number of staff allocated to training from the project staff should be reduced and more electronic means of keeping staff up to date introduced. Failure would be more likely if these parameters are not addressed.

Very slow and very fast changes are limited in their action due to being out of phase with the actions.

It is possible to allow for changes in requirements in this version of the model and also allow any changes to staffing fatigue etc. while the project is being run.

Future research should allow a prediction based on the size of project, error rates, and staff levels to be developed in a graphical form for initial estimates. The models used here do not contradict any of the work by other researchers, but merely add analytical support.

- Two simple SD models have been compared with the Abdel-Hamid SD model with good agreement of the cumulative tasks developed but not so good for tasks reworked.
- The real problems with these simple models are:
  - In the way the rework problem is identified and added to the total tasks to be worked
  - The computation of work needed in terms of staff input
- The final simplified model, rsm6, with 5 states is a good match for the prime states of the TAH model, the NASA data and compares favourably to the Ruiz model
- A linear control system model was developed after these two SD models and has a much simpler structure, even though it has the same limitations. It does not require as many empirical data inputs and is therefore more suited to preliminary estimates of project performance.

The next stage of the research is to develop the control system model to be able to represent agile processes.

REFERENCES

Abdel–Hamid, T. K., & Madnick, S. E. (1989). Lessons learned from modelling the dynamics of software development. *Communications of the ACM*, *32*(12), 1426–1437. doi:10.1145/76380.76383

Abdel-Hamid, T. K., & Madnick, S. E. (1991). *Software Project Dynamics*. Prentice-Hall.

Bérard, C. (2010). Group Model Building Using System Dynamics: An Analysis of Methodological Frameworks. *The Electronic Journal of Business Research Methods*, *8*(1), 35–45.

Boateng, P., Chen, Z., Ogunlana, S., & Ikediashi, D. (2012). A system dynamics approach to risk description in megaprojects development. *Int J Technology and Management in Construction*, *4*(3), 593–603.

Cangussu, J. W., DeCarlo, R. A., & Mathur, A. P. (2002). A formal model of the software test process. *IEEE Transactions on Software Engineering*, *28*(8), 782–796. doi:10.1109/TSE.2002.1027800

Cantwell, P. (2012). The effect of Using a systems approach to project control within the U.S. defense industry. In *Proceedings of IEEE Systems Conference*. IEEE.

Cao, L., Ramesh, B., & Abdel-Hamid, T. (2010). Modeling Dynamics in Agile Software Development. *ACM Transactions on Management, Information Systems*, *1*(1), 5.1-5.26.

Disney, S. M., & Towill, D. R. (2002). A discrete transfer function model to determine the dynamic stability of a vendor managed inventory supply chain. *International Journal of Production Research*, *40*(1), 179–204. doi:10.1080/00207540110072975

Eveleens, J. L., & Verhoef, C. (2010, January-February). The Rise and fall of the Chaos Report Figures. *IEEE Software*. doi:10.1109/MS.2009.154

Ford, D. (2009). *System Dynamics for Large Complex Projects*. Retrieved from http://131.215.239.80/workshop9/ford.pdf

Forrester, J. (1961). *Industrial Dynamics*. Cambridge, MA: MIT Press.

Gilb, T. (2005). *Competitive Engineering*. Oxford, UK: Elsevier.

Glass, R. (2006). The Standish Report: Does it really describe a software crisis? *Communications of the ACM*, *49*(8), 15–16. doi:10.1145/1145287.1145301

Häberlein, T. (2004). Common Structures in System Dynamics Models of Software Acquisition Projects. *Journal of Software Process Improvement and Practice*, *9*, 67–80. doi:10.1002/spip.197

Hansen, G. (1996, January). Simulating Software development processes. *IEEE Computer*, 73-77.

Houston, D., Ferreira, S., Collofello, J., Montgomery, D., Mackulak, G., & Shunk, D. (2001). Behavioral characterization: finding and using the influential factors in software process simulation models. *Journal of Systems and Software*, *59*, 259–270. doi:10.1016/S0164-1212(01)00067-X

Jiang, J. J., Klein, G., & Discenza, R. (2002). Pre-project partnering impact on an information system project, project team and project manager. *European Journal of Information Systems*, *11*(2), 86–97. doi:10.1057/palgrave/ejis/3000420

Johnson, C. (1999). Why human error modelling has failed to help systems development. *Interacting with Computers*, *11*(5), 517–524. doi:10.1016/S0953-5438(98)00041-1

Johnston, S., Peterson, D., & Swank, G. (2006). *Project of the Future Vision: Using System Dynamics to achieve 'model-in-the-loop' Project Planning and execution*. System Dynamics Conference. Retrieved from http://www.systemdynamics.org/conferences/2006/proceed/papers/JOHNS423.pdf

Jones, C. (1996, April). Large Software Systems Failures and Successes. *American Programmer*, 3-9.

Lewis, M. W., Welsh, M. A., & Dehler, G. E. (2002). Product development tensions: Exploring contrasting styles of project management. *Academy of Management Journal, 45*(3), 546–564. doi:10.2307/3069380

Lin, C. Y., & Levary, R. R. (1989). Computer Aided Software Development Process Design. *IEEE Transactions on Software Engineering, 15*(9), 1025–1037. doi:10.1109/32.31362

Lyneis, J., Cooper, K., & Els, S. (2001). Strategic management of complex projects: a case study using system dynamics. *System Dynamics Review, 17*(3), 237–260. doi:10.1002/sdr.213

Lyneis, J., & Ford, D. (2007). System Dynamics applied to project management: a survey, assessment and directions for future research. *System Dynamics Review, 23*(2/3), 57–189.

Mingers, J., & White, L. (2009). *A Review of the Recent Contribution of Systems Thinking to Operational Research and Management science*. University of Kent Working Paper 197. Retrieved from http://kar.kent.ac.uk/22312/

Moore, B. (1981). Principal Component Analysis in Linear Systems: Controllability, Observability and Model Reduction. *IEEE Transactions on Automatic Control, 26*, 17–31. doi:10.1109/TAC.1981.1102568

Roberts, E. B. (1964). *The Dynamics of Research and Development*. New York: Harper & Row.

Rodrigues, A., & Bowers, J. (1996). System Dynamics in Project Management: a comparative analysis with traditional methods. *System Dynamics Review, 12*, 121–139. doi:10.1002/(SICI)1099-1727(199622)12:2<121::AID-SDR99>3.0.CO;2-X

Royal Academy of Engineering. (2004). *The challenges of Complex IT projects*. Report of working group of RAE and BCS.

Ruiz, M., Ramos, I., & Toro, M. (2001). A Simplified model of software project dynamics. *Journal of Systems and Software, 59*, 299–309. doi:10.1016/S0164-1212(01)00070-X

Ruparelia, N. (2010). Software Development Lifecycle Models. *ACM Sigsoft Software Engineering Notes, 35*(3), 8–13. doi:10.1145/1764810.1764814

Smith, J. (2002, June). The 40 root causes of troubled IT projects. *Computing and Control Journal*, 109-112.

Standish Group International Inc. (2009). *Standard Group CHAOS Report*. Author.

Sterman, J. D. (2000). *Business Dynamics*. Boston: McGraw-Hill.

Sundarraj, R. P. (2002). An optimisation approach to plan for reusable software components. *European Journal of Operational Research, 142*(1), 128–137. doi:10.1016/S0377-2217(01)00285-5

Trammell, T., Madnick, S., & Moulton, A. (2013). *Using System Dynamics to Analyze the Effect of Funding Fluctuations on Software Development* (Working Paper CISL#2013-06). Sloan School of Management, MIT.

Ventana Systems Inc. (1999). *Vensim DSS Modeling Guide*. Author.

Von Zedtwitz, M. (2002). Organisational learning through post-project reviews in R & D. *R & D Management, 32*(3), 255–268. doi:10.1111/1467-9310.00258

White, A. S. (2006). External Disturbance control for software project management. *International Journal of Project Management, 24*, 127–135. doi:10.1016/j.ijproman.2005.07.002

White, A. S. (2011). A control system project development model derived from System Dynamics. *International Journal of Project Management, 29,* 696–705. doi:10.1016/j.ijproman.2010.07.009

White, A. S. (2012). Towards a Minimal Realisable System Dynamics Project Model. *International Journal of Information Technologies and Systems Approach*, *5*(1), 57–73. doi:10.4018/jitsa.2012010104

White, A. S., & Censlive, M. (2006). Observations on modelling strategies for vendor managed inventory. *Journal Manufacturing Technology Management*, *17*(4), 496–512. doi:10.1108/17410380610662915

Yeo, K. T. (2002). Critical failure factors in information system projects. *International Journal of Project Management, 20,* 241–246. doi:10.1016/S0263-7863(01)00075-8

Zhang, X., Wu, Y., Shen, L., & Skitmore, M. (2014). A prototype system dynamics model for assessing the sustainability of construction projects. *International Journal of Project Management, 32*(1), 66–76. doi:10.1016/j.ijproman.2013.01.009

APPENDIX

List of Symbols

a: Limit to rework.

A: State matrix for control system.

b: Delay to recognise rework.

B: Control matrix.

C: Output matrix.

ctrlsw: Switch allowing overtime in TAH model.

c_1: Hiring delay.

c_3: Assimilation delay.

c_6: Average employment time.

CUMSD: Cumulative staff days (cost) (state).

CRPRG: Cumulative real progress rate (state).

cmtkdv: Cumulative tasks developed (TAH model).

DURW: Desired rework (state).

fsat: Fraction satisfactory (measure of QA).

gprod: Gross average productivity.

IPD: Initial Project Development (tasks).

q: Delay in recognising effect of rework on schedule.

SCD: Scheduled completion date (state).

scdn: Initial estimate of scheduled completion date.

tdrwm: Detection time for undiscovered rework (based on past experience).

tdwfs: Adjustment time for workforce sought (based on HR policy and experience).

tkdscv: Tasks discovered in TAH model.

tms: Adjustment of schedule due to undiscovered rework.

Tr2: Delay to recognise workforce needed.

URW: Undetected rework (state).

WF: Workforce (state).

Wfat: Workforce adjustment time.

wfn: Initial workforce available.

WFSa: Workforce sought due to delayed limit (state).

WFSb: Workforce sought due to perceived workload (state).

wfpr: Workforce perceived required base on perception of project size.

x: States of the linear system.

y: Outputs of the linear system.

Chapter 5
Modeling a Simple Self–Organizing System

Nicholas C. Georgantzas
Fordham University, USA

Evangelos Katsamakas
Fordham University, USA

ABSTRACT

This chapter presents a System Dynamics (SD) simulation model that not only replicates self-organizing system uncertainty results but also looks at self-organization causally. The SD simulation and model analysis results show exactly how distributed control leads positive feedback to explosive growth, which ends when all dynamics have been absorbed into an attractor, leaving the system in a stable, negative feedback state. The chapter's SD model analysis helps explain why phenomena of interest emerge in agent-based models, a topic crucial in understanding and designing Complex Adaptive Self-Organizing Systems (CASOS).

INTRODUCTION

A multitude of systems, including biological ecosystems (Kauffman 1995) and markets (Arthur *et al* 1997, Ormerod 1999) are complex, adaptive, self-organizing systems (CASOS). In these systems, as in ant colonies and swarms of bees, beautiful patterns of behavior emerge without central control. Instead, global coherent patterns emerge out of local agent interactions and distributed control among system components. Some of these components are feedback loops.

CASOS ideas also provide an emerging framework for business and economics (Beinhocker

2006). Internet users self-organize to create social networks (e.g. Facebook or LinkedIn), to produce knowledge (e.g., Wikipedia), to trade goods (e.g., eBay), to fund projects (crowdfunding) and to develop software (e.g., open source software communities). Taking advantage of global Internet connectivity, these communities have attracted business interest because they demonstrate the capacity of self-organizing systems to innovate and to create economic value.

Most importantly CASOS concepts inspired by nature can provide the framework for solving a wide variety of distributed computing and engineering problems (Bonabeau *et al* 1999, Dorigo

DOI: 10.4018/978-1-4666-6098-4.ch005

and Stutzle 2004). Mamei and Zambonelli (2007) propose a system exploiting digital pheromones to coordinate autonomous agents in pervasive environments making use of RFID tags. We propose that CASOS concepts inspired by nature and biology can motivate *biologically-inspired* IS research.

Understanding, designing or even influencing systems that combine individual autonomy with global order is not a trivial task, as systems tend to run down from order to disorder. Kugler and Turvey (1987) argue, for example, that to contain disorder in a multi-agent system, one must couple that system to another, in which disorder increases. Accordingly, Parunak and Brueckner (2001) simulate an ant pheromone-driven CASOS and measure Shannon's statistical entropy or uncertainty at the ant agent and pheromone molecule levels, showing an entropy-based view of self-organization.

The focal contribution of our chapter is looking at self-organization causally, i.e., looking at the causes that make self-organization emerge. The culmination of Parunak and Brueckner's (2001) ant pheromone-driven self-organizing system into a system dynamics (SD) model, allows unearthing exactly how circular feedback-loop relations determine emergent phenomena in self-organizing systems. Cast as a methodological contribution to understanding CASOS, this chapter explains *why* phenomena of interest emerge in agent-based models. Our chapter demonstrates the value of system dynamics modeling in analyzing the behavior of natural and social CASOS. This may help the community design better "artificial swarm-intelligence" systems and motivate the future use of SD modeling in the analysis of distributed-computing CASOS.

The chapter uses the loop polarity and dominance ideas from the system dynamics literature (e.g., Rahmandad and Sterman 2008, Richardson 1995) to explain complex agent dynamics. The ant-pheromone SD model analysis results show that three feedback loops become prominent in generating the ant pheromone-driven dynamics, two balancing or negative loops at the pheromones level and one reinforcing or positive loop at the ant agent level.

As *shifting loop polarity (slp)* determines system behavior (Richardson 1995), distributed, as opposed to central, control leads positive feedback relations to explosive growth, which ends when all dynamics gets absorbed into an attractor, leaving the system in stable, negative feedback. What is unique and interesting here is that, following prior work on CASOS, this chapter goes a step further in explicitly analyzing a CASOS in terms of the causal feedback-loop relations responsible for its dynamics.

Below is a brief overview of SD model analysis. Then the chapter moves on to model description, through the listing of the SD model equations, to experimental simulation and model analysis results, and to a brief discussion.

SYSTEM DYNAMICS (SD) MODEL ANALYSIS

Influenced by engineering control theory, SD calls for simulation modeling that provides a rigorous understanding of system behavior through time. The SD modeling process helps articulate exactly how the structure of feedback loop relations among variables in a system determines its performance through time (Sterman 2000).

Two types of diagrams help formalize system structure: causal loop diagrams (CLDs) and stock and flow diagrams. CLDs depict relations among variables (see Figure 4a for example). Complementary to CLDs, stock and flow diagrams are graphical representations of differential equations. They show how flow variables accumulate into stocks. There is a one-to-one correspondence between SD model diagrams and equations in the *iThink®* software, thus this chapter only lists the equations on Tables 2 and 3, since they completely describe the underlying causal system structure.

In complex systems, behavior through time depends on which of the numerous feedback loops dominate through time. A loop's dominance can change through time because of non-linearities (Richardson 1995). To understand a system, one must try to understand how loop dominance changes endogenously, i.e., detect *shifting loop polarity* and *dominance*. Computational tools from discrete mathematics and graph theory help to simplify and then to automate model analysis (Mojtahedzadeh et al. 2004, Oliva 2004), mostly by linking feedback loop strength to system eigenvalues (Forrester 1983).

The algorithm supporting the analysis of this chapter's SD model is the pathway participation metric (PPM) implemented in the *Digest*® software (Mojtahedzadeh *et al*. 2004). This software, which accepts the *iThink*® SD model equations as its input, first slices a selected variable's time path or trajectory into discrete time-phases. In each time phase, the selected variable maintains the same sign for the first and second time derivative, corresponding to one of seven possible behavior patterns through time: balancing growth or decline, linear growth or decline, reinforcing growth or decline and equilibrium, either static or dynamic (Mojtahedzadeh *et al*. 2004). Then using a recursive heuristic approach, the PPM detects compact structures of causal paths and loops that contribute the most to the performance of the selected variable within each time phase.

Specifically, given a small change in a selected stock, the PPM computes how much the net flow of the selected stock or state variable would change; this is the total participation metric. Then this metric is partitioned among the pathways that affect the net flow. The most influential pathway, i.e., sequence of causal links or arrows, is the one with the largest participation magnitude and the same sign as the total participation metric (Mojtahedzadeh *et al*. 2004). *Digest*® then produces as output the most prominent causal paths drawn as CLDs (see Figure 5 for an example).

MODEL DESCRIPTION

Ant colonies are pheromone-driven CASOS (Parunak 1997, Parunak and Brueckner 2001) that provide the context for this chapters' model. Figure 1 shows two ant agents, one fixed and one mobile, who desire to be together (coordinate). Neither agent knows the location of the other. If only it knew where to go, the mobile agent or walker ant (*wa*) would travel to the destination of the stationary one. To find each other, the ants use scent markers called pheromones. The stationary agent or target ant (*ta*) deposits pheromone molecules at its location. As pheromone molecules (*pm*) diffuse through the environment and create the *pm* grid that walker ants can follow to locate the target ant. So pheromone molecules provide a *coordination mechanism* for self-organization that is similar to the "field-based coordination" concept (Mamei and Zambonelli 2006), and the analysis that follows can be seen more generally as analysis of the CASOS coordination problem.

By depositing pheromones, agents change their environment through their action. The environment in turn mediates self-organization through processes that generate physical structures, i.e., pheromone diffusion and evaporation, which the agents perceive, thus permitting ordered behavior on the agent grid. At the same time, these processes increase disorder on the *pm* grid, so that the system as a whole becomes less ordered with more (location) uncertainty through time. Parunak and Brueckner (2001) measure Shannon's information entropy (Shannon and Weaver 1949) or uncertainty (Tribus and McIrvine 1971) on the ant agent and *pm* (pheromone molecule) grids. Entropy is calculated as:

$$U = -\sum_{i=1}^{n} p_i \log p_i \tag{1}$$

where *i* ranges over all possible outcomes *n* and p_i is the probability of finding an agent in state

Figure 1. A pheromone-driven CASOS, with pheromone molecule (pm) and ant (ta and wa) agent grids (see Tables 1, 2 and 3 for variable acronyms and definitions; the differently colored points on the pm grid correspond to 30 different simulation runs)

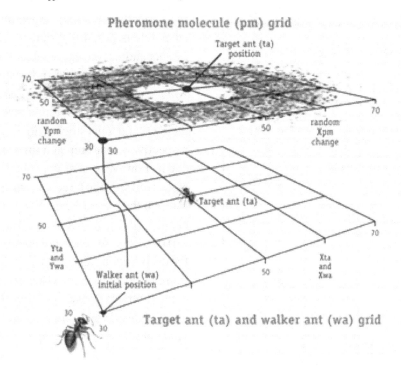

i. Unlike Parunak and Brueckner, however, this chapter's simulation results clearly separate the walkers' unguided, random motion from their pheromone-guided, deterministic motion.

Developed using the *iThink® Software* (Richmond *et al.* 2009), the system dynamics (SD) model incorporates two major parts or sectors. Table 1 shows the most pertinent variable acronyms and brief definitions used in the model and simulation results.

The Pheromone Molecule (Pm) Grid Model Sector

Table 2 shows the pheromone molecule (*pm*) grid model sector equations, which include level (stock), rate (flow) and auxiliary variables. The

target ant (*ta*) agent remains stationary at its fixed (50, 50) location (Figure 1), where it always deposits one pheromone molecule per time unit. Like the walker ant agents, each *pm* agent also moves by computing a random angle, i.e., random *pm* ∂ $\in$ [0, 2π] (Equation 2.16), relative to its current position.

Each *pm* agent then takes a step in the resulting direction, every cycle of the simulation (Equation 2.16). Both pheromone molecules and walker ants can find themselves at any real-valued (*X, Y*) location on their respective grids (Figure 1). Pheromone molecules move, however, every cycle of the simulation with a *pm* step = 2 (Equation 2.15), while ants take only one step every five cycles of the simulation. Altogether then, pheromone molecules move ten times faster than ant agents do.

Table 1. Pertinent variable acronyms and brief definitions

Variable	Definition
average Xpm	Pheromone molecule (pm) average x-coordinate on the pm agent grid
average Ypm	Pheromone molecule (pm) average y-coordinate on the pm agent grid
pm	Pheromone molecule (pm) on the pm agent grid
Ppm	Pheromone molecule (pm) average location probability on the pm agent grid
Pwa	Walker ant (wa) location probability on the ant agent grid
ρ	Walker ant (wa) perceptual radius (wa radius)
ta	Target ant on the ant agent grid
Upm	Pheromone molecule (pm) average location uncertainty on the pm grid
Uwa	Walker ant (wa) location uncertainty on the ant agent grid
wa	Walker ant on the ant agent grid
Xpm	Pheromone molecule (pm) x-coordinate on the pm agent grid
Xta	Target ant (ta) x-coordinate on the ant agent grid
Xwa	Walker ant (wa) x-coordinate on the ant agent grid
Ypm	Pheromone molecule (pm) y-coordinate on the pm agent grid
Yta	Target ant (ta) y-coordinate on the ant agent grid
Ywa	Walker ant (wa) y-coordinate on the ant agent grid

The CASOS environment aggregates pm deposits into the Pheromone Molecules stock (Equation 2.1). These pm agents evaporate (Equation 2.5) randomly through time, depending on the time to evaporate $\in$ [10, 40] parameter (Equation 2.17).

Depending on aggregated Pheromone Molecules' random heading and position, the random Xpm change and random Ypm change flows (Equations 2.7 and 2.9) either increase or decrease the Xpm and Ypm stocks (Equations 2.2 and 2.3), respectively, one step at a time (t). Each new pm agent, however, once deposited, it biases these stocks towards the target ant (ta) agent's location, through the biased Xpm change and biased Ypm change flows, respectively (Equations 2.6 and 2.10). Lastly, for each pm agent that evaporates, the evaporation caused Xpm change and evaporation caused Ypm change flows (Equations 2.8 and 2.11) subtract the average Xpm and average Ypm coordinates (Equations 2.12 and 2.13) from the Xpm and Ypm stocks, respectively.

Table 2. The pheromone molecule (pm) grid model sector equations

	Equation #
Level or State Variables (Stocks)	
Pheromone Molecules(t) = Pheromone Molecules(t - dt) + (pm production - pm evaporation) * dt	(2.1)
INIT Pheromone Molecules = time to evaporate * pm production {unit: pm}	(2.1.1)
Xpm(t) = Xpm(t - dt) + (biased Xpm change + random Xpm change	(2.2)
- evaporation caused Xpm change) * dt	(2.2.1)
INIT Xpm = Pheromone Molecules * Xta {unit: pm * step}	(2.3)
Ypm(t) = Ypm(t - dt) + (random Ypm change + biased Ypm change	(2.3.1)
- evaporation caused Ypm change) * dt	
INIT Ypm = Pheromone Molecules * Xta {unit: pm * step}	
Rate Variables (Flows)	
pm production = 1 {unit: pm / t}	(2.4)
pm evaporation = Pheromone Molecules / time to evaporate {unit: pm / t}	(2.5)
biased Xpm change = pm production * Xta {unit: pm * step / t}	(2.6)
random Xpm change = (COS(random pm ∂) * pm step) * Pheromone Molecules {unit: pm * step / t}	(2.7)
evaporation caused Xpm change = average Xpm * pm evaporation {unit: pm * step / t}	(2.8)
random Ypm change = (SIN(random pm ∂) * pm step) * Pheromone Molecules {unit: pm * step / t}	(2.9)
biased Ypm change = pm production * Yta {unit: pm * step / t}	(2.10)
evaporation caused Ypm change = average Ypm * pm evaporation {unit: pm * step / t}	(2.11)
Auxiliary Variables and Constants (converters)	
average Xpm = Xpm / Pheromone Molecules {unit: step}	(2.12)
average Ypm = Ypm / Pheromone Molecules {unit: step}	(2.13)
Monte Carlo Dummy = 1 {unit: dimensionless}	(2.14)
pm step = 2 {unit: step}	(2.15)
random pm ∂ = RANDOM (0, 2 * PI) {unit: radian}	(2.16)
time to evaporate = RANDOM (10, 40) {unit: t}	(2.17)

Table 3. The walker ant (wa) grid model sector equations

Level or State Variables (Stocks)	Equation #
Xwa(t) = Xwa(t – dt) + (random Xwa change + biased Xwa change) * dt	(3.1)
INIT Xwa = 30 {unit: step}	(3.1.1)
Ywa(t) = Ywa(t - dt) + (random Ywa change + biased Ywa change) * dt	(3.2)
INIT Ywa = 30 {unit: step}	(3.2.1)
Rate Variables (Flows)	
random Xwa change = IF (distance > wa radius) THEN (COS (random wa ∂) * wa step)	(3.3)
ELSE (0) {unit: step / t}	(3.4)
biased Xwa change = IF (distance <= wa radius) THEN ((difference in X / distance) * wa step)	(3.5)
ELSE (0) {unit: step / t}	(3.6)
random Ywa change = IF (distance > wa radius) THEN (SIN (random wa ∂) * wa step)	
ELSE (0) {unit: step / t}	
biased Ywa change = IF (distance <= wa radius) THEN ((difference in Y / distance) * wa step)	
ELSE (0) {unit: step / t}	
Auxiliary Variables and Constants (converters)	
difference in X = average Xpm - Xwa {unit: step}	(3.7)
difference in Y = average Ypm - Ywa {unit: step}	(3.8)
distance = SQRT((difference in X^2) + (difference in Y^2)) {unit: step}	(3.9)
random wa ∂ = RANDOM (0, 2*PI) {unit: radian}	(3.10)
wa radius = 25 {Parunak and Brueckner's (2001) ρ; unit: step}	(3.11)
wa step = GRAPH(MOD (TIME, 5) {unit: step})	(3.12)
(1.00, 1.00), (2.00, 0.00), (3.00, 0.00), (4.00, 0.00), (5.00, 0.00)	

The Walker Ant (Wa) Grid Model Sector

While the *pm* agents always execute an unbiased random walk, the walker ant (*wa*) computes its heading from two inputs (Table 3). Either it executes an unbiased random walk too, or it generates a vector from its current location to the average *pm* location.

It all depends on the *wa* radius (ρ) parameter (Equation 3.11). If the walker ant's distance (Equation 3.9) from the average *pm* location is strictly larger than $\rho = 25$, then *wa* executes an unbiased random walk. *First*, it computes a random angle, i.e. random *wa* $\partial \in [0, 2p]$ (Equation 3.10), relative to its current position. *Then*, it takes a step in the resulting direction, once every five cycles of the simulation (Equation 3.12: a recurring graphical table function, with wa step = 1 at t = 1 and zero elsewhere). Depending on *wa*'s random heading and position, the random X*wa* change and random Y*wa* change flows (Equations 3.3 and 3.5) either

increase or decrease the X*wa* and Y*wa* stocks (Equations 3.1 and 3.2), respectively, one step every five time (*t*) units.

EXPERIMENTAL RESULTS

The results shown here entail 30 random simulation runs, implemented through the '*Sensi Specs*' *iThink®* command. Each run's specifications are as follows: simulation *TIME* $\in$ [0, 250], with a computation interval *dt* = 1 and Euler's integration method.

The little arrows on the phase plot of Figure 2a show how the pheromone molecules' average location, i.e., average X*pm* coordinate and average Y*pm* coordinate, changes through time. While stationary, the target ant (*ta*) deposits one molecule at its fixed (50, 50) location every time step. As the pheromone molecules diffuse through the CASOS environment, they create a gradient that *wa* can follow.

Figure 2. Pheromone molecule (pm) average (a) dispersion and (b) location probability (Ppm), along with (c) ensemble of guided walker ant (wa) paths and (d) their final location probability (Pwa). The differently colored average pm dots on Figure 2a and wa paths on Figure 2c correspond to the 30 different simulation runs.

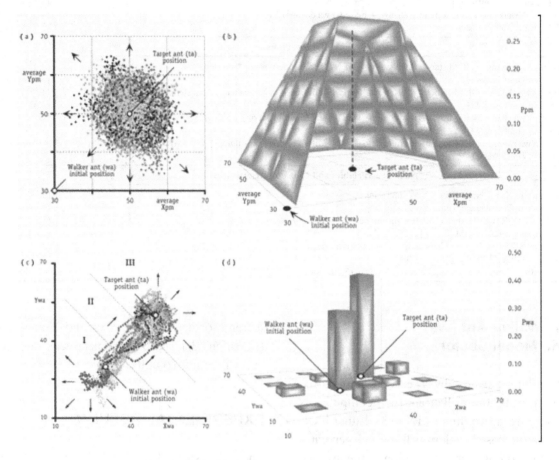

Each dot on Figure 2a shows the pheromone molecule average location on the *pm* agent grid. Figure 2c shows the color-coded trajectories of an ensemble of 30 *wa* agents with perceptual radius $\rho = 25$. Model's walker ants follow three distinct path groups (Figure 2c and Table 4) like in Parunak and Brueckner's (2001) experimental results.

Based on 30 simulation runs, the surface plot on Figure 2b shows the *pm* average location probability (Ppm) over a 4×4 tiling *pm* grid. Although pheromone molecules diffuse through the environment and evaporate (Equation 2.5), Figure 2b shows that the walker has a fair chance to find its target (*ta*). The 3D column chart on Figure 2d

shows the walker ants' location probability (Pwa) values, distributed over the 4×4 tiling *wa* grid. These Pwa values help compute the walker ant's normalized location uncertainty (Uwa), while the Ppm values determine the also normalized *pm* average location uncertainty (Upm) through time (Figure 3a).

The typical uncertainty about the *pm* average location (Upm) on Figure 3a increases through time until it saturates at one, its normalized upper bound. The more pheromone molecules enter the system and disperse, the higher Upm grows.

Similarly, the typical walker initially wanders randomly around its origin. Unguided, as if un-

Figure 3. Location uncertainty (U) in the pheromone-driven system: (a) ta is stationary and (b) shows an experimental extension where ta turns mobile

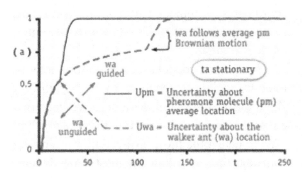
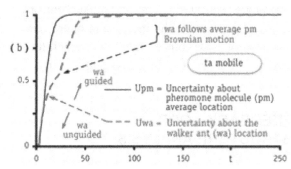

coupled from the pheromone molecule grid, its behavior is identical to that of the typical average *pm*. Consequently, U*wa* is initially identical to U*pm* (Figure 3a). But once *wa* senses the *pm* average inside its perceptual radius ρ, then it follows the pheromone molecule average, now guided by the *pm* grid that its target creates. Although the guided U*wa* continues to rise, it does so at a lower rate than when *wa* is unguided. There is less uncertainty on the ant agent grid about *wa*'s whereabouts when the *pm* grid that *ta* creates guides *wa*.

Once in *ta*'s region, the walker seems to meander again as if performing a random walk because *ta*'s *pm* average executes its random Brownian motion continuously throughout each simulation run. Faithfully following the pheromone molecules' random walk, the walker emulates their random behavior. So, like U*pm*, U*wa* also rises rapidly and *concomitantly*, until U*wa* too saturates at its maximum value of one. With *wa* still guided, the uncertainty about its whereabouts now matches the uncertainty about the pheromone molecules' average location, i.e., U*wa* = U*pm* = 1 (one).

U*pm* and U*wa* can equal each other as long as walker ants stay unguided. While *ta* remains stationary, U*wa* can stay concomitant to U*pm* longer because the average *pm* takes a long time to reach each walker's perceptual radius when ρ is small (e.g., $\rho = 1$). Even then, however, U*wa* stays rather consistently less than or equal to U*pm*

because their small ρ makes it virtually impossible for walkers to make an early run for *ta*'s location.

With $\rho = 25$ (Figure 2c), some walkers sometimes perceive their target early, before pheromone molecules have a chance to diffuse far enough from *ta*'s initial location. When that happens, the average *pm* location guides walkers early and U*wa* can exceed U*pm* for a while. Eventually, however, whether early or late, walkers always fall prey to the average pheromone's Brownian motion and the inevitable happens: U*wa* = U*pm* = 1. Both the *pm* and the *wa* CASOS grids become equally uncertain about their respective agents' location.

An interesting experimental extension entails turning the stationary *ta* mobile (Figure 3b). Mobile target agents cause the pheromone molecules they emit to diffuse more vigorously through the environment. Because of their initial random walk around their origin, walkers in different runs again will be at different locations when they start to sense *ta* and will follow slightly different paths to their target. But the excess *pm* randomness on the pheromone grid, while it still seems to be sequestering uncertainty (entropy) on the *wa* agent grid, it does so for a shorter time. It shortens both the time a typical *wa* stays unguided and the time it takes a walker to move to a now enlarged *ta* region. The system as a whole moves faster to U*wa* = U*pm* = 1.

Assessing entropy in the overall CASOS, Parunak and Brueckner (2001, p. 129) ask whether seemingly sequestering "macro [walker] entropy is causally related to the increase in micro [*pm*] entropy, or just coincidental". Feedback-loop analysis sheds light to this important question.

FEEDBACK-LOOP STRUCTURE ANALYSIS

In a nutshell, the answer to Parunak and Brueckner's question is that the normalized sub-system entropy measures are causally related, not coincidental. The phase plots on Figure 4 through Figure 6 highlight causal relations among variables embedded in feedback loops. The pathway participation metric helps detect and confirm the

shifting link polarity and prominence of these loops. Within each sector, the X and Y location coordinates are embedded in symmetric loops, so the experimental results shown mostly entail the X coordinate.

The *pm* grid model sector contains a total of three balancing '–' feedback loops or pathways about the X dimension, with negative links that emanate from outflows. The PPM algorithm, used to detect the most influential or prominent pathways that contribute the most to the dynamics of a variable of interest, shows that the two pathway sets on Figure 4—their negative links so marked—are the most prominent balancing pathways or causal loops for the Pheromone Molecules and X*pm* stocks.

On the left panel of Figure 4, loop polarity depends on time to evaporate (Equation 2.17), an

Figure 4. The most prominent feedback-loop pathways for the pheromone molecules and Xpm stocks, with phase plots. The differently colored dots on the phase plots correspond to the 30 different simulation runs.

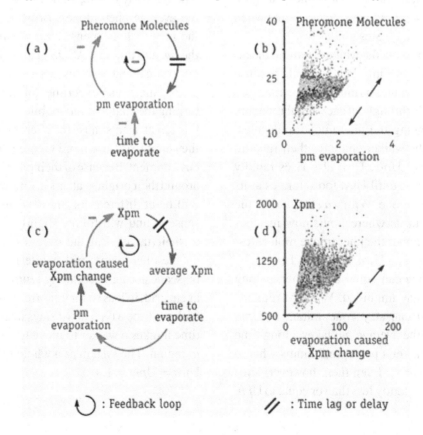

Figure 5. The walker ant (wa) sector prominent (outside feedback loop #1) and nested non-prominent (feedback loops #2 and #3) pathways about the Xwa and Ywa stocks, with phase plots. The differently colored points on the phase plots correspond to the 30 different simulation runs.

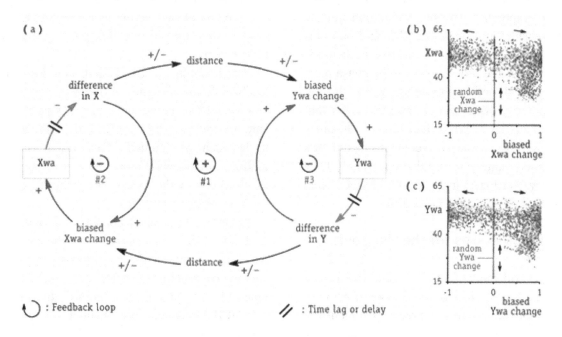

Figure 6. Top panel: shifting loop polarity (slp) along walker ant (wa) path groups I and II ($\rho = 25$). Foot panel: shifting loop polarity (slp) along walker ant (wa) path groups II and III ($\rho = 50$). The differently colored wa paths on the phase plots (left panel) correspond to the 30 different simulation runs.

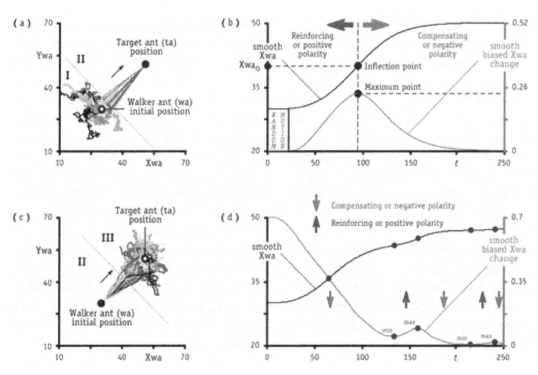

exogenous random parameter whose sign is set by the CASOS environment outside the loops. Although the nonlinear negative relation between time to evaporate and the *pm* evaporation outflow plays outside these loops, it can (Richardson 1995) and does turn negative links positive, as the positive slope of the little arrows on the phase plots on Figure 4b and Figure 4d show. So, shifting loop polarity drives the *pm* average so far that the walkers never sense their targets. Or, alternatively, it brings the *pm* average inside the *wa*'s perceptual radius ρ so fast that uncertainty U*wa* about walker location can at times exceed U*pm* on the pheromone molecules grid.

Feedback Loops for the Wa Sector

The *wa* grid model sector contains five nested feedback loops. Three of these loops affect *wa*'s X location dimension and three its Y dimension. Four of the loops have bipolar links. According to the PPM, two of these bipolar loops form the composite reinforcing '+' loop #1, which the X*wa* and Y*wa* stocks share (Figure 5a). Once *wa* senses the pheromone molecules, this outer composite loop #1 becomes the most prominent pathway, which contributes the most to the dynamics of *wa*'s X and Y location dimensions.

It is possible to tell exactly when the bipolar links of the reinforcing loop on Figure 5a have their polarities shift. According to the PPM, for example, between $t = 226$ and $t = 231$, the polarity of the link from difference in X to distance is positive '+', and so is the polarity of the link from difference in Y to distance. Then, between $t = 232$ and $t = 237$, the polarity of both these arrows changes to negative '–'.

Concurrently, between $t = 226$ and $t = 231$, the polarity of the link from distance to biased Y*wa* change is positive '+', and so is the polarity of the link from distance to biased X*wa* change. Then again, between $t = 232$ and $t = 237$, the polarity of both these latter arrows changes to negative '–'.

As the polarity of all these pathway pairs changes simultaneously, the polarity of the walker location feedback loop on Figure 5 remains positive '+', thereby always acting as a reinforcing '+' loop, despite the shifting link polarity that the PPM detects.

Worth noting on the nested, non-dominant feedback loops of Figure 5a (loops #2 and #3) is how the relation between the biased X*wa* change flow and the X*wa* stock confirms the orthogonality between *wa*'s guided or biased and random motion components (Figure 5b). And so does the relation between the biased Y*wa* change flow and the Y*wa* stock (Figure 5c).

Together, the nested feedback loops of the *wa* grid model sector determine *wa*'s behavior once it senses *ta* though the continuously random-walking *pm* grid that the latter agent creates. And much like its random counterparts, the biased or guided component loops behind *wa*'s motion can also turn positive. That is how they bias, i.e., reinforce, walkers to go meet their target fast. So fast, in fact, that pheromone molecules might not diffuse far enough from *ta*'s initial location for U*pm* to seemingly sequester U*wa* (Figure 3). These nested loops cause *wa* to respond to the *pm* average location through the average X*pm* effect on the difference in X (Figure 5). Then together, the difference in X and difference in Y co-determine distance, which, closing the circle(s), causes X*wa* to always have a negative effect on the difference in X, just as Y*wa* does on the difference in Y.

The relation between the walker's biased motion and uncertainty about its whereabouts prompts an in-depth model analysis that splits *wa*'s biased motion into two. *First*, one must look for *slp* (shifting loop polarity) during walkers' transition between their distinct path groups I and II (Table 4 and Figure 2c) *Second*, to reassess *slp* during the transition between distinct path groups II and III (Table 4 and Figure 2c). In both cases, both the PPM and Richardson's (1995) work help examine *slp* rigorously.

Table 4. Three distinct walker ant (wa) path groups

Path Group	Description
I	Initially, each *wa* wanders randomly around its (30, 30) origin until the average *pm* wave front, diffusing and evaporating from its (50, 50) origin, enters *wa*'s perceptual radius ρ. In this Brownian motion region, walkers have no guidance because they cannot yet sense *ta*'s pheromone molecules (lower left of the phase plot on Figure 2c).
II	When walkers sense the *pm* average inside their ρ, then they stop wandering and move swiftly from their initial (30, 30) region toward *ta*'s (50, 50) region. They can now sense *ta* and deterministically follow the *pm* average grid (middle of the phase plot on Figure 2c).
III	When they reach *ta*'s (50, 50) region, walkers seem to meander again as if performing a random walk. *But as our analysis shows walkers now deterministically follow ta's pheromone molecules, which continue executing a random walk under Brownian motion* (upper right of the phase plot on Figure 2c).

Transition from Path Group I to Path Group II

Treating *wa*'s Ywa coordinate as if it were an auxiliary constant, yields a *ceteris paribus* examination of the nested feedback loops that implicate *wa*'s Xwa location dimension. To isolate *slp* during *wa*'s transition along its distinct path groups I and II, *ta*'s Xta and Yta coordinates replace the average Xpm and average Ypm converters. This way, once walkers sense their target through pheromones, the former agents abandon their random motion and head directly to *ta*'s location, as opposed to following the *pm* grid. Because of their initial random walk, walkers in different runs are at different locations when they sense *ta* and follow slightly different paths, but ones that immediately converge to *ta*'s location (Figure 6a).

The actual dynamics of the typical walker's biased motion turns *wa*'s (30, 30) origin into an unstable equilibrium point outside its random motion region. Positive or reinforcing feedback dominates the system in the region where biased Xwa change has a positive slope (Figure 6b).

Balancing or negative feedback is dominant where biased Xwa change has a negative slope. Once outside its random motion region I, *wa*'s biased motion rate initially rises nearly linearly and then, while still below Xwa_0, i.e., the Xwa value where *slp* takes place, the system's behavior resembles pure exponential growth. As walkers approach *ta*'s location in region II (Figure 6a), their biased motion continues to rise, but at a declining rate (Figure 6b).

At Xwa_0, the biased Xwa change rate reaches a maximum. The peak of *wa*'s biased motion curve corresponds to the inflection point on the trajectory of Xwa, i.e., the point at which the smooth Xwa stock is rising at its maximum rate. Beyond the inflection point on Figure 6b, *wa*'s biased motion, while still positive, drops, falling to zero just when the walker reaches the target ant's (50, 50) location, the system's new stable equilibrium point.

Inside walkers' random motion region or path group I (Figure 6a), uncertainty about their location rises orthogonally to their smooth biased Xwa change rate (Figure 5b). Once the pheromone agents drive walkers' biased motion, Uwa abandons its vertical climb and begins to rise concomitantly with the walkers' smooth biased Xwa change (Figure 3a and Figure 6b). But once the walkers' biased, guided motion rate begins to resemble pure exponential growth, still below Xwa_0, Uwa also begins to rise faster again. By now walkers are far inside their path group II, so uncertainty about their location rises fast.

Then, just before it reaches its maximum, smooth biased Xwa change begins to rise at a declining rate (Figure 6b). Uwa again matches the biased motion's declining rise until it saturates at $Uwa = 1$ (Figure 3a). By now (Figure 6b), smooth biased Xwa change has reached its maximum and starts to decline toward zero. When inside walkers' perceptual radius, *ta*'s pheromones reveal its existence and cause walker agents to move orderly toward its location. This self-organizing behavior that the pheromones trigger seem to sequester U*wa* on the system's ant agent grid (Figure 3a).

Transition from Path Group II to Path Group III

To reassess *slp* along path groups II and III (Figure 6c), the average X*pm* and average Y*pm* converters must be restored, and the walkers' perceptual radius must increase drastically, i.e., $\rho = 50$. Now walkers sense the target through the *pm* grid it creates at the outset, before they have a chance to meander under their own Brownian motion. But, as opposed to heading directly to their target's location, they deterministically follow the pheromone molecules' random motion. Under all 30 color-coded simulation runs on Figure 6c, walkers are at the same initial location when they sense *ta*. But they follow divergent paths because of the pheromones' continuous random walk around *ta*'s location.

The experimental results on Figure 6c help to see how loop polarity shifts. The typical walker now leaves its initial (30, 30) location to go where it perceives its stationary target to be from the *pm* grid that the target creates. Negative or compensating feedback dominates as the negative slope of *wa*'s smooth biased X*wa* change shows in the time domain (Figure 6d). Initially, the walker's biased motion rate drops nearly linearly and the X*wa* stock begins to grow as it accumulates *wa*'s gain along the horizontal axis of Figure 6c. This negative feedback prominence (Figure 6d) has the potential to close the gap between the walker and the *pm* average location. The smooth biased X*wa* change rate is falling at a locally maximum rate that corresponds to an inflection point on the trajectory of smooth X*wa*, where the smooth X*wa* stock is rising at a locally maximum rate (Figure 6d).

But the *pm* average that the walkers aim for is a moving target, so the walkers' transition along their distinct path groups II and III ends soon. Just before time $t = 150$, a sudden, discontinuous random shift in the walker's goal causes positive or reinforcing feedback to dominate *wa*'s deterministic motion. Its smooth biased X*wa* change rate now shows a positive slope on Figure 6d as the walker begins to follow the pheromone molecules' random walk inside the distinct path group III.

In walkers' transition along their distinct path groups II and III, the continuously moving pheromones cause the *wa* agents to move orderly toward their perceived target. This orderly biased motion that the pheromones trigger seemingly sequesters U*wa* on the system's ant agent grid. Within *wa*'s path group II, as the walkers' smooth biased X*wa* change decreases, it seems to sequester uncertainty about their location. The less walkers walk, the less they change their location, the smaller the uncertainty about their location becomes. But once inside path group III, walkers fall prey to the pheromones' random motion, following them around deterministically. Uncertainty about their location now rises fast, eventually matching uncertainty about the *pm* average location, i.e., U*wa* = U*pm* = 1 (Figure 3a).

When inside walkers' perceptual radius, the pheromones reveal the target agent's existence and cause the walker ant agents to move orderly toward its location. This orderly, self-organizing behavior that the pheromones trigger is what seems to sequester U*wa* on the system's ant agent grid.

SUMMARY

This chapter presents a dynamic simulation model that looks at self-organization causally, helping to see exactly how CASOS' feedback-loop relations produce nonlinear dynamics spontaneously out of their local interactions. The experimental results show that as shifting loop polarity determines system behavior, distributed control leads positive feedback relations to explosive growth, which ends when all dynamics has been absorbed into an attractor, leaving the system in a stable, negative feedback state.

Assessing *shifting loop polarity* separately in walkers' transition, *first* between their distinct path groups I and II, and *then again* between groups II and III, helps explain the dynamics of the relation between walkers' biased motion rate and location uncertainty U*wa*. When walkers abandon their random walk to go meet their target, then the relation between their biased motion and U*wa* becomes positive. But when they deterministically follow the Brownian motion of the pheromones that their target emits, then the same relation turns negative. In the *first* case, the walkers change their location under reinforcing or positive feedback. In the *second* case, they change their location under balancing or negative feedback. In both cases, U*wa* rises because the walkers' location changes.

Interestingly, as agents move from random disorder to self-organizing order with deterministic rules, then it is positive feedback that causes the relation between their rate of motion and location uncertainty to become positive. Conversely, when agents move, again deterministically, from static order to random disorder, then it is negative feedback that causes the relation between their rate of motion and location uncertainty to become negative.

CONCLUDING REMARKS

Simulation modeling of complex systems is indispensable in understanding and improving system performance (e.g., Lattila *et al.* 2010, Cools *et al.* 2013). This chapter contributes a lucid insight in the context of CASOS: *Explicitly considering the feedback-loop structure of a complex self-organizing system, and using system dynamics for feedback analysis, is a promising direction for researchers interested in understanding **why** CASOS behave the way they do.* This approach can explain, intuitively, *why* phenomena of interest emerge in agent-based models, a topic of great importance in the understanding of CASOS and the design and analysis of artificial CASOS.

Applied scientists, who are responsible for the design and analysis of artificial CASOS, might also find this lucid insight useful. Looking at self-organization causally might come in handy, for example, in a situation where a client requests the design and implementation of a real system with distributed, as opposed to central, control. Client confidence and trust might increase dramatically, if a designer team takes that extra step of explicitly analyzing a CASOS in terms of the causal feedback-loop relations responsible for its dynamics. While looking for alternative policies to implement in a real system, without making pertinent feedback-relations explicit, it might be tempting to latently ascribe interesting CASOS dynamics to 'emergence'. Before that, however, consider looking at self-organization causally. Perhaps making cause-and-effect relations explicit in all applied science, might help the design of more robust, valuable and sustainable systems.

REFERENCES

Arthur, B., Lane, D., & Durlauf, S. (Eds.). (1997). *The Economy as an Evolving Complex System II*. Addison-Wesley.

Beinhocker, E. (2006). *The Origin of Wealth: Evolution, Complexity and the Radical Remaking of Economics*. Harvard Business School Press.

Bonabeau, E., Dorigo, M., & Theraulaz, G. (1999). *Swarm Intelligence*. Oxford University Press.

Cools, S. B., Gershenson, C., & D'Hooghe, B. (2013). Self-organizing traffic lights: A realistic simulation. In *Advances in Applied Self-Organizing Systems* (pp. 45–55). Springer London. doi:10.1007/978-1-4471-5113-5_3

Dorigo, M., & Stutzle, T. (2004). *Ant colony optimization*. MIT Press. doi:10.1007/b99492

Forrester, N. (1983). Eigenvalue analysis of dominant feedback loops. In *Plenary Session Papers Proceedings of the 1st International System Dynamics Society Conference*. Paris, France: Academic Press.

Kauffman, S. (1995). *At home in the universe: The search for the laws of self-organization and complexity*. Oxford University Press.

Kugler, P. N., & Turvey, M. T. (1987). *Information, Natural Law, and the Self-Assembly of Rhythmic Movement*. Lawrence Erlbaum.

Lättilä, L., Hilletofth, P., & Lin, B. (2010). Hybrid simulation models–when, why, how? *Expert Systems with Applications*, *37*(12), 7969–7975. doi:10.1016/j.eswa.2010.04.039

Mamei, M., & Zambonelli, F. (2007). Pervasive pheromone-based interaction with RFID tags. *ACM Transactions of Autonomous and Adaptive Systems*, *2*(2), 4. doi:10.1145/1242060.1242061

Mojtahedzadeh, M. T., Andersen, D., & Richardson, G. P. (2004). Using Digest® to implement the pathway participation method for detecting influential system structure. *System Dynamics Review*, *20*(1), 1–20. doi:10.1002/sdr.285

Oliva, R. (2004). Model structure analysis through graph theory: partition heuristics and feedback structure decomposition. *System Dynamics Review*, *20*(4), 313–336. doi:10.1002/sdr.298

Ormerod, P. (1999). *Butterfly economics: A new general theory of social and economic behavior*. Pantheon Books.

Parunak, H. V. D. (1997). Go to the ant: engineering principles from natural agent systems. *Annals of Operations Research*, *75*, 69–101. doi:10.1023/A:1018980001403

Parunak, H. V. D., & Brueckner, S. (2000). Ant-like missionaries and cannibals: Synthetic pheromones for distributed motion control. In *Proceedings of the Fourth International Conference on Autonomous Agents* (pp. 467-474). Academic Press.

Parunak, H. V. D., & Brueckner, S. (2001). Entropy and self-organization in multi-agent systems. In *Proceedings of the International Conference on Autonomous Agents*. Montreal, Canada: Academic Press.

Rahmandad, H., & Sterman, J. D. (2008). Heterogeneity and network structure in the dynamics of diffusion: comparing agent-based and differential equation models. *Management Science*, *54*(5), 998–1014. doi:10.1287/mnsc.1070.0787

Richardson, G. P. (1995). Loop polarity, loop dominance, and the concept of dominant polarity. *System Dynamics Review*, *11*(1), 67–88. doi:10.1002/sdr.4260110106

Richmond, B. (1980). A new look at an old friend. In *Plexus*. Hanover, NH: Dartmouth College.

Richmond, B., et al. (2009). *iThink® Software (Version 9.1.2)*. iSee Systems™.

Shannon, C. E., & Weaver, W. (1949). *The Mathematical Theory of Communication*. University of Illinois.

Sterman, J. D. (2000). *Business Dynamics: Systems thinking and modeling for a complex world*. Irwin McGraw-Hill.

Tribus, M., & McIrvine, E. C. (1971). Energy and information. *Scientific American*, *224*, 178–184.

Chapter 6
The Role of Standards in the Development of New Informational Infrastructure

Vladislav V. Fomin
Vytautas Magnus University, Lithuania

Marja Matinmikko
VTT Technical Research Centre of Finland, Finland

ABSTRACT

In this chapter, the authors inch towards better understanding of the notion of informational infrastructure and the role of standards in the development of infrastructures in the new information age. Specifically, the authors consider the standardization process as pertaining to informational infrastructure development. They focus on two particular aspects of standardization: temporal dynamics and the social organization. Using Bauman's concept of liquid modernity, the authors argue that standards often become hybrids of solid and liquid modernities linking together different scales of time, space, and social organization. To better illustrate theoretical concepts, they draw on practical examples from the development of informational standards, infrastructures, and services, particularly from the domain of Cognitive Radio Systems (CRS), a new generation of "paradigm changing" communication technologies and services. The aim of this chapter is to offer the scholars of standards and innovation a fresh, non-mainstream perspective on the social and temporal dynamics of standardization and infrastructure development processes, to bring forth new understandings of the complexity of relationships between business, technology, and regulatory domains in the formation of informational infrastructure.

INTRODUCTION

Today the political rhetoric of the European Union (EU) is focused on the transformation from service/industrial to Information Society – the concept emphasizing the role of national and global information infrastructures in the economic development of the state (Castells, 1996). Guided by the vision as laid out in European Commission's (EC) programme "eEurope", European societies and economies are accelerating the use of information and communication technologies (ICT) in

DOI: 10.4018/978-1-4666-6098-4.ch006

a hope to be able to fully exploit the potential of the new informational economy, which is expected to bring not less than a "tremendous potential for growth, employment and inclusion" (Council of the European Union 1999, 4).

More recently, the EC has developed its growth strategy "Europe 2020" for the coming decade aiming to make the EU a smart, sustainable and inclusive economy. Within Europe 2020 strategy, the Digital Agenda for Europe (DAE) launched in 2010 aims to reboot Europe's economy and help Europe's citizens and businesses to get the most out of digital technologies (European Commission 2012).

Similar to the processes of interconnecting roads and railways, bolts and nuts in the formation of the industrial economies, building informational economy requires networking of myriad of disparate information systems and resources on different levels of social organizing. Inter-operating informational resources and systems, making a "workable whole" out of disparate local implementations, brings about new requirements and dynamics unknown in the construction of industrial age infrastructure – the instantaneity of production and delivery of services, the inter-modality of different infrastructures (such as e.g., cellular mobile, the Internet, TV, radio, GPS) (Edwards 1998), consistency of informational resources (Gill and Miller 2002), a host of security-, safety- and privacy-related issues – just few to mention.

With new unthinkable levels of complexity in assuring interoperability of informational tools and resources, scholars of standardization and infrastructure development are operating with theories on standards competition and interoperability based on the knowledge of pre-informational age, and the validity of the extant theories is tried and often refuted as new cases of informational age are studied. To take few examples, competition of Open Document Format (ODF) and Microsoft's Office Open XML (OOXML) file formats is not like typical standards contests as we know from the literature – VHS vs. Beta, Mac vs. Windows, BluRay vs. HD DVD (West and Fomin 2011). And the development and introduction of a new audio-visual codec standard, needed to enable delivery of audio-visual content over the Internet, TV, and mobile services, does not follow the "common wisdom" of dominant design theory (Shapiro and Varian 1999; Fomin, Su, and Gao 2011).

In this essay we inch towards better understanding of the notion of *informational infrastructure* and the role of standards in the development of infrastructures in the new *informational age*. Specifically, we focus on two particular aspects of standardization-as-infrastructure-development – temporal dynamics and the social organization. Using Bauman's (2000) concept of *liquid modernity*, we argue that standards to fulfill on their function of enabling interoperability in the *global informational infrastructure* often become hybrids of solid and liquid modernities linking together different scales of time, space, and social organization (Edwards 2003). Our work is motivated by the need for novel theorizing on standards and standardization, as suggested by an increasing amount of research which questions and/or refutes the common knowledge of the industrial age (Gill and Miller 2002; Liu et al. 2008; West and Fomin 2011).

STANDARDS, INFRASTRUCTURES, AND MODERNITY

The industrial revolution created the conditions for booming economies in many countries of the world. The national economies grew as local markets became regional and eventually international. This was facilitated by new means of transport (roads, steam trains, harbors, and steam boats), new means of energy (steam, later electrification, diesel engines, turbines, etc.), and new means of communication (telegraph and telephony). Industrialization, therefore, developed a range of interdependencies. It was particularly due to the *network effects* of power supply from utilities, telecommunication networks, and governments active in promoting their industries internationally. Technological progress meant agreements between industrialists to accept certain *standards* needed to connect machines, to apply utensils, to rig boats and vessels, and to connect private, local operating telephony networks into national networks (Pedersen, Fomin, and Vries 2009).

A key turning point in the development of *informational networks* can be attributed to the first, focused statement of national policy for information infrastructure development – the Clinton Administration's policy initiative on National Information Infrastructure (NII), published as The National Information Infrastructure: Agenda for Action of September 15, 1993 (The White House 1993). It encompassed everything that produces, contains, processes, or uses information, in whatever form, or whatever media, as well as the people who develop the information, applications, and services, etc. (Kahin 1997, 193). Six years after the publication of NII's Agenda for Action, the EC presented a program eEurope aimed at accelerating the process of exploiting the potential of the new informational economy (Council of the European Union 1999, 4). Recently, the EC has published its growth strategy, Europe 2020, for the coming decade to make the EU a smart, sustainable and inclusive economy with a flagship initiative of DAE to get the most out of informational infrastructure and the services it can afford (European Commission 2012).

By the turn of the last century, the state informatization efforts seemed to gain a substantial momentum, with many countries deploying the "brand name" of "Information Society" (Ministry of Research and Information Technology 1996) to depict the state of informational infrastructure development in their respective territories.

The legacy of standards and standardization being carried over from the industrial to informational economy is profound – by the turn of the century some 80 percent of global trade (equivalent to around $4 trillion annually) was affected by standards or associated technical regulation (OECD, 1999, p.4). Today standards are important in both product and service markets, playing increasingly a central role as instruments of regional and international trade liberalization (Garcia, 1992; Mattli, 2001, p.328). At the same time, standardization increasingly becomes "a battleground", where a variety of interests are juxtaposed and powers tried (Bousquet, Fomin, and Drillon 2011; Stewart et al. 2011). Increasingly, theorizing about infrastructural development requires seeking new lenses and concepts (Edwards 2003; Edwards et al. 2009), as the extant theories can't accommodate the complexity of the informational age interdependencies (Fomin, Su, and Gao 2011, 753–4).

New Age Requirements for Information Infrastructures

To live in an informational society is to recognize essential dependencies of that society on a particular kind of infrastructure: "infrastructures produce and distribute a continuous flow of essential goods and services" (U.S. President's Commission on Critical Infrastructure Protection (PCCIP), quoted in Edwards 2003, 187). Given the essentiality of heterogeneous flows supporting the daily needs of private and business lives, Edwards argued infrastructures are "best defined negatively, as those systems without which contemporary societies can not function" (2003, 187). Thus, in their strive to establish "information society", European policymakers are creating critical dependencies on a variety of informational infrastructures and their resources.

Modern societies and economies are operating with help of a combination of systemic, technologically supported infrastructures on the one hand, infrastructures which are critically depend on standards, (Edwards 2003, 188). The number of informational infrastructures we depend on is large – post and telecommunications, Internet and financial services, TV and Global Positioning System (GPS), even contemporary transportation services and energy infrastructures cannot function without the "informational" component – smart grids, control and distribution systems are all dependent on informational flows.

If in the industrial age citizens could opt to live outside the reach (and without being dependent on) their supporting technology infrastructures (e.g., railway, electric grid, telephony), then in the informational age the dependencies of society to a variety of informational infrastructures are much stronger and the relationship between a citizen and an infrastructure is much more complex. At the same time, it seems like scholars' understanding of the processes leading to the creation of infrastructures and their critical constituents – standards – has not been brought up to date.

Our dependency on infrastructures means they have long been regarded as "public good". However in recent years many of the service infrastructures in Europe have been privatized – from railway to water supply – creating a venue for a "perpetual juxtaposition" of public and private interests – infrastructural services as a public good vs. infrastructure build-out and maintenance as a private business. The very understanding of the role of standards as serving the purpose of "public good" has been changing, too. There are examples of the opposite move – from private to public – as e.g., in the case of radio spectrum access for the provision of wireless communications services. The emerging concepts of and technologies for Dynamic Spectrum Access (DSA) and Cognitive Radio Systems (CRS) are promising to bring the new paradigm of shared, opportunistic access to the radio spectrum, as a complementary approach to the old one under which spectrum usage rights were assigned to individual/private users on long-term non-cooperative basis.

In the past, government-endorsed (the so-called *de jure*) standardization was seen as the process aimed at creating products of "collective mind", supposed to reflect generalized scientific or technical view to the specific problem and the encompass the expression of *the best good practices* in solving the problem. Thus, development of "public-good" standards presumed a process by which the government objectively chose the superior alternative through an incorruptible process of truth seeking (West and Fomin 2011, ii). Today *de jure* standardization reflects merely the endorsement by a government (or government-authorized) agency of one or more private interests (West and Fomin 2011, ii) in a process where political and diplomacy skills of competing claimants becomes more important than the merits of their respective claims (West and Fomin 2011; Isaak 2006; Bousquet, Fomin, and Drillon 2011).

Industrial age infrastructures were subject to different temporal dynamic than what we experience today. Production cycles of physical objects are much longer than those for informational (intangible) products. Lifetime of a steel rail is much longer than a lifetime of a telephone switch not for the reason of durability of materials used (Lovelock 1995), but due to much faster obsolescence of the latter technology. Path dependencies in physical infrastructures create much more pronounced rigidities, than in informational ones. Left lane driving still exists in the UK, India, Australia, and one could hardly imagine having these countries switch overnight to the right lane driving. Yet, the behemoth of online video file sharing – YouTube – with its billion-large user base and global reach was able to change the coding of the video content overnight once and is changing it again, as new, more efficient codecs are developed.

Inter-modality in the industrial age infrastructures is problematic – one of the minor exceptions is the ship container logistics infrastructure, which permits changing container transportation modalities from ship, to truck, to rail. In the informational age, informational content can be carried across different infrastructures – e.g., TV broadcast, Internet, radio broadcast – by appropriate for each particular infrastructure software containers (also referred to as *matroska*). These software containers become alike the ships, the trucks and the trains of the industrial age infrastructures, and the containers the transportation vehicles carried become an analog of data in the digital ICT infrastructures.

Finally, the industrial age infrastructures had a different spatial dynamics than the contemporary informational ones. In the past, different standards for railway gauge, electricity voltage and frequency, driving rules could be developed and sustained at the local or regional level, and today we still see disparate infrastructures with incompatible sets of standards existing in different locales. In the contemporary global ICT standardization arena there is little, if any, possibility for the development and sustain-ability of local standards (Kwak, Lee, and Fomin 2011) in the presence of competing global ones.

The seeming flexibility of the informational age infrastructures as presented above – the instantaneity of change, advanced interoperability, global reach – is what it is – only in appearance. In practice, to attain this flexibility, interoperability and instantaneity requires development and implementation of relevant standards in the first place – a complex process, understanding of which has been recently changing, and which today yields more questions than answers.

In the following, we briefly introduce Bauman's (2000) concept of *liquid modernity* and a number of illustrating examples to tap into the complexity of contemporary standards development. We will argue that standards effectively became hybrids, which abridge, level out, or absorb the juxtapositions, tensions and irregularities created by massive and uneven development of informational infrastructures on the global scale. While not offering any fine-tuned novel theoretical framework to the reader, we hope our essay will trigger some form of "creative imagination" (Weick, 1989) ultimately contributing to the novel theorizing about standards and standardization in the informational age.

CONTEMPORARY STANDARDIZATION THROUGH THE LENS OF LIQUID MODERNITY

Bauman (2000) developed a set of concepts describing the contemporary world as living in the state of *liquid modernity*. The lens of liquid modernity are specifically helpful in developing critical reflections on the dependencies between the individual and public spheres – the dependencies which shape conditions of modernity (Edwards 2003), and which are so typical in the context of infrastructural development.

The Solid and the Liquid Modernity: Bauman's Thesis

Bauman (2000) brings forth two concepts of *solid* and *liquid* modernity to juxtapose the difference in the *mutual dependencies* between the public and private spheres in the past and as seen today. Solid modernity of the industrial age, according to Bauman, was characterized by relatively stable social dynamics, as constituted by rules, norms and structures. Another distinguishing character was a clear boundary between the private and public spheres of the society (see Table 1).

If the social order in Bauman's solid modernity of the industrial past is stable, then in our current phase of modernity "the key characteristic is not simply of sweeping things away, but doing so continuously and obsessively; change is constant and iterative... The word 'liquidity' evokes the idea of flow, constant movement, of change... The movement is itself the objective ..." (Bryant, 2007, pp.127-8).

The mutual dependencies between the social entities in either types of *modernity* centre around the concept of *domination* – the strive of one or another social entity to *regulate* the social, political, and economic process. If in the solid modernity it was the 'bigger' player who was setting the rules, in the liquid modernity, "the game of domination... is... played between the quicker

Table 1. The social dynamics of the solid and the liquid modernity

	Solid Modernity	**Liquid Modernity**
Social world	Stable	Unstable
Social and temporal dynamics	Rules, norms and structures are enduring.	Rules, norms, structures can not keep their shape.
Public-private sphere relationship	Clear boundaries between the two domains	Boundaries between the two domains are fuzzy.

and the slower. Those who are able to accelerate beyond the catching power of their opponents rule" (Bauman 2000, 188).

While the concept of liquid modernity may reflect well the contemporary social dynamics, the concept itself does not provide any keys for managerial action in the new environment. Bauman "is throwing down a challenge: how can we start to understand liquid modernity and hence consider and devise possibilities and appropriate modes of action?" (Bryant, 2007, p.128).

Given the challenge, we draw on the "privileged" concept – that of standard – one that transcended the two modernity paradigms without losing its prominence. The shift of production and social paradigm must have effectively changed the way the race for domination unfolds in the society and in the standardization arena (Williams et al. 2011; Fomin, West, and Lyytinen 2001). We can see that standards and standardization came to play important, but not always well understood role in the race.

Critical Reflections on Standardization: Standards as Hybrids

We would like to defend the idea that contemporary standards and standardization processes combine elements of both liquid and solid modernity – they are hybrids. In the following, we explore some of these oppositions.

Individual vs. Public Domain

In liquid modernity public has no importance anymore – individual, private gains the power. Historically, standardization organizations were established to develop public, technically optimal standards through collective action of technical experts (Frary, 2008; ISO, 2008). In standardization today, the *private* stakeholders strive to promote their interests – specific standard specification, Intellectual Property Rights (IPRs), etc. At the same time, we see the growing concern for the public good, public safety, environmental friendliness integrated into the private strategies of individual standard's promoters – all concerns too easily associated with "public" rather than "individual" or "private".

In its recent move, Microsoft corporation opted to *open* its Office Documents formats to the general public by means of formal international standardization. Microsoft's action can be characterized as a *belated* move to establish the private-public hybrid in order to counter competition from the Open Office public initiative (West and Fomin, 2011).

The recent action of Microsoft's bitter rival Apple Inc. shows a *preemptive* move to establish the private-public interest hybrid. Apple developed a revolutionary computational paradigm *Khronos*, just to give away what could have served as a strategic IPR the private interest of Apple, to make it open (public) consortium standard, with an aspiration that the *private* value to Apple will grow exponentially as the *public* appreciation of the technology grows.

Other typical examples of the fuzzy boundary between the private and the public spheres are when e.g., IBM corporation is opening up its patented technologies to the open source community to attract "free public development" to its product line, or Google Inc. is releasing to the market a royalty free audio-video codec WebM, which is used to compete in the online media distribution with rivals using royalty-bearing codecs, such as H.264/MPEG4 (Fomin, Su, and Gao 2011).

The emerging paradigm of CRS technology in wireless communications provides a rich source of examples for our essay. To start with, the radio spectrum itself is an exciting hybrid, linking the private and public domains. Unseen and unfelt by humans, radio waves are subject to strict global and national regulation with regard to access rights and use patterns. To be more precise, the regulation concerns the specific "radio bands" designating a range of frequencies or wavelengths used in radio transmission. While the radio ether can hardly be imagined to be treated as a subject of private use, national regulatory authorities grant "access" rights to private and public entities for *exclusive* use of specific radio bands. Such regulatory paradigm was adopted soon after the radio waves were discovered. Today, however, with the growing demand for radio spectrum contrasted by the limited amount of "useful" radio bands, the practice of exclusive spectrum assignment is being challenged. The CRS technology can facilitate more efficient spectrum use by allowing sharing of this valuable resource between different wireless systems in situations where it was not foreseen to be feasible in the past, i.e., can help transition the inherently public resource from its current private use pattern to (a bit more) public one. Technology standards will play a crucial role in this endeavor, as the transition can not be accomplished without implementing critical to service provisioning enablers and controls (e.g., quality of service (QoS), non-interference, billing, etc).

Slow vs. Fast Change (Solid vs. Liquid Structures)

Some standards are anticipatory – developed ahead of the services/products they'd be applied to. Major technology standards can take a decade to develop (as, for example, in the field of cellular mobile telephony – the cases of NMT and GSM standards (Fomin, 2001; Manninen, 2002)). However, once standard is developed, standard-based products and services can reach market rapidly, even before the final version of the standard was published. New versions of the 802.11 wireless Internet standard is a good example here.

As an example, the CRS technology can give good insight into the pace of standardization and adoption of new technology. Recently, the use of so called Television White Spaces (TV WS) by CRS devices has been standardized in several standards bodies. The TV WS refers to frequency channels within the band used by the TV broadcasting service that have been left unused due to e.g., providing guard bands between active broadcast channels or limited deployment in some geographic areas. Some administrations have allowed or are considering to allow the provisioning of different wireless services in these TV WSs on a non-interfering basis.

Recognizing the potential business opportunities stemming from TVWS utilization, supporting technology implementations and standards followed shortly, such as e.g., IEEE 802.22, ECMA 392 and Weightless standards. However, contrary to the expectations of the technologists, business was reluctant to invest in the TVWS operation. The lack of commercial interest, in a turn, became a demotivating factor in national spectrum regulatory authorities' decision-making on issuing permissions for commercial operation of TVWS. Commercialization of TVWS services has not yet gained big momentum – currently, only in a limited number of countries such permissions have been granted.

On the other hand, the pace of CRS standards adoption can be reversed, if, for example, they become included into the technology portfolio of cellular mobile communication systems via such standardization consortia as 3GPP. Such inclusion, however, is likely to take a long time, as the vision for technology use cases has to be developed first. However, this development has already emerged to make mobile communication systems the next remarkable application area for the CRS technology.

Reversing the slow-fast hybrid, we can refer to standards that are created to limit the number of existing technology solutions in the market. Such standardization usually is rapid, but results in "rigidifying" the standardized solution, thus slowing down the innovation cycle. Perhaps, a good example here would be, again, of Microsoft Corp. pushing its proprietary OOXML document format through the formal SDO to make it open standard. With support of immense lobbying, immature standard reached the market far too quickly, causing a wave of mistrust and resistance to the standard among potential adopters (Egyedi and Koppenhol 2010; West and Fomin 2011).

Taking a firm's perspective, a firm that is first to adopt a technology standard may need a substantial time to change the organizational structures and procedures to meet the new standard. A reversed hybrid can be found in a firm that is late to adopt: using the lessons from the first-movers to have a rapid re-organization/adaptation of the organizational structure. This is especially visible in the case of ISO 9001 series quality management system standards. For the early adopters, a substantial learning time and consultancy time was required to pass standard's certification. Today, certifying organization for ISO 9001 often is a quick, straightforward process.

Rigid vs. Fragile Structures

The formal international SDOs are 60-140 years old organizations, with established culture and procedures (de Vries, 1999). Yet the most important decisions are made "behind the scenes", through non-procedural action, lobbying, etc. (Isaak 2006).

Liquid organizational structures of Asian manufacturing entrepreneurs have to comply with very solid, "unbreakable" rules imposed by standards and associated legal issues/procedures established by the Western organizations. Patents and IPRs imbedded in standards by the Western standards' developers impose a form of "neocolonialism" (Updegrove, 2007) to the manufacturers and users of standard-using ICT products in the *rest of the world*.

If we look at the "inner" side of standardization, the "dominant" standards are these, which are stable, i.e., non-changing, or *solid*, if to use Bauman's terms. Pure non-malleability (stability) of standard is normally associated with negative effects, such as lock-in effect. The desired *positive* stability of standards is actually *afforded by malleability* – updateability of the specifications, scalability – a hybrid of liquid-solid matter, which is being melted when and frozen many times depending on the needs of the designers.

CRS technology comes handy again in providing an example of rigid-fragile hybrid. The advent of CRS technology is widely believed to bring forth a paradigm shift in spectrum access, as was explained above. What has been an example of rigid business structures and business models – the operation of mobile telecommunications markets – could undergo a radical change, become highly dynamic, lowering entry barriers to new entrants, allowing opportunistic business operation, etc. At the same time, at the international level, the International Telecommunication Union Radiocommuniation sector (ITU-R), while having acknowledged the advantages of CRS and the changes it can bring to the markets, is not about to change the basic principles of the global spectrum use policy.

According to the ITU-R, a CRS is not a radiocommunication service, but a system that employs technology that can be implemented in a wide range of applications and it must operate in accordance with the Radio Regulations governing the use of a particular frequency band (ITU-R 2011). This indicates that the high level basic principles for spectrum access are still valid and remain unchanged. In the lower level, however, the national administrations have the flexibility to accommodate CRS technology with case specific rules and conditions to respond to the spectrum needs. With this example, we can see how a technology standard permits maintaining a balance between rigidity and dynamics, or help transition from one to another.

Temporal vs. Social Dynamics

Tensions and juxtapositions take place not only within temporal or social dimensions separately from one another. Local and global, micro and macro can clash across time-space continuum. The standards, as products of standardization, are expression of the needs of contemporary society – they are developed yesterday to serve today's and tomorrow's needs. But standards are also developed to be compatible with earlier versions of technology – the phenomenon referred to as *path dependency*. Thus, the past, the present, and the future may clash. A peculiar dynamics can be observed when special and social order is added to the temporal dimension. For example, contemporary geographical standards are the expression of contemporary geographical knowledge. However, in the historical geography we can find a different understanding of the subject matter. The standardized digital mapping of administrative territories is done by delineating an unbroken (solid) geographical portion of a country. This means that a contemporary administrative territory can be mapped in a geographical information system (GIS) as a polygon, which has clear boundaries with other polygons representing other administrative territories. In the past, however (e.g., in the XVI century in Lithuania) the administrative territory was the economical unit (set of villages) that was scattered in an approximate large geographical territory and (in the same territory) interblended with villages from the other sets. Consequently, the contemporary standardized understanding of administrative territory and contemporary standardized GIS tools can't be used for mapping of historical territories.

The rules and conditions in business, technology and regulatory domains are changing over time, co-influencing one another (Nelson and Winter 1982). For example, in the case of the CRS, the development of the CRS technology and the regulatory rules and conditions for using the technology are highly interrelated (Fomin, Medeišis, and Vitkutė-Adžgauskienė 2011). Initial rules and conditions for the deployment of CRS standards may turn out to be overcautious in ensuring that the incumbent spectrum users remain free from harmful interference. As CRS technologies mature over time and allow for more sophisticated control, those requirements are likely to be relaxed.

There are differences in the pace at which changes in business, technology development and regulatory domains take place. For example, the basic principles in spectrum use have remained unchanged for a long time and the basic spectrum allocation process at the ITU-R in its World Radiocommunication Conferences (WRCs) has followed a similar pattern with relatively long preparatory times (Takagi 2008). The business domain is changing at higher pace and sees the CRS technology as a potential means for accelerating the process of gaining access to new spectrum in parallel to the traditional approach.

CONCLUSION

In this work we aimed at exploring certain dependencies in the technology innovation in general, and standards-making in particular. Our work is motivated by the political vision for the (economic) development of Europe, which appears to be strongly grounded in the idea of digital (informational) infrastructure development and the use of services this infrastructure will afford (European Commission 2012), on the one hand, and by the lack of scholarly and/or managerial understanding on the interplay between technology standards, the build-out of digital infrastructures they contribute to, and the (commercial) services, which become afforded due to the standards and infrastructures, on the other hand.

Obtaining a better understanding of the governing principles for modern standardization arena becomes a crucial issue for scholars, managers and policy-makers, as international standards effectively rose to have a dominant role in international trade and policy, as standardization became a form of law-making or regulation (Hosein, Tsiavos, and Whitley 2003; Jarvenpaa, Tiller, and Simons 2003; Lessig 1999a; Lessig 1999b).

As the reach of informational infrastructures and dependencies they create become increasingly pronounced (Castells, 1996; Edwards, 2003) so does the realization that the knowledge of standards we derived from the lessons of infrastructural development of the industrial age may be partial or altogether irrelevant in explaining the role of standards in the development of contemporary informational infrastructures (Liu et al. 2008; West and Fomin 2011).

In this essay we focused on two particular concepts of Bauman's (2000) *liquid* modernity – temporal dynamics and the social organization – in order to understand how technology standards become *hybrids* capable of leveling out, bridging, reconciling the peculiarities, tensions, and juxtapositions created by the clash of the governing principles of the old and the new infrastructures, the old and the new political systems and economies, etc.

To better illustrate theoretical concepts, we drew on practical examples from the development of informational standards, infrastructures, and services. In doing this, the case of Cognitive Radio Systems (CRS) became for us a particular source of inspiration. CRS technologies are often referred to as "paradigm changing", as enablers of novel business models and services (Fomin, Medeišis, and Vitkutė-Adžgauskienė 2012) – in this we see them as being particularly suitable example in the discussion on the principles governing the formation of the new informational infrastructure and the services it can support.

Just as the transitioning from the solid to liquid modernity requires re-thinking and re-building the relationships between the social, political, and economic order, the development of CRS standards and commercialization of CRS-enabled services require re-conceptualizing and re-designing the long-standing constellation of technology, business, and regulatory entities.

While not offering any definite answers, the concepts and examples we used here can help further theorize business-technology-regulatory relationships in the formation of informational infrastructure.

ACKNOWLEDGMENT

The author acknowledges contribution of François-Xavier de Vaujany to the discussion on Bauman's liquid modernity and to James Stewart for critical comments. The examples on digital mapping standards were kindly provided by Rimvydas Laužikas. Collaboration of the authors was partially supported by ESF COST Action IC0905 "TERRA."

REFERENCES

Bauman, Z. (2000). *Liquid Modernity*. Polity Press Ltd.

Bousquet, F., Fomin, & Drillon. (2011). Anticipatory Standards Development and Competitive Intelligence. *International Journal of Business Intelligence Research*, 2, 16–30. doi:10.4018/jbir.2011010102

Castells, M. (1996). *The Rise of the Network Society* (Vol. 1). Oxford, UK: Blackwell Publishers, Ltd.

Council of the European Union. (1999). *eEurope: An Information Society for All*. Retrieved from http://europa.eu.int/information_society/eeurope/action_plan/index_en.htm

Edwards, P. N. (1998). Y2K: Millennial Reflections on Computers as Infrastructure. *History and Technology*, *15*, 7–29. doi:10.1080/07341519808581939

Edwards, P. N. (2003). Infrastructure and Modernity: Force, Time, and Social Organization in the History of Sociotechnical Systems. In *Modernity and Technology* (pp. 185–226). Cambridge, MA: MIT Press.

Edwards, P. N., Bowker, Jackson, & Williams. (2009). Introduction to the Special Issue: An Agenda for Infrastructure Studies. [JAIS]. *Journal of the Association for Information Systems*, *10*, 364–374.

Egyedi, T. M., & Koppenhol. (2010). The Standards War Between ODf and OOXML: Does Competition Between Overlapping ISO Standards Lead to Innovation? [JITSR]. *International Journal of IT Standards and Standardization Research*, *8*, 41–52. doi:10.4018/jitsr.2010120704

European Commission. (2012). *Communication from the Commission to the European Parliament, the Council, the European Economic and Social Committee and the Committee of the Regions: A Digital Agenda for Europe.* COM(2012) 784 final. Brussels, Belgium: European Commission. Retrieved from http://ec.europa.eu/information_society/newsroom/cf/dae/document.cfm?doc_id=1381

Fomin, V. V. West, & Lyytinen. (2001). Technological Regimes, Government Policies, and Contingency in the Development, Deployment, and Commercial Success of Cellular Mobile Communications on Three Continents. In *Proceedings of the 6th Asia-Pacific Regional Conference of International Telecommunications Society (ITS 2001)*, (pp. 146–157). Hong Kong: Hong Kong University of Science and Technology. Retrieved from www.hkust.hk/its2001

Fomin, V. V. Medeišis, & Vitkutė-Adžgauskienė. (2011). The Role of Policy in the Development of Cognitive Radio Systems: Co-Evolutionary Perspective. In *Proceedings of the 7th International Conference on Standardisation and Innovation in Information Technology (SIIT 2011)*, (pp. 79–90). Berlin: Mainz Publishing, Aachen.

Fomin, V. V., Su, & Gao. (2011). Indigenous Standard Development in the Presence of Dominant International Standards: The Case of the AVS Standard in China. *Technology Analysis and Strategic Management*, *23*(7), 745–758. doi:10.1080/09537325.2011.592270

Fomin, V. V. Medeišis, & Vitkutė-Adžgauskienė. (2012). In Search of Sustainable Business Models for Cognitive Radio Evolution. Technological and Economic Development of Economy, *18*(2), 230–247. doi: doi:10.3846/20294913.2012.663415

Gill, T., & Miller. (2002). Re-inventing the Wheel? Standards, Interoperability and Digital Cultural Content. *D-Lib Magazine*, *8*, 12–19. doi:10.1045/january2002-gill

Hosein, I., Tsiavos, & Whitley. (2003). Regulating Architecture and Architectures of Regulation: Contributions from Information Systems. *International Review of Law Computers & Technology*, *17*, 85–97. doi:10.1080/1360086032000063147

Isaak, J. (2006). The Role of Individuals and Social Capital in POSIX Standardization. *International Journal of IT Standards and Standardization Research*, *4*, 1–23. doi:10.4018/jitsr.2006010101

ITU-R. (2011). *Introduction to Cognitive Radio Systems in the Land Mobile Service.* M.2225. Geneva, Switzerland: International Telecommunication Union (ITU). Retrieved from http://www.itu.int/pub/R-REP-M.2225

Jarvenpaa, S. L., Tiller, & Simons. (2003). Regulation and the Internet: Public Choice Insights for Business Organizations. *California Management Review, 46,* 72–85. doi:10.2307/41166232

Kahin, B. (1997). The U.S. National Information Infrastructure Initiative: The Market, the Net, and the Virtual Project. In *National Information Infrastructure Initiatives: Vision and Policy Design* (pp. 150–189). Cambridge, MA: MIT Press.

Kahin, B. (1998). Beyond the National Information Infrastructure. In *Investing in Innovation. Creating Reseacrh and Innovation Policy That Works* (pp. 339–360). Cambridge, MA: MIT Press.

Kwak, J., Lee, & Fomin. (2011). The Governmental Coordination of Conflicting Interests in Standardisation: Case Studies of Indigenous ICT Standards in China and South Korea. *Technology Analysis and Strategic Management, 23*(7), 789–806. doi:10.1080/09537325.2011.592285

Lessig, L. (1999a). *Code and Other Laws of Cyberspace.* New York: Basic Books.

Lessig, L. (1999b). The Law of the Horse: What Cyberlaw Might Teach. *Harvard Law Review, 113,* 501–549. doi:10.2307/1342331

Liu, C. Z. Kemerer, Slaughter, & Smith. (2008). *Standards Competition In The Presence Of Digital Conversion Technology: An Empirical Analysis Of The Flash Memory Card Market.* Tepper School of Business. Retrieved from http://ssm.com/abstract=1021352

Lovelock, C. H. (1995). *Technology: Servant or Master in the Delivery of Services?.* doi:10.1016/S1067-5671(95)04019-6

Ministry of Research and Information Technology. (1996). *The Info-Society for All - the Danish Model. Copenhagen: Ministry of Research and Information Technology.* Retrieved from http://www.fsk.dk/fsk/publ/1996/it96-uk/

Nelson, R. R., & Winter. (1982). *An Evolutionary Theory of Economic Change.* Cambridge, MA: Harvard University Press.

Pedersen, M. K. Fomin, & de Vries. (2009). The Open Standards and Government Policy. In *ICT Standardization for E-Business Sectors: Integrating Supply and Demand Factors,* (pp. 188–199). Hershey, PA: IGI Global. Retrieved from http://www.igi-global.com/chapter/information-communication-technology-standardization-business/22931

Shapiro, C., & Varian. (1999). The Art of Standards Wars. *California Management Review, 4*(2), 8–32. doi:10.2307/41165984

Stewart, J., Shen, Wang, & Graham. (2011). From 3G to 4G: Standards and the Development of Mobile Broadband in China. *Technology Analysis and Strategic Management, 23,* 773–788. doi:10.1080/09537325.2011.592284

Takagi, H., & Walke (Eds.). (2008). *Spectrum Requirement Planning in Wireless Communications : Model and Methodology for IMT-Advanced.* Chichester, UK: Wiley.

West, J., & Fomin. (2011). Competing Views of Standards Competition: Response to Egyedi & Koppenhol. [JITSR]. *International Journal of IT Standards and Standardization Research, 9,* i–iv. doi: doi:10.4018/IJITSR

White House. (1993). *The Administration's Agenda for Action.* Retrieved from http://www.ibiblio.org/nii/NII-Agenda-for-Action.html

Williams, R., Graham, Jakobs, & Lyytinen. (2011). China and Global ICT Standardisation and Innovation. *Technology Analysis and Strategic Management, 23*(7), 715–724. doi:10.1080/09537325.2011.592265

Chapter 7
Development Framework Pattern for Pervasive Information Systems

José Eduardo Fernandes
Polytechnic Institute of Bragança, Portugal

Ricardo J. Machado
Universidade do Minho, Portugal

ABSTRACT

During last decade, the world watched a social acceptance of computing and computers, enhanced information technology devices, wireless networks, and Internet; they gradually became a fundamental resource for individuals. Nowadays, people, organizations, and the environment are empowered by computing devices and systems; they depend on services offered by modern Pervasive Information Systems supported by complex software systems and technology. Research on software development for PIS-delivered information, on issues and challenges on software development for them, and several other contributions have been delivered. Among these contributions are a development framework for PIS, a profiling and framing structure approach, and a SPEM 2.0 extension. This chapter, revisiting these contributions, provides an additional contribution: a pattern to support the use of the development framework and profiling approach on software development for PIS. This contribution completes a first series of contributions for the development of PIS. This chapter also presents a case study that allowed demonstrating the applicability of these contributions.

INTRODUCTION

The dissemination of computing and heterogeneous devices and platforms, the high pace of technological innovations and volatile requirements, the size and complexity of software systems characterize the software development context today. This context challenges the way software is developed for emerging forms of information systems. A world full of smart devices and the widespread adoption of pervasive technologies as basis for new systems and applications lead to the need of effectively design information systems that properly fulfil the goals they were designed for.

DOI: 10.4018/978-1-4666-6098-4.ch007

These Pervasive Information Systems (PIS) and the applications that constitute them need to be able to accommodate the permanent technological evolutions/innovations of the heterogeneous devices and the requirements changes that result from a faster and intense world of business competition. Software Development Processes (SDPs), as well as generalized adoption of models, are fundamental to efficient development efforts of successful software systems.

Software engineering has been, since its existence, subject of research and improvement in several areas of interest, such as software development processes (SDPs) whose process models evolved from waterfall and nowadays may assume several forms (Ruparelia, 2010). The development of large software systems is another area of interest that has been, for decades, subject of research work; several topics can be pointed out such as the exploration of issues related to the management of large scale software development (Benincasa, Daneels, Heymans, & Serre, 1985; Kay, 1969), software architecture (Gorton & Liu, 2010; Laine, 2001; Mirakhorli, Sharifloo, & Shams, 2008), model-driven development (Heijstek & Chaudron, 2009; Mattsson, Lundell, Lings, & Fitzgerald, 2007), among others. Not directly related with large projects, Medvidovic (2005) points the relevance of software architecture in leveraging the pervasive and ubiquitous area. Model-Based/Driven Development (hereafter in this document, unless otherwise stated, simply referred as MDD) is another area that gains an increasing focus. MDD constitutes an approach to software design and development that strongly focuses and relies on models (Fernandes, Machado, & Carvalho, 2004). It automates, as much as possible, the transformation of models and the generation of the final code. This enables higher independence from the technological platform that supports the realization of the system.

This document structures its content in the following sections: an introduction section that synthesizes pervasive information systems, its issues and the benefits of a model-based/driven development based approach; a software development for PIS section that provides a background into related research works for PIS; a development framework pattern section that presents the pattern as the contribute in this work; a section case study section that presents a case study wherein the contributions are demonstrated; and a last section that presents the conclusions and finishes this document.

Pervasive Information Systems

Pervasive Computing, also called Ubiquitous Computing (Weiser, 1993b; Weiser, Gold, & Brown, 1999), represents a new direction on the thinking about the integration and use of computers in people's lives. It aims to achieve a new computing paradigm, one in which there is a high degree of pervasiveness and availability of interconnected computing devices in the physical environment. Ubiquitous (computing embodies a philosophy different of that inherent to the personal computers of the 70s. In essence, it sustains that computing technology should not be the focus of attention of the user activity. It even does not require the need of carrying around any personal computer or PDA to access information; in this world, fully of connected devices, information is available and accessible everywhere (Weiser, 1993a). The data, once entered in a computing system, is readily available whenever and wherever needed (Ark & Selker, 1999), being accessible in an intuitive way through the use of devices eventually different from that one through which the data was entered. Decreasing emphasis of focus on the personal computer has already occurred with the emergence of the World Wide Web. For many users the computer is just a machine that provides a portal to the digital world where they have presence through their homepage, their email, or chat. In this way, computers are 'disappearing' and the focus goes beyond them (Davies & Gellersen, 2002). Ubiquitous computing brings then "the end of dominance of the traditional computing" (Ark & Selker, 1999), being computing embedded in more things than just our personal computer.

Considering the vision about ubiquitous computing, there are key characteristics of ubiquitous computing systems that differentiate these from traditional computing systems. Among these are: decentralization (autonomous small devices, taking over specific tasks and functionality, cooperate and establish a "dynamic network of relationships"), diversification (there is a move from universal computers to diversified devices for specific purposes), connectivity (different type of devices connect among themselves to exchange data and applications) and simplicity (pervasive devices, being specialized tools, should be easy and intuitive to use – "complex technology is hidden behind a friendly user-interface") (Hansmann, Merck, Nicklous, & Stober, 2003). In ubiquitous computing, the environment take a relevant place in computing: in "contrast with most traditional computing, in which the environment is mostly irrelevant, the environment plays a fundamental role for ubiquitous computing; the environment has influence on the 'semantics' of computing" (Ciarletta & Dima, 2000). There is a need of perceptual information about the environment (Saha & Mukherjee, 2003) and about the location of people and devices: such information enables for an enhanced interaction with users, allowing applications to adapt themselves to their environment, and constitutes an enabler element for the so-called invisible computing.

Beyond the traditional media, the web has emerged as a new fundamental and valuable global information system, being widely adopted not only by organizations but also by people. Today, the web is easily accessible in all developed countries, in schools, in private and public organizations, at home, and inside or outside buildings. Also notable has been the widespread adoption of cellular phones that, along with increasing computing resources, have acquired improved communication capabilities and new multimedia features. They allowed a new and quick way to contact and interchange information with people, to access to the World Wide Web everywhere, and to interconnect computing devices all around the world (even in the most inhospitable places). The advent of accessible commercial wireless networks and communications systems further contributed to dissemination of computing. The embedding of computing devices in objects or places for monitoring or control, enabled us to envision a "real" physical world enhanced with information and computing capabilities. These capabilities can be used to facilitate and pleasure human life in its diverse facets (as the personal or social) or to improve businesses or other organizational processes. Want, Pering, Borriello and Farkas (2002) consider that the "four most notable improvements in hardware technology" during the last decade that directly affected ubiquitous computing are: wireless networking, processing capability, storage capability, and high quality displays. These factors, among others, contributed for a culture characterized not only by having an easy access to information, but also by demanding for information availability; consequently there is an implicit acceptance of surrounding and permanent computing or other IT devices. Nowadays, there is an increasing feeling that information is omnipresent (we just need an IT device to access it) and that computing devices or applications are naturally part of our daily lives.

From a business perspective, ubiquitous computing brings the opportunity to introduce changes in the way business and consumers interact with each other (Fano & Gershman, 2002). It allows for an improvement on mutual intercommunications, richer and innovative interactions, and closer relationships. People become able to interact with services not only through telephone or PC but also through products. What was initially confined in developing technology to make pervasive computing out of a vision (Lyytinen & Yoo, 2002), surpassed the initial restricted frontiers to reach the development of applications for organizational domains, enabling for enhancements of current business processes or even to assist the development of new business models (Langheinrich, Coroama, Bohn, & Rohs, 2002). Business benefits and ubiquitous computing technologies have a mutual influence in each other: ubiquitous computing technologies are seen has offering support for potential business benefits to organization efficiency, and those potential benefits constitute a driving force and key factors to further research and deployment of ubiquitous computing technologies (Bohn, Coroamã, Langheinrich, Mattern, & Rohs, 2004); this leads to a permanent, vigorous, and rapid proliferation of information technology. Aware of those business benefits potentially offered by ubiquitous computing technologies, the industry has set their attention to the deployment of those technologies in supporting applications in diverse domains, pursuing imagined business benefits. Government agencies, insurance companies, organizations of several domains have been developing projects aiming to collect the potential gains of deployment of ubiquitous computing.

Widespread availability of affordable and innovative information technologies represents a potential opportunity for improvement/innovation on business processes or for enhancement of life quality of individuals. Among other things (such as social concerns), this opportunity promotes the attention to the efficiency and effectiveness of information management regarding to the way they acquire, process, store, retrieve, communicate, use, and share information. To take full benefits of the opportunities offered by modern information technologies, these devices need to be "appropriately integrated within organizational frameworks" (Sage & Rouse, 1999). Therefore, Pervasive Information Systems (PIS) (Fernandes, Machado, & Carvalho, 2008) orchestrate these devices in order to achieve a set of well-established goals. In this way, PIS not only provide a solid basis to sustain the needed information to achieve effectiveness at both individual and organizational levels, but also leverages the investment on those

information technologies or other organizational resources. In order to explore the potential offered by pervasive computing and to maximize the revenue of these kinds of systems, a PIS, as any other information system, must be designed, developed and deployed attending to its nature (these systems may potentially accommodate a large quantity of heterogeneous devices and be subject of frequent updates/evolutions).

Model-Driven Development

Since antiquity engineering disciplines have the activity of modelling as a fundamental technique to cope with complexity ("The use of engineering models is almost as old as engineering itself." (Selic, 2003)). Modelling provides a way to facilitate the understanding, reasoning, construction, simulation, and communication about complex systems (usually composed by smaller parts) (Thomas, 2004). Software engineering, in comparison with other forms of engineering, is on a privileged position to attain benefits from modelling, as it is one whereby an "abstract high-level model can be gradually evolved into the final product without requiring a change in skills, methods, concepts, or tools" (Selic, 2003).

There have been, and there will always be, several efforts in order either to improve the way and the cost of development of software systems, or to achieve a better satisfaction on accomplishment of systems requirements and expectations. One area of these efforts of improvement is on raising the abstraction at which software developers mainly work. Several examples of such rising of abstraction are the movements from binary languages to assembly languages and from assembly languages to higher-level languages. The new abstractions, initially introduced as novel concepts, were later adopted and supported, and tools were developed "to map from one layer to the next automatically" (Miller et al., 2004). Nowadays, there is a promotion of another rising of abstraction at which development occurs: this one is based on changing of the main development efforts from code and programming to models and modelling. This raise of abstraction at which software is written (the shift of the level of abstraction from code and programming languages, to models and model languages (Sendall & Kozaczynski, 2003)) implies that a software system will be mainly and fully (as possible) expressed by models. The models are the main artefacts of the development effort rather than computer programs (Selic, 2003). The raise of abstraction subjacent to the use of models allows for productivity improvement: "it's cheaper to write one line of Java than write 10 lines of assembly language. Similarly, (…) it's cheaper to build a graphical model in UML, say, than to write in Java" (Mellor, Clark, & Futagami, 2003). Synthetically, models, in a descriptive or a prescriptive form, can then be used to: (i) understand or communicate a problem, an existing system, or a proposed solution; (ii) analyze, or predict on changes, systems properties or risk failures; (iii) productivity improvement; (iv) reduction of system's development costs.

Albeit some opinions consider that there is no "universally accepted definition of MDD is and what support for it entails" (Atkinson & Kuhne, 2003), it can be said that MDD carries the notion that it can be possible to build, with modelling languages, a model that entirely represents the intended software system. This model can then be transformed, through well-defined transformation rules, into the "real thing" (Mellor et al., 2003). Nonetheless, it's noteworthy to point out that, to achieve or undertake model-driven development, "not all models need to be executable or even formal, but those that are can benefit from automation" (Mellor et al., 2003) and models do not need to be complete, as "it incompleteness or high degree of abstraction do not equate to imprecision" (Mellor et al., 2003).

As models are the primary artefact in model-driven development approach, it is necessary that "a clear, common understanding of the semantics of our modelling languages is at least as important

as a clear, common understanding of the semantics of our programming languages." (Seidewitz, 2003). The Unified Modelling Language (UML) specifies the primary notation used in the current practice of modelling. UML allows for the creation of models that capture different perspectives of the system. Regarding to the development of software systems, the Object Management Group (OMG, 2005) introduced in 2001 the Model Driven Architecture (MDA) (OMG, 2003), an open and vendor neutral architectural framework to the construction of software systems. MDA constitutes a software development approach that, through the focus on models and defined standards, separates the specification of the functionality of a system from the specification of its implementation on target technological platforms, providing a set of guidelines framing these specifications (Appukuttan, Clark, Reddy, Tratt, & Venkatesh, 2003). It enables the detachment of business-oriented decisions from technological issues of eventual specific platforms into which the system could be targeted, allowing for "a greater flexibility on the evolution of the system" (Brown, 2004). Model-driven architecture is considered a "model-driven" approach in the sense "code is (semi-) automatically generated from more abstract models, and which employs standard specification languages for describing those models and the transformations between them" (Brown, 2004).

MDD has the potential to offer key pathways that enable software developers to cope with complexity inherent to PIS. A proper PIS construction demands an approach that recognizes particularities of PIS and that benefit from MDD orientation.

SOFTWARE DEVELOPMENT FOR PIS

Research performed on pervasive information systems and model-driven development (Fernandes, Machado, & Carvalho, 2007) brought several contributions on the application of MDD concepts and techniques to software of PIS. Among these contribution are a development framework (able to sustain an approach for software development of PIS that take into account MDD potential and PIS characteristics, particularly, heterogeneity and functional variability), a profiling and framing structure approach, and a SPEM extension. The following subsections present a brief overview of these contributions.

Development Framework for PIS

The *development framework* (Fernandes et al., 2008) for PIS introduces and describes new conceptions framed on three perspectives of relevance to the development, called *dimensions*. Based in these dimensions, the development framework considers two additional main perspectives of

development: one concerning the overall development process, and a second concerning to individual development processes. Figure 1 illustrates a schema of the framework. The following paragraphs give an overview of these dimensions and development perspectives.

The three dimensions considered are: resources, functional, abstraction. The *resources dimension* sets up the several categories of devices with similar characteristics and capabilities. The *functional dimension* sets up the different functionality needed by the system and that can be assigned to resources in the system for its concretization. The assignment of a specific functional profile to a specific resource category results in a specific *functional profile instance* that is realized by devices in that resource category. Each functional profile instance has a corresponding *development*

Figure 1. Development framework for PIS

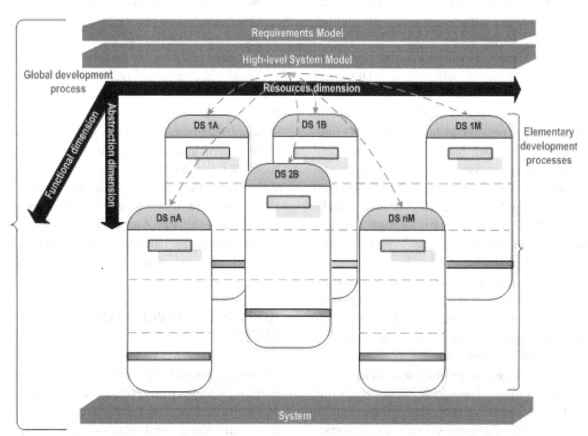

structure which embodies an elementary development process aiming to realize that instance. The *abstraction dimension* respects, in an MDD context, to the levels of abstraction that elementary development process may have (from platform-independent model (PIM), passing by platform-specific model (PSM), to generated code).

The development framework structures the development in a global development process and several elementary development processes. The *global development process* is responsible for modeling requirements and for establishing high-level and global system models. Based on these models, it sets up functional profiles and categories of resources, as well as, high-level PIM for each functional profile instance that shall exist. The global development process has the responsibility for making all the necessary arrangements for integration of the several artifacts that result from elementary development processes and for final composition, testing, and deployment of the system. *Elementary development processes* are responsible for the software development of parts of the system that realize specific functionalities for specific categories of resources. For each of the development structures, an adequate software development process can be chosen, as long as it respects the principles of the approach globally adopted. MDD concepts and techniques may be applied in order to improve the development and the quality of those resulting parts of the system. The implicit strategy to this development framework enables the adoption of development process and techniques most suitable to development of that individual development structure. It also eases the assignment of those structure units to different collaborating teams and, eventually, the outsourcing of the development. Therefore, the global process and the elementary process are not prescribed to be performed by any particular existent development process, being the choice of process development left to the developer. Besides the traditional documentation, the development approach should provide documentation for each development structure. Among this documentation, it is expected to be found information about the platform independent models (PIMs) at the top model-level, the PSMs at the intermediate model-level, the PSM at the bottom model-level, the mappings (either vertical or horizontal) and inherent transformation techniques used on the model's transformations, as well as information regarding to code generation. It becomes clear that it is convenient the use of suitable CASE tools to support global and individual development process developments as herein proposed. It is also expected the use of well-established standards on languages and techniques for modelling (models and transformations models), support for code generation, change management, and documentation of all artefacts and design decisions.

Profiling and Framing Structures

In the context of the previously presented development framework, Fernandes et al. (Fernandes, Machado, & Carvalho, 2012a, 2012b) provided an approach to effectively and consistently apply it in PIS development projects, independently of its size. The next paragraphs start by presenting some considerations regarding functional profile instantiation, and modeling levels in development structures; then they illustrate the concept of framing structure, giving emphasis on the way of using it in the context of large projects.

The assignment of a functional profile to a resource corresponds to an instantiation of the functional profile, carrying the meaning of responsibility assignment to that resource. Figure 2 illustrates an example of instances resulting from the assignment of functional profiles to resource categories. The result of an instantiation process is an instance profile that has subjacent a kind of platform independent model (or depending of the perspective, it may be seen as a PSM) as it is expected to be later subject of possible model transformations into intermediate platform specific models (or eventually directly subject to code generation). Further development takes place based on this model, giving origin to a specific development structure related to that specific functional profile instance. Each development structure reflects a pathway of software development in order to realize a functional profile assigned to a category of resources.

Figure 3 illustrates these development structures as well, as the modeling levels that can be found inside them. These modeling levels respects to the abstraction dimension, one of the three dimensions previously exposed. Depending from the point of view, an intermediate model can be seen as a PIM or a PSM: a model can be seen as a PSM when looking from a preceding higher abstraction model level, and can be seen as a PIM when looking from lower abstraction model level. For some development structures these levels may eventually not exist, as it is possible to directly generate the bottom-level PSM or even the code itself.

Considering the schema of the development framework and the schemas related to functional profiles instantiation, an overall conceptual representation of conceptions involved in the development framework can be schematized into a

conceptual framing structure that allows the definition and framing of functional profile instances. This conceptual structure can be expressed by a schema similar to the one presented in Figure 4.

Figure 4 illustrates the high-level and low-level models/specifications/artifacts produced by starting and ending activities of the global development process (it is important to notice that in parallel with the elementary development process activities, there may be in course other global development processes activities). All relevant functional profiles are listed at the left side of the framing structure, and the resources categories identified are listed at the middle top. The definition of functional profile instances are signaled in the proper intersections of lines of functional profile with the columns of resource categories. For each functional profile instance there is an associated development framework (as depicted in Figure 3); for each of these development frameworks there will be a corresponding elementary development process (as depicted by Figure 1).

Considering that systems vary in size and complexity, there may be large projects of systems involving the definition of large subsystems, for which there is the interest to define their own

Figure 2. Functional profile instances

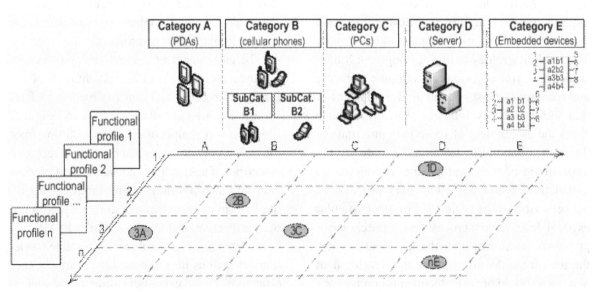

Figure 3. Modeling levels in development structures (abstraction dimension)

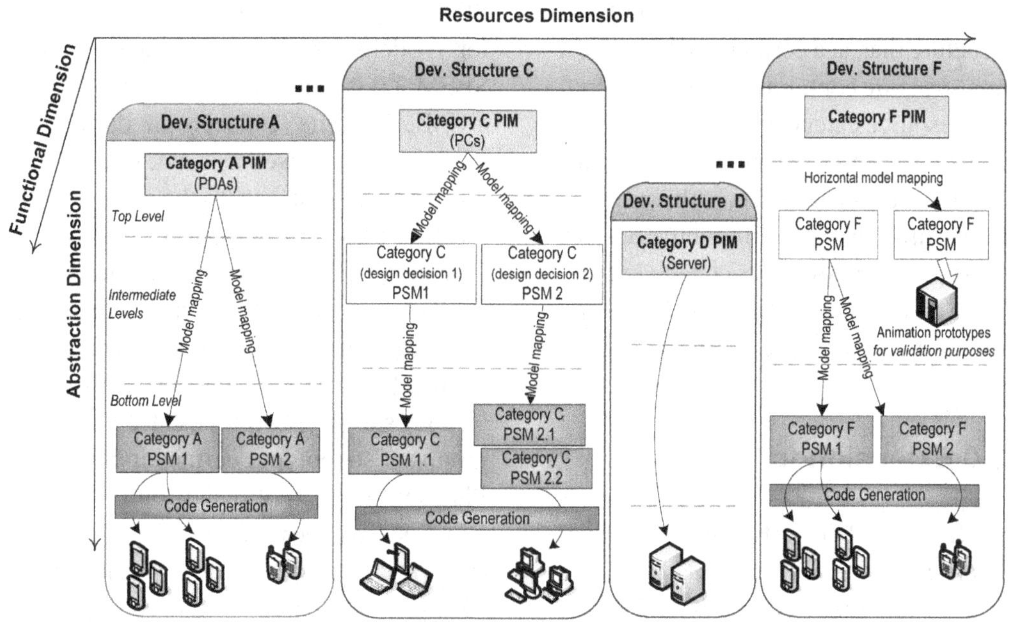

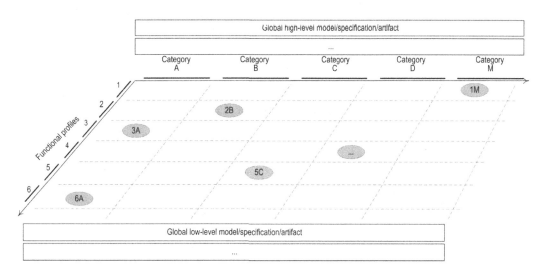

Figure 4. Framing structure for a project

functional profiles and resources categories. For such cases, the framing structure has an extended way of use. A framing structure is defined for the system and, for each of the identified subsystems, there is an additional framing structure; this will bring to existence nested framing structures. The system framing structure will contain elements (functional and resources) with a system level granularity, while each of the subsystem framing structures will have its own suitable subsystem level granularity. This situation may be recursive and a subsystem may be composed by its own subsystems; is this case, for each of the subsystems, there will be again a corresponding framing structure that, at a certain point, will be a leaf framing structure containing final functional profiles and resource categories.

The recursive nesting of framing structures allows dealing with any system size. In this process, each of the framing structures implicitly defines its own namespace for naming its constituent elements. Figure 5 shows an example of the nesting of the framing structures to deal with the size of large projects.

SPEM 2.0 Extension for PIS

Software & Systems Process Engineering Meta-Model Specification (SPEM) (OMG, 2008) is a current standard published by the OMG (OMG) for the description of systems and software processes. SPEM provides, to process engineers, conceptions for modeling method contents and processes. SPEM 2.0 is defined as a meta-model as well as a UML 2 Profile (concepts are defined as meta-model classes as well as UML stereotypes). This section briefly introduces the extension to SPEM (version 2.0) Base Plug-In Profile proposed by Fernandes and Machado (Fernandes & Machado, 2012) that includes stereotypes needed to support a suitable structural process organization for MDD approaches aiming to develop software for PIS.

The stereotypes proposed extend two main groups of stereotypes defined in SPEM 2.0 Base Plug-in: the "ActivityKind" and "WorkProduct-Kind" stereotypes. Figure 6 and Figure 7 illustrate, respectively, the new "ActivityKind" and "WorkProductKind" stereotypes (white boxes

Figure 5. Nesting of framing structures for large projects

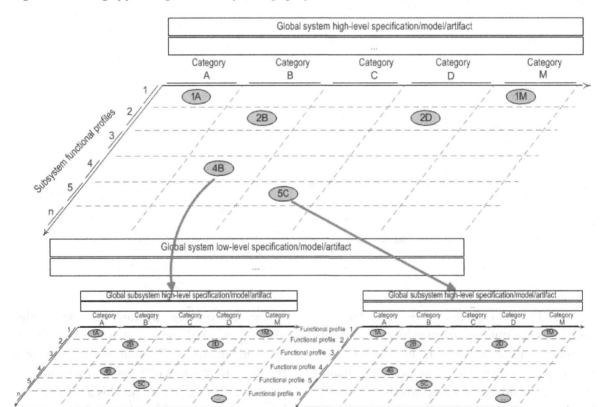

contain the predefined kinds; grey boxes contain the proposed additional kinds). The following paragraphs describe these new stereotypes, grouped by each of those kinds.

Regarding to "ActivityKind" stereotypes (Figure 6), in addition to the predefined "Process", "Phase", and "Iteration" stereotypes, there are the stereotypes "FrameworkSupport" and "Transformation" along with its specializations "ModelTransformation" and "CodeGeneration.

Additionally, to the "Process" of "ActivityKind", come to existence as specializations the "GlobalProcess" and "ElementaryProcess" stereotypes. The purpose of each of these "ActivityKind" stereotypes is explained in the following paragraphs.

The "GlobalProcess" stereotype allows the representation of the global process that encompasses the overall development of the system (as considered in the development structure). The convenience of this stereotype arises since an ap-

Figure 6. New "ActivityKind" stereotypes

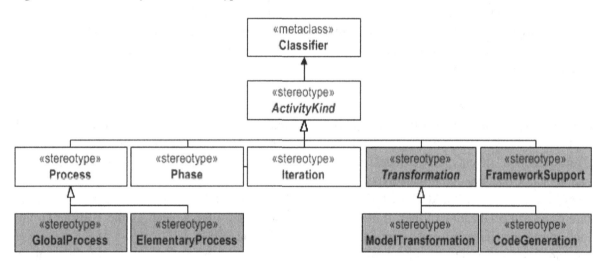

Figure 7. New "WorkProductKind" stereotypes

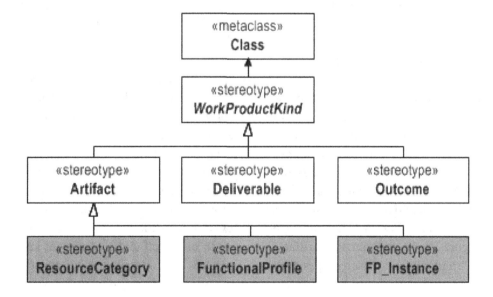

proach consistent to the development structure will have two major types of processes: a global process and several elementary development processes. This stereotype allows representing such overall process and also to relate with the overall main activities. The "ElementaryProcess" stereotype allows the representation of an elementary development process that exists for a Development structure associated with each functional profile instance. The convenience of this stereotype is analogous to the "GlobalProcess" stereotype: this stereotype allows the representation of an elementary development process and of the relationships of its inherent main activities. The "Transformation" stereotype is an abstract generalization that represents the activities of transformation models or other artifacts. Model-based/driven approaches are rich on these transformations; the specializations of this abstract stereotype allow to represent such transformations and to give further emphasis on its formalization. Specializations of this the "Transformation" stereotype are "ModelTransformation" and "CodeGeneration" stereotypes, which are next described. The "ModelTransformation" stereotype, a specialization of the "Transformation" stereotype, intends to represent activities that transform models into other kinds of model. The "CodeGeneration" stereotype intends to represent activities that transform models into code, or any other suitable artifact into code (for example, source code into executable code). The "FrameworkSupport" stereotype has a particular use. It does not map into any element of the development structure, but is essential for the overall structuring of development structure. The "FrameworkSupport" stereotype intends to represent any special activity related to the organization and deployment of the development framework, such as assisting the definition of the resources categories, functional profiles, functional profile instances, or elementary development processes.

Regarding to the "WorkProductKind" stereotypes (Figure 7), in addition to "Artifact", "Deliverable", and "Outcome" stereotypes, there are the "FunctionalProfile", "ResourceCategory", and "FP_Instance" stereotypes. These stereotypes aim to represent work products directly related to the development structure. These stereotype are convenient as they allow the representation of structural elements of the development structure.

DEVELOPMENT FRAMEWORK PATTERN

Designing software for complex systems is not easy, and reuse of workable solutions for recurrent problems is fundamental: "One thing expert designers know not to do is solve every problem from first principles. Rather, they reuse solutions that have worked for them in the past" (Gamma, Helm, Johnson, & Vlissides, 1995). Patterns, as general solutions for common problems, are important when crafting complex systems and can also be used to perceive the quality of system constructions. Being used in several disciplines, the use of patterns in software development has been promoted for years through conferences, books, and groups such as the Hillside Group (HillSide, 2013).

The pattern herein presented represents a technique and a set of actions to assist the process of software development for pervasive information systems. It facilitates the organization and documentation of requirements/analysis and design decisions regarding the (de)composition of functional responsibilities/profiles among the several sub-systems and devices of a PIS. The pattern is to be adopted at initial phase of the software development process, and is not meant to give origin to code directly. The foundational concepts, semantics, notational elements needed for its adoption were already set by the previous contributions of the development framework, the profiling and framing approach, and SPEM 2.0 extension for PIS.

In order to build a consistent knowledge on patterns and to facilitate their adoption, patterns are organized into pattern catalogues containing groups of patterns set through classification schemes. There are several classification schemes, each using well-defined criteria setting-up the relevant characteristics that sustain the classification and grouping of patterns. One of these classification schemes is proposed by Azevedo *et al.* (Azevedo, Machado, Bragança, & Ribeiro, 2011) that takes a multilevel and multistage classification approach based on Rational Unified Process (RUP) and OMG Four-Layer Architecture. This scheme considers a discipline dimension, a

stage dimension, a level dimension, and a domain nature attribute; it also considers a set of pattern type. Observing this scheme, this PIS pattern is considered as follows: regarding the *Discipline dimension*, this pattern can be adopted both within RUP's Requirements and Analysis and Design Disciplines; regarding the *Stage dimension* this pattern can be adopted at both RUP's Inception and Elaboration Stages); regarding the *Level Dimension*, this pattern is at M2-Level (see Figure 8); regarding the *Domain nature* this patterns is agnostic, as it is applicable to both vertical and

Figure 8. Structural development pattern for PIS

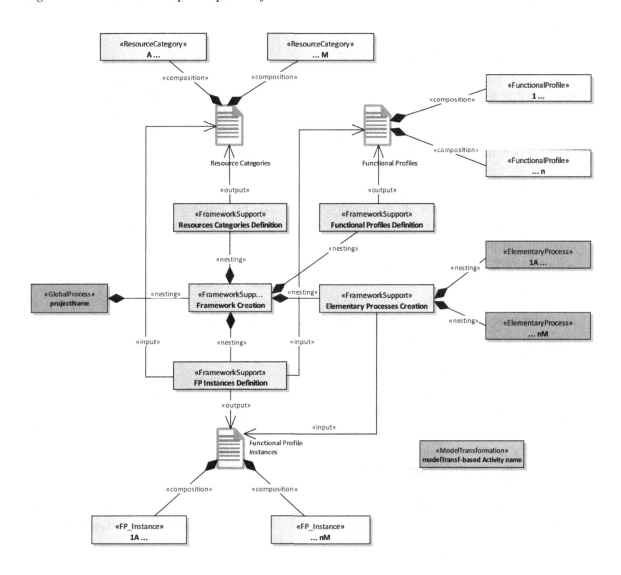

horizontal domains; regarding the *Pattern type*, none of the pattern types presented are applicable (it is a process pattern type, whose main target is not the system or part of it, but the development process itself).

Pattern Structure

- As state previously, the PIS Development Framework Pattern assumes the context PIS and the conceptions aforementioned, such as the development framework, the profiling and framing approach and the SPEM 2.0 Plug-In extension for PIS. This pattern assist in the task of defining or restructuring a SPEM-based software development process for PIS. Figure 8 illustrates the pattern for organizing the process elements according to the development framework for PIS; as it can be seen, the pattern makes use of the extending SPEM stereotypes. This pattern arranges the extending stereotypes in the following way:

- An activity kind instance stereotyped as «global process», named with project's name. It includes, besides all the major activities of the project that are deemed as being global process activities, a special activity named "Framework creation" that is stereotyped as «FrameworkSupport».

- An activity kind instance stereotyped as «FrameworkSupport», named as "Framework Creation". This is instance central to the incorporation of the several concepts of development framework. It includes activities for resources categories definition, functional profiles definition, functional profiles instances definition, and elementary process creation.

- An activity instance stereotyped as «FrameworkSupport», named as "Resources Categories Definition". This activity instance has the responsibility to provide the definition of the resources cat-

egories, which is materialized by the artefact "Resource Categories" that includes a work product instance stereotyped as «ResourceCategory» for each of the resource categories (symbolically named as A, ..M).

- An activity instance stereotyped as «FrameworkSupport», named as "Functional Profiles Definition". This activity instance has the responsibility to provide the definition of the functional profiles, materialized by the artefact "Functional Profiles", which includes a work product instance stereotyped as «FunctionalProfile» for each of the functional profile (symbolically named as 1, ...n).

- An activity instance stereotyped as «FrameworkSupport», named as "FP Instances Definition". This activity instance has the responsibility to provide the definition of the functional profiles instances, materialized by the artefact "Functional Profile Instances", which includes a work product instance stereotyped as «FP_Instance» for each of the functional profile instance (symbolically named in the pattern as 1A..., ...nM). This activity has as input the artefacts "Functional Profiles" and "Resource Profiles".

- An activity instance stereotyped as «FrameworkSupport», named as "Elementary Processes Creation". This activity instance has the responsibility to provide the creation of the elementary processes. It includes one activity instance stereotyped as «ElementaryProcess» for each of the defined functional profile instances, and each giving origin to a conceptual development structure (these elementary processes are symbolic named in the pattern as 1A..., ...nM). This activity has as input the artefact "Functional Profiles Instances".

Complementing the presentation, and belonging to the definition of this pattern, some notes are stated about the use of the pattern application and, additionally, some guidance actions are also provided. First, it is possible to intersperse activities among the patterns activities. For example, in the redefinition of a SPEM diagram of a development process, it is possible to put an existing major development activity between the «GlobalProcess» activity and the «FrameworkSupport» activity named "FrameworkCreation". Nonetheless, the structural organization of the pattern should be present and recognized in the overall SPEM model. Second, the realization of this pattern is considered complete after the identification of the transformations. Third, after the complete realization of the pattern, other actions can be undertaken, being these ones out of the scope of this pattern definition.

Guidelines for Applying the Pattern

For the realization of the pattern, some guidance actions are provided. Table 1 list these steps, grouped in four tasks; each of this task has a variable number of steps.

These guidance actions for pattern realization can be also formalized in a SPEM 2.0 model, using the concepts of activity, tasks, and steps. Figure 9 depicts the pattern realization SPEM 2.0 model.

CASE STUDY

This section starts by briefly introducing the USE-ME.GOV (USability-drivEn open platform for MobilE GOVernment), a project that aimed to create an open platform for mobile government services. Then, it illustrates the application of the development framework in this project. Attending

Table 1. Guidance steps for pattern application

Task Id.	Task Name Step id. – Step name. Step description
1	*Elements identification* S1.1: Identify global process activities. Identify the activities that should be considered as belonging to the scope of global process. S1.2: Identify elementary process activities. Identify the activities and respective structure that shall be considered as belonging to elementary processes. S1.3: Identify resources categories. S1.4: Identify functional profiles. S1.5: Define functional profile instances. Define the functional profile instances that shall come to existence. You may use a framing structure to visualize the functional profile instances.
2	*Pattern creation* S2.1: Create the pattern structure. Create in the SPEM diagram, the raw pattern structure, materializing the «GlobalProcess», «ResourceCategory», «FunctionalProfile», «FP_Instance», and «ElementaryProcess» stereotype instances with the information available. All «FrameworkSupport» can be materialized with the name used in the pattern (nonetheless, if deemed relevant, other names can be given).
3	*Pattern framing* S.3.1: Include global process activities. Include in the «GlobalProcess» activity instance, all the identified global process activities. S3.2: Include elementary process activities. Include each of the «ElementaryProcess» activity instances, as well as any corresponding activity structures of them. Make the adaptions and rearrangements needed.
4	*Transformations identification* S4.1: Identify transformations. After the (re)arrangements for proper pattern framing, it should be identified the existing activities that are susceptible to be classified as a transformation; for the ones that are validated as such, replace the activity by and activity instance stereotyped as «ModelTranformation» or «CodeGeneration» as appropriate. S4.2: Formalize the transformations. For each of the transformations, formalize, in a separate SPEM diagram, the transformation.

Figure 9. SPEM diagram of pattern realization

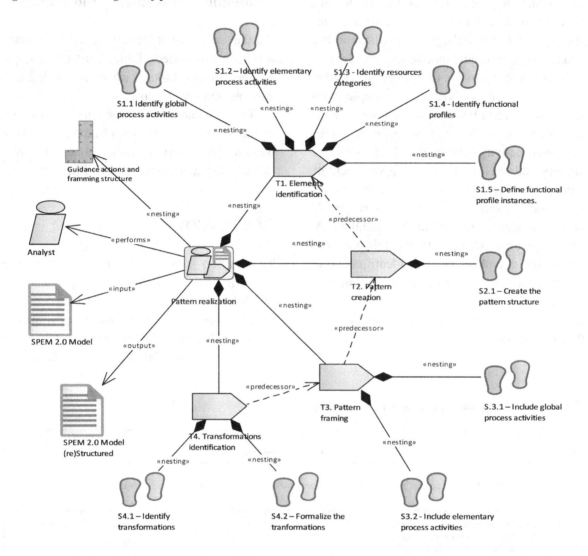

to the project dimension, only a part of the model (where appropriate) will be used for illustration purposes (this does not affect the rationale to be taken for the whole model). This section ends by exposing some issues pertinent to a proper project definition for PIS.

The USE-ME.GOV Project

The USE-ME.GOV project (USE-ME.GOV, 2003) focused on the development of an open platform for mobile government services. This platform facilitates the access of authorities to the mobile market by allowing them to share common modules of the platform and to deal with multiple mobiles operators independently of each one's interface. USE-ME.GOV system general architecture is illustrated by Figure 10.

The USE-ME.GOV Platform basically consists of two separate application system: (i) Core Platform, which is responsible for user's platform access, user and terminal management; (ii) Service Repository, which is a central registry of services. The USE-ME.GOV system also contains what is

Figure 10. USE-ME.GOV system general architecture (from (USE-ME.GOV, 2006))

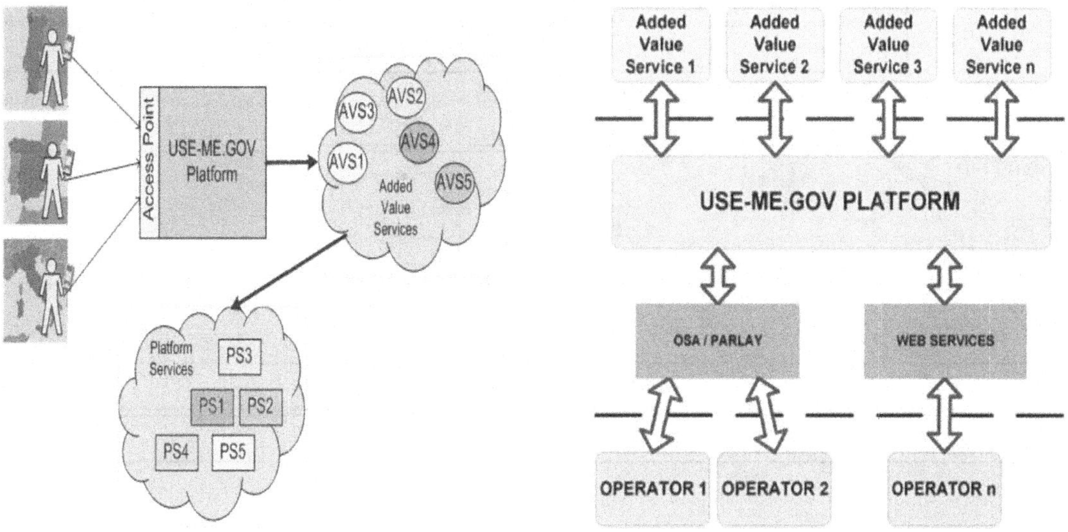

designated by "platform services". Platform services included in the USE-ME.GOV system are: (i) Context Provision and Aggregation Services; (ii) Localization Service; (iii) Content Provision and Aggregation Service. These services enable the use of user's context, user's localization, and access and aggregation of data form external sources.

The USE-ME.GOV project is extensive and includes several subsystems services. In the light of the profiling and framing approach, these subsystems can be seen as a system for which a whole development process can be applied. As such, the project will have a contextual system framing structure identifying the major subsystem's functional profiles and subsystem's resource category groupings. Then, for each of the subsystem functional profile instances (the crossing of subsystem's functional profile with subsystems' resources category grouping) is developed a new framing structure, at a subsystem level. In this framing structure the high-level model corresponds to the one regarding to the specific subsystem's functional profile instance in the preceding framing structure. In each subsystem's

functional profile instance related framing structure, there will be functional profiles and resources categories, as expected (unless there is another level of subsystems, in which case, the rationale is applied again). The following paragraphs show the system framing structure of USE-ME.GOV. For one of the identified subsystem's functional profile instances, the respective nested framing structure is illustrated. Further nested framing structures of this last one will not be presented here.

Figure 11 illustrates the framing structure at the system level. It shows the subsystem's functional profile instances that get existence in the project. As it can be seen in Figure 11, the framing structure has two major subsystem functional profiles: "Platform" and "Pilot Services". The resource categories related to subsystem functional profiles (as it also happens at the system level), have symbolic names of "Category group A", "Category group B", and so on. In these cases, it is acceptable to make no explicit identification/characterization of the resources categories. The framing structure assigns each of the subsystem functional profiles to only one resource group, giving origin to a single subsystem functional profile. The "Platform" and

Figure 11. Framing structure at system level for USE-ME.GOV project

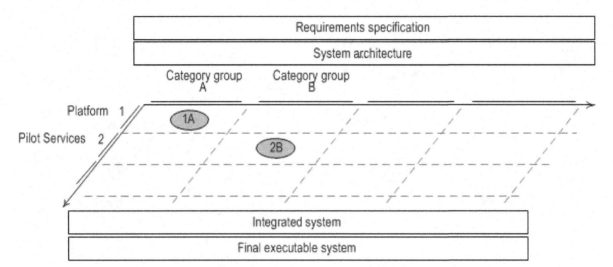

"Pilot Services" functional profile instances have also corresponding framing structures.

Figure 12 illustrates the framing structure related do "Pilot Services". The Pilot Services has several subsystems, one for each of the services of "Complaint Information Broadcasting", "Mobile Student", "Healthcare Information", and "Citizen Complaint". Again, as before in the preceding framing structure, there are resource category groups; for each of the subsystems, there will be again a corresponding framing structure. Symbolic names identify the several elements of the framing structure. Note that there is no conflict on the names used for resource categories groupings, functional profiles, or functional profiles instances as the framing structure implicitly defines a namespace.

Figure 12. Framing structure for Pilot Services subsystem of USE-ME.GOV

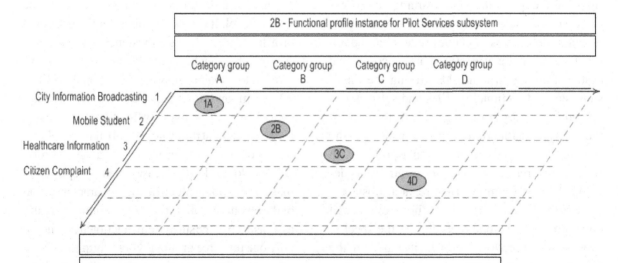

The Pattern in USE-ME.GOV

The following paragraphs present the use of the pattern related to the framing structure at system level (Figure 13). For the remaining framing structures, the rationale of the corresponding realizations of the development framework patterns is identical to this pattern or to the one already presented in the earlier project. For the realizations of the patterns in the SPEM model, the approach reorganizes, modifies, or properly creates the existing activities.

The global process activity of "Project Management" includes "Project Coordination" and "Project Assessment" activities. "Recommenda-tions" global process activity includes "Business Planning", "Implementation Planning", and "Standardization and Regulations" activities. The restructuration has to distribute (and eventually to redefine) the activities of "Preliminary Design & Mock-Up", "Detailed Design ad Specification", and "Implementation and Integration" by the several elementary processes regarding diverse subsystems.

Figure 14 illustrates the nesting of a framing structure achieved through new realization of the development framework pattern in connection to an elementary process of a higher framing structure. This elementary process assumes in the pattern the place usually allocated to the

Figure 13. USE-ME.GOV's after pattern adoption (major structuring elements at system level)

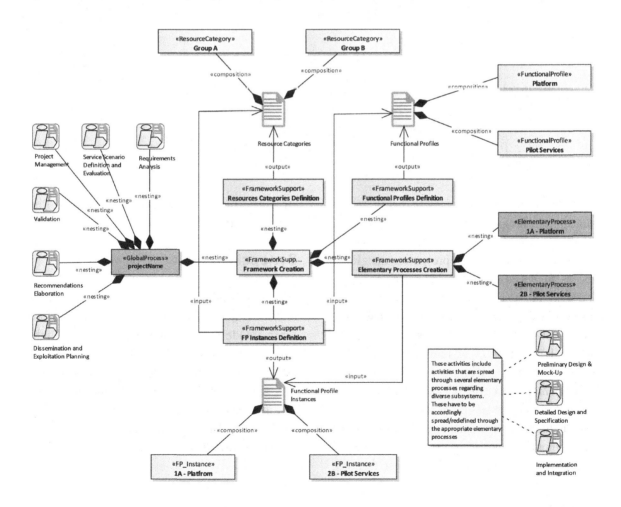

Figure 14. USE-ME.GOV after pattern adoption (major structuring elements at Platform subsystem level)

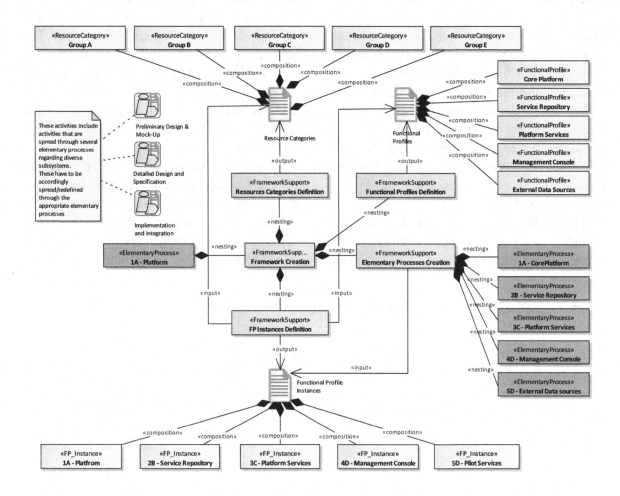

global development process. Note that there is a namespace established by the framing structure, reflected in this case by the symbolic designation of the element that is representing the global process, in this case the elementary process "1A-Platform". As such, the absolute name of another relative identified element in the diagram will be, its element's type reference followed by a tag in the form 1A.relative_id_of_diagramElement. For example, "elementary process 1A.3C" refers to the elementary process "3C-Platform Services".

Figure 15 illustrates another nesting of a framing structure, through further realization of the development framework pattern in connection to an elementary process of a higher framing structure. In this case, it respects to the "Pilot Services" subsystem.

Synopsis

The case study USE-ME.GOV promoted the reasoning about the design of project structures for the model-driven development of PIS. In this context, several factors/needs emerged as being pertinent to the design of project structures to accommodate MDD for PIS in order to achieve a proper, efficient, and resilient development and final system. The following paragraphs state some of these factors/needs of influence.

Figure 15. USE-ME.GOV after pattern adoption (major structuring elements at Pilot Services subsystem level)

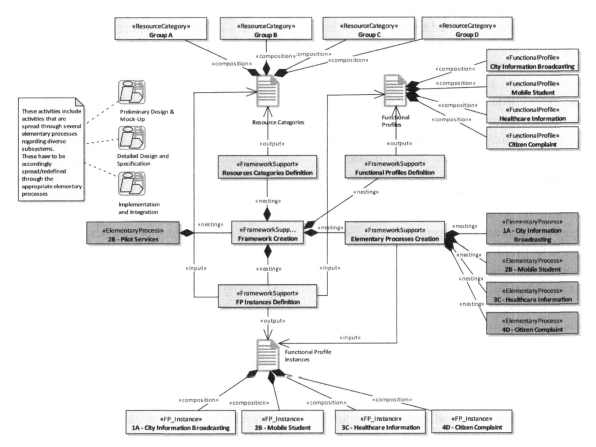

Project structures should be designed to support PIS. The way the elements are structured can have a positive impact in coping with heterogeneity in devices and in functionalities of PIS. The development framework (jointly with the profiling and framing approach) and the pattern herein presented, provide techniques to deal with pervasive characteristics such as heterogeneity of devices and changing functionalities.

Projects need an explicit manifestation of a model-driven approach. The projects must have, in the project design, a clear strategy to accommodate a model-driven approach making use of models beyond of schematic or documentation purposes in the several phases of the project.

Project elements must be properly defined. It is important to pay attention to several issues that may occur in the definition of project elements. Among these, are the lack of explicit artefacts, activities, or relationships; the inconsistent or improper naming; the incoherent sequence activities; or the misused of conceptions. The attention given to them is important as they are at a core level where it is fundamental to assure its correctness in order to pursuit, at higher levels of abstraction, the goals of model-driven development.

Projects should formalize activities as model transformations and other elements with semantic correctness. Without having a coherent, consistent, and clear formalization of the several projects constituents' elements, it will not be possible to establish, with an acceptable quality, a model-based/driven process development. Without the existence of coherently interconnected and precise process elements, it is hard, even impossible, to achieve a model-based/driven development orientation at a large extent and depth of the process. This is the consequence of the difficulties in: (i) incorporating new activities or optimizing the existing ones with model transformations techniques; (ii) reorganizing or redefining the process in order to pursuit a clearer and enhanced model-based/driven quality.

Projects should seek for model-driven semantic continuity/visibility. How much model-based/driven is a software development process? When does a software development project go from being model-"based" to being model-"driven"? It is important to reason about the robustness of process and the suitability of activities and artefacts regarding its use on a model-based/driven orientation. The usability of an artefact is related to its expression and ability to be consumed/reused on subsequent modelling tasks. The suitability of an activity is related to its ability to incorporate formal/explicit model transformation techniques that (optionally) consume models and produce models. The robustness of the process is related to the degree of the modelling semantic continuity provided by the chains of activities, from the beginning to the end of the development process. The links among model artefacts and model transformation activities (or well-structured and formalized activities) of the process define the visibility. The longer the path, the more model-driven is the development process. So, to enhance model-based/driven visibility, it is needed to pay attention to activities (or tasks) and the realization and flow of models.

The activities and artifacts of development process, either at global of elementary process, can be described using the Software & Systems Process Engineering Meta-model Specification (SPEM) 2.0 (OMG, 2008). SPEM provides to process engineers a conceptual framework for modelling method contents and processes, and as such, it is used to define software and systems development processes and their components. SPEM can be an important auxiliary tool for the definition (or diagnosis or optimization) of processes.

CONCLUSION

Pervasive forms of information system are increasingly predominating on landscape of software systems development. Among others, resources heterogeneity, increased number of functionalities that may be simultaneously accomplished by distinct resources, high pace of changes on resources and requirements characterizes PIS. These have to be taken into account by a suitable approach to software development for PIS. Some properties of process structures should be seek in order to achieve robustness of a development process definition, such as the comprehensiveness and depth of the structure of the process, semantic correctness, naming coherency and consistency, activity flows and input/output clearness, work unit's robustness, overall rationale, and model-based/driven visibility. Satisfaction of these properties contributes for the perception of a solid ground for project development. This document revisited development structures and techniques for the development of PIS and presented a development framework pattern for the software development of PIS. Those structures, techniques, and pattern allow the organization of the functionality that can be assigned to computational devices in a system and of the corresponding development structures and models. The proposed approach allows accommodating the profiling of functionalities that can be assigned to several resource categories and enables a structural approach to PIS development. Through a real case study, we have concluded that the strategy inherent to this development pattern and its inherent conceptions reveals as being able to cope with systems composed of several subsystems, while keeping the capacity to deal with heterogeneous devices and to accommodate model-based/driven approaches.

REFERENCES

Appukuttan, B., Clark, T., Reddy, S., Tratt, L., & Venkatesh, R. (2003). A model driven approach to model transformations. In *Proceedings of Model Driven Architecture: Foundations and Applications* (pp. 1–12). Enschede, The Netherlands: University of Twente.

Ark, W. S., & Selker, T. (1999). A look at human interaction with pervasive computers. *IBM Systems Journal, 38*(4), 504–507. doi:10.1147/sj.384.0504

Atkinson, C., & Kuhne, T. (2003). Model-driven development: a metamodeling foundation. *Software, IEEE, 20*(5), 36–41. doi:10.1109/MS.2003.1231149

Azevedo, S., Machado, R. J., Bragança, A., & Ribeiro, H. (2011). Systematic use of software development patterns through a multilevel and multistage classification. In J. Osis, & E. Asnina (Eds.), *Model-Driven Domain Analysis and Software Development: Architectures and Functions* (pp. 304–333). IGI Global.

Benincasa, G. P., Daneels, A., Heymans, P., & Serre, C. (1985). Engineering a large application software project: The Controls of the CERN PS Accelerator Complex. *Nuclear Science. IEEE Transactions on, 32*(5), 2029–2031.

Bohn, J., Coroamã, V., Langheinrich, M., Mattern, F., & Rohs, M. (2004). Living in a world of smart everyday objects - social, economic, and ethical implications. *Human and Ecological Risk Assessment, 10*(5). doi:10.1080/10807030490513793

Brown, A. W. (2004). Model driven architecture: Principles and practice. *Software & Systems Modeling, 3*, 314–327.

Ciarletta, L., & Dima, A. (2000). A conceptual model for pervasive computing. In *Proceedings of Parallel Processing* (pp. 9–15). Washington, DC: IEEE Computer Society.

Davies, N., & Gellersen, H.-W. (2002). Beyond prototypes: challenges in deploying ubiquitous systems. *Pervasive Computing, IEEE, 1*, 26–35. doi:10.1109/MPRV.2002.993142

Fano, A., & Gershman, A. (2002). The future of business services in the age of ubiquitous computing. *Communications of the ACM, 45*(12), 83–87. doi:10.1145/585597.585620

Fernandes, J. E., & Machado, R. J. (2012). SPEM 2.0 Extension for pervasive information systems. *WSEAS Transactions on Computers, 11*(9), 10.

Fernandes, J. E., Machado, R. J., & Carvalho, J. (2004). Model-driven methodologies for pervasive information systems development. In *Proceedings of MOMPES'04, 1st International Workshop on Model-Based Methodologies for Pervasive and Embedded Software* (pp. 15-23). Turku, Finland: TUCS.

Fernandes, J. E., Machado, R. J., & Carvalho, J. (2007). Model-Driven Software Development for Pervasive Information Systems Implementation. In *Proceedings of the 6th International Conference on Quality of Information and Communications Technology* (pp. 218-222). Washington, DC: IEEE Computer Society.

Fernandes, J. E., Machado, R. J., & Carvalho, J. (2008). Model-driven development for pervasive information systems. In S. K. Mostefaoui, Z. Maamar, & G. M. Giaglis (Eds.), *Advances in Ubiquitous Computing: Future Paradigms and Directions* (pp. 45–82). IGI Publishing. doi:10.4018/978-1-59904-840-6.ch003

Fernandes, J. E., Machado, R. J., & Carvalho, J. (2012a). A Case studies approach to the analysis of profiling and framing structures for pervasive information systems. *International Journal of Web Portals, 4*(2), 18. doi:10.4018/jwp.2012040101

Fernandes, J. E., Machado, R. J., & Carvalho, J. (2012b). Profiling and framing structures for pervasive information systems development. In G. Putnik, & M. Cruz-Cunha (Eds.), *Virtual and Networked Organizations, Emergent Technologies and Tools* (Vol. 248, pp. 283–293). Springer. doi:10.1007/978-3-642-31800-9_29

Gamma, E., Helm, R., Johnson, R., & Vlissides, J. (1995). *Design patterns - Elements of reusable object-oriented software*. Boston, MA: Addison-Wesley.

Gorton, I., & Liu, Y. (2010). Advancing software architecture modeling for large scale heterogeneous systems. In *Proceedings of the FSE/SDP Workshop on Future of Software Engineering Research* (pp. 143-148). New York, NY: ACM.

Hansmann, U., Merck, L., Nicklous, M. S., & Stober, T. (2003). *Pervasive computing* (2nd ed.). New York, NY: Springer-Verlag.

Heijstek, W., & Chaudron, M. R. V. (2009). Empirical investigations of model Size, complexity and effort in a large scale, distributed model driven development process. In *Proceedings of the 2009 35th Euromicro Coonference on Software Engineering and Advanced Applications* (pp. 113-120). Washington, DC: IEEE Computer Society.

HillSide. (2013). *The Hillside Group*. Retrieved from http://hillside.net/

Kay, R. (1969). The management and organization of large scale software development projects. In *Proceedings of the May 14-16, 1969, Spring Joint Computer Conference* (pp. 425-433). New York, NY: ACM.

Laine, P. K. (2001). The role of SW architectures in solving fundamental problems in object-oriented development of large embedded SW systems. In *Proccedings of the Working IEEE/IFIP Conference on Software Architecture* (pp. 14-23). Washington, DC: IEEE Computer Society.

Langheinrich, M., Coroama, V., Bohn, J., & Rohs, M. (2002). *As we may live – Real-world implications of ubiquitous computing: Distributed Systems Group, Institute of Information Systems*. Swiss Federal Institute of Technology.

Lyytinen, K., & Yoo, Y. (2002). Introduction [Issues and challenges in ubiquitous computing]. *Communications of the ACM, 45*(12), 62–65. doi:10.1145/585597.585616

Mattsson, A., Lundell, B., Lings, B., & Fitzgerald, B. (2007). Experiences from representing software architecture in a large industrial project using model driven development. In *Proceedings of the Second Workshop on SHAring and Reusing Architectural Knowledge Architecture, Rationale, and Design Intent* (pp. 6-6). Washington, DC: IEEE Computer Society.

Medvidovic, N. (2005). Software architectures and embedded systems: a match made in heaven? *Software, IEEE, 22*(5), 83–86. doi:10.1109/MS.2005.136

Mellor, S. J., Clark, A. N., & Futagami, T. (2003). Model-driven development - Guest editor's introduction. *Software, IEEE, 20*(5), 14–18. doi:10.1109/MS.2003.1231145

Miller, G., Ambler, S., Cook, S., Mellor, S., Frank, K., & Kern, J. (2004). Model driven architecture: the realities, a year later. In *Companion to the 19th Annual ACM SIGPLAN Conference on Object-oriented Programming Systems, Languages, and Applications* (pp. 138-140). New York, NY: ACM.

Mirakhorli, M., Sharifloo, A., & Shams, F. (2008). Architectural challenges of ultra large scale systems. In *Proceedings of the 2nd International Workshop on Ultra-large-scale Software-intensive Systems* (pp. 45-48). New York, NY: ACM.

OMG. (2003). *OMG's MDA Guide Version 1.0.1*. Retrieved from http://www.omg.org/docs/omg/03-06-01.pdf

OMG. (2005). *Object Management Group Home Page*. Retrieved from http://www.omg.org

OMG. (2008). *SPEM v2.0 - Software & Systems Process Engineering Meta-Model Specification v2.0*. Retrieved from www.omg.org/spec/SPEM/2.0/

Ruparelia, N. B. (2010). Software development lifecycle models. *SIGSOFT Softw. Eng. Notes*, *35*(3), 8–13. doi:10.1145/1764810.1764814

Sage, A. P., & Rouse, W. B. (1999). Information Systems Frontiers in Knowledge Management. *Information Systems Frontiers*, *1*(3), 205–219. doi:10.1023/A:1010046210832

Saha, D., & Mukherjee, A. (2003). Pervasive computing: a paradigm for the 21st century. *Computer*, *36*(3), 25–31. doi:10.1109/MC.2003.1185214

Seidewitz, E. (2003). What models mean. *Software, IEEE*, *20*(5), 26–32. doi:10.1109/MS.2003.1231147

Selic, B. (2003). Model-driven development of real-time software using OMG standards. In *Proceedings of the Sixth IEEE International Symposium on Object-Oriented Real-Time Distributed Computing* (pp. 4-6). Washington, DC: IEEE Computer Society.

Sendall, S., & Kozaczynski, W. (2003). Model transformation: the heart and soul of model-driven software development. *Software, IEEE*, *20*(5), 42–45. doi:10.1109/MS.2003.1231150

Thomas, D. (2004). MDA: Revenge of the modelers or UML utopia? *Software, IEEE*, *21*(3), 15–17. doi:10.1109/MS.2004.1293067

USE-ME.GOV. (2003). *Consortium Agreement - Annex I - Description of Work*. Author.

USE-ME.GOV. (2006). *D3.1 Recommendations*. Author.

Want, R., Pering, T., Borriello, G., & Farkas, K. I. (2002). Disappearing hardware [ubiquitous computing]. *Pervasive Computing, IEEE*, *1*, 36–47. doi:10.1109/MPRV.2002.993143

Weiser, M. (1993a). Hot topics-ubiquitous computing. *Computer*, *26*(10), 71–72. doi:10.1109/2.237456

Weiser, M. (1993b). Some computer science issues in ubiquitous computing. *Communications of ACM*, *36*(7), 75-84. doi: http://doi.acm.org/10.1145/159544.159617

Weiser, M., Gold, R., & Brown, J. S. (1999). The origins of ubiquitous computing research at PARC in the late 1980s. *IBM Systems Journal*, *38*(4), 693–696. doi:10.1147/sj.384.0693

Chapter 8
Neural Network–Based Spatial Modeling of Natural Phenomena and Events

Andreas Barth
Beak Consultants GmbH, Germany

Andreas Knobloch
Beak Consultants GmbH, Germany

Silke Noack
Beak Consultants GmbH, Germany

Frank Schmidt
Beak Consultants GmbH, Germany

ABSTRACT

Artificial Neural Networks (ANN) are used for statistical modeling of spatial events in geosciences. The advantage of this method is the ability of neural networks to represent complex interrelations and to be "able to learn" from known (spatial) events. The software advangeo® was developed to enable GIS users to apply neural network methods on raster geodata. The statistic modeling results can be developed and displayed in a user-friendly way within the Esri ArcGIS environment. The complete workflow is documented by the software. This chapter presents five case studies to illustrate the current possibilities and limitations of spatial predictions with the use of artificial neural networks, which describe influencing factors and the selection of known events of the phenomenon to be modeled. These applications include: (1) the prognosis of soil erosion patterns, (2) the country-wide prediction of mineral resources, (3) the vulnerability analysis for forest pests, (4) the spatial distribution of bird species, and (5) the spatial prediction of manganese nodules on the sea bottom.

DOI: 10.4018/978-1-4666-6098-4.ch008

INTRODUCTION

Natural phenomena and events are usually caused by a complex of interacting factors. An exact mathematical formulation of a geo-scientific task, however, with equations describing the dependence of a phenomenon on several main influencing factors, is rarely feasible. Typically, a model only refers to some aspects of the phenomenon in question. Due to the lack of data and knowledge of details of many geo-processes, mathematical models cannot be successfully defined and applied with reasonable certainty. This paper explores artificial neural networks (ANN) (Hassoun 1995, Kasabov 1996, Haykins 1998, Bishop 2008) as a means to provide a reliable tool to analyze causal relationships and to make the knowledge available for predictive processes. This approach differs from traditional methods in that viable results may be obtained with reasonable efforts invested in data processing, model design and computational time.

Results for five different case studies are discussed in this paper, following an introduction on the theoretical background of the neural network approach. The outcomes are predictive maps, which illustrate the favorabilities of occurrence for a given phenomenon. This forms an important basis for the planning of further (economic) activities. The case studies deal with various tasks in applied earth sciences and demonstrate the applicability of ANN/GIS approach. In particular, the following objectives applied to the case studies presented here are:

1. Spatial prediction of soil erosion channels to localize damages (on-site/off-site), and to model effects of mitigation measures;
2. Spatial prediction of the most promising locations for mineral exploration within a country, based on available geological data;
3. Spatial prediction of the most vulnerable forest stands in case of spreading bark beetle infections;

4. Prediction of spatial distribution of bird species according to a landuse/habitat map;
5. Spatial prediction of poly-metallic (manganese) nodules on the sea bottom.

Although the value of the application of neural network technologies in GIS environments was recognized in the past, actual application of this remained a challenge for standard users due to the lack of user-friendly tools (see separation of ANN and GIS in Lamothe (2009) and Brown et al. 2003). Thus, the overall goal of the case studies was to study the quality of model outputs and the general applicability of the ANN/GIS approach included in the software advangeo®.

RATIONALE AND OBJECTIVES OF THE STUDY: SELECTION OF AN APPROPRIATE MODELLING METHOD FOR SPATIAL EVENTS

The location of a spatial event both naturally or human induced is determined by a complex network of influential causes and subsequent effects. Hence, the relationships between the parameters are usually characterized by qualitative descriptors rather than quantifiable means if they can be described at all in a reasonable amount of time. In many cases, data rather than rules exist (Brown et al. 2003, Maier & Dandy 2000). This hampers the mathematical modeling and spatial prediction of natural phenomena. In general, spatial pattern of events can be modeled by two different approaches:

Firstly by conducting detailed studies of physical, chemical and other relations to establish an accurate quantitative model of the processes with mathematical-analytical methods, for example when using finite elements to model slope stability. With this approach, equations are used to parameterize and model natural processes. Equation calibration is usually accomplished by adjusting "constants", based on the comparison of modeled results and measured data.

Secondly by a statistical approach, whereby potentially influential factors are evaluated by multivariate methods, based on statistical correlations. The influence of several independent factors on the dependent variables is analyzed, for example regarding the development of a geo-hazard such as slope failure.

The calibration of analytical models is usually time-consuming (Huffman 2007) and associated with cost-intensive field studies. As a result, it is not uncommon that complex natural processes cannot be adequately described with derived physical equations for more extensive areas of interest. The statistical approach has the advantage of engendering usable results with much lower amounts of effort in terms of data capture and calibration (Hertwig et al. 2010). Well-known and widely used multivariate methods include regression, cluster and discriminant analyses (Stockburger 1998).

The ANN approach is a multivariate analysis method. With this method, it is possible for users to model complex non-linear relations without prior or initial knowledge of the relationships amongst the input layers. These relations are "investigated" by the ANN during a "learning process" during which a sizable amount of input data can be analyzed at various scales. However, type of data layers selected and the manner in which they are prepared by the user will influence the quality of outputs generated.

Various authors have successfully applied ANN to forecast the occurrence and extent of spatial events. Examples of applications have included the accurate identification of slope failure processes (Fernandez-Steeger 2002), the modeling of spatial air pollution patterns (Lin et al. 2004), the propagation of flood waves (Peters et al. 2006), the forecasting of water resources variables (Maier & Dandy, 2000), and the prediction of mineral deposits (Brown et al. 2000, Koike et al. 2002, Redford et al. 2004, Lamothe 2009). However, none of the previous studies involved the integration of ANN into a geographic information system to better facilitate the storage management

and display of the generated spatial information. The goal of this project was to address this with the development of a software product that can be applied by a GIS user within the standard GIS environment to facilitate the production of prediction maps for planning purposes.

METHOD: ARTIFICIAL NEURAL NETWORKS

Artificial Neural Networks (ANN) (Hassoun 1995, Kasabov 1996, Haykins 1998, Bishop 2008) can be used for the statistical modeling of spatial events. This method has proven to be capable of representing complex interactions (Brown et al. 2003, Lamothe 2009). Following training with such known events, ANN apply the "knowledge" to more extensive areas under similar boundary conditions. ANN help to detect the controlling factors for analyzed events and can also return a favorability value, which describes the likelihood of event occurrence for a particular location. These results are of vital importance, as they can inform about the nature of geo-hazards and aid in the planning and implementation of mitigation measures. In the case of mineral exploration, the analysis can help prospectors to minimize their efforts and expenditures by focusing resources and work on the most promising locations.

The main principle of the ANN approach is built on the concept of how networks of biological neurons are organized and function by imitating the properties of a real nervous system (Negnevitsky 2002). These systems are composed of many chemically interconnected neurons (nerve cells), which receive and process signals from other neurons. When these signals reach a certain threshold, sets of nerve cells (closest to the originating signals) are activated and forward the information to other connected neurons. Learning processes result from the constant adaptation of the interconnections amongst neurons, where the growth and strength of connections are directly related to their frequency of use and degenerate when rarely accessed.

The simulation of these biochemical processes in an ANN is done by artificial neurons, known as processing units. The connections are realized by directed interconnection weights w_{ij} Backhaus et al. (2003) and Kriesel (2009)). In general, an ANN may be described as an adaptive system, which changes its structure based on the flow of external or internal signals through the network.

Artificial neurons are usually organized in layers, comprised of:

- An input layer that receives input values (i.e. independent variables and crucial controlling factors related to the event to be modeled);
- Hidden layer(s) that process the signals and calculate the resultant value(s) by transforming them with the application of an activating function; and
- An output layer, created from the dependent variable to be modeled.

The network topology describes the way the neurons are interconnected. The direction of signal propagation (forward or backward), the level and the type of connection (completely connected or with shortcuts) are thus defined. Figure 1 shows the scheme of a completely connected feed-forward network with 4-3-1 topology. On the right-hand side, a processing unit (neuron) is sketched with its output function.

The weights increase or decrease the strength of the incoming signal and are adaptable during the learning process. By repeating the input of the training pattern, the intensity of the connections is modified such that the deviation or error between expected and actual outputs (between modeled and real data) are minimized.

There are different network paradigms such as the multi-layer perceptron (MLP), the radial basis function networks (RBF), Hopfield networks and self-organizing maps (SOM) (Negnevitsky 2002). The MLP paradigm is of particular interest for applications that involve supervised learning. The information processing that occurs is characterized as "feed forward". This network paradigm is an extension of earlier developments on the perceptron, which incorporates higher requirements for the modeling of complex relationships. A MLP consists of an input layer at least one hidden layer and an output layer as shown in Figure 1.

Another important network parameter is the activation function, which is used to calculate the output status of the neuron. Differentiable and non-linear functions are required for this purpose. Generally, sigmoid functions are applied.

Figure 1. General scheme of a feed forward network

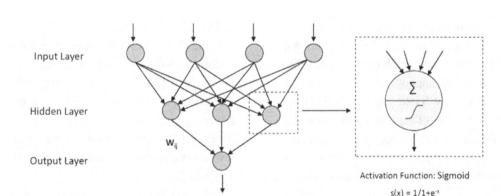

Activation Function: Sigmoid

$$s(x) = 1/1+e^{-x}$$

MLP are usually trained with a "back propagation" algorithm (Rumelhart et al. 1986, Rios 2010). "Back propagation of error" is a training algorithm, which adapts the weights (w_{ij}) by considering the degree of error from the output signal so that it may be minimized.

INTEGRATION OF THE METHOD INTO GIS

ANN have already been used for some time as an alternative to other multivariate, statistical methods and have been proven to produce adequate results (Brown et al. 2003). Although some ANN-based commercial products and class libraries are currently available, they usually require the manual generation of input data in a proprietary format. Some products have import interfaces, for instance Microsoft Excel spreadsheet structures. GIS users aiming to analyze numerous input data layers are faced with the organization and assessment of a sizable number of individual records. The identification of the spatial relation of the records (data layers) enables the GIS to derive information at any defined point and thus to define training data for the ANN across all data layers for the same location.

Up to now, the use of ANN to analyze spatial data has not been widespread in geosciences, due to the lack of user-friendly software that runs together with a standard GIS environment. Based on this observation, a software application was developed and used in this study, which provides users with tools to evaluate their spatial data with ANN within the Esri ArcGIS environment. This software, called advangeo® is comprised of two components namely "Data and Model Explorer" and "GIS Extension".The "Data and Model Explorer" (a stand-alone solution) provides support to the user as new projects are set up and assists in the systematic parameterization of the models with the workflow fully documented. The additional "GIS Extension" provides all of the necessary GIS functionalities in a user-friendly interface to facilitate the geodata with the ANN. Besides the availability of various functions to pre-process geodata, this extension also supports the automatic creation of output map layouts.

The "application meta data database" manages the project metadata, which includes calculations, embedded data, parameterized models and scenarios. Metadata are stored in a Microsoft SQL Server database as shown in Figure 2.The "project spatial data database" contains all of the spatial/thematic geodata and feature data for the build-up of the statistical models.

The setup of a consistent and reproducible statistical model for geodata analysis consists of a number of procedures, which formed the basis for the design and development of this software. The multiple stages include:

1. The exact formulation of the modeling objective and the delineation of the study area;
2. The description and compilation of source data, which represent the potentially influential factors with which predictions will be made;
3. The technical processing (from the scientific and IT point of view) and statistical pre-processing of the source data;
4. The setup and calculation of model scenarios for training, tests and applications;
5. The statistical post-processing and presentation of prediction results.

The "Data and Model Explorer" is the primary user interface where the main object types may be defined for modeling, organized with their respective metadata sets, modified and visualized. The processing of geodata and the presentation of subsequent results are supported by a GIS extension with a special toolbar and a project tree view option. The system architecture is illustrated in Figure 2.

Project definition is the first step of the modeling process and appears at the top of the "Data

Figure 2. System architecture of advangeo ®

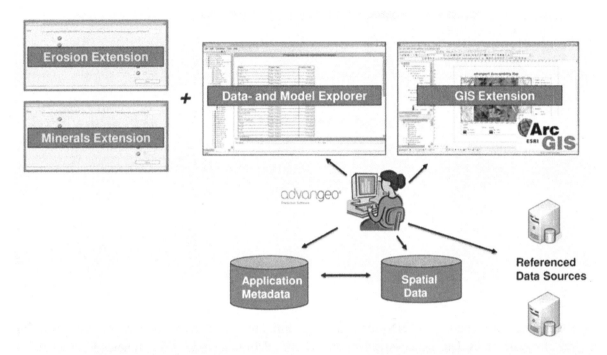

and Model Explorer" hierarchy. The levels are displayed in a tree view structure for easy navigation. By defining a project, the user sets the technical boundary of the intended task. The study training and test areas are delineated subsequently.

The basis of every modeling task is founded upon the ability to use various source data types. However, data usually have to be pre-processed, involving the conversion to a standard or recognizable format for a given application. Original source data are therefore unlikely to be used directly for calculations, but can be included in the project for documentation or reference purposes. Necessary processing procedures prior to modeling can include the calculation of field values, error identification and elimination, code adaption, scale transformations or data partitioning. The "processed source data" are transformed and saved as spatially compatible raster layers. Taking the extent of the project area into consideration, the data are transformed to "model input data" layers,

in the next step. This process is required to ensure a spatially consistent set of raster data.

Following the data processing procedures, a parameterized model is set up and used for the calculation (see below). Model input data, training and model parameters are then determined in a training scenario (Figure 3). Currently, the MLP approach is used in advangeo® along with various adaptable training algorithms and parameters. This procedure was realized with the open source library FANN (Nissen 2009). The user may opt to retain the standard default values at the beginning of the model parameterization stage. The model calculation results in a trained network within the defined training area. The initial run returns a preliminary estimation of the model quality. The GIS extension provides further functions for the statistical validation of model results. The trained network can then be applied to other study areas. The calculations may also be displayed in a semi-automatically generated prediction map within the GIS environment. The special, new and innovative

Figure 3. Training scenario with advangeo ®

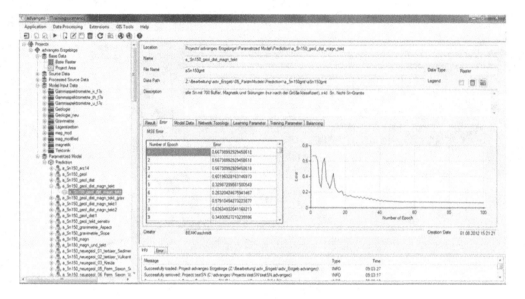

aspects advangeo® introduces in ANN processing are the integrated GIS data management in the standard GIS environment of Esri ArcGIS and the various tools to pre-process data, tools to assess the model quality and a customized map printing function as shown in Figure 7.

CASE STUDY 1: EROSION PATTERN PREDICTION

Precipitation with long duration and/or high intensity causes the dislocation of soil material in agricultural fields. Topsoil, which contains the greatest amount of nutrients, is most vulnerable to dislocation. Seeds may also be carried away. This reduces the potential yield of the land. These types of adverse effects are known as "on-site damages" (Favis-Mortlock 2005). "Offsite-damages", on the contrary, occur where soil is deposited or accumulated and can spoil water bodies and cause damages to human infrastructure. The prediction of the probability of erosion events along with a quantitative estimation of soil dislocation forms an important basis for the planning of preventative measures. Analytical equations to predict the

amount of dislocated soil have been derived and used for many years (Wischmeier & Smith 1978; de Vries et al. 1998). Other soil parameters have already been predicted successfully with ANN and the MLP approach in particular recently by Behrens et al. (2005), Alavi et al. (2010), Knobloch et al. (2010), Metelka et al. (2011) and, in case of soil contamination pattern, by Hertwig et al. (2010). The goal of this case study was to test the accuracy of the prediction with ANN in the Weisseritz catchment in the South of Eastern Germany.

Source Data and Pre-Processing

The main controlling factors governing soil erosion were well known for the study area, due to a number of existing algorithms developed for the parameterization of mathematical models. Factors include:

- Terrain attributes (slope and flow accumulation; to a lesser extent aspect, profile and plan curvature and flow length),
- Percent composition of top soil (soil particle size – fine, medium, coarse) and

- Land use (such as arable land, pastures, forests, urban areas).

Data sources comprised of a digital elevation model (DEM) with 20 m raster size (DGM 25), the soil concept map of the Free State of Saxony at a scale 1:25,000 and ATKIS land use data at the same scale. These data layers were pre-processed with selected GIS tools to create consistent raster layers. Various terrain attributes were calculated and tested based on the standard DEM derivations (Wilson & Gallant 2000). In order to include the influence of linear elements such as roads and hedgerows, which function as barriers to erosional processes, an "apparent enhancement" of the spatial resolution was realized by resampling the data to a 5 m grid. Metric data layers were then normalized to fall between 0 and 1. Nominal scales for layers containing data on the presences of forests, roads and geological units were reclassified as binary layers. Training data were manually digitized from scanned ortho-photos, which were taken after the severe rainfalls of August 2002. The accuracy of the data was also partially verified during site visits as shown in Figure 4.

The combination of slope and flow accumulation explained most of the observed erosion patterns. Other terrain attributes (derived from the DEM) did not enhance the results significantly, whereas top soil composition and land use (arable land, pastures, forest, urban areas) contributed to enhanced results. So these layers were selected for the further processing.

Network Parameterization

The previously described pre-processed data were used as input data for the model calculation. The model was defined with the described procedures and trained with the existing, verified training objects. Training was completed in a part of the defined study area. For modeling, a MLP approach was used. It was trained with various learning

Figure 4. Training area, field validation

algorithms, activation functions and parameters. Acceptable results were attained with the Resilient Back Propagation (RPROP) algorithm in combination with a sigmoid activation function.

Validation

The training was repeated several times with the same parameters. Comparable results (with only slight deviations acquired following a similarly defined training process) were observed. This confirmed the reproducibility and robustness of the network and is an important parameter for the assessment of the modeling result. The trained network was then applied on a separated, secondary test site and validated. The network accurately identified approximately 90% of the test records. The threshold for the decision "erosion/no erosion" was set to $p > 0.75$ and was derived from statistical calculations of confirmed erosion sites. Using this threshold value, the optimum of event recognition (96% of the test points) was reached. A lower threshold lead to noisy results whereas a higher threshold produced less than 96% of the test points. This result was confirmed in the field. Figure 5 shows water logging after high precipitation as well as erosion channels at locations of dark cell values indicating high erosion probability.

Planning of Preventative Measures and Presentation of Results

The trained network was later on used to plan for the introduction and implementation of erosion prevention measures. Additional barriers including landscape elements such as hedgerows were added into the digital terrain model on slopes that were especially susceptible to erosional processes. This was accomplished by modifying the input layers. Figure 6 shows that the erosion probability (dark cell values, dominated by the

factors flow accumulation and slope on arable land) is significantly reduced by introducing three barriers to cut of the major flow lines parallel to the elevation contours. The subsequent network run confirmed the successful mitigation of the predicted erosion processes. With this approach, prevention measures could be optimized (number and location of barriers) thereby facilitating the conservation of funds.

The integrated function for automatic map generation helped to display the prediction results in a user-friendly way. Figure 9 is an example of a prediction map with the following content: erosion channel probability (in color) on top of the DEM, hillshade display (top left), and on top of the aerial image (top right). The bottom line represents detailed maps on the same background data (as indicated in the overview map). The right-hand side diagrams explain the used factors of influence

Figure 5. Visual field inspection of predicted results

Figure 6. Mitigation of erosion processes by landscape elements (barriers) on a southwest exposed slope

Figure 7. Prediction map for soil erosion probability (original in color, indicating high erosion probability in red lines/areas)

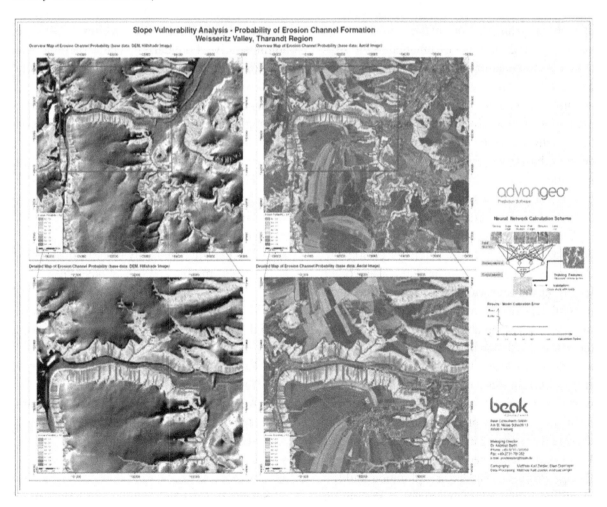

and display the model calibration error (training function). The overall erosion probability is given in a color scale and values from 0 – 1.

CASE STUDY 2: COUNTRY-WIDE PREDICTION OF MINERAL RESOURCES

The ability of ANN to analyze complex and non-linear combinations of multiple (raster) input data was tested for the interpretation of mineral occurrences in order to generate high quality prediction maps of mineral resources. Such maps are crucial especially for developing countries where positive results may be used to attract investment interest in their respective mineral sectors. The identification of exploration targets is one of the most ambitious tasks in geology as it is instrumental to the strategic development of companies and sometimes even countries and is generally tied to significant amounts of financial resources. The successful prediction of mineral occurrences plays a key role in the selection of further exploration tasks and defines a basis for which investment decisions can be made in many countries. Traditional methods of mineral prospectivity mapping with GIS are described e.g. in Carranza (2009).

Currently, analytical models cannot adequately describe the complex interactions of geological, tectonic, geochemical, geo-mechanical and other factors in the timescale that is required to form mineral deposits. Only single aspects of it can be modeled with acceptable levels of precision when there are fixed boundary conditions (how ore minerals attach to geochemical barriers) (Bougrain et al. 2003). In this case study, input data layers were selected based on existing knowledge about influencing factors of ore genesis, which was derived from geological maps. The study area of 11,000 km^2 was located in Kosovo in southeastern Europe. Promising targets for exploration could be identified at this scale of investigation. In addition to the already known deposits of lead, zinc, bauxite,

chromium, nickel and coal, the results indicated significant potential for gold and platinum metals.

Source Data and Pre-Processing

Between 2003 and 2007, existing geo-scientific data were compiled, reviewed, completed and transformed into a consistent set of digital maps, under the supervision of the "Independent Commission for Mines and Minerals" (ICMM). All necessary data layers for the prediction of mineral resources (especially geology, tectonics, known deposits, metallogeny, aero-geophysics) were made to be available at scales of 1:100,000 and 1:200,000, respectively (Barth et al. 2010). For modeling purposes, a raster cell size of 50m was estimated to be sufficient resulting in approximately 4,400,000 cell values within the Kosovo administrative boundaries. The structural and lithological relationships within the lead/zinc deposits were presented by Anković et al. (2003) and further explored in a study by Legler et al. (2008). The main controlling factors for the localization of ore deposits included:

- The tectonic elements in the NNW – SSE direction striking;
- The proximity of Cenozoic volcanic rocks; and
- The presence of highly reactive host rocks, such as marble and calcareous schist.

The following datasets were identified to be crucial for the generation of the prediction map:

- Known deposits and occurrences,
- Tectonic data (lineaments and faults),
- Aero-geophysical data (gamma spectrometry of elements U, Th and K, magnetics, and electromagnetics), and
- Lithological data

Selected influencing factors were derived from the geological map and transformed to a 50 m grid (see example of tectonic data preparation in Figure 8). In the cases involving the consideration of lineaments/faults and Cenozoic volcanic rocks, the distance from each cell to the nearest relevant structure was calculated, which functions as a viable potential indicator of deposits.

Network Parameterization

The training stage was completed for the test area illustrated in Figure 9. For the cross-validation stage, a subset of the known deposits within the test area was used for a second training scenario while the remaining known deposit locations that had been removed beforehand, were used to validate the trained results.

The training results were further assessed by an iterative process that involved the consideration of a greater number of input layers. In this case further investigation began with 3 layers (aero-radiometric layers Uranium (U), Thorium (Th) and Potassium (K)) and increased to the use of 6 layers, which included volcanic, tectonic and electromagnetic data. For modeling, the MLP approach was applied.

Validation

Training was repeated several times with the same parameters, which produced almost identical results to previous training runs. These results gave insight into how robust and reproducible the network-based training runs were. The trained network was then applied to the full extent of Kosovo with the exception of the northern and northwestern border where no geophysical data were available. Some known deposits, identified on the prediction map with probabilities of less than 0.5 were not used for the training exercise.

Presentation of Results

The results of the modeling stage were semi-automatically transformed into a prediction map within the GIS. This kind of map can be used to display the modeled results in a manner that can be easily used by potential investors in the mineral sector or other interested parties (Mining Journal 2009).

Figure 8. Pre-processing of tectonic data: Calculation of distances to potentially relevant lineaments/faults

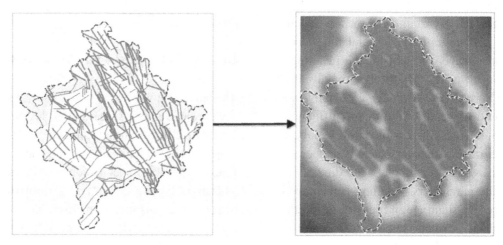

Figure 9. Training area and known deposits (dots)

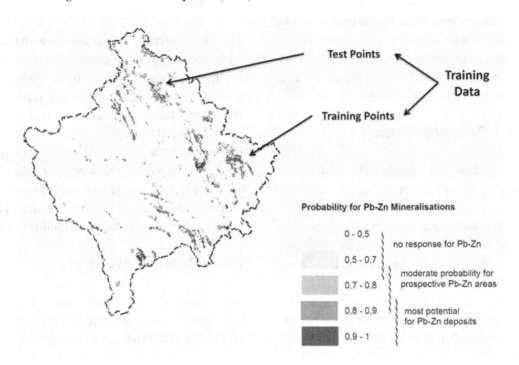

CASE STUDY 3: FOREST PEST VULNERABILITY ANALYSIS

Mass reproduction of the European Spruce Bark Beetle (*Ips typographus*) can lead to severe forest dieback since their larvae feed on the inner bark of trees at different life stages and in various degrees of deterioration (Seidl et al. 2007). Knowledge of controlling factors pertaining to the reproductive cycle of *I. typographus* is crucial for successful forest management and for the planning of mitigation measures. The beetles mainly affect Norway Spruce (*Picea abies*), especially older homogeneous stands. Significant influencing factors for the mass dispersion of this bark beetle include climate parameters such as temperature sequences, wind strength and wind direction, as well as site parameters including percentage of spruce present, stand age and density. In addition, topographical attributes such as terrain and soil conditions can influence the development of *I. typographus* populations. The goal of this study

was to test if the ANN approach with advangeo® is suitable for the spatial prediction of how susceptible a specific site is to future infections and the mass reproduction of this beetle species. Various approaches and models have been available for the analysis and prediction of the spread of *I. typographus*, as described in Baier et al. (2007), Seidl et al. (2007) and Netherer & Nopp-Mayr (2005).

Source Data and Pre-Processing

The study site was located in Saxony, Germany. Source data comprised of a digital elevation model (DEM) in 20 m resolution and ecological forest site map at 1:10,000 with soil and soil water data and forest stand data on species composition, stand age and height. For the ANN training, known locations of *I. typographus* infections from the years 2003 and 2008 were available as field data for the site of interest. The data layers were pre-processed based on the knowledge on influential factors of elevation and terrain attributes such as slope, aspect, curvature and the topographic wetness index and were subject to a scale transformation (Noack & Otto 2010). Soil data were processed to generate maps differentiating between *i)* fine and coarse soil particle sizes and *ii)* wetness classes.

A statistical evaluation of 16 site parameters and three forest stand parameters was conducted prior to the processing. Histograms were produced at the end of the evaluation, which helped to delineate data ranges and were used to estimate the potential influence of aforementioned factors, with the consideration of previous stand infections by *I. typographus* in 2003 and 2008. Highly correlated and potentially influential factors were identified to reduce the number of factors for subsequent training stages. For example, flow length and flow accumulation were found to be directly correlated (r=0.92). Therefore, they were not used simultaneously as input layers in order to avoid distortions or bias in the results. Furthermore, a logarithmic function was applied to the flow accumulation, which was notably skewed to the left to approximate a standard distribution of the range of its values (Noack & Otto 2010). Data normalization to values between 0 and 1 was carried out for most layers. Ordinal and nominal scales were transformed to binary grids. This is exemplified in the extraction of soil type data from maps and their conversion into single binary layers, where values of 1 or 0 were assigned for the presence or the non-existence of certain attributes (gley: yes/no or podsol: yes/no). This means reclassifying the data facilitated the evaluation of their significance as potential factors of influence.

Network Parameterization

The training algorithm was executed for the "Tharandter Wald" located in Saxony as well as within parts of the study area. The model was systematically set up with various input layers

representing factors of influence by using MLP coupled with a RPROP algorithm and a sigmoid activation function.

Validation

To validate the results, several parameters were evaluated. First, the "rate of matches" was calculated, which is the percentage of predicted sites to known sites of infection not used for training. In addition, the "prediction error sum of squares" (PRESS) was calculated. The determination of the quadratic difference of the values (known infections and predicted results) at infected locations described the quality of the predictions. In addition, a fourfold cross-validation assessment was conducted for the model. For this purpose, the training data were separated into two exclusionary subsets (training and test subsets) and used as input data on a rotational basis until each element was a part of the test subset for at least one time. The results showed that the model outputs were notably similar, which indicates that a successful learning process occurred during the network training stage.

The correlation between predicted and known values at infected locations raised some questions about the modeling quality. It was observed that 60-70% of the infected locations retained an infection probability at 0.5. There were few probabilities > 0.8 at all calculated by the model, even for infected locations. However, by visual inspection, the general spatial pattern (when looking at lower probabilities) showed a more accurate prediction trend. Results for 2003 (a rather dry year) were significantly better than those for 2008.

The low rates of matches between the two datasets were caused by the validity and accessibility of data on the positional accuracy of the training points (infected stands). This in turn was primarily influenced by different scales at which data were collected and made to be available for use. Additional factors that could significantly enhance the model quality include information about previous infections and forest management measures, more detailed forest stand parameters, information about neighboring stands and wetness. Another aspect was the absence of important climatic parameters such as duration of insolation, wind direction and precipitation, which may explain the differences of the results obtained between 2003 and 2008.

A common parameter set (in terms of potential factors of influence) for the 2003 and 2008 data turned out to be inefficient. The different environmental conditions, particularly differences in the climate, notably influenced the behavior of the beetle. It is hypothesized that the period of drought in 2003 extended the range of beetle dispersion into previously healthy forest stands indicating that stress caused by droughts led to higher susceptibility to infections. In the beginning of this study, a grid with an overall resolution of 5 m was used. Later on a resolution of 20 m was determined to be sufficient considering the quality of data that were available. This change in grid size was reflected in the calculation time and the output quality.

Presentation of Results

In order to compare the model output, the same classes were used to describe the probability of infection for each model run, where:

- No susceptibility: 0 – 0.5
- Low susceptibility: >= 0.5 – 0.6
- Average susceptibility: >= 0.6 – 0.7
- High susceptibility: >= 0.7 – 0.8
- Very high susceptibility: >= 0.8 (dark values on the color scale)

Figure 10 shows the model output with the susceptibility (probability of infection) as the mean value of 15 different model runs. Dark values indicate the highest of 5 probability classes (>= 0.8) and allow a quick overview to target actions in case of starting mass reproduction of the beetles. White areas represent other land use classes (villages, pastures, arable land, streams and forest roads). Finally, a quantitative prediction was calculated (in m³/infected location). Using the input layers for 2008, the following parameters were selected as the best (most representative) input datasets:

Figure 10. Mean values of 15 model runs with 5 probability classes (from very high to no susceptibility to infections by I. typographus)

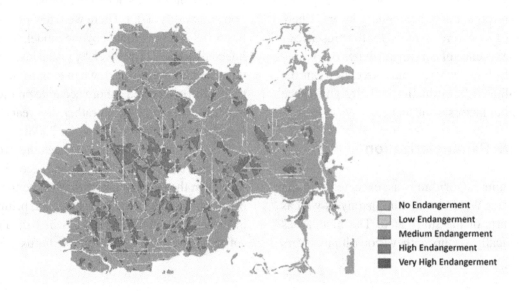

- Percentage of spruce (species composition of the forest stand).
- Forest stand age,
- Soil composition:
  ○ Percentage of coarse soil,
  ○ Percentage of silt percentage of sand,
- Appearance of gley soils,
- Soil moisture levels (soil type),
- Slope angle,
- Slope position,
- Aspect.

The general applicability of the approach to analyze and predict forest infections by I. typographus was proven by this study. Both qualitative and quantitative analysis of infections was possible with ANN and methods of supervised learning. By incorporating further spatial data layers into the ANN, an enhancement of the prediction model was reached.

CASE STUDY 4: PREDICTION OF BIRD SPECIES DISTRIBUTION AND FREQUENCY

In Germany, most bird species and their habitats are protected by either European or national regulations. For all development projects requiring a change in land use, an assessment of the impacts on the environment is mandatory. A prediction of species distribution and frequency of the individual species can help to target mapping campaigns for large areas, e.g. for restricted sites such as contaminated former military areas or sites with limited ground stability along flooded former opencast mines. It can be assessed how the species composition might change with an altered land use or natural succession. As a by-product, the dependencies between species and their habitats, represented by background data sets such as

vegetation or land use can be studied. For larger scales, studies with regression methods have been conducted successfully for birds of prey with vegetation and elevation data in Scotland (Austin et al. 1996) and in the North-East of Greece (Poirazidis et al. 2003), including known nesting and foraging sites, geomorphological features, vegetation and distances to rivers. The influence of pixel size in bird-landscape models was studied by Gottschalk et al. (2011). A grain size of 1-3 m was recommended to include important habitat features such as hedgerows and small streams. Neural networks were applied for species distribution mapping by various authors. For example, Goethals et al. (2007) give an overview of ANN applications in prediction of invertebrates in freshwater. Manel et al. (1999) compared methods (including ANN) to predict spatial bird species distribution along rivers in Himalaya. Maravelias et al. (2003) used ANN and other methods to predict presence or non-presence of fish species in the Mediterranean Sea and demonstrated that ANN work more efficient than linear methods.

The special task of this study was to test a model with detailed bird census data in high resolution for a rather urban area and to apply the neural network then to a rural environment to predict both, species composition and frequency with a user friendly, GIS based tool (advangeo®).

Source Data and Pre-Processing

The network was trained within a 33 km² map sheet in the Northwestern edge of Dresden, a city with approx. 500,000 inhabitants. It was then applied to the town of Freital and its rural surroundings, approx. 10 km South of Dresden (same map sheet size). The used bird census data were compiled by the Saxon State Office for the Environment, Agriculture and Geology after a country-wide mapping project between 2004 and 2007. Bird populations were mapped by several local ornithologists. The country-wide land use and habitat map (captured from color-infrared images of 2005 at a scale of 1:5,000, see LfULG 2012) was made for use at the same scale. The pre-processing of both data sets for this study was done by Römer (2012) with ArcGIS and advangeo®. As additional data, the cadaster of sealed surfaces of the city of Dresden was used to further differentiate the land use map, especially in urban land use classes. The task of pre-processing was mainly done to reduce the high number of habitat and land use types (study sheet: from 153 to 33), to convert it from vector to raster data (one layer per land use type) and to ensure a common coordinate system and raster size. Additional data layers were calculated from the habitat map such as the distance to streams and the distance to hedgerows.

In order to understand and assess the data quality, the 6247 mapped territories of the birds were analyzed according to the fractions of habitat/land use classes contained within one territory. The results (preferred habitat combinations per species) were compared to regional standard literature and showed a high conformity (Sühnel & Schmidt, 2012).

Network Parameterization

The training of the network was conducted in 5 m raster size for various bird species (occurrence raster map) with 33 land use/habitat type raster layers, a grid with distance to hedgerows and a grid with distance to streams, as well as a sealed surface raster (6 levels of sealing from 0% to 100%). For each grid cell (i.e. 25 m^2), a probability measure from 0 to 1 was calculated to indicate if the respective bird species might occur within this grid cell (based on the combination of the grids listed above). This was completed for 27 selected bird species to gain the "calibrated models". The result of the training compared (greyscale) to the mapped territories (circles) is shown for the Blackbird (*Turdus merula*) in Figure 11. All areas within the city center which showed a high density of this common bird were well captured and consisted of all relevant habitat preferences such as trees and shrubs in combination with lawns. All patches that were not populated were interpreted correctly as well (sealed places, river).

For training, the 100 hectares site including the St. Pauli cemetery was left out to have an

Figure 11. Mapped occurrences of Blackbird (Turdus merula) as circle and modeled probability of occurrence (greyscale) as result of training; city center of Dresden

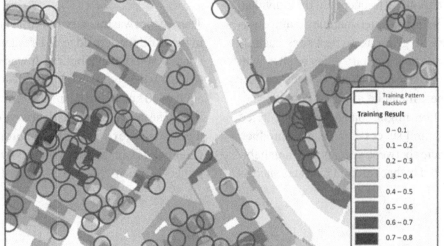

independent test site for the application of the network (Figure 12, again for Blackbird).

This test confirmed that the neural network had "learned" the relations between the occurrence of the specific bird species and the parameters from the input layers that represent the factors controlling the occurrence.

Following the training, the network was applied to the application area 10 km south of the training site.

A crucial issue to be solved was to establish a criterion for the occurrence of a territory (to be displayed as binary grid) based on the "probability grid". This was done individually for each bird species by use of a threshold value obtained during the training. The most accurate criterion was identified as median value of the histograms (probability value versus number of pixels) and differed for each species, usually between the values of p = 0.6 – 0.8.

Thus, the number of breeding pairs could be assessed with a reproducible method: After eliminating fragmented single pixels, the remaining connected pixels above the threshold were counted. The added size of these pixels was divided by the previously determined average size for a territory of the respective species (based on regional studies).

Validation

Following a visual inspection of the probability map in conjunction with the mapped territories in two available 100 hectares test sites (one in each map sheet; not included in the training of the network), a correlation between the number of territories (modeled and mapped) was analyzed for the 100 hectares site St. Pauli and the full map sheet Freital (33 km²; estimated ranges of territories were available from the 2004-07 mapping campaign). Both calculations returned similar R^2 values between 0.84 and 0.89 (see Figure 13).

Presentation of Results

The results of the study were presented as prediction maps indicating the probability of occurrence for each bird species for the map sheet and as tabular data, showing the estimated number of breeding pairs for each species.

A further result was the average composition of the territories for each species in terms of land use and habitat types. Local peculiarities for individual species were detected and discussed. The method to model bird species distribution with neural networks and GIS was generally suited but required a high initial data pre-processing supported by a local ornithologist in order to avoid nonsense correlations and to assess the data quality. The method seems to help planning large-scale bird census or to estimate bird populations in areas with restricted access. However, a comprehensive set of local training data is required.

Figure 12. Modeling results for Blackbird (Turdus merula) for test area (circles: mapped territories). Dark pixels: a cemetery/park within the densely populated city.

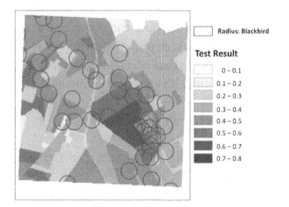

Figure 13. Correlation of the number of modeled and mapped bird territories on St. Pauli test site

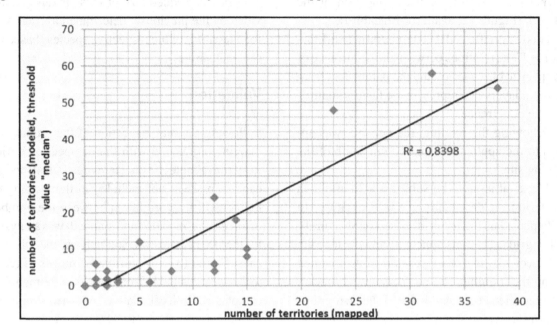

CASE STUDY 5: QUANTITATIVE PREDICTION OF MANGANESE NODULES COVERAGE DENSITY

The Federal Institute for Geosciences and Natural Resources of Germany (BGR) was contracted by the Federal Government of Germany to investigate the distribution and the economic exploitation potential of manganese nodules within two areas in the Pacific Ocean. For the assessment of the commercial value of the manganese nodule deposits in the Pacific Ocean, the knowledge of the absolute resource inventories and their spatial distribution is essential.

Since the density of the available data is not sufficient for a resource estimation using conventional methods and since it was not possible to retrieve significant relationship rules of the coverage density of manganese nodules based on the available data (bathymetry and sonic resistance), artificial neural networks were tested to estimate the mineral resources.

This case study intended to investigate the general applicability and efficiency of neural network methods with advangeo® to simulate the spatial distribution of manganese nodules. The aim of the project was to derive a methodology that enables a resource assessment of other areas with manganese nodules with the same environment conditions using the already trained artificial neural network.

Source Data and Pre-Processing

The following base data served as input data layers for the further processing and development of a prediction model/scenario. All data were provided under copyright by the Federal Institute for Geosciences and Natural Resources of Germany (BGR):

- Digital terrain model/bathymetry, in 100 meter resolution,
- Sonic resistance/backscatter, in 100 meter resolution,
- Measurement data of 39 samples of the seafloor taken by BGR with parameter coverage density in kg/m² and different element concentrations,

- Measurement data of 140 samples of the seafloor taken by PREUSSAG with parameter coverage density in kg/m^2 and different element concentrations,
- Test tracks/ship routes of measurement and sampling campaigns.

The study area is located in the tropical North Pacific Ocean and has a total area of 75,000 km^2. For further processing of the data in the frame of the project, a smaller area with a size of 23.400 km^2 was selected as pilot study area.

The data itself were available as grid data (bathymetry, backscatter) and vector data (measured tracks, measurement points). For further processing, all raster data were mapped to a uniform base grid in the coordinate system UTM zone 11N with a grid resolution of 100 m. The raster data of the absolute values of the bathymetry and the sonic resistance/ hardness were smoothed with an averaging filter to reduce the noise of the data. For the bathymetry, a 3x3 filter was used, whereas for the sonic resistance/hardness a 5x5 filter was used.

In the next processing step, the various derivatives, such as slope (first derivative), aspect and curvature (second derivative) were calculated based on absolute values of the bathymetry and sonic resistance/hardness. Furthermore, for aspect two separate grid data sets for N/S- and W/E-direction were calculated. Three variations for curvature were calculated: slope curvature (i.e. vertical curvature, curvature in the direction of the steepest gradient), aspect curvature (i.e. horizontal curvature, curvature in the direction of the contour lines), and maximum curvature. In addition, two grid data sets representing the potential morphological flow direction and flow accumulation were calculated and derived from the bathymetry.

The baseline of seamounts and the distribution of linear tectonic structures on the seafloor were digitized for the model area with the help of the bathymetry data and its derivatives. Based on these vector data, raster data were created by

calculating the Euclidian distance for each pixel representing the distance to the nearest seamount or lineament, respectively.

With respect to the raster data of the sonic resistance/hardness, a significant interference of the absolute values of the sonic resistance/hardness along the documented ship tracks/routes was observed during the data processing. For further use, and in particular the prevention of the negative influence of these values on the model result, the grid values measured along the documented ship tracks were masked with a width of 100 meters (1 pixel).

Network Parameterization

The coverage density of manganese nodules on the seafloor in kg/m^2 was modeled with the advangeo® prediction software. For this purpose, a neural networks with MLP (multi-layer-perceptron) network paradigm was trained in a supervised learning process at the location of the 29 measurement points of the coverage density executed by BGR using the areal available base data (bathymetry, backscatter, and their derivations) as model input data in a training scenario and later applied in an application scenario across the whole model area. At the beginning, simple artificial neural networks were used with just one of the available base data layers as input data. Thus, the sensitivity of the single input data layer and the direct correlation to the training data points was estimated. Based on this approach, the input data layers of the absolute value, the N/S-aspect, the flow accumulation and the vertical curvature of the bathymetry and the Euclidian distance to the seamounts and the linear tectonic structures showed the highest correlation and were used as primary input data layers in the next steps, in which different combinations of input data layers were used to set up the artificial neural network.

Finally, two model scenarios were developed based on different combination of model input data within the artificial neural network. For both model scenarios, the absolute value, the slope, the vertical curvature, the aspect in N/S-direction and the flow accumulation of the bathymetry as well as the absolute value of the backscatter data was used. In addition, for the first final model scenario, the Euclidian distance to the lineaments on the seafloor was used. For the second final model scenario, the Euclidian distance to the lineaments as well as the Euclidian distance to the seamounts was used – both with a maximum distance of 10 km.

The trained artificial neural network was then applied for both model scenarios across the whole model area and two raster files were created with a resolution of 100 meters and cell values for the coverage density in kg/m². Based on the calculation result of the spatial distribution of the coverage density in kg/m² for the whole area, it was possible to estimate the overall resources of Mn, Cu, Ni, Co, Mo, Fe and Zn in the model area. This was calculated based on the measured average metal content in the taken samples of the manganese nodules and calculated reserves of manganese nodules (Figure 14).

Validation

Both models were then compared to each other. Even though that there were differences in the spatial distribution, the total accumulated coverage density of manganese nodules within the model area only differed with less than 20% of total resources of manganese nodules in tons.

Presentation of Results

The applicability of the method of the neural networks to estimate the reserves of manganese nodules on the basis of the available measurements and base data was shown in this study.

A further improvement of the results of the modeling can be generally achieved through:

Figure 14. Prediction map of coverage density of manganese nodules in a selected part of the model area

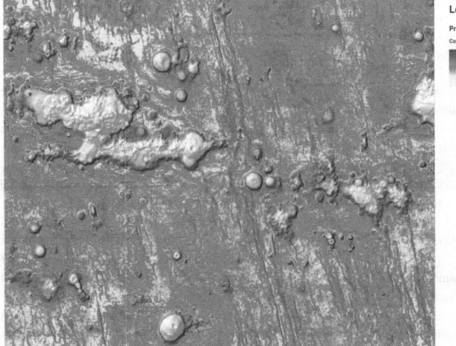

- Usage of a larger number of data for coverage density: use of photo-graphic data of the seafloor, taking new samples in a specific sampling pattern,
- Usage of advanced filtering techniques to reduce the effects in the backscatter data,
- Usage of additional input data representing other potentially influencing parameters such as sea water flow field, temperature gradients, bioactivity etc.

CONCLUSION

The case studies demonstrated that the multilayer-perceptron approach (MLP) is suitable for the analysis and prediction of various applications of spatially-dependent natural and human induced phenomenon, including the assessment of soil erosion, the identification of potential mineral occurrences, the spread of forest pests, and the distribution of bird species. The stepwise generation of model scenarios with advangeo® supported the derivation of information while taking the sensitivity of controlling factors into consideration. However, one disadvantage to this approach is its inadequate ability to explain results where the specific influences of single parameters cannot be directly retraced. All interrelations amongst factors of influence and the final result were revealed through the course of the training process. With this process, "erroneous learning" cannot be excluded. As a result, it remains a challenge to define the boundaries of neural network applications. This had already been stressed by Maier & Dandy (2000). It will be a continuing challenge for the ANN community in research to develop guidelines for ANN modelers. More emphasis must be put on sensitivity analysis (Yeung et al. 2010) and on a critical evaluation of the results with reproducible statistical measures.

To evaluate the quality of individual components of training goals and ability to generalize the input events, "expert knowledge" and the means to critically assess the outputs of the modeling process are required in addition to the generation of statistical figures on the proximity of predicted and measured values alone. The most significant advantage of the ANN is the relatively small amount of effort required for data pre-processing, model calibration and short model run times. As such the new tool used for the five case studies enables standard GIS users to apply ANN approaches that are fully integrated with their already familiar work environment.

ACKNOWLEDGMENT

The authors sincerely thank the Independent Commission for Mines and Minerals (ICMM) in Kosovo, the German Federal Institute for Geosciences and Natural Resources (BGR), the Staatsbetrieb Sachsenforst (State Agency for Forestry of Saxony/Germany) and the Landesamt für Umwelt, Landwirtschaft und Geologie (Saxon State Office for the Environment, Agriculture and Geology) for their expressed authorization to present proprietary project data and figures in this article. The research project was supported by the Federal Ministry of Economics and Technology, Germany (project identification number IW072061).

REFERENCES

Alavi, A. H., Gandomi, A. H., Mollahassani, A., Heshmati, A. A., & Rashed, A. (2010). Modeling of maximum dry density and optimum moisture content of stabilized soil using artificial neural networks. *Journal of Plant Nutrition and Soil Science, 173*, 368–379. doi:10.1002/jpln.200800233

Anković, S., Jelenković, R., & Vujić, S. (2003). *Mineral Resources and Potential Prognosis of metallic and non-metallic mineral raw materials in Serbia and Montenegro at the end of the XXth Century*. Engineering Academy of Serbia and Montenegro, Section of Mining and Geology Sciences.

Austin, G. E., Thomas, C. J., Houston, D. C., & Thompson, D. B. A. (1996). Predicting the Spatial Distribution of Buzzard Buteo buteo Nesting Areas Using a Geographical Information System and Remote Sensing. *Journal of Applied Ecology*, *33*(6), 1541–1550. doi:10.2307/2404792

Backhaus, K., Erichson, B., Plinke, W., & Weiber, R. (2003). *Multivariate Analysemethoden – eine anwendungsorientierte Einführung*. Berlin: Springer-Verlag.

Baier, P., Pennerstorfer, J., & Schopf, A. (2007). PHENIPS – A comprehensive phenology model of Ips typographus (L.) (Col., Scolytinae) as a tool for hazard rating of bark beetle infestation. *Forest Ecology and Management*, *249*(3), 171–186. doi:10.1016/j.foreco.2007.05.020

Barth, A., Noack, S., Legler, C., Seib, N., & Rexhaj, A. (2010). Rohstoffprognosekarten mit Verfahren der künstlichen Intelligenz – Fortschrittliche Identifizierung von Rohstoffpotentialen in Entwicklungs- und Schwellenländern. *Glück Auf*, *146*, 140–147.

Behrens, T., Förster, H., Scholten, T., Steinrücken, U., Spies, E., & Goldschmitt, M. (2005). Digital Soil Mapping using artifical neural networks. *Journal of Plant Nutrition and Soil Science*, *168*, 21–33. doi:10.1002/jpln.200421414

Bishop, M. C. (2008). *Neural Networks for Pattern Recognition*. Oxford University Press.

Bougrain, L., Gonzalez, M., Bouchot, V., Cassard, D., Lips, A. L. W., Alexandre, F., & Stein, G. (2003). Knowledge Recovery for Continental-Scale Mineral Exploration by Neural Networks. *Natural Resources Research*, *12*(3), 173–181. doi:10.1023/A:1025123920475

Brown, W., Groves, D., & Gedeon, T. (2003). Use of Fuzzy Membership Input Layers to Combine Subjective Geological Knowledge and Empirical Data in a Neural Network Method for Mineral-Potential Mapping. *Natural Resources Research*, *12*(3), 183–200. doi:10.1023/A:1025175904545

Brown, W. M., Gedeon, T. N., Groves, D. I., & Barnes, R. G. (2000). Artificial Neural Networks: A new method for mineral prospectivity mapping. *Australian Journal of Earth Sciences*, *47*, 757–770. doi:10.1046/j.1440-0952.2000.00807.x

Carranza, J. M. (2009). *Geochemical Anomaly and Mineral Prospectivity Mapping in GIS: Handbook of Exploration and Environmental Geochemistry* (Vol. 11). Elsevier. doi:10.1016/S1874-2734(09)70004-X

Favis-Mortlock. (2005). *Soil Erosion Site*. Retrieved October 24, 2010, from http://soilerosion.net/

Fernandez-Steeger, T. M. (2002). *Erkennung von Hangrutschungssystemen mit Neuronalen Netzen als Grundlage für Georisikoanalysen*. (Unpublished doctoral dissertation). Universität Karlsruhe.

Goethals, P. L. M., Dedecker, A. P., Gabriels, W., Lek, S., & De Pauw, N. (2007). Applications of artificial neural networks predicting macroinvertebrates in freshwaters. *Aquatic Ecology*, *41*, 491–508. doi:10.1007/s10452-007-9093-3

Gottschalk, T. K., Aue, B., Hotes, S., & Ekschmitt, K. (2011). Influence of grain size on species-habitat models. *Ecological Modelling*, 222(18), 3403–3412. doi:10.1016/j.ecolmodel.2011.07.008

Hassoun. (1995). *Fundamentals of Artificial Neural Networks*. MIT Press.

Haykins, S. (1998). *Neural Networks: A Comprehensive Foundation* (2nd ed.). Prentice Hall.

Hertwig, T., Müller, I., & Zeißler, K.-O. (2010). *Management of contaminated soils in urban areas in the ore mountains (Germany)*. Paper presented at ConSoil 2010, 11th International Conference on Management of Soil, Groundwater and Sediment. Salzburg, Austria. Retrieved October 24, 2010, from http://www.beak.de/advangeo/sites/default/files/file/CONSOIL_20100924_Presentation.pdf

Huffman, W. S. (2007). *Using neural networks to forecast flood events: A proof of concept*. (Doctoral Dissertation). Nova Southeastern University. Retrieved October 24, 2010, from www.wardsystems.com/Docs/Ward'sRevisedDissertation.doc

Kasabov, N. K. (1996). *Foundations of neural networks, fuzzy logic, and knowledge engineering*. MIT Press.

Knobloch, A., Schmidt, F., Zeidler, M.K., & Barth, A. (2010). *Creation of high resolution soil parameter data by use of artificial neural network technology (advangeo®)*. GeoFARMatics.

Koike, K., Matsuda, S., Suzuki, T., & Ohmi, M. (2002). Neural Network-Based Estimation of Principal Metal Contents in the Hokuroku District, Northern Japan, for Exploring Kuroko-Type Deposits. *Natural Resources Research*, 11(2), 135–156. doi:10.1023/A:1015520204066

Kriesel, D. (2009). *A Brief Introduction to Neural Networks*. Retrieved December 30, 2009, from http://www.dkriesel.com

Lamothe, D. (2009). *Assessment of the mineral potential for porphyry Cu-Au ± Mo deposits in the Baie-James region*. Document published by Géologie Québec (EP 2009-02). Retrieved October 24, 2010, from http://collections.banq.qc.ca/ark:/52327/bs1905189

Legler, C., Knobloch, A., & Barth, A. (2008). *Map of Minerals – Metallogenic / Minerogenic Map (1: 200,000) - Final Report – Map Description*. Beak Consultants GmbH.

LfULG. (2012). *Biotoptypen- und Landnutzungskartierung (BTLNK): Interactive map and link to dissemination of digital data*. Retrieved April 2012 from http://www.umwelt.sachsen.de/umwelt/natur/25140.htm

Lin, S.-W., Sun, C.-H., & Chen, C.-H. (2004). Temporal Data Mining using Genetic Algorithm and Neural Network: A Case Study of Air Pollutant Forecasts. *Geospatial Information Science*, 3, 31–38. doi:10.1007/BF02826674

Maier, H. R., & Dandy, G. C. (2000). Neural networks for the prediction and forecasting of water resources variables: A review of modelling issues and applications. *Environmental Modelling & Software*, 15, 101–124. doi:10.1016/S1364-8152(99)00007-9

Manel, S., Dias, J. M., Buckton, S. T., & Ormerod, S. J. (1999). Alternative methods for predicting species distribution: an illustration with Himalayan river birds. *Journal of Applied Ecology*, 36(5), 734–747. doi:10.1046/j.1365-2664.1999.00440.x

Maravelias, C. D., Haralabous, J., & Papaconstantinou, C. (2003). Predicting demersal fish species distributions in the Mediterranean Sea using artificial neural networks. *Marine Ecology Progress Series*, 255, 249–258. doi:10.3354/meps255249

Metelka, V., Baratoux, L., Jessell, M., Barth, A., & Naba, S. (2011). *Regolith landform mapping in western Burkina Faso, using airborne geophysics and remote sensing data in a neural network*. Retrieved January 21, 2013, from http://www.beak.de/advangeo/sites/default/files/file/CAG23/Abstracts_Metelka_CAG23%20final_updated.pdf

Mining Journal. (2009, July 17). Kosovo ready to roll. *Mining Journal,* 14-15.

Negnevitsky, M. (2002). *Artificial intelligence: a guide to intelligent systems*. Pearson Education Ltd.

Netherer, S., & Nopp-Mayr, U. (2005). Predisposition assessment systems (PAS) as supportive tools in forest management – rating of site and stand-related hazards of bark beetle infestation in the High Tatra Mountains as an example for system application and verification. *Forest Ecology and Management, 207*, 99–107. doi:10.1016/j.foreco.2004.10.020

Nissen, S. (2009). *Fast Artificial Neural Network Library (FANN)*. Retrieved December 30, 2009, from http://leenissen.dk/fann/

Noack, S., & Otto, L.-F. (2010). *Erste Ergebnisse einer Prognose der Befallswahrscheinlichkeit von Waldbeständen durch den Buchdrucker (Ips typographus L.) mittels eines künstlichen neuronalen Netzes*. Paper presented at Forstwissenschaften: Grundlage nachhaltiger Waldbewirtschaftung. Göttingen, Germany. Retrieved October 24, 2010, from http://www.beak.de/advangeo/advangeo_prediction/news/fowi_2010

Penning de Vries, F. W. T., Agus, F., & Kerr, J. (Eds.). (1998). *Soil erosion at multiple scales: Principles and methods for assessing causes and impacts*. CABI Publishing.

Peters, R., Schmitz, G., & Cullmann, J. (2006). Flood routing modelling with Artificial Neural Networks. *Advances in Geosciences, 9*, 131–136. doi:10.5194/adgeo-9-131-2006

Poirazidis, K., Goutner, V., Skartsi, T., & Stamou, G. (2003). Modelling nesting habitat as a conservation tool for the Eurasian black vulture (Aegypius monachus) in Dadia nature Reserve, northeastern Greece. *Biological Conservation, 118*, 235–248. doi:10.1016/j.biocon.2003.08.016

Redford, S., Lipton, G., & Ugalde, H. (2004). Predictive Ore Deposit Targeting Using Neural Network Analysis. *Society of Exploration Geophysicists (SEG). Expanded Abstracts, 23*, 1198.

Rios, D. (2010). *Neural networks: A requirement for intelligent systems*. Retrieved August 10, 2010, from http://www.learnartificialneuralnetworks.com/backpropagation.html

Römer, T. (2012). *GIS-gestützte Analyse der Beziehungen zwischen Biotop- und Landnutzungstypen sowie Brutvorkommen ausgewählter Vogelarten*. (Unpublished Master Thesis). Hochschule für Technik und Wirtschaft (University of Applied Sciences for Engineering and Economy), Dresden, Germany.

Rumelhart, D. E., Hinton, G. E., & Williams, R. J. (1986). Learning internal representations by error propagation. In *Parallel distributed processing: explorations in the microstructure of cognition*. MIT Press.

Seidl, R., Baier, P., Rammer, W., Schopf, A., & Lexer, M. J. (2007). Modelling tree mortality by bark beetle infestation in Norway spruce forests. *Ecological Modelling, 206*, 383–399. doi:10.1016/j.ecolmodel.2007.04.002

Stockburger, D. W. (1998). *Multivariate Statistics: Concepts, Models, and Applications*. Missouri State University. Retrieved October 24, 2010, from http://www.psychstat.missouristate.edu/multibook/mlt00.htm

Sühnel, T., & Schmidt, F. (2013). Analyse der Zusammenhänge zwischen Biotoptyp- u. Landnutzungsdaten sowie Revieren verschiedener Vogelarten mit Hilfe von Geo-Informationssystemen und neuronalen Netzen. *Actitis, 47*.

Wilson, J. P., & Gallant, J. C. (Eds.). (2000). *Terrain Analysis: Principles and Applications.* New York: Wiley.

Wischmeier, W. H., & Smith, D. D. (1978). Predicting rainfall erosion losses – a guide to conservation planning. In USDA Agriculture Handbook (No. 537, pp. 1-58). USDA.

Yeung, D. S., Cloete, I., Shi, D., & Ng, W. W. Y. (2010). *Sensitivity Analysis for Neural Networks: Natural Computing Series VIII.* Springer Science and Business Media. doi:10.1007/978-3-642-02532-7

Chapter 9
Multidimensional Data Analysis Based on Links:
Models and Languages

Paulo Caetano da Silva
Salvador University, Brazil

ABSTRACT

Analytical processing (OLAP) tools typically only deal with relational data. Hence, the analytical processing systems on XML data do not have all the functionality provided by OLAP tools to traditional data (i.e. relational). In addition, current commercial and academic OLAP tools do not process XML data that contains XLink. Therefore, there is a need to develop a solution for OLAP systems in order to assist in the strategic analysis of the organizational data represented in XML format. Aiming at overcoming this issue, this chapter proposes an analytical system composed by LMDQL (Link-Based Multidimensional Query Language), an analytical query language; XLDM (XLink Data Metamodel), a metamodel given to model cubes of XML documents with XLink and to deal with syntactic, semantic, and structural heterogeneities commonly found in XML documents; and XLPath (XLink Path Language), a navigation language for XML documents connected by XLink. As current W3C query languages for navigating in XML documents do not support XLink, XLPath is discussed in this chapter to provide features for the LMDQL query processing and a prototype system enabling OLAP queries over XML documents linked by XLink and XML schema. This prototype includes a driver, named sql2xquery, which performs the mapping of SQL queries into XQuery in a relational OLAP server. In order to validate the proposed system, a case study and its performance evaluation are presented to analyze the impact of analytical processing over XML/XLink documents.

INTRODUCTION

The current software applications usually have to deal with multiple sources and data formats. To minimize this problem, XML - eXtensible Markup Language (XML, 1998) was adopted as a way to integrate the data into a standard format. The use of XML as an alternative to integration of heterogeneous data sources has become this technology a de facto standard for data exchange on the Internet. XML documents are a rich source of information for organizational decision mak-

DOI: 10.4018/978-1-4666-6098-4.ch009

ing. Similarly, the use of Data Warehouses (DW) (Kimball, 2002) and OLAP (On-Line Analytical Processing) tools (Chaudhuri, 1997) allows the identification of tendencies and standards, in order to conduct better strategic decisions for companies businesses. However, the use of these technologies, together, is still in development process.

In XML, it is possible to represent information semantically similar in different ways. This leads to three kinds of data heterogeneity: (i) semantic, where similar information is represented through different names, e.g. enterprise and company, or dissimilar information through equal names, e.g. virus in the informatics field and in the health field; (ii) syntactic, where the semantically equal content is represented in several ways. For example, in different languages or in diverse measure units, e.g. meters and feet; and (iii) structural, in which data is organized in different structures, e.g. in different kinds of hierarchies, in attributes, or in elements (Näppilä, 2008). This representation flexibility is important, however, it makes the use of OLAP concepts in XML data a complex task. Applications and technologies, derived from XML, use XLink (XML Linking Language) (XLink, 2001) as an alternative for representing the information semantic and structure, expressing relationships between concepts. An example of how the data semantic is represented using XLink is XBRL (eXtensible Business Reporting Language) (Hernández-Ros, 2006), an international standard for representing financial reports that uses extended links for modeling financial concepts. A problem that occurs when processing documents, which have XLink and correspond to chains of links, is that the W3C (World Wide Web Consortium) available query languages (i.e. XQuery (XQuery, 2007) and XPath (XPath, 2007)) do not provide support for navigating on them. Although XPath has been widely adopted as query standard in XML documents, it does not provide such navigation functionality. Several proposals have been developed for performing the analytical queries (OLAP) over XML data (Beyer, 2005;

Bordawekar, 2005; Näppilä, 2008; Wang, 2007; Jian, 2007). However, these proposals do not take the use of XLink in XML documents into account.

In conventional OLAP server, the data cube is mapped from a relational DW. Queries on the data cube, which are usually expressed through MDX - Multidimensional Expressions (MDX, 2008), an industry standard, are converted into SQL queries that are executed directly in relational DBMS (Databases Management System). However, for information extraction in XML documents, OLAP solutions or for transaction processing (OLTP - Online Transaction Processing) are still poorly developed.

This chapter presents an analytical processing system for XML documents supported by XLink. This system is based on XLDM (XLink-based Multidimensional Metamodel), a metamodel suitable for solving XML heterogeneities, XLPath (Silva, 2010), a navigational language, an XPath extension for navigation over links, LMDQL (Link-based and Multidimensional Query Language) (Silva, 2009b), a multidimensional query language, and a process to convert SQL into XQuery queries, implemented by the *sql2xquery* driver. With the purpose of providing analytical processing of XML data, the *mondrain* OLAP server (Mondrian, 2008) has been extended by incorporating this driver. The choice of this tool is due to the fact of being an open source OLAP server used in various solutions for Business Intelligence (BI) and be extended and developed in Java, which makes it independent of computer platform. Another reason for choosing this server is that it is compatible with MDX, an industry standard for OLAP queries.

From the analysis of the related proposals discussed in this article, the existence of a query language to XML data, which allows the following, has not been verified: (i) uses a collection of XML documents; (ii) considers the existence of linkbases, as groups of links and source of information; (iii) is based on a data model, defined by XML Schema and XLink, to solve heterogeneity conflicts in XML. For these reasons, the development of an OLAP system for XML, which uses XLink, consists in the motivation to perform this research.

Following some of the most important OLAP proposals for XML data and SQL translators for XQuery are discussed and the metamodel XLDM, XLPath language and LMDQL query language specification are presented. The analytical system for XML and XLink is detailed together with a driver to convert SQL queries into XQuery. After approaches a case study and performance results are discussed. Conclusions and future work are given at the end of this paper.

OLAP FOR XML DOCUMENTS

In this section, some proposals for analytical processing in XML data are discussed. In order to make easier the selection of an appropriated model when designing applications that combine OLAP and XML technologies, Ravat et al. (Ravat, 2010) discuss different proposals that use these technologies. This discussion covers since the use of XML data incorporated in traditional data warehouses until those that use XML as a complete solution for warehousing processes. In this proposal, Ravat et al consider two types of documents, those based on data and those based on textual information (data-centric XML documents and document-centric XML documents, respectively). The documents based on data have a regular structure, as occurs in relational data. The text centered documents, however, are less structured than the first ones. They are rich text documents and are not adapted to the information exchange among applications. Based on this document classification, the distinction between two types of data warehouses based on XML is made: (i) XML data warehouse, which uses XML documents based on data and (ii) XML document warehouse, whose documents are based on texts. The work presented in this text focuses on the first approach.

In XQ-Cube (Park, 2005), a data warehouse data model based on a set of XML documents is presented. However, it is not defined how the data are structured in the documents for the data cube specification. A query language, named XML-MDX, is also presented, using XQuery expressions to handle numeric and textual data. XAggregation (Wang, 2007), based on XPath expressions, allows performing queries in different hierarchic structures. Therefore, the aggregation operation in XML documents is done using XPath expressions that take into account hierarchic differences. Jian et al. present IX-Cube (Jian, 2007), a data cube derived from XML documents, and methods to handle it. Since this approach is based on XPath, easiness is provided to users, for building XML data cubes and for analytical queries specification. However, this work requires the user's previous knowledge about possible hierarchic structures, and a multidimensional scheme for XML documents has not been defined. Also, queries are related to a single XML document, but not to a document collection, as occurs in many database applications. Bordawekar (2005) present an OLAP-XML proposal, which comprehends two kinds of queries: based on values or on structure. The first kind specifies the contents of an XML document, which can be the value of attributes or text-type nodes. The second one specifies query standards based on possible existing paths found in XML documents. The operator X^3, presented in (Wiwatwattana, 2007), has been defined to consider possible structure variations in XML document trees. Then, operators to handle hierarchic structures were established and XQuery was extended to use such operators. However, all the proposals outlined so far have the common characteristic of not approaching the use of XLink in XML documents, and some of them do not perform queries in more than one document, nor on the schema of a data cube.

Many papers analyses how to design a better data warehouse for XML data, some of them show systematic steps to build a XML data warehouse and others consider developing a model for designing and representations issues of it. For example, Taniar et al (Taniar, 2004, 2005a, 2005b, 2006, 2009, 2011) proposes a methodology on building XML data warehouses covering data warehousing processes such as extracting XML data from object-relational database, data cleaning and integration, summarization and updating and creating fact tables. These papers refers to modeling XML data warehouse based on XML documents linked. Forthwith, two proposals for data cube modeling, based on XML, are approached. X-Cube is a standardization proposal for XML documents (Hümmer, 2003), in which schemas are presented for dimensions, facts and cubes representation. It has the inherent advantages to a standardized environment, making easy the re-use of documents in different application domains. The syntactic content difference is partially solved in X-Cube, by the use of the units attribute, which represents information that have different units. However, the treatment given to similar contents, written in different languages, is not shown, thus partially solving data syntactic heterogeneity. XBRL Dimensions (Hernández-Ros, 2006) is a specification that models a cube based on financial data. This method is based on: (i) a vocabulary definition, specified through XML Schema (XML Schema, 2004); and (ii) relationships, based on linkbases and XLink, which express the document hierarchic structure, the dimensions and its members, labels in several languages for each vocabulary element and other kinds of relations. However, the use of linkbases is not mandatory, which implies the partial solution of XML data heterogeneity problems. XCube and XBRL Dimensions propose a multidimensional model for XML data cubes, though, do not approach the analytical process over such data. A data cube model pXCube was proposed to avoid join operation between dimension and fact data by determining unity path with dimension computation, reducing query cost (Liu

et al., 2012). A calculation method was presented to get unity path and some common OLAP algorithms in pXCube. However, heterogeneity in XML data has not been addressed in this cube.

In Table 1, a comparison among the proposals analyzed in this section is presented, regarding the issues of the data model and the treatment given to the heterogeneity existent in XML. Although the structural heterogeneity was considered on proposals XQ-Cube, OLAP XML X^3 Cube and pXCube, it is restricted to only one XML document. The proposals XCube, XBRL *Dimensions* and Xaggregation seek to solve this issue to allow the accomplishment of analytical queries in more than one document, but do not approach all the heterogeneity issues existent in XML data. The proposals XQ-Cube and XQuery extension have not solved the structural heterogeneity. One may observe that IX-Cube, OLAP XML, X^3 Cube, and XQuery extension approaches do not propose or make use of a data model for OLAP cubes and for the XML document. In spite of XQ-Cube present a solution for the data cube creation, for the XML document, a model to be adopted is not defined. It implicates the heterogeneity problems occurrence in XML data.

Table 2 presents a comparison among the proposals regarding the OLAP queries over XML documents. This comparison is carried out based on the characteristics considered relevant for the development of an OLAP solution for XML. X-Cube and XBRL *Dimensions* do not approach the issues related to the OLAP queries, for that, they were excluded from this comparative table. The other proposals have the common characteristic of do not consider the use of *links* among XML documents, since the technologies used, XPath and XQuery, for the solutions elaboration, do not navigate among XML documents.

Although X-Cube does not consider the XLink use, it uses cube, dimensions and fact, as done in the metamodel proposed here. XBRL Dimensions

Table 1. XML data heterogeneity treatment in OLAP- XML proposals

Correlate Proposals	Semantic Heterogeneity	Syntactic Heterogeneity of Content	Structural Heterogeneity	Data Model for the Data Cubes	Data Model for the XML Document
X – Cube	No	Partially	Yes	Yes	Yes
XBRL *Dimensions*	Partially	Partially	Partially	Yes	Yes
XQ – Cube	No	No	No	Yes	No
Xaggregation	No	No	Yes	No	No
IX – Cube	No	No	Yes	No	No
OLAP-XML	No	No	Yes	No	No
X^3 Cube	No	No	Yes	No	No
XQuery Extension	No	No	No	No	No
pXCube	No	No	Yes	No	No

Table 2. Queries characteristics in OLAP: XML proposals

Correlate Proposal	Queries Based on Value	Queries Based on Structure	Queries Over More than One XML Document	Queries Over Data Cube	Queries Based on MDX	Queries Based on XLink
XQ – Cube	Yes	No	Yes	Yes	Yes	No
Xaggregation	Yes	Yes	Yes	No	No	No
IX – Cube	Yes	Yes	No	Yes	No	No
OLAP-XML	Yes	Yes	No	No	No	No
X^3 Cube	Yes	Yes	No	No	No	No
XQuery Extension	Yes	No	Yes	No	No	No
pXCube	Yes	Yes	No	Yes	No	No

uses XLink, however it has its model designed for a specific domain application. Also, all the other proposals discussed here are not able to integrate the multidimensional data model with XML, so that the problems regarding XML heterogeneity are not solved.

As it can be seen, none of the above mentioned proposals allow the representation and processing of multidimensional data cubes based on both XML documents and XLink to solve the heterogeneity problems of semi-structured data. The present work proposes an analytical tool to process XML documents and XLink that are modeled as multidimensional data cubes.

CONVERTING SQL IN XQUERY

Some translators SQL to XQuery are found in the literature, but they are proprietary and the source code is not available: Aqualogic (BEA, 2013), Rox (Halverson, 2004), IBM DB2 (IBM, 2010), QuiLogic (QuiLogic's, 2001), Ipedo XIP (Ipedo Inc., 2013), SparQL (Fishcer et al., 2011).

The SQL Server DBMS, with paid license and unavailable code, and Postgres, open source, provide resources (functions) for performing the process of converting SQL queries to XQuery. Both support the XML data type and support XQuery. The DBMS MySQL, open source, suit the need of executing XQuery expressions on XML data, simulates via XPath expressions in String data type doing serialization of the content of the XML files, compromising their native semantic structure. These DBMSs do not support directly MDX expressions, suitable for OLAP queries.

Translators with XQuery interface are found in the literature: Ope XQSQL (Ope XQSQL, 2011), Zorba XQuery (Zorba, 2012), Saxon 7.5 (Kay, 2003), Relational XQuery 1.6 (Relational XQuery, 2006), all with available code and license free use. However, since OLAP tools use MDX expressions, which are converted to SQL expressions, these translators were not deemed appropriate tools for the proposed environment, due to its native XQuery interface. The Optiq translators (Hyde, 2012), MongoSQL (Schnable, 2013), MongoJDBCDriver (Manning, 2013), also open source, despite possessing SQL interface were not considered because the conversion process to JSON expressions (JavaScript Object Notation), which are used in databases oriented to JSON documents such as MongoDB and CouchDB (Apache CouchDB, 2013).

The work of Rodrigues et al. (Rodrigues, 2012) and Chang et al. (Chang et al., 2011) present solutions for the mapping of SQL to XQuery based on abstract syntax trees (AST). However, these works do not include the mapping of the AST generated by SQL queries from MDX expressions. The *sql2xquery* driver, presented in this work, considers the multidimensional queries environment, which allows that OLAP queries, i.e. MDX, are directly converted into XQuery expressions.

MODELING AND QUERYING XML AND XLINK

Aiming at performing analytical queries in XML documents that use XLink to express semantic relationships, it is proposed a computation environment based on: (i) a data metamodel that solves XML data heterogeneity issues, called XLDM; (ii) XLPath, a language for navigation

in links, created from XML Schema and XLink technologies; and (iii) an analytical query language, namely LMDQL.

The XLDM Metamodel

Gotlob (2003) defines a data model based on XML documents and a set of binary relations to propose an algorithm that evaluates XPath (XPath, 2007) expressions and optimizes the queries on these documents, regarding time and storage space needed to perform them. XML document is described as a non-classified tree, i.e. a tree with an arbitrary number of children, ordered and labeled, in which each child node is ordered, and each node has a label. The document tree is represented by a set of binary relations, whose axes are the ones from XPath language (e.g. self, child, parent, descendent). As a result, the data model defined allows the navigation in XML documents, performed by XPath language, which is the core mechanism for XML nodes addressing from other technologies, such as XQuery (Libkin, 2003) and XPointer (Grosso, 2003). Motivated by the use of XML applications, Barceló´ (2005) and Libkin (2003, 2006) analyze query languages for XML trees, based on the same document definition given before, and presents a group of definitions to handle XML data. These authors refer to several other papers that consider naturally modeled XML data as non-classified trees, and also conceptualize an XML document. Boussaid (2006) proposes a technology that specifies data warehouses, whose data model is based on a mathematic formalization performed through XML Schema, for star and snow-flake models logical definition.

The concepts presented by Gotlob, Libkin and Boussaid define the XML document, navigation functions and a formalization for data warehouse typical models, i.e. star schema and snowflake schema. These definitions are considered, in this paper, for the multidimensional metamodel based on XML Schema and XLink. They were extended to include the relations among two or more documents, through links, and to allow that new definitions be given to represent the existence of relationships between XML documents.

A multidimensional metamodel is presented for applications that use XML as an information source. Initially, mathematical definitions, which allow a non-ambiguous metamodel specification, are given. Then the set of XML documents, based on XML Schema and XLink, that compose the XLDM specifications proposed here is discussed.

Formal Definitions for XLDM

Definition 1: A rooted tree, ordered and non-classified, is a tree with unlimited child quantity, on which to each node is given a unique label, and that is an N* element (i.e. a finite string of natural numbers). Then, a rooted, ordered, labeled and non-classified tree T is defined as $(D, <_{pre})$ where:

1. The element $\varepsilon \in D$ (an empty string) is the root;
2. D is a set of nodes, named tree domain, which is a subset of N*, such $g \in D$, implies $b \in D$, if and only if $b <_{pre} g$. The relation $<_{pre}$ defines the order of the document, i.e. is the pre-fixed relation with the elements of D, being $b <_{pre} g$, if and only if the only way from the root to g goes through b.

Besides the relationship between nodes, in a given XML document, the relationships between nodes of two different documents are also defined. That is why the inclusion of Rσ is necessary in the XML document definition, which is a data structure that can be defined as follows.

Definition 2: An XML document d is represented as a 5-tuple $(T, \beta, \lambda, R\chi, R\sigma)$, where:

1. $T = (D, <_{pre})$ is the rooted, ordered, labeled and non-classified tree;

2. β is a set of tags (XML elements);
3. $\lambda: D \rightarrow \beta$ is a function that assigns a node in T on each XML tag;
4. $R\chi$ is a set of binary relations on β, e.g. parent, child and sibling;
5. $R\sigma$ is a set of binary relations on $\beta' x \beta''$, where β' and β'' are groups of tags from distinct XML documents, d' and d'', respectively, with $d' \neq d''$, $d' \subset D$ and $d'' \subset D$.

Definitions 1 and 2 are exemplified in Figure 1, assuming that the trees shown in this figure represent the documents d' and d'', the nodes ε and b are elements which have a binary relationship $\chi_{\varepsilon-b} \in R\chi$, such as *parent-child relationship*, and among the documents there is a relationship $\sigma_{b-a'} \in R\sigma$, established by the elements b and a'.

Definition 3: Taking into account that d is an XML document $(T, \beta, \lambda, R\chi, R\sigma)$, in a relation to $\chi \in R\chi$, and $\rho(\beta)$ as a subset of β, the function $f_\chi: \rho(\beta) \rightarrow P(\beta)$ is defined, with $f_\chi(X) = \{y \in \beta \mid \exists x \in X$, such that $(x,y) \in \chi\}$. Then the relation name could be overridden, such as $f_{child.}$

Definition 4: Being d' and d'' two XML documents $(T', \beta', \lambda', R\chi', R\sigma')$ and $(T'', \beta'', \lambda'', R\chi'', R\sigma'')$, respectively. For a relation $\sigma \in R\sigma'$ in d', the function $g_\sigma: P(\beta') \rightarrow P(\beta'')$ is defined by $g_\sigma(X) = \{y \in \beta'' \mid \exists x \in X$, such that $(x,y) \in \sigma\}$.

An XML document consists of element structures, which contain sub-elements and attributes. The attributes are added to the elements opening declarations (tag). Between an opening and a closing tag, there may be any number of sub-elements. The attributes can be used to make reference among elements or between elements and other XML documents. According to these properties, the following definitions are used to represent the data cube metamodel proposed in this work.

Figure 1. Relationships between the documents d´ and d´´ and among their elements

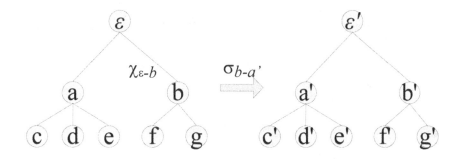

Definition 5: Being (F,S) a data warehouse (DW) schema, where F is a set of facts having *m* measures, {F.M_q, $1 \leq q \leq$ m), and a set of independent dimensions *r*, S = {S_s, $1 \leq s \leq$ r), where each S_s contains a group of i domains, {$S_s.I_j$, $1 \leq j \leq$ i} and each I_j contains a group of n members, {$I_j.N_p$, $1 \leq p \leq$ n}. The (F, S) schema is composed of schemas and linkbases documents.

1. F defines a set of fact tags;
2. S defines a set of dimension tags;
3. I defines a set of domain tags of a dimension;
4. N defines a set of member tags of a domain;
5. H defines a set of hypercube tags;
6. M defines a set of measures for a fact;
7. L is a set of linkbases documents, represented as a 5-tuple (*T*, β, λ, *R*χ, *R*σ);
8. ∀s ∈ {1,...,r}, S_s defines elements associated to facts f ∈ F;
9. ∀s ∈ {1,...,r} and ∀i ∈ {1,..., i_j}, $S_s.I_j$ defines relationships between dimensions and domains.
10. ∀i ∈ {1,..., i_j} and ∀n ∈ {1,..., n_p}, $I_j.N_p$ defines relationships between domains and members.

As the definition of XLink allows types of relationships between elements, by the use of the attribute *xlink:arcrole*, this is used for the defini-

tion of relationships between elements representing members, domains, dimensions, facts and cubes (Definition 6).

Definition 6: Considering *l* ∈ L, a linkbase (*T*, β, λ, *R*χ, *R*σ), the following relations are defined in *l*.

1. Domain-member: ∀n ∈ N, f_χ(n) = {i ∈ I | ∃n∈N, such that (n,i) ∈χ};
2. Dimension-domain:∀i ∈ I, f_χ(i) = {s ∈ S | ∃i∈I, such that (i,s) ∈χ};
3. Hypercube-dimension:∀s ∈ S, f_χ(s) = {h ∈ H | ∃s∈S, such that (s,h) ∈χ};
4. *All* and *not-all*: ∀n ∈ N, f_χ(n) = {f ∈ F | ∃n∈ N, tal que (n,f) ∈χ}.

Figure 2 shows how the relationships defined by Definition 6 can be established. Each circle represents a node, which correspond to an XML element. The lines that connect the nodes represent the possible relationship types that can exist between the elements. The *domain-member* relationship connects elements that are part of a domain. The *dimension-domain* relationship links the domain to the dimension. The *hypercube-dimension* relationship connects the fact to the dimension. Lastly, the relationships *all* and *not-all* state, for a given fact, if or not all domain members are part of the hypercube. These relationships are established in the XLDM metamodel through linkbases.

Figure 2. Relationships between the trees that represent the documents d´ and d´´

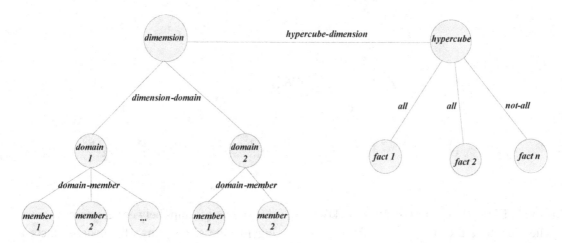

Definition 7: Allow d to be an XML document (T, β, λ, $R\chi$, $R\sigma$). An hypercube is defined as $\{\forall h \in H \mid H \subseteq d\}$ and $\{\forall f \in F \mid F \subseteq d\}$, and there is a function $f_\chi(f) = \{h \in H \mid \exists f \in F$, such that $(f,h) \in \chi\}$.

The XML formalism allows inserting sub-elements multi-levels into an XML element and establishing relationships, through XLink, which define hierarchies among elements. Thus, the definition of the *domain-member* relationship allows building hierarchies in a dimension. For example, one dimension *country* can have a *domain-member* relationship with the element *Brazil*, then, this one can have the same kind of relationship with other elements, e.g. *Brazil and south*, *Brazil* and *northeast*. Based on the definitions discussed in this section, documents that compose the XLDM metamodel specification were created. Next, the XLDM document specifications are discussed.

XLDM Documents

It is noticed that, due to the inherent XML technology flexibility, different data cube metamodels for data warehouses based on XML can be specified. For this reason, XML data heterogeneity problems are made evident. However, the use of XLink and

XML Schema can solve such problems through the specification of dimensions, facts and cubes. The proposed multidimensional metamodel is based on the definitions presented in section "Formal Definitions for XLDM" and extend XBRL *Dimensions* concepts. To do so, *instance-schema.xsd* and linkbase-*schema.xsd* documents have been specified, based on these definitions, and are available at http://www.cin.ufpe.br/~pcs3/XLDM/Spec.

An XML database with Xlink is made of schemas, linkbases and XML instances, i.e. XML documents with data. The first ones specify the elements that represent the facts, the dimensions, the dimension members and the cubes. The linkbases define the relationships between members, dimensions and facts, establishing combinations of cubes that can exist in the instance. In the instance, the facts occur and, combined with dimension members, determine a data cube.

The XML instance document, which may contain one or more cubes, has a structural dimension, where the contexts are presented with the dimension members. There is also a non-dimensional structure, with the facts measures. Figure 3 shows the UML components diagram for the XLDM metamodel proposed in this section. This figure illustrates the data organization

Figure 3. The XLDM multidimensional metamodel

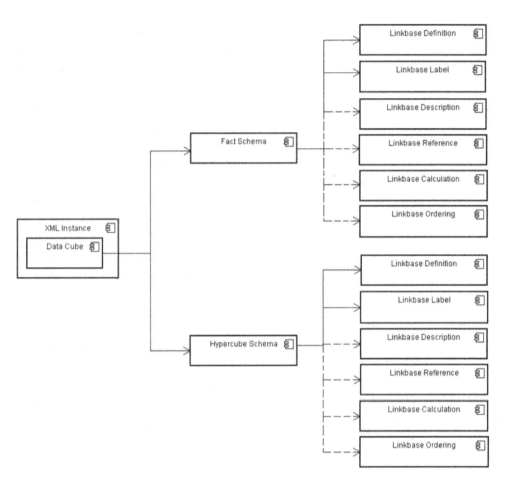

according to this model. Based on XML Schema, the vocabulary, i.e. a set of elements to be used in the XML instance, is specified. The relationships among the instance elements and among them and other resources are expressed in linkbases. The specified data types are common to a variety of domains. This was done in order to broaden the model applicability. However, it is possible to create types for a specific domain.

The attributes and elements declarations, which can be found in XLDM instances, are made in *instance-schema.xsd*. An element declaration of particular importance, the instance root element, is shown in Box 1. The presence of *xldm* root element and of child elements in the instance is based on Definitions 1, 2 and 3. Initially, the element naming is performed. In XLDM, two alternatives

are given for this element identification, in order to name it according to the domain where it is being applied:

1. Changing its declaration in the *instance-schema.xsd* document;
2. Without changing its declaration in the *instance-schema.xsd* document, in which a label can be created for this element, specifying it in the linkbase Label and creating a relationship between two documents ($R\sigma$, Definitions 2 and 4).

Thus, the instance *xldm* element has a label, for domain application, specified on the linkbase label. Next, there is the element description. After this, the declarations of the references to schemas,

Box 1. Definition of an XLDM root element

```
<element name="xldm">
. . .
<complexType>
<sequence>
<element ref="link:schemaRef" minOc-
curs="1"
maxOccurs="unbounded"/>
<element ref="link:linkbaseRef" min-
Occurs="2"
maxOccurs="unbounded"/>
<element ref="link:roleRef" minOc-
curs="0"
maxOccurs="unbounded"/>
<element ref="link:arcroleRef" minOc-
curs="0"
maxOccurs="unbounded"/>
<choice minOccurs="0"
maxOccurs="unbounded">
<element ref="xdmi:item"/>
<element ref="xdmi:tuple"/>
<element ref="xdmi:context"/>
<element ref="xdmi:unit"/>
<element ref="link:footnoteLink"/>
</choice></sequence>
</complexType></element>
```

linkbases, roles and arcroles are performed. To do so, *schemaRef*, linkbase*Ref*, *roleRef* and *arcroleRef* elements were specified to allow the establishment of relationships among documents ($R\sigma$) as shown in Definitions 2 and 4. A significant characteristic is the obligatoriness of two linkbases (namely Definition and Label, which will be discussed later). Thus, the number of minimum occurrences in the linkbase*Ref* element is defined as two. Finally, the elements that can occur in the instance are declared, such as *item* and *tuple*. From the *instance-schema. xsd* definitions, the documents *Fact Schema* and *Hypercube Schema* are created, which define, respectively, the elements that represent the facts and the dimensions members. For organization

purposes, these schemas can be specified in the same document or in distinct documents. In the instance documents the presence of *contextRef* and *unitRef* attributes in the elements that represent the facts is mandatory, which make reference to the dimensional context and the fact unit, represented by the elements *context* and *unit*, found in the multidimensional structure. The declaration of these two attributes and elements establishes the binary relations ($R\chi$) described in Definitions 2 and 3 and its use is illustrated at the extract of the XLDM instance document shown in Box 1.

Linkbases are defined to conform to the relationships that can be present in a great variety of domains. The definitions occur by roles specification for the *arcrole* attribute, besides the inclusion of elements and attributes. Box 2 shows the arcrole *multiplication-item* specification and, in Box 3, the Description linkbase definitions illustrated. XLDM proposes some linkbases and extends others from XBRL *Dimensions*, they are presented next.

1. The *Definition* linkbase, considered mandatory, allows the creation of the hierarchical element structure. With this, the problem of structural heterogeneity is treated. For the structural aspects, the relationship definition among dimensions, members and cubes is performed by this linkbase. The relationship expressed by the arcrole *domain-member* lists the possible members of a domain, which is associated to the dimension through the arcrole *dimension-domain*. The cross product between the dimensions and the facts, to establish the possible cubes to be used in the instance, is defined by the arcrole *hypercube-dimension*. To include the measures in the cube, the arcrole *all* is used. To exclude the member of a domain in a cube specification, the arcrole *notAll* is used. These relations, based on the Definitions 5, 6 e 7, determine the relationship among members, dimensions, facts, cubes and

Box 2. The multiplication-item Arcrole definition

```
<arcroleType id="multiplication-item"
  cyclesAllowed="undirected"
  arcroleURI="http://www.example.br/arcrole/multiplication-item">
<definition>Target (a primary item declaration) is a multiplication
  factor which composes the value of the source (a primary item
  declaration)</definition>
<usedOn>calculationArc</usedOn>
</arcroleType>
```

Box 3. The description linkbase definition

```
<element name="descriptionlLink"
  substitutionGroup="xl:extended">
<annotation>
<documentation>
  descriptionLink element definition.
</documentation>
</annotation>
<complexType>
<complexContent>
<restriction base="xl:extendedType">
<choice minOccurs="0"
maxOccurs="unbounded">
<element ref="xl:title"/>
<element ref="link:documentation"/>
<element ref="link:loc"/>
<element ref="link:descriptionArc"/>
</choice>

                    . . .

</complexContent>
</complexType>
</element>
```

possible values for the attribute *arcrole*, so that a data multidimensional model may be created. These relationships are shown in Figure 2. Besides these relationships, illustrated in Box 5, other relationships are specified. Their definition occurs with the following arcroles: (a) *main*, which defines a relationship between a concept and another as main, e.g. in a model for a health treatment, a medical procedure is defined as the main one for a disease treatment; (b) *secondary*, which defines a relationship as secondary. In the health treatment example, there may be the main procedure and the secondary ones. Then, the attribute *order* indicates the order in which the secondary procedures should be performed; (c) *substitution*, which determines the possibility of substitution of a concept with another one, e.g. a procedure can be replaced by another. The attribute *order* indicates the order in which the concepts can be replaced, e.g. it defines the order in which the procedures replace the main one;

2. The *Label* linkbase allows the use of different labels for the same element, which can be specified in different languages through the attribute *xml:lang*. It is mandatory, so that the semantic and syntactic heterogeneities can be avoided;

3. The *Ordering* linkbase, being optional, was defined to determine not only the elements presentation order in the instance, but also their processing order, which can differ from the presentation. For the definition of links aiming at specifying the presentation orders, an extended link element *presentationLink* is

used. For processing purposes, the element *processingLink* is used;

4. The *Description* linkbase, being optional, was introduced in this metamodel in order to supply a relationship textual description. For example, the relationship between a disease and its description is represented by these linkbase arcs. Placing the descriptions in a different linkbase contributes to the model modularity;

5. The *Reference* linkbase is optional and is used with the definition, by the user, of the elements that represent references;

6. The *Calculation* linkbase expresses arithmetic relations. It was defined so that, besides the sum operation, the arithmetic operations of multiplication, division, exponentiation and n-th root are specified. To do so, values are defined for the *arcrole* attribute. Box 4 shows the possible arcroles for this linkbase, which vary due to the arithmetic operation. Attributes are also defined, with proper domains, for each kind of operation. For example, the attribute *weight* changes its domain due to the operation. For sum, the domain varies from -1 to 1, which means that its value is completely or partially used in the addition, which results in the parent element value. This attribute domain for multiplication is the set of real numbers. Regarding the exponentiation and n-th root operations, there are the attributes *exponent* and *index*, whose domain is the set of natural numbers. For division, only the *arcrole* values are used in the numerator and denominator specification.

XLPATH SPECIFICATION

The language XLPath is specified to allow navigation on XLDM documents and extract information expressed by XLink links. XLink provides two types of links. The first one, the simple type, may be considered as a simplification of the extended link. A simple link associates exactly two resources, one local and one remote, with an arc going from the former to the latter. The second type corresponds to the extended links. In this case, separated documents are created, called linkbases, in which the links are grouped. Using extended links it is possible to associate an arbitrary number of resources. In order to provide such flexibility, the structure of extended links contains four types of elements that: (1) point to remote resources through an URI – xlink:type="locator"; (2) consist of local resources - xlink:type="resource", used for encapsulating information inside the link; (3) define arc traversing rules - xlink:type="arc". An arc connects two resources and provides information about the link traversing, such as the navigation direction and the application behavior regarding the traversing; and (4) provides descriptive information regarding the link - xlink:type="title". In this paper, the terms locator, resource, arc and title refer to the homonym type sub-elements.

In this section, the language proposed will permit navigation over these kinds of links. For this, the requirements identified as a guide to XLPath specification are given, two approaches are discussed to perform queries in XLPath and the language syntax and semantic are detailed.

XLPath Requirements

From the need verified regarding the navigation over links, as well as XLink conceptual approaches, it is possible to compile a series of requirements that have guided the XLPath construction:

1. **Conceptual distinction between arcs and connections, and the elements that define them**: From XLPath point of view, an arc or a connection must be taken as an "act" of an element refer another, through a label present in the attributes *from* and *to* of XLink, or

Table 3. Attribute arcrole in calculation Linkbase

Attribute Arcrole Name	Meaning
<link:calculationArc xlink:type="arc" xlink:arcrole="http://www.example.br/arcrole/ summation-item" xlink:from="A" xlink:to="B" weight="1.0"/>	The total value of concept B contributes for the formation of concept A.
<link:calculationArc xlink:type="arc" xlink:arcrole="http://www.example.br/arcrole/ multiplication-item" xlink:from="A" xlink:to="B" weight="3.0"/>	Three times the value of B is a multiplication factor to compose the value of A.
<link:calculationArc xlink:type="arc" xlink:arcrole="http://www.example.br/arcrole/ numerator-item" xlink:from="A" xlink:to="B"/>	The value of B is the numerator of the division that compose the value of A.
<link:calculationArc xlink:type="arc" xlink:arcrole="http://www.exemplo.br/arcrole/ denominator-item" xlink:from="A" xlink:to="C"/>	The value of C is the denominator of the division that composes the value of A.
<link:calculationArc xlink:type="arc" xlink:arcrole="http://www.example.br/arcrole/ exponentiation-item" xlink:from="A" xlink:to="B" expoent="3.0"/>	The value of A corresponds to the value of the third exponent of B.
<link:calculationArc xlink:type="arc" xlink:arcrole="http://www.example.br/arcrole/ nthroot-item" xlink:from="A" xlink:to="B" index="2.0"/>	The value of A corresponds to the n-th root of B.

through an URI in the *href* attribute. Thus, it is correct to affirm that, when regarding queries based on this language, an arc may start from an element locator to an element arc, or vice-versa;

2. **Navigation in different levels of abstraction**: The main purpose of a query language over links is allowing the navigation through the network formed by the existing references between distinct elements. However, references through URI (href) constitute the only possible path between two elements that refer themselves in this way. Thus, XLPath must provide the option of abstracting these connections, decreasing the quantity of steps necessary to reach the query final purpose;

3. **Approach for simple links as their extended equivalents**: Aiming to avoid a very long syntax, XLPath must be capable of navigating over simple links based on the same syntax used for extended links. To do so, this language must start from an approach that assimilates the simple links as their extended equivalents;

4. **Identification of implicit arcs**: In situations in which links are declared without the occurrence of arcs, or that, in the occurrence of them, the attributes from and/or to have been omitted, XLPath must be capable of identifying the occurrence of implicit arcs, maintaining, thus, the conformity with the XLink specification;

5. **Similarity with the XPath syntax**: The language proposed here for navigation over links must have the maximum possible number of similarities with the XPath syntax, in order to facilitate the assimilation for the users;

6. **Conditions for queries refinement**: Placed that may exist an arbitrary number of links referring a given element, XLPath must enable refinement conditions to be applied to the query, in order to allow the distinction among the different elements that constitute these links, starting from their names or values of attributes; and

7. **Absolute and relative path, and query performed in steps**: Just like it happens in XPath, XLPath follows the concept of query in steps, where each step selects a list of nodes that is passed as an input parameter for

the next step until the execution of the last step and obtainment of the final result. The initial step may start from a document root (absolute path), or from a specific internal node (relative path).

Graphical View

One way of analyzing how the structure formed by extended links may be explored by a query language is representing it graphically. We introduce two different approaches to represent the links, *Low Level Approach* and *High Level Approach.* These approaches are exemplified through a link illustrated in Box 4, adopting the symbolism presented in Table 4.

Box 4 illustrates a code excerpt for an extended link of the type *third-party.* This code was extracted from the XBRL taxonomy of project COREP (COREP, 2005), an initiative of CEBS (*Committe of European Banking Supervisors*) to provide a framework of financial reports for some institutions from European Union. In this code, elements locators were declared to refer the elements *d-ba_BankingActivitiesDomain*, *d-ba_TotalBankingActivities* and *d-ba_Total-BankingActivitiesSubjectBIA*, found in the scheme *d-ba-2006-07-01.xsd*. In addition, arcs are used to establish relationships of the type *domain-member* between these elements. In virtue of the increasing usage of XML as a mean for storing data, query languages carry out a base role, allowing access to data and metadata that compose the semi-structured data files. However many languages with this purpose exist, as XQL (Robie, 1999) and XML-QL (Deutsch, 2010), the languages constructed by W3C, XQuery and XPath, attend the main needs of access to databases and XML documents. The main use of XQuery is the performance of queries to data stored in native XML databases. The XPath use query expressions called *location path*, which determine a navigation path between the document parts, called nodes, exploring the relationships characteristic of the

tree formed by these nodes (e. g. parent, child, sibling). In extended links case, once they are XML base data, it is possible to explore them under the nodes tree perspective through XPath. Figure 4 shows a simplified nodes tree (without the attributes) that characterizes the extended link showed in the Box 4.

Low Level Approach: The low level approach offers a detailed view of the link, considering all the elements involved in the existing references, which includes elements locators, arcs and resources. The advantage of this approach for a query language is to allow the access to all these elements. Figure 5 shows the link of Box 4 represented in low level. To differentiate elements of the same kind and with the same name, numbers corresponding to the order in which each element appears in Box 4 are used as labels.

High Level Approach: In an extended link, a type locator element has the function of being the local representation of certain remote resource. Due to it, for each remote resource there will be only one locator referring it. The high level approach offers a simplified vision of the link, where the locators are omitted and the arcs make direct reference to the correspondent remote resource. For a query language, it would result in the formulation of simpler queries to do a link crossing (when we navigate from one resource to another passing by the link). Figure 6 shows the representation in high level for the link shown in Box 4.

Syntax and Semantic

This section presents the XLPath sintactic mechanisms, accompanied of examples that demonstrate their interpretation. The basic structure of an XLPath query expression is similar to the *location path* of XPath, including the axis elements, element specification – analogue to the node specification of XPath – and predicate. Besides those, to enjoy the advantages of the two navigation approaches, the XLPath query expressions make use of a mechanism that indicates the level of abstraction.

Box 4. Example of an extended link

```
<link:definitionLink xlink:type="extended"
   xlink:role="http://www.xbrl.org/2003/role/link">
 <link:loc xlink:type="locator" xlink:label="BankingActivitiesDomain"
   xlink:href="d-ba-2006-07-01.xsd#d-ba_BankingActivitiesDomain"
   xlink:title="BankingActivitiesDomain" />
 <link:loc xlink:type="locator" xlink:label="TotalBankingActivities"
   xlink:href="d-ba-2006-07-01.xsd#d-ba_TotalBankingActivities"
   xlink:title="TotalBankingActivities" />
 <link:definitionArc xlink:type="arc"
   xlink:arcrole="http://xbrl.org/int/dim/arcrole/domain-member"
   xlink:from="BankingActivitiesDomain"
   xlink:to="TotalBankingActivities"
   xlink:title="definition: BankingActivitiesDomain to
            TotalBankingActivities" order="1.0" />
 <link:loc xlink:type="locator"
   xlink:label="TotalBankingActivitiesSubjectBIA"
   xlink:href="d-ba-2006-07-01.xsd#
                      d-ba_TotalBankingActivitiesSubjectBIA"
   xlink:title="TotalBankingActivitiesSubjectBIA"/>
 <link:definitionArc xlink:type="arc"
   xlink:arcrole="http://xbrl.org/int/dim/arcrole/domain-member"
   xlink:from="TotalBankingActivities"
   xlink:to="TotalBankingActivitiesSubjectBIA"
   xlink:title="definition: TotalBankingActivities to
      TotalBankingActivitiesSubjectBIA" use="optional" order="1.0" />
                      . . .
</link:definitionLink>
```

Thus, expressions preceded by *LL* navigate through the extended links structures according to the low level approach, while expressions preceded by *HL* navigate in high level.

Axis Specification: The basic blocks of an expression location path of XPath are the location steps, which determine the paths that conduct to the desired information in an XML document. These paths are directed by the axis, which, in XPath, correspond mainly to the traditional relationships between nodes of XML documents trees. In XLPath, the same principle is used, however with the difference of the paths, in this case, are

determined by the references among the elements that compose the links networks. Graphically, these references correspond to the lines and ar-

Table 4. Simbology for extended links

Symbol	Representation
⬭	Element of extended link
▢	Remote resource
⬡	sub-element arc
⬠	sub-element locator
—	reference through URI
→	reference through label

Figure 4. Extended link nodes tree

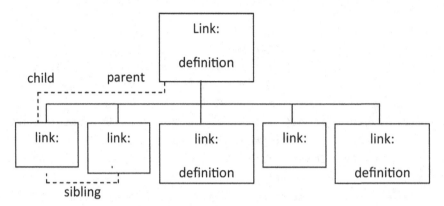

Figure 5. Low level representation of an extended link

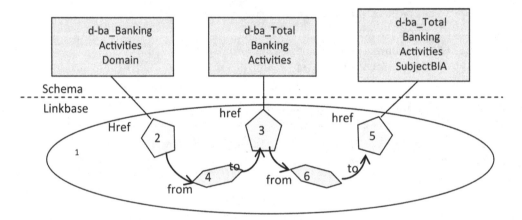

rows that connect the elements as given in Figure 5 and in Figure 6.

It is possible to realize that elements of the type arc are always associated to two link references: one through the attribute xlink:from and another through the attribute xlink:to, each one of them represented by an arrow, which identifies the directional character of this type of association. An important detail is that, from XLPath perspective, each one of these arrows is considered an arc. It means that there is a distinction between arcs and elements of the arc type. This distinction is made to allow that XLPath access elements of the arc type like nodes of the links networks, navigating

until them through arcs, i.e. references originating from elements of the arc type. Thus, XLPath axes are used to specify the type of existing association between the context element – equivalent to the context node of XPath – and the elements connected to it. These axes are:

1. **Linked axis:** directs the query to all the elements that refer or are referred by context element, including references by label and by URI;

2. **Arc-source axis:** directs the query to all the elements that are target nodes of arcs whose context element is the source;

Figure 6. High level representation of an extended link

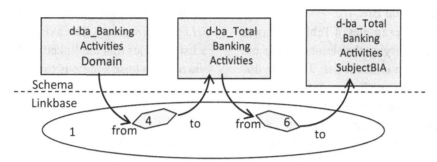

3. **Arc-destination axis:** directs the query to all the elements that are source nodes of arcs whose context element is the target.

The first axis, *linked*, is the most generic. Graphically, the result of its application is equivalent to propagate the query through all the lines and arrows connected to the context element. The other axes, *arc-source* and *arc-destination* propagate the query through arrows whose context element is source or target, respectively. Table 5 exemplifies the axes application, in different levels of abstraction, to the elements of Box 4. To differentiate elements with repeated names, the same numeration used as labels in Figures 4 and 5 were superscribed on them.

Element Specification: The element specification determines which elements in the axis direction will be selected. The selection criteria may be the type and the name of each element,

determined, respectively, by the parameter of the function *elementType(elementName)*. XLPath provides the following element specification:

1. **Locator(elementName):** Selects elements of locator type with the name *elementName*;
2. **Arc(elementName):** Selects elements of arc type with the name *elementName*;
3. **Resource(elementName):** Selects elements of resource type with the name *elementName*;
4. **Remote(elementName):** Selects remote resources with the name *elementName*;
5. **Element(elementName):** Selects elements of any type with the name *elementName*.

When the parameter *elementName* is not provided, the filtering is made based only on the type of element. Thus, the function *element()* may be used to put all the elements back in the direction of an axis, regardless the name and the type. Table 6

Table 5. Examples of abstraction levels and axis

Context Element	Level and Axis	Identified Elements
d-ba_TotalBankingActivities	LL::linked	link:loc³, link:definitionArc⁴, link:definitionArc⁶
d-ba_TotalBankingActivities	HL::linked	link:definitionArc⁴, link:definitionArc⁶
link:loc³	LL::arc-source	link:definitionArc⁶
d-ba_BankingActivitiesDomain	HL::arc-source	link:definitionArc⁴
link:definitionArc⁶	LL::arc-destination	link:loc⁵

shows examples of element specification applied to elements showed on Box 4.

Predicate: In the examples of Table 6, in some situations, even specifying the element name and type, the result is an element list. To filter this result, one may use predicates, which consist in conditions tested on each element on the list. Just like in XPath, the usage of predicates is not mandatory. Table 7 exemplifies the predicates to filter the list of elements extracted from Figure 1. XLPath provides the following conditions:

1. Attribute(attributeName)='attributeValue': Tests if the element has an attribute *attributeName* with the value *attributeValue*;
2. Text()='textValue': Tests if the text content of the element equals *textValue*;
3. Link(linkName): Tests if the element belongs to the link *linkName*.

XLPath was developed from the XPath+ (Silva, 2008, 2009a), aiming to redress its deficiencies with regard to queries with higher level of refinement. However, for certain applications, the mechanisms that allow XPath+ queries retrieve the nodes of certain links may be useful and, therefore, were kept in the specification of XLPath. These mechanisms include the axes *link-source* and *link-destination* and the functions *isLinkSource()* and *isLinkDestination()*. The axis *link-source* selects a list of nodes that are linked to the context node via a link whose source is the context node. The axis *link-destination* selects the list of nodes that have links pointing to the context node. An extract of the XLPath grammar is showed at Figure 7, all of this is in appendix A. It is described through representation based on an EBNF (Extended Backus–Naur Form).

LMDQL Operators

LMDQL is composed by specific operators, which allow the acquisition of information regarding relations expressed in links for XML documents multidimensional analysis. To perform navigation on links and recover information contained in linkbases, LMDQL uses XLPath. XLPath is a language that supports navigation on links defined in the XLink standard. The LMDQL syntax is based on MDX, with changes performed to become suitable to the XML documents context with XLink support. Important characteristics of the language LMDQL are:

Table 6. Examples of element specification

Context Element	Element Specification	Selected Elements
d-ba_TotalBankingActivities, link:loc[3]	locator()	link:loc[3]
link:loc[3], link:definitionArc[4], link:definitionArc[6]	arc()	link:definitionArc[4], link:definitionArc[6]
link:definitionArc[4], link:definitionArc[6]	arc(link:definitionArc)	link:definitionArc[4], link:definitionArc[6]
d-ba_TotalBankingActivities, d-ba_BankingActivitiesDomain	remote(d-ba_Total BankingActivities)	d-ba_Total BankingActivities
link:loc[3],link:definitionArc[4], d-ba_BankingActivitiesDomain	element()	link:loc[3], link:definitionArc[4], d-ba_BankingActivitiesDomain

Table 7. Examples of predicates

Context Element	Predicate	Filtered Elements
link:definitionArc[4], link:definitionArc[6]	attribute(title)='definition:BankingActivitiesDomain to TotalBankingActivities'	link:definitionArc[4]
link:loc[3]	link(link:definitionLink)	link:loc[3]

Figure 7. XLPath EBNF

```
XLPathExpr   ::=   AbsLocationPath | RelLocationPath
AbsLocationPath  ::=   "/" RelLocationPath
RelLocationPath  ::=   Step | RelLocationPath "/" Step
Step      ::=   LevelSpec AxisSpec ElementSpec Predicate*
LevelSpec ::=   ("HL" | "LL") "::"
AxisSpec  ::=   ("arc-destination" | "arc-source" | "linked" |
                "link-part-child" | "link-part-descendant") "::"
ElementSpec  ::= ElementName "(" QName? ")"
ElementName  ::= "arc" | "element" | "locator" | "remote" |
                "resource"
 Predicate   ::= "[" Operator Spec"]"
 OperatorSpec  ::=   AttributeSpec | LinkSpec | TextSpec
 AttributeSpec  ::=   "attribute(" QName ")=" Value
 LinkSpec  ::=    "link(" QName ")"
 TextSpec  ::=  "text()=" Value
```

- Consult a collection of XML documents, so that the information obtained may be distributed in more than one document;
- Perform queries based on value or the structure of the XML document. In addition to performing queries against a data value, it is necessary to consider different structures of XML instances;
- Consider the existence of links as a source of information, since the representation of semantic information about the data can occur in documents connected to the instance;
- Having the representation of the data cube column that expresses in percentage terms the relationship between the values of another column, and
- Process XML data without conflicts of heterogeneity.

The grammar of this language, which is based on EBNF, is described in Appendix B.

Query Sentence

LMDQL queries are represented by the set of elements illustrated in Box 5. A query returns a subset data cube on which it is applied, called cube result. For specify a query the following informations are necessary: axes or sets of hierarchies, members of each dimension to be included on each axis of the query, the name of the cube that sets the context of the query, members of an axis on which the data are extracted.

The LMDQL queries extend MDX to perform queries based on the value or on the XML document structure. To do so, the clause $VARIABLE has been specified, which declares the paths that will be used on recovering the members of the document. The statement *variable_specification* defines the paths to be used for recovery of the

Box 5. LMDQL query structure

```
($VARIABLE variable_specification)?
(WITH formula_specification)?
SELECT axis_specification_list
FROM cube_specification
(WHERE slice_specification)?
(CELL PROPERTIES cell_props)?
```

Box 6. LMDQL query statement

```
$VARIABLE [e] = [assetsBanks] |
  [assetsBanks].[privateBank] |
  [assetsBanks].[governmentBank]
WITH
MEMBER [Measure].[totalAssets] AS
'SUM ([e].Members)'
SELECT {[Measure].[totalAssets] ON
Axis(0)}
FROM Banks
```

members in the hierarchical structure of the document. The others clauses of the query forming expression remain as originally defined in MDX. One query based on the structure can be evaluated through the trees shown in Figure 8, displaying two representations of bank assets, considering that, in the tree on the left, the classification between public and private banks occurs. The LMDQL query, shown in Box 6, is performed on a collection of XML documents, named Banks, so as to recover the total of the banks assets in both structures.

MDQL Operators

Before listing the LMDQL operators, it is important to highlight some definitions that will be used in their specification (as shown in Table 8). For these definitions, the instance element defined in the schema, or a label related to the element is considered as a member.

The language operators are categorized due to the need of having operators that allow the query performance based on comparative values, once the use of indexes is of great importance in any

domain. However, the MDX language does not cover this kind of analysis completely, because it does not define an operator that allows the use of the Separatrix, a statistic position measure. On the other hand, the use of Xlink implies the need of an operator category that allows the navigation through linkbases. Thus, the LMDQL operators were categorized the following way: (i) Relative Evaluation Operators, which allow the creation of operators for determining indexes and the performance of horizontal and vertical analyses based on statistics information; and (ii) Navigation Operators, which allow the recovery of the information based on the document structure and on the linkbases.

Relative Evaluation Operators: The use of indexes is justified when the analysis of certain relations is more significant than the direct analysis on data. The LMDQL language allows the user to construct operators that express any relations, and its applications in analysis techniques. In this work, the horizontal, vertical and standard index

Figure 8. Organizational structure tree representations

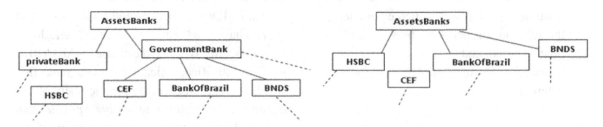

Table 8. Definitions used for specifying LMDQL

<MemberSet>	Set of members in a cube
<Member>	One member in a cube
<DimensionName>	Dimension name (e.g. [Location])
<MemberName>	A member name (e.g. [Location].[state].[Bahia])
<NumericExpression>	Any numeric value
<IntegerExpression>	Any Integer value
<NumericSet>	A set of any numeric values
<IntegerSet>	A set of any integer values

techniques are considered. The horizontal analysis highlights the variation of certain information over the time. The vertical analysis allows one to identify the participation percentage of certain information on the composition of another. The standard index analysis determines the relative location of information in a statistic distribution.

In MDX, the creation of operators through the use of calculated members can be performed. However, it is not possible to save the created operators, leading to redefinitions, in case they are necessary for further use. This feature is available in LMDQL. The LMDQL Relative Evaluation Operators are described below.

1. **OperatorDefinition (String, String [, param(String+)])**: Given two strings, one for defining the expression that specifies the relation between the members of a cube, and another one that identifies the new operator, this operator creates another one based on the previous relation given. Optionally, parameters to be used in the given expression can be supplied. The operator creation occurs

in execution time, allowing the immediate use of just created operators. The operators can be created in the internal context of a query or as an independent statement. In both cases, the operators created are stored in the operator library for future use. Box 7 illustrates the use of this operator for creating and using the *assetsReturn* operator. This operator allows the definition of a measure calculated in an XML cube, based on XLDM definitions. To do so, it is specified in the linkbase Calculation the relationship between the created operator and the other query members that are part of its definition. Thus, a taxonomy for specific groups of operators can be created. Box 8 exemplifies a linkbase Calculation with the definition of an operator created by *Operator*Definition.

2. **HAnalysis (MemberSet, MemberSet^{+2}, [NumericSet] *)**: Given a reference set, two or more sets of members and, optionally, the indexes for correcting value in each set, this operator calculates each set's evolution in relation to the reference. Box 9 shows the use of this operator.

3. **VAnalysis (Member, MemberSet)**: Given a reference member and a set of members, this operator calculates the percentage of each member in relation to the referenced one. In Box 10, the use of VAnalysis is illustrated.

4. **Separatrix (MemberSet, Member, IntergerExpression)**: From a set of members, a member to be evaluated and an integer that represents the separatrix, this operator determines the intervals for this set and returns the evaluation member relative posi-

Box 7. Use of the operator definition operator

```
OperatorDefinition('([Net Profit]/[Assets])', assetsReturn)
SELECT {[Time].[2007]} ON COLUMNS,
{Descendants ({[company].Children}, [geographic].[São Paulo])} ON ROWS FROM
Banks WHERE (assetsReturn)
```

Box 8. Linkbase calculation with operator definition

```
<xldm:linkbase xmlns:xldm="http://www.cin.ufpe.br/~pcs3/XLDM"
xmlns:xlink="http://www.w3.org/1999/xlink">
<xldm:calculationLink xlink:type="extended" xlink:role="http://www.xldm.org/
role/link">
<xldm:operator xlink:type="resource" xlink:label="SalesMedia"
    id="SalesMedia" xlink:role="http://www.xldm.org/role/calculation/operator"
  xldm:memberRef="[Measures].[Sales Media]">Sales Media</xldm:operator>
<xldm:member xlink:type="locator" xlink:label="StoreSales" id="StoreSales"
 xldm:memberRef="[Measures].[Store Sales]"
 xlink:href="//sales_fact_1997/store_sales"/>
<xldm:member xlink:type="locator" xlink:label="UnitSales" id="UnitSales"
 xldm:memberRef="[Measures].[Unit Sales]"
 xlink:href="//sales_fact_1997/unit_sales"/>
<xldm:calculationArc xlink:type="arc"
    xlink:arcrole="http://www.xldm.org/arcrole/numerator-item"
    xlink:from="SalesMedia" xlink:to="StoreSales"/>
<xldm:calculationArc xlink:type="arc" xlink:from="SalesMedia"
    xlink:to="UnitSales" xlink:arcrole="http://www.xldm.org/arcrole/denomina-
tor-item"/>
</xldm:calculationLink></xldm:linkbase>
```

Box 9. LMDQL query for horizontal analysis

```
SELECT {[Time].Members} ON COLUMNS,
{HAnalysis([Time].[2006],{[Measure]. [Assets].Children},1)}ON ROWS
FROM Banks WHERE ([bank].[BankOfBrazil],
    [geographic].[São Paulo].)
```

tion. The intervals are calculated through the members ordering, which are divided according to the integer value given as parameter. The use of this operator is exemplified in Box 11, where the query returns the position of Bank of Brazil assets in relation to the position of other banks from Brazil.

Navigation Operators: The operators presented next allow the retrieval of information contained in the relations expressed in linkbases, schemas and instances. For example, it is possible to find instances with different elements, but with the same meaning and same label. Then, the query is performed by checking the elements that relate with the label.

5. **Cross (Member, String*):** Given a reference member, this operator returns the members that have relation with it. Optionally, the kind of relation to return can be specified. This is given by the names of the linkbases. One example of the Cross operator is illustrated in Box 12.

Box 10. LMDQL Query for vertical analysis

```
SELECT {[Time].[2008]} ON COLUMNS, {VAnalysis([Measure].[Assets].[Operational
Assets], [Measure].[Assets].[Operational Assets].Children}}} ON ROWS FROM Banks
```

Box 11. Use of the Separatrix operator

```
SELECT {assetsReturn} ON COLUMNS,
{Separatrix({[company].Children, [geographic].[Brazil]},[bank].[BankOfBra-
zil],3)}ON ROWS FROM Banks
```

6. **NNearestValues (Member, IntergerExpression [,String])**: From a reference member and a precision numeric value (N), this operator returns the closest N members to the reference member. Optionally, it is possible to define, using ASC or DESC, whether this amount of members refers to the members with closest values above or below the reference value. One example of the use of this operator is shown in Box 13.

LMDQL Processor Architecture

The architecture of the LMDQL processor, which can be seen in Figure 9, is divided into three layers, which perform the interface function with the user, LMDQL query processing and data acquisition. These architecture layers are: (i) *Interface*, which contemplates the GUI used for command submission in LMDQL. The two components from this *Interface* layer are the *Query Editor*, that validates the queries and forwards them to the *Processor* layer, and the *Query Viewer*, that displays the results; (ii) *Processor*, where the analytic-dimensional processing mechanism is. It contains the modules *Query Processor*, *XPath+ Processor*, which can be viewed on the right of Figure 3, and the *Optimizer*, which contains optimization mechanisms. The *Query Processor* is meant to perform the lexical and syntactic analysis on the query and send it to the execution manager, which will be detailed in next section. *XPath+ Processor* is responsible for controlling the query performance, receiving requirements in the XPath+ expression form, performing them and retrieving the necessary data to query execution; (iii) *Data*, data acquisition layer, composed by: (a) *Data Cube*, stores the instance documents; (b) *Metadata Repository*, the repository of metadata, in which *schemas* and *linkbases* are; and (c) *Operators Library*, where the operators created by the user are stored.

Box 12. Use of the cross operator

```
SELECT {[Time].[2007], [Time].[2007]} ON COLUMNS,
{Cross([Measure].[Assets], 'Definition')} ON ROWSFROM Banks
```

Box 13. Use of the NNearestValues operator

```
SELECT {[Time].[2005].Children} ON COLUMNS,
{NNearestValues([Measure].[BankOfBrazil].[Assets], 3, DESC)
ON ROWS FROM Banks
```
(vii) NNearestValuesPercentual (Member, NumericExpression [,String]): given a reference member and a numeric value (N), this operator returns the present members at a percentage variation rate (N%) based on the reference value. Optionally, the ASC or DESC values are also used. Box 14 illustrated the use of this operator in one LMDQL query.

AN ANALYTICAL SYSTEM FOR XML AND XLINK

An analytical processing environment based on open source code tools was developed aimed at making the analysis over XML data accessible to a large number of users. The *mondrian* middleware (*Mondrian*, 2008) was chosen to compose the desired environment since it is an OLAP server used in several Business Intelligence (BI) solutions, and is developed in Java, which makes it computational platform independent. Another

Figure 9. Architecture of the LMDQL processor

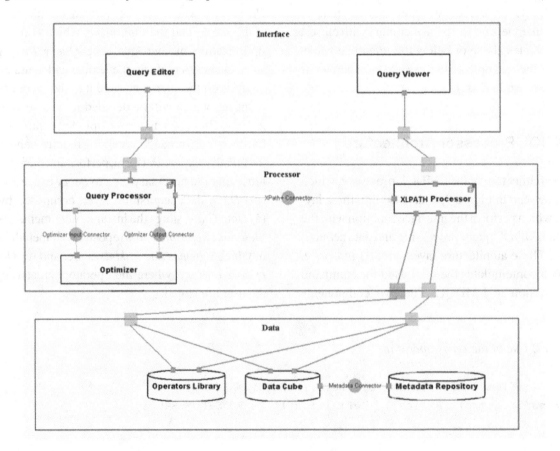

Box 14. Use of the NNearestValuesPercentual operator

```
SELECT {[Time].[2005].Children} ON COLUMNS,
{NNearestValuesPercentual([Measure].[BankOfBrazil].[Assets], 10)
ON ROWS FROM Banks
```

aspect that has influenced this decision was the use, by this server, of the MDX query language, a market pattern for analytical queries which provides resources that allow performing a great variety of queries on multidimensional data.

The *mondrian* architecture is formed by four layers: (i) the presentation layer that allows interaction with the user, (ii) the layer of dimension that parses, validates and executes MDX queries. This layer is stored the metadata file, an XML document that describes and maps the cube in a relational model, (iii) the third layer, which is responsible for maintaining the aggregated data in cache memory. The dimension layer sends requests to the cube cells, whether these cells are not cached and are not deductible from any data stored in the cache, the aggregation manager sends a request to the storage layer, and (iv) fourth layer, which consists of the database that contains the table of facts, dimensions and aggregated data.

The *mondrian* extension occurred in the database layer which contains the facts and dimensions tables, once LMDQL acts on XML. Then three DBMS XML, with distinct structures of XML documents storage, were used to evaluate the analytical environment for XML and XLink proposed in this paper: (i) eXist (eXist, 2010), an open code native XML DBMS, of public domain and independent of platform; (ii) IBM DB2 Express C (IBM, 2010), a relational DBMS that stores XML documents in tables with columns defined by XML data types; and, (iii) Oracle Berkeley DB XML (Oracle, 2010), which stores XML documents in only one data file. Another extended layer was the dimension layer, which analyses grammatically, validates and executes MDX queries. The metadata stored in this layer,

represented by an XML document, describe the data cube in a relational model. From this cube, a MDX query is transformed in different SQL queries, which are processed in a relational DBMS. This SQL query returns the values from the cube cells and the dimension members of the cube. The LMDQL query processing keeps the current cube mapping system. The LMDQL processor intercepts the SQL queries generated and converts them into XQuery, using XLPath expressions. This was the main challenge of this approach, since XQuery and SQL are based on different data paradigms (i.e. ordered sequences versus tuples sets). The correspondence among the tables, columns, dimensions and measures, defined in *mondrian* metadata, using the elements and attributes of a XML file, occurs through a configuration file, which is elaborated based on the linkbase Definition. Figure 10 illustrates the proposed solution for this mapping. SQL queries interception procedure and its conversion into XQuery are performed in the Query Processor module, from the LMDQL Processor layer, through a driver, namely *sql2xquery*.

The alternative adopted for query processing is the mapping of XML data to the relational model of *mondrian* and later converting SQL queries into XQuery. It is understood that this solution causes a smaller coupling to this OLAP server. This choice is justified by the possibility of using the driver *sql2xquery* in other BI applications that make use or not of *mondrian*, but that have as processing step SQL queries generation. Thus, models for XML data warehouses can be used in conjunction with this solution, just mapping the data cube on the mondrian, e.g. XLDM (Silva et al., 2011) and XML data warehouses (DW-XML)

(Baril and Bellahsène, 2004; Boussaidet et al., 2006a; Boussaid et al., 2006b; Darmont et al., 2003; Golfarelli et al., 2001; Jensen et al., 2001; Messaoud et al., 2006; Nassis et al., 2004; Pokorny, 2001; Pedersen et al., 2002a and 2002b;. Trujillo et al., 2004). Thus, it is transparent to the user the fact that the data repository is relational or based on any solution of DW-XML.

The *mondrian*, as well as other OLAP servers, requires that the fact tables and dimension tables that map the cube are specified. This requirement precludes the completion of the mapping of a data warehouse based on XML because this model of data warehouse is not formed by relational tables. To solve this problem, extract the sets of XML data from XML DW, containing elements equivalent to the tables' structures in *mondrian* and carried out the mapping in the *mondrian*'s metadata. For example, in Figure 11 is shown a model of DW relational for the sales area. The Figures 12 show sets of XML data equivalent to the structures of the data warehouse relational tables, shown in Figure 11.

SQL2XQUERY Driver

Aiming at performing the translation of SQL queries into XQuery, a translation process was defined. This process is illustrated in Figure 13,

Figure 10. Mapping SQL to XQuery

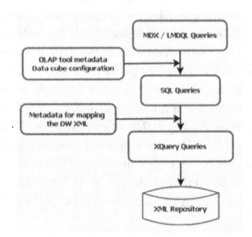

and consists in 2 tasks: generation of SQL query syntactic tree, necessary to recognize SQL query elements, and creation of XQuery queries. These tasks are discussed follow.

Generation of the syntax tree: The generation of the SQL query syntax tree is the first step in converting SQL queries into XQuery. The purpose of this step is to provide for the subsequent step the conditions specified in the SQL query. To this, was defined for the parser driver, a grammar similar of the language SQL SELECT command, from which the syntactic analysis of the queries will be held.

The Box 15 contains the formal specification of this syntax represented in EBNF. This specification is limited to the syntax of the SQL SELECT command, because this command is used for queries. To ensure compatibility with *mondrian*, an analysis was performed on the source code of this server to insert in the grammar the elements of the SQL syntax that are used on that server. Below are listed some features of this Grammar:

1. The return columns of the query must be specified in the SELECT command preceded by the table name ("*tableName. columnName*");
2. The join conditions must be specified in the WHERE clause, not being accepted operators UNION and JOIN;
3. The functions accepted are: *SUM, AVG, COUNT, MAX, MIN, UPPER, LOWER* and *ISNULL*;
4. Beyond relational operators and logical operators NOT, AND and OR will be accepted the operators IN, IS and BETWEEN.

The generation of the syntax tree starts with the lexical analysis of the SQL query, from which is generated the sequence of tokens that constitute the query. The parser builds the syntax tree of the query from the relationships between tokens of this sequence, using the grammar rules defined. Figure 14 illustrates the syntax tree generated

Figure 11. Relational model of sales data warehouse

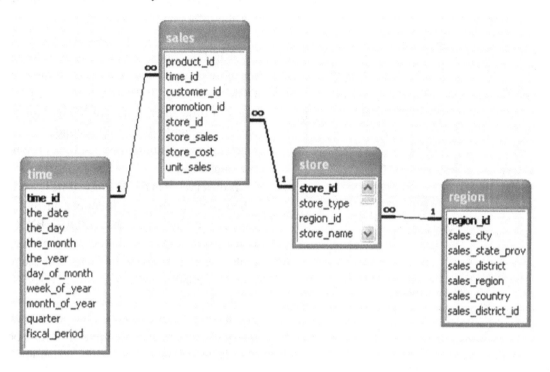

Figure 12. Sets of XML data equivalent to sales and time tables of the sales DW

```
<?xml version="1.0" encoding="UTF-8">
<table name="sales">
  <row>
    <product_id>804</product_id>
    <time_id>632</time_id>
    <customer_id>7543</customer_id>
    <promotion_id>0</promotion_id>
    <store_id>2</store_id>
    <store_sales>2.21</store_sales>
    <store_cost>0.7072</store_cost>
    <unit_sales>1</unit_sales>
  </row>
  <row>
    <product_id>15</product_id>
    <time_id>632</time_id>
    <customer_id>2180</customer_id>
    <promotion_id>0</promotion_id>
    <store_id>2</store_id>
    <store_sales>6.87</store_sales>
    <store_cost>3.0228</store_cost>
    <unit_sales>3</unit_sales>
  </row>
  ...
</table>
```

```
<?xml version="1.0" encoding="UTF-8"?>
<table name="time">
  <row>
    <time_id>367</time_id>
    <the_date>1997-01-01T00:00:00</the_date>
    <the_day>Wednesday</the_day>
    <the_month>January</the_month>
    <the_year>1997</the_year>
    <day_of_month>1</day_of_month>
    <week_of_year>2</week_of_year>
    <month_of_year>1</month_of_year>
    <quarter>Q1</quarter>
  </row>
  <row>
    <time_id>368</time_id>
    <the_date>1997-01-02T00:00:00</the_date>
    <the_day>Thursday</the_day>
    <the_month>January</the_month>
    <the_year>1997</the_year>
    <day_of_month>2</day_of_month>
    <week_of_year>2</week_of_year>
    <month_of_year>1</month_of_year>
    <quarter>Q1</quarter>
  </row>
  ...
</table>
```

Figure 13. Translation process

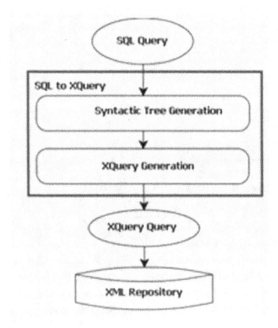

from the SQL query shown in Table 2. On the syntax tree are identified the restrictions of the query as junction tables, the where clause filters and grouping conditions.

Creation of XQuery queries: From the syntax tree created, is built the XQuery query. The literal translation of SQL queries is relatively trivial, this because the XQuery language has a set of clauses and a structure similar to SQL. A basic difference in the structure of these languages is that, while in SQL a single expression is used to perform queries in XQuery is necessary to associate various FLWOR expressions, acronym for For, Let, Where, Order By and Return, (XQuery, 2007) to find the same results. Therefore, it is possible that for a given SQL expression, several sets of XQuery expressions produce the same result. So, is necessary identification of the best set of XQuery expressions, e.g. with shorter execution time, especially when the SQL queries use group functions (SUM, AVG, MAX, MIN, COUNT) or involve more than one table for the grouping fields. Thus, the same SQL query can generate various

XQuery expressions that return the same result, but the difference between the response time of each can be relevant. An SQL query usually takes a few milliseconds, or hundreds of milliseconds for more complex queries. We used the MySQL DBMS (MySQL, 2013) for the comparative study of time and results. An XQuery query can vary from hundreds of milliseconds to seconds reaching up to minutes or even hours to provide the same result.

Is observed that the response time is increased when is used grouping functions in SQL queries, especially when the GROUP BY clause is used with data distributed in more than one table. Another aggravating factor was the use of complex conditional expressions (HAVING or WHERE). The SELECT DISTINCT clause was also a complicating factor for the performance of query execution. The high response time occurs mainly in XQuery expressions generated with use of many clauses "distinct-values", "for" and "where". Since the use of "distinct-values" is a problem for the performance, we adopted the strategy called DVPR (Distinct Values Pos Run). The DVPR not generate "distinct-values" in XQuery expressions (except into groupings GROUP BY), the filtering of duplicate results is made on the results generated after the implementation of the XQuery expression. That is, the "distinct-values" is made by the conversion process after obtaining the data in XML documents. With this procedure, the execution time decreases considerably, especially in XQuery expressions generated with SQL expressions formed with the SELECT DISTINCT clause.

An optimization to reduce the execution time, was incorporated into the group functions (SUM, AVG, MAX, MIN, COUNT) using XPath expression in each "for" or "let", especially if associated with the clause "distinct-values", and the elimination of conditional items within the "where" of the FLWOR expression. But this can only be done when the conditional items are connected

Box 15. EBNF grammar for generating the syntax tree of the SQL query

```
selectStmt::=
"SELECT" columnItemList
"FROM" fromClause
["WHERE" whereClause]
["GROUP" "BY" groupByClause ["HAVING" havingClause]]
["ORDER" "BY" orderByClause]
columnItemList::= ["ALL" | "DISTINCT"] columnItem ("," columnItem)*
columnItem::= (columnRef | setFunctionItem) [["AS"] columnAlias]
columnRef::= [databaseName "."] tableName "." columnName
setFunctionItem::= setFunction "(" ["DISTINCT" | "ALL"] columnRef | "*" |
constValue ")"
setFunction::= "SUM" | "AVG" | "COUNT" | "MAX" | "MIN" | "UPPER" | "LOWER" |
"ISNULL"
fromClause::= tableRef ("," tableRef)*
tableRef::= [databaseName "."] tableName [["AS"] tableAlias]
whereClause::= conditItemList
havingClause::= conditItemList
conditItemList::= conditItem ("AND"| "OR" conditItem)*
conditItem::= relatComp | betweenComp | inComp | isComp | "(" conditItemList
")"
| "NOT" conditItemList
relatComp::=          columnItemrelatOper (columnItem | constValue)
betweenComp::= columnItem ["NOT"] "BETWEEN" constValue "AND" constValue
inComp::= columnItem ["NOT"] "IN" "(" constValue ("," constValue)* ")"
isComp::= columnItem "IS" ["NOT"] "NULL"
relatOper::= "=" | "<>" | "<" | ">" | "<=" | ">="
groupByClause::= columnRef ("," columnRef)*
orderByClause::=         columnItem ("," columnItem)* ["ASC "| "DESC"]
```

with ANDs, without ORs or NOTs. This is what happens more in the the behavior of *mondrian*. Studies should be conducted to improve the performance of queries generated by the driver.

The *driver sql2xquery* processes any XML structure (i.e. elements, sub-elements of various levels, attributes). For this, the structure to be processed must be declared in the configuration file that maps the XML datawarehouse. Box 17 illustrates a structure of XML documents to be processed, XBRL documents, whose mapping to the *mondrian* relational environment is

done in the configuration file sql2xquery.xml illustrated in Box 18. The "entity" tag informs, through the "tagName" attribute, the set of XML document data (Box 17) to be processed and the corresponding tables in this set, in the *mondrian* configuration file, attribute "tableName". The tags "field" informs the elements, sub-elements and attributes to be processed. The value of the attribute "name" of this tag indicates the property referenced in the the *mondrian* configuration file and the "value" attribute the path in which data is found in the XML document. The property in

Figure 14. Syntax tree of SQL query

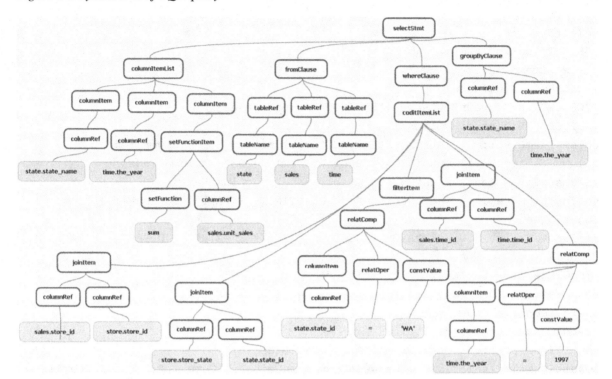

the metadata refers to the columns of the fact and dimension tables.

The Box 19 shows an excerpt of the XQuery query generated after this step, which is equivalent to that of SQL query showed on the Box 16.

Sql2xquery Architecture

The *sql2xquery* is a JDBC driver coded in Java. The architecture of the driver *sql2xquery*, which can be seen in Figure 15, is divided into three layers, which play the role of interface with OLAP server, converting SQL queries in XQuery and XML DBMS interface. The layers of this architecture are described below.

1. Interface, which includes the interface to the OLAP server. This layer aims to receive requests from the MDX query through the SQL statements generated by mondrian, refer them to the processing layer and return

the result generated by them, in an object of type ResultSet, provided by the access layer to data;

2. SQL2XQuery, which is the mechanism for converting SQL queries to XQuery. It contains the components SQL, XQuery and exception. SQL has a function to perform the lexical and syntactic analysis of the SQL query to generate the syntax tree of this query. XQUERY has the responsibility to create XQuery queries from tokens of the SQL query and the metadata that maps the cube defined in the OLAP server for XML-DW. The exception component has the function of address the errors occurred at the conversion processing, and

3. XMLDBAccess, layer of interface with the XML DBMS on which are managed and established connections to the database and return the result of the query;

Box 16. SQL query to generate the syntax tree

```
SELECT state.state_name, time.the_year, sum(sales.unit_sales)
FROM state, sales, time
WHERE           sales.store_id = store.store_id AND
                store.store_state = state.state_id AND
                state.state_id = 'WA' AND
                sales.time_id = time.time_id AND
                time.the_year = 1997
GROUP BY  state.state_name, time.the_year
```

Box 17. Kind of XML document that can be processed by driver sql2xquery

```
<xbrli:unit id="u1">
  <xbrli:measure>iso4217:USD</xbrli:measure>
</xbrli:unit>
<xbrli:unit id="u2">
  <xbrli:divide>
    <xbrli:unitNumerator>
      <xbrli:measure>iso4217:USD</xbrli:measure>
    </xbrli:unitNumerator>
    <xbrli:unitDenominator>
      <xbrli:measure>xbrli:shares</xbrli:measure>
    </xbrli:unitDenominator>
  </xbrli:divide>
</xbrli:unit>
```

Box 18. Excerpt of the configuration file sql2xquery.xml.

```
<entity tableName="unit"
tagName="db2-fn:xmlcolumn('FBR.INSTANCE.INFO')//xbrli:unit">
<field name="id" value = "@id" />
<field name= "unitNumerator"
value= "xbrli:divide/xbrli:unitNumerator/xbrli:measure" />
<field name= "unitDenominator"
value= "xbrli:divide/xbrli:unitDenominator/xbrli:measure" />
<field name= "measure" value = "xbrli:measure" />
</entity>
```

Box 19. XQuery query resulting from the translation process

```
for $store_store_state in distinct-values(db2-fn:xmlcolumn('FOODMART.STORE.
INFO')//store[store_state = 'WA']/store_state)
for $time_by_day_the_year in distinct-values(db2-fn:xmlcolumn('FOODMART.TIME_
BY_DAY.INFO')//time_by_day[the_year = 1997]/the_year)
let $store:= db2-fn:xmlcolumn('FOODMART.STORE.INFO')//store[store_state =
$store_store_state and store_state = 'WA']
let $time_by_day:= db2-fn:xmlcolumn('FOODMART.TIME_BY_DAY.INFO')//time_by_
day[the_year = $time_by_day_the_year and the_year = 1997]
let $sales_fact_1997:= db2-fn:xmlcolumn('FOODMART.SALES_FACT_1997.INFO')//
sales_fact_1997[store_id = $store/store_id and time_id = $time_by_day/time_id]
let $sum:= sum($sales_fact_1997/unit_sales)
where $sales_fact_1997
return
<line>
<store_state>{$store_store_state}</store_state>
<the_year>{$time_by_day_the_year}</the_year>
<sum>{$sum}</sum>
</line>
```

The sql2xquery driver was specified by object-oriented modeling, using the UML class diagram. The SQL and XQuery architecture components are described below:

- **SQL Component**: Composed of a set of classes illustrated in Figure 16, which represents the EBNF grammar of SQL query specified in Box 15. His classes are:
- **SQLQuery**: Allows the MDX query submitted be divided into several small SQL queries, defined from the EBNF grammar;
- **SelectStmt**: Class that represents the SQL command of the query. Have objects of all classes that make up the SQL queries: *SelectClause, FromClause, WhereClause, GroupByClause, HavingClause* e *OrderByClause*;
- **ColumnItem**: Represents an item of column, which can be a function or a column reference;

- **ColumnRef**: Class that represents a column reference, necessarily represented by the table name and column name;
- **FunctionItem**: Represents a function item, which can identify and represent the

Figure 15. Driver sql2xquery architecture

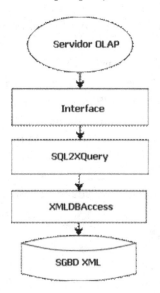

Figure 16. SQL component class diagram

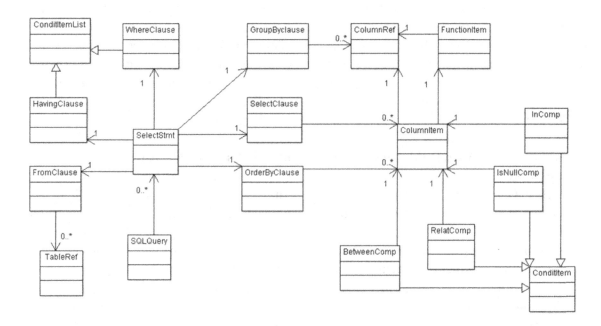

following functions: SUM, AVG, COUNT, MAX, MIN, UPPER, LOWER, ISNULL;

- **SelectClause**: Class that represents all the items listed in the SELECT statement of the SQL query, verifies the DISTINCT or ALL handling. It is a collection of *ColumnItem*;
- **TableRef**: Represents a table;
- **FromClause**: Class that represents the FROM clause of the SQL query. It is a collection of *TableRef*;
- **OrderByClause**: Represents the ORDERBY clause of the SQL query. It is a collection of *ColumnItem*;
- **GroupByClause**: Represents the GROUPBY clause of the SQL query. It is a collection of *ColumnRef*;
- **ConditItem**: Abstract super class of all conditional items;
- **RelatComp**: Derived from *ConditItem* is a class that represents a comparison conditional item, based on the smaller, larger, equal or different symbols. Allows comparison of one item from column

(*ColumnItem*) with another item or a constant;

- **BetweenComp**: Derived from *ConditItem*, represents a conditional item comparing a *ColumnItem* with a range of values;
- **InComp**: Derived from *ConditItem*, represents a conditional item that checks if a *ColumnItem* belongs to a list of constants;
- **IsNullComp**: Derived from *ConditItem*, represents a conditional item that checks if a *ColumnItem* is null;
- **ConditItemList**: Class that represents a collection of expressions/conditional items, represented by a collection of *ConditItem* and its derived classes. Conditional items can be separated or preceded by operators AND, OR or NOT;
- **WhereClause**: Derived from *ConditItemList*, represents the WHERE clause of a SQL query;
- **HavingClause**: Derived from *ConditItemList*, represents the HAVING clause of a SQL query.

- **XQUERY Component**: Formed by a set of classes that interpret an SQL expression, converts into XQuery expressions and make access to the database returning the result of the original MDX query. The class diagram of this component is shown in Figure 17. Its classes are:

- **XQuery**: Manage the process of converting SQL to XQuery expressions, promoting its execution at the XML DBMS. Provides results in XQResultSet;

- **XQueryGenerator**: Class that contains all the business rules, as well as its execution flow for converting SQL to XQuery;

- **XQWhere**: Class for handling of conditional expressions on FLWOR expressions. Specialisation of *ConditItemList*.

- **XQJoinCondition**: Class that verifies and optimizes conditional expressions from table joins in SQL query (the SQL JOIN clause);

- **XQueryRunner**: Class that manages the execution of XQuery queries in XML database getting and refining the results (i.e. handling duplication of results due to the not inclusion of distinct-value clause on XQuery expressions);

- **XQResultSet**: Class that implements the ResultSet interface to ensure compatibility with the return of queries in relational DBMS, also written in ResultSet objects. Facilitates the selection of query execution in relational or XML DBMS, implemented on this extension *mondrian*;

- **XQResultSetMetaData**: Class that provides the metadata of the data from the result of XQuery queries. This information is not useful in the conversion and implementation of XQuery process, however it is used in *mondrian* decisions for execution flow.

Besides these classes, there is Util class of the driver *sql2xquery* which contains useful and common functions to most classes. The exception classes present in *sql2xquery.exception* contain exceptions triggered by the driver. They are subclasses of the Exception class, from the API (Application Programming Interface) standard Java language.

Mondrian Integration

The driver integration with *mondrian* OLAP server was conducted through changes on the source code of this tool. The main changes were implemented in the *execute* method of the *SQLStatement* class, which is invoked by the *executeQuery* method of the *RolapUtil* class, which are part of *Mondrian. rolap* package. This method is responsible for executing, through an object from the *Statement* class, the SQL queries generated by *mondrian*.

The Interface layer is an extension of the second layer of the *mondrian*, with the overhead of the *SQLStatement* class to process MDX queries on data represented in XML.

The driver performs the cube mapping defined in the OLAP server for the XML documents through a metadata, which are represented by a configuration file. The configuration of the mondrian's metadata file is performed only once for each DW-XML. From the identification of the query elements at the metadata, we seek on the configuration file the property corresponding. For property in the metadata, it is understood, for the relational environment, the columns of the fact or dimension tables, which correspond to the XML elements, sub-elements or attributes.

After translating the SQL queries, the driver applies the resulting XQuery queries on the corresponding XML documents stored in the XML DBMS and sends the returned data from these queries to the OLAP server. However, before performing this conversion process, the LMDQL

Figure 17. XQUERY component class diagram

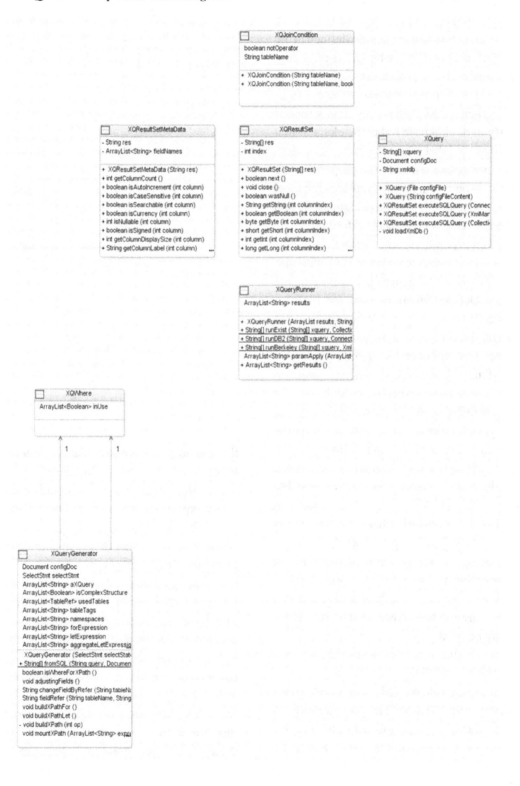

processor evaluates the MDX expression to check if it is composed by the properties names, which represent measures and dimensions, defined in the server configuration file, or by labels regarding these properties. If the properties names given in the query expression are not found in this configuration file, then the XLPath processor is activated to identify in the linkbase Label the element that is relative to the label. Once the element is identified, the processor retrieves the property name from the configuration file and replaces the label by the property name in the query expression, and then, the conversion process is performed.

For the incorporation of the LMDQL language processor in the *mondrian* server, it was necessary: (i) to implement the language operators using the UDF (User-Defined Functions) resource; (ii) to integrate the *driver sql2xquery*, for the conversion of SQL queries in XQuery; and (iii) to retrieve the operators created by the operator *OperatorDefinition* and found in the linkbase Calculation. *mondrian* metadata configuration is performed only once for each data warehouse, while the navigation on the linkbase Label, however, is performed each time the query elements are not found in this metadata. The approach chosen for the *mondrian* extension has the advantage of causing the smallest possible coupling to this OLAP server. Also, in addition to the XLDM metamodel, other data warehouses data models for XML (e.g.without XLink) can be used, being enough the cube mapping in the *mondrian*. Thus, it is important to notice that it is transparent for the user if the database is relational or not and any multidimensional data model for XML may be used.

Figure 18 illustrates the activities diagram refers a LMDQL/MDX query execution in a data warehouse based on XML and XLink, modeled according to XLDM. The configuration of *Mondrian* metadata is performed only once for each *data warehouse*, on the other hand, the navigation on linkbase Label is performed every time that the query elements are not found on

Figure 18. Activities diagram for MDX/LMDQL query execution

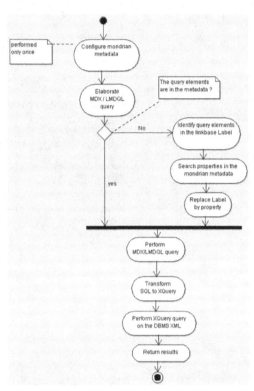

this metadata. After that, the XLPath processor is activated to search on linkbase Label the element correspondent to the Label provided in the query expression. Once the element is identified, it searches on *Mondrian* configuration file the property correspondent to it, substituting the Label of the user's XQuery expression by the value of the property found on *Mondrian* metadata. For the relational environment, these properties consist in columns of facts or dimensions tables, which correspond, in the XML environment, to the elements, subelements or attributes. Forthwith, it is carried out the MDX/LMDQL query execution following the process of conversion *Mondrian* from this expression in SQL expressions. After that, the *driver sql2xquery* actuates converting these SQL expressions in XQuery expressions and executing them on DBMS XML.

A CASE STUDY

The ideas discussed on this work and their main contributions, XLDM, XLPath and LMDQL are evaluated by three case studies. The first case study has as a goal to evaluate the XLDM model in a medical area context. The second one contemplates financial databased on XBRL *Dimensions* documents, which is a context that uses a varied number of indicators to measure companies financial and economic situation, and, for that, allows illustrating XLPath and LMDQL *OperatorDefinion* operator application, which allows the creation of financial indexes. In the end, it is discussed a case study based on a data warehouse over data of OLAP *mondrian* tool tests. Such data was converted from the relational model to XML, with the creation of XML instances, data schema, based on XML *Schema,* and linkbase*s*, all of this based on XLDM. Additionally, it is presented a performance evaluation, relative to the queries execution time. In this evaluation were performed tests in three DBMS that store XML documents differently. The purpose of this test was to identify the behavior of driver *sql2xquery* in different storage environments. Comparative tests were carried out to evaluate the execution time of queries that need to obtain information on linkbases in relation to those that do not use this resource and tests to compare the execution time of LMDQL and MDX queries that produce the same result.

The case studies were performed in different data warehouses XML, in order to show that the solution of analytical process over XML data can perform queries over XML documents maintained in different DBMS and different application domains.

An XLDM Metamodel Application

Figure 19 shows UML components diagram for the data cube model used in this case study. The *TreatmentCube* hypercube has four dimensions:

Patient, Procedure, Medication and Disease. They relate to the hypercube through the arcroles *hypercube-dimension.* There is also the relationship of the cube with the *Dosage* measure, made with the use of the arcrole *all.* The schema created is shown in Box 20. It contains the definition of the data cube *TreatmentCube,* of the dimension *PatientDimension,* of the domain *PatientDomain* and of a member of this domain (*Patient1*). Finally, the specification of the *Dosage* measure is made. The use of the attribute *abstract,* in some elements, indicates that these are used only for structural organization purposes, not being possible to be used in the instance document.

Box 21 illustrates some elements of the Definition linkbase, in which the definitions of the hierarchic relations occur. For the relationship between the TreatmentCube cube and the Dosage measure, the arcrole all is used. The dimensions are linked to the cube through the arcrole hypercube-dimension. Besides, the dimensions also relate to its domains, through the arcrole dimension-domain. Finally, the arcrole domain-member provides the representation of the hierarchies in the dimensions.

The Label linkbase, used to create labels for the members, can be seen in Box 22. There are the labels specification, to represent the medicine commercial names, and the ICD-10 code, an international standard for diseases. In this example illustrated in Box 22, the attribute *lang* indicates that the drug name is specified in the English language. These relations use the arcrole *concept*-Label.

For the health area, it is necessary to specify an order for performing certain procedures in the disease treatment. In the proposed data model, it is possible to express this by ordering representation using the Ordering linkbase. This linkbase can be seen in Box 23, which uses a processingLink element to define that the first element that should be processed is the cube, followed by the dimension, the domain and the member. This is done by the numerical value of the attribute *order.*

Figure 19. The data model for the treatment cube

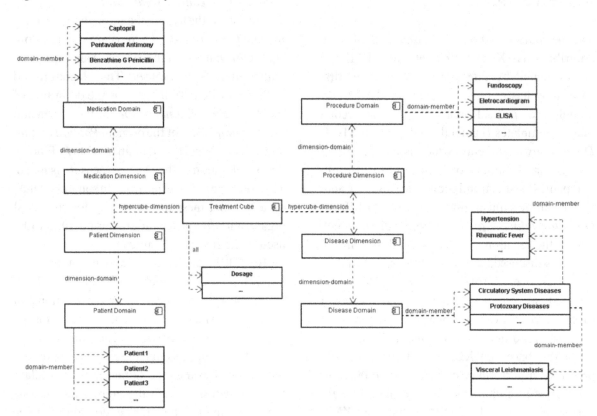

Box 20. Schema document

```
<element id="TreatmentCube" name="TreatmentCube"
    type="xldmi:stringItemType"
    abstract="true" substitutionGroup="xldmdt:hypercubeItem"/>
<element id="PatientDimension" abstract="true" name="PatientDimension"
    type="xldmi:stringItemType" substitutionGroup="xldmdt:dimensionItem"/>
<element id="PatientDomain" name="PatientDomain"
    type="xldmi:stringItemType"
    abstract="true"  substitutionGroup="xldmi:item"/>
<element id="Patient1" name="Patient1" type="xldmi:stringItemType"
    substitutionGroup="xldmi:item"/>
<element id="Dosage" name="Dosage" type="xldmi:stringItemType"
    substitutionGroup="xldmi:item"/>
```

The *Description* linkbase is used to provide textual descriptions related to a certain concept. Box 24 shows the description made for an element that represents the disease Rheumatic Fever. In Box 25, the use of a linkbase of type *References* illustrated, in this example the elements *ref:Name*, *ref:Number*, *ref:Chapter* and *ref:URI* are used to establish a reference representation for the element *Hypertension*, defined in the data schema *treatment.xsd*.

The only arithmetic operation seen in XBRL *Dimensions* is addition. Box 26 puts in evidence the use of this operation in a different context from the financial, showing the composition of a medicine manipulated by the relation between the formula components and the medicine. However, the changes performed in linkbase Calculation regard the extensions that allow the use of other arithmetic operations besides addition, which will be seen in the case study performed for the financial area.

An extract of the instance document is illustrated in Box 27, illustrating a data cube, where the context Patient1_Hypertension is defined. In this context, the dimension members PatientDimension, ProcedureDimension, MedicationDimension and DiseaseDimension are given. The temporal view of the fact is established by the element period, with sub-elements for the starting and ending date for which the fact is valid. A temporal

Box 21. Definition linkbase

```
<definitionLink xlink:type="extended"
  xlink:role="http://www.example.br/xldm/treatment">
<loc xlink:type="locator" xlink:label="lbl_TreatmentCube"
  xlink:href="treatment.xsd#TreatmentCube"/>
<loc xlink:type="locator" xlink:label="lbl_Dosage"
  xlink:href="treatment.xsd#lbl_Dosage" />
<definitionArc xlink:type="arc"
  xlink:arcrole=http://www.exemple.br/arcrole/all
  xlink:from="lbl_Dosage" ink:to="lbl_TreatmentCube"/>
<loc xlink:type="locator" xlink:label="lbl_PatientDimension"
  xlink:href="treatment.xsd#lbl_PatientDimension" />
<definitionArc xlink:type="arc"
  xlink:arcrole="http://www.example.br/arcrole/hypercube-dimension"
  xlink:from="lbl_TreatmentCube" xlink:to="lbl_PatientDimension"/>
<loc xlink:type="locator" xlink:label="lbl_PatientDomain"
  xlink:href="treatment.xsd#lbl_PatientDomain"/>
<definitionArc xlink:type="arc"
  xlink:arcrole=http://www.example.br/arcrole/dimension-domain
  xlink:from="lbl_PatientDimension" xlink:to="lbl_PatientDomain"/>
<loc xlink:type="locator" xlink:label="lbl_Patient1"
  xlink:href="treatment.xsd#lbl_Patient1" />
<definitionArc xlink:type="arc"
  xlink:arcrole="http://www.example.br/arcrole/domain-member"
  xlink:from="lbl_PatientDomain" xlink:to="lbl_Patient1"/>
</definitionLink>
```

Box 22. Label linkbase

```
<labelLink xlink:type="extended"  xlink:role="http://www.exemplo.br/xldm/
treatment">
<loc xlink:type="locator" link:label="lbl_Captopril"
xlink:href="treatment.xsd#Captopril" />
<label xlink:type="resource" xml:lang="en" xlink:label="lbl_Capitopril_Comer-
cial"
     xlink:role="http://www.example.br/role/label">Capoten</label>
<labelArc xlink:type="arc" xlink:arcrole="http://www.example.br/arcrole/con-
cept-label"
xlink:from="lbl_Captopril" xlink:to="lbl_Capitropil_Comercial"/>
</labelLink>
```

Box 23. Ordering linkbase

```
<processingLink xlink:type="extended"
  xlink:role="http://www.examplE.br/xldm/treatment">
<loc xlink:type="locator"  xlink:label="lbl_TreatmentCube"
   xlink:href="treatment.xsd#lbl_TreatmentCube"/>
<loc xlink:type="locator" xlink:label="lbl_PatientDimension"
   xlink:href="treatment.xsd#lbl_PatientDimension"/>
<processingArc xlink:type="arc" xlink:from="lbl_TreatmentCube"
   xlink:to="lbl_PatientDimension" order="1"
xlink:arcrole="http://www.exemplo.br/arcrole/parent-child"/>
<loc xlink:type="locator" xlink:label="lbl_PatientDomain"
   xlink:href="treatment.xsd#lbl_PatientDomain" />
<processingArc xlink:type="arc" xlink:from="lbl_PatientDimension"
    xlink:to="lbl_PatientDomain"
    xlink:arcrole="http://www.example.br/arcrole/parent-child
    "order="2"/>
<loc xlink:type="locator" xlink:label="lbl_Patient1"
   xlink:href="treatment.xsd#lbl_Patient1"/>
<processingArc xlink:type="arc"
  xlink:arcrole="http://www.example.br/arcrole/parent-child"
  xlink:from="lbl_PatientDomain" xlink:to="lbl_Patient1" order="3"/>
</processingLink>
```

hierarchy can be established by other sub-elements, e.g. elements for year or semester. The element unit defines the measure unit, in the example, the unit referring to the fact is miligrams per day, i.e. for patient1, which is undertaking the fundoscopy treatment, in the period from January 1st, 2007 to December 31st, 2007, for the disease hypertension, the daily dose of the medicine Captopril is 50mg.

The members of each dimension are identified according to the characteristic of the dimension

Box 24. Description linkbase

```
<descriptionLink xlink:type="extended"
  xlink:role="http://www.example.br/xldm/treatment">
<loc xlink:type="locator" xlink:label="lbl_Rheumaticfever"
  xlink:href="treatment.xsd#RheumaticFever"/>
<description xlink:type="resource"
  xlink:role="http://www.example.br/role/description"
  xlink:label="desc_RheumaticFever">
Rheumatic fever is an inflammatorydisease that may develop two to three weeks
after a Group A streptococcal infection such as strep throat or scarlet fe-
ver). It is believed to be caused by antibodycross-reactivity and can involve
the heart,joints, skin,
And brain. Acute rheumatic fever commonly appears in children ages 5 through
15, with only 20% of first time attacks occurring in adults  </description>
</descriptionLink>
```

Box 25. Linkbase reference

```
<referenceLink xlink:type="extended"
  xlink:role="http://www.example.br/role/link">
<loc xlink:type="locator" xlink:label="lbl_Hypertension"
  xlink:href="treatment.xsd#Hypertension" />
<referenceArc xlink:type="arc"
  xlink:arcrole="http://www.example.br/arcrole/concept-reference"
  xlink:from="lbl_Hypertension" xlink:to="ref_Hypertension"/>
<reference xlink:type="resource" xlink:label="ref_Hypertension"
  xlink:role="http://www.example.br/role/reference">
<ref:Name>International Classification of Diseases</ref:Name>
<ref:Number>I10</ref:Number>
<ref:Chapter>IX</ref:Chapter>
<ref:URI>
http://apps.who.int/classifications/apps/icd/icd10online/gi10.htm </ref:URI>
</reference></referenceLink>
```

to which they belong to. Two types of dimensions are originally defined: *explicitMember*, illustrated in Box 27, in which all the domain members are discreetly grouped; and *typedMember*, in which the elements quantity cannot be expressed by a finite number, as in longitude and latitude cases, in a geographic context.

With this data structure for the *data warehouse*, based on XLDM, the heterogeneity problems do not exist, once the measure unit is defined by the attribute *unit*, Label*s* for the elements are specified in the linkbaseLabel, the elements and their names are defined in the data schema, based on XML *Schema*, and the elements hierarchic structure is defined in the linkbase Definition.

Box 26. Calculation linkbase

```
<calculationLink xlink:type="extended"
 xlink:role="http://www.example.br/treatment">
<loc xlink:type="locator" xlink:label="lbl_Hydralazine"
 xlink:href="treatment.xsd#Hydralazine" />
<loc xlink:type="locator" xlink:label="lbl_SodiumNitroprussiate"
 xlink:href="treatment.xsd#SodiumNitroprussiate" />
<calculationArc xlink:type="arc"
 xlink:arcrole="http://www.example.br/arcrole/summation-item"
 xlink:from="lbl_Hydralazine" xlink:to="lbl_SodiumNitroprussiate"
 weight="0.05"/>
<loc xlink:type="locator" xlink:label="lbl_IsotonicGlucoseSolution"
    xlink:href="treatment.xsd#IsotonicGlucoseSolution"/>
<calculationArc xlink:type="arc"
 xlink:arcrole="http://www.example.br/arcrole/summation-item"
 xlink:from="lbl_Hydralazine" xlink:to="lbl_IsotonicGlucoseSolution"
 weight="0.25"/>
</calculationLink>
```

Box 27. XLDM instance

```
<context id="Patient1_Hypertension">
<entity>
<segment>
<xldmdi:explicitMember dimension="trat:PatientDimension">
      trat:Patient1</xldmdi:explicitMember>
<xldmdi:explicitMember  dimension="trat:ProcedureDimension">
      trat:Fundoscopy</xldmdi:explicitMember>
<xldmdi:explicitMember dimension="trat:MedicationDimension">
      trat:Captopril</xldmdi:explicitMember>
<xldmdi:explicitMember dimension="trat:DiseaseDimension">
       trat:Hypertension</xldmdi:explicitMember>
</segment>
</entity>
<period><startDate>2007-01-01</startDate>
<endDate>2007-12-31</endDate></period>
</context>
<unit id="mg_day"><divide>
<unitNumerator>mg</unitNumerator>
<unitDenominator>day</unitDenominator></divide>
</unit>
<trat:Dosage contextRef="Patient1_Hypertension" unitRef="mg_day">50</
trat:Dosage>
```

OLAP for the Financial Analysis

Currently, in the financial area one may find a relevant application for LMDQL language, since XBRL *Dimensions* is a technology based on XML *Schema* and XLink and most of the Central Banks and regulating institutions in the stock market have been adopting this technology as a means for financial information interchange. Thus, examples of XLPath language use and examples in which financial operators based on XLDM are presented, besides the use of other LMDQL operators.

To justify the need for navigating in links, the use of XLPath language in the financial environment is discussed showing the XLPath use by navigation in steps, similar to XPath. It is approached the use of the operator *OperatorDefinition* in the financial analysis environment, creating XLDM documents for representing the financial indexes. Besides that, it is presented the use of LMDQL operators in XBRL documents.

Examples of XLPath Queries

As an example of XPath expression, the following location path may be used to find, from the linkbase document showed in Box 4, the element locator whose label is "BankingActivitiesDomain":

*/descendant-or-self::link:*DefinitionLink*/ child::link: loc[@xlink:*Label=*"BankingActivit iesDomain"].*

The query resulting from the computation of this expression is performed in stages called *location steps* (isolated by "/"), whose general form is: *axis::nodeSpecification[Predicate]*. The axis indicates in each direction from one reference node – called *context node* – the query must be performed, placed that in majority of cases this direction regards to one of the relationships of the XML tree. The *node specification* determines which nodes in this direction must be selected. Besides that, it is possible to filter the result using

a predicate (optional), which consists in a boolean test applied to the selected node: when the result is true, the node is maintained; otherwise, it is discarded. The expression organization in successive *location steps* allows any node in the tree to be accessed, making XPath an ideal tool for navigating in this type of structure. XPath has been seen as a de facto standard in the XML query research area. However, it does not provide a means of navigating through XLink links. As a result, both the semantics and the processing issues concerning link data are compromised.

When the interest is exploring the information according to the extended links perspective, this solution appears to be insufficient. For example, to formulate a query whose purpose is to *select all the targets elements of arcs, whose source is the element d-ba_TotalBankingActivities*, two important issues must be considered: (i) differently from a traditional XML tree, the data structure resulting from references established by the links characterize a network; and (ii) there is no restriction regarding the location of a referred resource, which may be in any part of the XML document or, yet, in a distinct document. Thus, exploring the information related by the extended link using XPath, when it is not possible (in the case of references between distinct XML documents), demands a formulation of complex queries. With XQuery the situation is not different, since mechanisms as FLWOR clauses (XQuery, 2007) are not proper for navigation in links. It is evident, therefore, the need for a query language specialized in the extended links mechanism. However, it is important to ponder that the development of a language based on a completely new syntax would cause a bigger difficult assimilation from the users who are already familiar with XPath syntax. To minimize this impact, it is desirable the existence of a proximity between these syntaxes. The XLPath language is based on *location path* expressions of XPath, in which new axis, node tests and predicates were developed aiming the navigation through the networks formed by extended links. This query, besides other examples, is solved bellow through XLPath:

Select all arcs targets elements whose element d-ba_TotalBankingActivities is the source.

```
/d-ba_
TotalBankingActivities::HL::arc-
source::arc()/HL::arc-
source::element()
```

Select the locator belonging to the link:DefinitionLink that connects itself to the element d-ba_BankingActivitiesDomain.

```
/d-ba_BankingActivitiesDom
ain::LL::linked::locator()
[link(link:definitionLink)]
```

Select the remote resource that attends the following conditions: (i) be connected to the locator whose Label *is "TotalBankingActivities";*

and (ii) be the source of the arc whose element db-a_TotalBankingActivitiesSubjectBIA is target.

```
/d-ba_TotalBankingActivitiesSubjec
tBIA::HL::arc-destination::arc()/
LL::arc-destination::locator()[attrib
ute(xlink:label)='TotalBankingActivit
ies']/LL::linked::remote()
```

Execute the link crossing from the element d-ba_BankingActivitiesDomain to the element d-ba_TotalBankingActivities.

```
/d-ba_
BankingActivitiesDomain::HL::arc-
source::arc()/HL::arc-source::
remote(d-a_TotalBankingActivities)
```

These examples show how XLPath perform queries in XML documents interconnected by XLink. Figure 20 illustrates a query performed in the scheme *d-ba-2006-07-01.xsd*. This docu-

Figure 20. XLPath processor console

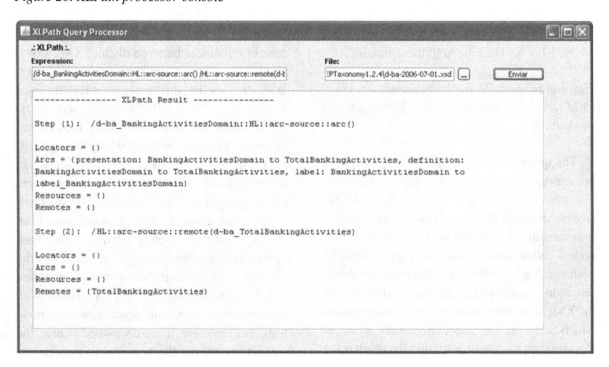

ment contains elements referred by the link *link:*Definition*Link*, which is in a linkbase. During the query execution, the XLPath expression identifies these references and, automatically, identifies the corresponding linkbase. This type of query cannot be performed by the languages XPath or XQuery. Thus, the main contribution of XLPath is the ability to perform queries in XML documents interconnected by extended links.

Example of *OperatorDefinition*

There is a large quantity of information that may be extracted from financial statements. This information organization, according to financial analysis literature, allows the analysis that starts from generic to particular evaluations. With LMDQL operator *OperatorDefinition,* it is possible to create operators specific for business evaluation, including performance analysis, shares evaluation and models defined by statistic studies, followed by those for cashier management analysis and, in the end, by the profit management ones (Brigham, 2007; Damondaran, 2007; Helfert, 1997; Matarazzo, 2003). In the creation of the operators by the operator *OperatorDefinition*, the linkbases Definition, Calculation and Label are generated to represent the relationships that compose the definition of these operators, and in addition, the created operators are defined in a XML Schema document. Thus, a taxonomy based on XLDM for financial indexes is created.

The syntax and semantic of some of these financial operators are presented at http://www. cin.ufpe.br/~pcs3/XLDM/FinancialDataModel, as well as an XLDM taxonomy developed to represent these operators (Silva, 2010). This taxonomy based on XLDM allows representing results from financial analysis extracted from data represented in XBRL, complementing the information contained on financial statements.

The operators created through the operator *OperatorDefinition* are stored in a library of operators of the metadata repository (LMDQL Ar-

chiteture) for future use. This approach facilitates the management of these operators according to the area in which they are embedded and enables its use in different contexts. In the creation of these operators, the linkbase Definition and Label and the elements specification that represent the operators (XML *Schema*) allow the solution of XML data heterogeneity problems. Besides that, the arithmetic relation among the elements that constitute the operator is represented in the linkbase Calculation. To exemplify the use of the *OperatorDefinition*, it was created an index that represents a relation among the members *"Exposure Value"* and *"Credit Risk capital requirements"*. Figure 21 illustrates the creation of this operator and Figure 22 shows the use of the created operator by the *OperatorDefinition*.

Figure 23 shows the linkbase Calculation, generated by the operator *OperatorDefinition*, which represents the created index.

The metamodel XLDM, besides having a bigger scope of domains than XBRL *Dimensions*, also provides a bigger expressivity. It may also be seen with the use of the new *arcroles* proposed for the linkbase Calculation. Box 28 shows a portion of a linkbase Calculation in which there is the specification of another financial index named *"debtComposition"*. It is composed by the relation between the concepts *"currentLiabilities"* and *"OthersCapital"*. In the original definition of this linkbase, in XBRL *Dimensions*, it is not possible to express this type of relationship. Thus, XLDM contribution in the financial field extends the possibilities offered by XBRL *Dimensions*.

Sales Data Warehouse: Foodmart

Aiming at validating the LMDQL operators, a data warehouse based on the *mondrian* sample dataset was converted from the relational model to XML by creating XML instances and using the XLDM data scheme. FoodMart dataset contains corporate sales performance indicators. Linkbases Label was created to establish relationships between

Figure 21. Index creationfrom the operator OperatorDefinition

Operator Definition

```
with operatordefinition(' [Measures].[ExposureValue]/[Measures].
[CreditRiskCapitalRequirements]',ExposureRiskIndex)
```

Create Operator Definition

List of Operator Definition

```
#ExposureRiskIndex# --> member [Measures].[ExposureRiskIndex] as '[Measures].[ExposureValue]/[Measures].[CreditRiskCapitalRequirements]'
#AcumulativeExposure# --> member [Measures].[AcumulativeExposure] as '1.00*[Measures].[ExposureValue]+1.00*[Measures].[CreditRiskCapitalRequirements]'
```

Figure 22. Use of operator created by the operator OperatorDefinition

Ad-Hoc MDX Queries

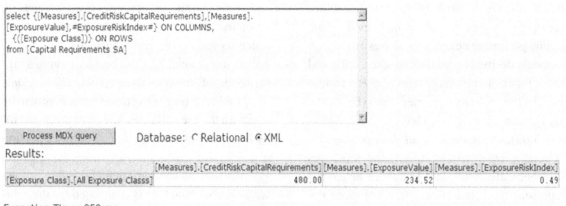

```
select {[Measures].[CreditRiskCapitalRequirements],[Measures].
[ExposureValue],#ExposureRiskIndex#} ON COLUMNS,
 {([Exposure Class])} ON ROWS
from [Capital Requirements $A]
```

Process MDX query   Database: ◦ Relational ● XML

Results:

	[Measures].[CreditRiskCapitalRequirements]	[Measures].[ExposureValue]	[Measures].[ExposureRiskIndex]
[Exposure Class].[All Exposure Classs]	480.00	234.52	0.49

Execution Time: 859 ms.

labels and the XML instances elements. Others associations can be of type Definition or Calculation, as specified in the XLDM metamodel. Box 29 illustrates an excerpt of linkbase Label, which specifies labels for XML documents elements. The LMDQL queries used in our performance tests are based on this collection of documents. They were executed using the *mondrian* OLAP tool integrated with the driver *sql2xquery* and the LMDQL/XLPath processors. Figure 24 ex-

emplifies an LMDQL query with the use of the *OperatiorDefinition* operator. The query of this figure does not need to navigate on a linkbase Label to search for information. To illustrate the use of a linkbase navigation resource, another query was considered in our experiments, which replace measures and dimensions names by labels defined for the Portuguese language and found in a linkbase Label. Figure 25 gives this query that illustrates the use of *Separatrix* operator as well.

Figure 23. Linkbase calculation, created by the operator OperatorDefinition

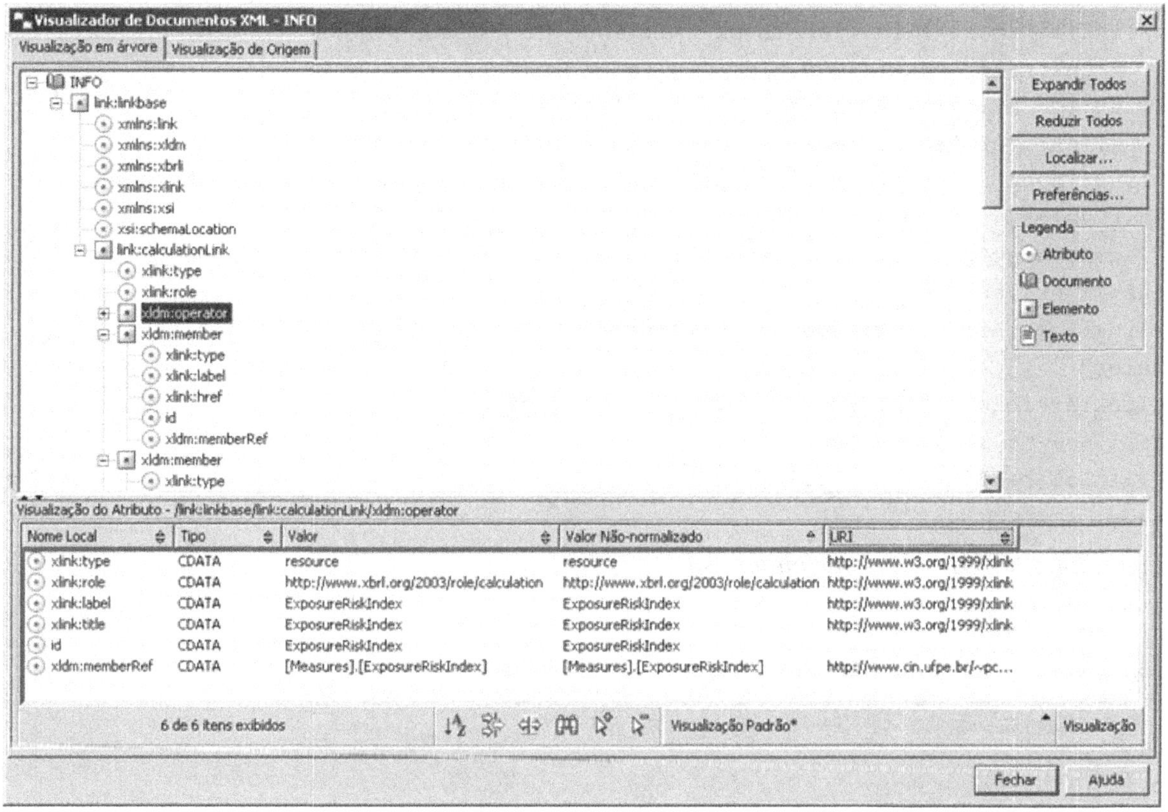

Box 28. Specification of debt composition índex

```
<calculationLink xlink:type="extended"
  xlink:role="http://www.example.br/financial">
<loc xlink:type="locator" xlink:label="lbl_currentLiabilities"
    xlink:href="financial.xsd#currentLiabilities"/>
<loc xlink:type="locator" xlink:label="lbl_debtComposition"
    xlink:href="financial.xsd#debtComposition"/>
<calculationArc xlink:type="arc"
    xlink:arcrole="http://www.exemplo.br/arcrole/numerator-item"
    xlink:from="lbl_debtComposition" xlink:to="lbl_currentLiabilities"/>
<loc xlink:type="locator" xlink:label="lbl_OthersCapital"
    xlink:href="financial.xsd#OthersCapital"/>
<calculationArc xlink:type="arc"
    xlink:arcrole=http://www.exemplo.br/arcrole/denominator-item"
    xlink:from="lbl_debtComposition" xlink:to="lbl_OthersCapital"/>
</calculationLink>
```

Box 29. Linkbase label

```
</link:linkbase><link:labelLink xml:lang="pt" xlink:type="extended"
    xlink:role="http://www.xldm.org/role/link">
<link:loc xlink:type="locator" xlink:label="unit_sales"
    xlink:href="xquery:db2-fn:xmlcolumn('LINKBASE.TAXONOMY.INFO')#unit_sales"/>
<link:label xlink:type="resource" id="label_unit_sales" xlink:label="label_
unit_sales"
    xml:lang="pt" xlink:role="http://www.xldm.org/role/label">Vendas Unitar-
ias</link:label>
<link:labelArc xlink:type="arc" xlink:from="unit_sales" xlink:to="label_unit_
sales"
xlink:arcrole="http://www.xldm.org/arcrole/concept-label"/>
                        . . .
</link:labelLink></link:linkbase>
```

Figure 24. LMDQL operatordefinition use

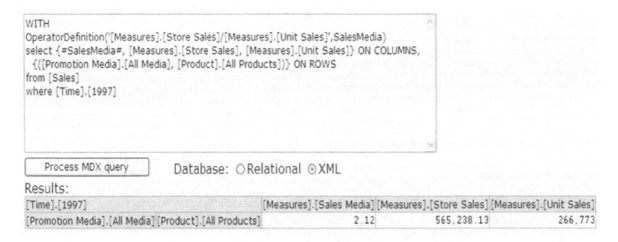

PERFORMANCE EVALUATION

The performance evaluation aimed at evaluating the elapsed time of the proposal presented in this paper for the analytical processing of XML documents. The size of the database and the metadata repository (linkbases and schema) were 160 and 256 MB, respectively. The workbench was composed by the operational system Windows XP, 32 bits, service Pack 3, computer with processor Intel Pentium Core 2 Duo 1.7GHZ, 1.5GB RAM. Each evaluated query was executed 20 times, with the operational system, the DBMS and the application server being restarted for avoiding the reuse of previously fetched data. Through this procedure, the result derived from possible intermediary data stored in cache was avoided. Performance tests were executed to: (i) evaluate the elapsed time to process queries that transform SQL expressions into XQuery; (ii) investigate the elapsed time of analytical queries that search for data in linkbases; and, (iii) examine the elapsed times spent to process both a MDX query and its corresponding LMDQL query (Figure 26, Figure 27).

Figure 25. Separatrix operator query with labels

```
select{[Measures].[Vendas Unitarias]} on columns,
{Separatrix({Descendants([Store].[Store Country].[USA], 2)},
          [Store].[Store Country].[USA].[CA].[Beverly Hills], 10)} on rows
from Sales
```

Process MDX query   Database: ⊂ Relational ⊙ XML

Results:

	[Measures].[Unit Sales]								
	2202,30	2236,60	11490,90	23590,20	24575,50	25010,80	25662,10	26078,40	35256,70
[Store].[All Stores].[USA].[CA].[Beverly Hills]				21.333					

Figure 26. Mondrian query

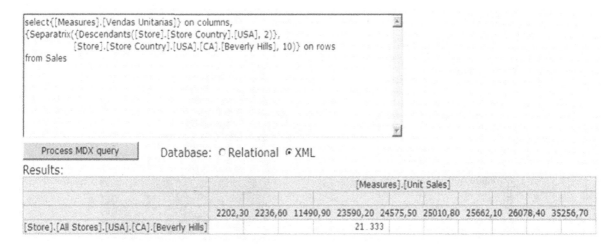

Test Query uses Mondrian OLAP

Promotion Media	Product	Measures		
		Unit Sales	Store Cost	Store Sales
⊕All Media	−All Products	266.773	225.627,23	565.238,13
	−Drink	24.597	19.477,23	48.836,21
	−Alcoholic Beverages	6.838	5.576,79	14.029,08
	−Beer and Wine	6.838	5.576,79	14.029,08
	−Beer	1.683	1.348,14	3.400,45
	⊕Good	269	198,21	500,18
	⊕Pearl	385	218,30	549,85
	⊕Portsmouth	362	412,24	1.067,17
	⊕Top Measure	306	141,94	343,04
	⊕Walrus	361	377,45	940,21
	⊕Wine	5.155	4.228,64	10.628,63
	⊕Beverages	13.573	11.069,53	27.748,53
	⊕Dairy	4.186	2.830,92	7.058,60
	⊕Food	191.940	163.270,72	409.035,59
	⊕Non-Consumable	50.236	42.879,28	107.366,33

Slicer: [Year=1997]

1. **sql2xquery driver performance**: Driver performance tests were run in four XML database managing systems MySQL, DB2 Express C, eXist-DB and Berkeley, on the first one was evaluated the runtime on a relational data model, i.e. the XML data was mapped and loaded into relational database tables and the others are XML DBMS. The evaluation was performed using six LMDQL/MDX queries. These generated 8, 11, 15, 18, 22 and 26 SQL queries, respectively. The sixth query on the *mondrian* can be seen in Figure 26, whose MDX query is shown in Box 30. The elapsed time of the

Figure 27. Global time of queries execution

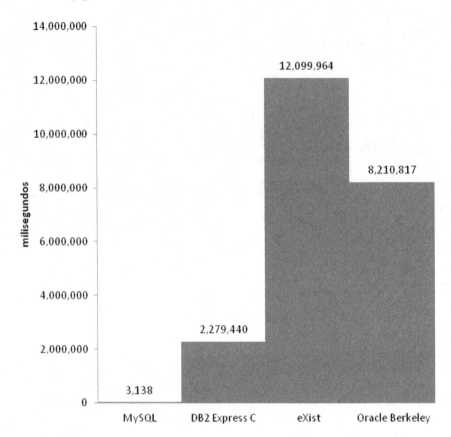

Box 30. MDX query

```
select {[Measures].[Unit Sales], [Measures].[Store Cost], [Measures].[Store
Sales]} ON COLUMNS,
   Hierarchize(Union(Union(Union(Union(Union(Crossjoin({[Promotion Media].[All
Media]}, {[Product].[All Products]}), Crossjoin({[Promotion Media].[All Me-
dia]}, [Product].[All Products].Children)), Crossjoin({[Promotion Media].[All
Media]}, [Product].[All Products].[Drink].Children)), Crossjoin({[Promotion Me-
dia].[All Media]}, [Product].[All Products].[Drink].[Alcoholic Beverages].Chil-
dren)), Crossjoin({[Promotion Media].[All Media]}, [Product].[All Products].
[Drink].[Alcoholic Beverages].[Beer and Wine].Children)), Crossjoin({[Promotion
Media].[All Media]}, [Product].[All Products].[Drink].[Alcoholic Beverages].
[Beer and Wine].[Beer].Children))) ON ROWS
from [Sales] where [Time].[1997]
```

26 SQL queries, that were transformed into XQuery expressions by the driver *sql2xquery* and were submitted to XML DBMS, is given in Figure 27. For MySQL, the SQL expressions generated by *mondrian* were used, with no conversion to XQuery expressions by *sql2xquery* driver. DB2 Express C showed an average processing time of 2279.4 seconds, the eXist processed the query about 12099.9 seconds and Oracle Berkeley in 8210.8 seconds, while in the relational DBMS, MySQL, the execution time was 3 seconds. The difference in execution time of these three XML DBMS can be attributed to different ways of storing XML documents, since no change in driver *sql2xquery* to process queries on them. Due to DBMS eXist and Oracle Berkeley's low performances in comparison with DB2 Express C, the remaining tests were executed using the DB2 Express C only. Based on this evaluation, it can be concluded that the XQuery expressions, obtained through the driver sql2xquery and submitted at the three XML DBMS, have lower performance than SQL queries submitted in relational DBMS (without driver intervention). In the best case of queries executed in XML DBMS, i.e. DB2 Express C, there was a significant increase in execution time with respect to queries made in MySQL DBMS, this can be associated with the efficient performance of the indexes in relational DBMS, an issue yet to be settled in XML DBMS.

2. **Performance results for queries with XLink:** To compare the execution of queries that do not need to recover information in linkbases, with those that need, it was performed a test with queries illustrated in Figure 28. The only difference among the queries is the fact that the later searches for information regarding the elements that refer to the labels written in Portuguese in the query expression. This analysis was performed in a linkbases linked sequence, in which seven labels found in the query expression were distributed on the first linkbase, or on the second, and successively until the eighth linkbase. Thus, we created five test configurations: (C0) the expression query has no labels, so no need for navigation in linkbase, (C1) the labels are retrieved in the first linkbase, (C2) the labels are recovered in the second linkbase, (C4) the labels are recovered in the fourth linkbase and (C8): the labels are recovered in the eighth linkbase. The total execution time of the queries with the search on linkbases may be seen on Table 7. It is relevant to notice that there is only a small difference between the queries elapsed times, indicating that the additional processing to search information in linkbases Label is not relevant. This test result may be an indication that the increased computation cost related to the processing of links did not impair the performance of OLAP queries over XML data with XLink. This is the first study of this nature and our performance results should be interpreted in this light. Nevertheless, this additional cost for processing XML documents with XLink did not seem to be related to high performance losses indicating that it may be compensated by the facility of representing multidimensional data cubes, dealing with XML data heterogeneity issues and performing OLAP queries over XML documents with XLink.

3. **Performance results for queries written in MDX versus LMDQL:** A comparative assessment of the elapsed time of a LMDQL query with the same query written in MDX was carried out using the horizontal analysis operator of LMDQL, namely HAnalysis. The average running time of these queries were respectively 165,376 and 166,317 milliseconds, indicating a very small difference between the two approaches investigated. The specifications of these queries can be

viewed in Figures 29 and 30. It is important to note that the LMDQL query sentence is simpler and more concise than the MDX sentence. In this example, for the MDX query specification, we had to create eight calculated members and write specific expressions for determining the result that represents the information needed for computing the horizontal analysis. In queries of this type that requires a greater amount of information, the MDX expression clearly will be more extensive and complex. Further investigation is still needed but such complexity may be the reason why no performance impact was found in our performance evaluation tests.

CONCLUSION

In this paper, we presented a query environment for multidimensional data, which is based on XML data interconnected by links. This environment is composed of: (i) a data multidimensional metamodel, named XLDM; (ii) a language for navigation on XML data interconnected by links, XLPath; (iii) based on this approaches, a query language for multidimensional data, LMDQL, was specified, which allows the elaboration of queries over interconnected XML data; and (iv) to do so,

it was implemented a driver, which maps expressions of SQL queries into XQuery and extends an open code OLAP server. Thus, it was possible to perform queries using the operators defined in LMDQL and the traditional multidimensional operators as well. This proposal was founded on standards widely diffused as MDX, XML Schema, XLink and XPath and it is not known, until now, the existence of a multidimensional query language for XML documents interconnected by links.

A data model for XML based on relationships among elements and on the definition of a data schema provides resources for performing different types of queries. Since the solution adopted in this work for the navigation of XML documents with links is based on XPath, the execution of queries based on XML documents nodes ordering and on the document structure (i.e. in path patterns) are addressed. Issues like semantic similarity (i.e. elements with different names and even meanings or elements semantically different with the same name) may be solved by the specification of relationships that name the elements. In the same way, the elements semantic ordering may be established through their specification in relationships. These relationships may define the order in which the elements may be processed or that may be present in the XML instance.

Figure 28. LMDQL query expression with and without labels

```
LMDQL query without label

select {[Measures].[Unit Sales], [Measures].[Store Cost],
[Measures].[Store Sales]} on columns,{VAnalysis([Store].[Store
Country].[USA], {[Store].[Store Country].[USA].Children})} on rows
from [Sales] where [Time].[1997]


LMDQL query with label

select {[Measures].[Vendas Unitarias], [Measures].[Custo da Loja],
[Measures].[Vendas da Loja]} on columns,
 {VAnalysis([Loja].[Pais da Loja].[USA], {[Loja].[Pais da
Loja].[USA] .Children})}
on rows from [Vendas] where [Tempo].[1997]
```

Figure 29. LMDQL query expression for horizontal analysis

```
select {[Time].[1997].Children} on columns,
{HAnalysis([Store].[Store Country].[USA], {[Store].[Store
Country].[USA].Children},"1.05,1.10,1.15")} on rows from Sales
```

Figure 30. MDX query expression for horizontal analysis

```
With member [Measures].[AH Q1] AS '(([Time].[1997].[Q1] *
100)/[Time].[1997].[Q1])'
member [Measures].[AH Q2] AS '1.05*(([Time].[1997].[Q2] *
100)/[Time].[1997].[Q1])'
member [Measures].[AH Q3] AS '1.10*(([Time].[1997].[Q3] *
100)/[Time].[1997].[Q1])'
member [Measures].[AH Q4] AS '1.15*(([Time].[1997].[Q4] *
100)/[Time].[1997].[Q1])'
member [Measures].[US Q1] AS '[Time].[1997].[Q1]'
member [Measures].[US Q2] AS '[Time].[1997].[Q2]'
member [Measures].[US Q3] AS '[Time].[1997].[Q3]'
member [Measures].[US Q4] AS '[Time].[1997].[Q4]'
select {[Measures].[US Q1],[Measures].[AH Q1],[Measures].[US
Q2],[Measures].[AH Q2],[Measures].[US Q3],[Measures].[AH Q3],
[Measures].[US Q4],[Measures].[AH Q4]} on columns,{[Store].[Store
Country].[USA].Children} on rows from Sales
```

Table 9. Execution time of queries having to search on linked linkbases

Test Configuration	C0	C1	C2	C4	C8
Average	159.497	159.733	159.928	160.696	161.569
Percentage Variation	-	0,15%	0,12%	0,48%	0,54%

We also presented a formalism whose definitions helped in the creation of a multidimensional metamodel of data interconnected by XML documents. Mathematic definitions were given to indicate in a non ambiguous way how linkbases, elements, attributes and relationships may be used to represent cubes, dimensions, hierarchies, levels and members. From these formalizations, a multidimensional metamodel for interconnected XML data, was proposed and specified. It was discussed an example of XLDM use in the medical area, however, the metamodel was also applied in other domains, as financial and sales, illustrating its scope of use. Once the given formalization explicit in a non ambiguous way how the XML components themselves relate, its application may reach different domains and avoid the occurrence of heterogeneity in the data, through the mandatory use of some linkbases. Thus, OLAP queries are performed based on data schema, linkbases and XML instances.

Further, we specified XLPath language, an extension of XPath language, for allowing the navigation over links. The specification and implementation of XLPath language allow, from an XML document, to navigate in other documents interconnected for obtaining additional information. In this proposal, XLPath was used on LMDQL language processor. Based on XLDM and XLPath, it was presented the specification of the multidimensional query language LMDQL (Link-based Multidimensional Query Language) for the analytical processing in XML documents interconnected.

For the LMDQL processor implementation was defined a process for executing queries on XML documents and linkbases. The definition of this process allowed the specification of a driver, named *sql2xquery* for mapping SQL queries in XQuery. So, was possible hold a LMDQL query on a traditional OLAP server. For this, the *mondrian* server was extended to allow the execution of analytical queries on XML documents with support for XLink. Despite the implementation of this work has been carried out within the *mondrian* architecture, the ideas proposed are independent of this architecture and can be implemented in other works that aim at the development of analytical processing over XML data linked. The driver implementation *sql2xquery* was performed such that allowed its integration with *mondrian* OLAP server by intercepting the SQL queries generated by the server, and converting them into XQuery. The development of the driver occurred so that the way to access the data present on XML documents is the same that is used to access relational databases, i.e. through MDX queries. Thus, it is indifferent to OLAP server the environment of the database to perform the queries, XML or relational.

LMDQL language, besides introducing operators for performing queries based on proximity of data values and on techniques of horizontal, vertical and supported on the separatrix statistic measure analysis, it enables, also, the operator creation by the user. Such functionality allows the analyst, for instance, to perform analysis through indexes over XML documents. A characteristic example of this operator use was discussed in the case study based on XBRL Dimensions documents, which

application area uses different types of financial indexes. The operator *OperatorDefinition* has enough flexibility to allow the user creating new indexes and constructing its own business evaluation model. This way, LMDQL provides a generic mechanism to create users' specific operators, making flexible the accomplishment of analysis based on relations originally unforeseen.

The main differential of this work in relation to correlate proposals is the fact that it considers links for obtaining additional information, besides the definition of a multidimensional data metamodel, which solve the data heterogeneity problem, as well as LMDQL operators. Besides that, for having the implementation based on open and extensible patterns, the reuse and evolution of the ideas here proposed may be performed in an easier way.

With this proposal development, one may understand that the following contributions were achieved:

1. **Specification of XLDM multidimensional metamodel**. XML data models containing *links* for expressing relationships and additional information to the documents of instances may be created for different application domains. This metamodel is based on standard technologies, such as XML *Schema* and XLink. Further issues related to the heterogeneities in XML could be solved;

2. **Specification of XLPath**. With this language it is possible to navigate and extract information in XML documents interconnected by *links*. It allowed the provision of this resource in LMDQL. Besides that, since XLPath is a language extended from XPath, XLPath enables its use by other query languages, like XQuery, which currently do not have resources for performing queries in XML documents interconnected;

3. **Specification of LMDQL language for OLAP queries**, which allowed:

a. Information acquisition on linkbase*s*, through the integration of XLPath with LMDQL;

b. Accomplishment of analytical queries in more than one XML document;

c. Accomplishment of queries based on the value or on the structure of the XML document;

d. Creation of operators based on other operators; and

e. Accomplishment of horizontal, vertical, through separatrix and based on proximity of data values.

4. **Specification of the *driver sql2xquery***: The specification of this *driver* enabled the incorporation of LMDQL processor in an open code OLAP server. This incorporation allowed analyzing the practical viability of the proposed ideas, besides guaranteeing the use of multidimensional operators already existent on the server; and,

5. **Evaluation of LMDQL processor performance**: The tests allowed, in a preliminary way, investigating:

a. The impact of *links* processing in LMDQL queries in the OLAP *mondrian* server;

b. The *driver sql2xquery* processing time in three different XML DBMS and one relational DBMS;

c. Comparing the execution of a LMDQL query with another MDX that produces the same result.

In our tests results, it was observed that the processing over linkbases did not significantly influence the query performance over the DBMS. This may be caused by the execution flow related to query processing in *mondrian*, which performs the search on the linkbase before sending the query for processing on OLAP server when the query conversion on XQuery expressions is performed and the query is submitted to a XML DBMS.

We also had a large variation on the query execution time for the three XML DBMS considered in our preliminary tests. This may be a hint that studies for explaining these differences and for designing indexing structures based on XML documents interconnected by XLink must be carried out. We are currently investigating this issue. Considering the result of XQuery queries, is characterized as future work, a study addressing the improvement of the performance of XQuery queries in XML repositories, as well as measure the influence of the driver sql2xquery in query performance. The extension of LMDQL functionalities to incorporate operators for performing OLAP queries on XML document warehouses can be seem as another indication of future work. In order to complement the investigation of the linked XML documents effects, we are also planning to run new experiments using increasing data volumes and different database management systems. The design of a data warehouse benchmark for XML/XLink documents to enable further query performance investigation is another interesting work to be performed. Increase the numbers of operators LMDQL for the financial domain, for example for forensic analysis, is another objective to be achieved.

REFERENCES

Apache Couch, D. B. (2013). *Versaion 1.5.0*. Retrieved from http://couchdb.apache.org/

Barceló, P., & Libkin, L. (2005). Temporal Logics over Unranked Trees. In *Proceedings of the 20th Annual Symposium on Logic in Computer Science*. Chicago, IL: Academic Press.

BEA AquaLogic Data Services Platform™ 2.5. (n.d.). Retrieved from http://docs.oracle.com/cd/E13167_01/aldsp/docs25/

Beyer, K., Chamberlin, D., Colby, L., Ozcan, F., Pirahesh, H., & Xu, Y. (2005). Extending XQuery for Analytics. In *Proceedings of SIGMOD 2005*. Baltimore, MD: ACM.

Bordawekar, R. R., & Lang, C. A. (2005). Analytical Processing of XML Documents: Opportunities and Challenges. *SIGMOD Record, 34*(2). doi:10.1145/1083784.1083790

Boussaid, O., Messaoud, R. B., Choquet, R., & Anthoard, S. (2006). X-Warehousing: An XML-Based Approach for Warehousing Complex Data. *LNCS, 4152*, 39–54.

Brigham, E. F., & Ehrhaedt, M. C. (2007). *Financial Management: Theory and Practice* (12th ed.). Mason, OH: Thomson South-Western College.

Chang, H. J., Liu, Z. H., & Warner, J. W. (2011). *Rewriting node reference-based XQuery using SQL/SML*. Retrieved from http://www.google.com.br/patents/US7870124?dq=xquery+with+sql+2011

Chaudhuri, S., & Dayal, U. (1997). An overview of data warehousing and olap technology. *SIGMOD Record, 26*(1), 65–74. doi:10.1145/248603.248616

COREP XBRL Project. (2005). Retrieved from http://www.eurofiling.info/index.html

Damondaran, A. (2007). *Avaliação de empresas*. São Paulo, Brazil: Prentice Hall.

Deutsch, A., Fernandez, M., Florescu, D., Levy, A., & Suciu, D. (1998). *XML-QL: a query language for XML*. Retrieved from http://www.w3.org/TR/NOTE-xml-ql/

eXist Open Source Native XML Database. (2010). Retrieved from http://exist-db.org/exist/apps/homepage/index.html

Fishcer, P., Florescu, D., Kaufmann, M., & Kossmann, D. (2011). *Translating SPARQL and SQL to XQuery*. Retrieved from http://archive.xmlprague.cz/2011/presentations/sparql-sql-xquery.pdf

Gottlob, G., Koch, C., & Pichler, R. (2003). XPath query evaluation: improving time and space efficiency. In *Proceedings of 19th International Conference on Data Engineering*. Bangalore, India: Academic Press.

Grosso, P., Male, E., Marsh, J., & Walsh, N. (2003). *XPointer Framework W3C Recommendation*. Retrieved from http://www.w3.org/TR/xptr-framework/

Halverson, A., Josifovski, V., Lohman, G., Pirahesh, H., & Mörschel, M. (2004). *ROX: Relational Over XML*. Retrieved from http://www.vldb.org/conf/2004/RS7P2.PDF

Helfert, E. A. (1997). *Techniques of Financial Analysis: A Practical Guide to Measuring Business Performance*. New York, NY: McGraw-Hill.

Hernández-Ros, I., & Wallis, H. (2006). *XBRL Dimensions*. Retrieved from www.xbrl.org/Specification/XDT-REC-2006-09-18.htm

Hümmer, W., Bauer, A., & Harde, G. (2003). XCube – XML for Data Warehouses. In *Proceedings of the 6th ACM Intl Workshop on Data Warehousing and OLAP*, (pp. 33–40). Bologna, Italy: ACM.

Hyde, J. (2012). *Optiq- Extensible query-planning framewor*. Retrieved from http://sourceforge.net/projects/optiq/

IBM DB2 Express Server Ed. (2010). Retrieved from http://www-01.ibm.com/software/data/db2/express/

Ipedo Inc. (2010). *Ipedo XIP 4.0*. Retrieved from http://www.ipedo.com/

Jian, F. M., Pei, J., & Fu, A. W. (2007). *IX-Cubes: Iceberg Cubes for Data Warehousing and OLAP on XML Data*. Paper presented at CIKM'07. Lisboa, Portugal.

Kay, M. H. (2003). *Saxon 7.5*. Retrieved from http://saxon.sourceforge.net/saxon7.5/

Kimball, R., & Ross, M. (2002). *The Data Warehouse Toolkit*. New York, NY: John Wiley and Sons.

Libkin, L. (2006). Logics For Unranked Trees: An Overview. *Logical Methods in Computer Science, 2* (3:2), 1–31.

Libkin, L., & Neven, F. (2003). Logical Definability and Query Languages over Unranked Trees. In *Proceedings of LICS 2003*. IEEE Computer Society.

Liu, W., Sun, D., Ren, P., & Xiong, H. (2012). Path-Calculation-Based XML Data Cube Model. In *Proceedings of Convergence and Hybrid Information Technology: 6th International Conference*, ICHIT 2012. Daejeon, Korea: ICHIT.

Manning, R. (2013). *Mongo JDBC Driver - A minimal JDBC driver implementation for MongoDB*. Retrieved from http://sourceforge.net/projects/mongojdbcdriver

Matarazzo, D. C. (2003). *Análise financeira de balanços*. São Paulo, Brazil: Editora Atlas.

MDX Function Reference. (2008). Retrieved from msdn.microsoft.com/en-s/library/ms145506.aspx

Mondrian. (2008). Retrieved from http://community.pentaho.com/projects/mondrian/

MySQL. (2013). Retrieved from http://www.mysql.com/

Näppilä, T., Järvelin, K., & Niemi, T. (2008). A tool for data cube construction from structurally heterogeneous XML documents. *Journal of the American Society for Information Science and Technology, 59*(3), 435–449. doi:10.1002/asi.20756

Ope, X. Q. S. Q. L. (2011). *XQuery SQL-Client (XQSQL) for XQuery Ope*. Retrieved from http://xqsql.sourceforge.net/

Oracle Berkeley DB XML. (2010). Retrieved from www.oracle.com/technology/documentation/berkeley-db/xml/index.html

Park, B. K., Han, H., & Song, I. Y. (2005). XML-OLAP: A Multidimensional Analysis Framework for XML Warehouses. In *Proceedings of 7th International Conference in Data Warehousing and Knowledge Discovery* (LNCS), (vol. 3589, pp. 32–42). Copenhagen, Denmark: Springer.

QuiLogic. (2001). *In Memory SQL / XML Database Technology for Universal Data Management*. Retrieved from http://www.quilogic.cc

Ravat, F., Teste, O., Tournier, R., & Zurfluh, G. (2010). Finding an application-appropriate model for XML data warehouses. *Information Systems, 35*, 662–687. doi:10.1016/j.is.2009.12.002

Relational XQuery. (2006). Retrieved from http://www.software112.com/products/relational-xquery.html

Robie, J. (1999). *XQL (XML Query Language)*. Retrieved from http://www.ibiblio.org/xql/xql-proposal.html

Rodrigues, T., Sauer, C., & Galante, R. (2012). *Executing SQL Queries with an XQuery Engine*. Retrieved from http://www.lume.ufrgs.br/bitstream/handle/10183/54129/000855691.pdf?sequence=1

Schnable, K. (2013). *MongoSQL - A friendly SQL UI for MongoDB*. Retrieved from http://www.mongosql.com

Silva, P. C., Aquino, I. J. S., & Times, V. C. (2008). *A Query Language for Navigation Over Links*. Paper presented at the XIV Brazilian Multimedia Systems and Web Symposium. Vila Velha, Brazil.

Silva, P. C., Santos, M. M., Cruz, M. S. H., & Santos, A. A. (2010). XBRL Taxonomy for Indexes of Financial Analysis. In *Proceeding of the 7th CONTECSI International Conference on Information Systems and Technology Management*. São Paulo, Brazil: CONTECSI.

Silva, P. C., Santos, M. M., & Times, V. C. (2010). *XLPATH: XML Linking Path Language*. Paper presented at the IADIS International Conference. Timisoara, Romania.

Silva, P. C., & Times, V. C. (2009a). *XPath+: A Tool for Linked XML Documents Navigation*. Paper presented at XSym 2009 - Sixth International XML Database Symposium at VLDB'09. Lyon, France.

Silva, P. C., & Times, V. C. (2009b). LMDQL: link-based and multidimensional query language. In *Proceeding of the ACM twelfth international workshop on Data warehousing and OLAP (DOLAP'09)*. Hong Kong, China: ACM.

Taniar, D., Nguyen, H., Rahayu, J. W., & Nguyen, K. (2011). Double-layered schema integration of heterogeneous XML sources. *Journal of Systems and Software*, *84*(1), 63–76. doi:10.1016/j.jss.2010.07.055

Taniar, D., Pardede, E., & Rahayu, J. W. (2005b). Preserving Conceptual Constraints During XML Updates. *International Journal of Web Information Systems*, *1*(2), 65–82. doi:10.1108/17440080580000084

Taniar, D., Pardede, E., & Rahayu, J. W. (2006). Object-relational complex structures for XML storage. *Information and Software Technology*, *48*(6), 370–384. doi:10.1016/j.infsof.2005.12.015

Taniar, D., Rusu, L. I., & Rahayu, J. W. (2004). On Building XML Data Warehouses. In *Proceedings of the 5th International Conference on Intelligent Data Engineering and Automated Learning* (IDEAL 2004), (LNCS), (vol. 3177, pp. 293-299). Springer.

Taniar, D., Rusu, L. I., & Rahayu, J. W. (2005a). A Methodology for Building XML Data Warehouses. *International Journal of Data Warehousing and Mining*, *1*(2).

Taniar, D., Rusu, L. I., & Rahayu, J. W. (2009). Partitioning methods for multi-version XML data warehouses. *Distributed and Parallel Databases*, *25*(1-2), 47–69. doi:10.1007/s10619-009-7034-y

Wang, H., Li, J., He, Z., & Gao, H. (2007). Flexible and Effective Aggregation operator for XML Data. *Information Technology Journal*, *6*(5), 697–703. doi:10.3923/itj.2007.697.703

Wiwatwattana, N., Jagadish, H., Lakshmanan, L., & Srivastava, D. (2007). *X^3: A cube operator for xml olap*. Paper presented at the 23rd International Conference on Data Engineering (ICDE'07). Istanbul, Turkey.

XBRL Consortium. (2006). Retrieved from http://www.xbrl.org

XLink - XML Linking Language. (2001). Retrieved from www.w3.org/TR/xlink

XML Schema W3C Recommendation. (2004). Retrieved from www.w3.org/TR/xmlschema-1

XPath - XML Path Language W3C Recommendation. (2007). Retrieved from www.w3c.org/tr/xpath20/

XQuery 1.0: An Xml Query Language. (2007). Retrieved from www.w3.org/TR/xquery

Zorba. (2012). *ZorbaNoSQL Query Processor (Version 3.0)*. Retrieved from http://www.zorba.io

APPENDIX A: XLPATH EBNF

LocationPath	::= RelativeLocationPath
	|AbsoluteLocationPath
AbsoluteLocationPath	::= '/' RelativeLocationPath?
	| AbbreviatedAbsoluteLocationPath
RelativeLocationPath	::= Step
	| RelativeLocationPath '/' Step
	| AbbreviatedRelativeLocationPath
Step	::= AxisSpecifierNodeTestPredicate*
	| LevelSpec AxisSpecifier NodeTest Predicate*
	| AbbreviatedStep
LevelSpec	::= ('HL' | 'LL') '::'
AxisSpecifier	::= AxisName '::'
	| AbbreviatedAxisSpecifier
AxisName	::= 'ancestor'
	| 'ancestor-or-self'
	| 'attribute'
	| 'child'
	| 'descendant'
	| 'descendant-or-self'
	| 'following'
	| 'following-sibling'
	| 'namespace'
	| 'parent'
	| 'preceding'
	| 'preceding-sibling'
	| 'self'
	| **'link-destination'**
	| **'link-source'**
	|**'arc-destination'**
	| **'arc-source'**
	| **'linked'**
	| **'link-part-child'**
	| **'link-part-descendant'**
NodeTest	::= NameTest
	| NodeType '(' ')'
	| 'processing-instruction' '(' Literal ')'
	| ElementSpec
ElementSpec	::= ElementName '(' QName? ')'
ElementName	::= 'arc'
	| 'element'

	'locator'
	'remote'
	'resource'
Predicate	::= '[' PredicateExpr ']'
	'[[' PredicateExpr ']]'
PredicateExpr	::= Expr
	OperatorSpec
OperatorSpec	::= AttributeSpec
	LinkSpec
	TextSpec
AttributeSpec	::= 'attribute(' QName ')=' Value
LinkSpec	::= 'link(' QName ')'
TextSpec	::= 'text()=' Value
Abbreviated	
AbsoluteLocationPath	::= '//' RelativeLocationPath
	'///' RelativeLocationPath
AbbreviatedRelative	
LocationPath	::= RelativeLocationPath '//' Step
AbbreviatedStep	::= '.'
	'..'
	'...'
AbbreviatedAxis	
Specifier	::= '@'?
Expr	::= OrExpr
PrimaryExpr	::= VariableReference
	'(' Expr ')'
	Literal
	Number
	FunctionCall
FunctionCall	::= FunctionName '(' (Argument (',' Argument)*)? ')'
Argument	::= Expr
UnionExpr	::= PathExpr
	UnionExpr '|' PathExpr
PathExpr	::= LocationPath
	FilterExpr
	FilterExpr '/' RelativeLocationPath
	FilterExpr '//' RelativeLocationPath
FilterExpr	::= PrimaryExpr
	FilterExprPredicate
OrExpr	::= AndExpr
	OrExpr 'or' AndExpr
AndExpr	::= EqualityExpr
	AndExpr 'and' EqualityExpr

EqualityExpr	::= RelationalExpr
	| EqualityExpr '=' RelationalExpr
	| EqualityExpr '!=' RelationalExpr
RelationalExpr	::= AdditiveExpr
	| RelationalExpr '<' AdditiveExpr
	| RelationalExpr '>' AdditiveExpr
	| RelationalExpr '<=' AdditiveExpr
	| RelationalExpr '>=' AdditiveExpr
AdditiveExpr	::= MultiplicativeExpr
	| AdditiveExpr '+' MultiplicativeExpr
	| AdditiveExpr '-' MultiplicativeExpr
MultiplicativeExpr	::= UnaryExpr
	| MultiplicativeExprMultiplyOperator UnaryExpr
	| MultiplicativeExpr 'div' UnaryExpr
	| MultiplicativeExpr 'mod' UnaryExpr
UnaryExpr	::= UnionExpr
	| '-' UnaryExpr
ExprToken	::= '(' | ')' | '[' | ']' | '.' | '..' | '@' | ',' | '::' | '...' | '[[' | ']]'
	| NameTest
	| NodeType
	| Operator
	| FunctionName
	| AxisName
	| Literal
	| Number
	| VariableReference
Literal	::= '"' [^"]* '"'
	| "'" [^']* "'"
Number	::= Digits ('.' Digits?)?
	| '.' Digits
Digits	::= [0-9]+
Operator	::= OperatorName
	| MultiplyOperator
	| '/' | '//' | '///' | '|' | '+' | '-' | '='
	| '!=' | '<' | '<=' | '>' | '>='
OperatorName	::= 'and' | 'or' | 'mod' | 'div'
MultiplyOperator	::= '*'
FunctionName :	:= QName - NodeType
VariableReference	::= '$' QName
NameTest	::= '*'
	| NCName ':' '*'
	| QName
NodeType	::= 'comment'
	| 'text' | 'processing-instruction' | 'node'
ExprWhitespace :	:= S

APPENDIX B: LMDQL EBNF

```
<MDX_statement>::= <select_statement>
                 | <create_formula_statement>
                 | <drop_formula_statement>
<select_statement>::= [$VARIABLE <variable_specification>]
                      [WITH <formula_specification>]
                      SELECT [<axis_specification>
                             [, <axis_specification>...]]
                      FROM [<cube_specification>]
                      [WHERE [<slicer_specification>]]
                      [<cell_props>]
<variable_specification>::= <member>.<identifier>
                            [<or><member>.<identifier>…]
<or>::= |
<formula_specification>::= <single_formula_specification>  [<single_formula_
specification>...]
<single_formula_specification>::= <member_specification>   | <set_specifica-
tion>
<member_specification>::= MEMBER <member_name> AS <value_expression>
                          [, <solve_order_specification>]  [, <member_prop-
erty_definition>...]
<member_name>::= <member>.<identifier> | <cube_name>.<member>.<identifier>
<solve_order_specification>::= SOLVE_ORDER = <unsigned_integer>
<member_property_definition>::= <identifier> = <value_expression>
<set_specification>::= SET <set_name> AS <set>
<set_name>::= <identifier> | <cube_name>.<identifier>
<axis_specification>::= [NON EMPTY] <set> [<dim_props>] ON <axis_name>
<axis_name>::= COLUMNS
             | ROWS
             | PAGES
             | CHAPTERS
             | SECTIONS
             | AXIS(<index>)
<dim_props>::= [DIMENSION] PROPERTIES <property> [, <property>...]
cube_specification>::= [<cube_name> [,<cube_name>...]]
<slicer_specification>::= {<set> | <tuple>}
<cell_props>::= [CELL] PROPERTIES <cell_property> [, <cell_property>...]
<cell_property>::= <mandatory_cell_property>
                 | <optional_cell_property>
                 | <provider_specific_cell_property>
<mandatory_cell_property>::= CELL_ORDINAL | VALUE | FORMATTED_VALUE
```

```
<optional_cell_property>::= FORMAT_STRING
                         | FORE_COLOR
                         | BACK_COLOR
                         | FONT_NAME
                         | FONT_SIZE
                         | FONT_FLAGS
<provider_specific_cell_property>::= <identifier>
<create_formula_statement>::= CREATE [<scope>]<formula_specification>
<drop_formula_statement>::= <drop_member_statement>
                         | <drop_set_statement>
<drop_member_statement>::= DROP MEMBER <member_name>
                                     [, <member_name>...]
<drop_set_statement>::= DROP SET <set_name> [, <set_name>...]
<scope>:= GLOBAL | SESSION
<identifier>::= <regular_identifier> | <delimited_identifier>
<regular_identifier>::= <alpha_char> [{<alpha_char> | <digit>
                                     | <underscore>}...]
<delimited_identifier>::=
<start_delimiter>{<double_end_delimiter> | <nondelimit_end_symbol>}
     [{<double_end_delimiter> | <nondelimit_end_symbol> }...]
<end_delimiter>
<start_delimiter>::= <open_bracket>
<end_delimiter>::= <close_bracket>
<double_end_delimiter>::= <end_delimiter><end_delimiter>
<nondelimit_end_symbol>::= !! Any character except <end_delimiter>
<cube_name>::= [ [ [ <data_source>.] <catalog_name>.][<schema_name>.]
<identifier>
<data_source>::= <identifier>
<catalog_name>::= <identifier>
<schema_name>::= <identifier>
<dim_hier>::= [<cube_name>.]<dimension_name>
| [[<cube_name>.]< dimension_name>.]<hierarchy_name>
<dimension_name>::= <identifier>
                 | <member>.DIMENSION
                 | <level>.DIMENSION
                 | <hierarchy>.DIMENSION
<dimension>::= <dimension_name>
<hierarchy>::= <hierarchy_name>
<hierarchy_name>::= <identifier>
                 | < member>.HIERARCHY
                 | <level>.HIERARCHY
<level>::= [<dim_hier>.]< identifier>
         | <dim_hier>.LEVELS(<index>)
```

```
| <member>.LEVEL
<member>::= [<level>.]<identifier>
          | <dim_hier>.<identifier>
          | <member>.<identifier>
          | <member_value_expression>
<property>::= <mandatory_property> | <user_defined_property>
<mandatory_property>::= CATALOG_NAME
                      | SCHEMA_NAME
                      | CUBE_NAME
                      | DIMENSION_UNIQUE_NAME
                      | HIERARCHY_UNIQUE_NAME
                      | LEVEL_UNIQUE_NAME
                      | LEVEL_NUMBER
                      | MEMBER_UNIQUE_NAME
                      | MEMBER_NAME
                      | MEMBER_TYPE
                      | MEMBER_GUID
                      | MEMBER_CAPTION
                      | MEMBER_ORDINAL
                      | CHILDREN_CARDINALITY
                      | PARENT_LEVEL
                      | PARENT_UNIQUE_NAME
                      | PARENT_COUNT
                      | DESCRIPTION
<user_defined_property>::= <dim_hier>.<identifier>
                         | <level>.<identifier>
                         | <member>.<identifier>
<tuple>::= <member>
         | (<member> [, <member>...])
         | <tuple_value_expression>
<set>::= <member>:<member>
       | <set_value_expression>
       | <open_brace>[<set>|<tuple> [, <set>|<tuple>...]]<close_brace>
       | (<set>)
<open_brace>::= {
<close_brace>::= }
<open_bracket>::= [
<close_bracket>::= ]
<open_parenthesis>::= (
<close_parenthesis>::=)
<underscore>::= _
<alpha_char>::= a | b | c |...| z | A | B | C |.. | Z
<digit>::= 0 | 1 | 2 | 3 | 4 | 5 | 6 | 7 | 8 | 9
```

```
<value_expression>::= <numeric_value_expression>
                    | <string_value_expression>
<numeric_value_expression>::= <term>
                            | <numeric_value_expression> {<plus> | <minus>}
<term>
<term>::= <factor> | <term> {<asterisk> | <solidus>| <exponentiation> | <root>}
<factor>
<factor>::= [<sign>] <numeric_primary>
<sign>::= + | -
<plus>::= +
<minus>::= -
<asterisk>::= *
<solidus>::= /
<exponentiation>::= ^
<root>::= root
<numeric_primary>::= <value_expression_primary>
                   | <numeric_value_function>
<value_expression_primary>::= <unsigned_numeric_literal>
                            | (<value_expression>)
| <character_string_literal>
| [<cube_name>.]<tuple>[.VALUE]
| <property>[.VALUE]
| <conditional_expression>
<conditional_expression>::= <if_expression> | <case_expression>
<if_expression>::= IIF(<search_condition>, <true_part>, <false_part>)
<true_part>::= <value_expression>
<false_part>::= <value_expression>
<case_expression>::= <simple_case> | <searched_case> | <coalesce_empty>
<simple_case>::= CASE <case_operand>
<simple_when_clause>...
                    [<else_clause>]
                  END
<searched_case>::= CASE
<searched_when_clause>...
                    [<else_clause>]
                  END
<simple_when_clause>::= WHEN <when_operand> THEN <result>
<searched_when_clause>::= WHEN <search_condition> THEN <result>
<else_clause>::= ELSE <value_expression>
<case_operand>::= <value_expression>
<when_operand>::= <value_expression>
<result>::= <value_expression>
<coalesce_empty>::= COALESCEEMPTY (<value_expression>,
```

```
<value_expression>
                                   [, <value_expression> ]...)
<unsigned_numeric_literal>::= <exact_numeric_literal>
                      | <approximate_numeric_literal>
<exact_numeric_literal>::= <unsigned_integer>[.<unsigned_integer>]
| <unsigned_integer>.
|.<unsigned_integer>
<unsigned_integer>::= {<digit>}...
<approximate_numeric_literal>::= <mantissa>E<exponent>
<mantissa>::= < exact_numeric_literal>
<exponent>::= [<sign>]<unsigned_integer>
<string_value_expression>::= <value_expression_primary>
                      | <string_value_expression>
<concatenation_operator>
<value_expression_primary>
<character_string_literal>::=<quote>[<character_representation>...]
<quote>
<character_representation>::= <nonquote_character> | <quote_symbol>
<nonquote_character>::= !!
                Any character in the character set other than <quote>
<quote_symbol>::= <quote><quote>
<quote> ::= `
<concatenation_operator>::= ||
<index>::= <numeric_value_expression>
<percentage>::= <numeric_value_expression>
<set_value_expression>::= <dim_hier>.MEMBERS
                      | <level>.MEMBERS
                      | <member>.CHILDREN
                      | BOTTOMCOUNT(<set>, <index>
                       [, <numeric_value_expression>])
                      | BOTTOMPERCENT(<set>, <percentage>,
<numeric_value_expression>)
                      | BOTTOMSUM(<set>, <numeric_value_expression>,
<numeric_value_expression>)
                      | CROSSJOIN(<set>, <set>)
| DESCENDANTS(<member>, <level> [,<desc_flags>])
                      | DISTINCT(<set>)
                      | DRILLDOWNLEVEL(<set> [, <level>])
                      | DRILLDOWNLEVELBOTTOM(<set>, <index>
                       [,[<level>], <numeric_value_expression>])
                      | DRILLDOWNLEVELTOP(<set>, <index>[, [<level>]
                      , <numeric_value_expression>])
                      | DRILLDOWNMEMBER(<set>, <set>[, RECURSIVE])
```

```
                        | DRILLDOWNMEMBERBOTTOM(<set>, <set>, <index>
                          [, <numeric_value_expression>], RECURSIVE])
                        | DRILLDOWNMEMBERTOP(<set>, <set>, <index>
                          [, [<numeric_value_expression>], RECURSIVE])
                        | DRILLUPLEVEL(<set>[, <level>])
                        | DRILLUPMEMBER(<set>, <set>)
                        | EXCEPT(<set>, <set> [, [ALL]])
| EXTRACT(<set>, <dim_hier>[, <dim_hier>...])
| FILTER(<set>, <search_condition>)
                        | GENERATE(<set>, <set> [, [ALL]])
                        | HIERARCHIZE(<set>)
                        | INTERSECT(<set>, <set> [, [ALL]])
                        | LASTPERIODS(<index> [, <member>])
                        | MTD([<member>])
                        | ORDER(<set>, <value_expression>
                          [, ASC | DESC | BASC | BDESC])
                          | PERIODSTODATE([<level>[, <member>]])
                        | QTD([<member>])
                        | TOGGLEDRILLSTATE(<set1>, <set2>[, RECURSIVE])
                | TOPCOUNT(<set>, <index> [, <numeric_value_expression>])
                        | TOPPERCENT(<set>, <percentage>, <numeric_value_ex-
pression>)
                        | TOPSUM(<set>, <numeric_value_expression>, <numeric_
value_expression>)
                        | UNION(<set>, <set> [, [ALL]])
                        | WTD([<member>])
                        | YTD(<member>)
                | OPERATORDEFINITION (<string_value_expression>,
                            <string_value_expression>
                              [,PARAM<open_parenthesis>
                            <string_value_expression>...
                            <close_parenthesis>])
                | HANALYSIS (<set>, <set><set>[<set>] [,<unsigned_numeric_lit-
eral>...])
                | VANALYSIS (<member>, <set>)
                | CROSS (<member>[, <string_value_expression>...])
                | NNEARESTVALUES (<member>, <unsigned_integer> [, ASC | DESC])
                | NNEARESTVALUESPERCENTUAL (<member>, <unsigned_numeric_literal>
[,
                                            ASC | DESC])
<desc_flags>::= SELF
                | AFTER
                | BEFORE
```

```
                      | BEFORE_AND_AFTER
                      | SELF_AND_AFTER
                      | SELF_AND_BEFORE
                      | SELF_BEFORE_AFTER
<member_value_expression>::= <member>.{PARENT | FIRSTCHILD | LASTCHILD
                                    | PREVMEMBER | NEXTMEMBER}
                          | <member>.LEAD(<index>)
                          | <member>.LAG(<index>) | <member>.{FIRSTSIBLING |
LASTSIBLING}
                          | <dimension>[.CURRENTMEMBER]
                          | <dimension>.DEFAULTMEMBER
                          | <hierarchy>.DEFAULTMEMBER
                          | ANCESTOR(<member>, <level>)
                          | CLOSINGPERIOD(<level>[, <member>])
                          | COUSIN(<member>, <member>)
                          | OPENINGPERIOD(<level>[, <member>])
                          | PARALLELPERIOD([<level>[, <index> [, <member>]]])
<tuple_value_expression>::= <set>.CURRENTMEMBER
                          | <set>[.ITEM]({<string_value_expression>
                                    [, <string_value_expression>...]}
                          | <index>)
<boolean_primary>::= <value_expression><comp_op><value_expression>
alter_statement::= <create_statement> | <remove_statement> | <move_statement>
|
<update_statement>
<create_statement>::= CREATE DIMENSION MEMBER <member_spec>,
                    KEY='<key_value>' [[, <property_name>='<value>'] [,
<property_name>='<value>']...]
<remove_statement>::= DROP DIMENSION MEMBER <member_spec> [WITH DESCENDANTS]
<move_statement>::= MOVE DIMENSION MEMBER <member_spec>
                    [WITH DESCENDANTS]
                    UNDER <member_spec>
<update_statement>::= UPDATE DIMENSION MEMBER <member_spec>
                    [AS '<mdx_expression>', ] |
<property_name>='<value>' [[, <property_name>='<value>']...]
<numeric_value_function>::=
AGGREGATE(<set> [, <numeric_value_expression>])
AVG(<set>[, <numeric_value_expression>])
CORRELATION(<set>, <numeric_value_expression>  [, <numeric_value_expression>])
COVARIANCE(<set>, <numeric_value_expression>  [, <numeric_value_expression>])
COUNT(<set>[, INCLUDEEMPTY])
LINREGINTERCEPT(<set>, <numeric_value_expression>  [, <numeric_value_expres-
sion>])
```

```
LINREGPOINT(<numeric_value_expression>, <set>, <numeric_value_expression>
[,<numeric_value_expression>])
LINREGR2(<set>, <numeric_value_expression> [, <numeric_value_expression>])
LINREGSLOPE(<set>, <numeric_value_expression> [, <numeric_value_expression>])
LINREGVARIANCE(<set>, <numeric_value_expression> [, <numeric_value_expres-
sion>])
MAX(<set>[, <numeric_value_expression>])
MEDIAN(<set>[, <numeric_value_expression>])
MIN(<set>[, <numeric_value_expression>])
RANK(<tuple>, <set>)
STDEV(<set>[, <numeric_value_expression>])
SUM(<set>[, <numeric_value_expression>])
VAR(<set>[, <numeric_value_expression>])
SEPARATRIX (<set>, <member>, <unsigned_integer>)
<search_condition>::= <boolean_term>  | <search_condition> {OR | XOR} <bool-
ean_term>
<boolean_term>::= <boolean_factor> | <boolean_term> AND <boolean_factor>
<boolean_factor>::= [NOT] <boolean_primary>
<boolean_primary>::= <value_expression><comp_op><value_expression>
                    | ISEMPTY(<value_expression>)
                    | (<search_condition>)
<comp_op>::= <equals_operator>
           | <not_equals_operator>
           | <less_than_operator>
           | <greater_than_operator>
           | <less_than_or_equals_operator>
           | <greater_than_or_equals_operator>
<equals_operator>::= =
<not_equals_operator>::= <>
<greater_than_operator>::= >
<less_than_operator>::= <
<greater_than_or_equals_operator>::= >=
<less_than_or_equals_operator>::= <=
```

Chapter 10
A Scouting–Based Multi–Agent System Model to Deal with Service Collaboration in Cloud Computing

Mauricio Paletta
Universidad Nacional Experimental de Guayana (UNEG), Venezuela

ABSTRACT

Cloud computing addresses the use of scalable and often virtualized resources. It is based on service-level agreements that provide external users with requested services. Cloud computing is still evolving. New specific collaboration models among service providers are needed for enabling effective service collaboration, allowing the process of serving consumers to be more efficient. On the other hand, Scout Movement or Scouting has been a very successful youth movement in which the collaboration of its members can be observed. This motivated a previous work aiming to design MAS-Scout, a framework that defines Multi-Agent Systems based on the principles of Scouting. In this chapter, MAS-Scout is used to design a system to deal with service collaboration in a cloud computing environment focusing on the premise that Scouting has been a very successful social movement in the world and that collaboration is part of its principles. The results presented in this chapter show that MAS-Scout, which is based on the Scouting principles, can be satisfactorily used to automate cloud computing needs.

1. INTRODUCTION

Cloud Computing (CC) is emerging as a new distributed system that works towards providing reliable, customized and "quality of service" guaranteed dynamic computing environments for end-users (Weiss, 2007). It is primarily based on service-level agreements that provide external users with requested services. The success of achieving this goal in proper time (efficiency) and/or to obtain higher quality results (effectiveness) in these dynamic and distributed environments depends on implementing an appropriate collaboration model between service providers in the cloud. The following are some definitions of CC given by different authors, the last one being

DOI: 10.4018/978-1-4666-6098-4.ch010

a definition given by the National Institute of Standards and Technology (NIST):

- "Cloud is a parallel and distributed computing system consisting of a collection of inter-connected and virtualized computers that are dynamically provisioned and presented as one or more unified computing resources based on service-level agreements (SLA) established through negotiation between the service provider and consumers" (Buyya et al, 2009).
- "Clouds are a large pool of easily usable and accessible virtualized resources (such as hardware, development platforms and/or services). These resources can be dynamically reconfigured to adjust to a variable load (scale), allowing also for an optimum resource utilization. This pool of resources is typically exploited by a pay-per-use model in which guarantees are offered by the Infrastructure Provider by means of customized Service Level Agreements" (Vaquero et al, 2009).
- "Cloud Computing is the evolution of a variety of technologies that have come together to alter an organization's approach to building out an information technology infrastructure. Like the Web a little over a decade ago, there is nothing fundamentally new in any of the technologies that make up cloud computing" (Reese, 2009).
- "At its simplest, cloud computing is the dynamic delivery of information technology resources and capabilities as a service over the Internet. Cloud computing is a style of computing in which dynamically scalable and often virtualized resources are provided as a service over the Internet. It generally incorporates infrastructure as a service (IaaS), platform as a service (PaaS), and software as a service (SaaS)" (Sarna, 2011).

- "Cloud computing is a model for enabling convenient, on-demand network access to a shared pool of configurable computing resources (e.g., networks, servers, storage, applications, and services) that can be rapidly provisioned and released with minimal management effort or service provider interaction. This cloud model promotes availability and is composed of five essential characteristics: on-demand self-service, broad network access, resource pooling, rapid elasticity, and measured service; three service models: infrastructure as a service, platform as a service, and software as a service; and four deployment models: private, community, public, and hybrid" (Mell & Grance, 2009).

Distributed computing system, computing resource, service, negotiation, and infrastructure provider are keywords extracted from these definitions and are related with CC technology. As we will see in Section 3 these keywords are relevant to discover the relationship between CC systems and multi-agent based collaboration distributed systems. Moreover, this relationship can also be analyzed by identifying the key characteristics of CC (Armbrust et al, 2009):

1. The illusion of infinite computing resources.
2. The elimination of an up-front commitment by cloud users.
3. The ability to pay for use as needed.

Additionally, (Voorsluys et al, 2011) present the following features desired for a cloud:

1. **Self-Service:** Consumers of CC services expect on-demand, nearly instant access to resources. For that reason clouds must allow the use of services without human intervention (Mell & Grance, 2009).
2. **Per-Usage Metering and Billing:** CC eliminates up-front commitment by users.

Services must be priced on a short-term basis and released as soon as they are not needed (Armbrust et al, 2009). This means that the users will only pay for what is used.

3. **Elasticity:** CC gives the illusion of infinite computing resources available on demand (Armbrust et al, 2009), so that users expect clouds to provide a quantity of resources at any time efficiently (rapidly) and effectively (with quality).

4. **Customization:** A great disparity between user needs is common in a multi-tenant cloud. So then, resources must be highly customizable.

Moreover, (Rochwerger et al, 2011) enumerate the basic principles of CC by highlighting the fundamental requirement from the providers of CC that allows virtual applications to freely migrate, grow, and shrink:

1. **Federation:** Service providers in a CC environment have a finite capacity. In order to grow beyond this capacity, "Cloud Computing providers should be able to form federations of providers such that they can collaborate and share their resources".

2. **Independence:** Service providers in a CC environment should be able to manage their infrastructure without exposing internal details to their customers or partners so that users should be able to use the services of the cloud without relying on any specific tool. Therefore, "services need to be encapsulated and generalized such that users will be able to acquire equivalent virtual resources at different providers".

3. **Isolation:** Users in a CC environment need warranties from services providers so that their personal computer items are completely isolated from others. "Users must be ensured that their resources cannot be accessed by others sharing the same cloud and that ad-

equate performance isolation is in place to ensure that no other user may possess the power to directly affect the service granted to their application".

4. **Elasticity:** It is the CC ability to provide or release resources on-demand. This ability should be enacted automatically by CC providers to meet demand variations.

5. **Business Orientation:** CC providers should develop mechanisms to ensure quality of service and proper support for service-level agreements.

6. **Trust:** Establishing trust is one of the most critical issues to be addressed before CC can become the preferred computing paradigm. Therefore, the mechanisms that allow building and maintaining trust between consumers and providers, as well as between providers are essential for the success of CC systems.

To complete this brief review about CC it is important to remember the three service models that compose CC established by NIST (Jha et al, 2011):

1. **Software as a Service (SaaS):** It provides ready-to-run services that are deployed and configured for the user.

2. **Platform as a Service (PaaS):** It provides the ability to deploy custom applications on the infrastructure of the CC providers. These applications are developed using the programming languages and the application programming interfaces defined by the provider.

3. **Infrastructure-as-a-Service (IaaS):** It provides low-level, virtualized resources, such as storage, networks, and other fundamental computing resources via self-services to the user. In general, the user can deploy and run arbitrary software, which usually includes operating systems as well as applications.

"From a technology viewpoint, as of today, the IaaS type of cloud offerings have been the most successful and widespread in usage. However, the potential of PaaS has been high: All new cloud-oriented application development initiatives are based on the PaaS model. The significant impact of enterprises leveraging IaaS and PaaS has been in the form of services whose usage is representative of SaaS on the cloud" (Mohan, 2011).

Aiming to define appropriate collaboration mechanisms for enabling effective service collaboration in CC systems, a MAS-based model with emphasis in agent collaboration may be an interesting way to deal with it (Paletta & Herrero, 2010a). Moreover, an important question to be considered is this: what is the right MAS framework that can be used to implement a CC system taking into account all or most of the subjects identified above?

Services providers, collaboration, negotiation and task distribution encourage us to focus on the principles of the Scout Movement or Scouting in order to define a MAS framework for implementing CC. Scouting is a globally known connotation for a youth movement in which organization, cooperation, trust, leadership, learning, communication, roles, rules, obligations, prohibitions, hierarchy and so on are presented. Therefore, this article uses MAS-Scout (Paletta, 2012a & 2012b), a MAS framework designed for the organization of Intelligent Agents (IA) in MASs by means of the worldwide known Scout Movement, in order to adequately address the relevant issues previously mentioned related to CC.

The main goal is to consider MAS-Scout as a strategy that can be used for designing a CC system and for defining the way in which tasks can be resolved by distribution. Due to the fact that this strategy is based on Scouting, the cooperation between agents is the key to achieving the desired total goals. In this regard, the main contribution of this work is to study the majority of the aspects related to Scouting in order to organize a Multi-Agent System (MAS) and to

define a cooperation mechanism that would help achieve common goals.

The remainder of the article is organized as follows. Some related work is given in Section 2. Section 3 contains the motivational aspects involved in a MAS-based CC system. Details of the MAS-Scout framework are showed in Section 4. In Section 5 the design of a CC system by using the MAS-Scout framework is presented. Section 6 contains details of the implementation and results of some experimental tests. Finally, the last section includes the conclusions and outgoing and future research related to this work.

2. RELATED WORK

This section presents a number of previous works related with CC combined with at least one of the following items: IAs, MAS, negotiation, collaboration and communication. The end of the section contains a table with summary and personal comments that compare these previous works with what is presented in this article. The following are excerpts from related works that use IAs aiming to improve any process of the CC system:

- An agent-based cloud service composition approach to:
  - Dynamically contracting service providers, setting service fees on a supply-and-demand basis, and
  - Dealing with incomplete information regarding cloud resources (e.g., location and providers) (Gutierrez & Sim, 2010).
- A flexible servicing architecture within the CC by using the agent platform called UBIWARE, where various components and systems can configure, run and reuse intelligent cloud services to provide higher degree of flexibility and interoperability for their applications (Nikitin et al, 2010).

- A reliable integrated model of cloud and client computing to take full advantage of all nodes' resources. The model adopts an agent to encapsulate the behaviors and resources of a node to achieve more efficient resource sharing and collaboration goals (Xu et al, 2010).

- AMBAR-C (an Awareness-based Learning model for Service Collaboration in Cloud Computing), designed to allow nodes in a distributed environment to accomplish an effective collaboration among service providers in a "cloud" by means of a multi-agent architecture in which agents are aware of its surroundings throughout a parametrical and flexible use of this information. AMBAR-C makes use of heuristic strategies to improve effectiveness and efficiency in collaborations of these particular environments (Paletta & Herrero, 2010a).

On the other hand, the following two works deal with giving "intelligence" to a CC without using IAs:

- In (Zhang et al, 2010) authors present a version of intelligent CC based on data warehouse technology, which is used to record the inside and outside data of the system for data analysis and data mining. In this sense, a certain number of tactics of the CC performance optimization can be found and problems such as resource allocation policies, infrastructure development plan, and the management of capabilities among others can be quantified through analyzing all data mentioned above.

- In (Chen, 2010) the author adopted both the swarm intelligence and CC for a learning system, and developed friendly human-computer-interface software for

users to employ as personal computers or notebooks.

Related with the specific topic of negotiation the following previous works can be mentioned:

- Sim, 2010 that contains: 1) the design of a cloud negotiation mechanism that supports negotiation activities in interrelated markets: a cloud service market between consumer agents and broker agents, and multiple cloud resource markets between broker agents and provider agents, and 2) the design of the contracting and coordination algorithms for the concurrent negotiation activities between broker and provider agents in multiple cloud resource markets.

- Yoo & Sim, 2010 which contains the proposal of a business model supporting a multilateral price negotiation for trading cloud services. The authors state that trading cloud services between consumers and providers is a complicated issue of cloud computing because a consumer can negotiate with multiple providers to acquire the same service and each provider can receive many requests from multiple consumers, to facilitate the trading of cloud services among multiple consumers and providers.

- Nepal & Zic, 2008, in which CNA (Conflict Neighboring Algorithm) is presented as a contract negotiation algorithm used in dynamic collaboration environments to share resources as services. Here, the authors take into account that sharing such resource services requires that the participants agree to the terms and conditions of their responsibilities, as well as access to information and policies regulating their behavior within the collaboration.

- Song et al, 2009, which contains an evaluation approach used to select the partner in the formation of dynamic collaboration among cloud providers. This proposal uses Back Propagation Neuron Network (BPNN) instead of any fixed objective function and both, an individual and a collaborative performance of partner candidates are considered (Table 1).

3. MULTI-AGENT SYSTEMS AND INTELLIGENT CLOUDS

This section presents the motivational aspects involved in the implementation of CC by mean of MAS-based frameworks. In this regard, Service-Oriented Architecture (SOA) is extensively used at present for the design of development models of Internet systems, being the Web Services (WS) technology[1], one of the most important technolo-

Table 1. Summary of the MAS-Scout framework related work

Work	Description	Comments
(Gutierrez & Sim, 2010)	Agent-based cloud service composition.	It considers incomplete information about cloud participants and its combination with dynamic service selection mechanisms. It is an interesting MAS-based framework proposal but the architecture is quite complex and there are different kinds of agents. Moreover, it lacks a learning strategy.
UBIWARE	CC architecture.	A defined set of rules and politics is needed. In MAS-Scout these are based on Scouting principles.
(Xu et al, 2010)	Agent based model focuses on the efficient use of resources.	The definition of a cloud-coins-based incentive mechanism is also included in the work. MAS-Scout proposal framework is simpler because it is not necessary to extend roles, organizations, and environments for it to work since they are well defined based on the Scout movement.
AMBAR-C	MAS-based model focuses on the collaboration and learning processes.	Considering all the items presented in this table this is perhaps the work that is closely related to MAS-Scout. One aspect of MAS-Scout that stands out is the organization of agents in the MAS.
(Zhang et al, 2010)	Database intelligent strategy for designing rules and politics.	Even if IAs are not used in this proposal, this work offers an interesting point that can be used to add new abilities to IA-Scouts of the MAS-Scout model.
(Chen, 2010)	Learning strategy.	It can be considered as an alternative learning strategy in a collaboration model like MAS-Scout.
(Sim, 2010)	Negotiation mechanism.	It can be considered as an alternative negotiation strategy in a collaboration model like MAS-Scout.
(Yoo & Sim, 2010)	Negotiation mechanism.	It can be considered as an alternative negotiation strategy in a collaboration model like MAS-Scout.
CNA	Negotiation mechanism.	It can be considered as an alternative negotiation strategy in a collaboration model like MAS-Scout.
(Song et al, 2009)	Selection strategy to identity the service providers.	It can be considered as an alternative selection strategy in a collaboration model like MAS-Scout. For example, to select the IA-Scouts aiming to solve specific tasks.

gies that exist. In a SOA, software resources are packaged as "services," which are well-defined, self-contained modules that provide standard business functionality and are independent of the state or context of other services. Services are described in a standard definition language and have a published interface (Papazoglou & Van den Heuvel, 2007). In reference (Weerawarana et al, 2005) the following three items of the SOA triangle are indicated (see Figure 1) in order to: 1) provide an abstract definition of the service; 2) publish details of services so that those who want to use them can understand what they do and can obtain the information necessary to connect and to use them; 3) find a way to discover what services that meet the required needs are available.

The emergence of WS open standards has significantly contributed to improve advances in the domain of software integration (Papazoglou & Van den Heuvel, 2007). "WS can glue together applications running on different messaging product platforms, enabling information from one applica-

tion to be made available to others" (Voorsluys et al, 2011). While some WSs are published with the intent of serving end-user applications, their true power resides in WS's interface being accessible by other services. An enterprise application that follows the SOA paradigm is a collection of services that together perform complex business logic (Papazoglou & Van den Heuvel, 2007).

It can be clearly seen that there is a relationship between CC and SOA. It is natural then to use WS as the base of an implementation of a CC system. On the other hand, WS-based systems and MAS share a motivation in trying to find information systems that are flexible and adaptable. That is why it is natural to consider a conceptual relation among these technologies in the following common themes (Dickinson & Wooldridge, 2005):

- **No conceptual distinction:** There is no conceptual difference between a WS and an IA because both are active building blocks in a loosely-coupled architecture.

Figure 1. The SOA triangle (Weerawarana et al, 2005)

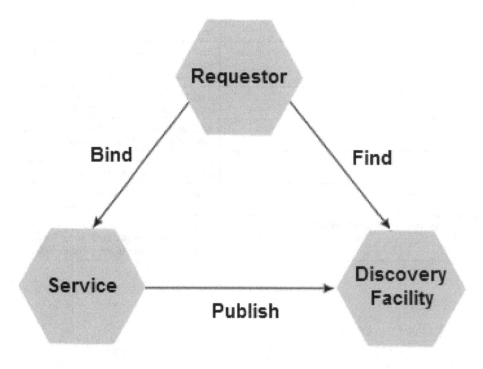

- **Bi-directional integration:** IAs and WSs can interoperate with each other by initiating communications.
- **IA invokes WS:** WSs are invoked by agents as component behaviors, while the IA level is represented by autonomy and intent.

Besides the relationship between CC and WS along with the relationship between WS and MAS, there exist a number of other factors influencing the implementation of CC by using a MAS:

- In order to meet the principle of "federation" there exist collaboration models utilized in MASs that can be used to form federations of services providers.
- To meet the principle of "independence" that CC should have, the autonomy that IAs have is an important factor.
- The principle of "isolation" can be met by managing the characteristics of delegation that IAs can have.
- To make "elasticity" of the CC system possible, any combination of the following characteristics can be used: autonomy, personality, communication, degradation in style, cooperation and expectations.
- "Business orientation" can be focused through the IA's task-resolution strategies because the domain of an agent is flexible.
- "Trust" in CC can be achieved as there is trust with IAs. Trust in IAs is derived from the characteristics of autonomy and delegation of the agents.

On the other hand, by considering the cloud of a CC as the environment of a MAS, the following can be said about the cloud:

- It is accessible because all services are available.
- It is deterministic because agents know which services are provided by other agents.
- It is episodic because the task an agent has to perform depends on a discrete number of services.
- It is dynamic because the environment changes while agents are collaborating.
- It is discrete because the number of possible services is finite and fixed.

In order to implement a CC based on IAs a MAS-based collaboration model is needed. Any node in the cloud environment (both service requestor and provider) is endowed with an IA of the MAS. The needs of a particular requestor are autonomously managed by the corresponding agent. The collaboration and negotiation between service providers made to meet all the requesting services are also autonomously managed by the corresponding agent of each provider. The following observations should be noted about the processes that MAS platforms should allow:

- Adding or removing nodes in a CC system implies the creation and termination of agents respectively.
- The unique identification address of any node in the cloud environment is the unique identification address any agent in a MAS needs.
- WS technology provides a registration system where agents can publish their capabilities.
- The necessary communication channel that nodes in a CC system have is the communication channel that agents in a MAS need.

The name "Intelligent Cloud" (Paletta, 2012c) derives from the fact that it is a CC system managed by IAs. In order to show more details of this type of scenario, the next section presents the MAS-based collaboration model called MAS-Scout.

4. MAS-SCOUT: MAS BY MEANS OF SCOUT MOVEMENT

This section contains the definitions and other details related to the MAS-Scout framework starting with a brief explanation of Scouting.

4.1 Scout Movement

Scout movement or Scouting is a global connotation that refers to a youth movement which stated goal is to support young people in their physical, mental, and spiritual states so that they can play a constructive role in society. Scouting dates back to 1907, when Robert Baden-Powell, Lieutenant General of the British Army, held the first Scout camp on Brownsea Island in England. After that, Baden-Powell wrote the principles of Scouting in *Scouting for Young People* (Baden-Powell, 1908). During the first half of the 20th-century, the movement grew to encompass three major groups for boys: Cub Scout (Pack), Boy Scout (Troop), and Rover Scout (Clan). In 1910, a new organization, Girl Guides, was created for girls.

In the words of its founder: "Scouting is a game of boys, led by them, and for which older brothers can give to younger ones a healthy environment, and encourage them to indulge in those activities that are conducive to healthily awaken the virtues of citizenship". This method makes use of motion scout, a non-formal education program with emphasis on practical outdoor activities such as camping, woodcraft, aquatics, hiking, walking, and sports. Another feature of this method is the movement that recognized the mandatory use of the Scout uniform. This movement intends to hide all social differences and struggles for equality.

Scouting principles remain common throughout the world, where all Scouting associations are joined together to respect the same values and laws. The emphasis on "learning by doing" provides members with experiences that serve them as a practical method of learning and building confidence. These experiences, coupled with an emphasis on honesty and personal honor, help members develop responsibility, character, confidence, reliability, and willingness leading to collaboration and leadership. Various activities and games carried out outdoors provide not only a fun way to develop skills such as dexterity, but also provide interaction with the natural environment.

In the same order of ideas, principles and laws of the scouts are the same worldwide. Many of such principles and laws derived from the code followed by medieval knights of the Middle Ages. Therefore, the organization ensures the homogeneity of global processes. The precepts to be observed by scouts are: 1) a Scout puts his honor aside in order to be trustworthy; 2) a Scout is loyal; 3) a Scout is useful and helpful to others without thought of reward; 4) a Scout is everyone's friend, and brother to all other Scouts without distinction of creed, race, nationality or social class; 5) a Scout is courteous and gentlemanly; 6) a Scout sees in nature the work of God, he protects animals and plants; 7) a Scout obeys without question and does nothing by halves; 8) a Scout smiles and sings through difficulties; 9) a Scout is economical, hard-worker, and concerned for the good of others; 10) a Scout is clean and healthy, pure in thoughts, words, and actions.

A Scout group consists of different members grouped in organized units that still maintain the original hierarchical structure. Groups are made up of three divisions. A fourth division exists in order to support new activities to society. The first three divisions (pack, troop and clan) are designed to train young people and consist of young people between ages 6-11, 11-16 and 16-21 years old respectively.

Because of the age differences between the boys, each subgroup/division is organized somewhat differently. However, they always have a guide or leader to guide them. All guides must submit a plan in advance that the young Scouts must meet in order to obtain medals and for personal growth. The number and name of each medal is defined by each National organization.

Likewise, the effort made among the leaders of each subgroup and the young members is not the same. In a pack, 100% of the initiative and responsibility lies in the leader. In a troop, responsibility is divided by 50% between the leaders and the members, as the boys are more grown-up and should be given some responsibility as well as discipline, always under adult supervision. Somewhat similarly, Scouts in a clan are older and therefore have more freedom and because of that they are expected to propose activities and to be oriented by their leader.

A troop is a unit of Scouts that brings together Scout patrols. A Scoutmaster and his assistants run a troop (Baden-Powell, 1908). The troops are formed by patrols and every Scout belongs to a patrol. A patrol is made up of a maximum of eight members and each patrol must have a name in order to be distinguished within the troop. Every Scout in the patrol is properly identified with a number. The leader (guide) of the patrol is identified with the number 1, the sub-guide or second in command is identified by the number 2, and so on. These guides and sub-guides are elected by the entire patrol and they are responsible for the performance of the patrol at the same time as they are responsible to report to the Scoutmaster. On the other hand, Scouts can only accomplish assigned goals in pairs or groups. According to Baden-Powell, a Scout Patrol is the basic unit of Scouting because it is the base needed for members to learn how to work in teams towards the satisfaction of common goals.

All the members of the patrol elect number 1 or the Patrol Leader. Number 1 is the leader and, therefore, the link between the patrol members

and the Scoutmaster (troop's leader). In addition, within each troop a court of honor is defined. A court of honor deals with all matters related with any patrol (work programs, rewards, punishments, etc.). It consists of the Scoutmaster and the patrol leaders. Decisions are made by secret ballot and the Scoutmaster does not vote. Moreover, without the Scoutmaster the patrol leaders are responsible for making decisions for the troop.

In summary, organization, communication, cooperation, trust, learning, and leadership are features related to Scouting that can be used to organize a MAS.

4.2 Basic Definitions

To help understand the MAS-based framework MS-Scout, various terminologies are defined below:

Definition 1- Activity: Is any action A_i that is necessary to do in order to achieve a main goal (or task).

Definition 2- Level of complexity: Is denoted by $\rho(A_i)$ and it is measured by a number between 1 and 3 that indicates whether A_i is easy, average, or difficult respectively.

Definition 3- Skill: Is denoted by $\Pi(A_i) = \{s_1, \ldots, s_k\}$ and it represents the set of skills/abilities s_i needed to accomplish the activity A_i. It is worth noting that there is a finite set of possible pre-defined skills s_i that can be in $\Pi(A_i)$.

It is also worth noting that, as there is a set of skills $\Pi(A_i)$ related with any activity A_i, there is also a set of skills $\Pi(a)$ associated to an IA-Scout agent a. Initially, agents in the systems do not have to or have not learned any skill ($\Pi(a) = \varnothing$). Skills will be acquired by each agent a through a learning process (see details bellow in this section).

Definition 4- Completion time: Is the amount of time expressed in milliseconds necessary to complete the activity A_i; it is denoted by $\tau(A_i)$.

Definition 5- Task: Is the representation of a main goal and it consists of a set of activities A_i i.e. $T = (A_1, ..., A_n)$.

Definition 6- IA-Scout: Is any of the IA that is part of the MAS defined by means of the MAS-Scout framework.

Definition 7- IA-Scout age: Related with the IA-Scout a, it is the agent execution time $\Gamma(a)$.

Definition 8- Organization: Is the way in which IA-Scout agents in a MAS-Scout system are arranged. This is done in the same way as Scouts are organized in Scouting. This means that there are three kinds of groups: clan, troops, and patrols. There are also three kinds of patrols: MAS-Pack, MAS-Troop, and MAS-Clan patrols. Initially all IA-Scouts have an execution time equal to 0 ($\Gamma(a) = 0$), which makes them part of a MAS-Pack patrol.

Starting from the lowest position in the hierarchy, the ascending line of command is as follows: a MAS-Pack patrol member; a MAS-Pack patrol sub-leader; a MAS-Pack patrol leader; a MAS-Troop patrol member; a MAS-Troop patrol sub-leader; a MAS-Troop patrol leader; a MAS-Clan patrol member; a MAS-Clan patrol sub-leader; a MAS-Clan patrol leader; a Troop leader; a Clan leader.

As agents are incorporated into the system and, due to the fact that they are at this moment beginners (($\Gamma(a) = 0$), they are incorporated into an incomplete MAS-Pack, i.e. a patrol that does not have the maximum of eight members a patrol should have. Initially, when there is not a Scout in the MAS-Scout organization, the first agent to be incorporated to the system becomes the number 1 (leader) of the Clan. The second agent to join the system will be the leader of the first Troop. The next agent will be the leader of the first MAS-Pack patrol and so on until 6 more members are added to the system completing the patrol. It is worth mentioning that, although eight is the maximum number of members that a patrol

can have according to Scouting, in MAS-Scout this is a parameter and therefore this value can be changed depending on run conditions such as, for example, the number of agents in the MAS or agent society.

When another agent needs to be incorporated into the MAS-Scout and all current patrols are full, it must form a new MAS-Pack and this requires selecting a leader. The new MAS-Pack leader is selected by using the probability presented in (2) and applied to the current MAS-Pack patrols' sub-leaders. The same occurs when selecting a sub-leader for a new patrol, which is selected from the remaining members of each current MAS-Pack patrol. When the sub-leader of a patrol X is selected to be a leader of a new patrol Y, the new sub-leader of X is selected from the remaining members of X. This movement of agents results in vacant spaces on patrols that are later occupied by new agents added into the MAS.

Figure 2 summarizes the way in which IA-Scout agents in a MAS-Scout system are organized based on Scouting organization. Note that there is no limit on the amount and type of patrols of each troop and there is also no limit on the amount of troops in the clan. The MAS-Scout is really organized within a Clan with a single leader.

Definition 9- Court of honor: Is a tribunal constituted by Troop leaders and, as it happens in Scouting, it deals with the following matters as they happen in any patrol in MAS-Scout: rewards, promotions, and punishments.

Definition 10- Promotion: Is the process in which a specific IA-Scout is ascended from its current group to a higher level in the same or in another group. It is determined by calculating a probability of distribution inspired in the Boltzmann distribution (Metropolis et al, 1953). An energy functional $E_t(a)$ of an IA-Scout agent a at time t is defined as shown in (1).

Figure 2. MAS-Scout organization

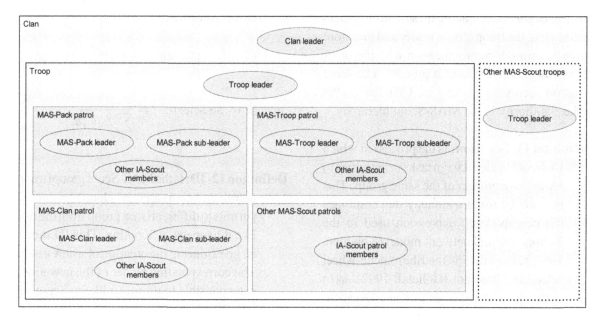

$$E_t(a) = \alpha \times \Gamma(a) + \beta \times P(a)$$
$$\alpha + \beta = 1 \tag{1}$$

$$\Delta E_t(a) = E_{t2}(a) - E_{t1}(a)$$
$$prob(a \text{ to be promoted}) = 1 - e^{-\Delta E_t(a)} \tag{2}$$

P(a) represents the accumulation of merit / awards / medals received by agent a from the moment that part of the MAS-Scout started to form. The weights α and β are coefficients expressed in the range [0, 1] and used to establish a degree of importance between the "age" of the agent $\Gamma(a)$ and its "merits" P(a).

Either increasing the run-time of the IA-Scout agent or the awards the agent has received during its execution can be factors that contribute in increasing the energy accumulated by the agent at any time t. Therefore, the difference or change that energy increases between two instants of time t_1 and t_2 is required to determine the IA-Scout promotion. It can be logically deduced then that, the greater the difference in energy $\Delta E(a)$ the higher is the probability that the agent will be promoted. An IA-Scout is selected to ascend a hierarchy level when $prob(a$ to be promoted) > random(0, 1). Expression (2) is used to calculate this probability.

P(a) is calculated based on the set of activities A_i an IA-Scout agent has accomplished since the last calculation of P(a) was completed. The aim is to reward those agents who have completed complex activities in a short period of time and to punish agents when simple tasks are performed during a long period of time. This is inversely proportional to the age of the agent. Expression (3) is used to calculate P(a).

$$P(a) = \frac{1}{\Gamma(a)} \sum_{i=1} \frac{\rho(A_i)}{\tau(A_i)} \tag{3}$$

From time to time (based on the MAS-Scout parameter ϖ) by convening a court of honor, the patrol leaders have to consider the promotion of corresponding patrol members according to the ascending line of command mentioned before. Occasionally, a Troop might be without a leader so that, a leader must be chosen from all current

MAS-Clan patrol leaders in the system. This process begins once one of these patrol leaders realizes that the troop has no leader and therefore initiates, through communication with the other patrol leaders, this selection process. The same situation occurs for electing the Clan leader, the highest authority in the MAS-Scout hierarchy.

Definition 11- Selection: Is the process in which IA-Scout leaders assign tasks or activities to IA-Scout members of the same group. This is made by using a strategy that combines the neighborhood expression used in the Kohonen neural network model (Kohonen, 1982; Kohonen, 1984) and the roulette-wheel selection algorithm (Holland, 1992). $\varphi(b)$ is the quantity of times that any IA-Scout leader a receives a request as part of the communication between an IA-Scout and its leader from the corresponding IA-Scout member b being led by a. The $\varphi(b)$ numbers are counted for each leader. The idea is to calculate a probability in which b is selected depending on the difference between $\varphi(b)$ and $\varphi(b^*)$, b^* being the IA-Scout that has sent more requests and therefore has the bigger value of $\varphi(b)$. Therefore, this probability is directly proportional to their $\varphi(b)$. To do this, the Kohonen neighborhood expression $\Delta(b,b^*)$ is used (see expression (4)) aiming for those IA-Scouts that have sent more requests to have the higher probability of being selected, but also giving an opportunity to those IA-Scouts that have sent fewer requests and therefore have a lower probability to be selected. After that and by using these probabilities, the roulette-wheel selection algorithm performed by the leader is used to select the IA-Scout that will be assigned a specific task that has to be done. σ in (4) is a parameter of width that determines how great the difference between $\varphi(b)$ and $\varphi(b^*)$ should be. It is recommended to start with a value of about 25% of the space to

be measured and to gradually decrease the value over time.

$$\Delta(b,b^*) = \exp\left[\frac{-(\phi(b) - \phi(b^*))^2}{\sigma^2}\right]$$

$$prob(b \text{ to be selected}) = \frac{\Delta(b,b^*)}{\sum_j \Delta(b_j,b^*)} \quad (4)$$

Definition 12- ID: Is the MAS-Scout group (troop, patrol, and clan) form of identification that permits to differentiate a group from the rest, like it happens in Scouting. This ID should be given during the creation of a new group. The corresponding leader of the new group is responsible to do so. Unlike in Scouting, where group names are mainly related to animal names (tiger, lion, squirrel, and so on), in MAS-Scout the name of each group is formed according to a numerical sequence based on the group's level in the organization. So that, the ID of the MAS-Clan is 1, the ID of an MAS-Troop is for example 1-1, 1-2, 1-3, and so on. In the case of MAS-Scout patrols, the character P, T, or C is added at the end of the ID to indicate if the patrol is related with a Pack (P), a Troop (T), or a Clan (C). Therefore, a valid ID for a MAS-Scout patrol is for example 1-2-1-T (a MAS-Troop patrol identified with number 1 depending on the Troop 2 of the Clan).

Having an ID to differentiate a group from another is important for the communication process between MAS-Scout agents. Details of this process are presented in the next section.

4.3 Communication

Communication between agents in MAS is essential. What is more, service sharing in a CC is implemented by using IAs. In this regard, for communication to occur in MAS-Scout the following interactions between the agents that make up the system are needed: 1) between members of the same patrol; 2) between an IA-Scout and its leader; 3) between an IA-Scout leader and the members of the group in which he is the leader; 4) between patrol leaders, including the leader of the troop selected by the convening a court of honor; 5) between troop leaders. Details of these five different MAS-Scouts' inter-agents' communication scenarios are presented below. First, it is important to mention that communication between IA-Scout agents in MAS-Scout systems is done by the exchange of messages between agents. Any message can be sent either to a particular IA-Scout by using its ID (peer-to-peer / P2P) or to all the current agents in the MAS-Scout system (broadcast). Note that broadcast messages allow simulating, a process that in Scouting is the blackboard that allows communication among Scouts. In order to know which agent is sending a message the message packet must have both, the sender's ID and rank, and the name of the group to which the sender belongs.

Communication between IA-Scout members of the same patrol is necessary for establishing the possible cooperation needed to solve a particular task assigned by the patrol leader. This exchange of messages is performed as follows: 1) IA-Scout a sends a message to all other members of the group to which a belongs looking for cooperation; 2) IA-Scout b sends to a the confirmation that it will cooperate with a; a sends to b the task it wants b to carry out (this can be given to more than one agent, depending on the complexity of the task and on the decision taken by a; see Section 4.4 for details); 3) a can receive confirmation from other agents and, if it does not require more collaboration, it sends a response that cooperation is no longer required; 4) b sends to a an answer related with the task given to it by a.

Communication between an IA-Scout and its leader usually starts from a patrol member and ends with the clan leader. It is mainly carried out in order to periodically request activities to perform.

This request is made only when the IA-Scout is without an activity/task at any given time or, in the case it is a leader, when there is a member in its group without an activity/task. The request is also used to check that a leading group exists. In this regard, it is possible to have the following scenarios: 1) a patrol without a leader, for which the number 2 on the patrol takes the lead and it is necessary to wait for the next court of honor to elect a new number 2; 2) a troop without a leader, for which a court of honor must convene urgently (see communication between patrol leaders below); 3) there is no leader for the clan and therefore a clan leader must be elected from current troop leaders (see communication between troop leaders below). Communication between an IA-Scout and its leader also occurs when the IA-Scout sends replies to its leader regarding the task assigned for it to solve.

Communication between an IA-Scout leader and the members of the group in which he is the leader is required for the assignation of tasks or activities starting from the Clan leader to the patrol members.

Communication between patrol leaders including the leader of the troop occurs in order to convene or convoke a court of honor. In this regard, any patrol leader is responsible to guarantee whether or not any of the patrol members has to be rewarded, promoted, or punished. To do this, and because leaders in general have all the information about satisfied activities, i.e. the level of complexity $\rho(A_i)$ of the activities and the times $\tau(A_i)$ in which each activity A_i was completed, leaders must keep track of these statistics in the manner shown bellow.

By using expression (2) each leader calculates the probability of promoting of each of its members. Once the number of members selected (i.e. $prob(a$ to be promoted$) > random(0, 1)$) exceeds a parameter ϖ the corresponding patrol leader sends a message to the other patrol leaders to convoke a court of honor. Once the court of honor has been convoked each leader sends the best candidate that exists in their corresponding patrol to the rest. The best candidate is the one that has the highest probability of being promoted (expression (2)). In the case of the leader who convened the court of honor, it must select the best candidate from the list of ϖ members selected. After that, each leader has as many candidates as there are patrols in the specific troop, each candidate with its probability of being promoted. Therefore, a roulette-wheel selection algorithm is performed by each patrol leader to select the IA-Scout that should be elected according to each patrol leader. Information about the IA-Scout selected is then sent to the troop leader. Finally, once the troop leader receives all the candidates from the patrol leaders it makes the final decision based on the greatest number of votes or selections made in favor of a candidate. In the event of a tie, all IA-Scout involved are promoted. By using the IA-Scout's ID, the troop leader informs the corresponding patrol leaders about these promotions. It should be remembered that promotions might lead to the formation of other patrols.

Communication between troop leaders is necessary only when the Clan does not have a leader. In this regard, once a troop leader realizes that the Clan does not have a leader, the troop leader is responsible for the process of selecting a new Clan leader and for that it sends a message to the rest of the troop leaders. The selection process is similar to what is explained above. Starting with the troop leader exchanging the candidates' corresponding probabilities of being promoted and ending with the counting of votes conducted by those responsible of the process, the Clan leader is elected. In this case, and due to the fact that there should be only one Clan leader, possible ties must be resolved randomly. The agent responsible for running the process is also involved in the election process and, unless it was selected, the process ends when it sends a message to the troop leader chosen informing it about its promotion.

Table 2 summarizes the extent of the messages exchanged between MAS-Scout agents indicating both the type of message (broadcast or P2P) and the data required to send the message.

4.4 Cooperation, Trust, Learning and Leadership

Cooperation is the process that occurs between IA-Scout agents aiming to accomplish a certain amount of activities. It is established through the communication between IA-Scout members of the same patrol. As part of this process, the calculation of the following two probabilities is necessary: 1) the probability to look for cooperation related to any activity; and 2) the probability of rejecting to cooperate in relation to a specific activity. The probability to look for cooperation related to any activity A_i is used by an agent a when it receives the assignment of a task $T = (A_1, ..., A_n)$ (see expression (5)). This probability depends on the agent's age $\Gamma(a)$ (the younger a is the more help it will need), the complexity of the activity $\rho(A_i)$ (the more complex the activity is the more cooperation it will require), and the skills $\Pi(a)$ agent a has related to skills $\Pi(A_i)$ activity A_i requires (the less skills a has the more cooperation it will require). It is worth noting that $\Gamma(a) \neq 0$ (a has started executing before receiving any assignment).

$$\kappa(a, A_i) = \frac{\rho(A_i) * \left[\left| \Pi(A_i) \right| - \left| \Pi(A_i) \cap \Pi(a) \right| \right]}{\Gamma(a)}$$

$prob(a$ has to look for cooperation

$$\text{related to } A_i) == \frac{\kappa(a, A_i)}{\sum_j \kappa(a, A_j)}$$

$$(5)$$

The probability of rejecting to cooperate in relation to a specific activity depends on the current workload $\omega(a)$ agent a has (the more work-

Table 2. Summary of the messages exchanged between MAS-Scout agents

Between	Message type	Description	Data
Members of the same group	Broadcast	Look for cooperation	Task information
	P2P	Confirm cooperation	Activity
	P2P	Inform that cooperation is no longer required	No
	P2P	Send a task that must be accomplished	Task information
	P2P	Send the response to the tasks that were given to be solved	Response information
An IA-Scout and its leader	P2P	Request activities to perform	No
	P2P	Send the response to the tasks that were given to be solved	Response information
IA-Scout leader and the members of the group	P2P	Assign tasks or activities to be performed	Task information
Between patrol leaders	Broadcast	To convoke a court of honor	No
	Broadcast	To inform about the best candidate of the troop	IA-Scout information
Between a patrol leader and its troop leader	P2P	To inform about the candidate selected to be promoted	IA-Scout information
Between the troop leader and the corresponding patrol leaders	P2P	To inform which IA-Scout should be promoted	IA-Scout information
Between troop leaders	Broadcast	To inform that a Clan leader must be selected	Troop leader responsible for the process
	Broadcast	To send the information of each troop leader needed for the selection process	Troop leader information
	P2P	To inform the troop leader candidate to be selected to be the Clan leader	Troop leader information
	P2P	To inform a particular troop leader about its promotion	No

load a has, the more likely it is that a will refuse cooperation). Expression (6) shows the way this probability is calculated; $\hat{A}_i$ refers to activities that a is currently performing and A_i is the activity for which a has to decide whether to accept or reject in response to a request for cooperation.

$$\omega(a) = \sum_i \kappa(a, \hat{A}_i)$$

$prob$(to reject cooperation related to A_i) ==
$0.75 * \omega(a) + 0.25 * \kappa(a, A_i)$

(6)

The cooperation process between IA-Scouts follows the guidelines stated next (being a the agent which is assigned the task $T = (A_1, ..., A_n)$):
1) a must perform at least one activity A_i and this activity must have the highest level of complexity $\rho(A_i)$ from all activities of T; 2) a can look for collaboration with more than one other agent b at a time but only a single activity can be assigned to b; 3) any activity that a might be working on as a result of cooperation with any other agent b at time of receiving T has to be completed before starting to accomplish T; 4) probability shown in (5) is used to look for cooperation related to a

particular activity; 5) an agent's decision about with which agent to cooperate is made randomly; 6) once *a* receives the assignment of *T* it rejects any cooperation requests coming from any other agent in order to give priority to the completion of *T*; and 7) in addition to the previous scenario, an agent can also refuse cooperation based on the amount of activities being undertaken and the amount of skills of the agent, for which the probability of rejecting cooperation shown in (6) is used.

As noted, depending on the current conditions of the patrol, an IA-Scout *a* may either get no help from another IA-Scout that can cooperate with it—for which *a* will have to perform all assigned activities—or *a* can get help from other agents in relation to all assigned activities, but at least one of them has to be necessarily performed by *a*.

It is important to emphasize that the cooperation mechanism is one of the most significant characteristics of the MAS-Scout proposal. The way in which Scouts cooperate with each other in order to achieve goals from activities that are conducted in groups is taken into account to define this mechanism. Unlike other proposals (in which the cooperation between agents is possible but without agents being able to learn) in MAS-Scout all agents clearly know: 1) with which other agents to look for cooperation; 2) how agents must cooperate with other agents; 3) how to distribute the activities of any task properly; 4) how agents have to communicate with each order in order to cooperate; and 5) how learning improves future cooperation between agents.

Trust is essential in Scouting and therefore it is also essential in MAS-Scout. We have an example of trust when an agent *a* assigns a task to a fellow patrol member *b* knowing that the duration in which *b* accomplishes that task as well as the quality of the response can help agent *a* in its promotion. Therefore, *a* trusts *b* to finish the assigned activities as soon and with the best quality as possible. Another example of trust is presented in the election process.

In MAS-Scout any IA-Scout must learn the necessary skills needed to perform the tasks. Therefore, the learning process is used to increase / add abilities to the set $\Pi(a)$ of any IA-Scout *a*. In this regard, for each skill s_i pre-defined in MAS-Scout and each skill that can be part of $\Pi(a)$ there is a learning factor $\xi(s_i)$ that determines how much of the skill s_i (initially $\xi(s_i) = 0$ for all s_i) agent *a* has learned. Being $\xi(s_i)$ a factor measured between 0 and 1 where 0 indicates that the agent has not learned anything about s_i, the decision to add s_i to $\Pi(a)$ is given by the relation $\xi(s_i) > H$ where H is a learning factor level, another parameter of the MAS-Scout.

The learning process occurs as follows. Each time an IA-Scout agent *a* accomplishes an activity A_i, whether it belongs to a task assignment to *a* or A_i is related to the cooperation *a* has given to another agent, an adjustment factor $\Delta\xi(s_i)$ associated with the learning of all skills s_i relating to A_i is calculated ($s_i \in \Pi(A_i)$). $\Delta\xi(s_i)$ is then applied to the accumulation factor $\xi(s_i)$ and relation $\xi(s_i) > H$ is evaluated. If the relational expression is true then s_i is added to $\Pi(a)$ indicating that *a* has learned the skill s_i. Expression (7) is used to calculate $\Delta\xi(s_i)$. It is assumed that 3 is the highest value for $\rho(A_i)$ and 0.1 the smallest value that $\tau(A_i)$ can have i.e. the learning constant λ ($0 \leq \lambda \leq 1$) is the maximum value $\Delta\xi(s_i)$ can have. Note that, as the agent execution time $\Gamma(a)$ is greater, learning is slower. Note also that this learning process was inspired by the Scouting slogan "learning by doing".

$$\Delta\xi(s_i) = \lambda \frac{1}{\Gamma(a)} \frac{\rho(A_i)}{30*\tau(A_i)}; \quad s_i \in \Pi(A_i)$$

$$(7)$$

Leadership is one of the basic principles of Scouting. Communication is a basic process needed to guarantee leadership. Leadership is guaranteed in MAS-Scout because all messages have the ID of the IA-Scout that is sending the message and because the ID has both, the number (rank) of the IA-Scout and the knowledge of which group level the IA-Scout belongs to. All agents must obey orders that come from messages sent by other IA-Scouts with a higher rank. An example of this is the assignment of tasks.

By using the definitions presented in Section 4.2 and by guaranteeing all: cooperation, trust, learning and leadership, the MAS-Scout framework has all the necessary elements to implement a CC system for enabling effective service collaboration. Next section presents the details regarding this assertion.

5. SERVICE COLLABORATION IN CLOUD COMPUTING BY MEANS OF MAS-SCOUT BASE MODEL

This section presents details of how theoretical aspects of MAS-Scout presented in the previous section are used to establish service collaboration in CC. All the main aspects related to CC and described in Section 1 are explained by means of MAS-Scout model. Let's give the name CCS-Scout to this CC System by means of an MAS-Scout model.

5.1 The Basic CC Elements

A CC service is represented in CCS-Scout as a Task (see Definition 5). Therefore, a service consists of a set of activities each of which has a level of complexity and requires a set of skills to be completed. Notice that the level of complexity and/or the required skills any activity has can be used to determine a value to this specific activity. This value could be an amount that may be charged for the completion of the activity. Therefore, a cost estimation of one service may be calculated by totalizing the cost of all the corresponding activities. Related to this, expression (8) calculates the cost $\varsigma(T)$ to achieve service/task $T = (A_1, ..., A_n)$

based on the costs to achieve activities A_i, $\varsigma(A_i)$ that are calculated based on the corresponding skills $\Pi(A_i)$. It is worth noting that since $\Pi(A_i)$ is a set of specific skills s_j, $\varsigma(A_i)$ may be calculated by using a weighted average expression aiming to express the importance of each skill $s_j \in \Pi(A_i)$. Therefore, the more specialized the skill, the greater its influence will be on the calculation of $\varsigma(A_i)$.

$$\varsigma(T) = \sum_{i=1}^{n} \varsigma(A_i); \quad \varsigma(A_i) = p_1\varsigma(s_1) + p_2\varsigma(s_2) + ... + p_k\varsigma(s_k); \quad s_j \in \Pi(A_i) \quad (8)$$

Each node in the CCS-Scout cloud (either client or service provider) is endowed with a MAS-Scout patrol, which means that any node has one or more IA-Scouts responsible for both requesting for the termination of services required as well as for providing the solution for requested services.

Moreover, service providers that deal with the same subject or business are grouped in MAS-Scout troops so that all the collaboration needed between them is guaranteed because this is a natural process in MAS-Scout (see Section 4.4). These groups should be seen like consortiums of companies who help each other meet each other's needs. Even different consortiums or MAS-Scout troops could collaborate together if it was needed because they are organized in a MAS-Scout clan.

In order to inform the account of the services rendered among nodes in CCS-Scout by means of MAS-Scout patrols, and because all services needs are handled by the MAS-Scout troop leader (see Section 4.3 for details), these troop leaders maintain a table with account balances indicating how much to pay or reimburse each patrol leader. Troop leaders then hold a bag of money and make periodical collections or distributions of goods accordingly. To do that, the following three exchange messages between IA-Scout troop leaders and IA-Scout patrol leaders have to be carried out:

- A P2P message from a patrol leader to its troop leader aiming to ask the patrol leader's balance account. This message does not have any data.

- A P2P message from a troop leader to the leader of one of its patrols responding the previous message. The corresponding data of this message has the details of the quantity that the patrol leader has to pay to the troop leader or get as reimbursement from it.

The manner in which debts between patrol leaders and troop leaders are settled is previously defined before the CCS-Scout system starts, for example, by using credits cards, pay for services rendered, and free.

Initially, the entire CCS-Scout system could be disordered. In this case a process of self-organization is needed. In this regard, reference (Paletta, 2012a) contains a proposal of self-organization of a MAS-Scout based system that includes the way in which all leaders are selected.

5.2 Characteristics, Features, Principles, and Models

Does the CCS-Scout support all the characteristics, features, principles, and models associated to CC and indicated in Section 1? Let's do a brief review of each of these elements.

Because collaboration between patrols (or nodes) in the same troop (or consortium) and collaboration between troops in the entire CC system (or clan) is possible, all services or resources required can be satisfied giving to the clients the *illusion of infinite computing resources*. This collaboration process is carried naturally and automatically so that the *elimination of an up-front commitment by cloud users* is guaranteed. Clients request the completion of a service and they receive a response without knowing which node made it. Moreover, expression (8) defines the *ability to pay for use as needed*.

The following points offer a brief explanation related to the desired features of a cloud: 1) because the use of services in CCS-Scout by means of the collaboration process described in Section 4.4 can be carried out without human intervention, *Self-Service* is a feature present in CCS-Scout; 2) because the cost of the service is calculated based on the cost of just the activities included in the service and based on the skills needed to accomplish any activity (see (8)), clients will only pay for what is used and therefore the *Per-Usage metering and billing* feature is presented in CCS-Scout; 3) because CCS-Scout can grow without limit according to Definition 8 and because there are also no limitations in the collaboration process in the sense that all services required should be provided (no rejections), clients expect to be provided with any quantity of resources at any time and for that *Elasticity* is presented in CCS-Scout; 4) because MAS-Scout troops are associated with different kinds of businesses and because nodes of different troops can also collaborate with each other in the same way nodes of the same troop collaborate among them, services' requirements in CCS-Scout are highly customizable so that *Customization* is present as well.

Regarding the basic principles of CC, in CCS-Scout, *Federations* are formed by providers in as much a quantity as they can organize in MAS-Scout troops. Moreover, all services in CCS-Scout enjoy of *Independence* because activities, skills and all other parameters related with them are encapsulated. On the other hand, the collaboration process between users and service providers that occurs in CCS-Scout (see Section 4.4) guarantees the *Isolation* of the resources. CCS-Scout has also the abilities of *Elasticity* and *Business Orientation* because there are no limitations on the quantity and quality of services that can be demanded at any time. Finally, as it was mentioned in Section 4.4, trust is presented in MAS-Scout because it is a Scouting principle, so that nodes in CCS-Scout *Trust* each other.

Furthermore, CCS-Scout not only provides ready-to-run services (clients do not have to wait for a requirement to be sent) but also provides the ability to deploy custom services (new services can be added at any time) as well as low-level virtualized resources (clients ask for services unaware of who or how these services will be solved, clients just wait for the completion of the services). Therefore, there are no limitations in CCS-Scout for implementing the three service models that compose CC: SaaS, PaaS, and IaaS.

According to what is presented in this section, CCS-Scout is capable of implementing a CC system with all the characteristics, features, principles and models CC should have. Next section contains some details on the way in which MAS-Scout was implemented and on how to derive to a CCS-Scout implementation by using MAS-Scout.

6. IMPLEMENTATION AND EVALUATION

This section presents details of an implementation of the MAS-Scout description presented in Section 4. SOFIA (SOA-based Framework for Intelligent Agents) (Paletta & Herrero, 2009; Paletta & Herrero, 2010b) is the general agent architecture used to develop the IA-Scout agents (see Section 5.1

for details). This section also presents the way in which CCS-Scout is defined by using MAS-Scout and some experimental results related with the implementation of the CCS-Scout done.

6.1 The Agent Architecture

SOFIA focuses on the design of a common framework for intelligent agents with the following characteristics: 1) it merges interdisciplinary theories, methods, and approaches, 2) it is extensible and open as to be completed with new requirements and necessities, and 3) it highlights the agent's learning processes within the environment. SOFIA's general architecture contains four main components (see Figure 3):

1. The Embodied Agent (IA-EA) or the "body": It is a FIPA-based structure (FIPA, 2002) because it has a Service Directory element that provides a location where specific and correspondent descriptions of services can be registered. The IA-EA encloses the set of services related to the abilities of sensing stimuli from the environment and interacting with it.

2. The Rational Agent (IA-RA) or the "brain": This component represents the agent's intelligent part and therefore, it encloses the set

Figure 3. SOFIA's general architecture

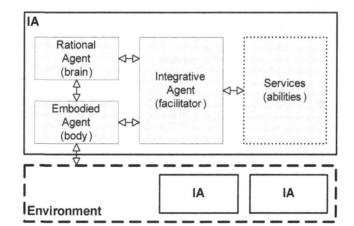

of services used by the agent to implement the processes associated with these abilities. It is also a FIPA-based structure.

3.　The Integrative/Facilitator Agent (IA-FA) or the "facilitator": It plays the role of simplifying the inclusion of new services into the system as well as the execution of each of them when necessary. The basic function of the IA-FA is to coordinate the integration of the IA-SV the rest of the IA components. This integration is needed when a new service is integrated within the IA and therefore it is registered into the corresponding Service Directory, even when an existing service is being executed.

4.　The IA Services or "abilities" (IA-SV): It is a collection of individual and independent software components integrated to the system (the IA) that implement any specific ability either to the IA-EA or the IA-RA.

6.2 Implementation Details

Because it is FIPA-compliant as well as an open-source (based on Java), IA-Scout agents were implemented in JADE (Bellifemine et al, 1999) by using SOFIA architecture. In addition to having a class to define the agents (IAScouts) and a class to represent the MAS-Scout environment in which the necessary parameters for the system are represented, other classes were defined as it is shown in Figure 4 and explained in Table 3. On the other hand, Table 4 not only shows a summary of the required parameters but also shows the values used for the simulation presented in this section. The pre-defined skill set is also found in the class used to represent the MAS-Scout environment.

In order to perform the MAS-Scout simulation in a hypothetical scenario, an application from which some screenshots are shown in Figure 5 and Figure 6 was used. The hypothetical scenario

Figure 4. MAS-Scout class model

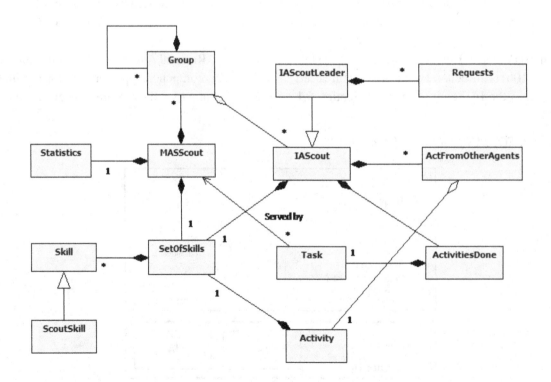

Table 3. MAS-Scout classes

Class	Description
IAScout	Represents a common IAScout agent.
IAScoutLeader	An IAScout specialized in being a leader.
MASScout	Represents the MAS environment
Group	Represents all Scout groups: clan, troop, or patrol.
Statistics	Keeps the statistics obtained from the MAS execution.
Skill	Represents a particular skill that a Scout could have or an activity it could offer.
ScoutSkill	A Skill that is specialized in order for Scouts to learn it.
SetOfSkills	Contains a set of objects of type Skill.
Requests	Contains the requests for tasks Scouts sent to their leaders.
Activity	Represents an activity Scouts can perform.
Task	Represents a set of activities to be performed by Scouts of the MAS-Scout system.
ActFromOtherAgents	Represents the activities Scouts are performing in collaboration other Scouts.
ActivitiesDone	Keeps all the activities Scouts have finished.

presented below has the following characteristics: 1) IA-Scouts (agents) were added to the MAS randomly; 2) tasks were assigned randomly to the Clan leader of the MAS-Scout system; 3) for each task, the quantity of activities and the level of difficulty of these activities were also defined randomly; and 4) the duration of the completion of any activity was also random. Figure 5 shows the MAS organization by using a tree-shaped structure. Note that the first agent in each group is the group leader, represented in the Figure 5 with a different icon from the rest of the agents that are not leaders. Also note that some of the Scouts have the activities they are currently performing.

The corresponding ID and level of difficulty of each activity is also shown. On the other hand, Figure 6 shows the statistics obtained during the simulation. The statistics reflect the activities performed by the agents, the promotions given, the total number of court of honors convened, and the total number of Scouts removed from the MAS.

In summary, and by using the strategies explain in Section 4, the implementation of the MAS-Scout framework includes the following aspects:

1. As Scouts are added to the MAS they are automatically organized following the Scouting structure.

Table 4. Summary of the MAS-Scout parameters

Parameter	Description	Value
α	Level of importance of $\Gamma(a)$ in expression (1)	0.5
β	Level of importance of $P(a)$ in expression (1)	0.5
η	Maximum number of members a patrol can have	5
ϖ	Number of members that should be selected in order to initiate the process of convening a court of honor	2
H	The learning factor level used for determining that a skill has been learned	0.9
λ	Learning factor used to calculate $\Delta\xi$	0.125

Figure 5. Screenshot of the application used to perform the MAS-Scout simulation showing the MAS organization

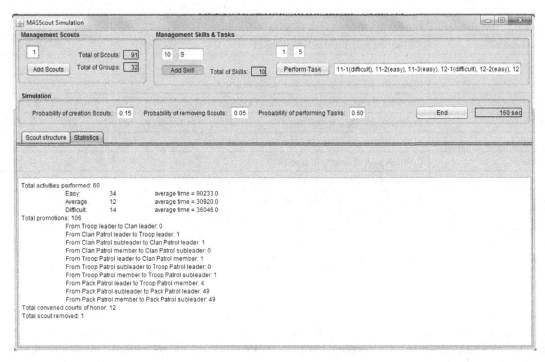

Figure 6. Screenshot of the application used to perform the MAS-Scout simulation showing the statistics

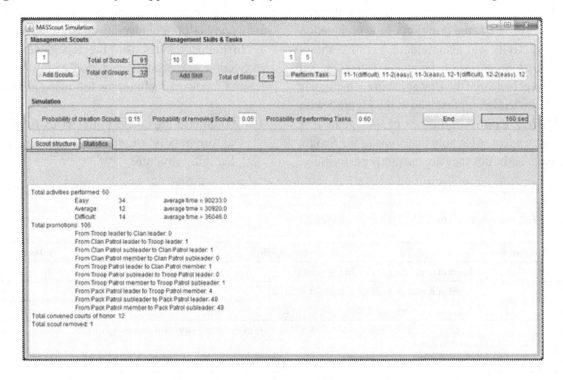

2. Groups are created automatically as they are required.

3. Starting from the Clan leader, leaders in general assign tasks or activities to other members of the group.

4. Scouts of the same patrols can collaborate with each other to solve the assigned tasks.

5. As Scouts perform the tasks assigned to them they learn the skills associated with the corresponding activities.

6. The patrol leaders automatically convene the court of honour when the required conditions are present in the MAS.

7. Scouts' promotions, including the need to fill vacancies in the structure, are handled automatically.

8. It is possible to remove Scouts from the structure, including the Clan leader.

The screenshot shown in Figure 5 contains the necessary elements needed to control the simulation. In this regard, the simulation can be done both manually and automatically. In order to be done automatically both, the probabilities for adding and removing Scouts to and from the MAS, as well as the probability for assigning tasks by the Clan leader, can be dynamically changed.

6.3 CCS-Scout by Means of MAS-Scout

In CCS-Scout the concept of Service is defined by a Task specialized in adding the definition of the service's cost (see Section 5.1). CCS-Scout is a MAS-Scout specialization that adds the new exchange messages for handling the account for services rendered.

Therefore, in order to implement CCS-Scout by means of MAS-Scout two more classes have to be incorporated to the MAS-Scout class model presented in Figure 4 (see Figure 7): 1) a specialization of the class "MAS-Scout" that represents "CCS-Scout" objects by adding the new features to handle the account for services rendered; and 2) a specialization of the class "Task" that represents a "Service".

6.4 Case Study and Experimental Results

In order to test the CCS-Scout model based on a case study, the MAS-Scout simulation explained in Section 6.2 was modified according to the specializations presented in the previous section. The case study is related to reservations made

Figure 7. CCS-Scout class model by using MAS-Scout model

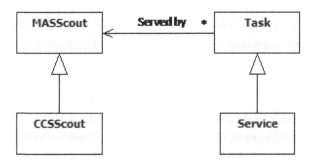

for a trip and all the possible items involved, such as transport, room and board, and tourist attractions by means of a CCS. This case refers to a distributed system that possesses nodes that collaborate with each other to offer a combined package that satisfies the needs of the traveler. The application is developed searching to design a package of combined trips made for diverse purposes (tourism, business and pleasure among others). Traveling agencies or related businesses are benefited from this application. Generally, a package of combined travels involves a series of items such as: room and board, hotel, transportation, vehicle rental, and tickets to shows or tourist attractions among others. Occasionally, clients that chose this type of businesses to request a travelling package are offered an incomplete package because the business finds it impossible to include some of the items in the package. As a consequence the client must work on some of the remaining arrangements separately.

It is necessary then to have an application that allows businesses that work in the travelling area to collaborate with each other so as complete the requested travelling packages. If this happened then a company that could not complete a package because it cannot offer a certain item can then complete the package by asking for the missing item to other companies that offer it. Companies benefit from this because their profits rise by participating as a whole in combined packages that are requested in any of them and their clients receive a complete package without having to work on some of the missing items individually.

In this scenario, MAS-Scout patrols or nodes are formed by those businesses (travel agencies) that offer one or more services related to the elements that can be a part of a combined travelling package and that wish to participate in this collaboration system. The quantity of nodes allowed to be in the system at the beginning is unlimited. A combined travelling package is represented by

a service with activities that are those elements that can be a part of a combined travelling package and the related operations such as: making reservations, cancelling reservations, changing a reservation or purchase and payment of an item. For example, for an item related with transportation the following activities are at hand: making reservations for a certain kind of transportation, cancelling a reservation, changing a previously made reservation or purchase, purchasing tickets for a certain kind of transportation, and so on. The quantity of elements to be considered to become part of a combined travelling package is unlimited. Moreover, MAS-Scout troops re-consortiums formed by travel agencies.

After running the simulation automatically for a long period of time (approximately 24 hours), and after continuously changing the probabilities to add / remove Scouts and interchange service's needs between nodes in the system, the experimental results can be summarized as follows:

1. The MAS remains correctly organized following the Scouting structure once each Scout is added to or removed from the system.
2. The assigned services are distributed fairly among the different groups that form part of the MAS.
3. Collaborations often occur between Scouts that are members of the same patrol aiming to solve activities that form part of the services required and that this specific patrol can solve based on its current resources and skills.
4. Collaborations also occur between patrols that form part of a troop aiming to solve those activities that patrols cannot solve by themselves and therefore they have to send the corresponding requirements to the CC environment in order for other patrols of the same troop to collaborate.

5. Based on random values established initially during the definition of skills, troop leaders calculate the balance of each patrol's account and the exchange of message sharing of this information done in the CC system.

7. CONCLUSION AND ONGOING WORK

In this article, a MAS-based framework called MAS-Scout, defined by means of theoretical aspects of Scouting is used aiming to define the CCS-Scout model. CCS-Scout, a new proposal for implementing CC, focuses on the premise that Scouting has been a very successful social movement where collaboration, organization and teamwork are basic principles.

Although CCS-Scout has not yet been tested in real applications and there exists no comparison with other similar proposals, CCS-Scout has been designed to be suitable for real CC environments where service-level agreements that provide external users with requested services is achieved. In fact, the results obtained from experimental scenarios and validation over simulated conditions show that the behavior of the MAS or CC organized as Scouting is as expected. From the way it is framed, CCS-Scout can be successfully extended to real scenarios satisfying the main CC goals in a reasonable time (looking for efficiency) and/or to obtain higher quality results (looking for effectiveness).

On the other hand, a theoretical validation through using different aspects related with CC is also included in this article showing the way in which all these issues can be satisfied by using CCS-Scout. In other words, CCS-Scout proves to cover almost all if not all CC theoretical aspects.

Both: 1) testing the CCS-Scout model in real applications, particularly in distributed environments where agents of a MAS should be organized and collaboration is required; and 2) defining a new protocol for exchanging messages between the Scouts in order to reduce the message traffic, are some ongoing work related with this research.

ACKNOWLEDGMENT

This research was supported by the Center for Research in Informatics and Computer Technology (CITEC – from the Spanish "Centro de Investigación en Informática y Tecnología de la Computación") at the Universidad Nacional Experimental de Guayana (UNEG) of Venezuela.

REFERENCES

Armbrust, M., Fox, A., Griffith, R., Joseph, A. D., & Katz, R. (2009). *Above the Clouds: A Berkeley View of Cloud Computing* (UC Berkeley Reliable Adaptive Distributed Systems Laboratory White Paper). Berkeley, CA: University of California.

Baden-Powell, R. (1908). *Scouting for Boys*. London: Windsor House.

Bellifemine, F., Poggi, A., & Rimassa, G. (1999). JADE-A FIPA-compliant agent framework. In *Proceedings of International Conference on Practical Applications of Agents and Multi-Agent Systems (PAAM'99)* (pp. 97-108). London, UK: The Practical Application Company Ltd.

Buyya, R., Yeo, C. S., Venugopal, S., Broberg, J., & Brandic, I. (2009). Cloud computing and emerging IT platforms: Vision, hype, and reality for delivering computing as the 5th utility. *Future Generation Computer Systems, 25*(6), 599–616. doi:10.1016/j.future.2008.12.001

Chen, L. (2010). Application of cloud computing to learning. *African Journal of Business Management, 4*(14), 3217–3225.

Dickinson, I., & Wooldridge, M. (2005). Agents are not (just) web services: considering BDI agents and web services. In *Proceedings of 2005 Workshop on Service-Oriented Computing and Agent-Based Engineering (SOCABE'2005)*. Utrecht, The Netherlands: HP Technical Reports.

Gutierrez, J. O., & Sim, K. M. (2010). Self-organizing agents for service composition in cloud computing. In *Proceedings of 2nd IEEE International Conference on Cloud Computing Technology and Science (CloudCom)* (pp. 59-66). Indianapolis, IN: IEEE Press.

Holland, J. (1992). *Adaptation in natural and artificial systems*. Cambridge, MA: MIT Press.

Jha, S., Katz, D. S., Luckow, A., Merzky, A., & Stamou, K. (2011). Understanding Scientific Applications for Cloud Environments. In R. Buyya, J. Nroberg, & A. Goscinski (Eds.), *Cloud Computing: Principles and Paradigms* (pp. 345–372). John Wiley & Sons, Inc. doi:10.1002/9780470940105.ch13

Kohonen, T. (1982). Self-Organized Formation of Topologically Correct Feature Maps. *Biological Cybernetics, 43*, 59–69. doi:10.1007/BF00337288

Kohonen, T. (1984). *Self-Organization and Associative Memory*. Berlin, Germany: Springer-Verlag.

Mell, P., & Grance, T. (2009). The NIST Definition of Cloud Computing. *Computer and Information Science, 53*(6), 50.

Metropolis, N., Rosenbluth, A. W., Rosenbluth, M. N., Teller, A. H., & Teller, E. (1953). Equations of state calculations by fast computing machines. *The Journal of Chemical Physics, 21*(6), 1087–1091. doi:10.1063/1.1699114

Mohan, T. S. (2011). Migrating into a Cloud. In R. Buyya, J. Nroberg, & A. Goscinski (Eds.), *Cloud Computing: Principles and Paradigms* (pp. 43–56). John Wiley & Sons, Inc. doi:10.1002/9780470940105.ch2

Nepal, S., & Zic, J. (2008). A conflict neighbouring negotiation algorithm for resource services in dynamic collaborations. In *Proceedings of IEEE International Conference on Services Computing (SCC)* (pp. 283-290). Honolulu, HI: IEEE Press.

Nikitin, S., Terziyan, V., & Nagy, M. (2010). Mastering intelligent clouds - Engineering intelligent data processing services in the cloud. In *Proceedings of 7th International Conference on Informatics in Control, Automation and Robotics (ICINCO)* (pp. 174-181). Madeira, Portugal: SciTePress – Science and Technology Publications.

Paletta, M. (2012a). Self-Organizing Multi-Agent Systems by means of Scout Movement. [CSENG]. *Recent Patents on Computer Science, 5*(3), 197–210. doi:10.2174/2213275911205030197

Paletta, M. (2012b). MAS-based Agent Societies by Means of Scout Movement. [IJATS]. *International Journal of Agent Technologies and Systems, 4*(3), 29–49. doi:10.4018/jats.2012070103

Paletta, M. (2012c). Intelligent Clouds – By means of using multi-agent systems environments. In L. Chao (Ed.), *Cloud Computing for Teaching and Learning: Strategies for Design and Implementation*. Hershey, PA: IGI Global. doi:10.4018/978-1-4666-0957-0.ch017

Paletta, M., & Herrero, M. P. (2009). Awareness-based learning model to improve cooperation in collaborative distributed environments. In *Proceedings of 3rd International KES Symposium on Agents and Multi-agents Systems Technologies and Applications (KES-AMSTA 2009)* (pp. 793-802). Uppsala, Sweden: Springer.

Paletta, M., & Herrero, M. P. (2010a). An awareness-based learning model to deal with service collaboration in cloud computing. In N. T. Nguyen, & R. Kowalczyk (Eds.), *Transactions on Computational Collective Intelligence I* (pp. 85–100). Berlin, Germany: Springer-Verlag. doi:10.1007/978-3-642-15034-0_6

Paletta, M., & Herrero, M. P. (2010b). Collaboration in Distributed Systems by means of an Awareness-based Learning Model. [CSENG]. *Recent Patents on Computer Science*, *3*(2), 1–21. doi:10.2174/2213275911003020127

Papazoglou, M. P., & Van den Heuvel, W. J. (2007). Service oriented architectures: Approaches, technologies and research issues. *The VLDB Journal*, *16*(3), 389–415. doi:10.1007/s00778-007-0044-3

Reese, G. (2009). *Cloud Application Architectures: Building Applications and Infrastructure in the Cloud*. Sebastopol, CA: O'Reilly Media, Inc.

Rochwerger, B., Vazquez, C., Breitgand, D., Hadas, D., Villari, M., Massonet, P., & Galán, F. (2011). An Architecture for Federated Cloud Computing. In R. Buyya, J. Nroberg, & A. Goscinski (Eds.), *Cloud Computing: Principles and Paradigms* (pp. 393–412). John Wiley & Sons. doi:10.1002/9780470940105.ch15

Sarna, D. E. Y. (2011). *Implementing and Developing Cloud Computing Applications*. Boca Raton, FL: CRC Press.

Sim, K. M. (2010). Towards complex negotiation for Cloud economy. In P. Bellavista, R. S. Chang, H. C. Chao, S. F. Lin, & P. M. Sloot (Eds.), *Advances in Grid and Pervasive Computing* (pp. 395–406). Berlin, Germany: Springer-Verlag. doi:10.1007/978-3-642-13067-0_42

Song, B., Mehedi, H. M., Tian, Y., & Huh, E. N. (2009). A back propagation neural network for evaluating collaborative performance in cloud computing. *Communications in Computer and Information Science*, *63*, 57–64. doi:10.1007/978-3-642-10549-4_8

Vaquero, L. M., Rodero-Merino, L., Caceres, J., & Lindner, M. (2009). A break in the clouds: Towards a cloud definition. *ACM SIGCOMM Computer Communications Review*, *39*, 50–55. doi:10.1145/1496091.1496100

Voorsluys, W., Broberg, J., & Buyya, R. (2011). Introduction to Cloud Computing. In R. Buyya, J. Nroberg, & A. Goscinski (Eds.), *Cloud Computing: Principles and Paradigms* (pp. 3–42). John Wiley & Sons, Inc. doi:10.1002/9780470940105.ch1

Weerawarana, S., Curbera, F., Leymann, F., Storey, T., & Ferguson, D. (2005). *Web Services Platform Architecture*. Prentice Hall PTR.

Weiss, A. (2007). Computing in the Clouds. *Networker*, *11*(4), 16–25. doi:10.1145/1327512.1327513

Xu, X., Cheng, C., & Xiong, J. (2010). Reliable integrated model of cloud & client computing based on multi-agent. *Journal of Computer Information Systems*, *6*(14), 4767–4774.

Yoo, D., & Sim, K. M. (2010). A multilateral negotiation model for cloud service market. *Communications in Computer and Information Science*, *121*, 54–63. doi:10.1007/978-3-642-17625-8_6

Zhang, Y. H., Zhang, J., & Zhang, W. H. (2010). Discussion of Intelligent Cloud Computing System. In *Proceedings of 2010 International Conference on Web Information Systems and Mining (WISM)* (pp. 319-322). Jiangsu, China: IEEE Press.

ENDNOTES

[1] http://www.w3.org/2002/ws/

Chapter 11
Power Quality Improvement using Improved Approximated Fuzzy Logic Controller for Shunt Active Power Filter

Asheesh K. Singh
Motilal Nehru National Institute of Technology Allahabad, India

Rambir Singh
Inderprastha Engineering College, India

ABSTRACT

This chapter presents the design approach of an Improved Approximated Simplest Fuzzy Logic Controller (IASFLC). A cascade combination of simplest 4-rule Fuzzy Logic Controller (FLC) and an nth degree polynomial is proposed as an IASFLC to approximate the control characteristics of a 49-rule FLC. The approximation scheme is based on minimizing the sum of square errors between the control outputs of a 49-rule FLC and a simplest 4-rule FLC in the entire range of Universe Of Discourse (UOD). The coefficients of compensating polynomial are evaluated by solving instantaneous square error equations at various test points in the entire UOD. This IASFLC maps the output of a 49-rule FLC with absolute deviation of less than 5%. The proposed IASFLC is used to control the dc link voltage of a three-phase shunt Active Power Filter (APF). A detailed analysis is performed during transient and steady state conditions to check Power Quality (PQ) and dynamic performance indices under randomly varying balanced and unbalanced loading conditions. The performance of proposed IASFLC is compared with a 49-rule FLC and Approximated Simplest Fuzzy Logic Controller (ASFLC) based on minimization of the deviation at central values of Membership Functions (MFs). It is found comparatively better for harmonic and reactive compensation with a comparable dynamic response. The memory requirement and computational time of proposed IASFLC are even lesser than the ASFLC.

DOI: 10.4018/978-1-4666-6098-4.ch011

INTRODUCTION

Fuzzy logic controllers (FLCs) have been successfully used for the control of shunt active power filter (APF) due to their ability to handle complex control tasks at randomly varying operating conditions. With remarkable increase in the applications of semiconductor devices, the issues of harmonic contamination, poor voltage regulation, poor power factor, low system efficiency, and interference in nearby communication system etc are need to be addressed. All these issues in some form or other affect the power quality. Shunt APF has emerged as an undisputed solution for current harmonics mitigation and reactive power compensation.

Bose (1994) in his invited paper has explored the possibilities of expert system, fuzzy logic and neural network applications in power electronics and motion control. This work has opened a new space of opportunities for control engineers. It is now an established fact that an FLC based shunt APF shows better dynamic response and higher control precision as compared with the PI controller as concluded by Dixon et al. (1999), Jain et al. (2002), Singh et al. (2007), An et al. (2009), Karuppanan & Mahapatra (2011), Panda & Mikkili (2013), Benassia et al. (2013), and Agarwal & Bhuria (2013). In all these papers a 49-rule FLC is used with uniform or non uniform distribution of membership functions (MFs) in the entire universe of discourse (UOD). Due to large number of rules a 49-rule FLC is structurally more complex, required more memory and large computation time to execute a desired control action.

Some studies regarding approximation and reduction of rule base size have been reported in literature. Zeng & Singh (1994, 1995) proposed a mathematical description of approximation theory of fuzzy systems for single input single output (SISO) and multi input multi output (MIMO) cases. These papers were mainly focusing on the approximation capabilities of the fuzzy systems for approximating a mathematical polynomial rather

than on the rule reduction. Hampel & Chaker (1998) provided analyses for minimization of number of variable parameters for optimization of fuzzy controller and concluded that reduction of variable parameter does not necessarily result in a restriction in the quality of an FLC. Moser & Navara (2002) proposed a fuzzy controller with conditionally firing rules. In this work numbers of rules were not minimized but the degree of overlapping of MFs was replaced by the truth value of a conditional statement. So the conditions of firing a particular rule were reduced rather than rule base size. Bezine et al. (2002) explained some issues on design and rule base size reduction for the fuzzy control of robot manipulators. Ciliz (2005) explained some concepts regarding resizing of rule base by removing inconsistent and redundant rules for the application of vacuum cleaner. These two studies were application specific.

Arya (2006) has proposed a process independent simplest FLC using approximation for unit step response analysis of two different processes of second and third order. A robust and application independent ASFLC was given by Singh et al. (2011) for a multi-objective and highly complex control application of shunt active power filter. The methodology was based on comparing the output of 49-rule FLC with 4-rule FLC at central values of MFs and then designing the compensating factors to minimize the deviation between the responses of two controllers. The ASFLC exhibited better dynamic performance than conventional PI controller and harmonic compensation was comparable with 49-rule FLC during transient state and even better during steady state operation of shunt APF. The response of ASFLC was compared with a 49-rule FLC at six points in the entire UOD and based on that six compensating factors were designed. The approach is analogues to a piecewise linearization of a nonlinear function. To achieve exact behavioral mapping of a 49-rule FLC by a 4-rule FLC the entire UOD need to be analyzed at more locations than at merely six distinct points. This is what exactly motivated the authors to put forward a new approach, for designing of proposed IASFLC.

In the proposed work entire UOD is partitioned in much fine segments, which results in more accurate approximation. Further, the six compensating factor used in the ASFLC are replaced by a single compensating polynomial in proposed IASFLC resulting in less complex approximation structure. The IASFLC is used to control a voltage source inverter (VSI) based shunt APF. The application of shunt APF for harmonic and reactive power compensation has been discussed by Akagi et al. (1984), Peng et al. (1990), Grady et al. (1990), Singh et al.(1999a,1999b), Grady & Santoso (2001), Singh et al.(2007), and Singh et al. (2011). A control scheme proposed by Dixon et al. (1999), which requires minimum sensing variables for generation of reference current, is used in this work.

The improved approximation using proposed IASFLC is reflected in better harmonic and reactive power compensation performance of shunt APF.

The rest of the chapter is organized in the following sequence. Next section covers the basic compensation principle and control scheme of shunt APF with proposed IASFLC. The simplest 4-rule FLC and 49-rule FLC are discussed in the subsequent section. Thereafter, the proposed approximation technique and derivation of compensating polynomial are discussed. Simulation results and comparison of performances of proposed scheme with 49-rule FLC and ASFLC are finally discussed prior to conclusion.

SHUNT ACTIVE POWER FILTER

The single line diagram shown in Figure 1, represent the compensation principle of shunt active power filter. The rectifier fed R-L load introduces the current harmonics in the source current. The compensation of these current harmonics is achieved by injecting equal and phase opposite harmonic compensating current from the shunt APF as described by Dixon et al. (1999), Singh

Figure 1. Single line diagram representing compensation principle of shunt APF

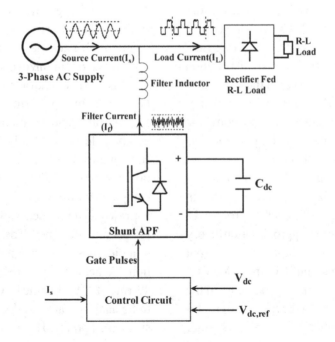

et al.(1999a,1999b), Jain et al. (2002), Singh et al. (2007), An et al. (2009), Kumar & Mahajan (2009), Karuppanan & Mahapatra (2011), Singh et al. (2011), Trinh &Lee (2013), Rahmani et al. (2013) and Chang et al (2014). A shunt APF behaves like a current source, the phase shifted current component injected by shunt APF cancels the harmonic component present in source current, resulting in purely sinusoidal source currents, which are in phase with the respective phase voltages.

Working Principle and Control Scheme

The schematic diagram of control scheme of VSI based shunt APF with the proposed IASFLC is shown in Figure 2. The shunt APF is connected in parallel with the nonlinear load. In voltage control loop, the dc link voltage of APF is compared with a set reference value. The error (e) and change in error (ce) between actual and reference values of dc link capacitor voltages are used as the input variables to the IASFLC. The output of controller will be the incremental change δI_{max} (t) in peak value of reference source current I_{max}. The peak value of current is obtained by adding the incremental change δI_{max} (t) with the peak value of current at previous sampling instant to introduce the integrating effect in FLC.

$$I_{max}(t) = I_{max}(t\text{-}1) + \delta I_{max}(t) \qquad (1)$$

Figure 2. Schematic diagram of control scheme of shunt APF with proposed IASFLC

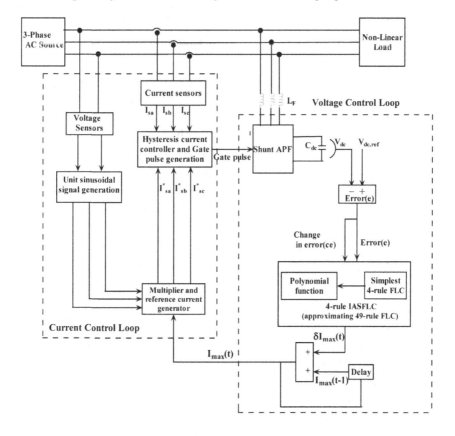

where

I_{max} (t) is the peak value of reference source current at instant t,

I_{max} (t-1) is the peak value of reference source current at instant (t-1), and

δI_{max} (t) is incremental change in reference peak current at instant t.

In current control loop, the reference source currents are compared with actual source currents and the error signals are processed through hysteresis current controllers for generating the desired gate signals for shunt APF. To achieve an efficient harmonic compensation the source currents must be sinusoidal and for reactive power compensation it should be in phase with the source voltage. For this the instantaneous value of reference current template can be given as:

$$\left.\begin{array}{l} i_{sa}{}^*(t) = I_{max}\sin \omega t \\[2em] i_{sb}{}^*(t) = I_{max}\sin(\omega t\text{-}2\pi/3) \\[2em] i_{sc}{}^*(t) = I_{max}\sin(\omega t\text{+}2\pi/3) \end{array}\right\} \quad (2)$$

where, $i_{sa}{}^*(t)$, $i_{sb}{}^*(t)$, $i_{sc}{}^*(t)$ are the instantaneous values of reference source currents of phase a, b and c respectively, and ω is the supply frequency in rad/sec.

The maximum value of reference current template can be obtained by regulating the dc link voltage of shunt APF and the respective phase angles can be derived from the unit sinusoidal signals obtained from source voltage. The current controller loop forces the actual source currents to follow the reference current template, resulting in a purely sinusoidal source current operating at unity power factor, irrespective of actual nature of load.

FUZZY LOGIC CONTROLLER (FLC)

Fuzzy logic controller (FLC) imitates the human decision making with varying degree of possibilities, an approach different from conventional logic theory. The FLCs are able to incorporate human experience, intuition and heuristics into the system instead of relying on mathematical models. In this chapter an attempt is made to reduce the complexity of a 49-rule FLC by approximating it with a 4-rule IASFLC without compromising its control performance.

Simplest FLC

The simplest FLC refers to a minimal possible configuration of parameters in terms of number of input variables, fuzzy sets and fuzzy rules of a fully functional FLC as discussed by Ying (2000). To realize a simplest FLC two triangular MFs are used for each input variable i.e. error e(t) and change in error ce(t) and three triangular MFs are used for output variable $\delta I_{max}(t)$. The UOD for inputs and output variables is taken as (-1, 1). The centroid method of defuzzification is used. The MFs for input variables use two linguistic variables negative (N) and positive (P), while output variable also include zero (ZE) as shown in Figure 3.

Let x is the instantaneous value of any input variable e(t) and ce(t) at sampling instant t. The membership grades of MFs for both the input variables can be given as:

$$\mu_{N,x} = \begin{cases} 1, & \text{for } x \leq -1 \\ \dfrac{1-x}{2}, & \text{for } -1 < x < 1 \\ 0, & \text{for } x \geq 1 \end{cases} \quad (3)$$

$$\mu_{P,x} = \begin{cases} 0, & \text{for } x \leq -1 \\ \dfrac{1+x}{2}, & \text{for } -1 < x < 1 \\ 1, & \text{for } x \geq 1 \end{cases} \quad (4)$$

Figure 3. Membership functions for (a) error, (b) change in error and (c) output δI_{max} of simplest FLC

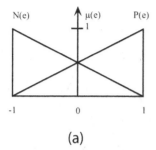
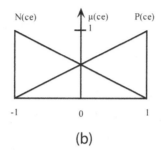
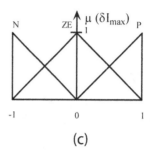

(a)   (b)   (c)

Similarly the membership grades of triangular output MFs can be given as:

$$\mu_{N,\delta I_{max}} = \begin{cases} 1, & \text{for } \delta I_{max} \leq -1 \\ -\delta I_{max}, & \text{for } -1 < \delta I_{max} < 0 \\ 0, & \text{for } \delta I_{max} \geq 0 \end{cases}$$

(5)

$$\mu_{P,\delta I_{max}} = \begin{cases} 1, & \text{for } \delta I_{max} \geq 1 \\ \delta I_{max}, & \text{for } 0 < \delta I_{max} < 1 \\ 0, & \text{for } \delta I_{max} \leq 0 \end{cases}$$

(6)

$$\mu_{ZE,\delta I_{max}} = \begin{cases} 1-\delta I_{max}, & \text{for } 0 \leq \delta I_{max} \leq 1 \\ 1+\delta I_{max}, & \text{for } -1 < \delta I_{max} < 0 \\ 1, & \text{for } \delta I_{max} = 0 \end{cases}$$

(7)

The four rules covering the entire range of system behaviour using simplest FLC explained by Ying (2000) are given below:

Rule 1: If e is negative (N) and ce is negative (N) then δI_{max} is negative (N).

Rule 2: If e is negative (N) and ce is positive (P) then δI_{max} is zero (ZE).

Rule 3: If e is positive (P) and ce is negative (N) then δI_{max} is zero (ZE).

Rule 4: If e is positive (P) and ce is positive (P) then δI_{max} is positive (P).

49-Rule FLC

In 49-rule FLC, seven triangular MFs are used for both input and output variables to cover entire UOD as shown in Figure 4 (a) and (b). The linguistic variables used are negative large (NL), negative medium (NM), negative small (NS), zero (ZE), positive small (PS), positive medium (PM) and positive large (PL). The range of UOD and defuzzification method employed is similar to a 4-rule simplest FLC. The Control rules for 49-rule FLC are shown in Table 1. The membership grades of input and output variables can also be defined for 49-rule FLC, similar to that of 4-rule FLC.

APPROXIMATION PRINCIPLE

The outputs of a 49-rule FLC and a 4-rule simplest FLC are compared at regular intervals in the entire range of input variables to find the deviation in the responses of two controllers. The approximation is based on evaluating a compensating polynomial such that its series combination with simplest FLC approximately maps the output of the 49-rule FLC. This cascaded arrangement of simplest FLC with compensating polynomial is termed as improved approximated simplest fuzzy logic controller

Figure 4. Membership function for (a) input variables error and change in error (b) output δI_{max} of 49-rule FLC

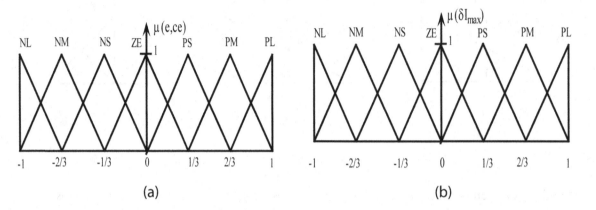

(a)   (b)

Table 1. Rule base for 49 rules FLC

e ce	NL	NM	NS	ZE	PS	PM	PL
NL	NL	NL	NL	NL	NM	NS	ZE
NM	NL	NL	NL	NM	NS	ZE	PS
NS	NL	NL	NM	NS	ZE	PS	PM
ZE	NL	NM	NS	ZE	PS	PM	PL
PS	NM	NS	ZE	PS	PM	PL	PL
PM	NS	ZE	PS	PM	PL	PL	PL
PL	ZE	PS	PM	PL	PL	PL	PL

(IASFLC). Figure 5 represents the comparison of control output for 4-rule FLC and 49-rule FLC at various points of input variables.

Let $u(t)$ and $u_1(t)$ are the outputs of a 49-rule FLC and 4-rule FLC respectively. Then the deviation or error can be given as:

$$e(t) \;=\; u(t) - u_1(t) \tag{8}$$

Now the sum of square error (SSE) can be represented as:

$$SSE = \sum_{t=1}^{N} e^2(t) \tag{9}$$

To understand the least square fitting process, let us consider N data points on which the error in responses is measured. Now to implement the approximation scheme, an nth order polynomial will be used in cascade with the 4-rule FLC such that this combination maps the output of a 49-rule FLC with least square error.

The output of IASFLC in terms of nth order polynomial of $u_1(t)$ is given as:

Figure 5. Comparison of outputs of 49-rule FLC and 4-rule FLC

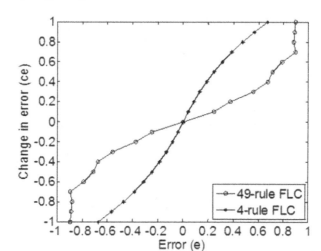

$$u_2(t) = a_n u_1^n(t) + a_{n-1} u_1^{n-1}(t) + \ldots\ldots + a_1 u_1(t) + a_0 \tag{10}$$

where, $u_1(t)$ and $u_2(t)$ are the outputs of 4 rule FLC and proposed IASFLC, respectively. $a_0, a_1, a_2, \ldots a_n$ are the coefficients of nth order polynomial.

Now sum of square errors is represented as:

$$SSE = \sum_{t=1}^{N} \{u(t) - u_2(t)\}^2 \tag{11}$$

$$SSE = \sum_{t=1}^{N} [u(t) - \{a_n u_1^n(t) + a_{n-1} u_1^{n-1}(t) + \ldots\ldots + a_1 u_1(t) + a_0\}]^2 \tag{12}$$

To minimize SSE, its partial derivatives with respect to each unknown coefficients is equated to zero to get as many equations as the number of unknown coefficients. The solution of these equations gives the values of these unknown coefficients. The flow chart to find the unknown coefficients $a_n, a_{n-1}, a_{n-2}, \ldots a_1$ and a_0 of compensating polynomial is shown in Figure 6.

The order of compensating polynomial plays a critical role in approximation. A large order polynomial is also avoided due to the following reasons:

1. A large order polynomial needs more computer time and memory, which defeats the basic objective of designing a reduced rule approximated FLC.
2. Higher order polynomial can be highly oscillatory and an order larger than the exact fit case may lead to multiple solutions resulting in a confusing state for software as well as operator to select one solution.

On the other hand a lower order may not provide the sufficient approximation. This situation leads towards maintaining a tradeoff between the order of polynomial and degree of fitness for adequate approximation.

Kishor et al. (2007) has proposed that the generalization capabilities of two data sets can be checked using two performance indices, i.e., variance account for (VAF) and root mean square error (RMSE), given by (13) and (14).

Figure 6. Implementation of proposed scheme with flow chart

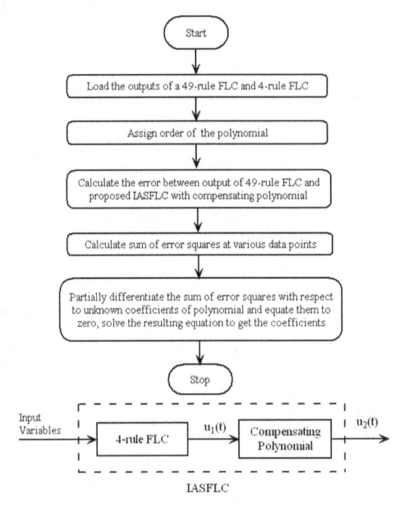

$$VAF \ (\%) = \left[1 - \frac{\text{var}(y_i - \hat{y}_i)}{\text{var}(y_i)} \right] \times 100 \qquad (13)$$

$$RMSE = \sqrt{\frac{\sum\limits_{i=1}^{N} (y_i - \hat{y}_i)^2}{N}} \qquad (14)$$

where, var stands for variance, y_i, $\hat{y}_i$ are actual

and reference data set output values (in this case, output of proposed approximated FLC is consid-

ered as actual output and output of 49-rule FLC is taken as reference output).

A higher VAF or conversely smaller RMSE indicates better closeness in approximation. The variation of these performance indices is analyzed with variation of order of polynomial as shown in Figure 7 and Figure 8, respectively, to select an optimum order for compensated polynomial. In Figure 7, a pattern of variation is clearly visible as the percentage VAF of pair of first order and second order, third order and fourth order, fifth order and sixth order, and seventh order and eighth order are same. It indicates that in a pair the lower

Figure 7. Variation of VAF with order of polynomial

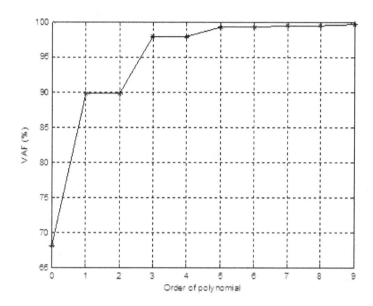

Figure 8. Variation of RMSE with order of polynomial

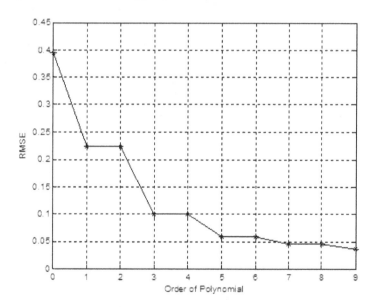

order (having odd number) polynomial is equally capable to map the response with same level of accuracy as its even numbered counterpart. So the optimum choice of order of polynomial is lower order polynomial out of the pair having similar VAF values. The percentage VAF of third order polynomial onwards is more than 95%, whereas, the RMSE value is less than 0.1 or 10%. To maintain comparatively better closeness and less RMSE, the criterion used here is to keep VAF more than 95% and RMSE less than 0.05 or 5%.

The polynomial orders satisfying this criterion are 7th and 9th order. However the 9th order polynomial exceeds in complexity level, in terms of required computational memory. Therefore, the 7th order polynomial derived using the concept of minimization of SSE, as given in (15), is selected to maintain the VAF above 95%, and RMSE below 5%.

$$u_2(t) = -61.2748u_1^7(t) + 60.8078u_1^5(t)$$
$$- 21.4164u_1^3(t) + 4.2446u_1(t)$$

$$(15)$$

A comparison of control output of 49-rule FLC and IASFLC is presented in Figure 9. The control performance of IASFLC approximately maps the output of a 49-rule FLC. The percentage absolute deviation in the response of 4-rule FLC and IASFLC with respect to a 49-rule FLC is shown in Figure 10.

With the proposed IASFLC maximum deviation is ±0.0762 corresponding to the input data sets of (0.1, 0.1) and (-0.1, -0.1) respectively. It amounts 3.81% on entire UOD i.e. (-1, 1), whereas maximum deviation of 4-rule FLC is ±0.5071 (i.e. 25.36%).

Comparative Analysis of Computational Memory

For comparative analysis of computational memory requirement, an FLC is functionally divided into following three sections:

1. Fuzzification,
2. Fuzzy inference and knowledge base, and
3. Defuzzification.

A 4-rule FLC require minimum computational memory but suffers with large deviation in control action as compared with 49-rule FLC as shown in Figure 5. The IASFLC overcomes this drawback with proposed approximation technique as shown in Figure 9. In IASFLC, some additional memory is required to perform approximation than a 4-rule FLC. Even after this additional requirement, total memory requirement of IASFLC is less than a 49-rule FLC and ASFLC. A comparison of memory requirements of various controllers is presented in Table 2.

Figure 9. Mapping of outputs of 49-rule FLC and proposed IASFLC

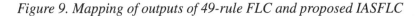
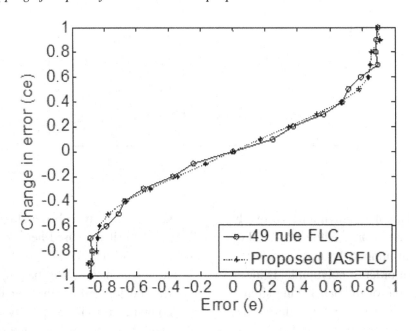

Figure 10. Comparison of absolute deviations in control outputs of a 4-rule FLC and proposed IASFLC with respect to a 49-rule FLC

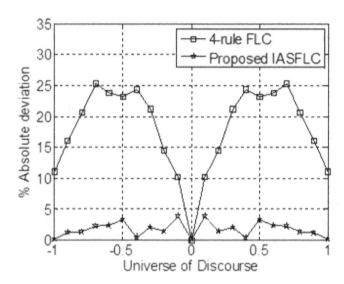

Table 2. Comparison of computational memory requirement, in terms of 'm', the memory requirement of each MF

Sl. No.	Module	Parameter	49-rule FLC	ASFLC	IASFLC
1.	Fuzzification	No. of input variables	2	2	2
		Number of MF for each input	7	2	2
		Memory units required	14 * m	4* m	4* m
2.	Fuzzy Inference and Knowledge Base	Number of rules	49	4	4
		Number of antecedent	7	4	4
		Number of consequent	7	4	4
		Memory units required	686	4*(4+4)=32	32
3.	Defuzzification	Number of output variable	1	1	1
		MF for output variable δI_{max}	7	3	3
		Memory units required	7 * m	3* m	3* m
4.	Approximation	Number of comparators	-	6	-
		Number of multipliers	-	2	9
		Number of adders	-	11	3
		Number of terms with non zero coefficients	-	-	4
		Memory units required	-	19	16
Total Memory requirement			21*m+686	7*m+51	7*m+48

SIMULATION RESULTS

The simulation results are obtained with three different FLCs in voltage control loop i.e. 49-rule FLC, ASFLC and proposed IASFLC. The simulation is performed on MATLAB Simulink®. The system parameters for simulation studies are presented in Table 3. The performance is analyzed both under balanced and unbalanced loading Conditions

Operation Under Balanced Loading Conditions

The performance of shunt active power filter is analyzed for the following three cases:

Case 1

In case-1 the dynamic behaviour of three FLCs is analyzed during switch on response.

The shunt APF is switched on at 0.05 sec, with load a rectifier fed series connected R-L, where R = 30Ω, L = 20mH. This load is connected for 10 cycles (0.2 sec). The dynamic response of shunt APF using 49-rule FLC, ASFLC and IASFLC are presented in Figure 11(a), (b), and (c) respectively. The source current becomes sinusoidal from a stepped wave shave as soon as the filter is switched on. The peak overshoot /undershoot in dc link voltage and its settling time (to settle

Table 3. System parameters

System Parameter	Value
Source voltage(V_s)	230 V (rms/phase)
System frequency(f)	50 Hz
Source impedance(R_s,L_s)	0.1Ω, 0.5mH
Filter impedance (R_F,L_F)	0.4Ω, 3.35mH
Reference DC link voltage ($V_{dc,ref}$)	680 V
DC link capacitance (C_{dc})	2000μF

within ±1% band of reference value) for these controllers is compared in Table 4.

The THD profile of source current is analyzed for every cycle (0.02 sec) of entire loading period and results are depicted in Figure 12. The THD of source current reduces from 28.26% (prior to compensation) to approx. 2% within one cycle and maintains it within 2%, thereafter. The proposed

Figure 11. Switch ON response (a) 49-rule FLC, (b) ASFLC and (c) IASFLC at 0.05 sec

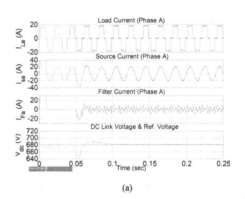

(a)

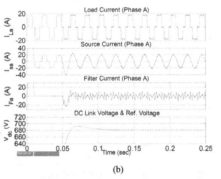

(b)

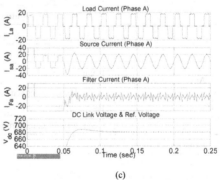

(c)

Table 4. Comparison of dynamic response of different controllers

Load	% Peak Overshoot / Undershoot			Settling Time (cycles)		
	49-rule FLC	**ASFLC**	**IASFLC**	**49-rule FLC**	**ASFLC**	**IASFLC**
Case-1	1.32	1.79	1.31	1.81	2.30	2.15
Case-2	2.05	2.14	2.14	1.80	2.00	2.03
Case-3	1.17	1.25	1.27	0.47	0.55	0.55

Figure 12. THD profile with three different controllers after filter is switched on at 0.05 sec

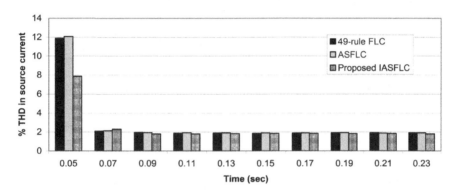

IASFLC has exhibited excellent harmonic compensation capability, particularly at the instant of load change and even maintain it throughout the steady state performance.

Case 2

In case-2, load resistance is changed from 30Ω to 60Ω at 0.25 sec. As a result the load current is reduced from 13.83 A (rms) to 6.95 A (rms). Figure 13 (a) to (c) represent the load perturbation response of three controllers under consideration. The source current reduces in magnitude but maintains the sinusoidal nature, the dc link voltage momentarily increases but the control action brings it back to reference value within two cycles. The comparative details are given in Table 4. The THD profile of source current with three different controllers for the next 10 cycles after load perturbation at 0.25 sec is shown in Figure 14. THD of source current maintains within 2% after one cycle for all the controllers. In this case

also the proposed IASFLC dominates the other two controllers, which validates the effectiveness of approximation technique.

Case 3

In this case, the load resistance is again changed from 60Ω to 45Ω at 0.45 sec. Due to load change, the load current is increased from 6.95 A (rms) 9.26 A (rms). Figure 15 shows the effect of load change and the responses of various controllers to regulate the dc link capacitor voltage. In this case also the dynamic responses of all the three controllers are comparable as shown in Table 4. The THD in source current remains well within the 5% limit imposed by IEEE-519 standards (IEEE Industry Application Society /Power Engineering Society, 1993) even during the first cycle of load change. The THD maintains below 2% thereafter for all the controllers, but comparatively IASFLC exhibits better compensation capabilities as shown in Figure 16.

Figure 13. Load perturbation response (a) 49-rule FLC, (b) ASFLC and (c) IASFLC at 0.25 sec

Figure 15. Load perturbation response (a) 49-rule FLC, (b) ASFLC and (c) IASFLC at 0.45 sec

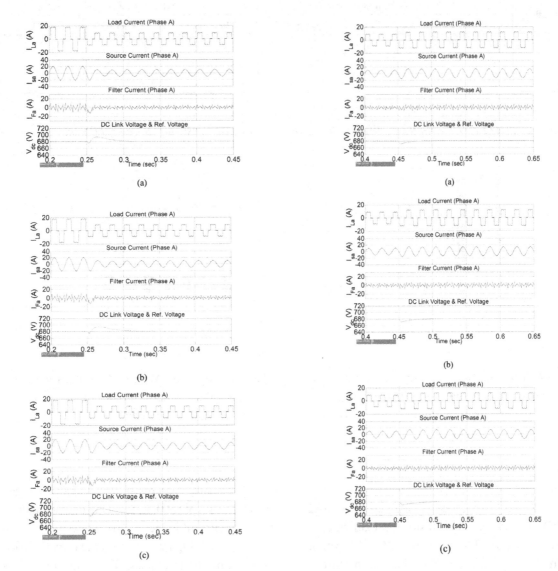

Figure 14. THD profile with three different controllers during load perturbation response at 0.25 sec

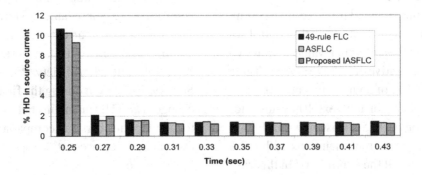

Figure 16. THD profile with three different controllers during load perturbation response at 0.45 sec

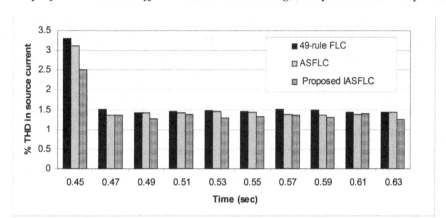

Reactive Power Compensation

Most of the practical loads used in industry are inherently inductive in nature. These inductive loads require reactive power for proper operation from the source. This increases the amount of current drawn from source through distribution lines and leads to increased line loss. If reactive power can be supplied near the load, the line current and line loss can be reduced and voltage regulation can be improved. By providing reactive power compensation using shunt APF, the reactive power component from source current is reduced or almost eliminated. Figure 17, represents the reactive power required from source with and without compensation. Without any reactive power compensation device the source has to supply the reactive power demand of 783.64 volt ampere reactive (var) in case-1. While in case-2 reactive power demand goes as high as 1780 var and then settles at 277 var.

Figure 17. Reactive power supplied by source with compensation using IASFLC and without compensation

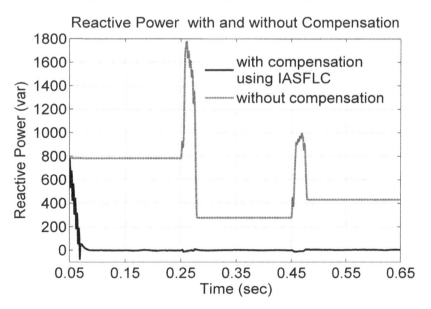

The maximum var demand in case-3 reaches up to 998.8 var with steady state value of 431.01 var. When the filter is switched on at 0.05 sec, the var supplied from source is quite close to zero.

A comparative analysis of 49-rule FLC, ASFLC and proposed IASFLC in terms of reactive power compensation for all the three cases of load patterns is presented in Figure 18.

The peak reactive power supplied by source at any time including transient /steady state in all three cases of switch on and load change condi-

tions using the above discussed controllers is compared in Table 5. The control action of proposed IASFLC brings back the var requirement from source close to zero faster than ASFLC and almost similar to 49-rule FLC which is lucidly presented in Figure 18.

This explanation helps in concluding that:

1. Proposed IASFLC provides more efficient reactive power compensation with faster response than ASFLC.

Figure 18. Reactive power compensation (a) for case-1, (b) for case-2 and (c) for case-3 using 49-rule FLC, ASFLC and IASFLC for each case

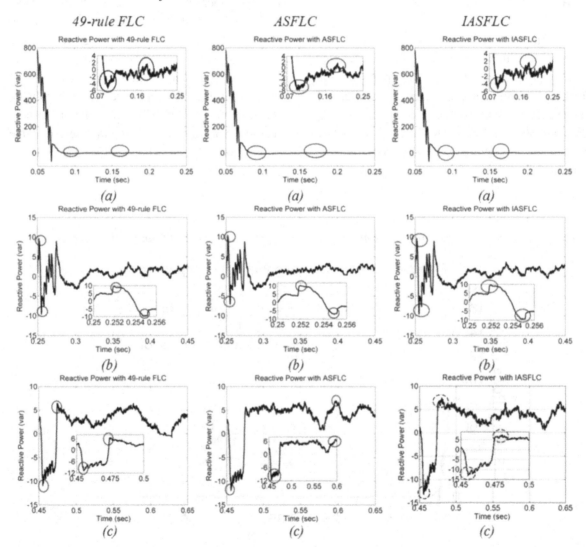

Table 5. Comparison of reactive power compensation of 49-rule FLC, ASFLC and IASFLC

Load	Peak Reactive Power (var) Supplied by Source During Transient / Steady State Conditions		
	49-rule FLC	ASFLC	IASFLC
Case-1	1.75	1.76	1.76
Case-2	9.60	10.44	9.68
Case-3	6.54	7.03	7.04

2. IASFLC also maintains close similarity with a 49-rule FLC in comparison to ASFLC during load change as well as in steady state.

Comparison of Performance Indices and Simulation Execution Time

A comparison of the integrated time averaged error (ITAE), integrated average error (IAE), integrated square error (ISE), integrated time square error (ITSE) and simulation execution time during the entire simulation period (i.e.325000 samples) is demonstrated in Table 6. This comparison clearly establishes the effectiveness of proposed control scheme, i.e. IASFLC over 49-rule FLC and ASFLC.

The proposed IASFLC is comparable with the other two controllers in terms of performance indices based on various errors. There is a considerable reduction in simulation execution time due to the reduced complexity of IASFLC. The proposed IASFLC performs equally well to meet all performance indices in close proximity of a 49-rule FLC and ASFLC with considerable lesser computational efforts and reduced complexity.

Operation Under Unbalanced Loading Conditions

The control scheme and performance of shunt APF under unbalanced loading condition is realized by connecting rectifier fed R-L and R-C loads between any two phases, in addition to original balanced nonlinear load. The waveforms of three-phase load, source and filter currents along with dc-link voltage are shown in Figure 19. The shunt APF is switched on at 0.05 sec with balance nonlinear load as discussed in case-1 of previous case study. The source currents become sinusoidal due to the compensation provided by shunt APF.

At 0.25 sec, sudden load unbalanced is created by connecting two rectifier fed R-L loads between phases a-b, and c-a. The unbalance in load currents is depicted in Figure 19. The rms values of unbalanced load currents change from 13.83 A (per phase) to 21.51 A, 17.29 A, and 18.26 A, for phase a, b and c, respectively, as depicted in Figure 20. However, the effective compensation maintains the source currents in all the three phases almost balanced with values 19.55 A, 19.11 A, and 19.81 A, correspondingly, as shown in Figure 21.

Table 6. Comparison of controllers on the basis of performance indices

Performance Index	49-rule FLC	ASFLC	IASFLC
ITAE	0.36	0.36	0.36
IAE	7.62	7.64	7.65
ISE	1970.76	1971.53	1971.97
ITSE	11.88	12.01	12.02
Simulation execution time (sec)	399.43	243.06	211.06

Figure 19. Dynamic response of proposed approximated FLC based shunt APF with balanced and unbalanced nonlinear load

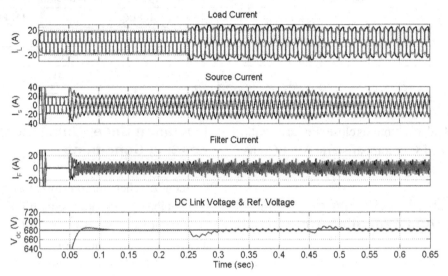

At 0.45 sec, the rectifier fed R-L load connected between phases a-b is switched off and another rectifier Fed R-C load is connected between phases b-c. The compensated source currents are found almost balanced, irrespective of abrupt changes in unbalanced load currents, as evident from Figure 19, Figure 20 and Figure 21.

Due to the above discussed cases of unbalance, the THD of load currents varies drastically. The variations in the THD of three-phase load and source currents are shown in Figure 22 and Figure 23, in that order.

The THD in source currents remain almost constant due to compensation provided by shunt APF and is maintained within 5% limit of IEEE-519-1992 [20] standard just after one cycle of load change.

Figure 20. Load currents profile of different phases under balanced and unbalanced nonlinear loading conditions

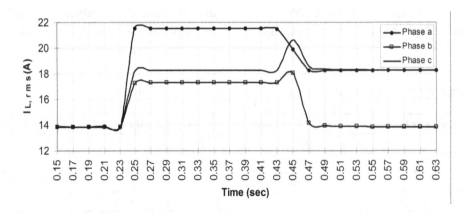

Figure 21. Source current profile of different phases under balanced and unbalanced nonlinear loading conditions after compensation using proposed approximated FLC based shunt APF

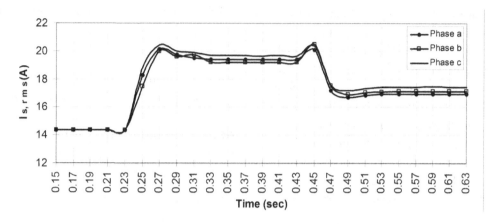

Figure 22. THD profile of three phase load currents under balanced and unbalanced nonlinear loading conditions

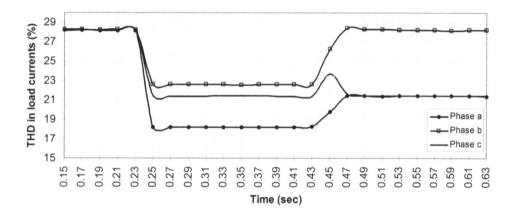

Figure 23. THD profile of three phase source currents under balanced and unbalanced nonlinear loading conditions after compensation using proposed approximated FLC based shunt APF

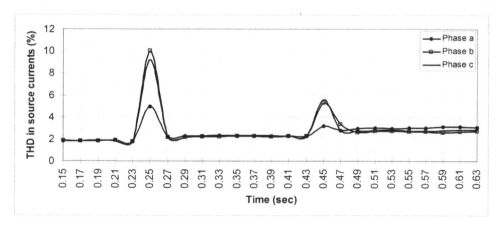

CONCLUSION

The aim of this chapter is to propose an improved approximation of a 49-rule FLC, given as IAS-FLC, to control a shunt APF providing harmonic mitigation along with reactive power compensation. In the proposed IASFLC, the input-output behavioural mapping of a 49-rule FLC is achieved through a cascade combination of 4-rule FLC with a compensating polynomial. The proposed IAS-FLC maintains the absolute deviation in control action below 3.81% with respect to 49-rule FLC, which signifies the effectiveness of approximation strategy.

The performance of the proposed IASFLC has been extensively investigated for a wide range of load variations under balanced as well as unbalanced loading conditions. Results are provided to justify the superior performance of APF with the proposed IASFLC over ASFLC in terms of better reactive power compensation and harmonic mitigation, especially at the instants of load change. During compensation, it exhibits faster response than ASFLC with more similarity to 49-rule FLC, due to comparatively better partitioned UOD than ASFLC. Additionally, the reduced memory requirement and decision-making computational time are also the advantages of IASFLC. The performance of proposed IASFLC justifies its suitability as a potential and worthy alternative of 49-rule FLC. The future work targets the on-line tuning of scaling factors to further improve the dynamic response of the IASFLC.

REFERENCES

Agarwal, S., & Bhuria, V. (2013). Shunt active power filter for harmonic mitigation using fuzzy logic controller. *Int. Jour. of Advanced Research in Computer Engineering & Technology*, 2(6), 1950–1954.

Akagi, H., Kanajawa, Y., & Nabae, A. (1984). Instantaneous reactive power compensator comprising switching devices without energy storage components. *IEEE Trans. Ind. Appl., I-A-20* (3), 625-630.

An, L., Zhikang, S., Wenji, Z., Ruixiang, F., & Chunming, T. (2009). Development of hybrid active power filter based on adaptive fuzzy dividing frequency-control method. *IEEE Transactions on Power Delivery*, 24(1), 424–432. doi:10.1109/TPWRD.2008.2005877

Arya, R. K. (2006). Approximations of Mamdani type multi-fuzzy sets fuzzy controller by simplest fuzzy controller. *Int. Jour. of Comp. Cog.*, 4, 35–47.

Benaissa, A., Rabhi, B., & Moussi, A. (2013). *Power quality improvement using fuzzy logic controller for five-level shunt active power filter under distorted voltage conditions*. Frontiers in Energy.

Bezine, H., Derbel, N., & Alimi, A. M. (2002). Fuzzy control of robotic manipulator: some issues on design and rule base size reduction. *Engineering Applications of Artificial Intelligence*, 15, 401–416. doi:10.1016/S0952-1976(02)00075-1

Bose, B. K. (1994). Expert systems, fuzzy logic, and neural network applications in power electronics and motion control. *Proceedings of the IEEE*, 82(8), 1303–1323. doi:10.1109/5.301690

Chang, G. W., Hong, R.-C., & Su, H.-J. (2014). An efficient reference compensation current strategy of three-phase shunt active power filter implemented with processor-in-the-loop simulation. *International Transactions on Electrical Energy Systems*, 24, 125–140. doi:10.1002/etep.1763

Ciliz, M. K. (2005). Rule base reduction for knowledge based fuzzy controller with application to vacuum cleaner. *Expert Systems with Applications*, 28, 175–184. doi:10.1016/j.eswa.2004.10.009

Dixon, J. W., Contrado, J. M., & Morán, L. A. (1999). A fuzzy-controlled active front-end rectifier with current harmonic filtering characteristics and minimum sensing variables. *IEEE Transactions on Power Electronics*, *14*(4), 724–729. doi:10.1109/63.774211

Grady, W. M., Samotyj, M. J., & Noyola, A. H. (1990). Survey of active power line conditioning methodologies. *IEEE Transactions on Power Delivery*, *5*(3), 1536–1542. doi:10.1109/61.57998

Grady, W. M., & Santoso, S. (2001). Understanding power system harmonics. *IEEE Power Engineering Review*, *21*(11), 8–11. doi:10.1109/MPER.2001.961997

Hampel, R., & Chaker, N. (1998). Minimizing the variable parameters for optimizing the fuzzy controller. *Fuzzy Sets and Systems*, *100*, 131–142. doi:10.1016/S0165-0114(97)00059-6

IEEE Standard 519-1992. (1993). *IEEE Recommended Practices and Requirements for Harmonic Control in Electrical Power Systems, IEEE Industry Application Society /Power Engineering Society*. New York: IEEE Press.

Jain, S. K., Agrawal, P., & Gupta, H. O. (2002). Fuzzy logic controlled shunt active power filter for power quality improvement. *Proc. Electr. Power Appl.*, *149*(5), 317–328. doi:10.1049/ip-epa:20020511

Karuppanan, P., & Mahapatra, K. K. (2011). PLL with fuzzy logic controller based shunt active power filter for harmonic and reactive power compensation. In *Proc. India International Conference on Power Electron. (IICPE)*, (pp. 1-6). IICPE. DOI: 10.1109/IICPE.2011.5728073

Kishor, N., Singh, M., & Raghuvanshi, A. S. (2007). Particle Swarm Optimization based Neural-Network Model for Hydro Power Plant Dynamics. *IEEE Congress on Evolutionary Computation*, 2725-2731.

Kumar, P., & Mahajan, A. (2009). Soft computing techniques for the control of an active power filter. *IEEE Transactions on Power Delivery*, *24*(1), 452–461. doi:10.1109/TPWRD.2008.2005881

Moser, B., & Navara, M. (2002). Fuzzy controllers with conditionally firing rules. *IEEE Transactions on Fuzzy Systems*, *10*(3), 340–349. doi:10.1109/TFUZZ.2002.1006437

Panda, A. K., & Mikkili, S. (2013). FLC based shunt active filter (p–q and Id–Iq) control strategies for mitigation of harmonics with different fuzzy MFs using MATLAB and real-time digital simulator. *Electrical Power and Energy Systems*, *47*, 313–336. doi:10.1016/j.ijepes.2012.11.003

Peng, F. Z., Akagi, H., & Nabae, A. (1990). Study of active power filters using quad series voltage source PWM converters for harmonic compensation. *IEEE Transactions on Power Electronics*, *5*(1), 9–15. doi:10.1109/63.45994

Rahmani, S., Hamadi, A., Al-Haddad, K., & Alolah, A. I. (2013). DSP-based implementation of an instantaneous current control for a three-phase shunt hybrid power filter. *Mathematics and Computers in Simulation*, *91*, 229–248. doi:10.1016/j.matcom.2012.09.013

Singh, B., Al-Haddad, K., & Chandra, A. (1999b). A review of active power filters for power quality improvement. *IEEE Transactions on Industrial Electronics*, *46*(5), 960–969. doi:10.1109/41.793345

Singh, B., Chandra, A., & Al-Haddad, K. (1999a). Computer aided modeling and simulation of active power filters. *Elect. Mach. Power Syst.*, *27*, 1227–1241. doi:10.1080/073135699268687

Singh, G. K., Singh, A. K., & Mitra, R. (2007). A simple fuzzy logic based robust active power filter for harmonic minimization under random load variation. *Electric Power Systems Research*, *77*, 1101–1111. doi:10.1016/j.epsr.2006.09.006

Singh, R., Singh, A. K., & Arya, R. K. (2011). Approximated simplest fuzzy logic controlled shunt active power filter for current harmonic mitigation. [IJFSA]. *International Journal of Fuzzy System Applications*, *1*(4), 18–36. doi:10.4018/ijfsa.2011100102

Trinh, Q.-N., & Lee, H.-H. (2013). An Advanced Current Control Strategy for Three-Phase Shunt Active Power Filters. *IEEE Transactions on Industrial Electronics*, *60*(12), 5400–5410. doi:10.1109/TIE.2012.2229677

Ying, H. (2000). *Fuzzy Control and Modeling: Analytical foundations and applications*. New York: IEEE Press. doi:10.1109/9780470544730

Zeng, X., & Singh, M. G. (1994). Approximation theory of fuzzy systems-SISO case. *IEEE Transactions on Fuzzy Systems*, *2*(2), 162–194. doi:10.1109/91.277964

Zeng, X., & Singh, M. G. (1995). Approximation theory of fuzzy systems-MIMO case. *IEEE Transactions on Fuzzy Systems*, *3*(2), 219–235. doi:10.1109/91.388175

Compilation of References

Abdel–Hamid, T. K., & Madnick, S. E. (1989). Lessons learned from modelling the dynamics of software development. *Communications of the ACM, 32*(12), 1426–1437. doi:10.1145/76380.76383

Abdel-Hamid, T. K., & Madnick, S. E. (1991). *Software Project Dynamics*. Prentice-Hall.

Abowd, G. D., Atkenson, C. G., Hong, J., Long, S., Kooper, R., & Pinkerton, M. (1997). Cyberguide: a mobile context-aware tour guide. *Journal of Wireless Networks, 3*(5), 421–433. doi:10.1023/A:1019194325861

Agarwal, S., & Bhuria, V. (2013). Shunt active power filter for harmonic mitigation using fuzzy logic controller. *Int. Jour. of Advanced Research in Computer Engineering & Technology, 2*(6), 1950–1954.

Ahn, Y. A., & Park, J. S. (2008). Spatio-Temporal Context Manager in an Open Context Awareness Framework. *Fourth International Conference on Networked Computing and Advanced Information Management. 2*, pp. 681-684. Gyeongju, Korea: IEEE.

Ahn, Y.-A. (2009). *Context awareness inference engine for location based applications. 2009 International COnference on Hybrid Infromation Technology* (pp. 213–216). New York: ACM.

Akagi, H., Kanajawa, Y., & Nabae, A. (1984). Instantaneous reactive power compensator comprising switching devices without energy storage components. *IEEE Trans. Ind. Appl., I-A-20* (3), 625-630.

Alavi, A. H., Gandomi, A. H., Mollahassani, A., Heshmati, A. A., & Rashed, A. (2010). Modeling of maximum dry density and optimum moisture content of stabilized soil using artificial neural networks. *Journal of Plant Nutrition and Soil Science, 173*, 368–379. doi:10.1002/jpln.200800233

Almeida, J. P., Iacob, M.-E., Jonkers, H., & Quartel, D. (2006). Model-Driven Development of Context-Aware Services. In *Distributed Applications and Interoperable Systems* (Vol. 4025, pp. 213–227). Oslo, Norway: Springer. doi:10.1007/11773887_17

Anderson, B. (1991). *Imagined communities: Reflections on the origin and spread of nationalism* (rev. ed.). London, UK: Verso.

Anguita, D., Ghio, A., Oneto, L., Parra, X., & Reyes-Ortiz, J. L. (2012, 12). *UCI Machine Learning Repository.* Retrieved from UCI Machine Learning Repository: http://archive.ics.uci.edu/ml/datasets/Human+Activity+Recognition+Using+Smartphones

Anguita, D., Ghio, A., Oneto, L., Parra, X., & Reyes-Ortiz, J. L. (2012). Human Activity Recognition on Smartphones Using a Multiclass Hardware-Friendly Support Vector Machine. In *Ambient Assisted Living and Home Care* (Vol. 7657, pp. 216–223). Vitoria-Gasteiz, Spain: Springer. doi:10.1007/978-3-642-35395-6_30

Anković, S., Jelenković, R., & Vujić, S. (2003). *Mineral Resources and Potential Prognosis of metallic and non-metallic mineral raw materials in Serbia and Montenegro at the end of the XXth Century.* Engineering Academy of Serbia and Montenegro, Section of Mining and Geology Sciences.

An, L., Zhikang, S., Wenji, Z., Ruixiang, F., & Chunming, T. (2009). Development of hybrid active power filter based on adaptive fuzzy dividing frequency-control method. *IEEE Transactions on Power Delivery, 24*(1), 424–432. doi:10.1109/TPWRD.2008.2005877

Apache Couch, D. B. (2013). *Versaion 1.5.0.* Retrieved from http://couchdb.apache.org/

Appukuttan, B., Clark, T., Reddy, S., Tratt, L., & Venkatesh, R. (2003). A model driven approach to model transformations. In *Proceedings of Model Driven Architecture: Foundations and Applications* (pp. 1–12). Enschede, The Netherlands: University of Twente.

Aristotle, . (1941). *The basic works of Aristotle* (R. McKeon, Ed.). New York, NY: Random House.

Ark, W. S., & Selker, T. (1999). A look at human interaction with pervasive computers. *IBM Systems Journal*, *38*(4), 504–507. doi:10.1147/sj.384.0504

Armbrust, M., Fox, A., Griffith, R., Joseph, A. D., & Katz, R. (2009). *Above the Clouds: A Berkeley View of Cloud Computing* (UC Berkeley Reliable Adaptive Distributed Systems Laboratory White Paper). Berkeley, CA: University of California.

Arthur, B., Lane, D., & Durlauf, S. (Eds.). (1997). *The Economy as an Evolving Complex System II*. Addison-Wesley.

Arya, R. K. (2006). Approximations of Mamdani type multi-fuzzy sets fuzzy controller by simplest fuzzy controller. *Int. Jour. of Comp. Cog.*, *4*, 35–47.

Atkinson, C., & Kuhne, T. (2003). Model-driven development: a metamodeling foundation. *Software, IEEE*, *20*(5), 36–41. doi:10.1109/MS.2003.1231149

Austin, G. E., Thomas, C. J., Houston, D. C., & Thompson, D. B. A. (1996). Predicting the Spatial Distribution of Buzzard Buteo buteo Nesting Areas Using a Geographical Information System and Remote Sensing. *Journal of Applied Ecology*, *33*(6), 1541–1550. doi:10.2307/2404792

Azevedo, S., Machado, R. J., Bragança, A., & Ribeiro, H. (2011). Systematic use of software development patterns through a multilevel and multistage classification. In J. Osis, & E. Asnina (Eds.), *Model-Driven Domain Analysis and Software Development: Architectures and Functions* (pp. 304–333). IGI Global.

Backhaus, K., Erichson, B., Plinke, W., & Weiber, R. (2003). *Multivariate Analysemethoden – eine anwendungsorientierte Einführung*. Berlin: Springer-Verlag.

Baden-Powell, R. (1908). *Scouting for Boys*. London: Windsor House.

Badii, A., Crouch, M., & Lallah, C. (2010). A Context-Awareness Framework for Intelligent Networked Embedded Systems. *Third International Conference on Advances in Human-Oriented and Personalized Mechanisms, Technologies and Services* (pp. 105-110). Reading, UK: IEEE.

Baier, P., Pennerstorfer, J., & Schopf, A. (2007). PHENIPS – A comprehensive phenology model of Ips typographus (L.) (Col., Scolytinae) as a tool for hazard rating of bark beetle infestation. *Forest Ecology and Management*, *249*(3), 171–186. doi:10.1016/j.foreco.2007.05.020

Barbosa, V., & Andrade, M. T. (2009). Multicao: A semantic approach to context-aware adaptation decision taking. *10th Workshop on Image Analysis for Multimedia Interactive Services* (pp. 133-136). London, UK: IEEE.

Barceló, P., & Libkin, L. (2005). Temporal Logics over Unranked Trees. In *Proceedings of the 20th Annual Symposium on Logic in Computer Science*. Chicago, IL: Academic Press.

Barth, A., Noack, S., Legler, C., Seib, N., & Rexhaj, A. (2010). Rohstoffprognosekarten mit Verfahren der künstlichen Intelligenz – Fortschrittliche Identifizierung von Rohstoffpotentialen in Entwicklungs- und Schwellenländern. *Glück Auf*, *146*, 140–147.

Bauman, Z. (2000). *Liquid Modernity*. Polity Press Ltd.

BEA AquaLogic Data Services Platform™ 2.5. (n.d.). Retrieved from http://docs.oracle.com/cd/E13167_01/aldsp/docs25/

Behn, R. D. (1995). The big questions of public management. *Public Administration Review*, *55*(4), 313–324. doi:10.2307/977122

Behrens, T., Förster, H., Scholten, T., Steinrücken, U., Spies, E., & Goldschmitt, M. (2005). Digital Soil Mapping using artifical neural networks. *Journal of Plant Nutrition and Soil Science*, *168*, 21–33. doi:10.1002/jpln.200421414

Beinhocker, E. (2006). *The Origin of Wealth: Evolution, Complexity and the Radical Remaking of Economics*. Harvard Business School Press.

Bellifemine, F., Poggi, A., & Rimassa, G. (1999). JADE-A FIPA-compliant agent framework. In *Proceedings of International Conference on Practical Applications of Agents and Multi-Agent Systems (PAAM'99)* (pp. 97-108). London, UK: The Practical Application Company Ltd.

Benaissa, A., Rabhi, B., & Moussi, A. (2013). *Power quality improvement using fuzzy logic controller for five-level shunt active power filter under distorted voltage conditions*. Frontiers in Energy.

Benincasa, G. P., Daneels, A., Heymans, P., & Serre, C. (1985). Engineering a large application software project: The Controls of the CERN PS Accelerator Complex. *Nuclear Science. IEEE Transactions on*, *32*(5), 2029–2031.

Bérard, C. (2010). Group Model Building Using System Dynamics: An Analysis of Methodological Frameworks. *The Electronic Journal of Business Research Methods*, *8*(1), 35–45.

Bernini, D., Micucci, D., & Tisato, F. (2010). A platform for interoperability via multiple spatial views in open smart spaces. *2010 IEEE Symposium on Computers and Communications (ISCC)* (pp. 1047-1052). Riccione, Italy: IEEE.

Beyer, K., Chamberlin, D., Colby, L., Ozcan, F., Pirahesh, H., & Xu, Y. (2005). Extending XQuery for Analytics. In *Proceedings of SIGMOD 2005*. Baltimore, MD: ACM.

Bezine, H., Derbel, N., & Alimi, A. M. (2002). Fuzzy control of robotic manipulator: some issues on design and rule base size reduction. *Engineering Applications of Artificial Intelligence*, *15*, 401–416. doi:10.1016/S0952-1976(02)00075-1

Bhattacharya, A. (1943). On a measure of divergence between two statistical populations defined by their probability distributions. *Bulletin of the Calcutta Mathematical Society*, *35*, 99–109.

Bishop, M. C. (2008). *Neural Networks for Pattern Recognition*. Oxford University Press.

Blaha, M., & Rumbaugh, J. (2005). *Object-Oriented Modeling and Design with UML*. Pearson.

Blum, M. L. (2005). *Real-time Context Recognition*. Zurich: Swiss Federal Institute of technology (ETH).

Boateng, P., Chen, Z., Ogunlana, S., & Ikediashi, D. (2012). A system dynamics approach to risk description in megaprojects development. *Int J Technology and Management in Construction*, *4*(3), 593–603.

Bohn, J., Coroamã, V., Langheinrich, M., Mattern, F., & Rohs, M. (2004). Living in a world of smart everyday objects - social, economic, and ethical implications. *Human and Ecological Risk Assessment*, *10*(5). doi:10.1080/10807030490513793

Boman, M., Bubenko, J., Johannesson, P., & Wangler, B. (1997). *Conceptual Modeling*. New York: Prentice-Hall.

Bonabeau, E., Dorigo, M., & Theraulaz, G. (1999). *Swarm Intelligence*. Oxford University Press.

Booch, G., Rumbaugh, J., & Jacobson, I. (1999). *The Unified Modeling Language User Guide*. Addison Wesley Longman, Inc.

Bordawekar, R. R., & Lang, C. A. (2005). Analytical Processing of XML Documents: Opportunities and Challenges. *SIGMOD Record*, *34*(2). doi:10.1145/1083784.1083790

Bose, B. K. (1994). Expert systems, fuzzy logic, and neural network applications in power electronics and motion control. *Proceedings of the IEEE*, *82*(8), 1303–1323. doi:10.1109/5.301690

Bougrain, L., Gonzalez, M., Bouchot, V., Cassard, D., Lips, A. L. W., Alexandre, F., & Stein, G. (2003). Knowledge Recovery for Continental-Scale Mineral Exploration by Neural Networks. *Natural Resources Research*, *12*(3), 173–181. doi:10.1023/A:1025123920475

Bousquet, F., Fomin, & Drillon. (2011). Anticipatory Standards Development and Competitive Intelligence. *International Journal of Business Intelligence Research*, *2*, 16–30. doi:10.4018/jbir.2011010102

Boussaid, O., Messaoud, R. B., Choquet, R., & Anthoard, S. (2006). X-Warehousing: An XML-Based Approach for Warehousing Complex Data. *LNCS*, *4152*, 39–54.

BPMN. (2004). *Business Process Modelling Notation*. Retrieved June 9, 2009, from http://www.bpmn.org

Brdiczka, O., Crowley, J. L., & Reignier, P. (2007). Learning Situation Models for Providing Context-Aware Services. In *Universal Access in Human-Computer Interaction. Ambient Interaction* (pp. 23–32). Beijing, China: Spinger. doi:10.1007/978-3-540-73281-5_3

Brigham, E. F., & Ehrhaedt, M. C. (2007). *Financial Management: Theory and Practice* (12th ed.). Mason, OH: Thomson South-Western College.

Brown, A. W. (2004). Model driven architecture: Principles and practice. *Software & Systems Modeling, 3*, 314–327.

Brown, W. M., Gedeon, T. N., Groves, D. I., & Barnes, R. G. (2000). Artificial Neural Networks: A new method for mineral prospectivity mapping. *Australian Journal of Earth Sciences, 47*, 757–770. doi:10.1046/j.1440-0952.2000.00807.x

Brown, W., Groves, D., & Gedeon, T. (2003). Use of Fuzzy Membership Input Layers to Combine Subjective Geological Knowledge and Empirical Data in a Neural Network Method for Mineral-Potential Mapping. *Natural Resources Research, 12*(3), 183–200. doi:10.1023/A:1025175904545

Bruce, R. R. (2011). What is organization: Governing by imperatives of regulated freedoms. In *Proceedings of the 7th Annual International Conference for Public Administration* (Vol. 1, pp. 734-743). Chengdu, China: University of Electrical Science and Technology China Press.

Bruce, R. R. (2013). *New ways of seeing things, Nature's laws for energy evolving toward self-government*. Paper presented at COMPACT Work II Conference on Challenges of Making Public Administration and Complexity Theory Work. La Vern, La Vern, CA.

Bruce, R. R., & Kirk. (2007). Three-way partnership for economic development, the public, private and academic sectors, Sri Lanka. In *Proceedings of 2007 international conference on public administration*. Chengdu, China: UESTC Press.

Bruce, R., & Wyman. (1998). *Changing Organizations, Practicing Action Training and Research*. Thousand Oaks, CA: Sage Publications Inc.

Bruce, R. R. (1997). *Work as organization: A theory*. Helsinki, Finland: Hallinnon Tutkimuksen.

Bruce, R. R., & Cote. (2002). Taming wicked problems: theory and practice, a practical lesson in how to tackle the multi-faceted problems in the workplace. *Public Management, 31*(3), 39–46.

Bulfoni, A., Coppola, P., Mea, V. D., Gaspero, L. D., Mischis, D., Mizzaro, S., et al. (2008). AI on the Move: Exploiting AI Techniques for Context Inference on Mobile Devices. *18th European Conference on Artificial Intelligence* (pp. 668-672). Amsterdam, The Netherlands: ACM.

Bunge, M. A. (1979). Treatise on Basic Philosophy, vol. 4, Ontology II: A World of Systems. Reidel Publishing Company.

Buyya, R., Yeo, C. S., Venugopal, S., Broberg, J., & Brandic, I. (2009). Cloud computing and emerging IT platforms: Vision, hype, and reality for delivering computing as the 5th utility. *Future Generation Computer Systems, 25*(6), 599–616. doi:10.1016/j.future.2008.12.001

Cangussu, J. W., DeCarlo, R. A., & Mathur, A. P. (2002). A formal model of the software test process. *IEEE Transactions on Software Engineering, 28*(8), 782–796. doi:10.1109/TSE.2002.1027800

Cantrell, C. D. (2000). *Modern Mathematical Methods for Physicists and Engineers*. Cambridge, UK: Cambridge University Press.

Cantwell, P. (2012). The effect of Using a systems approach to project control within the U.S. defense industry. In *Proceedings of IEEE Systems Conference*. IEEE.

Cao, J., Xing, N., Chan, A. T., Feng, Y., & Jin, B. (2005). Service adaptation using fuzzy theory in context-aware mobile computing middleware. *11th IEEE International Conference on Embedded and Real-Time Computing Systems and Applications* (pp. 496-501). Hong Kong: IEEE.

Cao, L., Ramesh, B., & Abdel-Hamid, T. (2010). Modeling Dynamics in Agile Software Development. *ACM Transactions on Management, Information Systems, 1*(1), 5.1-5.26.

Cao, Y., Klamma, R., Hou, M., & Jarke, M. (2008). Follow Me, Follow You - Spatiotemporal Community Context Modeling and Adaptation for Mobile Information Systems. *9th International Conference on Mobile Data Management* (pp. 108 - 115). Beijing, China: IEEE.

Cardelli, L., & Gordon, A. D. (2001). Mobile Ambients. In *Foundations of Software Science and Computation Structures* (pp. 140–155). Lisbon, Portugal: Springer.

Carranza, J. M. (2009). *Geochemical Anomaly and Mineral Prospectivity Mapping in GIS: Handbook of Exploration and Environmental Geochemistry* (Vol. 11). Elsevier. doi:10.1016/S1874-2734(09)70004-X

Castells, M. (1996). *The Rise of the Network Society* (Vol. 1). Oxford, UK: Blackwell Publishers, Ltd.

Chang, H. J., Liu, Z. H., & Warner, J. W. (2011). *Rewriting node reference-based XQuery using SQL/SML.* Retrieved from http://www.google.com.br/patents/US7870124?dq=xquery+with+sql+2011

Chang, G. W., Hong, R.-C., & Su, H.-J. (2014). An efficient reference compensation current strategy of three-phase shunt active power filter implemented with processor-in-the-loop simulation. *International Transactions on Electrical Energy Systems, 24*, 125–140. doi:10.1002/etep.1763

Chaudhuri, S., & Dayal, U. (1997). An overview of data warehousing and olap technology. *SIGMOD Record, 26*(1), 65–74. doi:10.1145/248603.248616

Chavarriaga, R., Sagha, H., Roggen, D., & Ferscha, A. (2011). Opportunity activity recognition challenge: Results and conclusions. *2011 IEEE International Conference on Systems, Man, and Cybernetics (IEEE SMC 2011).* Anchorage, USA: IEEE.

Cheng, H.-T., Buthpitiya, S., Sun, F.-T., & Griss, M. L. (2010). *OmniSense: A Collaborative Sensing Framework for User Context Recognition Using Mobile Phones. Proceedings of HotMobile 2010* (p. 1). Annapolis: ACM.

Chen, H., Finin, T., & Joshi, A. (2003). An Intelligent Broker for Context-Aware Systems (CoBrA). *Proceedings of Ubicomp, 2003*, 12–15.

Chen, L. (2010). Application of cloud computing to learning. *African Journal of Business Management, 4*(14), 3217–3225.

Chester, M., & Athwall, A. (2002). *Basic Information Systems Analysis and Design.* London: McGraw-Hill.

Cheung, R., Yao, G., Cao, J., & Chan, A. (2008). A fuzzy service adaptation engine for context-aware mobile computing middleware. *International Journal of Pervasive Computing and Communications, 4*(2), 147–165. doi:10.1108/17427370810890256

Cheverst, K., Mitchell, K., & Davies, N. (1999). Design of an Object Model for a Context Sensitive Tourist GUIDE. *Computers & Graphics, 23*(6), 883–891. doi:10.1016/S0097-8493(99)00119-3

Chihani, B., Bertin, E., Suprapto, I. S., Zimmermann, J., & Crespi, N. (2012). Enhancing Existing Communication Services with Context Awareness. *Journal of Computer Networks and Communications, 2012*, 1–10. doi:10.1155/2012/493261

Chopra, A. K., Mylopoulos, J., Dalpiaz, F., Giorgini, P., & Singh, M. P. (2010). Requirements as Goals and Commitments Too. In *Intentional Perspectives on Information System Engineering.* Springer. doi:10.1007/978-3-642-12544-7_8

Ciarletta, L., & Dima, A. (2000). A conceptual model for pervasive computing. In *Proceedings of Parallel Processing* (pp. 9–15). Washington, DC: IEEE Computer Society.

Cicero, M. T. (45BC). *Tusculan Disputations.* Retrieved from http://www.gutenberg.org/files/14988/14988-h/14988-h.htm#page-7

Ciliz, M. K. (2005). Rule base reduction for knowledge based fuzzy controller with application to vacuum cleaner. *Expert Systems with Applications, 28*, 175–184. doi:10.1016/j.eswa.2004.10.009

Cioara, T., Anghel, I., Salomie, I., & Dinsoreanu, M. (2009). A generic context model enhanced with self-configuring features. *Journal of Digital Information Management, 7*, 159–165.

Cockburn, A. (2000). *Writing Effective Use Cases.* Addison-Wesley Professional.

Cools, S. B., Gershenson, C., & D'Hooghe, B. (2013). Self-organizing traffic lights: A realistic simulation. In *Advances in Applied Self-Organizing Systems* (pp. 45–55). Springer London. doi:10.1007/978-1-4471-5113-5_3

COREP XBRL Project. (2005). Retrieved from http://www.eurofiling.info/index.html

Council of the European Union. (1999). *eEurope: An Information Society for All.* Retrieved from http://europa.eu.int/information_society/eeurope/action_plan/index_en.htm

Damondaran, A. (2007). *Avaliação de empresas.* São Paulo, Brazil: Prentice Hall.

Dargie, W. (2009). Adaptive audio based context recognition. *IEEE Transactions on Systems, Man, and Cybernetics, 39*(4), 715–725. doi:10.1109/TSMCA.2009.2015676

Davies, N., & Gellersen, H.-W. (2002). Beyond prototypes: challenges in deploying ubiquitous systems. *Pervasive Computing, IEEE, 1*, 26–35. doi:10.1109/MPRV.2002.993142

de Deugd, S., Carroll, R., Kelly, K. E., Millett, B., & Ricker, J. (2006). SODA: Service-Oriented Device Architecture. *IEEE Pervasive Computing / IEEE Computer Society [and] IEEE Communications Society, 5*(3), 94–96. doi:10.1109/MPRV.2006.59

De, S., & Moessner, K. (2008). Ontology-based context inference and query for mobile devices. *IEEE 19th International Symposium on Personal, Indoor and Mobile Radio Communications* (pp. 1-5). Cannes: IEEE.

Denning, P. J., & Medina-Mora, R. (1995). Completing the Loops. *Interfaces, 25*, 42–57. doi:10.1287/inte.25.3.42

Dennis, A., Wixom, B. H., & Tegarden, D. (2010). *Systems Analysis and Design with UML* (3rd ed.). Wiley.

Deutsch, A., Fernandez, M., Florescu, D., Levy, A., & Suciu, D. (1998). *XML-QL: a query language for XML.* Retrieved from http://www.w3.org/TR/NOTE-xml-ql/

Dey, A. K., & Abowd, G. D. (1999). *The Context Toolkit: Aiding the Development of Context-Aware Applications. SIGCHI conference on Human factors in computing systems* (pp. 443–441). Pittsburgh, USA: ACM.

Dickinson, I., & Wooldridge, M. (2005). Agents are not (just) web services: considering BDI agents and web services. In *Proceedings of 2005 Workshop on Service-Oriented Computing and Agent-Based Engineering (SOCABE'2005)*. Utrecht, The Netherlands: HP Technical Reports.

Dietz, J. L. G. (2006). *Enterprise Ontology: Theory and Methodology*. Springer. doi:10.1007/3-540-33149-2

Disney, S. M., & Towill, D. R. (2002). A discrete transfer function model to determine the dynamic stability of a vendor managed inventory supply chain. *International Journal of Production Research, 40*(1), 179–204. doi:10.1080/00207540110072975

Dixon, J. W., Contrado, J. M., & Morán, L. A. (1999). A fuzzy-controlled active front-end rectifier with current harmonic filtering characteristics and minimum sensing variables. *IEEE Transactions on Power Electronics, 14*(4), 724–729. doi:10.1109/63.774211

Dori, D. (2002). *Object-Process Methodology: A Holistic System Paradigm*. Springer. doi:10.1007/978-3-642-56209-9

Dorigo, M., & Stutzle, T. (2004). *Ant colony optimization.* MIT Press. doi:10.1007/b99492

Dreyfus, H. L., & Rabinow, P. (1983). *Michel Foucault: Beyond structuralism and hermeneutics* (2nd ed.). Chicago, IL: University of Chicago Press.

Duggal, A., Misra, M., & Srinivasaraghavan, R. (2012). Categorising Context and Using Short Term Contextual Information to Obtain Long Term Context. *11th International Conference on Trust, Security and Privacy in Computing and Communications* (pp. 1771 - 1776). Liverpool, UK: IEEE.

Durkheim, E. (1993). *The division of labor in society.* New York, NY: Macmillan.

Eddington, S. A. (1958). *The nature of the physical world.* Ann Arbor, MI: The University of Michigan Press.

Edwards, P. N. (1998). Y2K: Millennial Reflections on Computers as Infrastructure. *History and Technology, 15*, 7–29. doi:10.1080/07341519808581939

Edwards, P. N. (2003). Infrastructure and Modernity: Force, Time, and Social Organization in the History of Sociotechnical Systems. In *Modernity and Technology* (pp. 185–226). Cambridge, MA: MIT Press.

Edwards, P. N., Bowker, Jackson, & Williams. (2009). Introduction to the Special Issue: An Agenda for Infrastructure Studies.[JAIS]. *Journal of the Association for Information Systems, 10*, 364–374.

Egyedi, T. M., & Koppenhol. (2010). The Standards War Between ODf and OOXML: Does Competition Between Overlapping ISO Standards Lead to Innovation?[JITSR]. *International Journal of IT Standards and Standardization Research, 8*, 41–52. doi:10.4018/jitsr.2010120704

Encyclopedia Britannica. (2012). *Ctesibius of Alexandria.* Retrieved February 29, 2012, from http://www.britannica.com/EBchecked/topic/145475/

European Commission. (2012). *Communication from the Commission to the European Parliament, the Council, the European Economic and Social Committee and the Committee of the Regions: A Digital Agenda for Europe.* COM(2012) 784 final. Brussels, Belgium: European Commission. Retrieved from http://ec.europa.eu/information_society/newsroom/cf/dae/document.cfm?doc_id=1381

Eveleens, J. L., & Verhoef, C. (2010, January-February). The Rise and fall of the Chaos Report Figures. *IEEE Software.* doi:10.1109/MS.2009.154

Evermann, J., & Wand, Y. (2009). Ontology Based Object-Oriented Domain Modeling: Representing Behavior. *Journal of Database Management, 20*(1), 48–77. doi:10.4018/jdm.2009010103

eXist Open Source Native XML Database. (2010). Retrieved from http://exist-db.org/exist/apps/homepage/index.html

Fahy, P., & Clarke, S. (2004). CASS: A Middleware for Mobile Context-Aware Applications. *Second International Workshop on Context Awareness* (pp. 1-6). Boston, USA: ACM.

Fano, A., & Gershman, A. (2002). The future of business services in the age of ubiquitous computing. *Communications of the ACM, 45*(12), 83–87. doi:10.1145/585597.585620

Favis-Mortlock. (2005). *Soil Erosion Site.* Retrieved October 24, 2010, from http://soilerosion.net/

Feng, Y. H., Teng, T. H., & Tan, A. H. (2009). Modelling Situation Awareness for Context-aware Decision Support. *Expert Systems with Applications, 36*(1), 455–463. doi:10.1016/j.eswa.2007.09.061

Fernandes, J. E., Machado, R. J., & Carvalho, J. (2004). Model-driven methodologies for pervasive information systems development. In *Proceedings of MOMPES'04, 1st International Workshop on Model-Based Methodologies for Pervasive and Embedded Software* (pp. 15-23). Turku, Finland: TUCS.

Fernandes, J. E., Machado, R. J., & Carvalho, J. (2007). Model-Driven Software Development for Pervasive Information Systems Implementation. In *Proceedings of the 6th International Conference on Quality of Information and Communications Technology* (pp. 218-222). Washington, DC: IEEE Computer Society.

Fernandes, J. E., & Machado, R. J. (2012). SPEM 2.0 Extension for pervasive information systems. *WSEAS Transactions on Computers, 11*(9), 10.

Fernandes, J. E., Machado, R. J., & Carvalho, J. (2008). Model-driven development for pervasive information systems. In S. K. Mostefaoui, Z. Maamar, & G. M. Giaglis (Eds.), *Advances in Ubiquitous Computing: Future Paradigms and Directions* (pp. 45–82). IGI Publishing. doi:10.4018/978-1-59904-840-6.ch003

Fernandes, J. E., Machado, R. J., & Carvalho, J. (2012a). A Case studies approach to the analysis of profiling and framing structures for pervasive information systems. *International Journal of Web Portals, 4*(2), 18. doi:10.4018/jwp.2012040101

Fernandes, J. E., Machado, R. J., & Carvalho, J. (2012b). Profiling and framing structures for pervasive information systems development. In G. Putnik, & M. Cruz-Cunha (Eds.), *Virtual and Networked Organizations, Emergent Technologies and Tools* (Vol. 248, pp. 283–293). Springer. doi:10.1007/978-3-642-31800-9_29

Fernandez-Steeger, T. M. (2002). *Erkennung von Hangrutschungssystemen mit Neuronalen Netzen als Grundlage für Georisikoanalysen.* (Unpublished doctoral dissertation). Universität Karlsruhe.

Ferrario, R., & Guarino, N. (2008). Towards an Ontological Foundation for service Science. In *Proceedings of First Future Internet Symposium.* Vienna, Austria: Springer.

Fishcer, P., Florescu, D., Kaufmann, M., & Kossmann, D. (2011). *Translating SPARQL and SQL to XQuery.* Retrieved from http://archive.xmlprague.cz/2011/presentations/sparql-sql-xquery.pdf

Fomin, V. V. Medeišis, & Vitkutė-Adžgauskienė. (2011). The Role of Policy in the Development of Cognitive Radio Systems: Co-Evolutionary Perspective. In *Proceedings of the 7th International Conference on Standardisation and Innovation in Information Technology (SIIT 2011),* (pp. 79–90). Berlin: Mainz Publishing, Aachen.

Fomin, V. V. Medeišis, & Vitkutė-Adžgauskienė. (2012). In Search of Sustainable Business Models for Cognitive Radio Evolution. Technological and Economic Development of Economy, 18(2), 230–247. doi: doi:10.3846/20 294913.2012.663415

Fomin, V. V. West, & Lyytinen. (2001). Technological Regimes, Government Policies, and Contingency in the Development, Deployment, and Commercial Success of Cellular Mobile Communications on Three Continents. In *Proceedings of the 6th Asia-Pacific Regional Conference of International Telecommunications Society (ITS 2001)*, (pp. 146–157). Hong Kong: Hong Kong University of Science and Technology. Retrieved from www.hkust. hk/its2001

Fomin, V. V., Su, & Gao. (2011). Indigenous Standard Development in the Presence of Dominant International Standards: The Case of the AVS Standard in China. *Technology Analysis and Strategic Management, 23*(7), 745–758. doi:10.1080/09537325.2011.592270

Ford, D. (2009). *System Dynamics for Large Complex Projects*. Retrieved from http://131.215.239.80/workshop9/ford.pdf

Forrester, N. (1983). Eigenvalue analysis of dominant feedback loops. In *Plenary Session Papers Proceedings of the 1st International System Dynamics Society Conference*. Paris, France: Academic Press.

Forrester, J. (1961). *Industrial Dynamics*. Cambridge, MA: MIT Press.

Fowler, M. (1997). *Analysis Patterns: Reusable Object Models*. Menlo Park, CA: Addison-Westley.

Frank, K., Röckl, M., & Robertson, P. (2008). The Bayeslet Concept for Modular Context Inference. *Proceedings of the 2008 The Second International Conference on Mobile Ubiquitous Computing, Systems, Services and Technologies* (pp. 96-101). Valenica: ACM.

Fulbright Senior Specialist Program. (2006). *Project ID 2303*. University of Moratuwa.

Füller, M., Nüßer, W., & Rustemeyer, T. (2012). Context driven process selection and integration of mobile and pervasive systems. *Pervasive and Mobile Computing, 8*(3), 467–482. doi:10.1016/j.pmcj.2011.03.002

Gamma, E., Helm, R., Johnson, R., & Vlissides, J. (1995). *Design patterns - Elements of reusable object-oriented software*. Boston, MA: Addison-Wesley.

Gane, C., & Sarson, T. (1979). *Structured System Analysis*. Prentice Hall.

Gardner, N. (1974). Action training and research: Something old and something new. *Public Administration Review, 34*(2), 106–115. doi:10.2307/974933

Ghadiri, N., Baraani-dastjerdi, A., Ghasem-aghaee, N., & Nematbakhsh, M. A. (2011). A Human-Centric Approach To Group-Based Context-Awareness. *International Journal of Network Security and its Applications, 3* (1), 47-66.

Gilb, T. (2005). *Competitive Engineering*. Oxford, UK: Elsevier.

Gill, T., & Miller. (2002). Re-inventing the Wheel? Standards, Interoperability and Digital Cultural Content. *D-Lib Magazine, 8*, 12–19. doi:10.1045/january2002-gill

Glass, R. (2006). The Standish Report: Does it really describe a software crisis? *Communications of the ACM, 49*(8), 15–16. doi:10.1145/1145287.1145301

Glinz, M. (2000). Problems and Deficiencies of UML as a Requirements Specification Language. In *Proc. of the 10-th International Workshop on Software Specification and Design*. Academic Press.

Goethals, P. L. M., Dedecker, A. P., Gabriels, W., Lek, S., & De Pauw, N. (2007). Applications of artificial neural networks predicting macroinvertebrates in freshwaters. *Aquatic Ecology, 41*, 491–508. doi:10.1007/s10452-007-9093-3

Golsa, M. P., Troped, P. J., & Evans, J. J. (2013). Environment feature extraction and classification for Context aware Physical Activity monitoring. *IEEE Sensors Applications Symposium (SAS)* (pp. 123-128). Galveston, TX, USA: IEEE.

Gordijn, J., Akkermans, H., & van Vliet, H. (2000). Business Process Modeling is not Process Modeling.[LNCS]. *Proceedings of Conceptual Modeling for E-Business and the Web, 1921*, 40–51. doi:10.1007/3-540-45394-6_5

Gorton, I., & Liu, Y. (2010). Advancing software architecture modeling for large scale heterogeneous systems. In *Proceedings of the FSE/SDP Workshop on Future of Software Engineering Research* (pp. 143-148). New York, NY: ACM.

Gottlob, G., Koch, C., & Pichler, R. (2003). XPath query evaluation: improving time and space efficiency. In *Proceedings of 19th International Conference on Data Engineering*. Bangalore, India: Academic Press.

Gottschalk, T. K., Aue, B., Hotes, S., & Ekschmitt, K. (2011). Influence of grain size on species-habitat models. *Ecological Modelling*, *222*(18), 3403–3412. doi:10.1016/j.ecolmodel.2011.07.008

Gould, S. J. (2004). The evolution of life on Earth: Dinosaurs and Other Monsters. *Scientific American*, *14*, 93.

Grady, W. M., Samotyj, M. J., & Noyola, A. H. (1990). Survey of active power line conditioning methodologies. *IEEE Transactions on Power Delivery*, *5*(3), 1536–1542. doi:10.1109/61.57998

Grady, W. M., & Santoso, S. (2001). Understanding power system harmonics. *IEEE Power Engineering Review*, *21*(11), 8–11. doi:10.1109/MPER.2001.961997

Grosso, P., Male, E., Marsh, J., & Walsh, N. (2003). *XPointer Framework W3C Recommendation*. Retrieved from http://www.w3.org/TR/xptr-framework/

Gu, T., Pung, H. K., & Zhang, D. Q. (2004). A Middleware for Building Context-Aware Mobile Services. *IEEE 59th Vehicular Technology Conference. 5*, pp. 2656-2660. IEEE: Los Angeles, USA.

Gu, T., Pung, K. H., & Zhang, D. (2008). Peer-to-Peer Context Reasoning in Pervasive Computing Environments. *Sixth Annual IEEE International Conference on Pervasive Computing and Communications* (pp. 406-411). Singapore: IEEE.

Guan, D., Yuan, W., Lee, S., & Lee, Y.-K. (2007). Context Selection and Reasoning in Ubiquitous Computing. *The 2007 International Conference on Intelligent Pervasive Computing* (pp. 184-187). Jeju City: IEEE.

Guo, H., Gao, G., Ma, J., Li, Y., & Huang, R. (2008). *Reserach of an Adaptive System in Mobile Learning Environment*. Biejing, China: R&D Center for Knowledge Engineering, Beijing Normal University.

Gustafsson, J., & Höglund, J. (2009). The Common Model of an Enterprise's Value Objects: Presented in Relevant Business Views. In A. Persson & J. Stirna (Eds.), Lecture Notes in Business Information Processing: Vol. 39: The Practice of Enterprise Modeling: Second IFIP WG 8.1 Working Conference, PoEM 2009, (pp. 23-37). New York: Springer.

Gustas, R. (1998). Integrated Approach for Modelling of Semantic and Pragmatic Dependencies of Information Systems. In *Proceedings of 17th International Conference on Conceptual Modeling* (ER'98). Singapore: Springer.

Gustas, R. (2010b). Conceptual Modeling and Integration of Static and Dynamic Aspects of Service Architectures. In *Proceedings of International Workshop on Ontology, Conceptualization and Epistemology for Information Systems, Software Engineering and Service Sciences*. Hammamet, Tunisia: Springer.

Gustas, R. (2011b). *Overlaying Conceptualizations for Managing Complexity of Scenario Specifications*. Paper presented at the IFIP WG8.1 Working Conference on Exploring Modeling Methods for Systems Analysis and Design. London, UK.

Gustas, R., & Gustiene, P. (2009). Service-Oriented Foundation and Analysis Patterns for Conceptual Modelling of Information Systems. In C. Barry, K. Conboy, M. Lang, G.Wojtkowski, & W. Wojtkowski (Eds.), *Information Systems Development: Towards a Service Provision Society: Proceedings of the 17th International Conference on Information System Development* (ISD2008), (pp. 157-165). New York: Springer.

Gustas, R. (2010a). A Look behind Conceptual Modeling Constructs in Information System Analysis and Design. *International Journal of Information System Modeling and Design*, *1*(1), 79–108. doi:10.4018/jismd.2010092304

Gustas, R. (2011a). Modeling Approach for Integration and Evolution of Information System Conceptualizations. *International Journal of Information System Modeling and Design*, *2*(1), 45–73. doi:10.4018/jismd.2011010103

Gustas, R., & Gustiene, P. (2008). Pragmatic-Driven Approach for Service-Oriented Analysis and Design. In *Information Systems Engineering - from Data Analysis to Process Networks*. IGI Global. doi:10.4018/978-1-59904-567-2.ch005

Gustas, R., & Gustiene, P. (2012). Conceptual Modeling Method for Separation of Concerns and Integration of Structure and Behavior. *International Journal of Information System Modeling and Design, 3*(1), 48–77. doi:10.4018/jismd.2012010103

Gustiené, P. (2010). *Development of a New Service-Oriented Modelling Method for Information Systems Analysis and Design.* (Doctoral Thesis). Karlstad University Studies.

Gustiene, P., & Gustas, R. (2011). Modeling Method for Bridging Pragmatic and Semantic Dimensions of Service Architectures. In *Proceedings of International Conference on Information System Development.* Springer.

Gustiene, P., & Gustas, R. (2013). A Method for Data Minimization in Personal Information Sharing. In D. Mouromtsev, C. Pchenichniy, & D. Ignatov (Eds.), *Proceedings of the MSEPS 2013 (Modeling States, Events, Processes and Scenarios) Workshop associated with the 20th International Conference on Conceptual Structures* (pp. 33-34). Mumbai, India: ICCS. Retrieved from http://iccs2013.hbcse.tifr.res.in/workshops/copy_of_text.pdf

Gutierrez, J. O., & Sim, K. M. (2010). Self-organizing agents for service composition in cloud computing. In *Proceedings of 2nd IEEE International Conference on Cloud Computing Technology and Science (CloudCom)* (pp. 59-66). Indianapolis, IN: IEEE Press.

Häberlein, T. (2004). Common Structures in System Dynamics Models of Software Acquisition Projects. *Journal of Software Process Improvement and Practice, 9*, 67–80. doi:10.1002/spip.197

Halverson, A., Josifovski, V., Lohman, G., Pirahesh, H., & Mörschel, M. (2004). *ROX: Relational Over XML.* Retrieved from http://www.vldb.org/conf/2004/RS7P2.PDF

Hammer, M. (1990). Reengineering work: Don't Automate, Obliterate. *Harvard Business Review*, 104–112.

Hamming, W. R. (1950). Error Detecting and Error Correcting Codes. *The Bell System Technical Journal, 26*(2), 147–160. doi:10.1002/j.1538-7305.1950.tb00463.x

Hampel, R., & Chaker, N. (1998). Minimizing the variable parameters for optimizing the fuzzy controller. *Fuzzy Sets and Systems, 100*, 131–142. doi:10.1016/S0165-0114(97)00059-6

Hansen, G. (1996, January). Simulating Software development processes. *IEEE Computer*, 73-77.

Hansmann, U., Merck, L., Nicklous, M. S., & Stober, T. (2003). *Pervasive computing* (2nd ed.). New York, NY: Springer-Verlag.

Hardwick, C. S. (1977). *Semiotic and significs: the correspondence between Charles S. Peirce and Victoria Lady Welby.* Academic Press.

Harel, D. (1987). Statecharts: A Visual Formalism for Complex Systems. *Science of Computer Programming, 8*, 231–274. doi:10.1016/0167-6423(87)90035-9

Harmon, M. M., & Mayer, R. T. (1986). *Organization theory for public administration.* Boston, MA: Little Brown.

Hartmann, M., Zesch, T., Mühlhäuser, M., & Gurevych, I. (2008). Using Similarity Measures for Context-Aware User Interfaces. *Proceedings of the 2008 IEEE International Conference on Semantic Computing* (pp. 190-197). Washigton DC, USA: IEEE.

Hassoun. (1995). *Fundamentals of Artificial Neural Networks.* MIT Press.

Haykins, S. (1998). *Neural Networks: A Comprehensive Foundation* (2nd ed.). Prentice Hall.

Heidegger, M. (1977). *Science and reflection: The question concerning technology and other essays* (W. Lovitt, Trans.). New York, NY: HarperCollins.

Heijstek, W., & Chaudron, M. R. V. (2009). Empirical investigations of model Size, complexity and effort in a large scale, distributed model driven development process. In *Proceedings of the 2009 35th Euromicro Coonference on Software Engineering and Advanced Applications* (pp. 113-120). Washington, DC: IEEE Computer Society.

Helfert, E. A. (1997). *Techniques of Financial Analysis: A Practical Guide to Measuring Business Performance.* New York, NY: McGraw-Hill.

Hellinger, E. (1907). *Die Orthogonalinvarianten quadratischer Formen von unendlichvielen Variablen.* University of Göttingen: University of Göttingen.

Hernández-Ros, I., & Wallis, H. (2006). *XBRL Dimensions*. Retrieved from www.xbrl.org/Specification/XDT-REC-2006-09-18.htm

Hertwig, T., Müller, I., & Zeißler, K.-O. (2010). *Management of contaminated soils in urban areas in the ore mountains (Germany)*. Paper presented at ConSoil 2010, 11th International Conference on Management of Soil, Groundwater and Sediment. Salzburg, Austria. Retrieved October 24, 2010, from http://www.beak.de/advangeo/sites/default/files/file/CONSOIL_20100924_Presentation.pdf

Hettiarachchi, P. (2007). *Competence and Beyond a guide providing a holistic understanding of human capital in the apparel and textile industry*. Sri Lanka: Joint Apparel Association Forum.

HillSide. (2013). *The Hillside Group*. Retrieved from http://hillside.net/

Hofer, T., Pichler, M., Leonhartsberger, G., Altmann, J., & Werner, R. (2002). Context-Awareness on Mobile Devices – The Hydrogen Approach. *Proceedings of the 36th Annual Hawaii International Conference on System Sciences* (pp. 292-302). Hawaii: IEEE.

Holland, J. (1992). *Adaptation in natural and artificial systems*. Cambridge, MA: MIT Press.

Horkoff, J., & Yu, E. (2010). Interactive Analysis of Agent-Goal Models in Enterprise Modeling. *International Journal of Information System Modeling and Design*, *1*(4). doi:10.4018/jismd.2010100101

Hosein, I., Tsiavos, & Whitley. (2003). Regulating Architecture and Architectures of Regulation: Contributions from Information Systems. *International Review of Law Computers & Technology*, *17*, 85–97. doi:10.1080/1360086032000063147

Houston, D., Ferreira, S., Collofello, J., Montgomery, D., Mackulak, G., & Shunk, D. (2001). Behavioral characterization: finding and using the influential factors in software process simulation models. *Journal of Systems and Software*, *59*, 259–270. doi:10.1016/S0164-1212(01)00067-X

Huffman, W. S. (2007). *Using neural networks to forecast flood events: A proof of concept*. (Doctoral Dissertation). Nova Southeastern University. Retrieved October 24, 2010, from www.wardsystems.com/Docs/Ward'sRevisedDissertation.doc

Hümmer, W., Bauer, A., & Harde, G. (2003). XCube – XML for Data Warehouses. In *Proceedings of the 6th ACM Intl Workshop on Data Warehousing and OLAP*, (pp. 33–40). Bologna, Italy: ACM.

Hyde, J. (2012). *Optiq- Extensible query-planning framewor*. Retrieved from http://sourceforge.net/projects/optiq/

IBM DB2 Express Server Ed. (2010). Retrieved from http://www-01.ibm.com/software/data/db2/express/

IEEE Standard 519-1992. (1993). *IEEE Recommended Practices and Requirements for Harmonic Control in Electrical Power Systems, IEEE Industry Application Society/Power Engineering Society*. New York: IEEE Press.

Ipedo Inc. (2010). *Ipedo XIP 4.0*. Retrieved from http://www.ipedo.com/

Isaak, J. (2006). The Role of Individuals and Social Capital in POSIX Standardization. *International Journal of IT Standards and Standardization Research*, *4*, 1–23. doi:10.4018/jitsr.2006010101

ITU-R. (2011). *Introduction to Cognitive Radio Systems in the Land Mobile Service*. M.2225. Geneva, Switzerland: International Telecommunication Union (ITU). Retrieved from http://www.itu.int/pub/R-REP-M.2225

Jacobson, I., & Ng, P.-W. (2005). *Aspect-Oriented Software Development with Use Cases*. Pearson Education.

Jain, S. K., Agrawal, P., & Gupta, H. O. (2002). Fuzzy logic controlled shunt active power filter for power quality improvement. *Proc. Electr. Power Appl.*, *149*(5), 317–328. doi:10.1049/ip-epa:20020511

Jarvenpaa, S. L., Tiller, & Simons. (2003). Regulation and the Internet: Public Choice Insights for Business Organizations. *California Management Review*, *46*, 72–85. doi:10.2307/41166232

Jha, S., Katz, D. S., Luckow, A., Merzky, A., & Stamou, K. (2011). Understanding Scientific Applications for Cloud Environments. In R. Buyya, J. Nroberg, & A. Goscinski (Eds.), *Cloud Computing: Principles and Paradigms* (pp. 345–372). John Wiley & Sons, Inc. doi:10.1002/9780470940105.ch13

Jian, F. M., Pei, J., & Fu, A. W. (2007). *IX-Cubes: Iceberg Cubes for Data Warehousing and OLAP on XML Data.* Paper presented at CIKM'07. Lisboa, Portugal.

Jiang, J. J., Klein, G., & Discenza, R. (2002). Pre-project partnering impact on an information system project, project team and project manager. *European Journal of Information Systems, 11*(2), 86–97. doi:10.1057/palgrave/ejis/3000420

Johnson, C. (1999). Why human error modelling has failed to help systems development. *Interacting with Computers, 11*(5), 517–524. doi:10.1016/S0953-5438(98)00041-1

Johnston, S., Peterson, D., & Swank, G. (2006). *Project of the Future Vision: Using System Dynamics to achieve 'model-in-the-loop' Project Planning and execution.* System Dynamics Conference. Retrieved from http://www.systemdynamics.org/conferences/2006/proceed/papers/JOHNS423.pdf

Jones, C. (1996, April). Large Software Systems Failures and Successes. *American Programmer*, 3-9.

Jones, C. (2009). Positive and Negative Innovations in Software Engineering. *International Journal of Software Science and Computational Intelligence, 1*(2), 20–30. doi:10.4018/jssci.2009040102

Junker, H. (n.d.). *Context Database.* Retrieved from Institut für Pervasive Computing: http://www.pervasive.jku.at/Research/Context_Database/viewSubmission.php?key=5&action=View&keyname=b4a4&table=c0b0ad8dc8d0&db=9e8f8772

Kahin, B. (1997). The U.S. National Information Infrastructure Initiative: The Market, the Net, and the Virtual Project. In *National Information Infrastructure Initiatives: Vision and Policy Design* (pp. 150–189). Cambridge, MA: MIT Press.

Kahin, B. (1998). Beyond the National Information Infrastructure. In *Investing in Innovation. Creating Researh and Innovation Policy That Works* (pp. 339–360). Cambridge, MA: MIT Press.

Kaluža, B., Mirchevska, V., Dovgan, E., Luštrek, M., & Gams, M. (2010). An agent-based approach to care in independent living. *Proceedings of the First international joint conference on Ambient intelligence AmI'10* (pp. 177-186). Malaga, Spain: ACM.

Kaluža, B., Mirchevska, V., Dovgan, E., Luštrek, M., & Gams, M. (2010, 11). Retrieved from UCI Machine Learning Repository: http://archive.ics.uci.edu/ml/datasets/Localization+Data+for+Person+Activity

Karuppanan, P., & Mahapatra, K. K. (2011). PLL with fuzzy logic controller based shunt active power filter for harmonic and reactive power compensation. In *Proc. India International Conference on Power Electron. (IICPE)*, (pp. 1-6). IICPE. DOI: 10.1109/IICPE.2011.5728073

Kasabov, N. K. (1996). *Foundations of neural networks, fuzzy logic, and knowledge engineering.* MIT Press.

Kauffman, S. (1995). *At home in the universe: The search for the laws of self-organization and complexity.* Oxford University Press.

Kay, M. H. (2003). *Saxon 7.5.* Retrieved from http://saxon.sourceforge.net/saxon7.5/

Kay, R. (1969). The management and organization of large scale software development projects. In *Proceedings of the May 14-16, 1969, Spring Joint Computer Conference* (pp. 425-433). New York, NY: ACM.

Keen, W. O., & Bruce, R. R. (2000). *Keeping the public trust: The value of values in government.* Reston, VA: Keen Ideas.

Khalil, I., Ali, F. M., & Kotsis, G. (2008). A Datalog Model for Context Reasoning in Pervasive Environments. *International Symposium on Parallel and Distributed Processing with Applications* (pp. 452-459). Sydney, Austrailia: IEEE.

Kimball, R., & Ross, M. (2002). *The DataWarehouse Toolkit.* New York, NY: John Wiley and Sons.

Kishor, N., Singh, M., & Raghuvanshi, A. S. (2007). Particle Swarm Optimization based Neural-Network Model for Hydro Power Plant Dynamics. *IEEE Congress on Evolutionary Computation,* 2725-2731.

Knobloch, A., Schmidt, F., Zeidler, M.K., & Barth, A. (2010). *Creation of high resolution soil parameter data by use of artificial neural network technology (advangeo®).* GeoFARMatics.

Ko, K.-E., & Sim, K.-B. (2008). Development of context aware system based on Bayesian network driven context reasoning method and ontology context modeling. *International Conference on Control, Automation and Systems* (pp. 2309-2313). Seoul, Korea: IEEE.

Kohonen, T. (1982). Self-Organized Formation of Topologically Correct Feature Maps. *Biological Cybernetics, 43,* 59–69. doi:10.1007/BF00337288

Kohonen, T. (1984). *Self-Organization and Associative Memory.* Berlin, Germany: Springer-Verlag.

Koike, K., Matsuda, S., Suzuki, T., & Ohmi, M. (2002). Neural Network-Based Estimation of Principal Metal Contents in the Hokuroku District, Northern Japan, for Exploring Kuroko-Type Deposits. *Natural Resources Research, 11*(2), 135–156. doi:10.1023/A:1015520204066

Könönen, V., Mäntyjärvi, J., Similä, H., Pärkkä, J., & Ermes, M. (2010). Automatic feature selection for context recognition in mobile devices. *Journal of Pervasive and Mobile Computing, 6*(2), 181–197. doi:10.1016/j.pmcj.2009.07.001

Korpipaa, P., Mantyjarvi, J., Kela, J., Keranen, H., & Malm, E. J. (2003). Managing Context Information in Mobile Devices. *IEEE Pervasive Computing / IEEE Computer Society [and] IEEE Communications Society, 2*(3), 42–51. doi:10.1109/MPRV.2003.1228526

Krause, M., Linnhoff-Popien, C., & Strassberger, M. (2007). Concurrent Inference on High Level Context Using Alternative Context Construction Trees. *Proceedings of the Third International Conference on Autonomic and Autonomous Systems* (pp. 1-7). Athens, Greece: IEEE.

Kriesel, D. (2009). *A Brief Introduction to Neural Networks.* Retrieved December 30, 2009, from http://www.dkriesel.com

Kugler, P. N., & Turvey, M. T. (1987). *Information, Natural Law, and the Self-Assembly of Rhythmic Movement.* Lawrence Erlbaum.

Kumar, P., & Mahajan, A. (2009). Soft computing techniques for the control of an active power filter. *IEEE Transactions on Power Delivery, 24*(1), 452–461. doi:10.1109/TPWRD.2008.2005881

Kunz, W. & Rittel. (1970). Issues as elements of information systems. In *Center for Planning and Development Research* (Working Paper 131). Berkeley, CA: University of California, Berkeley.

Kuo, Y.-M., Lee, J.-S., & Chung, P.-C. (2010). A visual context-awareness-based sleeping-respiration measurement system. *IEEE Transactions on Information Technology in Biomedicine, 14*(2), 255–265. doi:10.1109/TITB.2009.2036168 PMID:19906594

Kurz, M., Holzl, G., Ferscha, A., Calatroni, A., Roggen, D., & Troster, G. et al. (2011). The OPPORTUNITY Framework abd Data Processing Ecosystem for Opportunistic Activity and Context Recognition. *International Journal of Sensors, Wireless Communication and Control, 1*(2), 102–125.

Kwak, J., Lee, & Fomin. (2011). The Governmental Coordination of Conflicting Interests in Standardisation: Case Studies of Indigenous ICT Standards in China and South Korea. *Technology Analysis and Strategic Management, 23*(7), 789–806. doi:10.1080/09537325.2011.592285

Laerhoven, K. V. (2004). *Context Database.* Retrieved 2011, from Institut für Pervasive Computing: http://www.pervasive.jku.at/Research/Context_Database/viewSubmission.php?key=1&action=View&keyname=b4a4&table=c0b0ad8dc8d0&db=9e8f8772

Laine, P. K. (2001). The role of SW architectures in solving fundamental problems in object-oriented development of large embedded SW systems. In *Proccedings of the Working IEEE/IFIP Conference on Software Architecture* (pp. 14-23). Washington, DC: IEEE Computer Society.

Lamothe, D. (2009). *Assessment of the mineral potential for porphyry Cu-Au ± Mo deposits in the Baie-James region.* Document published by Géologie Québec (EP 2009-02). Retrieved October 24, 2010, from http://collections.banq.qc.ca/ark:/52327/bs1905189

Langheinrich, M., Coroama, V., Bohn, J., & Rohs, M. (2002). *As we may live – Real-world implications of ubiquitous computing: Distributed Systems Group, Institute of Information Systems*. Swiss Federal Institute of Technology.

Lättilä, L., Hilletofth, P., & Lin, B. (2010). Hybrid simulation models–when, why, how? *Expert Systems with Applications, 37*(12), 7969–7975. doi:10.1016/j.eswa.2010.04.039

Lee, H., Choi, J. S., & Elmasri, R. (2009). A classification and modeling of the quality of contextual information in smart spaces. *IEEE International Conference on Pervasive Computing and Communications* (pp. 1-5). Galveston, TX: IEEE.

Lee, J., & Lee, H. (2008). A Sensor based context-aware inference algorithm for ubiquitous residential environments. *13th International Conference on Computer Aided Architectural Design Research in Asia*, (pp. 93-102). Chiang Mai.

Lee, K. (2010). Context recognition from incomplete situation with uncertainity management. *4th International Conference on New Trends in Information Science and Service Science* (pp. 481-484). Gyeongju: IEEE.

Legler, C., Knobloch, A., & Barth, A. (2008). *Map of Minerals – Metallogenic / Minerogenic Map (1: 200,000) - Final Report – Map Description*. Beak Consultants GmbH.

Lessig, L. (1999a). *Code and Other Laws of Cyberspace*. New York: Basic Books.

Lessig, L. (1999b). The Law of the Horse: What Cyberlaw Might Teach. *Harvard Law Review, 113*, 501–549. doi:10.2307/1342331

Lewin, K. et al. (1975). *Frustration and Regression: An Experiment With Young Children*. Iowa City, IA: University of Iowa Press.

Lewin, K. (1997). *Resolving social conflicts and field theory in social science*. Washington, DC: American Psychological Association. doi:10.1037/10269-000

Lewis, M. W., Welsh, M. A., & Dehler, G. E. (2002). Product development tensions: Exploring contrasting styles of project management. *Academy of Management Journal, 45*(3), 546–564. doi:10.2307/3069380

LfULG. (2012). *Biotoptypen- und Landnutzungskartierung (BTLNK): Interactive map and link to dissemination of digital data*. Retrieved April 2012 from http://www.umwelt.sachsen.de/umwelt/natur/25140.htm

Li, Y., Fang, J., & Xiong, J. (2008). A Context-Aware Services Mash-Up System. *Seventh International Conference on Grid and Cooperative Computing* (pp. 707-712). Shenzhen: IEEE.

Libkin, L. (2006). Logics For Unranked Trees: An Overview. *Logical Methods in Computer Science, 2*(3:2), 1–31.

Libkin, L., & Neven, F. (2003). Logical Definability and Query Languages over Unranked Trees. In *Proceedings of LICS 2003*. IEEE Computer Society.

Lin, C. Y., & Levary, R. R. (1989). Computer Aided Software Development Process Design. *IEEE Transactions on Software Engineering, 15*(9), 1025–1037. doi:10.1109/32.31362

Lin, S.-W., Sun, C.-H., & Chen, C.-H. (2004). Temporal Data Mining using Genetic Algorithm and Neural Network: A Case Study of Air Pollutant Forecasts. *Geospatial Information Science, 3*, 31–38. doi:10.1007/BF02826674

Liu, C. Z. Kemerer, Slaughter, & Smith. (2008). *Standards Competition In The Presence Of Digital Conversion Technology: An Empirical Analysis Of The Flash Memory Card Market*. Tepper School of Business. Retrieved from http://ssm.com/abstract=1021352

Liu, W., Sun, D., Ren, P., & Xiong, H. (2012). Path-Calculation-Based XML Data Cube Model. In *Proceedings of Convergence and Hybrid Information Technology: 6th International Conference*, ICHIT 2012. Daejeon, Korea: ICHIT.

Llewellyn, R. (2009). Stakeholder Management Overview. *The Project Management Hut*. Retrieved from http://www.pmhut.com/stakeholder-management-overview

Loke, S. W. (2010). Inceremental Awareness and Compositionality: A Design Philosophy For Context-Aware Pervasive System. *Journal of Pervasive and Mobile Computing, 6*(2), 239–253. doi:10.1016/j.pmcj.2009.03.004

Lovelock, C. H. (1995). *Technology: Servant or Master in the Delivery of Services?*. doi:10.1016/S1067-5671(95)04019-6

Lukowicz, P., Pirkl, G., Bannach, D., Wagner, F., Calatroni, A., Foerster, K., et al. (2010). Recording a Complex, Multi Modal Activity Data Set for Context Recognition. *23rd International Conference on Architecture of Computing Systems (ARCS)* (pp. 1-6). Hanover, Germany: IEEE.

Lyneis, J., Cooper, K., & Els, S. (2001). Strategic management of complex projects: a case study using system dynamics. *System Dynamics Review, 17*(3), 237–260. doi:10.1002/sdr.213

Lyneis, J., & Ford, D. (2007). System Dynamics applied to project management: a survey, assessment and directions for future research. *System Dynamics Review, 23*(2/3), 57–189.

Lyytinen, K., & Yoo, Y. (2002). Introduction[Issues and challenges in ubiquitous computing]. *Communications of the ACM, 45*(12), 62–65. doi:10.1145/585597.585616

Maciaszek, L. (2005). *Requirements Analysis and System Design: Developing Information Systems with UML.* London: Addison-Wesley.

Mahmud, U., Iltaf, N., Rehman, A., & Kamran, F. (2007). *Context-Aware Paradigm for a Pervasive Computing Environment (CAPP). WWW\Internet 2007* (pp. 337–346). Villa Real, Portugal: IADIS.

Mahmud, U., & Javed, M. Y. (2012). Context Inference Engine (CiE): Inferring Context.[IJAPUC]. *International Journal of Advanced Pervasive and Ubiquitous Computing, 4*(3), 13–41. doi:10.4018/japuc.2012070102

Maier, H. R., & Dandy, G. C. (2000). Neural networks for the prediction and forecasting of water resources variables: A review of modelling issues and applications. *Environmental Modelling & Software, 15*, 101–124. doi:10.1016/S1364-8152(99)00007-9

Mamei, M., & Zambonelli, F. (2007). Pervasive pheromone-based interaction with RFID tags. *ACM Transactions of Autonomous and Adaptive Systems, 2*(2), 4. doi:10.1145/1242060.1242061

Manel, S., Dias, J. M., Buckton, S. T., & Ormerod, S. J. (1999). Alternative methods for predicting species distribution: an illustration with Himalayan river birds. *Journal of Applied Ecology, 36*(5), 734–747. doi:10.1046/j.1365-2664.1999.00440.x

Manhattan Distance. (n.d.). (NIST) Retrieved 10 2011, from NIST: http://xlinux.nist.gov/dads//HTML/manhattanDistance.html

Manning, R. (2013). *Mongo JDBC Driver - A minimal JDBC driver implementation for MongoDB.* Retrieved from http://sourceforge.net/projects/mongojdbcdriver

Maravelias, C. D., Haralabous, J., & Papaconstantinou, C. (2003). Predicting demersal fish species distributions in the Mediterranean Sea using artificial neural networks. *Marine Ecology Progress Series, 255*, 249–258. doi:10.3354/meps255249

Martin, J., & Odell, J. J. (1995). *Object-Oriented Methods: A Foundation.* Prentice-Hall.

Marx, K. (1976). *Capital* (Vol. 1). London, UK: Penguin Books.

Maslow, A. H. (1996). A theory of human motivation. In *Classic readings in organizational behavior* (2nd ed., pp. 45–56). Belmont, CA: Wadsworth.

Matarazzo, D. C. (2003). *Análise financeira de balanços.* São Paulo, Brazil: Editora Atlas.

Mattsson, A., Lundell, B., Lings, B., & Fitzgerald, B. (2007). Experiences from representing software architecture in a large industrial project using model driven development. In *Proceedings of the Second Workshop on SHAring and Reusing Architectural Knowledge Architecture, Rationale, and Design Intent* (pp. 6-6). Washington, DC: IEEE Computer Society.

Maurer, M. (2011). *Skill Formation Regimes in South Asia: A Comparative Study on the Path-Dependent Development of Technical and Vocational Education and Training for the Garment Industr.* Komparatistische Bibliothek / Comparative Studies Series / Bibliotheque d'Etudes Comparatives Ser.

Mayrhofer, R. (2004). An Architecture for Context Prediction. *2nd International Conference on Pervasive Computing (Pervasive 2004)* (pp. 65-72). Vienna, Austria: Austrian Computer Society (OCG).

McKeever, S., Ye, J., Coyle, L., Bleakley, C., & Dobson, S. (2010). Activity recognition using temporal evidence theory. *Journal of Ambient Intelligence and Smart Environments, 2*(3), 253–269.

McLachlan, G. J. (1999). Mahalanobis Distance. *Resonance*, *4*(6), 20–16. doi:10.1007/BF02834632

MDX Function Reference. (2008). Retrieved from msdn.microsoft.com/en-s/library/ms145506.aspx

Medvidovic, N. (2005). Software architectures and embedded systems: a match made in heaven? *Software, IEEE*, *22*(5), 83–86. doi:10.1109/MS.2005.136

Mellor, S. J., Clark, A. N., & Futagami, T. (2003). Model-driven development - Guest editor's introduction. *Software, IEEE*, *20*(5), 14–18. doi:10.1109/MS.2003.1231145

Mell, P., & Grance, T. (2009). The NIST Definition of Cloud Computing. *Computer and Information Science*, *53*(6), 50.

Metelka, V., Baratoux, L., Jessell, M., Barth, A., & Naba, S. (2011). *Regolith landform mapping in western Burkina Faso, using airborne geophysics and remote sensing data in a neural network*. Retrieved January 21, 2013, from http://www.beak.de/advangeo/sites/default/files/file/CAG23/Abstracts_Metelka_CAG23%20final_updated.pdf

Metropolis, N., Rosenbluth, A. W., Rosenbluth, M. N., Teller, A. H., & Teller, E. (1953). Equations of state calculations by fast computing machines. *The Journal of Chemical Physics*, *21*(6), 1087–1091. doi:10.1063/1.1699114

Miller, G., Ambler, S., Cook, S., Mellor, S., Frank, K., & Kern, J. (2004). Model driven architecture: the realities, a year later. In *Companion to the 19th Annual ACM SIGPLAN Conference on Object-oriented Programming Systems, Languages, and Applications* (pp. 138-140). New York, NY: ACM.

Mingers, J., & White, L. (2009). *A Review of the Recent Contribution of Systems Thinking to Operational Research and Management science*. University of Kent Working Paper 197. Retrieved from http://kar.kent.ac.uk/22312/

Mining Journal. (2009, July 17). Kosovo ready to roll. *Mining Journal*, 14-15.

Ministry of Finance and Planning. (2006). *2006 Budget Speech*. Colombo: Ministry of Finance and Planning.

Ministry of Research and Information Technology. (1996). *The Info-Society for All - the Danish Model. Copenhagen: Ministry of Research and Information Technology*. Retrieved from http://www.fsk.dk/fsk/publ/1996/it96-uk/

Min, J.-K., & Cho, S.-B. (2011). A Hybrid Context-Aware Wearable System with Evolutionary Optimization and Selective Inference of Dynamic Bayesian Networks. In *Hybrid Artificial Intelligent Systems* (Vol. 6678, pp. 444–451). Wroclaw, Poland: Springer. doi:10.1007/978-3-642-21219-2_56

Minkowski, H. (1910). *Geometrie der Zahlen*. Leipzig: Teubner.

Mirakhorli, M., Sharifloo, A., & Shams, F. (2008). Architectural challenges of ultra large scale systems. In *Proceedings of the 2nd International Workshop on Ultra-large-scale Software-intensive Systems* (pp. 45-48). New York, NY: ACM.

Mitchell, T. (1997). *Machine Learning*. Maidenhead, UK: McGraw-Hill.

Mohan, T. S. (2011). Migrating into a Cloud. In R. Buyya, J. Nroberg, & A. Goscinski (Eds.), *Cloud Computing: Principles and Paradigms* (pp. 43–56). John Wiley & Sons, Inc. doi:10.1002/9780470940105.ch2

Mojtahedzadeh, M. T., Andersen, D., & Richardson, G. P. (2004). Using Digest® to implement the pathway participation method for detecting influential system structure. *System Dynamics Review*, *20*(1), 1–20. doi:10.1002/sdr.285

Mondrian. (2008). Retrieved from http://community.pentaho.com/projects/mondrian/

Moore, B. (1981). Principal Component Analysis in Linear Systems: Controllability, Observability and Model Reduction. *IEEE Transactions on Automatic Control*, *26*, 17–31. doi:10.1109/TAC.1981.1102568

Moser, B., & Navara, M. (2002). Fuzzy controllers with conditionally firing rules. *IEEE Transactions on Fuzzy Systems*, *10*(3), 340–349. doi:10.1109/TFUZZ.2002.1006437

MySQL. (2013). Retrieved from http://www.mysql.com/

Näppilä, T., Järvelin, K., & Niemi, T. (2008). A tool for data cube construction from structurally heterogeneous XML documents. *Journal of the American Society for Information Science and Technology, 59*(3), 435–449. doi:10.1002/asi.20756

Negnevitsky, M. (2002). *Artificial intelligence: a guide to intelligent systems*. Pearson Education Ltd.

Nelson, R. R., & Winter. (1982). *An Evolutionary Theory of Economic Change*. Cambridge, MA: Harvard University Press.

Nepal, S., & Zic, J. (2008). A conflict neighbouring negotiation algorithm for resource services in dynamic collaborations. In *Proceedings of IEEE International Conference on Services Computing (SCC)* (pp. 283-290). Honolulu, HI: IEEE Press.

Netherer, S., & Nopp-Mayr, U. (2005). Predisposition assessment systems (PAS) as supportive tools in forest management – rating of site and stand-related hazards of bark beetle infestation in the High Tatra Mountains as an example for system application and verification. *Forest Ecology and Management, 207*, 99–107. doi:10.1016/j.foreco.2004.10.020

Nguyen, T. V., & Choi, D. (2008). Context Reasoning Using Contextual Graph. *Proceedings of the 2008 IEEE 8th International Conference on Computer and Information Technology Workshops* (pp. 488-493). Sydney, Australia: IEEE.

Nietzsche, F. (1988). *Other worlds: Essays in cultural politics* (G. C. Spivak, Ed.). New York, NY: Routledge.

Nikitin, S., Terziyan, V., & Nagy, M. (2010). Mastering intelligent clouds - Engineering intelligent data processing services in the cloud. In *Proceedings of 7th International Conference on Informatics in Control, Automation and Robotics (ICINCO)* (pp. 174-181). Madeira, Portugal: SciTePress – Science and Technology Publications.

Niklas, K., Klaus, D., Sigg, S., & Beigl, M. (2010). DAG Based Context Reasoning: Optimised DAG Creation. *23rd International Conference on Architecture of Computing Systems* (pp. 1-6). Hannover, Germany: IEEE.

Nissen, S. (2009). *Fast Artificial Neural Network Library (FANN)*. Retrieved December 30, 2009, from http://leenissen.dk/fann/

Noack, S., & Otto, L.-F. (2010). *Erste Ergebnisse einer Prognose der Befallswahrscheinlichkeit von Waldbeständen durch den Buchdrucker (Ips typographus L.) mittels eines künstlichen neuronalen Netzes*. Paper presented at Forstwissenschaften: Grundlage nachhaltiger Waldbewirtschaftung. Göttingen, Germany. Retrieved October 24, 2010, from http://www.beak.de/advangeo/advangeo_prediction/news/fowi_2010

Oliva, R. (2004). Model structure analysis through graph theory: partition heuristics and feedback structure decomposition. *System Dynamics Review, 20*(4), 313–336. doi:10.1002/sdr.298

OMG. (2003). *OMG's MDA Guide Version 1.0.1*. Retrieved from http://www.omg.org/docs/omg/03-06-01.pdf

OMG. (2005). *Object Management Group Home Page*. Retrieved from http://www.omg.org

OMG. (2008). *SPEM v2.0 - Software & Systems Process Engineering Meta-Model Specification v2.0*. Retrieved from www.omg.org/spec/SPEM/2.0/

OMG. (2010). *Unified Modeling Language Superstructure, version 2.2*. Retrieved January 19, 2010, from www.omg.org/spec/UML/2.2/

Ope, X. Q. S. Q. L. (2011). *XQuery SQL-Client (XQSQL) for XQuery Ope*. Retrieved from http://xqsql.sourceforge.net/

Oracle Berkeley DB XML. (2010). Retrieved from www.oracle.com/technology/documentation/berkeley-db/xml/index.html

Ormerod, P. (1999). *Butterfly economics: A new general theory of social and economic behavior*. Pantheon Books.

Padovitz, A., Loke, S. W., & Zaslavsky, A. (2004). Towards a Theory of Context Spaces. *Proceedings of Second IEEE Annual Conference on Pervasive Computing and Communications Workshop* (pp. 38-42). Orlando, Florida, USA: IEEE.

Paganelli, F., Spinicci, E., & Giuli, D. (2008). ERMHAN: A Context-Aware Service Platform to Support Continuous Care Networks for Home-Based Assistance. *International Journal of Telemedicine and Applications, 2008*, 1–13. doi:10.1155/2008/867639 PMID:18695739

Paletta, M., & Herrero, M. P. (2009). Awareness-based learning model to improve cooperation in collaborative distributed environments. In *Proceedings of 3rd International KES Symposium on Agents and Multi-agents Systems Technologies and Applications (KES-AMSTA 2009)* (pp. 793-802). Uppsala, Sweden: Springer.

Paletta, M. (2012a). Self-Organizing Multi-Agent Systems by means of Scout Movement.[CSENG]. *Recent Patents on Computer Science, 5*(3), 197–210. doi:10.2174/2213275911205030197

Paletta, M. (2012b). MAS-based Agent Societies by Means of Scout Movement.[IJATS]. *International Journal of Agent Technologies and Systems, 4*(3), 29–49. doi:10.4018/jats.2012070103

Paletta, M. (2012c). Intelligent Clouds – By means of using multi-agent systems environments. In L. Chao (Ed.), *Cloud Computing for Teaching and Learning: Strategies for Design and Implementation*. Hershey, PA: IGI Global. doi:10.4018/978-1-4666-0957-0.ch017

Paletta, M., & Herrero, M. P. (2010a). An awareness-based learning model to deal with service collaboration in cloud computing. In N. T. Nguyen, & R. Kowalczyk (Eds.), *Transactions on Computational Collective Intelligence I* (pp. 85–100). Berlin, Germany: Springer-Verlag. doi:10.1007/978-3-642-15034-0_6

Paletta, M., & Herrero, M. P. (2010b). Collaboration in Distributed Systems by means of an Awareness-based Learning Model.[CSENG]. *Recent Patents on Computer Science, 3*(2), 1–21. doi:10.2174/2213275911003020127

Panda, A. K., & Mikkili, S. (2013). FLC based shunt active filter (p–q and Id–Iq) control strategies for mitigation of harmonics with different fuzzy MFs using MATLAB and real-time digital simulator. *Electrical Power and Energy Systems, 47*, 313–336. doi:10.1016/j.ijepes.2012.11.003

Pantsar-Syvaniemi, S., Simula, K., & Ovaska, E. (2010). Context-awareness in smart spaces. *IEEE Symposium on Computers and Communications (ISCC)* (pp. 1023-1028). Riccione: IEEE.

Papazoglou, M. P., & Van den Heuvel, W. J. (2007). Service oriented architectures: Approaches, technologies and research issues. *The VLDB Journal, 16*(3), 389–415. doi:10.1007/s00778-007-0044-3

Park, B. K., Han, H., & Song, I. Y. (2005). XML-OLAP: A Multidimensional Analysis Framework for XML Warehouses. In *Proceedings of 7th International Conference in Data Warehousing and Knowledge Discovery* (LNCS), (vol. 3589, pp. 32–42). Copenhagen, Denmark: Springer.

Partridge, E. (Ed.). (1958). *Origins: A short etymological dictionary of modern English*. New York, NY: Macmillan.

Parunak, H. V. D., & Brueckner, S. (2000). Ant-like missionaries and cannibals: Synthetic pheromones for distributed motion control. In *Proceedings of the Fourth International Conference on Autonomous Agents* (pp. 467-474). Academic Press.

Parunak, H. V. D., & Brueckner, S. (2001). Entropy and self-organization in multi-agent systems. In *Proceedings of the International Conference on Autonomous Agents*. Montreal, Canada: Academic Press.

Parunak, H. V. D. (1997). Go to the ant: engineering principles from natural agent systems. *Annals of Operations Research, 75*, 69–101. doi:10.1023/A:1018980001403

Pedersen, M. K. Fomin, & de Vries. (2009). The Open Standards and Government Policy. In *ICT Standardization for E-Business Sectors: Integrating Supply and Demand Factors*, (pp. 188–199). Hershey, PA: IGI Global. Retrieved from http://www.igi-global.com/chapter/information-communication-technology-standardization-business/22931

Peirce, C. S. (1888). *A Guess at the Riddle: The triad in physics, MS 909, EP1*. Retrieved 4/4/2013, from http://www.cspeirce.com/menu/library/bycsp/guess/guess.htm

Peng, F. Z., Akagi, H., & Nabae, A. (1990). Study of active power filters using quad series voltage source PWM converters for harmonic compensation. *IEEE Transactions on Power Electronics, 5*(1), 9–15. doi:10.1109/63.45994

Penning de Vries, F. W. T., Agus, F., & Kerr, J. (Eds.). (1998). *Soil erosion at multiple scales: Principles and methods for assessing causes and impacts*. CABI Publishing.

Perttunen, M., Kleek, M. V., Lassila, O., & Riekki, J. (2009). An Implementation of Auditory Context Recognition for Mobile Devices. *Tenth International Conference on Mobile Data Management: Systems, Services and Middleware* (pp. 424-429). Taipei, Taiwan: IEEE.

Peters, R., Schmitz, G., & Cullmann, J. (2006). Flood routing modelling with Artificial Neural Networks. *Advances in Geosciences*, 9, 131–136. doi:10.5194/adgeo-9-131-2006

Poirazidis, K., Goutner, V., Skartsi, T., & Stamou, G. (2003). Modelling nesting habitat as a conservation tool for the Eurasian black vulture (Aegypius monachus) in Dadia nature Reserve, northeastern Greece. *Biological Conservation*, *118*, 235–248. doi:10.1016/j.biocon.2003.08.016

Qiao, X., & Li, X. (2009). Bayesian Network-Based Service Context Recognition Model. *International Journal of Distributed Sensor Networks*, 5(1), 80–80. doi:10.1080/15501320802571830

QuiLogic. (2001). *In Memory SQL / XML Database Technology for Universal Data Management*. Retrieved from http://www.quilogic.cc

Rahmandad, H., & Sterman, J. D. (2008). Heterogeneity and network structure in the dynamics of diffusion: comparing agent-based and differential equation models. *Management Science*, *54*(5), 998–1014. doi:10.1287/mnsc.1070.0787

Rahmani, S., Hamadi, A., Al-Haddad, K., & Alolah, A. I. (2013). DSP-based implementation of an instantaneous current control for a three-phase shunt hybrid power filter. *Mathematics and Computers in Simulation*, *91*, 229–248. doi:10.1016/j.matcom.2012.09.013

Ranganathan, A., & Campbell, R. H. (2008). Provably Correct Pervasive Computing Environments. *2008 Sixth Annual IEEE Conference on Pervasive Computing and Communications (PERCOM '08)* (pp. 160 - 169). Hong Kong: IEEE.

Ravat, F., Teste, O., Tournier, R., & Zurfluh, G. (2010). Finding an application-appropriate model for XML data warehouses. *Information Systems*, *35*, 662–687. doi:10.1016/j.is.2009.12.002

Redford, S., Lipton, G., & Ugalde, H. (2004). Predictive Ore Deposit Targeting Using Neural Network Analysis. *Society of Exploration Geophysicists (SEG). Expanded Abstracts*, *23*, 1198.

Reese, G. (2009). *Cloud Application Architectures: Building Applications and Infrastructure in the Cloud*. Sebastopol, CA: O'Reilly Media, Inc.

Reid, B. P. (n.d.). *Linear Least Squares*. Retrieved from http://www.dartmouth.edu/~chemlab/info/resources/linear/linear.html

Relational XQuery. (2006). Retrieved from http://www.software112.com/products/relational-xquery.html

Riaz, M., Kiani, S. L., Lee, S., Han, S.-M., & Lee, Y.-K. (2005). Service Delivery in Context Aware Environments: Lookup and Access Control Issues. *11th IEEE International Conference on Embeded and Real-Time Computing Systems and Applications* (pp. 455-458). Hong Kong: IEEE.

Riboni, D. (2012, January). *Human activity recognition*. Retrieved from EveryWhere Lab: http://everywarelab.di.unimi.it/palspot

Riboni, D., & Bettini, C. (2009). Context-Aware Activity Recognition through a Combination of Ontological and Statistical Reasoning. *Proceedings of the 6th International Conference on Ubiquitous Intelligence and Computing UCI '09* (pp. 39-53). Brisbane, Austrailia: ACM.

Riboni, D., & Bettini, C. (2011). OWL 2 modeling and reasoning with complex human activities. *Journal of Pervasive and Mobile Computing*, 7(3), 379–395. doi:10.1016/j.pmcj.2011.02.001

Richardson, G. P. (1995). Loop polarity, loop dominance, and the concept of dominant polarity. *System Dynamics Review*, *11*(1), 67–88. doi:10.1002/sdr.4260110106

Richmond, B., et al. (2009). *iThink® Software (Version 9.1.2)*. iSee Systems™.

Richmond, B. (1980). A new look at an old friend. In *Plexus*. Hanover, NH: Dartmouth College.

Rios, D. (2010). *Neural networks: A requirement for intelligent systems*. Retrieved August 10, 2010, from http://www.learnartificialneuralnetworks.com/backpropagation.html

Rittel, H. W. (1972). *Second generation design methods*. J. Wiley and Sons.

Rittel, H. W.J., & Webber. (1973). Dilemmas in a General Theory of Planning. *Policy Sciences*, 4.

Roberts, E. B. (1964). *The Dynamics of Research and Development*. New York: Harper & Row.

Robie, J. (1999). *XQL (XML Query Language)*. Retrieved from http://www.ibiblio.org/xql/xql-proposal.html

Rochwerger, B., Vazquez, C., Breitgand, D., Hadas, D., Villari, M., Massonet, P., & Galán, F. (2011). An Architecture for Federated Cloud Computing. In R. Buyya, J. Nroberg, & A. Goscinski (Eds.), *Cloud Computing: Principles and Paradigms* (pp. 393–412). John Wiley & Sons. doi:10.1002/9780470940105.ch15

Rockl, M., Frank, K., Hermann, P. G., & Vera, M. (2008). Knowledge Representation and Inference in Context-Aware Computing Environments. *The Second International Conference on Mobile Ubiquitous Computing, Systems, Services and Technologies* (pp. 89-95). Valencia: IEEE.

Rodrigues, T., Sauer, C., & Galante, R. (2012). *Executing SQL Queries withanXQueryEngine*. Retrieved from http://www.lume.ufrgs.br/bitstream/handle/10183/54129/000855691.pdf?sequence=1

Rodrigues, A., & Bowers, J. (1996). System Dynamics in Project Management: a comparative analysis with traditional methods. *System Dynamics Review*, *12*, 121–139. doi:10.1002/(SICI)1099-1727(199622)12:2<121::AID-SDR99>3.0.CO;2-X

Rogers, C. (1951). *Client-centered therapy: Its current practice, implications and theory*. London, UK: Constable.

Roggen, D., Calatroni, A., Rossi, M., Holleczek, T., Forster, K., Troster, G., et al. (2010). Collecting complex activity datasets in highly rich networked sensor environments. *2010 Seventh International Conference on Networked Sensing Systems (INSS)* (pp. 233 - 240). Kassel: IEEE.

Román, M., Hess, C., Cerqueira, R., Campbell, R. H., & Nahrstedt, K. (2002). Gaia: A Middleware Infrastructure to Enable Active Spaces. *IEEE Pervasive Computing / IEEE Computer Society [and] IEEE Communications Society*, *1*(4), 74–82. doi:10.1109/MPRV.2002.1158281

Römer, T. (2012). *GIS-gestützte Analyse der Beziehungen zwischen Biotop- und Landnutzungstypen sowie Brutvorkommen ausgewählter Vogelarten*. (Unpublished Master Thesis). Hochschule für Technik und Wirtschaft (University of Applied Sciences for Engineering and Economy), Dresden, Germany.

Ross, D. H. (2009). *A Critical Companion to William butler Yeats, A Literary Reference to His Life and Work*. Facts on File.

Royal Academy of Engineering. (2004). *The challenges of Complex IT projects*. Report of working group of RAE and BCS.

Ruiz, M., Ramos, I., & Toro, M. (2001). A Simplified model of software project dynamics. *Journal of Systems and Software*, *59*, 299–309. doi:10.1016/S0164-1212(01)00070-X

Rumelhart, D. E., Hinton, G. E., & Williams, R. J. (1986). Learning internal representations by error propagation. In *Parallel distributed processing: explorations in the microstructure of cognition*. MIT Press.

Ruparelia, N. (2010). Software Development Lifecycle Models. *ACM Sigsoft Software Engineering Notes*, *35*(3), 8–13. doi:10.1145/1764810.1764814

Russell, N., Hofstede, A. H. M., Aalst, W. M. P., & Mulyar, N. (2006). *Workflow Control-Flow Patterns: A Revised View* (BPM Centre Report BPR-06-22). Retrieved September 11, 2008, from http://www.workflowpatterns.com/documentation/documents/BPM-06-22. pdf

Russell, S., & Norvig, P. (2010). *Artificial Intelligence: A Modern Approach* (3rd ed.). Berkley: Pearson Education.

Sage, A. P., & Rouse, W. B. (1999). Information Systems Frontiers in Knowledge Management. *Information Systems Frontiers*, *1*(3), 205–219. doi:10.1023/A:1010046210832

Saha, D., & Mukherjee, A. (2003). Pervasive computing: a paradigm for the 21st century. *Computer*, *36*(3), 25–31. doi:10.1109/MC.2003.1185214

Samulowitz, M., Michahelles, F., & Linnhoff-Popien, C. (2001). CAPEUS: An Architecture for Context-Aware Selection and Execution of Services. *Third International Working Conference on New Developments in Distributed Applications and Interoperable Systems* (pp. 23-40). Kraków, Poland: Springer.

Santos, A. C., Tarrataca, L., Cardoso, J. M., Ferreira, D. R., Diniz, P. C., & Chainho, P. (2009). Context Inference for Mobile Applications in the UPCASE Project. *Lecture Notes of the Institute for Computer Science. Social Informatics and Telecommunications Engineering*, *7*, 352–365.

Sarna, D. E. Y. (2011). *Implementing and Developing Cloud Computing Applications*. Boca Raton, FL: CRC Press.

Scalmato, A., Sgorbissa, A., & Zaccaria, R. (2013). Describing and Recognizing Patterns of Events in Smart Environments With Description Logic. *IEEE Transactions on Cybernetics*, *43*(6), 1882–1897. doi:10.1109/TSMCB.2012.2234739 PMID:23757579

Schilit, B. N., Hilbert, D. M., & Trevor, J. (2002). Context-Aware Communication. *IEEE Wireless Communication*, *9*(5), 46–54. doi:10.1109/MWC.2002.1043853

Schmidtke, H. R., & Woo, W. (2009). Towards ontology-based formal verification methods for context aware systems. In *Pervasive Computing* (pp. 309–326). Nara, Japan: Springer. doi:10.1007/978-3-642-01516-8_21

Schnable, K. (2013). *MongoSQL - A friendly SQL UI for MongoDB*. Retrieved from http://www.mongosql.com

Seidewitz, E. (2003). What models mean. *Software, IEEE*, *20*(5), 26–32. doi:10.1109/MS.2003.1231147

Seidl, R., Baier, P., Rammer, W., Schopf, A., & Lexer, M. J. (2007). Modelling tree mortality by bark beetle infestation in Norway spruce forests. *Ecological Modelling*, *206*, 383–399. doi:10.1016/j.ecolmodel.2007.04.002

Selic, B. (2003). Model-driven development of real-time software using OMG standards. In *Proceedings of the Sixth IEEE International Symposium on Object-Oriented Real-Time Distributed Computing* (pp. 4-6). Washington, DC: IEEE Computer Society.

Sendall, S., & Kozaczynski, W. (2003). Model transformation: the heart and soul of model-driven software development. *Software, IEEE*, *20*(5), 42–45. doi:10.1109/MS.2003.1231150

Shafritz, J. M., & Ott, S. J. (1996). Introduction. In *Classics of organization theory* (3rd ed.). Belmont, CA: Wadsworth.

Shannon, C. E., & Weaver, W. (1949). *The Mathematical Theory of Communication*. University of Illinois.

Shapiro, C., & Varian. (1999). The Art of Standards Wars. *California Management Review*, *4*(2), 8–32. doi:10.2307/41165984

Shin, C., & Woo, W. (2005). *Conflict Resolution Method utilizing Context History for Context-Aware Applications*. S. Korea: GIST U-VR Lab.

Siebra, S. A., Salgado, A. C., Tedesco, P. A., & Brézillon, P. (2005). *A Learning Interaction Memory using Contextual Information*. Retrieved 03 28, 2014, from http://www.cin.ufpe.br/~mbjn/D1.pdf

Silva, P. C., & Times, V. C. (2009a). *XPath+: A Tool for Linked XML Documents Navigation*. Paper presented at XSym 2009 - Sixth International XML Database Symposium at VLDB'09. Lyon, France.

Silva, P. C., & Times, V. C. (2009b). LMDQL: link-based and multidimensional query language. In *Proceeding of the ACM twelfth international workshop on Data warehousing and OLAP* (DOLAP'09). Hong Kong, China: ACM.

Silva, P. C., Aquino, I. J. S., & Times, V. C. (2008). *A Query Language for Navigation Over Links*. Paper presented at the XIV Brazilian Multimedia Systems and Web Symposium. Vila Velha, Brazil.

Silva, P. C., Santos, M. M., & Times, V. C. (2010). *XL-PATH: XML Linking Path Language*. Paper presented at the IADIS International Conference. Timisoara, Romania.

Silva, P. C., Santos, M. M., Cruz, M. S. H., & Santos, A. A. (2010). XBRL Taxonomy for Indexes of Financial Analysis. In *Proceeding of the 7th CONTECSI International Conference on Information Systems and Technology Management*. São Paulo, Brazil: CONTECSI.

Sim, K. M. (2010). Towards complex negotiation for Cloud economy. In P. Bellavista, R. S. Chang, H. C. Chao, S. F. Lin, & P. M. Sloot (Eds.), *Advances in Grid and Pervasive Computing* (pp. 395–406). Berlin, Germany: Springer-Verlag. doi:10.1007/978-3-642-13067-0_42

Singh, B., Al-Haddad, K., & Chandra, A. (1999b). A review of active power filters for power quality improvement. *IEEE Transactions on Industrial Electronics*, *46*(5), 960–969. doi:10.1109/41.793345

Singh, B., Chandra, A., & Al-Haddad, K. (1999a). Computer aided modeling and simulation of active power filters. *Elect. Mach. Power Syst.*, *27*, 1227–1241. doi:10.1080/073135699268687

Singh, G. K., Singh, A. K., & Mitra, R. (2007). A simple fuzzy logic based robust active power filter for harmonic minimization under random load variation. *Electric Power Systems Research*, 77, 1101–1111. doi:10.1016/j.epsr.2006.09.006

Singh, R., Singh, A. K., & Arya, R. K. (2011). Approximated simplest fuzzy logic controlled shunt active power filter for current harmonic mitigation.[IJFSA]. *International Journal of Fuzzy System Applications*, 1(4), 18–36. doi:10.4018/ijfsa.2011100102

Singh, S., Vajirkar, P., & Lee, Y. (2003). Context-Based Data Mining Using Ontologies. In *Conceptual Modeling - ER 2003* (pp. 405–418). Chicago, IL, USA: Springer. doi:10.1007/978-3-540-39648-2_32

Skinner, B. F. (1974). *About behaviorism.* New York, NY: Vintage Books.

Smith, J. (2002, June). The 40 root causes of troubled IT projects. *Computing and Control Journal*, 109-112.

Song, B., Mehedi, H. M., Tian, Y., & Huh, E. N. (2009). A back propagation neural network for evaluating collaborative performance in cloud computing. *Communications in Computer and Information Science*, 63, 57–64. doi:10.1007/978-3-642-10549-4_8

Song, I.-J., & Cho, S.-B. (2013). Bayesian and behavior networks for context-adaptive user interface in a ubiquitous home environment. *Expert Systems with Applications*, 40(5), 1827–1838. doi:10.1016/j.eswa.2012.09.019

Standish Group International Inc. (2009). *Standard Group CHAOS Report.* Author.

Sterman, J. D. (2000). *Business Dynamics: Systems thinking and modeling for a complex world.* Irwin McGraw-Hill.

Stewart, J., Shen, Wang, & Graham. (2011). From 3G to 4G: Standards and the Development of Mobile Broadband in China. *Technology Analysis and Strategic Management*, 23, 773–788. doi:10.1080/09537325.2011.592284

Stockburger, D. W. (1998). *Multivariate Statistics: Concepts, Models, and Applications.* Missouri State University. Retrieved October 24, 2010, from http://www.psychstat.missouristate.edu/multibook/mlt00.htm

Strobbe, M., Laere, O. V., Ongenae, F., Dauwe, S., Dhoedt, B., & Turck, F. D. et al. (2012). Novel Applications Integrate Location and Context Information. *Pervasive Computing*, 11(2), 64–73. doi:10.1109/MPRV.2011.60

Sühnel, T., & Schmidt, F. (2013). Analyse der Zusammenhänge zwischen Biotoptyp- u. Landnutzungsdaten sowie Revieren verschiedener Vogelarten mit Hilfe von Geo-Informationssystemen und neuronalen Netzen. *Actitis, 47.*

Sundarraj, R. P. (2002). An optimisation approach to plan for reusable software components. *European Journal of Operational Research*, 142(1), 128–137. doi:10.1016/S0377-2217(01)00285-5

Takagi, H., & Walke (Eds.). (2008). *Spectrum Requirement Planning in Wireless Communications : Model and Methodology for IMT-Advanced.* Chichester, UK: Wiley.

Taniar, D., Rusu, L. I., & Rahayu, J. W. (2004). On Building XML Data Warehouses. In *Proceedings of the 5th International Conference on Intelligent Data Engineering and Automated Learning* (IDEAL 2004), (LNCS), (vol. 3177, pp. 293-299). Springer.

Taniar, D., Nguyen, H., Rahayu, J. W., & Nguyen, K. (2011). Double-layered schema integration of heterogeneous XML sources. *Journal of Systems and Software*, 84(1), 63–76. doi:10.1016/j.jss.2010.07.055

Taniar, D., Pardede, E., & Rahayu, J. W. (2005b). Preserving Conceptual Constraints During XML Updates. *International Journal of Web Information Systems*, 1(2), 65–82. doi:10.1108/17440080580000084

Taniar, D., Pardede, E., & Rahayu, J. W. (2006). Object-relational complex structures for XML storage. *Information and Software Technology*, 48(6), 370–384. doi:10.1016/j.infsof.2005.12.015

Taniar, D., Rusu, L. I., & Rahayu, J. W. (2005a). A Methodology for Building XML Data Warehouses. *International Journal of Data Warehousing and Mining*, 1(2).

Taniar, D., Rusu, L. I., & Rahayu, J. W. (2009). Partitioning methods for multi-version XML data warehouses. *Distributed and Parallel Databases*, 25(1-2), 47–69. doi:10.1007/s10619-009-7034-y

Taylor, F. (1976). The principles of scientific management. In *Classics of organization theory* (9th ed., pp. 66–67). Belmont, CA: Wadsworth.

Thomas, D. (2004). MDA: Revenge of the modelers or UML utopia? *Software, IEEE, 21*(3), 15–17. doi:10.1109/MS.2004.1293067

Thyagaraju, G. S., & Kulkarni, U. P. (2012). Rough Set Theory Based User Aware TV Program and Settings Recommender. *International Journal of Advanced Pervasive and Ubiquitous Computing, 4*(2), 48–64. doi:10.4018/japuc.2012040105

Trammell, T., Madnick, S., & Moulton, A. (2013). *Using System Dynamics to Analyze the Effect of Funding Fluctuations on Software Development* (Working Paper CISL#2013-06). Sloan School of Management, MIT.

Tribus, M., & McIrvine, E. C. (1971). Energy and information. *Scientific American, 224*, 178–184.

Trinh, Q.-N., & Lee, H.-H. (2013). An Advanced Current Control Strategy for Three-Phase Shunt Active Power Filters. *IEEE Transactions on Industrial Electronics, 60*(12), 5400–5410. doi:10.1109/TIE.2012.2229677

USE-ME.GOV. (2003). *Consortium Agreement - Annex 1 - Description of Work* Author.

USE-ME.GOV. (2006). *D3.1 Recommendations*. Author.

Vaquero, L. M., Rodero-Merino, L., Caceres, J., & Lindner, M. (2009). A break in the clouds: Towards a cloud definition. *ACM SIGCOMM Computer Communications Review, 39*, 50–55. doi:10.1145/1496091.1496100

Ventana Systems Inc. (1999). *Vensim DSS Modeling Guide*. Author.

Vladoiu, M., & Constantinescu, Z. (2011). U-Learning Within A Context-Aware Multiagent Environment. [IJCNC]. *International Journal of Computer Networks & Communications, 3*(1), 1–15. doi:10.5121/ijcnc.2011.3101

Von Zedtwitz, M. (2002). Organisational learning through post-project reviews in R & D. *R & D Management, 32*(3), 255–268. doi:10.1111/1467-9310.00258

Voorsluys, W., Broberg, J., & Buyya, R. (2011). Introduction to Cloud Computing. In R. Buyya, J. Nroberg, & A. Goscinski (Eds.), *Cloud Computing: Principles and Paradigms* (pp. 3–42). John Wiley & Sons, Inc. doi:10.1002/9780470940105.ch1

Wagner, G. (2003). The Agent-Object-Relationship Metamodel: Towards Unified View of State and Behaviour. *Information Systems, 28*(5). doi:10.1016/S0306-4379(02)00027-3

Walsh, J. P., Meyer, A. D., & Schoonhoven, C. B. (2006). A future for organization theory: Living in and living with changing organizations. *Organization Science*, 657–671. doi:10.1287/orsc.1060.0215

Wand, Y., Storey, V., & Weber, R. (2000). An Ontological Analysis of the Relationship Construct in Conceptual Modeling. *ACM Transactions on Database Systems, 24*(4), 494–528. doi:10.1145/331983.331989

Wang, X., Rosenblum, D., & Wang, Y. (2012). Context-Aware Mobile Music Recommendation for daily activities. *Proceedings of the 20th ACM international conference on Multimedia MM'12* (pp. 99-108). Nara, Japan: ACM.

Wang, Y.-K. (2004). Context Awareness and Adaptation in Mobile Learning. *The 2nd IEEE International Workshop on Wireless and Mobile Technologies in Education* (pp. 154-158). Taiwan: IEEE.

Wang, H., Li, J., He, Z., & Gao, H. (2007). Flexible and Effective Aggregation operator for XML Data. *Information Technology Journal, 6*(5), 697–703. doi:10.3923/itj.2007.697.703

Want, R., Hopper, A., Falcao, V., & Gibbons, J. (1992). The Active Badge Location System. *ACM Transactions on Information Systems, 10*(1), 91–102. doi:10.1145/128756.128759

Want, R., Pering, T., Borriello, G., & Farkas, K. I. (2002). Disappearing hardware[ubiquitous computing]. *Pervasive Computing, IEEE, 1*, 36–47. doi:10.1109/MPRV.2002.993143

Weber, M. (1992). *The protestant ethic and the spirit of capitalism*. New York, NY: Routledge.

Weber, S. G., & Gustiené, P. (2013). Crafting Requirements for Mobile and Pervasive Emergency Response based on Privacy and Security by Design Principles. *International Journal of Information Systems for Crisis Response and Management, 5*(2), 1–18. doi:10.4018/jiscrm.2013040101

Weerawarana, S., Curbera, F., Leymann, F., Storey, T., & Ferguson, D. (2005). *Web Services Platform Architecture*. Prentice Hall PTR.

Weick, K. E. (1979). *The social psychology of organizing* (2nd ed.). New York, NY: Random House.

Wei, E. J., & Chan, A. T. (2012). CAMPUS: A Middleware for Automated Context-Aware Adaptation Decision Making at Run Time. *Pervasive and Mobile Computing*, *9*(1), 35–56. doi:10.1016/j.pmcj.2011.10.002

Weiser, M. (1993b). Some computer science issues in ubiquitous computing. *Communications of ACM, 36*(7), 75-84. doi: http://doi.acm.org/10.1145/159544.159617

Weiser, M. (1993a). Hot topics-ubiquitous computing. *Computer, 26*(10), 71–72. doi:10.1109/2.237456

Weiser, M., Gold, R., & Brown, J. S. (1999). The origins of ubiquitous computing research at PARC in the late 1980s. *IBM Systems Journal, 38*(4), 693–696. doi:10.1147/sj.384.0693

Weiss, A. (2007). Computing in the Clouds. *Networker, 11*(4), 16–25. doi:10.1145/1327512.1327513

West, J., & Fomin. (2011). Competing Views of Standards Competition: Response to Egyedi & Koppenhol.[JITSR]. *International Journal of IT Standards and Standardization Research, 9*, i–iv. doi: doi:10.4018/IJITSR

White House. (1993). *The Administration's Agenda for Action*. Retrieved from http://www.ibiblio.org/nii/NII-Agenda-for-Action.html

White, A. S. (2006). External Disturbance control for software project management. *International Journal of Project Management, 24*, 127–135. doi:10.1016/j.ijproman.2005.07.002

White, A. S. (2011). A control system project development model derived from System Dynamics. *International Journal of Project Management, 29*, 696–705. doi:10.1016/j.ijproman.2010.07.009

White, A. S. (2012). Towards a Minimal Realisable System Dynamics Project Model. *International Journal of Information Technologies and Systems Approach, 5*(1), 57–73. doi:10.4018/jitsa.2012010104

White, A. S., & Censlive, M. (2006). Observations on modelling strategies for vendor managed inventory. *Journal Manufacturing Technology Management, 17*(4), 496–512. doi:10.1108/17410380610662915

Wieringa, R. (2008). Operational Business-IT Alignment in Value Webs. In *Proceedings of 2-nd International United Information Systems Conference UISCON*. Springer.

Wieringa, R., & Gordijn, J. (2005). Value-Oriented Design of Service Coordination Processes: Correctness and Trust. In *Proc. of the 20-th ACM Symphosium on Applied Computing*. ACM Press.

Wijayasiri, J. (2008). *Case study 3: The ending of the multi-fibre agreement and 713 Ministry of Finance and Planning*. Colombo: Ministry of Finance and Planning.

Williams, R., Graham, Jakobs, & Lyytinen. (2011). China and Global ICT Standardisation and Innovation. *Technology Analysis and Strategic Management, 23*(7), 715–724. doi:10.1080/09537325.2011.592265

Wilson, J. P., & Gallant, J. C. (Eds.). (2000). *Terrain Analysis: Principles and Applications*. New York: Wiley.

Winograd, T., & Flores, R. (1986). *Understanding Computers and Cognition: A New Foundation for Design*. Norwood, NJ: Ablex.

Wischmeier, W. H., & Smith, D. D. (1978). Predicting rainfall erosion losses – a guide to conservation planning. In USDA Agriculture Handbook (No. 537, pp. 1-58). USDA.

Wiwatwattana, N., Jagadish, H., Lakshmanan, L., & Srivastava, D. (2007). *X^3: A cube operator for xml olap*. Paper presented at the 23rd International Conference on Data Engineering (ICDE'07). Istanbul, Turkey.

XBRL Consortium. (2006). Retrieved from http://www.xbrl.org

XLink - XML Linking Language. (2001). Retrieved from www.w3.org/TR/xlink

XML Schema W3C Recommendation. (2004). Retrieved from www.w3.org/TR/xmlschema-1

XPath - XML Path Language W3C Recommendation. (2007). Retrieved from www.w3c.org/tr/xpath20/

XQuery 1.0: An Xml Query Language. (2007). Retrieved from www.w3.org/TR/xquery

Xu, T., Zhou, Y., David, B., & Chalon, R. (2013). Supporting Activity Context Recognition in Context-Aware Middleware. *27th AAAI Conference on Artificial Intelligence* (pp. 61-70). Califoria: AAAI Press.

Xue, W., Pung, H. K., & Sen, S. (2013). Managing context data for diverse operating spaces. *Pervasive and Mobile Computing*, *9*(1), 57–75. doi:10.1016/j.pmcj.2011.11.001

Xu, X., Cheng, C., & Xiong, J. (2010). Reliable integrated model of cloud & client computing based on multi-agent. *Journal of Computer Information Systems*, *6*(14), 4767–4774.

Ye, J., Stevenson, G., & Dobson, S. (2011). A top-level ontology for smart environments. *Pervasive and Mobile Computing*, *7*(3), 359–378. doi:10.1016/j.pmcj.2011.02.002

Yeo, K. T. (2002). Critical failure factors in information system projects. *International Journal of Project Management*, *20*, 241–246. doi:10.1016/S0263-7863(01)00075-8

Yeung, D. S., Cloete, I., Shi, D., & Ng, W. W. Y. (2010). *Sensitivity Analysis for Neural Networks: Natural Computing Series VIII*. Springer Science and Business Media. doi:10.1007/978-3-642-02532-7

Ying, H. (2000). *Fuzzy Control and Modeling: Analytical foundations and applications*. New York: IEEE Press. doi:10.1109/9780470544730

Yoo, D., & Sim, K. M. (2010). A multilateral negotiation model for cloud service market. *Communications in Computer and Information Science*, *121*, 54–63. doi:10.1007/978-3-642-17625-8_6

Yordanova, K., Kruger, F., & Kirste, T. (2012). Tool Support for Activity Recognition with Computational Casual Behaviour Models. *35th German Conference on Artifical Intelligence* (pp. 108-112). Saarbrücken, Germany: Springer.

Yourdon, E., & Constantine, L. L. (1979). *Structured Design*. Prentice Hall.

Yuan, J., & Wu, Y. (2008). Context-Aware Clustering. *IEEE Conference on Computer Vision and Pattern Recognition* (pp. 1-8). Anchorage, AK: IEEE.

Yu, Z., Nakamura, Y., Zhang, D., Kajita, S., & Mase, K. (2008). Content Provisioning for Ubiquitous Learning. *Pervasive Computing*, *7*(4), 62–70. doi:10.1109/MPRV.2008.69

Zachman, J. A. (1987). A Framework for Information System Architecture. *IBM Systems Journal*, *26*(3). doi:10.1147/sj.263.0276

Zeng, X., & Singh, M. G. (1994). Approximation theory of fuzzy systems-SISO case. *IEEE Transactions on Fuzzy Systems*, *2*(2), 162–194. doi:10.1109/91.277964

Zeng, X., & Singh, M. G. (1995). Approximation theory of fuzzy systems-MIMO case. *IEEE Transactions on Fuzzy Systems*, *3*(2), 219–235. doi:10.1109/91.388175

Zentrum, E. T. H. Switzerland. (n.d.). *Opportunity*. Retrieved from http://www.opportunity-project.eu/

Zhang, D., Guan, H., Zhou, J., Tang, F., & Guo, M. (2008). iShadow: Yet Another Pervasive Computing Environment. *International Symposium on Parallel and Distributed Processing with Applications* (pp. 261-268). Sydney, Austrailia: IEEE.

Zhang, Q., & Izquierdo, E. (2008). Bayesian learning and reasoning for context exploitation in visual information retrieval. *5th International Conference on Visual Information Engineering* (pp. 170-175). Xian, China: IEEE.

Zhang, Y. H., Zhang, J., & Zhang, W. H. (2010). Discussion of Intelligent Cloud Computing System. In *Proceedings of 2010 International Conference on Web Information Systems and Mining (WISM)* (pp. 319-322). Jiangsu, China: IEEE Press.

Zhang, X., Wu, Y., Shen, L., & Skitmore, M. (2014). A prototype system dynamics model for assessing the sustainability of construction projects. *International Journal of Project Management*, *32*(1), 66–76. doi:10.1016/j.ijproman.2013.01.009

Zorba. (2012). *ZorbaNoSQL Query Processor (Version 3.0)*. Retrieved from http://www.zorba.io

About the Contributors

Mehdi Khosrow-Pour, D.B.A., received his Doctorate in Business Administration from the Nova Southeastern University (Florida, USA). Dr. Khosrow-Pour taught undergraduate and graduate information system courses at the Pennsylvania State University – Harrisburg for 20 years. He is currently Executive Editor at IGI Global (www.igi-global.com). He also serves as Executive Director of the Information Resources Management Association (IRMA) (www.irma-international.org) and Executive Director and President of the World Forgotten Children's Foundation (www.world-forgotten-children.org). He is the author/editor of over 20 books in information technology management. He is also the editor-in-chief of the *Information Resources Management Journal*, the *Journal of Cases on Information Technology*, the *Journal of Electronic Commerce in Organizations*, and the *Journal of Information Technology Research*, and has authored more than 50 articles published in various conference proceedings and scholarly journals.

* * *

Andreas Barth, born in the German Democratic Republic, studied Geochemistry at Moscow State University (Lomonosov University) in the former Soviet Union 1974 – 79. Dr. Barth earned a PhD in Geology at the Freiberg Mining Academy (Germany) in 1983. From 1979 – 1990, he worked mainly in geological exploration in Germany, Yemen and Mongolia. Since 1994, Dr. Barth is Managing Director of Beak Consultants GmbH, Germany, and managed projects in the area of mining, environment and development of information systems in Germany, Kosovo, Ghana, South Africa, Namibia, Tanzania, Rwanda, Yemen, Mongolia, Jordan, Albania, Kyrgistan, Bolivia, and other countries. Within the last 15 years, the focus of his work was on the design and implementation of geo-scientific information management systems for various state agencies, mainly in Africa and Germany. He is currently supervising mineral prediction projects with advangeo© in Germany's Ore Mountains and several African countries.

Raymon R. Bruce is Adjunct Professor for Embry-Riddle Aeronautical University and for the University of Electrical Science and Technology China. He was Transition Process Historian for the Clinton-Gore 1992 Presidential Transition Team. He was a Fulbright Senior Scholar in Kaunas, Lithuania (1995) and a Fulbright Senior Specialist in Beijing, P R China (2005), Colombo, Sri Lanka (2006), and the Republic of Slovakia (2006). He was and Invited Fellow at the Rajasthan University in Jaipur, India (2009). He holds a Ph.D. (1992) in Public Administration and Policy from Virginia Polytechnic Institute and State University, a Master of Science degree in Organization Development (1980) from Pepperdine University, a Master of Arts Degree in Theatre (1965), and BA degree in Foreign Language (1961) from the University of Montana. He has presented papers at International conferences. They have been published widely in many international journals in the field of public and private administration with a specialty in managing organization change and government transitions in the United States, Eastern and Central Europe, India Sub-Continent, P R China, and Micronesia. He is the lead author of *Changing Organizations: Practicing Action Training and Research*, from his mentor Neely Gardner's posthumous works (Sage 1998).

Paulo Caetano da Silva received the BS degree in chemical engineering from Federal University of Bahia, Brazil, in 1985. In 2003, he received the MS degree in computer science from the Salvador University, Brazil. He obtained his PhD degree in computer science from the Federal University of Pernambuco in 2010. He is currently a professor of the Master in Systems and Computing from Salvador University, Salvador, Brazil. In addition, he has worked as a computer system analyst at the Central Bank of Brazil since 1994. His research interests include XML, XBRL, data warehouse, Service-Oriented Architecture (SOA), software engineering, and financial information systems.

José Eduardo Fernandes is professor at the Department of Informatics and Communications, Polytechnic Institute of Bragança, Portugal. He holds a PhD in Information Systems and Technology, a master degree in Information Systems, and a degree in Informatics and Systems Engineering from University of Minho. He is a researcher at the SEMAG research group at the ALGORITMI Research Centre. His research and publications focus on software engineering, particularly model-driven development approaches for pervasive information systems. Currently, his interests include analysis and development of project structures for pervasive information systems, ontologies, standards in software engineering, and also software engineering education.

Vladislav Vladimirovich Fomin is a professor at the department of Applied Informatics at Vytautas Magnus University in Kaunas, Lithuania, and holds visiting positions at the University of Latvia and Turība University in Riga, Latvia. After earning his PhD degree in 2001, Vladislav V. Fomin held academic positions at the University of Michigan in Ann Arbor (2001-3), Copenhagen Business School (2004-6), Delft University of Technology (2006), Montpellier Business School (2007), and Rotterdam School of Management, Erasmus University (2008). Dr. Fomin has an extensive experience in international research and professional projects. Vladislav is serving on the editorial board of the *International Journal of IT Standards & Standardization Research* (JITSR) and *Baltic Journal of Modern Computing* (BJMC), is serving as a reviewer for many recognized journals, and is regularly invited to serve as a scientific committee member to recognized international conferences. Fomin is a member of European Academy of Standardization (EURAS) and The Association for Information Systems (AIS). Vladislav has over 70 scientific publications in journals, conferences, and as book chapters, including *Journal of Strategic Information Systems, Communications of the Association for Information Systems, International Journal of IT Standards & Standardization Research, Telecommunications Policy*, and *Knowledge, Technology, & Policy*. Conference publications and presentations include The International Conference on Information Systems, European Conference on Information systems, Hawaii International Conference on System Sciences, Academy of Management, and others.

Nicholas C. Georgantzas is Professor, Management Systems Area, and Director, System Dynamics Consultancy, Fordham University Business Schools, New York, NY, USA. Both an Associate and a Guest Editor, *System Dynamics Review,* he is also consultant to senior management, specializing in simulation modeling for learning in strategy, production, and business process (re) design. Author of *Scenario-Driven Planning* (Greenwood 1995), Dr. Georgantzas has published expansively in refereed scholarly journals, conference proceedings, and edited books. Mostly trans-disciplinary, his research interests, publications, and consulting entail systems thinking, knowledge technology, and strategy design, focusing on the necessary theory and modeling for learning in and about the dynamically complex systems in which we all live.

Remigijus Gustas is a full professor at the Department of Information Systems, Karlstad University. He holds a diploma in system engineering, a doctor and a docent diploma in the area of information systems. Remigijus Gustas has been involved in a number of industrial and European information technology projects. He was leading projects in the area of enterprise modeling, service-oriented analysis and design, e-business modeling, and software technologies. Remigijus Gustas has acted as a reviewer of contributions for several journals. He was chairing and serving as a program committee member in a number of international conferences. Remigijus Gustas is the author of 1 monograph and more than 80 publications. His research interests lie in the area of conceptual modeling, information system analysis and design, enterprise modeling, and integration. Remigijus Gustas is a founder and editor-in-chief of the *International Journal of Information System Modeling and Design.*

Prima Gustiené is an Assistant Professor at Karlstad Business School, at Karlstad University, Sweden. She holds a PhD in Information Systems from Karlstad University. Prima Gustiené is a member of the enterprise and systems architecture design group. Her research interests lie in the area of conceptual and enterprise modeling, graphical representation of e-business solutions, privacy enhancement, and security assurance issues. Prima Gustiené is the author of many publications in the area of information systems development.

Muhammad Younus Javed did his PhD in Adaptive Communication Systems from University of Dundee, Scotland, United Kingdom in 1991 and MS in Predictive Systems from the same university in 1988. He completed BE Electrical Engineering from UET Lahore, Pakistan, in 1982. He is Dean Faculty of Engineering in the College of Electrical and Mechanical Engineering, NUST, with over 20 years of teaching experience. His areas of interest are biometrics, parallel systems, operating systems, computer networks, digital image processing, database systems and design and application of algorithms. He has more than 250 national/international publications to his credit.

Evangelos (Evan) Katsamakas is Associate Professor and Area Chair of Information Systems, Gabelli School of Business and Graduate School of Business, Fordham University, New York. He is also the Associate Director of Fordham's Center for Digital Transformation. Professor Katsamakas holds a Ph.D. from the Stern School of Business, New York University and a M.Sc. from the London School of Economics. His research analyzes the business and economic impact of digital technologies, focusing on digital strategy, digital transformation, networks and platforms, and open innovation. His research interests include economics and game theory modeling, econometrics, and dynamic simulation of complex systems. Prof. Katsamakas' research has appeared in *Management Science, Journal of MIS, System Dynamics Review, International Journal of Medical Informatics,* and in other major academic journals, conference proceedings and books. He served as guest-editor of the Fall 2008 *System Dynamics Review* special issue on the *Dynamics of Information Systems.* Prof. Katsamakas has been teaching a variety of graduate and undergraduate business school courses including E-business Strategies and Applications, Cloud Computing, Tech Startups, Systems Development, and Systems Analysis and Design.

Andreas Knobloch studied Geology at Technische Universität Bergakademie Freiberg (Germany) and South Dakota School of Mines and Technology (US) from 1998 to 2004. He reached his MSc in Germany with a thesis about the numerical modelling of the saturated and unsaturated ground water flow in 2004 using FEMWATER and GMS. He joined Beak Consultants GmbH in 2005 and has been a project manager for various mineral exploration projects. Between 2005 and 2009, he has been involved in the mineral resource management and information system development in Kosovo. Since 2011, he is working in Rwanda for detailed survey and exploration in prospective mineral target areas. Besides this, he has been involved in the scientific research and processing of several projects using advangeo® Prediction Software (e.g. for gold deposits in Ghana or Rwanda, for coal fires in China, and for manganese nodules in the Pacific Ocean).

Ricardo J. Machado is Associate Professor with Habilitation at the Dept. of Information Systems and Director of the ALGORITMI Research Centre, University of Minho, Portugal. He leads the SEMAG research group and his research focuses on software engineering and management, namely on model-driven development, requirements engineering, and software quality, resulting in more than 100 publications. His current research projects focus on the development of multi-staged approaches in software product lines and on the integration of multi-standard models in software high maturity levels. He has been involved in the organization of various international events, including ACSD 2003/2011, DIPES 2006, IEEEXtreme 2008, QUATIC 2007/2010/2012/2014, ICSOB 2015, and he is the chair of the steering committee of the MOMPES international workshops series. Ricardo J. Machado received the 2009 IEEE MGA Achievement Award.

Umar Mahmud did his MS in Software Engineering from National University of Sciences and Technologies, (NUST) Pakistan in 2006 and BE in Computer Software from NUST in 2003. He is presently a Faculty Member in Military College of Signals, NUST with more than 7 years of teaching experience at UG level. His areas of interest are context-awareness, pervasive computing and machine learning. He has 10 research papers including a book to his credit.

Marja Matinmikko is senior scientist at VTT Technical Research Centre of Finland in Oulu, Finland. She received her M.Sc. degree in industrial engineering and management and Dr.Sc. degree in telecommunication engineering from University of Oulu, Finland, in 2001 and 2012, respectively. She is the coordinator of the Finnish project consortium on Cognitive Radio Trial Environment+ (CORE+) that demonstrated the world's first live Authorised Shared Access (ASA)/Licensed Shared Access (LSA) trial in April 2013 in Finland. She has actively participated in ITU-R activities on Cognitive Radio Systems (CRS) and IMT spectrum requirements and chairs the work on CRS at ITU-R WP5A. She received "Young Scientist of the Year 2013" award from Finnish Foundation for Technology Promotion for her active cooperation between the research, regulatory, and industry domains in mobile communications.

Silke Noack graduated in 2001 as Engineer for Mine Surveying and Geodesy at Freiberg Mining Academy (Germany). In 2002, she joined Beak Consultants GmbH as GIS and database developer and is now project manager for the development of the artificial neural network software advangeo©. Her main professional experiences cover the development of databases with GIS functionalities for various applications such as erosion prediction, agriculture, water management (registers of hydraulic engineering structures, digital document management system for a river barrage), and other geo-scientific applications in Germany, as well as for the Geological Survey of Namibia.

Mauricio Paletta is an Assistant Professor at the Universidad Nacional Experimental de Guayana and the Universidad Católica Andrés Bello (Guayana), in Venezuela. He earned a Ph.D. in Computer Science at the Universidad Politécnica de Madrid, in Spain. He was the co-founder of a Research Center in Computer Science at the UNEG (in Spanish: *Centro de Investigación en Informática y Ciencia de la Computación* – CITEC), and for more than two years, he has coordinated the research line named "intelligent and emergence computing" attached to the CITEC. His research interests include agents and multi-agent systems, emergence computing and object-oriented technology, and more recently, collaborative and cloud computing systems.

Frank Schmidt studied Land Management and Environmental Engineering at Rostock University (Germany) and in Newcastle-upon-Tyne (UK) from 1993 to 1999. He reached a PhD in Geoinformatics at Rostock University with a thesis about the generation and application of digital elevation models for agricultural purposes in 2003 and worked with RTK-GPS, laserscanning data, soil samples, geostatistical software, and was involved in GIS teaching. He joined Beak Consultants in 2003 and has been a project manager for various environmental impact assessments and planning projects and an ecological river basin development study. Since 2005, he has been involved in information system development projects in Africa (Ghana, Uganda). In 2012, he supervised a master thesis about the prediction of bird habitats with advangeo©.

Asheesh K. Singh is an Associate Professor in the Electrical Engineering Department, MNNIT, Allahabad, India. He received the Ph.D. degree from the Indian Institute of Technology, Roorkee, India, the M.Tech. degree from REC, Kurukshetra, India, and the B.Tech. degree from HBTI, Kanpur, India, in 2007, 1994 and 1991, respectively. Since 1995, he has been on the academic staff of MNNIT, Allahabad, India. His research interests include application of soft computing techniques in power systems, distributed generation, power quality, and reliability, etc.

Rambir Singh is associated with Electrical and Electronics Engineering Department, Inderprastha Engineering College, Ghaziabad, India. He has served the maintenance branch of Indian Air Force for more than 17 years. He has obtained his Ph.D. and M.Tech. degree in Electrical Engineering from MNNIT, Allahabad, India in 2013 and 2004, respectively, and Bachelor degree in Electrical Engineering from IEI, Calcutta, India in 2001. His research interests include power quality, active power filters, fuzzy logic control, artificial intelligence, and evolutionary algorithms.

Anthony S. White graduated in Aeronautical Engineering, working for Rolls Royce and Hawker Siddeley Dynamics. Since pursuing an academic career, he has been concerned with the development of Mechatronics, Robotics, and quality systems, as well as project management. He has implemented ISO9000 in a medium-size company and run short courses for senior managers in lean systems, JIT, QFD, Kaizan, and project management. He has initiated several project management degrees while at Middlesex. Dr. White has researched for some 12 years into software project system problems using System Dynamics and Control System methods. He has supervised numerous research degrees to completion as well as publishing over 200 papers. Prof. White was Dean of the School of Engineering Systems at Middlesex from 1997 to 2002.

Index

A

APF 310-314, 322, 325, 327-330
artificial neural networks 67, 186-188, 204-205
aspect-oriented software 2, 27-28

B

build-out 152, 157

C

CASOS 134-136, 138-139, 141-142, 144, 146-147
CBA 65-67, 94-95
CiE 65-66, 70-72, 74-75, 77, 79-81, 84-86, 89, 91,
    93-95, 97-101, 104
Cloud computing 282, 299
COAT 36, 50-51, 53-61
collaboration 158, 282-283, 285, 289-290, 295, 297,
    299-300, 306-307
Compensating Polynomial 310, 312, 315, 317, 330
Conceptual modeling 1-5, 7-8, 14, 29
Context Awareness 65, 67-68, 70
Control system models 115
crowdfunding 134
CRS 149, 152, 155-158

D

Dynamic Response 310-311, 322, 328, 330

E

eBay 134
ecosystems 134
eEurope 149, 151
eigenvalues 113, 118-119, 126, 129, 136
energy exchange 34-35, 38-39, 42-45, 48, 53, 62
entropy 44, 69, 135-136, 141-142
expressive power 1-2, 21, 29-30

F

Facebook 134
failure percentage 66, 79-81, 84, 91-104
feedback loops 114-115, 121, 134-136, 142-145
forest pests 186, 207
framework 37, 50, 134, 153, 161-162, 165-168, 172,
    175, 179-182, 226, 282, 285, 290-291, 299,
    301, 303, 307
Fuzzy logic 310-311, 314-315

H

Harmonic Compensation 311, 314, 323
heterogeneous devices 161-162, 164, 183

I

Improved Approximated Simplest Fuzzy Logic
    Controller 310, 315
industrial age 150, 152-153, 158
Information Systems 1, 29, 150, 161-162, 164-165,
    172, 288
interaction dependency 4
interaction loop 5-6, 10, 12, 15, 20-24, 26-29
inter-reaction 41, 45, 52, 55
iThink® 135-137, 139

J

jurisdictional domains 34-35, 48, 55, 62

K

kNN 70, 72, 80

L

LinkedIn 134
LMDQL 212-214, 217, 230-233, 235-237, 246, 248-
    249, 255, 257-258, 260, 264-267, 274